OVER-THINKING

The Protection of Personal Information Act

The last POPIA book you will ever need

OVER-THINKING

The Protection of Personal Information Act

The last POPIA book you will ever need

juta

Over-thinking The Protection of Personal Information Act

First published 2021

Juta and Company (Pty) Ltd
PO Box 14373, Lansdowne 7779, Cape Town, South Africa

ISBN: 978 1 48513 682 8

Production Specialist: Valencia Wyngaard-Arenz
Editor: Sarah De Jager
Proofreader: Andrew Scholtz
Cover design and illustrations: Nudge Studio
Typesetter: Elinye Ituba DTP Solutions
Indexer: Lexinfo (Adami Geldenhuys)

Typeset in ITC Garamond Std 10/13

ACKNOWLEDGEMENTS

This book would not have been possible without the patience and expertise of everybody around us.

Our spouses Anelde, Martin and Madelyn took the brunt of the decision to change a quick 100 page update to our old book to a 714 page colossus. Thank you for giving us the time and space to do this, keeping the home fires burning and for tolerating all of the complaining (during a pandemic no less!). To our children Mark, Katherine, Hannah and Stella: Thank you for leaving us alone when we asked you to. Hannah, we promise the next book will be about 'Princess Poppy from Trolls'. We are sorry we disappointed you.

The book wouldn't have been if it weren't for our parents. Thank you for giving us enquiring minds, stubborn streaks, a love of language, the urge to write things down and our senses of humour. A special word of thanks to Pieter Luttig for exposing Ilze to the law and for the season tickets to Newlands. None of this would have happened had it not been for those tickets. We miss you.

Our work family had to cope with the complaining and book-induced burnout. Ann, Liezl, and Sadieka thank you for patiently listening to the whining, all of the pep talks and the occasional ass-kicking. Liezl, Annie and Stef, thank you for the beautiful layout, cover design and illustrations – you outdid yourselves!

We benefited from the expertise of Elmien du Plessis, Celeste Schlebusch, Era Gunning, Francis Cronje and Luke Brodziak. Thank you for taking the time to read chapters and answer some very stupid questions.

A heartfelt thank you to our long suffering Juta team. Edmund, Marlinee, Stephen, Sarah and Valencia gave us an infinite amount of rope yet saved us from ourselves on many occasions. A special mention to Stephen who kept us going with a daily delivery of darkly hilarious memes at the end.

The co-authors also wanted to thank each other, but couldn't agree on what to say. We settled on 'Sorry!'

CONTENTS

FOREWORD

One of the biggest human rights challenges in the 21st century after climate change is probably the violation of data privacy. Innovation and the rapid evolution that characterises the fourth industrial revolution, coupled with Covid-19 which is accelerating online activities, have magnified this challenge. However, the law is struggling to keep pace with these technological developments. The drafters of the Protection of Personal Information Act 4 of 2013 (POPIA) were mindful of the difficult task of the effective regulation of personal information in the digital space. This is one of the reasons that they chose to take a principles-based approach when POPIA was drafted. The strengths and disadvantages of principles-based regulation was best summarised by the SA Law Reform Commission while it was researching and drafting the first version of POPIA:[1]

> '[Principles-based regulation] emphasises a "do the right thing" approach and promotes compliance with the spirit of the law. It, furthermore, provides flexibility through the statement of general principles that can be applied to new and changing circumstances. ... The disadvantages of a principles-based system centre on problems of ambiguity.'

South Africa is no stranger to the agony and ecstasy of principles-based regulation. We are used to the balancing act of weighing different, often competing, rights against each other; after all, that is what our Constitution requires. In performing this task, section 44(1)*(b)* of POPIA enjoins the Information Regulator to:

> '[H]ave due regard for the protection of all human rights and social interests that compete with privacy, including the general desirability of a free flow of information and the recognition of the legitimate interests of public and private bodies in achieving their objectives in an efficient way.'

What this underscores is the importance of fostering debate about the conditions for the lawful processing of personal information and approaching them, not just from the perspective of the data subjects we are tasked with protecting, but also the interests of public and private bodies. Luckily, we are not alone in this endeavour. We walk in the footsteps of the countries that have walked this path before and on whose shoulders POPIA was built.

---

[1] The SA Law Reform Commission Project 124 on Privacy and Data Protection is comprised of a 2005 Discussion Paper (available at https://www.justice.gov.za/salrc/dpapers/dp109.pdf) and their 2009 Report (available at https://www.justice.gov.za/salrc/reports/r_prj124_privacy%20and%20data%20protection2009.pdf).

The strength of this publication lies in the fact that it draws from so many different perspectives; the language of the legislation, the Constitution, the long title and preamble of POPIA, the materials taken into account by the drafters (as set out in the SA Law Reform Commission Project 124 on Privacy and Data Protection, which contains the research which informed POPIA and the first draft of the POPI Bill), international guidelines and foreign law, the authors' experience of working with private and public bodies (and of being data subjects), the insights of popular figures like Dolly Parton and even fictional ones, like Darth Vader. The comprehensive research that has gone into drafting this commentary is almost as valuable as the humour in which it is packaged.

Adv Pansy Tlakula
Chairperson: The Information Regulator
August 2021

ANOTHER FOREWORD

This POPIA book is not late. It arrived precisely when it meant to.

Gandalf the Grey
11 March 2021

The Undying Lands

Introduction: About this book

There is no better way to start this book than by reciting the Dunning-Kruger[1] prayer: 'Let me be smart enough to know how dumb I am and give me the courage to carry on anyway.' No, we are not calling the readers stupid, we are referring to our own stupidity when it comes to POPIA; writing this book was hard for a couple of reasons.

POPIA is new. Yes, it was drafted ages ago, but it has not been tested. So, this book is full of some (educated) guesses. It is important to acknowledge that. When we were guessing we marked it as a 'tricky area'. In the words of young Ms Boast, 'if she had a nickel for every tricky area ...'.

POPIA is old. The research that underpinned the first draft was published in 2005 and POPIA was enacted in 2013. Researching this book was a bit like an archaeological dig to determine what the drafters were thinking back then. That is why you will see us referring to repealed data protection legislation from time to time.

POPIA is complex. POPIA is comprised of a list of different principles that are linked in the most complicated way. Studying these principles as separate topics leads to confusion and some very bad advice. Hence, the book is not structured around the eight conditions of the lawful processing of personal information.

---

1 The Dunning-Kruger effect is a cognitive bias explained as follows by John Cleese: 'You see, if you're very, very stupid, how can you possibly realize that you're very, very stupid? You'd have to be relatively intelligent to realize how stupid you are … . [Knowing] how good you are at something requires exactly the same skills as it does to be good at that thing in the first place. Which means – and this is terribly funny – that if you're absolutely no good at something at all, then you lack exactly the skills that you need to know that you're absolutely no good at it.'

To help you navigate the book, here is a map to the chapters:

#	Chapter	What it is about	Main sections discussed
1	POPIA's place in the grand scheme of governance	We explain the relationship of POPIA to other governance areas, the different roles and responsibilities POPIA creates and how to document POPIA compliance.	Section 17 Sections 55 and 56 Regulation 4
2	The purpose and inter-pretation of POPIA	In this chapter we discuss principle-based legislation and what you must take into account when interpreting POPIA. We also discuss key concepts that are used in POPIA. They are: • The concept of reasonableness • What is reasonably practicable? • Taking legitimate interests into account • Transparency • The right to object • Consent (the c-word); and • Historical, statistical or research purposes. Lastly, we look at what happens when POPIA collides with other legislation.	The Constitution (privacy is a human right after all) Section 2 Section 3(2) to (4) The definition of consent
3	The application and scope of POPIA	In this chapter we will discuss when POPIA applies, when it doesn't apply, whether it applies retrospectively and when POPIA came into effect.	Section 3(1) Section 6 Section 7 Sections 36 to 38 Section 114 The definitions of: • Personal information • Processing • Record • Responsible party

➡

#	Chapter	What it is about	Main sections discussed
4	Who is held accountable for POPIA compliance	This chapter is about knowing who will be held liable for POPIA non-compliance. We look at the concepts of responsible parties, co-responsible parties and operators. We also look at managing POPIA compliance between organisations through contracts, binding corporate rules and third-party risk management.	Section 8 Section 20 Section 21 The definitions of: • Responsible party • Operator
5	Information security management	In this chapter we learn to speak Geek! We discuss the CIA triad and information security management and marry it to what POPIA requires in respect of information security. The chapter is also about what to do when the POPIA strikes the fan.[2]	Section 19 Section 22
6	Processing must be for a lawful purpose	In this chapter we answer the question 'is what we want to do with this personal information legal?' This is a two-step process: • determine the purpose for which the information was collected; and • apply one of the six legal justifications. If none of the six legal justifications apply, the processing is not lawful and must stop.	Section 9 Section 11 Section 13(1)

➡

2 There are many ways to pronounce POPIA. In certain parts of South Africa it does sound a little bit like 'papaya'.

#	Chapter	What it is about	Main sections discussed
7	Special personal information and children's personal information	Not all personal information is created equal. In this chapter we discuss special personal information and children's personal information and the additional rules that apply before an organisation can process it.	Sections 26 to 35
8	When the Information Regulator must be approached for prior authorisation	What fresh hell is this? Prior authorisation? There are certain high risk or large-scale forms of processing that require prior authorisation from the Information Regulator. In this chapter we discuss what processing is subject to this requirement and how to apply.	Sections 57 to 59
9	The principles of minimal processing and information quality	The Marie Kondo of POPIA principles.[3] In this chapter we discuss the role of minimality in data protection and what it means that personal information must be adequate, relevant and not excessive. We also discuss the requirement that information must be complete, accurate, not misleading and updated where necessary. Don't hang on to personal information that no longer sparks joy.[4]	Section 10 Section 16

➡

[3] Marie Kondo may as well be talking about information governance. Here is an example that applies to records management: 'But when we really delve into the reasons for why we can't let something go, there are only two: an attachment to the past or a fear for the future.' See '17 Marie Kondo Quotes That Will Help You Organise and Get Control of Your Life and Work', available at https://www.inc.com/peter-economy/17-marie-kondo-quotes-that-will-help-you-organize-get-control-of-your-life-work.html.

[4] More Marie Kondo.

#	Chapter	What it is about	Main sections discussed
10	Collecting and creating personal information	In this chapter we discuss the rule that is going to give nightmares to data brokers – organisations have to collect personal information directly from the data subject. There are exceptions to this rule and we will discuss those too. The chapter also discusses POPIA implications for personal information which is created by organisations.	Section 12
11	Notifying data subjects	Here we discuss effing the ineffable; notifying data subjects of what personal information is being collected and what it is used for. We look at what must be disclosed, when and how.	Section 18 Bits of the Promotion of Access to Information Act
12	Further processing of personal information (secondary use)	What happens if an organisation wants to use personal information for a new purpose; one that they had not thought about when the information was collected? That is referred to as 'further processing' and is what this chapter is about.	Section 15
13	Sharing personal information between organisations	In this chapter we will discuss how all of the conditions in POPIA apply to sharing in order to answer the question 'when can an organisation share personal information with third parties?' We will discuss the most common forms of sharing such as selling and buying personal information, sharing personal information in groups of companies and verifying personal information obtained from the data subject with third parties.	We apply all of the conditions (sections 8 to 25) to the sharing of information

#	Chapter	What it is about	Main sections discussed
14	Transborder information flows	In this chapter we will discuss when organisations are allowed to transmit personal information to third parties in foreign countries.	Section 72
15	Profiling and automated decision-making	In this chapter we will discuss when organisations are allowed to do profiling and make automated decisions about data subjects.	Section 71 We also apply all of the conditions (sections 8 to 25) to profiling and automated decisions
16	Direct marketing	In this chapter we will discuss how POPIA will impact direct marketing. We will not only look at the provisions that relate to direct marketing specifically, but also how the other principles in POPIA will impact on marketing activities.	Section 69 Regulation 6 and form 4
17	Records management	POPIA has an impact on what records that include personal information organisations can retain. In this chapter we will discuss what records can be retained, how they must be destroyed and the rules relating to the restriction of certain records.	Section 14
18	Data subject rights	POPIA gives data subjects a whole host of new rights. In this chapter we discuss what these rights are and how to give effect to them.	Section 5 Sections 23 to 25 Section 70 Section 71
19	Enforcement of POPIA	In this chapter we discuss the Information Regulator, its powers and the offences, penalties, fines and civil liability organisations who fall foul of POPIA can be exposed to.	Section 40 Section 43 Sections 60 to 68 Sections 73 to 99 Sections 100 to 109

#	Chapter	What it is about	Main sections discussed
20	How to implement a POPIA Programme	In this chapter we discuss: • (POPIA) compliance frameworks • personal information impact assessments • internal measures to process requests for access to information • providing training; and • privacy management software.	We have come full circle, back to section 55 and regulation 4

POPIA is overwhelming. We are campaigning to have 'POPIA paralysis' and 'POPIA fatigue' recognised as syndromes in the DSM-6.[5] In order to combat the almost inevitable paralysis, we also included 'key points'. These nuggets are the things that are (a) most important to understand and (b) most commonly misunderstood.

The last problem that we had to overcome was that POPIA (as with any law) can suck the joy out of life. To combat the tedium, we drew inspiration from our favourite people, books, movies and musicians. We did not do this to be funny. Receiving information 'when you are in a good mood, or even when you have a pencil stuck crosswise in your mouth to make you "smile", also induces cognitive ease'.[6] We tried to apply this principle from cover to cover (in the litteral sense). For those of you who haven't figured it out, none of the fictional characters on the cover of this book (or inside it) actually said any of the quotes we ascribe to them in the context of a POPIA book. This is their fault of course, as if they knew how gripping data protection could be we are sure they would have. We are hoping that you have fun reading this book, but if you don't we think that Justice Sachs said it best: 'The Constitution cannot oblige the dour to laugh. It can, however, prevent the cheerless from snuffing out the laughter of the blithe spirits among us.'"

5 American Psychiatric Association *Diagnostic and Statistical Manual of Mental Disorders*.

6 Paragraph 107, Laugh It Off Promotions CC v South African Breweries International (Finance) BV t/a Sabmark International and Another (CCT42/04) [2005] ZACC 7; 2006 (1) SA 144 (CC); 2005 (8) BCLR 743 (CC) (27 May 2005), available at http://www.saflii.org/za/cases/ZACC/2005/7.html

1 POPIA's place in the grand scheme of governance

1.1 WHAT TO EXPECT IN THIS CHAPTER

This chapter comes with a warning: 'One does not simply walk into Mordor.' This is not only a quote from Lord of the Rings, but also something one of our favourite business analysts used to say at the start of big POPIA projects. This chapter is for the information officer, deputy information officers, compliance officers and consultants who are responsible for POPIA strategy. It is about the relationship of POPIA to other governance areas (and how they depend on each other) and explains the different roles and responsibilities POPIA creates.

In this chapter we discuss the following:

- POPIA in the greater governance context
- Roles and responsibilities within the organisation
- Documenting processing activities

1.2 POPIA IN THE GREATER GOVERNANCE CONTEXT

The process of becoming POPIA compliant is not unlike looking in a funhouse mirror. The process reveals and amplifies every crack and imperfection in the governance of an organisation. This is because implementing POPIA in an organisation is heavily dependent on the maturity of existing governance functions. In the words of Dr Elizabeth Coombs, NSW Privacy Commissioner: 'Privacy is easiest when it is the organisation's standard mode of operation and monitoring is mainstreamed through existing governance mechanisms'.[1]

So, which governance functions need to be in place in order to implement POPIA? Here they are at a glance:

Corporate governance			
Compliance risk management	**Information governance**	**Data governance**	**Technology governance**
POPIA compliance (and risk) now has to be managed through a compliance framework.	POPIA is about the protection of personal information and privacy rights.	Good data governance is a prerequisite to good information governance.	Technology is the tool with which personal information is processed – it can enable or derail POPIA compliance.

In the remainder of this section, we will discuss the role of corporate governance, compliance risk management, information governance, data governance and technology governance in POPIA compliance.

1 Information Governance ANZ 'Privacy and data breaches – how information governance minimizes the risk', available at https://www.infogovanz.com/archive/privacy-and-data-breaches-how-information-governance-minimises-the-risk/.

Tricky area: If this book appears to be focused on large businesses with compliance departments and in-house lawyers, it is because to a large extent it is. This begs the question whether POPIA compliance looks different for small- to medium-sized enterprises? POPIA does not distinguish between different types of enterprises, by size or any other metric. In other words, on the surface, small businesses are subject to the same compliance requirements. However, a deeper look at POPIA reveals that many of the principles are based on a reasonableness standard. What will be reasonable to expect of a big corporate will not be the same for a small business.

However, it is important for smaller businesses to 'formalise' their POPIA compliance in a POPIA compliance framework and to perform personal information impact assessments. Both of these steps are discussed in chapter 20. There is also a section dedicated to small businesses in that chapter in paragraph 20.7.

1.2.1 Corporate governance

King IV defines corporate governance as 'the exercise of ethical and effective leadership by the governing body towards the achievement of the following governance outcomes: Ethical culture, good performance, effective control and legitimacy.'[2]

POPIA compliance is impossible without strong governance structures. For instance, it was telling that when the United States' Federal Trade Commission (FTC) imposed a historic USD5 billion civil penalty on Facebook for violations of a 2012 FTC order and section 5 of the Federal Trade Commission Act, the settlement order imposed 'significant structural reforms on how Facebook does business, including greater corporate accountability, more rigorous compliance monitoring and increased transparency'.[3] According to the FTC the 'order imposes a sea change in the way Facebook addresses consumers' privacy with a belt-and-suspender approach to compliance'.[4] The specific responsibilities of the board when it comes to POPIA compliance are discussed in paragraph 1.3.2 below.

Of course, whether there was a sea change or not is up for debate!

---

2 *King IV Report on Corporate Governance for South Africa* (2016).

3 Federal Trade Commission *Prepared Remarks of Chairman Joe Simons Facebook Settlement Press Conference, July 24, 2019*, 2, available at https://www.ftc.gov/system/files/documents/public_statements/1537170/simons_-_facebook_press_conference_7-24-19.pdf.

4 Federal Trade Commission *Prepared Remarks of Chairman Joe Simons Facebook Settlement Press Conference, July 24, 2019*, 3, available at https://www.ftc.gov/system/files/documents/public_statements/1537170/simons_-_facebook_press_conference_7-24-19.pdf.

1.2.2 Compliance risk management

Compliance risk management forms part of the broader discipline of enterprise risk management.[5] An independent compliance function must ensure that an organisation manages all of the compliance risk the organisation is exposed to continuously and effectively. The introduction of POPIA is a significant addition to most organisations' compliance burden.

Compliance risk is:

> 'the effect of uncertainty (including potential events and consequences of non-compliance) on an organisation's compliance objectives (adapted from ISO 19 600, 3.9). This includes the current and prospective risk of damage to the organisation's reputation and financial soundness arising from non-adherence to compliance obligations and failing to meet valid compliance-related expectations of key stakeholders such as clients, investors, staff members and society as a whole. Compliance risk therefore not only exposes the organisation to consequences such as fines, penalties, civil claims and a loss of authorisation to operate, but also to reputational damage. In many cases, compliance risk results from inadequate controls.'[6]

An organisation's approach to the management of compliance risk is referred to as a compliance risk framework which is in turn comprised of a compliance strategy, objectives, governance, policy, roles and responsibilities, risk appetite, process and techniques and reporting. Regulation 4(1)*(a)* of the POPIA Regulations prescribes that the information officer must 'ensure that ... a compliance framework is developed, implemented, monitored and maintained.'[7]

One of the core responsibilities of the compliance function is to implement a compliance risk management process. Below is the compliance risk management process[8] prescribed in the Compliance Institute of Southern Africa Generally Accepted Compliance Practice framework:

5 There are two families of ISO standards that govern these disciplines. ISO 31 000:2018 in respect of enterprise risk management, and ISO 19600:2014 in respect of compliance management systems.

6 See the definition of 'compliance risk' in the Compliance Institute of Southern Africa Generally Accepted Compliance Practice framework ('GACP').

7 This is discussed in chapter 20.

8 The compliance risk management process should not be confused with 'personal information impact assessments' (PIIAs) prescribed in regulation 4(1)*(b)* of POPIA. The PIIA process is an example of a compliance control used by organisations to achieve and maintain compliance with POPIA. PIIAs are discussed in chapter 20.

Phase I: Compliance risk identification
1. Identify all the compliance obligations that fall within the scope of the compliance risk for the entity as a whole. (This should be done first for the entity as a whole and thereafter for the individual divisions/subsidiaries.)
Phase II: Compliance risk assessment
2. Categorise the identified compliance obligations in terms of core/primary, secondary or topical/pertinent. **3.** Prioritise the identified compliance obligations by rating each in terms of Probability and Seriousness. (The provisions of each requirement should also be analysed and prioritised, if applicable, on the same basis.) **4.** Plot the compliance obligations according to the ratings on a scatter diagram (if needed). **5.** Classify compliance obligations into high, medium and low risks.
Phase III: Compliance risk management (control optimisation). Refer to the separate guideline on developing compliance risk management plans.
6. Based on the compliance obligations in the high-risk area as priority, develop a compliance risk management plan for each compliance obligation by identifying, inter alia, the following: • the provision(s) for each compliance obligation that has to be complied with • the control measure that will monitor compliance • the person responsible for implementing the control measure; and • the target date for implementing the control measure (if applicable). **7.** Include a compliance risk management plan in the compliance manual.
Phase IV: Compliance risk monitoring
8. Develop an effective review process to evaluate the implementation of the compliance risk management plan throughout the entity. This would include the development of a compliance risk monitoring plan. **9.** Monitor in terms of the review process and report findings to the relevant role-players.

Organisations that have mature compliance functions will add the obligations imposed by POPIA to the compliance obligations identified in phase I (in the table above) and implement POPIA via the existing compliance risk management process.

Key point: Organisations that do not have a mature compliance function should consider investing in this function before they implement POPIA. Why? If an organisation does not have a view on all of its compliance obligations, how does it know that POPIA is the biggest compliance risk it is faced with? In addition, many sections in POPIA justify the processing of personal information on the basis that the responsible party is subject to an obligation imposed 'by law'. It will be difficult for responsible parties to gauge whether they comply with POPIA if they are not aware of all of the legal obligations they are subject to.[9] This is often referred to as a compliance or regulatory universe.

1.2.3 Information governance

Information governance is 'the specification of decision rights and an accountability framework to ensure appropriate behaviour in the valuation, creation, storage, use, archiving and deletion of information. It includes the processes, roles and policies, standards and metrics that ensure the effective and efficient use of information in enabling an organisation to achieve its goals'.[10] Put differently, it is 'the activities and technologies that organisations employ to maximise the value of their information while minimising associated risks and costs'.[11]

Information governance concerns itself with all types of information, not just personal information. King IV defines information as 'all data, records and knowledge in electronic or any other format, which forms part of the intellectual capital used, transformed or produced by an organisation'.[12] Other forms of information that may be of value to organisations include all intellectual property (e.g. trademarks, designs, inventions, trade secrets, know-how, content or publications the organisation created and technical documents), financial information, contracts and information about contract negotiations, strategies and plans, policies, internal memoranda, minutes of meetings and agendas and research.

Robert Smallwood, one of the giants in information governance, describes it as a 'new and developing hybrid "super discipline" that crosses multiple functional boundaries, principally records management,

9 The phrase 'by law' appears in (amongst others) section 11(1)*(c)*, section 14(1)*(a)*, section 18(1)*(f)* and section 20. We are of the view that the phrase 'by law' includes the Constitution, legislation, common law, customary law and court decisions.

10 Gartner IT Glossary.

11 The Information Governance Initiative.

12 *King IV Report on Corporate Governance for South Africa* (2016).

information security, risk management, legal and e-discovery issues, information technology (IT), Big Data analytics, privacy and more'.[13] Information security and privacy are therefore seen as sub-disciplines of the larger field of information governance.

ARMA International has developed The Principles® Maturity Model which is used to measure an organisation's information governance maturity. Information governance maturity assessments help organisations to spot areas that are in need of improvement. In other words, an information governance maturity assessment can also be used to assess whether an organisation is mature enough to become POPIA compliant.[14]

Here are the different principles and the implications of a low level of maturity:

Information governance principle	The implications of a low level of maturity
Accountability Information governance is a priority for the organisation, and senior managers are responsible for it (and they know it!). Clear roles and responsibilities concerning information governance have been assigned throughout the organisation. Policies, standards and procedures have been put in place to ensure that the level of information governance can be audited.	How an organisation ranks on the accountability principle indicates whether information governance is a priority. Becoming POPIA compliant without looking at how all information is governed is not only difficult, it is also dangerous. It is entirely possible that the organisation is faced with more significant risks to other categories of information (e.g. its intellectual property). Organisations should consider starting an information governance project before its POPIA project. Compliance with POPIA can be one phase of the information governance project.

➥

[13] Robert Smallwood *Best Practices for Information Governance*, available at https://community.aiim.org/blogs/robert-smallwood/2015/04/29/best-practices-for-information-governance.

[14] Here is a link to an information governance maturity assessment which was adapted from the ARMA International Information Governance Maturity Model: https://novcon.co.za/2020/05/05/are-you-mature-enough-for-popia/.

<table>
<tr><th>Information governance principle</th><th>The implications of a low level of maturity</th></tr>
<tr><td>Standardisation[15]
There is an agreed way of working at the organisation.
Business processes and activities are well defined and documented in an open and verifiable way. The documentation must be available to employees and third parties who play a role in the processes and activities.</td><td>When POPIA compliance is assessed, organisations are assessing their policies, procedures and business processes.[16]
If there are no policies, procedures or processes, or if they are poorly implemented, we are in cowboy country. Given that it is not possible to monitor every employee all the time, POPIA compliance will become difficult, if not impossible, to assess.
Organisations should consider starting a corporate governance project, instead of a POPIA project.</td></tr>
<tr><td>Confidentiality
Information must be protected from unauthorised destruction, modification and loss.</td><td rowspan="3">Confidentiality, integrity and availability are referred to as the CIA triad, which is a concept used in information security management. It is also a requirement of POPIA.[17] This is closely related to the quality of the information which is regulated in section 16. Information quality is discussed in chapter 9.
If an organisation does not proactively protect the confidentiality of its information, have processes in place to ensure its integrity and have business continuity plans in place, it should consider starting an information security management project before it embarks on a POPIA project.</td></tr>
<tr><td>Integrity
The right processes are in place to guarantee that information is comprehensible, clear, consistent and reliable.</td></tr>
<tr><td>Availability
Policies and business continuity plans are in place to ensure that information, and the infrastructure the organisation needs to manage and use that information, is available to the appropriate people at the appropriate time.</td></tr>
</table>

[15] This is more commonly referred to as the transparency principle. Transparency or 'openness' is also one of the conditions for the lawful processing of personal information (see section 18 of POPIA). So, to avoid confusion, refer to this principle of information governance as 'standardisation'.

[16] We discuss the difference between policies, procedures, standards and guidelines in chapter 20 paragraph 20.2.6. People often use procedures and processes interchangeably. For us, a procedure is a formally agreed upon (e.g. by management) way of doing something, while a process is a series of actions taken in order to achieve a particular end, but is not necessarily formally agreed upon.

[17] Section 19.

Information governance principle	The implications of a low level of maturity
Compliance The organisation has structures, policies and processes in place to ensure that the organisation complies with all legislation, supervisory requirements created by regulators, codes of conduct and other standards that apply to the organisation. There is a continuous process through which compliance risks are identified, analysed (rated according to their impact and likelihood), addressed and monitored. This forms part of the organisation's enterprise risk management process.	Almost all types of information are regulated in some way or another. The introduction of POPIA creates significant regulatory compliance risk. Compliance risk management is discussed in paragraph 1.2.2 above. If an organisation does not have a reasonably mature compliance risk management function, POPIA compliance will be a challenge. Also, if the organisation is not currently managing compliance risk (or worse, not managing any type of risk whatsoever) there may be areas of non-compliance with other legislation that exposes the organisation to bigger risks than POPIA. The organisation should consider doing a compliance risk management project before it starts a POPIA project. If the organisation does not manage any form of risk, it should consider undertaking an enterprise risk management project.
Records management The organisation manages records (information maintained as evidence of actions or decisions). The organisation only retains information for as long as it is required by legal, regulatory, fiscal, operational and historical requirements.	A failure to maintain proper records (or keeping personal information indefinitely) will not only result in POPIA non-compliance,[18] but can also cause business disruption and inefficiency, including the ineffective use of staff time to recreate or retrieve records and unnecessary storage and retrieval costs. Organisations with poor records management will also fail to meet audit requirements and may be unable to defend themselves during investigations, disputes and litigation. Records management is discussed in chapter 17. The organisation should consider doing a records management project before it starts a POPIA project.

➥

18 Section 14.

Information governance principle	The implications of a low level of maturity
Change management and empowerment The organisation proactively manages change by assessing the impact of events and strategies on its existing policies, processes, infrastructure and people. The organisation's employees are empowered through training and skills development to work responsibly with information and to protect it.	POPIA is not an IT problem; it is a people problem.[19] The majority of information risks are either caused or exacerbated by human error. Organisations that do not have a strong culture of change management, training and skills development will find POPIA compliance difficult to achieve and maintain. Change management and POPIA training are discussed in chapter 20. The organisation should consider strengthening its change management, learning and skills development functions before starting a POPIA project.

Key point: We have found that the reason why many POPIA projects fail is a lack of information governance maturity. It does not mean that an organisation cannot become POPIA compliant; it just means that the focus of the project should be adjusted to achieve information governance maturity at the same time. This also ensures that an organisation gets the most value out of the project. For instance, why only look at the security of personal information if the organisation could improve the security of all types of information?

1.2.4 Data management

Data management is a collection of functions aimed at ensuring that an organisation's 'data' is accessible, reliable and useful.

1.2.4.1 What is the difference between 'data' and 'information'?

There has always been confusion about what constitutes 'information' versus what constitutes 'data'. The terms are often used interchangeably, with the unfortunate effect that they are mistaken for synonyms. The mistake is not without consequences as it has led to confusion about what is included in the related, but very much separate, fields of data governance and information governance.

19 For more on this statement, see paragraph 1.2.5 below.

So, what is the difference? 'Data' should be viewed as an unrefined element which, following processing, is turned into useful 'information'. The difference between data, information, knowledge and wisdom is often depicted using the DIKW pyramid:

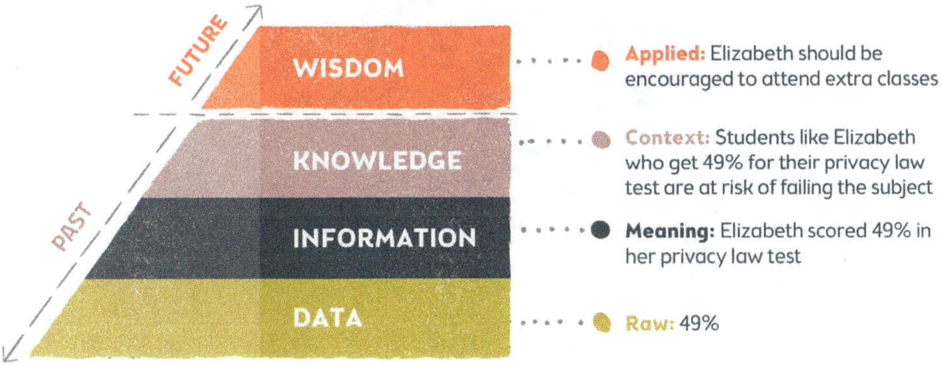

POPIA correctly refers to 'personal information', because in order for the 'information' to be 'personal' it has to relate to an identifiable (living) individual or (existing) juristic person.[20] In short, for POPIA to apply, the data must already be:

- transformed into information by putting it in a relational database that
- includes data that identifies (or could identify)[21] an individual or juristic person.

The European Union's General Data Protection Regulation 2016/679 (EU GDPR) incorrectly refers to 'personal information' as 'personal data'. Having said all of this, there is very little point in being a purist about this and running around scolding everybody for being wrong.[22] As long as you know what personal information is (and is not) and that the two separate fields of data governance and information governance are both important for POPIA compliance, everything will be okay in the end.

[20] See the definition of 'personal information' in section 1 of POPIA.

[21] The definition of 'personal information' must always be read with the definition of 'de-identify' which extends POPIA's scope to information that does not identify the individual or juristic person if there is a reasonably foreseeable method by which the individual or juristic person *could* be identified from the information (e.g. by linking it with other information). The definitions of 'personal information' and 'de-identification' are discussed in chapter 3.

[22] Even POPIA refers to 'data subjects'; presumably because personal information subjects sounds a bit silly. And, in section 14(6)*(d)* a reference to 'personal data' slipped in.

1.2.4.2 What are the ten major functions of data management

DAMA International[23] has defined ten major functions of data management, and data governance is identified as a central function:

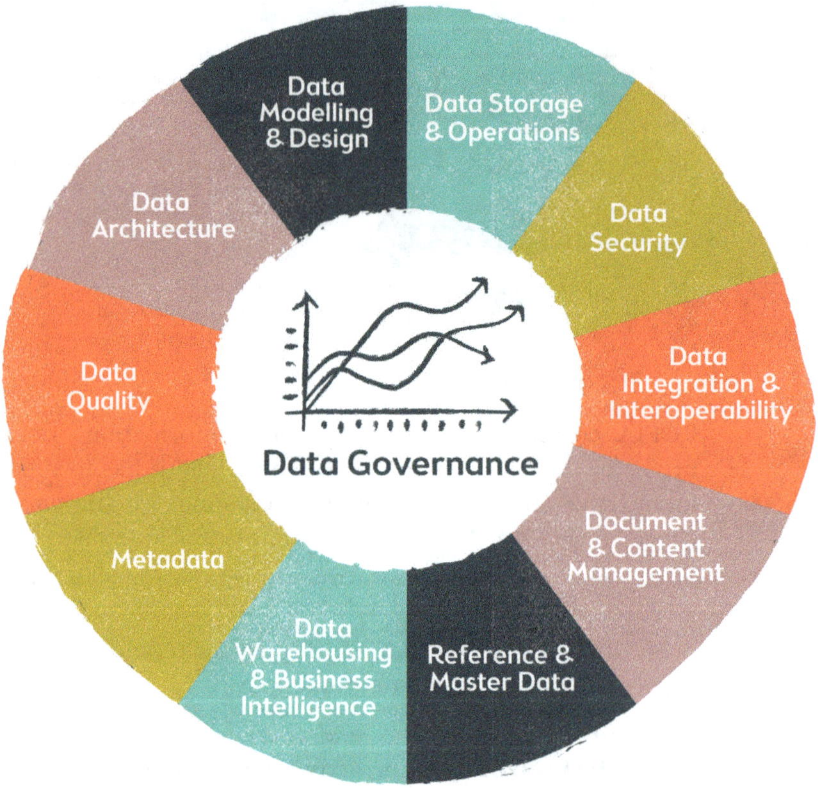

It is crucial that attorneys, compliance officers, information officers and their deputies learn to speak at least enough geek to recognise when a crucial part of the POPIA puzzle is missing. All ten of these functions have the potential to either aid in POPIA compliance, or, if done incorrectly, to frustrate POPIA compliance. However, some have a more direct impact than others. Here are the data governance functions that make POPIA compliance possible:

[23] DAMA stands for DAta MAnagement. Visit DAMA International's website here: https://www.dama.org/. They are responsible for the DAMA-MBOK (Data Management Book of Knowledge), a rather dramatic name.

Some definitions	What does it have to do with POPIA?
Data governance Data governance is defined as 'the exercise of authority, control and shared decision-making (planning, monitoring and enforcement) over the management of data assets'.[24]	Good data governance is a prerequisite for good information governance (see paragraph 1.2.3 above) as it ensures that the information compiled from data is of a high quality, and useful. There is an industry adage that reads 'garbage in, garbage out'.
Data security 'The planning, development, and execution of security policies and procedures to provide proper authentication, authorisation, access and auditing of data and information assets.'[25]	POPIA requires security safeguards. Information security management is discussed in chapter 5.
Data quality '[T]he planning, implementation, and control of activities that apply quality management techniques to data, in order to assure it is fit for consumption and meets the needs of data consumers.'[26] Dataversity lists the following 'data quality dimensions': • accuracy • completeness • consistency • integrity • reasonability • timeliness • uniqueness/deduplication • validity; and • accessibility.	POPIA requires information quality. This is discussed in chapter 9.

24 DAMA *The DAMA Dictionary of Data Management* (2008).

25 Dataversity *What is Data Security?* Available at https://www.dataversity.net/what-is-data-security/.

26 Dataversity *What is Data Quality?* Available at https://www.dataversity.net/what-is-data-quality/.

Some definitions	What does it have to do with POPIA?
Metadata Metadata 'includes information about technical and business processes, data rules and constraints, and logical and physical data structures.'[27] Put differently, metadata is '[d]ata about Data that unlocks the Who, How, Where, Why and What value of the data'. This quote from Dataversity is also useful: 'Think of it as a wrapper around data that describes it, like how packaging tells what food is in a box or container.' Dataversity lists three types of metadata: • Business metadata: It focuses on the content and condition of the data and defines terms in everyday language. • Technical metadata: It provides information about the format and structure of data for computer systems, e.g. 'physical database tables, access permissions, data models, backup rules, mapping documentation [and] data lineage'. • Operational metadata: It 'describes details of the processing and accessing of data', e.g. 'job execution logs, data sharing rules, error logs, audit results, various version maintenance plans, archive and retention rules'.	The term 'metadata' does not appear in POPIA. However, in order to demonstrate compliance with POPIA and to respond to data subject requests (discussed in chapter 18), organisations will have to document processing activities in a significant amount of detail. This is done, at least in part, through metadata management. Each chapter contains tips on documenting compliance.

➥

27 Dataversity *What is Metadata?* Available at https://www.dataversity.net/what-is-metadata/.

Some definitions	What does it have to do with POPIA?
Data architecture Data architecture 'includes specifications used to describe existing state, define data requirements, guide data integration, and control data assets as put forth in a data strategy'. It is often described as the bridge between business strategy and technical execution.[28] Here is a simpler definition, from Dataversity, attributed to Dr Peter Aiken: 'A set of rules, policies, and models that determine what kind of data gets collected, and how it gets used, processed and stored within a database system.'[29]	Data architecture is of significant strategic importance, but it also has practical value. One of the requirements of POPIA is to perform personal information impact assessments (PIIAs) (discussed in chapter 20). One of the steps in a PIIA is to describe the processing activity – this is done through data flow maps. Data architects are invaluable in this process.
Master and reference data Master data management is defined as 'control over Master Data values and identifiers that enable consistent use, across systems, of the most accurate and timely data about essential business entities'. This description from Dataversity's 2017 *Trends in Data Architecture Report* says it best: 'As more and more organizations struggle with obtaining a single, consistent view of core data such as Product, Customer, Vendor, and Location data, Master Data Management (MDM) is seeing a rise in implementation. Master Data Management is closely linked to other key initiatives … such as Data Governance and Data Quality, but is a practice in and of itself made up of diverse activities such as matching rules, gold record survivorship rules, and data migration or virtualisation.'[30]	POPIA's requirements in relation to information security (specifically integrity, which is discussed in chapter 5), data quality (discussed in chapter 9) and data subject requests (discussed in chapter 18) are almost impossible to achieve without some form of master data management, data integration and interoperability.

[28] Dataversity *What is Data Architecture?* Available at https://www.dataversity.net/what-is-dataarchitecture/.

[29] Dataversity *What is Data Architecture?* Available at https://www.dataversity.net/what-is-dataarchitecture/.

[30] Dataversity *What is Master Data Management?* Available at https://www.dataversity.net/whatis-master-data-management/. We discuss this concept in some detail in chapter 9 paragraph 9.6.5 in the context of the principles of minimality and information quality.

Some definitions	What does it have to do with POPIA?
Data integration and interoperability Integration 'refers to the process of combining multiple applications to function together as one uninterrupted system'. 'Interoperability refers to the basic ability of different computerised products or systems to readily connect and exchange information with one another.' In order to achieve this, the products or systems 'must be able to exchange, interpret, and present shared data in a way that is understood by the other. This is accomplished with the establishment of syntactic interoperability, which involves adopting a common data format and common data structure protocols, followed by semantic interoperability, which involves the addition of metadata that links each data element to a controlled, shared vocabulary.'[31]	

1.2.5 (Information) Technology governance

Technology governance is also known as information technology (IT) governance, but should it be?[32] In King IV 'it is recognised that information and technology overlap but are also distinct sources of value creation which pose individual risks and opportunities. It is to reinforce this distinction that [principle 12] in the King IV code now refers to technology *and* information instead of information technology.'[33]

Information governance was discussed in paragraph 1.2.3 above, but what is (information) technology governance? IT Governance 'is an element of corporate governance, aimed at improving the overall management of IT and deriving improved value from investment in information and technology'.[34] *CIO Magazine* defined it as follows:

---

31 Omni Sci 'Interoperability Definition', available at https://www.omnisci.com/technical-glossary/interoperability.

32 Alas, to learn more about technology governance it is still best to google IT governance.

33 *King IV Report on Corporate Governance for South Africa* (2016) 30.

34 www.itgovernance.co.uk is an enormously useful website on this topic. The definition of IT governance is available here: https://www.itgovernance.co.uk/it_governance. There are several IT governance frameworks: E.g. COBIT, ITIL and ISO 38500.

> 'Essentially, IT governance provides a structure for aligning IT strategy with business strategy. By following a formal framework, organisations can produce measurable results toward achieving their strategies and goals. A formal program also takes stakeholders' interests into account, as well as the needs of staff and the processes they follow. In the big picture, IT governance is an integral part of overall enterprise governance.'[35]

So, if privacy is part of information governance, does that mean that it has nothing to do with technology governance? No. Privacy is usually also one of the ethical principles that underpin the governance of technology. For instance, The Responsible Machine Learning Principles[36] include the 'trust by privacy' principle[37] which states that 'I commit to build and communicate processes that protect and handle data with stakeholders that may interact with the system directly and/or indirectly' and the 'data risk awareness' principle[38] which states that 'I commit to develop and improve reasonable processes and infrastructure to ensure data and model security are being taken into consideration during the development of machine learning systems'.

In addition, POPIA compliance is often enabled by technology. Specifically, section 19 requires that responsible parties put reasonable technical measures in place to secure the integrity and confidentiality of personal information. That said, it is a mistake to think of information security management as the exclusive domain of the IT department. Unfortunately, this mistake has led organisations to make POPIA compliance the IT department's responsibility. This is dangerous, for the following reasons:

- It affirms the mistaken impression that POPIA is just about protecting digital information from 'hackers'.[39] While cybersecurity is undoubtedly critical, there is a great deal more to POPIA than cybersecurity.
- Not all information risk can be mitigated through technology. In fact, high risk human behaviour is behind the lion's share of incidents. As Adrian Sanabria (one of the good hackers) put it '[t]he security problems we're now facing can't be fixed with

35 Kim Lindros 'What is IT governance? A formal way to align IT & business strategy' *CIO Africa*, available at https://www.cio.com/article/2438931/governanceit-governance-definition-and-solutions.html.

36 These were created by The Institute for Ethical Machine Learning. Read more about them at https://ethical.institute/principles.html.

37 Principle 7.

38 Principle 8.

39 There is a campaign to stop using the term 'hacker' pejoratively. You can read more about this campaign at https://www.hackingisnotacrime.org/.

products alone. We can't fix them with more security analysts any more than a retailer could fix shoplifting by assigning a security guard to watch every shopper as they wander around the store.' If your head of information security reports to the head of IT then there will be an inherent bias to either fix everything with an IT solution or to ignore the problem if it isn't IT related. Your head of Information Security should report to the risk committee instead to avoid these pitfalls.

- By relegating POPIA, and even information security, to IT you train your staff to think that it is not their responsibility, because 'someone else is taking care of it, right?'

Key point: POPIA supplements the role of the information officer (discussed in paragraph 1.3.5 below), which was first created by the Promotion of Access to Information Act (PAIA).[40] Before this, in 1980, the title of chief information officer was coined by William Synnott and William Gruber in their book *Information Resource Management: Opportunities and Strategies for the 1980s*. The title 'chief information officer' is now incredibly common and is usually the title of the head of the IT department.

This is problematic because it is difficult for employees, and the (chief) information officers themselves, to distinguish the one role from the other. This leads to misunderstandings and confusion about who is responsible for which aspects of POPIA compliance. Lastly, it leads to the absurd situation where a 'chief information officer' reports to an 'information officer'.

To avoid this Babylonian confusion, the title of the chief information officer should be changed to the chief technology officer or another title that best describes the role.

1.3 ROLES AND RESPONSIBILITIES WITHIN THE ORGANISATION

1.3.1 Roles and responsibilities at a glance

In risk and compliance management it is considered best practice to follow the three lines of defence model.[41] To properly comply

40 Act 2 of 2000.

41 We are aware that the three lines of defence model was broadened to the five lines of assurance model in King IV. The five lines are the board of directors, internal audit, specialist units (compliance officers, risk managers and the like), CEO and C-suite and work units (the business unit leaders). See Tim Leech and Conor Hanlon 'Three Lines of Defence versus Five Lines of Assurance:

with POPIA and manage POPIA risks, all three lines need to be functioning optimally.

This is how the three lines of defence model operates in the POPIA context:

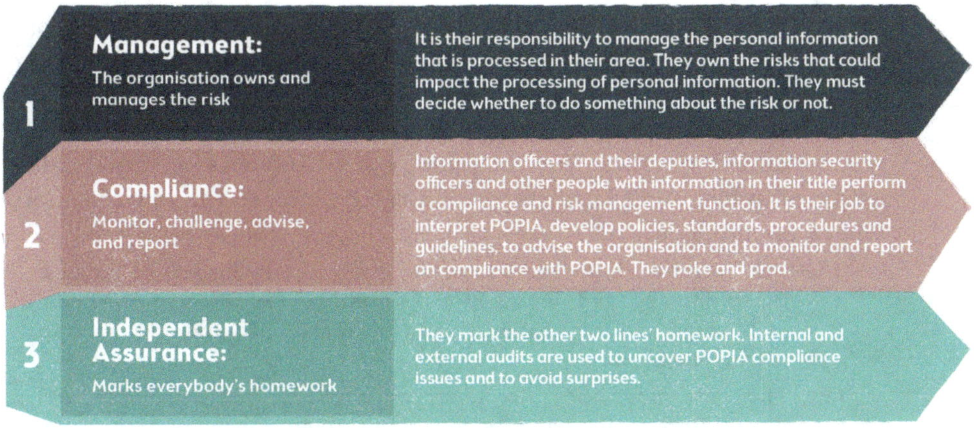

What is the role of the three lines in POPIA compliance?

1.3.2 The board (or other governing body)

In general, the role of a board (or other governing body) in compliance is 'to lead, control, and monitor the business of the organisation and to provide effective corporate governance, with the specific responsibility to oversee compliance with compliance obligations'.[42] In addition, principle 13 of King IV states that the board should 'govern compliance with applicable laws and adopt non-binding rules, codes and standards in a way that supports the organisation being ethical and a good corporate citizen'.[43]

This means that the board is ultimately accountable for compliance with POPIA even though it may delegate responsibility to the (POPIA) compliance function.[44] This principle was adopted in POPIA, as the information officer appointed by default in POPIA is the Chief Executive Officer (CEO) or 'head' of an organisation. The identity and responsibilities of the information officer are discussed in paragraph 1.3.5 below.

Elevating the Role of the Board and CEO in Risk Governance' in Richard Leblanc (eds) The Handbook of Board Governance: A Comprehensive Guide for Public, Private and Not for Profit Board Members (2016). So why still go with the three lines? It is just a little simpler for a POPIA book.

42 The Generally Accepted Compliance Practice framework ('GACP') 84.

43 *King IV Report on Corporate Governance for South Africa* (2016). See the recommended practices for compliance governance from 63.

44 The Generally Accepted Compliance Practice framework ('GACP') 91.

The task of monitoring compliance is usually delegated to an audit, compliance and risk committee(s). The information officer should have a reporting line into this committee(s), either directly or through the head of compliance.[45]

However, POPIA is not just about managing compliance risk; principle 12 of King IV states that 'the governing body should govern technology and information in a way that supports the organisation setting and achieving its strategic objectives'. King IV (at 62–63) lists the several recommended practices for technology *and* information governance, many of which will directly or indirectly impact the organisation's POPIA compliance:

> '10. The governing body should assume responsibility for the governance of technology and information by setting the direction for how technology and information should be approached and addressed in the organisation.
>
> 11. The governing body should approve policy that articulates and gives effect to its set direction on the employment of technology and information.
>
> 12. The governing body should delegate to management the responsibility to implement and execute effective technology and information management.
>
> 13. The governing body should exercise ongoing oversight of technology and information management and, in particular, oversee that it results in the following:
>
>   a. Integration of people, technologies, information and processes across the organisation.
>   b. Integration of technology and information risks into organisation-wide risk management.
>   c. Arrangements to provide for business resilience.
>   d. Proactive monitoring of intelligence to identify and respond to incidents, including cyber attacks and adverse social media events.
>   e. Management of the performance of, and the risks pertaining to, third-party and outsourced service providers.
>   f. The assessment of value delivered to the organisation through significant investments in technology and information, including the evaluation of projects throughout their life cycles and of significant operational expenditure.
>   g. The responsible disposal of obsolete technology and information in a way that has regard to environmental impact and information security.
>   h. Ethical and responsible use of technology and information.
>   i. Compliance with relevant laws.

[45] The Generally Accepted Compliance Practice framework ('GACP') 84.

14. The governing body should exercise ongoing oversight of the management of information and, in particular, oversee that it results in the following:
    a. The leveraging of information to sustain and enhance the organisation's intellectual capital.
    b. An information architecture that supports confidentiality, integrity and availability of information.
    c. The protection of privacy or personal information.
    d. The continual monitoring of security of information.
15. The governing body should exercise ongoing oversight of the management of technology and, in particular, oversee that it results in the following:
    a. A technology architecture that enables the achievement of strategic and operational objectives.
    b. The management of the risks pertaining to the sourcing of technology.
    c. Monitoring and appropriate responses to developments in technology, including the capturing of potential opportunities and the management of disruptive effects on the organisation and its business model.
16. The governing body should consider the need to receive periodic independent assurance on the effectiveness of the organisation's technology and information arrangements, including outsourced services.
17. The following should be disclosed in relation to technology and information:
    a. An overview of the arrangements for governing and managing technology and information.
    b. Key areas of focus during the reporting period, including objectives, significant changes in policy, significant acquisitions and remedial actions taken as a result of major incidents.
    c. Actions taken to monitor the effectiveness of technology and information management and how the outcomes were addressed.
    d. Planned areas of future focus.'

1.3.3 Management

This is how the GACP describes the role of management in compliance: 'Management are responsible for ensuring that compliance obligations are met on a day-to-day basis and that the organisation's compliance policy and framework are effectively implemented, supported and adhered to.'[46] By extension, it is the role of management to make sure that the organisation's POPIA obligations are met, that POPIA-related policies are followed, that PIIAs are performed and that employees receive adequate training and other support in the area of the organisation under their authority.[47] This is why management is referred to as the first line of

[46] The Generally Accepted Compliance Practice framework ('GACP') 38.

[47] POPIA-related policies and PIIAs are discussed in chapter 20.

defence in compliance and risk management. Management performs these tasks with the support of the information officer. Management must also report to the board on the level of compliance in their area.

Key point: It often comes as a surprise to management that they are responsible for day-to-day compliance and risk management. This indicates that the organisation has a low level of information governance maturity and should consider a compliance management project before it tackles POPIA. The impact of low information governance maturity is discussed in paragraph 1.2.3 above.

While management is ultimately accountable for compliance lapses in their areas, it is open to management to delegate the tasks involved in maintaining POPIA compliance to a subordinate(s). They are often referred to as custodians, data stewards or privacy champions.

1.3.4 Other employees

All employees are obligated 'to carry out their day-to-day duties and activities' in such a way 'that they adhere to compliance obligations that apply to their area of responsibility and implement the necessary controls to ensure compliance'.[48] In other words, all employees have a responsibility to follow the organisation's policies, procedures, processes and practices. This is why regulation 4(1)*(d)* of the POPIA Regulations prescribes that information officers must ensure that internal awareness sessions are conducted.[49]

1.3.5 Information officer

POPIA supplements the role of the information officer, which was first created by PAIA. In the case of a private body, the information officer will be the 'head' of the private body. 'Head' is defined in section 1 of PAIA. In the case of a juristic person this will be the 'chief executive officer or equivalent officer of the juristic person'.

In the case of a public body, the identity of the 'information officer' is determined by section 1 of PAIA. However, POPIA also states that the 'information officer' of a public body could also be a 'deputy information officer' designated in terms of section 17 of PAIA. Not confusing at all!

48 The Generally Accepted Compliance Practice Framework ('GACP') 40.

49 This obligation is discussed in chapter 20.

Tricky area: It is less than ideal that the information officer will by default also be the head of the public body or the CEO. Why was this a bad idea? An information officer cannot be a player and a referee. A CEO will often be involved in making decisions on behalf of a responsible part about how personal information will be processed. The role of a data privacy officer (as it is known in other parts of the world), is to assess these decisions. So what now?

Can the information officer appointed by law (e.g. the CEO of a juristic person) assign the role to someone else in the organisation? Some commentators have expressed the view that in the case of a private body, this is possible. This is due to the fact that the definition of 'head' in section 1 of PAIA provides that a person 'duly authorised' by the information officer can fulfil the role.[50]

The same is not true of an information officer of a public body.[51] However, in the case of a public body, the 'information officer' must designate 'such number of persons as are necessary to render the public body reasonably accessible' as deputy information officers in terms of section 17. The definition of 'information officer' in section 1 of POPIA provides that a deputy information officer appointed in terms of section 17 of PAIA, could be an information officer for purpose of POPIA.

If organisations cannot appoint an independent information officer, they should compensate for this conflict of interest by appointing independent deputy information officers, or by appointing a data privacy officer with a direct line to the governing body to 'guard the guardian' as Plato would say.

Even though the appointment of an information officer is automatic, section 55(2) of POPIA provides that the information officer must only take up their duties once they have been registered with the Information Regulator.[52]

[50] Francis Cronje & Eddie Laubscher *PAIA: What You Need to Know* (2016) 15.

[51] Francis Cronje & Eddie Laubscher *PAIA: What You Need to Know* (2016) 17.

[52] For a useful list of information officers of public bodies see Francis Cronje & Eddie Laubscher *PAIA: What You Need to Know* (2016) at Addendum K.

Key point: The Information Regulator developed a guidance note for the registration of information officers and deputy information officers.[53] See chapter 19 paragraph 19.4 for a discussion on the legal status of guidance notes.

Information officers have the following responsibilities:

Responsibilities of information officers	What does this responsibility mean?
Encourage compliance with POPIA.[54]	This is one of those 'catch all' responsibilities. It includes carrying out a risk assessment and developing, implementing and monitoring 'good policies, procedures and practices to protect personal information'.[55] Policy development and the types of policies required for POPIA compliance are discussed in chapter 20. In a sense, all of the other responsibilities of an information officer would fall under this umbrella.
Develop, implement, monitor and maintain a compliance framework.[56]	This firmly cements the place of the information officer in the so-called 'second line of defence', referred to in paragraph 1.3.1 above. In other words, information officers will employ many of the same strategies as a compliance officer. Compliance framework 'best practices' are discussed in detail in chapter 20.
Do a personal information impact assessment ('PIIA') to ensure that adequate measures and standards exist in order to comply with POPIA.[57]	The introduction of PIIAs in the POPIA Regulations is a welcome one indeed. It is akin to the Privacy Impact Assessments and Data Protection Impact Assessments in other jurisdictions. PIIAs are discussed in detail in chapter 20.
Conduct internal awareness sessions.[58]	Providing training is discussed in detail in chapter 20.

➡

53 They are available here: https://www.justice.gov.za/inforeg/docs/InfoRegSA-GuidanceNote-IO-DIO-20210401.pdf.

54 Section 55(1)*(a)*.

55 Section 109(3)*(g)*.

56 Regulation 4(1)*(a)* of the POPIA Regulations.

57 Regulation 4(1)*(b)* of the POPIA Regulations.

58 Regulation 4(1)*(c)* of the POPIA Regulations.

Responsibilities of information officers	What does this responsibility mean?
Develop internal measures and adequate systems to process data subject requests.[59]	The various types of data subject requests which an information officer might face are discussed in chapter 18.
Develop, monitor, maintain and make a PAIA manual available.[60]	The continued role of the PAIA manual is discussed in chapter 18.
Work with the Information Regulator in the event of an investigation for purposes of considering an application for prior authorisation.[61]	Applications for prior authorisation are discussed in chapter 8.

The information officer is part of the second line of defence. In other words, it is a compliance function. One of the implications of this is that the information officer must be independent. The GACP provides that '[t]he compliance function should be sufficiently independent of business activities to be able to discharge its responsibilities objectively'.[62] This is similar to how the role of the 'data protection officer' is described in the EU. The EU GDPR provides that the data protection officer (their equivalent of the information officer) must not 'receive any instructions regarding the exercise of [his or her] tasks' and 'should be in a position to perform their duties and tasks in an independent manner'.[63] The UK's Information Commissioner's Office (ICO) adds that the data privacy officer must perform their tasks 'without any conflicts of interest' and must not 'take any direct operational decisions about the manner and purposes of processing personal data' within the organisation.[64]

59 Section 55(1)*(b)* and regulation 4(1)*(d)* of the POPIA Regulations.

60 Regulation 4(1)*(e)* of the POPIA Regulations.

61 Section 55(1)*(c)*.

62 GACP 51.

63 Article 38(3) and recital 97. It can be useful to read guidelines on data protection officers (DPOs), but tread carefully. The EU GDPR is very different to POPIA in this respect. For instance, unlike POPIA, not all responsible parties have to appoint a DPO and the responsible party has a wider discretion about who to appoint. For guidelines on DPOs, see the Article 29 Data Protection Working Party's *Guideline on Data Protection Officers*, available at https://ec.europa.eu/newsroom/article29/item-detail.cfm?item_id=612048.

64 The ICO's *Accountability Framework* under 'appropriate reporting', available at https://ico.org.uk/for-organisations/accountability-framework/leadership-and-oversight/appropriate-reporting/.

Key point: The POPIA Regulations provide that the information officer must 'ensure' that a compliance framework is developed etc.[65] This does not mean that the information officer must do all of the work themselves. In fact, doing so may well compromise their independence. Instead, the information officer should provide advice to management on POPIA obligations, oversee implementation of compliance-related procedures (e.g. a personal information impact assessment procedure), report to the governing body on the level of compliance being achieved, liaise with the Information Regulator, resolve issues of non-compliance, assist with investigations and providing training.[66]

Much has been made about the potential for personal liability for information officers due to POPIA non-compliance.[67] Section 93*(b)* of POPIA provides that the enforcement committee can make recommendations about any 'action that should be taken against an information officer'. This sounds ominous for information officers, does it not? However, the bulk of the enforcement actions available to the Information Regulator will be aimed at the 'responsible party' and not the information officer of the responsible party.[68]

In addition, only certain types of non-compliance with POPIA and PAIA are offences and, in most cases, it is not the information officer that is mentioned, but 'any person'. These offences are listed in chapter 19 paragraph 19.10.1.

Of course, an information officer can be held personally liable by the organisation in terms of section 77 of the Companies Act 71 of 2008 which regulates civil claims against directors, prescribed officers, board committee members and members of the audit committee. In order to be successful, the organisation would have to show that the information officer did not meet the standard of conduct prescribed by the Companies Act or the common law.[69] The information officer may

65 Regulation 4(1) of the POPIA Regulations. This is discussed in chapter 20 paragraph 20.2.

66 The Generally Accepted Compliance Practice Framework ('GACP') 98.

67 The enforcement of POPIA is discussed in chapter 19.

68 For instance, administrative fines can only be levied against 'responsible parties' (section 109) and only the 'responsible party' is guilty of an offence if it fails to comply with an enforcement notice. Determining who the 'responsible party' is, is discussed in chapter 4. For more on the enforcement of POPIA, see chapter 19.

69 Section 76 of the Companies Act 71 of 2008 sets out the standard of conduct that can be expected from directors. Section 77 sets out the circumstances under which a director may be held personally liable.

potentially be liable for any loss, damages or costs sustained by the company – this could be a significant amount of money given the cost of the average data breach.

1.3.6 Deputy information officer

Section 17 of PAIA provides that information officers of public bodies 'must' appoint 'such number of persons as deputy information officers as are necessary to render the public body as accessible as reasonably possible' to data subjects. Section 56 of POPIA has made it possible for private bodies to designate deputy information officers too.

Tricky area: Is it mandatory to appoint a deputy information officer? In respect of public bodies, PAIA says that they 'must'.[70] Section 56 of POPIA, which applies to both public bodies and private bodies, provides that they must designate 'such number' of deputy information officers as is necessary to perform the duties of the information officer, but it also says 'if any'. So, it would appear that private bodies do not have to designate deputy information officers, if the information officer can discharge the duties. In respect of public bodies? Who knows. We are not asking who knows. We assume no one does.

We think for PAIA they must, but they don't necessarily have to appoint deputy information officers for POPIA.

POPIA provides that the deputy information officer 'performs' the duties of the information officer.[71]

Key point: The Information Regulator developed a guidance note for the registration of information officers and deputy information officers.[72] See chapter 19 paragraph 19.4 for a discussion on the legal status of guidance notes.

1.3.7 Independent assurance (internal and external audit)

The third line of defence in compliance management is independent assurance. POPIA itself requires that the information officer must

70 Section 17 of PAIA.

71 Section 56.

72 They are available here: https://www.justice.gov.za/inforeg/docs/InfoRegSA-GuidanceNote-IO-DIO-20210401.pdf.

ensure that a compliance framework is 'monitored and maintained'.[73] This is consistent with the principle in the GACP which states that '[t]he compliance function should ensure that it continually improves' through 'regular self-assessments and independent reviews'.[74] Self-assessment will probably not be enough; the information officer cannot mark his or her own homework. Independent reviews should be conducted, either by internal or external audit.

Once the reports are in, it is equally important to analyse the findings, do a root cause analysis to identify the reasons for adverse findings and to put plans in motion to address any shortcomings.

1.4 DOCUMENTING PROCESSING ACTIVITIES

In the coming chapters, it will become clear that behaving reasonably is at the heart of POPIA compliance. The words 'reasonable' and 'reasonably', appear 78 times in POPIA. What this means is that the context will determine what actions a responsible party should take to comply and that responsible parties should put themselves in a position where they can justify their actions, or inaction, when the Information Regulator launches an investigation.

In addition, section 17 of POPIA provides that responsible parties must keep a record of all processing activities under their control.

Here are examples of all the documents which an organisation can use to discharge this obligation:

Write it down!	What? Why?
A (POPIA) compliance framework	A compliance framework is where the organisation sets out its approach to the management of POPIA risks. It is not necessarily one document; it could be a collection of documents. Having said that, it is handy to have one place where all of the components of the approach are recorded. (POPIA) compliance frameworks are discussed in chapter 20.

➡

73 Regulation 4(1).

74 The Generally Accepted Compliance Practice framework ('GACP') 79.

Write it down!	What? Why?
Policies, procedures, standards and guidelines	Policies are where organisations agree what actions they will take to become compliant. They are often supported by procedures (how do we comply?), standards (what is required?) and guidelines. These documents are an important record of the organisation's approach to POPIA compliance. Policy development is discussed in chapter 20.
Agreements	Operator agreements, data protection clauses and other agreements aimed at regulating the responsibility for personal information shared between organisations are an important record of information sharing. How to manage POPIA risks between organisations is discussed in chapter 4. Information sharing is discussed in chapter 13. Responsible parties should keep a record of all of the third parties with whom information is shared, what information was shared, why and how it was shared. This can be combined with a register of agreements that involve the sharing of personal information. Having a register of agreements is also an important aspect of contract management, which is essential for POPIA compliance. POPIA requirements relating to contract management and third-party risk management are discussed in chapter 4. It is equally important for organisations to know which version of their standard terms and conditions were in force at any given time. One of the justifications for the processing of personal information is that it was necessary for the conclusion or performance of a contract.[75] It will only be possible to rely on this justification if the organisation has a record of which version of the standard terms were in place. The six justifications for the lawful processing of personal information are discussed in chapter 6.

➡

75 Section 11(1)*(b)*.

Write it down!	What? Why?
Versions of forms and consents	Forms (digital, paper-based or call-centre scripts) are the primary tools organisations use to collect personal information. By keeping track of which version of a form was in use at what time, organisations can create a record of what personal information they were collecting at what time. The collection of personal information is discussed in chapter 10. An organisation's forms should also contain any consents which the organisation may be relying on. In addition to maintaining a record of the wording of the consents, organisations must keep a record of which data subjects consented, as well as when and how they consented. If an organisation is relying on consent, the onus will be on the organisation to prove that it was legally obtained.[76] Consent is discussed in chapter 2 paragraph 2.6.6.
Privacy notices[77]	Privacy notices are used to meet POPIA's notification requirements. They are used to record all of the information that an organisation is required to disclose to data subjects.[78] If an organisation has a record of which version of its privacy notice was in force at a certain time, it will have a record of what information was being collected, the purpose for which it was collected, any law authorising or requiring the collection of the information, etc. Even though POPIA does not require that privacy notices must record what legal basis the organisation is relying on to justify processing the personal information, it is an ideal place to keep a record of compliance with section 11. Section 11 is discussed in chapter 6.

➡

76 Section 11(1)*(a)* read with the definition of consent in section 1.

77 These are sometimes referred to as 'privacy policies'. We prefer 'privacy notice', because people confuse a privacy policy with an internal privacy policy aimed at achieving POPIA compliance in an organisation. Privacy notices are often public documents and are necessary to comply with POPIA's notification requirements.

78 Section 18(1). Section 18 is discussed in chapter 11.

Write it down!	What? Why?
All aspects of PIIAs	In addition to having a documented PIIA procedure, it is important that a meticulous record is kept of: • presentations • questionnaires and their answers • risks that were identified • decisions on how the risks would be treated and the plan to treat them • recommendations from the information officer for remedial steps • correspondence • minutes of meetings; and • reports. Personal information impact assessments are discussed in chapter 20.
Reports	Organisations must keep a record of any monitoring activities. For instance, any reports generated by the information officer as a result of a self-assessment and any audit reports generated by internal or external audit. In addition to keeping a record of reports, a record should be maintained of the actions which the organisation will take to remedy the shortcomings revealed in the reports.

Write it down!	What? Why?
Memoranda and minutes of meetings	There are always a myriad of ways to treat POPIA risks. As discussed earlier in this section, POPIA by and large requires organisations to act reasonably. In order to demonstrate reasonableness organisations will have to show what they considered when they made decisions relating to POPIA compliance and POPIA risks.[79] This means that organisations should keep a meticulous record of the information the organisation took into account when making decisions (e.g. memoranda, legal opinions, advice from the information officer and other advice) and how it weighed the options (recorded in the minutes of its meetings). Identifying and evaluating risk is discussed in chapter 20. **Key point:** If there is ever an investigation, the Information Regulator will issue an information notice (information notices are discussed in chapter 19 paragraph 19.6.8.2). The Information Regulator cannot compel an organisation to provide communication between a professional legal adviser and their client 'in connection with the giving of legal advice on the client's obligations, liabilities or rights' under POPIA or 'in connection with or in contemplation of proceedings under or arising' out of POPIA.[80] A 'professional legal adviser' is defined as 'any legally qualified person, whether in private practice or not, who lawfully provides a client, at his or her or its request with independent, confidential legal advice'.[81] This definition would cover legal advisers in private practice, in-house counsel[82] and legal consultants. If the contentious issues have to be discussed (e.g. a data breach), invite the legal adviser to ensure that the record of the meeting is confidential.

79 Identifying and evaluating risk is discussed in chapter 20.

80 Section 90(6).

81 See the definition of 'professional legal adviser' in section 1.

82 There have been several cases in which it was found that privilege attaches to in-house counsel. See *Van der Heever v Die Meester* 1997 (3) SA 93 (T) and *Mohamed v President of the Republic of South Africa* 2001 (2) SA 1145 (C).

Write it down!	What? Why?
Job descriptions and key performance indicators	Roles and responsibilities are discussed in paragraph 1.3 above. When responsibilities are given to a individual within the organisation, this should be documented in the person's job description and key performance indicators should be defined. This will enable the organisation to manage the individual's performance, to ensure that skills deficits are addressed and that the person has the infrastructure (e.g. hardware, software, equipment or tools) to perform the required tasks. Organisations should keep a record of all performance management activities.
Training	POPIA requires organisations to train their employees. This requirement is discussed in chapter 20. In order to demonstrate compliance with this requirement, a record must be kept of the content of the training, who was trained and when they were trained. Assessments and the results should also be documented along with any remedial steps that were taken after the assessment.
Data flow maps and ROPAs	Data flow maps are used to document the collection, use, transfer, archiving or destruction of personal information. This is also called 'Tracking the Data Lifecycle'.[83] It is an essential step in performing personal information impact assessments, but is also a way to document how personal information was processed at a certain time. Personal information impact assessments are discussed in chapter 20. See paragraph 20.3. In the EU GDPR this is referred to as 'Records of processing activities'. Article 30 provides that a responsible parties and operators must maintain a ROPA. The ICO put it in human: 'It's a legal requirement to document your processing activities. Taking stock of what information you have, where it is and what you do with it makes it much easier for you to improve your information governance and comply with other aspects of data protection law (such as creating a privacy notice and keeping personal data secure). It is a clear way to show what you are doing in line with the accountability principle.' FN: See the very helpful guide the ICO developed at https://ico.org.uk/for-organisations/accountability-framework/records-of-processing-and-lawful-basis/.

➡

83 Jeremy Berkowitz, Michael Mangold & Stephen Sharon 'Data flow maps—increasing data processing transparency and privacy compliance in the enterprise' (2017) 73(2) *Washington and Lee Law Review Online* 802, available at https://scholarlycommons.law.wlu.edu/wlulr-online/vol73/iss2/11.

Write it down!	What? Why?
Metadata	The importance of metadata management is discussed in paragraph 1.2.4 above. Sufficient information about personal information must be retained to ensure that the organisation can answer questions such as how (and where) the personal information was obtained, and who has accessed, used, changed, deleted, or done anything else with personal information. This is known as operational metadata.

1.5 PRACTICAL ADVICE

It is important to ensure that your organisation is mature enough for POPIA, before starting a POPIA project. The fastest way to measure how mature an organisation is, is to perform an information governance maturity assessment.[84]

It is also important to view POPIA in the context of all of the risks facing the organisation. If an organisation does not have an enterprise risk management function, the organisation may have more important problems than POPIA without knowing it. In this case, establishing an enterprise risk management function may be more important.

[84] See paragraph 1.2.3 above.

2

Laws and sausages: The purpose and interpretation of POPIA

2.1 WHAT TO EXPECT IN THIS CHAPTER

This is a very important chapter; do not skip it! In the words of Leo McGarry: 'There's two things in the world you never want to let people see how you make 'em: laws and sausages.'[1] POPIA is probably no different, but we have learnt quite a lot about sections we previously thought were just odd by looking at previous drafts and the discussion paper and report on Privacy and Data Protection of the SA Law Reform Commission.[2]

---

1 We are fans of *The West Wing*, so we will go with this version, but this quote is usually attributed to Otto von Bismarck, but apparently that is not correct either (see Joe Amrheim 'Quote ... misquote' *New York Times*, available at https://www.nytimes.com/2008/07/21/magazine/27wwwl-guestsafire-t.html).

2 The SA Law Reform Commission Project 124 on Privacy and Data Protection is comprised of a 2005 Discussion Paper (available at https://www.justice.gov.za/salrc/dpapers/dp109.pdf) and their 2009

In this chapter we discuss the following:

- POPIA as principle-based legislation
- What you can take into account when you do 'purposive interpretation'
- Considering international guidelines and foreign law
- The (competing) purposes of POPIA
- Key concepts in POPIA that bring balance to the force
- When POPIA and other South African legislation collide

2.2 POPIA AS PRINCIPLE-BASED LEGISLATION

We often hear legal professionals complain that POPIA is vague and difficult to interpret, because it is replete with terminology such as 'reasonable' and 'satisfactory safeguards'. This is not surprising; many jurisdictions regulate privacy through a set of principles.[3] These are the hallmarks of principle-based regulation:[4]

- It relies on general principles to guide conduct and decisions rather than detailed prescriptive rules and processes.
- It prescribes the outcomes (goals) organisations must achieve, rather than precisely how organisations get to those outcomes.
- Organisations are free to find the most efficient and effective way of achieving the outcomes.
- It allows organisations to comply with the spirit of the law through policies that not only comply with the legislation, but also meet the needs of the organisation.
- Ethics and the culture of an organisation play an important role in compliance.
- As a bonus, the uncertainty leaves legal professionals way, way outside of their comfort zones.

The strength of principle-based regulation lies in its flexibility and ability to respond to new issues without needing to amend the legislation. It is also an appropriate approach to regulation where compliance involves balancing competing interests, rights and obligations.

Report (available at https://www.justice.gov.za/salrc/reports/r_prj124_privacy%20and%20data%20protection2009.pdf). In this book we have referenced the 2009 Report.

3 SA Law Reform Commission Project 124 on Privacy and Data Protection (2009 Report) 158.

4 SA Law Reform Commission Project 124 on Privacy and Data Protection (2009 Report) 159.

Its weakness is that it is inherently uncertain and ambiguous and subject to (mis)interpretation. It is also difficult to predict how a regulator will interpret the principles in a particular context.[5]

Bearing this in mind, this chapter is designed to help you become better at interpreting POPIA convincingly. We start with section 3(3) where POPIA itself provides guidance by prescribing 'purposive interpretation'.

2.3 WHAT YOU CAN TAKE INTO ACCOUNT WHEN YOU DO 'PURPOSIVE INTERPRETATION'

Section 3(3) provides that POPIA must be interpreted to give effect to the purposes set out in section 2. POPIA's purpose is not to protect privacy to the exclusion of all other rights and interests. Rather, it requires the balancing of competing interests.

The purposive method of interpretation has been described as a method which 'attributes meaning to a legislative provision in the light of the purpose which it seeks to achieve in the context of the instrument of which it forms part'.[6] But, this does not give us licence to ignore the language in POPIA. Instead: 'This requires the interpreter to utilise the various methods and presumptions of legislative interpretation in order to find the best answer in the given case (and to take responsibility for their interpretation).'[7] This is confirmed in case law:

> 'Interpretation is the process of attributing meaning to the words in [...] legislation [...] having regard to the context provided by reading the particular provision or provisions in the light of the document as a whole and the circumstances attendant upon its coming into existence. [...] [C]onsideration must be given to the language used in the light of the ordinary rules of grammar and syntax; the context in which the provision appears; the apparent purpose to which it is directed and the material known to those responsible for its production. Where more than one meaning is possible each possibility must be weighed in the light of all these factors. The process is objective and not subjective. A sensible meaning is to be preferred to one that leads to insensible or unbusinesslike results or undermines the apparent purpose of the document. Judges must be alert to, and guard against, the temptation to substitute what they regard as reasonable, sensible or businesslike for the words actually used. To do so in regard to a statute or statutory instrument is to cross the divide between interpretation and legislation. [...] The "inevitable point of departure is the language of the provision itself", read in context and having regard to the purpose of the provision and the background to the preparation and production of the document.'[8]

---

5 SA Law Reform Commission Project 124 on Privacy and Data Protection (2009 Report) 159.

6 Du Plessis *Re-Interpretation of Statutes* (2002) 96.

7 Du Plessis 'The (re-)systematization of the canons of and aids to statutory interpretation' (2005) 122 *SALJ* 591 at 612.

8 *Natal Joint Municipal Pension Fund v Endumeni Municipality* 2012 (4) SA 593 (SCA) paragraph 16.

The table below contains some things to think about when interpreting POPIA:

What you can take into account	Where you can find it
The language used in the legislation	Start with the language, because it is important. Guard against substituting what the legislation says with what you wish it said.[9] Read the language in light of the purpose of POPIA. If the purpose or the language is unclear, then look at the context – the context will often explain the purpose of the legislation.
The Constitution	The Constitution acts as a tie-breaker: Where there is more than one plausible interpretation, the 'one which brings the legislation within constitutional bounds must be preferred'.[10] However, in the case of POPIA, this is not an easy task given that there will often be conflicting rights involved. This is discussed in paragraph 2.5 below.
The purpose of the legislation	To apply purposive interpretation, one has to have a very firm grasp of the purposes of POPIA (see paragraph 2.5 below).
The context in which the specific provision appears	In the chapters to come, provisions of POPIA will be put in their proper context. IMHO.
The material known to those responsible for its production	An example of material known to the drafters is the SA Law Reform Commission Project 124 on Privacy and Data Protection, which contains the research which informed POPIA and the first draft of the Bill.[11]
International guidelines and foreign law	We discuss the use of international guidelines and foreign law as an aid to interpreting POPIA in paragraph 2.4 below.

9 There is a form of POPIA denial which people suffer from where they maintain that the legislation cannot possibly mean what it says, because it would put an end to a business practice. Privacy activists sometimes suffer from the same affliction - the legislation can't possibly protect rights and interests other than privacy. Our mothers and the Constitution would say to both sides 'too much of a good thing...'

10 *Daniels v Campbell* 2004 (5) SA 331 (CC).

11 SA Law Reform Commission Project 124 on Privacy and Data Protection (2009 Report).

2.4 CONSIDERING INTERNATIONAL GUIDELINES AND FOREIGN LAW

Data protection and privacy has been on the global agenda since the 1890s.[12] The question is to what extent we can learn from the experiences in other jurisdictions?

Section 44(1)*(d)* provides that the Information Regulator must 'consider any developing general international guidelines relevant to the better protection of individual privacy'. In addition, section 39(1) of the Constitution provides that when interpreting the Bill of Rights (which includes the right to privacy[13]), courts, tribunals or forums 'must consider international law' and 'may consider foreign law'.[14] Considering other jurisdictions is part and parcel of the purposive approach to interpretation. [15]

But perhaps the most persuasive argument for taking international guidelines and foreign law into account when interpreting POPIA is that the SA Law Reform Commission took international guidelines and foreign law into account when producing the first Bill. In fact, ensuring that POPIA is consistent with international instruments and foreign law was one of the Law Commission's priorities when they drafted the Bill. The SA Law Reform Commission emphasised that

> '[p]rivacy is therefore an important trade issue, as information privacy concerns can create a barrier to international trade. Considering international trends and expectations, information privacy or data legislation will ensure South Africa's future participation in the information market, if it is regarded as providing "adequate" information protection by international standards'.[16]

The reference to 'adequacy' here refers to the article in the EU Data Protection Directive[17] that dealt with transfers of personal information to other countries. In the Data Protection Directive, transfers were permissible if the country provided an 'adequate level of protection'.[18] It looks like the SA Law Reform

---

12 For a brief history of privacy, see this infographic: https://inplp.com/latest-news/article/a-brief-history-of-data-protection-how-did-it-all-start/.

13 Section 14 of the Constitution of the Republic of South Africa, 1996.

14 Section 39(1) of the Constitution.

15 Du Plessis 'The (re-)systematization of the canons of and aids to statutory interpretation' (2005) 122 *SALJ* 591 at 612.

16 SA Law Reform Commission Project 124 on Privacy and Data Protection (2009 Report) vii.

17 This is the predecessor of the EU GDPR. Directive 95/46/EC of the European Parliament and of the Council of 24 October 1995 on the protection of individuals with regard to the processing of personal data and on the free movement of such data (the Data Protection Directive).

18 Article 25(2). There were also other legal bases which a data controller could rely on in the event that the levels of protection were not adequate (see article 26). Under the EU GDPR, it is still permissible to transfer personal information to another country where the European Commission has decided that that country provides 'adequate levels of protection'; article 45 of the EU GDPR. The list of countries that are providing 'adequate protection' according to the European Commission can

Commission wanted to ensure that the levels of protection in South Africa would be adequate, which explains why the wording of POPIA is so close to the Data Protection Directive's wording in many instances.

Tricky area: The Data Protection Directive had a significant impact on the drafting of POPIA. However, the Data Protection Directive has since been replaced by the General Data Protection Regulation (the EU GDPR).[19] Which one should we take into account when interpreting POPIA? Project 124 was published in 2009. The European Commission's first communication on the reform of the Data Protection Directive was published in 2010.[20] POPIA was only enacted in 2013, which means that the drafters would have had the benefit of seeing the reforms taking place in Europe. In this book we attach some weight to the interpretation of those 'articles' (sections) in the EU GDPR where the wording corresponds closely to sections in POPIA. Those articles also tend to be the ones that were not changed fundamentally by the EU GDPR. Where a section of POPIA closely corresponds with the Data Protection Directive, we attached some weight to how the Directive was interpreted before it was replaced by the EU GDPR.

The SA Law Reform Commission did not only take the EU Data Protection Directive into account. Here are some of the other international instruments which feature in Project 124:[21]

- The Council of Europe's 1981 Convention for the Protection of Individuals with regard to the Automatic Processing of Personal Data.
- The 1981 Organization for Economic Cooperation and Development's Guidelines Governing the Protection of Privacy and Transborder Data Flows of Personal Data.
- United Nations Guidelines Concerning Computerised Personal Data Files (adopted on 14 December 1990) (since then the UN adopted the Personal Data Protection and Privacy Principles).

---

be found here: https://ec.europa.eu/info/law/law-topic/data-protection/international-dimension-data-protection/adequacy-decisions_en. Section 72 of POPIA deals with 'transborder information flows', but there is no provision for 'adequacy decisions' by the Information Regulator. Transborder information flows are discussed in chapter 14.

19 Project 124 was published in 2009. The European Commission's first communication on the reform of the Data Protection Directive was published in 2010.

20 European Commission *Communication from the Commission to the European Parliament, the Council, the Economic and Social Committee and the Committee of the Regions on 'A comprehensive approach on personal data protection in the European Union'* COM (2010) 609 final, available at https://eur-lex.europa.eu/LexUriServ/LexUriServ.do?uri=COM:2010:0609:FIN:EN:PDF.

21 SA Law Reform Commission Project 124 on Privacy and Data Protection (2009 Report) from 618.

The SA Law Reform Commission also considered the laws of the following jurisdictions:[22]

- United States of America
- Great Britain and Northern Ireland
- The Netherlands
- New Zealand
- Canada; and
- Commonwealth of Australia.

The fact that South Africa was behind in the data protection race did not mean that we blindly relied on the experiences of other countries when drafting POPIA. Here are some of the things the SA Law Reform Commission took into account when evaluating data protection in other jurisdictions:[23]

- the country's legal framework and whether privacy is recognised as an existing right
- cultural attitudes towards openness, privacy and the role of the government
- historical events that may have shaped the public's attitude to privacy; and
- the size of the population.

2.5 THE (COMPETING) PURPOSES OF POPIA

People skip the long title and preamble of legislation, but these can often provide insight into the soul of the legislation. POPIA's preamble contains what one might expect – references to section 14 of the Constitution (the right to privacy) and an explanation that the right to privacy 'includes a right to protection against the unlawful collection, retention, dissemination and use of personal information'.

The Constitution also provides that 'consonant with the constitutional values of democracy and openness, the need for economic and social progress, within the framework of the information society,[24] requires the removal of unnecessary

[22] SA Law Reform Commission Project 124 on Privacy and Data Protection (2009 Report) from 620.

[23] SA Law Reform Commission Project 124 on Privacy and Data Protection (2009 Report) 616.

[24] What is this 'information society'? IBM defines it as '[a] society characterised by a high level of information intensity in the everyday life of most citizens, in most organisations and workplaces; by the use of common or compatible technology for a wide range of personal, social, educational and business activities, and by the ability to transmit, receive and exchange digital data rapidly between places irrespective of distance'. See the IBM Community Development Foundation *The Net Result – Report of the National Working Party for Social Inclusion*. A project team in the Presidential National Commission on Information Society and Development (established in 2001)

impediments to the free flow of information, including personal information'. It goes on to provide that the right to privacy is subject 'to justifiable limitations that are aimed at protecting other rights and important interests'. Section 2*(a)* of POPIA provides that these justifiable limitations are aimed at 'balancing the right to privacy against other rights, particularly the right to access to information' and 'protecting important interests, including the free flow of information within the Republic and across international borders'.

The Information Regulator is required to take these competing purposes into account when exercising its functions. Section 44(1)*(b)* provides that the Information Regulator must 'have due regard for the protection of all human rights and social interests that compete with privacy, including the general desirability of a free flow of information and the recognition of the legitimate interests of public and private bodies in achieving their objectives in an efficient way'. Yes, the Regulator *must* take commercial objectives into account too.

In summary, these are the (competing) purposes of POPIA:

Protect the constitutional right to privacy including the unlawful collection, retention, dissemination and use of personal information.[25]	Economic and social progress (within the framework of the information society) which requires access to information and the free flow of personal information.[26] The interests of public and private bodies in achieving their objectives (yes, even the commercial ones) in an efficient way.[27]

➡

developed the National Information Society and Development Plan. The plan was referenced in the SA Law Reform Commission Project 124 on Privacy and Data Protection. This was the precursor to POPIA. If you are still reading this footnote, welcome to Nerdvana. Yes, we nerds will eventually inherit the Earth.

25 POPIA's preamble.

26 Section 2*(a)*.

27 Section 44(1)*(b)*.

	The public interest in: • freedom of expression[28] • national security[29] • the prevention, detection and prosecution of offences[30] • public health and safety[31] • research;[32] and • important economic and financial interests of a public body.[33]

2.6 KEY CONCEPTS IN POPIA THAT BRING BALANCE TO THE FORCE

It is safe to say that the drafters of POPIA knew they needed to balance data subject rights with other rights, the interests of the public, the public sector and even the private sector. There is evidence of the weighing exercise required to balance these seemingly competing purposes throughout POPIA. Even before POPIA was drafted, the South Africa Law Commission acknowledged this:

> 'In protecting a person's personal information consideration should, therefore, also be given to competing interests such as the administering of national social programmes, maintaining law and order, and protecting the rights, freedoms and interests of others, including the commercial interests of industry sectors such as banking, insurance, direct marketing, health care, pharmaceuticals and travel services. The task of balancing these opposing interests is a delicate one.'[34]

---

28 Section 7(1) and 37(2)*(f)*. If the processing is solely for the purpose of journalistic, literary or artistic expression, POPIA will not apply if 'such an exclusion is necessary to reconcile, as a matter of public interest, the right to privacy with the right to freedom of expression'. Exclusions are discussed in chapter 3.

29 Section 6(1)*(c)* and section 37(2)*(a)*. POPIA does not apply to processing by a public body that involves national security, but only if adequate safeguards have been established in legislation for the protection of the personal information being processed. Exclusions are discussed in chapter 3.

30 Section 37(2)*(b)*.

31 If the further processing of personal information is necessary to mitigate a serious and imminent threat to public health or safety or the life or health of a specific data subject, it will be allowed (without consent). Section 15(3)*(d)*. Further processing, i.e. processing personal information for a new or secondary purpose is discussed in chapter 12.

32 Section 37(2)*(e)*. There are also several examples where the principles of POPIA are relaxed when personal information is being used for 'historical, statistical or research purposes'. Here are some examples: records may be retained for longer (section 14(2)), further processing will be allowed (section 15(3)*(e)*), the data subject does not have to be notified (section 18(4)*(f)*) and the processing of special personal information or the personal information of a child will be allowed if it is in the public interest or it was impossible to ask for consent (sections 27(1)*(d)* and 35(1)*(d)*). For more on the impact of POPIA on research and biobanks, see Staunton & De Stadler 'Protection of Personal Information Act No. 4 of 2013: Implications for biobanks' (2019) 109(4) *South African Medical Journal* 232.

33 Section 37(2)*(c)*.

34 SA Law Reform Commission Project 124 on Privacy and Data Protection (2009 Report) vi.

There are key concepts aimed at performing this delicate balancing act, that form a golden thread that runs through POPIA:

- reasonableness and what could be considered reasonably practicable
- legitimate interests
- transparency
- the data subject's right to object; and
- consent.

2.6.1 The concept of reasonableness

The words 'reasonable' and 'reasonably', appear 78 times in POPIA. Probably the most important instance is in section 9 which states that '[p]ersonal information must be processed ... in a reasonable manner that does not infringe the privacy of the data subject'.[35] It is not just the responsible party that must be reasonable either. For instance, section 11(3)*(a)* provides that data subjects can object to certain types of processing, but only on 'reasonable grounds relating to his, her or its particular situation'. The right to object is discussed in chapter 18.

This of course begs the question of how 'reasonableness' will be evaluated by the Information Regulator and, eventually, by the courts.

It is important to recognise that POPIA did not introduce the right to privacy into South African law. Under the common law, the *actio iniuriarum* protects personality rights of which the right to privacy is one. The right to privacy was also enshrined in section 14 of the Constitution as a fundamental human right. In both instances, the right to privacy is not absolute.

Section 36(1) of the Constitution of South Africa provides that the right to privacy may only be limited (for instance, by POPIA) 'to the extent that the limitation is reasonable and justifiable in an open and democratic society based on human dignity, equality and freedom'. When determining whether a limitation is constitutional, all relevant factors must be taken into account, including:

- the nature of the right
- the importance of the purpose of the limitation
- the nature and extent of the limitation
- the relationship between the limitation and its purpose; and
- whether there were less restrictive means to achieve the purpose.

If we accept that all processing of personal information is an infringement of a person's privacy, then all processing should be measured

[35] Section 9*(b)*.

against these factors to determine whether it is justifiable. In other words, the entirety of POPIA is an exercise in determining whether the infringement of a person's privacy is reasonable. Ultimately, this comes down to the assessment of the necessity and proportionality of the processing of personal information for a specific purpose. These principles are not only relevant when assessing the constitutionality of a law that limits the right to privacy; they also feature in the South African common law as defences to claims for infringing a person's privacy.[36] The case law relating reasonableness in the context of section 36(1) and the common law inform each other, because the Constitution provides that when a court interprets any legislation or develops the common law, the 'spirit, purport and objects of the Bill of Rights' must be taken into account by the court.[37]

In the EU GDPR these principles are also not just used to assess the constitutionality of data protection legislation; data protection impact assessments (DPIA) must include 'an assessment of the necessity and proportionality of the processing operations in relation to the purposes'.[38] Over the years many guidelines have been developed to assess necessity and proportionality.[39] The ICO lists the following two main considerations:[40]

- Will the processing that you plan to do achieve your purpose for processing the personal information?[41]
- Is there any other reasonable [there is that word again] way to achieve the same result?

The second question is reminiscent of one of the factors considered in section 36(1) of the Constitution which considers whether 'there are less restrictive means to achieve the purpose'. This lies at the heart of necessity and proportionality and was written into POPIA as the

Chapter 2

---

36 SA Law Reform Commission Project 124 on Privacy and Data Protection (2009 Report) 26.

37 Section 39(2) of the Constitution.

38 Article 35(7)*(b)*. POPIA also requires personal information impact assessments, but provides no guidance on what they must include. PIIAs are discussed in chapter 20.

39 Article 29 Data Protection Working Party *Guidelines on Data Protection Impact Assessment (DPIA)*, Annexure A, available at https://ec.europa.eu/newsroom/article29/item-detail.cfm?item_id=611236; European Data Protection Supervisor 'EDPS Guidelines on assessing the proportionality of measures that limit the fundamental rights to privacy and to the protection of personal data', available at https://edps.europa.eu/sites/edp/files/publication/19-12-19_edps_proportionality_guidelines_en.pdf.

40 ICO 'How do we do a DPIA?', available at https://ico.org.uk/for-organisations/guide-to-data-protection/guide-to-the-general-data-protection-regulation-gdpr/data-protection-impact-assessments-dpias/how-do-we-do-a-dpia/#how9. See step 4.

41 You will see that the principle that personal information must only be collected for a 'specific, explicitly defined and lawful purpose' is at the heart of POPIA compliance. This is discussed in chapter 6.

principle of minimality (or data minimisation, as it is known in other jurisdictions), which states that '[p]ersonal information may only be processed if, given the purpose for which it is processed, it is adequate, relevant and not excessive'.[42]

2.6.2 What is reasonably practicable?

So far, we have discussed the general role of 'reasonableness' in POPIA. There are also multiple instances in POPIA where responsible parties will be held to what amounts to a 'reasonableness' standard when it comes to the implementation of specific principles. Here are some examples:

- A responsible party must take 'appropriate, reasonable technical and organisational measures' to secure personal information.[43]
- The principle that personal information must be collected directly from the data subject, does not apply if 'compliance is not reasonably practicable in the circumstances'.[44]
- A responsible party must destroy or delete personal information as soon as 'reasonably practicable' if the responsible party no longer has a legal or operational need to retain it.[45]
- A responsible party must take 'reasonably practicable steps' to ensure that the personal information is 'complete, accurate, not misleading and updated when necessary'.[46]
- A responsible party must take 'reasonably practicable steps' to notify the data subject of its processing activities.[47]
- A responsible party must also respond to data subject requests as 'soon as reasonably practicable'.[48]
- Section 99 deals with civil actions for damages resulting from a breach of certain sections of POPIA.[49] This liability attaches 'whether or not there is intent or negligence', but it is a defence if 'compliance was not reasonably practicable in the circumstances of the particular case'.

---

[42] Section 10. Minimality is discussed in chapter 9.

[43] Section 19(1). Information security management is discussed in chapter 5.

[44] Section 12(2)*(f)*.

[45] Section 14(4). Records management is discussed in chapter 17.

[46] Section 16(1). Information quality is discussed in chapter 9.

[47] Section 18(1). Notification is discussed in chapter 11.

[48] Section 24(2). Data subject rights are discussed in chapter 18.

[49] Section 99(1). Enforcement is discussed in chapter 19.

How do we determine what is reasonably practicable? POPIA does not give guidance on this question, apart from section 19 which relates to security safeguards. There, a risk-based approach is prescribed.[50] Another hint appears in section 109(3) which provides factors when the Information Regulator is considering an appropriate fine.[51]

South African courts have considered the concept of 'reasonably practicable' already, particularly in the area of health and safety. In *Pikitup (SOC) Ltd v SA Municipal Workers Union on behalf of Members & Others*[52] the Labour Appeal Court had to consider what 'reasonably practicable' meant in the context of the Occupational Health and Safety Act (OHSA).[53] The OHSA defines 'reasonably practicable' as:

> 'practicable having regard to–
> *(a)* the severity and scope of the hazard or risk concerned;
> *(b)* the state of knowledge reasonably available concerning that hazard or risk and of any means of removing or mitigating that hazard or risk;
> *(c)* the availability and suitability of means to remove or mitigate that hazard or risk; and
> *(d)* the cost of removing or mitigating that hazard or risk in relation to the benefits deriving therefrom[.]'

We can adapt this definition 'reasonably practicable' to POPIA to read:

> 'practicable having regard to–
> *(a)* the severity and scope of the data protection or privacy risk concerned;
> *(b)* the state of knowledge reasonably available concerning that data protection or privacy risk and of any means of removing or mitigating that hazard or risk;
> *(c)* the availability and suitability of means to remove or mitigate that data protection or privacy risk; and
> *(d)* the cost of removing or mitigating that data protection or privacy risk in relation to the benefits deriving therefrom[.]'

The *Pikitup* case also balanced the right of privacy of the workers with the need of the employer to ensure that its workers were sober while at work. The court cited the Canadian case of *Communications, Energy and Paperworkers Union of Canada v Irving Pulp & Paper, Limited* where the Canadian Supreme Court held that the imposition of a breathalyser test 'effects a loss of liberty and personal autonomy. These are at the heart of the right to privacy'.[54] As a result it rejected the employer's submission that breathalyser tests were the only

50 Section 19(2). Information security management is discussed in chapter 5.

51 Section 109(3)*(f)*. These factors are discussed in chapter 19 paragraph 19.10.3.

52 (2014) 35 *ILJ* 983 (LAC).

53 Act 85 of 1993.

54 2013 SCC 34 at paragraphs 49–50, available at https://scc-csc.lexum.com/scc-csc/scc-csc/en/item/13106/index.do.

'reasonably practicable' measure that it could take to ensure that its employees were sober as the intrusion into the data subject's privacy was too great.

In summary, we would argue that what is reasonably practicable should be considered against the following factors:

- Can the responsible party demonstrate that it performed a personal information impact assessment (PIIA) on the processing activity? Responsible parties should not rely on the defence that compliance was not reasonably practicable after the fact.[55] If it was impossible to perform a PIIA before processing takes place (e.g. it was an emergency), responsible parties should document why it was not possible as soon as they can.
- Can the responsible parties justify why it did not apply for an exemption in terms of section 37?[56]
- The risk posed to data subjects by the processing activity. This will often be determined by the type of personal information involved, the number of data subjects impacted and the likelihood of substantial damage or distress.[57]
- Any benefit to the data subject or public interest which is served by the processing activity.[58]
- The availability of technical or other measures to address the risk. In section 109(3)*(f)* the Regulator is required to consider whether the responsible party or a third party could have prevented the contravention.
- The cost of compliance for the responsible party. This will probably be controversial, but in some instances, the cost of compliance may be prohibitive. This argument is likely to be successful only in instances where non-compliance does not pose a substantial risk of damage or distress.[59]

---

55 Personal information impact assessments are prescribed in regulation 4(1)*(b)* of the POPIA Regulations. They are discussed in chapter 20.

56 Section 37. Exemptions are discussed in chapter 3.

57 These factors are all relevant when determining an appropriate fine in terms of section 109(3).

58 As discussed in paragraph 2.5, public interests carry a lot of weight.

59 Benefit to the data subject or a third party which outweighs interference with the privacy rights of the data subject is also a requirement for granting an exemption. Exemptions are discussed in chapter 3.

- Whether complying with the provision would hinder the 'free flow of information and the recognition of the legitimate interests of public and private bodies in achieving their objectives in an efficient way'.[60]

This last consideration brings us to the next concept that runs through POPIA: the limitation of the right to privacy by 'legitimate interests'.

2.6.3 Taking legitimate interests into account

The SA Law Reform Commission said it best:

> 'Any information privacy legislation will [...] have to find a balance between the data subject's fundamental right to privacy as set out in [section 14] of the Constitution on the one hand, and on the other hand, other persons' legitimate needs to obtain information about the data subject. These needs may be based on the person or institution's fundamental right to choose their trade, occupation or profession freely, their fundamental right to access to information, their fundamental right to freedom of expression, as well as other legitimate interests or rights.'[61]

The concept of 'legitimate interest' features prominently in POPIA. Here are some examples:

- Protecting the legitimate interest of the data subject is one of the lawful reasons to process personal information.[62]
- If a responsible party is processing personal information to pursue its own legitimate interests, or even that of a third party, the processing will also be lawful.[63]
- The principle that personal information must be collected directly from the data subject does not apply if collecting the information from another source 'would not prejudice a legitimate interest of the data subject' or if it is 'necessary to maintain the legitimate interests of the responsible party or of a third party'.[64]
- A responsible party does not have to notify a data subject of its processing activities if, 'non-compliance would not prejudice the legitimate interests of the data subject as set out in terms of this Act'.[65]

---

60 Section 44(1)*(b)*.

61 SA Law Reform Commission Project 124 on Privacy and Data Protection (2009 Report) 16.

62 Section 11(1)*(d)*. Having a legal justification for processing personal information is discussed in chapter 6.

63 Section 11(1)*(f)*. Having a legal justification for processing personal information is discussed in chapter 6.

64 Section 12(2)*(c)* and *(d)*(v). Collection is discussed in chapter 10.

65 Section 18(4). Notification is discussed in chapter 11.

- The Information Regulator must take 'the legitimate interest of public and private bodies in achieving their objectives in an efficient way' into account when exercising its powers.[66]
- The Information Regulator may extend the requirement of prior authorisation to more types of processing if the processing 'carries a particular risk for the legitimate interests of the data subject'.[67]
- Codes of conduct must protect the legitimate interests of data subjects when responsible parties use their personal information for automated decision-making.[68]

All of the examples above either involve the legitimate interest of:

- the data subject
- the responsible party; or
- of a third party.

Most of the discussion around what constitutes a legitimate interest has happened in the context of determining a legal basis for processing.[69]

> **Tricky area:** Some of the recitals to and commentary on the EU GDPR and its predecessor provide some guidance on what could constitute a legitimate interest, but these should be treated with care, because the EU GDPR wording is not identical to POPIA.

When it comes to the legitimate interest of the data subject, the EU GDPR refers to a 'vital' interest.[70] This is interpreted as an interest 'which is essential for the life of the data subject'.[71] Here are some examples:

- 'matters of life and death' such as sharing medical history with emergency responders when an individual has suffered life-threatening injuries[72]
- '[p]rocessing which is necessary for humanitarian purposes, including for monitoring epidemics and their spread';[73] and

66 Section 44(1)*(b)*.

67 Section 57(2). Prior authorisation is discussed in chapter 8.

68 Sections 60(4)*(a)*(ii) and 71(2)*(a)* and *(b)*. Automated decision-making is discussed in chapter 15.

69 Section 11(1)*(d)* and *(f)* of POPIA and article 6(1)*(d)* and *(f)* of the EU GDPR. Lawfulness is discussed in chapter 6.

70 Article 6(1)*(d)*.

71 Recital 46 of the EU GDPR.

72 ICO 'Vital Interests', available at https://ico.org.uk/for-organisations/guide-to-data-protection/guide-to-the-general-data-protection-regulation-gdpr/lawful-basis-for-processing/vital-interests/.

73 Recital 46 of the EU GDPR.

- 'situations of humanitarian emergencies, in particular in situations of natural and man-made disasters'.[74]

Of course, POPIA does not use the word 'vital', but rather 'legitimate'. The concept of a 'legitimate interest' of the data subject is broader than a 'vital interest'. In other words, a legitimate interest will not necessarily be a vital one. For instance, the processing may benefit the data subject financially, make products or services more accessible or more suited to the needs of the data subject. All of these interests are 'legitimate', but not necessarily 'vital'. The question in these instances will be whether the data subject's interests outweigh the harm which may result from the infringement of the data subject's rights.

The legitimate interest of the responsible party or a third party also features as one of the legal justifications for processing personal information.[75] The following legitimate interests of responsible parties and third parties have been recognised in the context of the EU GDPR:[76]

- processing which is strictly necessary for the purposes of preventing fraud
- processing for direct marketing purposes
- transmitting personal data within a group of organisations for internal administrative processes
- processing for the purpose of ensuring network and information security
- unsolicited non-commercial messages, e.g. from political campaigns or charitable fundraising
- debt collection or enforcement of other legal claims
- preventing misuse of services or money laundering
- employee monitoring for safety or management purposes
- whistle-blowing schemes
- processing for historical, scientific or statistical purposes
- processing for research purposes (including marketing research); and
- collecting the preferences of customers in order to better personalise offers.

Chapter 2

---

74 Recital 46 of the EU GDPR.

75 Section 11(1)*(f)*. This is discussed in chapter 6.

76 Article 29 Data Protection Working Party *Opinion 06/2014 on the Notion of Legitimate Interests of the Data Controller under Article 7 of Directive 95/46/EC,* available at https://ec.europa.eu/justice/article-29/documentation/opinion-recommendation/files/2014/wp217_en.pdf.

Key point: In South Africa, some of these activities would be justifiable on the basis that they comply with an obligation imposed by law (section 11(1)*(c)*). When this is the case, it is not necessary to rely on a legitimate interest justification. Legal justifications and how to decide which one is most appropriate are discussed in chapter 6.

However, just because a responsible party or third party has a legitimate interest in the processing, does not necessarily mean that (for instance) the processing will be lawful for purposes of section 11(1). The responsible party or third party must still show that the limitation of the data subject's right to privacy is reasonable.[77]

Tricky area: In the EU GDPR, this was explicitly recognised by adding the qualification that a responsible party or third party cannot rely on a legitimate interest 'where such interests are overridden by the interests or fundamental rights and freedoms of the data subject which require protection of personal data, in particular where the data subject is a child'.[78] Under its predecessor, the Data Protection Directive, the legal justification was also 'subject to an additional balancing test against the data subject's rights and interests'.[79] This led to the development of legitimate interest assessments, or LIAs, which are used to perform this balancing act.[80] They require a three-step process where the responsible party first identifies the legitimate interest, then applies the necessity test and then does a balancing test.

Even though this assessment is not explicitly required in POPIA, we would argue that section 36 of the Constitution would also trigger such an assessment given that the data subject's right to privacy is being limited.[81] LIAs are a useful way to document that such an assessment was done.

---

77 Section 36 of the Constitution. See the discussion of the concept of reasonableness in paragraph 2.6.1.

78 Article 6(1)*(f)*. Legitimate interest cannot be used as a justification for the processing of the personal information of children. This is discussed in chapter 7 paragraph 7.5.

79 Article 7*(f)* of the Directive 95/46/EC of the European Parliament and of the Council of 24 October 1995 on the protection of individuals with regard to the processing of personal data and on the free movement of such data.

80 ICO 'Legitimate interests', available at https://ico.org.uk/for-organisations/guide-to-data-protection/guide-to-the-general-data-protection-regulation-gdpr/lawful-basis-for-processing/legitimate-interests/.

81 This balancing exercise is also discussed in paragraph 2.6.2 above.

The ICO produced the following helpful guideline for responsible parties to performing a legitimate interest assessment:

> 'First, identify the legitimate interest(s). Consider:
>
> - Why do you want to process the data – what are you trying to achieve?
> - Who benefits from the processing? In what way?
> - Are there any wider public benefits to the processing?
> - How important are those benefits?
> - What would the impact be if you couldn't go ahead?
> - Would your use of the data be unethical or unlawful in any way?
>
> Second, apply the necessity test. Consider:
>
> - Does this processing actually help to further that interest?
> - Is it a reasonable way to go about it?
> - Is there another less intrusive way to achieve the same result?
>
> Third, do a balancing test. Consider the impact of your processing and whether this overrides the interest you have identified. You might find it helpful to think about the following:
>
> - What is the nature of your relationship with the individual?
> - Is any of the data particularly sensitive or private?
> - Would people expect you to use their data in this way?
> - Are you happy to explain it to them?
> - Are some people likely to object or find it intrusive?
> - What is the possible impact on the individual?
> - How big an impact might it have on them?
> - Are you processing children's data?
> - Are any of the individuals vulnerable in any other way?
> - Can you adopt any safeguards to minimise the impact?
> - Can you offer an opt-out?'[82]

Tricky area: Many of the questions above refer to 'individuals'. Always remember that POPIA also includes juristic persons in the definition of 'data subject'. This means that the personal information of organisations will be protected by POPIA too.

82 ICO 'Legitimate interests', available at https://ico.org.uk/for-organisations/guide-to-data-protection/guide-to-the-general-data-protection-regulation-gdpr/lawful-basis-for-processing/legitimate-interests/.

2.6.4 Transparency

POPIA is in large part underpinned by the notion that if data subjects are given information about what their personal information will be used for and control in the form of privacy settings that allows them to opt in and out, they will protect themselves. After all, Bill Gates once wrote for Microsoft:[83]

> 'Users should be in control of how their data is used. Policies for information use should be clear to the user. Users should be in control of when and if they receive information to make best use of their time. It should be easy for users to specify appropriate use of their information including controlling the use of emails they send.'

This was echoed in the EU GDPR which explicitly states that the EU GDPR is based on control and certainty and that individuals 'should have control of their own personal data'.[84]

In POPIA 'control' is given back to data subjects by demanding transparency. Section 18 of POPIA contains an extensive list of information which must be disclosed to data subjects. The section requires a high degree of transparency from responsible parties, unless one of the exceptions apply. Notification to the data subject is discussed in chapter 11.

But will all this transparency actually do us any good? Probably not. Researchers at Carnegie Mellon found that it would take the average internet user 76 working days to read the privacy notices they encounter on the internet in a year.[85] Even if people had the time and motivation to read all of these privacy policies, they cannot protect themselves effectively. Behavioural economists have been pointing out for years that information overload has a negative effect on the quality of consumers' decision-making due to 'the limited capacity of the human mind to evaluate every possible alternative and calculate the corresponding results'.[86] In other words, while transparency is alluring, it may have a detrimental effect on consumer decision-making.[87] We are not saying that responsible

---

83 Bill Gates 'Bill Gates: Trustworthy Computing' *Wired* (17 January 2002).

84 Recital 7 of the EU GDPR.

85 Aleecia M McDonald & Lorrie Faith Cranor 'The cost of reading privacy policies' (2008) *A Journal of Law and Policy for the Information Society*, available at https://lorrie.cranor.org/pubs/readingPolicyCost-authorDraft.pdf.

86 Iain Ramsay *Consumer Law and Policy: Texts and Materials on Regulating Consumer Markets* 3 ed (2012) 59; Hanneke Luth *Behavioural Economics in Consumer Policy: The Economic Analysis of Standard Terms on Consumer Contracts Revisited* (2010) 48.

87 Michael J Trebilcock 'Rethinking consumer protection policy' in Charles E F Rickett & Thomas G W Telfer (eds) *International Perspectives on Consumers' Access to Justice* (2003) 75; Geraint Howells & Stephen Weatherill *Consumer Protection Law* 2 ed (2005) 64; Hanneke Luth *Behavioural Economics*

parties should not be transparent, but merely that regulators should not fall for the fallacy that data subjects can protect themselves as long as they are well-informed. On the contrary, over-notification by the responsible party often simply results in the data subject ignoring the notification entirely.

2.6.5 The right to object

Similarly, we are wary of the ability of data subjects to protect themselves by exercising their right to object or opt out of processing.[88] Here are the instances where POPIA provides the data subject with an opportunity to object:

- If the responsible party is relying on one of the following grounds to justify the processing: *(a)* processing is necessary for pursuing the legitimate interest of the responsible party or a third party to whom the personal information is supplied, *(b)* processing protects a legitimate interest of the data subject; or *(c)* processing is necessary for the proper performance of a public law duty by a public body.[89]
- If the responsible party is using the personal information for direct marketing via telephone or other non-electronic communication channels.[90]
- If the responsible party is sending electronic direct marketing to its customers, they must (amongst other requirements), be given an opportunity to unsubscribe when their information is collected and each time they are contacted.[91]
- If the responsible party is not a spiritual or religious organisation (or an organisation founded on religious or spiritual beliefs), but is processing personal information relating to the data subject's religion or spiritual beliefs.[92]

---

in Consumer Policy: The Economic Analysis of Standard Terms on Consumer Contracts Revisited (2010) 36; Iain Ramsay *Consumer Law and Policy: Texts and Materials on Regulating Consumer Markets* 3 ed (2012) 101; PN Stoop 'The Consumer Protection Act 68 of 2008 and procedural fairness in consumer contracts' (2015) 18(4) *PELJ* 1091 at 1096.

88 Data subject rights are discussed in chapter 18.

89 Section 11(3)*(a)*. The lawful purposes for which personal information may be processed (and when the data subject can object), are discussed in chapter 6.

90 Section 11(3)*(b)*. If direct marketing is being done via 'electronic communication', the responsible party may need consent. Direct marketing is discussed in chapter 16.

91 Section 69(3). Direct marketing is discussed in chapter 16.

92 Section 28(1)*(c)*.

- If the responsible party is an insurance company, medical scheme, medical scheme administrator or a managed healthcare organisation and it is processing information relating to the data subject's health for purposes of risk assessments.[93]
- Data subjects who are subscribers to a printed or electronic directory of subscribers must be given a reasonable opportunity to object to the inclusion of their personal information in the directory.[94]

Even though data subjects have to be informed of the right to object or opt out,[95] data subjects are confronted with so many decisions relating to their 'privacy settings' that they suffer from 'decision paralysis' or inertia.[96] As Woodrow Hartzog so eloquently put it 'while you might remember to adjust your privacy settings on Facebook, what about Instagram, Twitter, Google, Amazon, Netflix, Snapchat, Siri, Cortana, Fitbit, Candy Crush, your smart TV, your robot vacuum cleaner, your WiFi-connected car, and your child's Hello Barbie?'[97]

In other instances, data subjects may fall prey to default or status quo bias. That is the phenomenon that people will choose doing nothing over doing something. So, the option set as the default will be hugely popular – Sunstein and Thaler refer to this as the 'yeah whatever' bias.[98] Companies deploy 'dark patterns' to nudge us to make the decision they want us to.[99] What does it mean to use 'dark patterns'? It is when the designers exploit human psychology and invert principles of user experience design to 'trick users into doing things they might not otherwise do'.[100]

To combat this, the EU GDPR explicitly requires that responsible parties practice data protection by design and default.[101] These are principles

---

93 Section 32(1)*(b)*(i).

94 Section 70(2).

95 Section 18(1)*(h)*(iv).

96 Hanneke Luth *Behavioural Economics in Consumer Policy: The Economic Analysis of Standard Terms on Consumer Contracts Revisited* (2010) 49; Iain Ramsay *Consumer Law and Policy: Texts and Materials on Regulating Consumer Markets* 3 ed (2012) 60.

97 Woodrow Hartzog 'Privacy and the dark side of control' (*IAI News*, 4 September 2017), available at https://iai.tv/articles/privacy-the-dark-side-of-control-auid-882.

98 Richard H Thaler & Cass R Sunstein *Nudge* (2009) 37.

99 Woodrow Hartzog 'The case against idealising control' (2018) 4 *European Data Protection Law Review* 423 at 427, available at https://edpl.lexxion.eu/data/article/13517/pdf/edpl_2018_04-006.pdf.

100 Harry Brignull 'Dark Patterns: Inside the interfaces designed to trick you' *The Verge*, available at https://www.theverge.com/2013/8/29/4640308/dark-patterns-inside-the-interfaces-designed-to-trick-you.

101 Article 25 of the EU GDPR.

that 'emphasize the need for built-in privacy enhancing technologies, default settings that minimise data processing, and the provision of the necessary tools that enable the highest possible protection of personal data'.[102] POPIA does not contain equivalent provisions,[103] but it is considered best practice not to be an a-hole.

2.6.6 Consent

This then brings us to consent, or 'the c-word' as we call it. One of the most enduring myths about POPIA is that as long as you have consent, you can do whatever you like with personal information. The number of blanket consents we see hidden in terms and conditions is nothing short of staggering. Most of these consents will be invalid. That is because POPIA defines consent as a 'voluntary, specific and informed expression of will'.[104] These are the elements of consent and what they mean in practice:

[102] European Data Protection Board *Guidelines 3/2019 on Processing of Personal Data through Video Devices* (2020) 30.

[103] Principles like 'minimality' (section 10) could be used to advocate for privacy by default. Minimality is discussed in chapter 9.

[104] See the definition of 'consent' in section 1 of POPIA.

Voluntary	It must be a genuine choice. The data subject has to be able to say no, but still continue with the activity (e.g. to purchase a product or service or apply for employment).[105] The consent should also not be bundled with terms and conditions – the data subject has to have the freedom to withhold consent, but still accept the terms and conditions.[106] In other words, no 'fit in or f-off' consents. **Key point:** Where there is a significant imbalance of power (e.g. in the employment relationship or if the responsible party is a public authority[107]), consent may not be appropriate at all. In a case adjudicated by the Hellenic Data Protection Authority it was held that consent in the context of an employment relationship cannot be regarded as freely given because of the imbalance of power between employers and employees.[108] The CNIL (French Data Protection Authority) recently concluded that consent in an employment relationship can only be regarded as freely given if there are no consequences for the employees if they do not consent. For instance, the recording of a promotional video in a workspace that shows identifiable employees may be based on the employees' consent if: (i) the employees have a real choice as to whether or not to appear in the recording; and (ii) the employees' choice has no impact on them (in particular with regard to working conditions, remuneration, advancement, etc).[109]

105 European Data Protection Board *Guidelines 05/2020 on Consent under Regulation 2016/679* 10, available at https://edpb.europa.eu/sites/edpb/files/files/file1/edpb_guidelines_202005_consent_en.pdf.

106 European Data Protection Board *Guidelines 05/2020 on Consent under Regulation 2016/679* 7 and 10, available at https://edpb.europa.eu/sites/edpb/files/files/file1/edpb_guidelines_202005_consent_en.pdf.

107 Recital 43 of the EU GDPR.

108 Greek DPA decision (No 26/2019). In this decision PWC was fined EUR 150 000 for relying on consent when it was inappropriate to do so. Also see European Data Protection Board *Guidelines 05/2020 on Consent under Regulation 2016/679* 9, available at https://edpb.europa.eu/sites/edpb/files/files/file1/edpb_guidelines_202005_consent_en.pdf.

109 Patrice Navarro and Julie Schwartz 'CNIL's new guidelines on HR processing', available at https://www.engage.hoganlovells.com/knowledgeservices/news/cnils-new-guidelines-on-hr-processing. For those of you who can read French, here is the actual text: https://www.legifrance.gouv.fr/jorf/

	Data subjects must be free to withdraw consent without undue effort and without any detrimental effects such as an increase in cost, a cessation of services or a decrease in service levels.[110] **Tricky area: Section 11(3)*(b)* states that a data subject may withdraw consent provided in terms of section 11(1)*(a)* at any time. The right to withdraw consent is not mentioned in section 27(1)*(a)* in respect of special personal information. However, we believe that data subjects also have the right to withdraw other consents due to the requirement that consent must be voluntary.[111]** The requirement that consent must be voluntary will often make consent inappropriate, because the processing activity in question is not optional. Luckily, there are other legal justifications (e.g. that the processing is necessary for the performance of a contract with the data subject) that will be appropriate.[112]
Specific	The consent must always relate to a specific, well-articulated purpose.[113] A blanket consent covering all purposes for which personal information is processed will be too vague to be valid. Instead, consents must be granular.[114]

id/JORFTEXT000041798580/ and some answers to questions here: https://www.cnil.fr/sites/default/files/atoms/files/referentiel_grh_novembre_2019_0.pdf.

110 European Data Protection Board *Guidelines 05/2020 on Consent under Regulation 2016/679* 13, available at https://edpb.europa.eu/sites/edpb/files/files/file1/edpb_guidelines_202005_consent_en.pdf.

111 Section 1 of POPIA.

112 This is discussed in chapter 6.

113 European Data Protection Board *Guidelines 05/2020 on Consent under Regulation 2016/679* 13, available at https://edpb.europa.eu/sites/edpb/files/files/file1/edpb_guidelines_202005_consent_en.pdf.

114 European Data Protection Board *Guidelines 05/2020 on Consent under Regulation 2016/679* 12, available at https://edpb.europa.eu/sites/edpb/files/files/file1/edpb_guidelines_202005_consent_en.pdf.

<table>
<tr><td>Informed</td><td>The consent must be worded in such a way that the data subject is put in a position to make an informed decision. This means that they must have an understanding of the facts of the situation and the implications of granting or withholding consent.

The European Data Protection Board is of the view that the following information must be provided for a consent to be valid:[115]
• the identity of all of the responsible parties who will be relying on the consent
• the purpose of each processing operation for which consent is asked
• the type of personal information that will be collected and used
• that the data subject can withdraw consent; and
• whether the information will be used for automated decision-making.

POPIA does not provide that responsible parties must use plain language. However, we would argue that a consent which is not in plain language will not meet the requirement that consent must be informed. In addition, the relationship between the responsible party and the data subject may be governed by the Consumer Protection Act 68 of 2008 which provides that '[t]he producer of a notice, document or visual representation that is required, in terms of [the Consumer Protection Act] or any other law [like POPIA]' must provide the notice in plain language.[116]

A consent will be in plain language 'if it is reasonable to conclude that an ordinary consumer of the class of persons for whom the [consent] is intended, with average literacy skills and minimal experience as a consumer of the relevant goods or services, could be expected to understand the content, significance and import of the [consent] without due effort'.[117]

The most important aspect of plain language is that responsible parties must take the target audience (also referred to as a market segment) into account. For instance, if the audience has lower levels of literacy, responsible parties must use simpler language.</td></tr>
</table>

➡

[115] European Data Protection Board *Guidelines 05/2020 on consent under Regulation 2016/679* 15, available at https://edpb.europa.eu/sites/edpb/files/files/file1/edpb_guidelines_202005_consent_en.pdf.

[116] Section 22(1) of the CPA.

[117] Section 22(2) of the CPA. For more on the definition of 'plain language' see Stoop 'Section 22' in Commentary on the Consumer Protection Act and De Stadler & Van Zyl 'Plain language contracts: challenges and opportunities' 2017(1) *SAMLJ* 95.

Expression of will	The consent must be explicit, which means that it has to be given by means of a clear, unambiguous, affirmative act. It cannot be given by default and silence or inactivity cannot be taken as consent. To avoid ambiguity, the action of giving consent must also be distinct from other actions such as agreeing to terms and conditions.[118]

There are several mentions of consent throughout POPIA. They are:

- consent to processing[119]
- consent to collection from a third party[120]
- consent to retention of a record[121]
- consent to processing of a stored record[122]
- consent to further processing[123]
- consent to waive notification[124]
- consent to processing of special personal information[125]
- consent to direct marketing[126]
- consent to transfer personal information overseas;[127] and
- consent to processing of account numbers.[128]

118 European Data Protection Board *Guidelines 05/2020 on consent under Regulation 2016/679* 18, available at https://edpb.europa.eu/sites/edpb/files/files/file1/edpb_guidelines_202005_consent_en.pdf.

119 Section 11(1)*(a)*.

120 Section 12(2)*(b)*.

121 Section 14(1)*(d)*.

122 Section 14(7).

123 Section 15(3)*(a)*.

124 Section 18(4)*(a)*.

125 Section 27(1)*(a)*. The processing of special personal information is discussed in chapter 7.

126 Section 69(1)*(a)*. Note that the Information Regulator has prescribed a specific form for consent for direct marketing by electronic means in the POPIA Regulations (regulation 6 read with form 4).

127 Section 72(1)*(b)*.

128 Section 106(1).

Tricky area: What should a responsible party do when they discover that they have been relying on an invalid consent? Since, in our opinion (which is supported by the approach in other jurisdictions), consent should only be used as justification if none of the other justifications applies, the responsible party cannot rely on any one of the other justifications as a fallback. The European Data Protection Board has gone so far as to say that (in the context of the EU GDPR): 'It is important to note here that if a controller chooses to rely on consent for any part of the processing, they must be prepared to respect that choice and stop that part of the processing if an individual withdraws consent. Sending out the message that data will be processed on the basis of consent, while actually some other lawful basis is relied on, would be fundamentally unfair to individuals.'[129] This means that a responsible party will have to stop processing until new, valid consent has been obtained from the data subject.

But, even if the consents are valid, we are still left with the uncomfortable truth that 'the problem with thinking of privacy as control is that if we are given our wish for more privacy, it means we are given so much control that we choke on it'.[130] Perhaps it is indeed time for lawmakers to 'ensure companies are trustworthy regardless of the control [data subjects] are given'.[131]

2.6.7 Processing 'for historical, statistical or research purposes'

The phrase 'for historical, statistical or research purposes' is sprinkled throughout POPIA. Notably in the context of an exemption from some of the conditions for lawful processing.[132]

---

129 European Data Protection Board *Guidelines 05/2020 on consent under Regulation 2016/679* 25.

130 Woodrow Hartzog 'The case against idealising control' (2018) 4 *European Data Protection Law Review* 423 at 429, available at https://edpl.lexxion.eu/data/article/13517/pdf/edpl_2018_04-006.pdf.

131 Woodrow Hartzog 'The case against idealising control' (2018) 4 *European Data Protection Law Review* 423 at 432, available at https://edpl.lexxion.eu/data/article/13517/pdf/edpl_2018_04-006.pdf.

132 You will find it in sections 14(2) (retention and restriction of records), 15(3)*(c)* (further processing, 18(4)*(f)*(ii) (notification), 27(1)*(d)* (authorisation concerning special personal information), 32(5)*(b)* (authorisation concerning data subject's health or sex life), 35(1)*(d)* (general authorisation concerning personal information of children), and 37(2)*(e)* (Regulator may exempt processing of personal information).

Where does this phrase come from? The EU GDPR, the UK's Data Protection Act,[133] New Zealand's Privacy Act[134] and Canada's Privacy Act[135] (amongst others) all contain a version of this exception, worded in slightly different ways and used in a variety of circumstances. POPIA is based on the versions of these acts in force in 2009 when the SA Law Reform Commission paper was drafted.

The EU GDPR uses the 'for scientific or historical research purposes or statistical purposes' phrase in relation to the retention of records[136] and further processing.[137] In POPIA, the phrase is used in the following contexts:

- Records may be retained for longer periods for historical, statistical or research purposes as long as there are appropriate safeguards in place to ensure that the records are not used for other purposes.[138]
- Personal information may be used for further processing if it is used for historical, statistical or research purposes and the responsible party ensures that the further processing is used solely for this purpose and will not be published in an identifiable form.[139]
- Responsible parties do not have to notify data subjects if their information will be used for historical, statistical or research purposes.[140]
- The use of special personal information or the personal information of children is generally authorised for historical, statistical or research purposes if the processing is necessary to serve a public interest or it would have been impossible or would involve a disproportionate effort to ask for consent. It will only be authorised if there are sufficient guarantees in place to ensure that 'the processing does not adversely affect the individual privacy of the data subject to a disproportionate extent'.[141]

Chapter 2

133 of 2018.

134 Act 31 of 2020.

135 R.S.C., 1985, c. P-21

136 Article 5(1)*(b)*.

137 Article 5(1)*(e)*.

138 Section 14(2).

139 Section 15(3)*(e)*.

140 Section 18(4)*(f)*.

141 Section 27(1)*(d)* and section 35(1)*(d)*. The processing of special personal information is discussed in chapter 7.

- Personal information concerning inherited characteristics can be processed if it is necessary for historical, statistical or research activity.[142]

The EU's Article 29 Data Protection Working Party opinion 'on purpose limitation' discussed the meanings of these terms.[143] The Working Party is firm that this exception 'should not be read as providing an overall exception from the requirement of compatibility, and it is not intended as a general authorisation to further process data in all cases for historical, statistical or scientific purposes'.[144] Essentially, this exception cannot be used as a free-for-all, and the personal information needs to actually be processed or retained for historical, statistical or research purposes, as the case may be.

Let's look at the meaning of each of these purposes individually.

2.6.7.1 Statistical purposes

The Article 29 Data Protection Working Party's opinion defines 'statistical purposes' as follows:

> '"Statistical purposes" in particular, cover a wide range of processing activities, from commercial purposes (e.g., analytical tools of websites or big data applications aimed at market research) to public interests (e.g. statistical information produced from data collected by hospitals to determine the number of people injured as a result of road accidents).'[145]

Recital 162 of the EU GDPR gives a further definition:

> 'Statistical purposes mean any operation of collection and the processing of personal data necessary for statistical surveys or for the production of statistical results. Those statistical results may further be used for different purposes, including a scientific research purpose. The statistical purpose implies that the result of processing for statistical purposes is not personal data, but aggregate data, and that this result or the personal data are not used in support of measures or decisions regarding any particular natural person.'[146]

---

142 Section 32(5)*(b)*.

143 Article 29 Data Protection Working Party 'Opinion 03/2013 on purpose limitation' at 28, available at https://ec.europa.eu/justice/article-29/documentation/opinion-recommendation/files/2013/wp203_en.pdf.

144 Article 29 Data Protection Working Party 'Opinion 03/2013 on purpose limitation' at 28, available at https://ec.europa.eu/justice/article-29/documentation/opinion-recommendation/files/2013/wp203_en.pdf.

145 Article 29 Data Protection Working Party 'Opinion 03/2013 on purpose limitation' at 29, available at https://ec.europa.eu/justice/article-29/documentation/opinion-recommendation/files/2013/wp203_en.pdf.

146 Recital 162 of the EU GDPR. Further processing is discussed in chapter 12.

2.6.7.2 Research purposes

The EU GDPR refers to 'scientific and historical research purposes'. Recital 159 of the EU GDPR defines 'scientific research' as follows:

> 'For this Regulation, the processing of personal data for scientific research purposes should be interpreted in a broad manner including for example technological development and demonstration, fundamental research, applied research and privately funded research ... Scientific research purposes should also include studies conducted in the public interest in the area of public health.'[147]

It is important to note that the EU GDPR's broad definition of scientific research means that 'scientific research' not only refers to research done by 'hard sciences' but in humanities and social sciences as well.[148]

POPIA refers to 'research purposes' which is a wider term than the EU GDPR's 'scientific research'. The National Health Research Ethics Council's glossary defines research as follows:

> '[Research] includes a range of activities conducted by many different disciplines that may use different methodologies and explanatory frameworks to extend knowledge through disciplined inquiry or systematic investigation.'[149]

Tricky area: How broad is the concept of 'research' in POPIA? Does it include market(ing) research and profiling? We do not think so. It is likely that our Information Regulator will agree that the exceptions created all over POPIA for research purposes should not be treated as a free-for-all.

2.6.7.3 Historical purposes

The term 'historical' is ordinarily defined as 'of or concerning history or past events'.[150]

The Article 29 Data Protection Working Party's opinion 'on purpose limitation' did not give a definition for 'historical purposes'. However, the opinion did state that many member states will have laws which require that personal information

147 Recital 159 of the EU GDPR.

148 Recital 157 of the EU GDPR.

149 NHREC 'Guidelines on Research Ethics' at 55, available at http://nhrec.health.gov.za/index.php/grids-preview.

150 Lexico 'historical', available at https://www.lexico.com/definition/historical.

is kept for longer than necessary for national archiving, to document recent history (for example of a recent oppressive regime) and court files kept by the judiciary.[151] While many of these historical purposes will be determined by legislation,[152] personal information which is decades old can still have an adverse impact on a data subject and still needs to be protected.[153]

Recital 160 of the EU GDPR does not refer to 'historical purposes' but refers to 'historical research purposes'. This Recital defines 'historical research purposes' as follows:

> 'This should also include historical research and research for genealogical purposes, bearing in mind that this Regulation should not apply to deceased persons.'[154]

2.7 WHEN POPIA AND OTHER SOUTH AFRICAN LEGISLATION COLLIDE

POPIA can be seen as the 'constitution' when it comes to the protection of personal information. What we mean by that is that if another piece of legislation 'regulates the processing of personal information' and that legislation is 'materially inconsistent' with one of the purposes or specific provisions of POPIA, POPIA will trump that legislation.[155]

Given that one of the purposes of POPIA is to give effect to the constitutional right to privacy, the question of whether another piece of legislation limits the right to privacy should be evaluated, not only against POPIA, but also against section 36 of the Constitution. As discussed in paragraph 2.6.1 above, when considering whether a limitation of the right to privacy is fair and justified, the importance of the purpose of the limitation, the nature and extent of the limitation, the relationship between the limitation and its purpose and whether there are less restrictive means to achieve the purpose, should be considered.[156]

151 Article 29 Data Protection Working Party 'Opinion 03/2013 on purpose limitation' at 29, available at https://ec.europa.eu/justice/article-29/documentation/opinion-recommendation/files/2013/wp203_en.pdf.

152 A local example is the National Archives and Record Service of South Africa Act 43 of 1996.

153 Article 29 Data Protection Working Party 'Opinion 03/2013 on purpose limitation' at 29, available at https://ec.europa.eu/justice/article-29/documentation/opinion-recommendation/files/2013/wp203_en.pdf.

154 Recital 160 of the EU GDPR.

155 Section 3(2)*(a)*.

156 Section 36(1) of the Constitution.

The *Amabhungane* case, where the constitutionality of the Regulation of Interception of Communications and Provision of Communication-related Information Act 70 of 2002 (RICA) was considered, is a good example of how limitations on the right to privacy will be evaluated.[157] In particular, in *Amabhungane* it was successfully argued that the secret monitoring of persons such as lawyers and journalists would have a chilling effect on free speech. In the Gauteng High Court Judge Sutherland issued six orders which included requiring that the (data) subject be notified of the interception order (consider the notification duty in POPIA which we discuss in chapter 11), further safeguards to be implemented to safeguard the independence of the designated judge, additional requirements to be set out where the person intercepted is a lawyer or journalist and a prohibition against bulk surveillance.

The relationship between POPIA and other legislation is also relevant when determining whether a responsible party has a legal basis for processing personal information. Processing personal information will be lawful where 'processing complies with an obligation imposed by law on the responsible party'.[158] In other words, where a piece of legislation requires that personal information must be processed by a responsible party, the processing will be justified as long as the responsible party only does what is necessary to comply and no more.

Tricky area: What happens if a responsible party is compelled by the government or a public body to do more processing than is required by the legislation in question? This will often put a responsible party between a rock and a hard place. Where a responsible party believes that the required processing activity is excessive, the responsible party should request that the Information Regulator assesses whether processing required by the government is compliant with POPIA.[159] When performing this assessment, the Information Regulator should (a) consider whether the legislation in question is materially consistent with POPIA, and (b) if it is, whether the government or public body's interpretation of the legislation and the requirements that are being imposed are adequate, relevant and not excessive.

[157] *Amabhungane Centre for Investigative Journalism NPC v Minister of Justice* 2020 (1) SA 90 (GP). The case is discussed in further detail in chapter 4 paragraph 4.4.2.

[158] Section 11(1)*(c)*. Determining lawfulness is discussed in chapter 6.

[159] Section 89.

New legislation can also be 'tested' against POPIA. The Information Regulator has the power to monitor and enforce compliance with POPIA by examining proposed legislation or government policy and report the results of the examination to the Minister of Justice and Constitutional Development.[160]

Lastly, POPIA also provides that if another piece of legislation provides more extensive provisions for the lawful processing of personal information, the other piece of legislation will prevail.[161]

2.8 PRACTICAL ADVICE

It is entirely possible, if not probable, that different responsible parties will have different interpretations of the principles in POPIA. There are no black and white answers. This begs the question as to how responsible parties are to cope with the uncertainty that this causes?

The answer lies in meticulous record-keeping and an ability to keep up with changes in how the law is interpreted. Responsible parties must ensure that they keep a record of the legal advice they receive and the basis for their interpretation of POPIA and change their behaviour if the advice changes. Responsible parties will also have to ensure that their interpretation remains current as case law and further guidance from the Regulator on the interpretation of POPIA will inevitably happen.

160 Section 40(1)*(b)*(iii).

161 Section 3(2)*(b)*.

3

The application and scope of POPIA

3.1 WHAT TO EXPECT IN THIS CHAPTER

When any organisation doing business in South Africa asks 'does POPIA apply to us?' it should lead to a very short legal opinion.[1] Yes. The reason for that is that even if an organisation does not use personal information to deliver its products or services, the organisation must have the personal information of its customers, employees and suppliers to function. Of course, it is a bit more complicated and nuanced than this.

In this chapter we discuss the following:

- When does POPIA apply?
- When does POPIA not apply?
- When did POPIA come into effect?
- Does POPIA apply retrospectively?

3.2 WHEN DOES POPIA APPLY?

POPIA applies to all 'processing' of 'personal information' which is entered into a record by a 'responsible party' who is domiciled in South Africa *or* makes use of automated or non-automated means in South Africa, except if those means are only used to forward the information through South Africa.[2]

It becomes easier to understand the application of POPIA if it is broken down into the following 'triggers' which will be discussed in the remainder of this section:

- Is the organisation 'processing' 'personal information'?
- Is the personal information entered into a 'record' (or in the case of non-automated processing a 'filing system')?
- Is the processing being done by or for a 'responsible party'?
- Is that 'responsible party' domiciled in South Africa? OR Is that 'responsible party' making use of automated or non-automated means in South Africa?

If the answer to all four questions is 'yes', POPIA will apply unless one of the exceptions applies. The exceptions are discussed in paragraph 3.3 below.

The triggers are discussed in the remainder of this section.

---

1 Of course, there is not really such a thing as a short legal opinion, but that is a story for another book.

2 Section 3(1).

3.2.1 Is the organisation 'processing' 'personal information'?

Understanding the definitions of 'personal information' and 'processing' is essential to understanding the scope of POPIA.

3.2.1.1 The definition of 'personal information'

Personal information is all information that can be linked to an identifiable living individual, or existing juristic person. The individual or juristic person to whom the personal information relates is referred to as the 'data subject'.[3]

Key point: South Africa is one of very few countries where the information of juristic persons is included in the definition of personal information. Most data protection and privacy regulations only apply to the information of individuals.

The SA Law Reform Commission explained its decision to include the personal information of juristic persons as follows:

> 'A juristic person, just like a natural person, has a sphere of privacy in which it has a legitimate interest and which is therefore worthy of legal protection. Juristic entities as well as natural persons are affected by the increased processing of information on them. It is therefore necessary to impose certain duties on persons processing information, while giving the subjects of such processing certain rights, to ensure that the processing of information on them does not harm their legitimate interests. ... The aim of privacy legislation is not to stem the flow of information, but to regulate it. This will also be the position regarding juristic personas. Worldwide, privacy legislation is regarded as an example of ordinary good business practice. If juristic persons were excluded from the application of the proposed data protection measures, credit bureaus, for example, would be in a position to collect and use information on the creditworthiness of companies without any constraint except perhaps those imposed by totally inadequate traditional common law data protection principles.'[4]

However, the definition of 'personal information' in the Promotion of Access to Information Act (PAIA)[5] does not include a reference to juristic persons, but only to natural persons.

Chapter 3

---

3 Section 1.

4 SA Law Reform Commission Project 124 on Privacy and Data Protection (2009 Report) 83.

5 Act 2 of 2000.

Tricky area: POPIA extends data subject rights to all data subjects in terms of section 23 or 24, but provides that the procedures for PAIA must be followed when it comes to access rights. Given that the definition of personal information in PAIA does not cover juristic persons, does this mean that they have different access rights to data subjects who are individuals? We don't think so. PAIA provides that a requester can be either an individual or a juristic person. However, the inconsistent definitions do cause trouble when it comes to the grounds on which a responsible party must refuse access (e.g. if providing access will disclose the personal information of a third party). We discuss this in chapter 18, paragraph 18.3.3.2.

There is a long list of personal information in the definition in section 1, but that list is not exhaustive. New, and increasingly creative, types of personal information are created all the time. For instance, Cambridge Analytica (the subject of Netflix's *The Great Hack*) claimed to have had 5 000 data points on over 220 million Americans. That is 5 000 pieces of personal information. We don't know 5000 things about ourselves. Do you? So, the definition in section 1 should not be treated as a checklist. Even things that are not on there can be personal information. Here is the list, broken up into categories and supplemented:

Type of personal information	Examples (there may be more)
Identifiers	A name, identity number, staff number, account number, customer number, company registration number, tax number, IP addresses, a phone's IMEI number and usernames on websites and social media. 'Unique identifiers' are also discussed in chapter 8 paragraph 8.2.1 in the context of prior authorisation.

Type of personal information	Examples (there may be more)
Biometric information	'Biometrics' is defined as 'a technique of personal identification that is based on physical, physiological or behavioural characterisation including blood typing, fingerprinting, DNA analysis, retinal scanning and voice recognition'.[6] Biometric information is considered 'special personal information'. This means that special principles will apply to it. For a more detailed definition see chapter 7 paragraph 7.2.7.
Demographic information	Race, gender, sex, pregnancy, marital status, nationality, ethnicity, sexual orientation, age, physical or mental health, disability, religion, conscience, belief, culture and language. Some demographic information will also be considered 'special personal information' and special principles will apply. For a full list of what is considered 'special' see chapter 7 paragraph 7.2.
Contact details and location	Physical and postal addresses, location information, email addresses, telephone numbers and social media handles.
Financial information	Bank and other account numbers, statements, account balances, financial records, salary information and credit histories. Misbehaving around account numbers has dire consequences. We discuss this in chapter 19 paragraph 19.10.2.
Background information	Educational, financial, employment, medical, criminal or credit history. Health information will also be considered 'special personal information' and special principles will apply. See chapter 7 paragraph 7.2.5 for a discussion on information relating to 'health and sex life'.
Behavioural information	Likes, dislikes, preferences, opinions, views, posts on social media, browser history, location information, shopping history and who you associate with.
Correspondence	Correspondence that is implicitly or explicitly of a private or confidential nature.
Opinions about the data subject	Opinions expressed about an individual or organisation, e.g. references, trade reference or reviews.
What's in a name	A name will be personal information if it appears with other personal information. A name on its own will also be personal information, if the name itself reveals information about the person.

6 New forms of biometrics are being concocted up all the time. For instance, smell recognition is now a thing. Not kidding. Odour biometrics is a thing. Google it, if you don't believe us (and stop sniffing people).

POPIA applies to personal information irrespective of the medium it is recorded on, e.g. paper, electronic, clay tablet. See the definition of 'record' in paragraph 3.2.2 below.

Key point: POPIA also applies to information that is in the public domain. A lot of personal information can be found in public records, on the internet or in other 'public domains'. There is a popular misconception that when this is the case, POPIA does not apply. This is not true. In fact, harvesting information from public records or the internet is considered a high-risk activity and often sits at the heart of non-compliance with data privacy regulations. This is discussed in chapter 10.

Not all personal information is treated in the same way. POPIA creates a category of personal information called 'special personal information'. This is personal information concerning religious or philosophical beliefs, race or ethnic origin, trade union membership, political persuasion, health or sex life, biometric information and information relating to the commission of an offence, or the proceedings about that offence.[7] There are also special rules that apply to special personal information and the information of children. Special personal information and the personal information of children are discussed in chapter 7.

While POPIA's definition of 'personal information' expressly refers to living individuals, PAIA does not. In terms of PAIA, 'personal information' includes the information of individuals who have been deceased for less than 20 years. This explains why PAIA requests will continue to include requests for access to records relating to deceased persons. PAIA requests are discussed in chapter 18.

---

7 Section 26.

Tricky area: Organisations do not see dead people. Most organisations do not keep track of who is dead or alive. So, at any given moment, most organisations would have no reliable and efficient way of knowing which data subjects are living individuals at all times (and they cannot check constantly). Organisations have no choice but to err on the side of caution and assume that all of the data subjects whose information they have are alive, until they receive reliable evidence to the contrary. Similarly, organisations must assume that juristic persons have not been de-registered or liquidated, although it is generally easier to get information about the status of juristic persons from the regulatory body governing companies, which is the Companies and Intellectual Property Commission (CIPC) in South Africa.

When is information identifiable? Recital 26 of the EU GDPR states that 'to determine whether a natural person is identifiable, account should be taken of all the means reasonably likely to be used' by the responsible party or another person to re-identify the data subject'. The recital also states that responsible parties can determine what is 'reasonably likely' by taking into account 'all objective factors, such as the cost of and the amount of time required for identification, taking into consideration the available technology at the time of the processing and technological developments'. The ICO says that a responsible party must consider what other information is out there, who it is available to, and whether it is likely to be used in a re-identification process. The other information could be information available to certain organisations, to certain members of the public or information that is available to everyone. The risk of re-identification increases as data linkage techniques and computing power develop, and as more information becomes publicly available.[8] De-identification is discussed again in paragraph 3.3.2.

---

[8] ICO *Anonymisation: managing data protection risk code of practice* 18, available at https://ico.org.uk/media/for-organisations/documents/1061/anonymisation-code.pdf. Also see Article 29 Data Protection Working Party *Opinion 05/2014 on Anonymisation Techniques* (https://ec.europa.eu/justice/article-29/documentation/opinion-recommendation/files/2014/wp216_en.pdf). Also see the definition of de-identification in paragraph 3.3.2 below.

Key point: Sometimes the data subject will be directly identifiable, and in other instances the identification happens indirectly through the use of unique identifiers. For an extensive discussion of this, see the Article 29 Data Protection Working Party *Opinion 4/2007 on the concept of personal data*.[9]

3.2.1.2 The definition of 'processing'

The definition of 'processing' in section 1 is equally wide.

Processing covers all activities that involve personal information – from collection to destruction. This includes to collect, receive, record, organise, collate, store, update, modify, retrieve, alter, consult, use, disseminate (transmit, distribute or make available), merge, link, restrict, degrade, erase or destroy the information. There is hardly a verb left on the board.

Key point: If an organisation has personal information, it is processing it.

3.2.2 Is the personal information entered into a 'record'?

In order for POPIA to apply, the personal information must be 'entered into a record'. 'Record' is defined in section 1. It refers to 'recorded information ... regardless of form or medium'. The definition includes the following examples of recorded information:

- writing on any material
- information produced, recorded or stored by means of a tape recorder,[10] a computer or other device (hardware or software) and 'any material subsequently derived from information'
- labels, markings or other writing that 'describes anything of which it forms part, or to which it is attached by any means'
- books, maps, plans, graphs or drawings
- photograph, film, negative, tape; and
- cave paintings, clay tablets and smoke signals.[11]

---

9 Available at https://ec.europa.eu/justice/article-29/documentation/opinion-recommendation/files/2007/wp136_en.pdf.

10 Remember those?

11 We made up this last bullet. The rest are listed in the definition of 'record' in section 1 of POPIA.

A record can be created by automated or non-automated means. 'Automated means' is defined in section 3(4) as 'any equipment capable of operating automatically in response to instructions given for the purpose of processing information'. This is a very convoluted way of saying that it does not matter whether the record is created by a computer or whether it is created by a person.

However, if the processing is taking place by non-automated means, it must form part of a 'filing system'. This term is also defined in section 1. It refers to a structured set of personal information 'which is accessible according to specific criteria' regardless of whether it is centralised, decentralised or all in the same place. An unsophisticated filing system would be a lever arch file. A more complex filing system would be multiple inter-related databases which can be accessed from anywhere in the world and can handle complex search queries.

Key point: POPIA applies to the personal information which is sitting in a database as well as personal information which is kept in a hard copy filing system.

3.2.3 Is the processing being done for or by a responsible party?

Section 3(1)*(a)* provides that the personal information must be entered into a record by or for a 'responsible party'. A responsible party is the 'person' who decides the purpose and means for processing personal information.[12] The person can either be a natural person (for example a sole proprietor) or a juristic person (for example a company). The responsible party must ensure POPIA compliance. While this definition makes it sound easy to work out who the responsible party is, in practice it is often much harder than you would expect. We deal with these difficulties in chapter 4.

3.2.4 Is the responsible party domiciled in South Africa, OR making use of means to process personal information in South Africa?

For POPIA to apply, the responsible party must:

- be domiciled (resident) in South Africa; or
- use automated or non-automated means (in other words 'any' means) to process the personal information in South Africa.

[12] See the definition of 'responsible party' in section 1.

3.2.4.1 Responsible parties who are domiciled in South Africa

If a responsible party is domiciled in South Africa, POPIA will apply to it. An organisation will be domiciled in South Africa if it is incorporated, established or formed in South Africa, or if it has its 'central management and control' in South Africa.[13]

3.2.4.2 When POPIA applies to foreign responsible parties

POPIA provides that a foreign responsible party (not domiciled in South Africa), can still be subject to POPIA if:

- the foreign organisation is the responsible party; and
- it uses automated or non-automated means in South Africa to process the personal information (unless those means are only used to forward personal information through South Africa).

'Means' is defined as 'any equipment', but equipment is not defined. When POPIA applies to a foreign organisation is very difficult to interpret. The wording is very similar to the EU Data Protection Directive and this is how it was interpreted back in its day:

> 'The Directive does not contain a definition of this term. According to the Collins English dictionary, "equipment" is defined as a set of tools or devices assembled for a specific purpose.
>
> Examples of equipment are personal computers, terminals and servers, which may be used for nearly all kinds of processing operations. The Directive makes clear that *equipment* as such can be automated or otherwise as far as it is not used only for transit of information through the territory of the Community.
>
> A typical case where equipment is used for transit only are the telecommunications networks (back bones, cables etc.), which form part of the Internet and over which Internet communications are travelling from the expedition point to the destination point.'[14]

'Making use' means that there must be some kind of activity by the responsible party and the intention to process personal information. It does not matter whether the responsible party owns the equipment. The question is whether they exercise control over the equipment. In the EU this was interpreted

---

[13] The definition of 'resident' in terms of section 1 of the Income Tax Act 58 of 1962.

[14] Article 29 Data Protection Working Party *Working document on determining the international application of EU data protection law to personal data processing on the Internet by non-EU based web sites* 9, available at https://ec.europa.eu/justice/article-29/documentation/opinion-recommendation/files/2002/wp56_en.pdf. The test of whether the equipment is used 'for transit only' is similar to the 'mere conduit' rule in section 73 of the Electronic Communications and Transactions Act 25 of 2002 which absolves internet service providers (ISPs) from liability when they act as a mere conduit for data.

to mean that 'the equipment should be at the disposal of the [responsible party], but that the responsible party does not have to exercise full control over the equipment. It also does not need to own the equipment in order for the legislation to apply'.[15] In order for it to apply, 'there needs to be some kind of activity undertaken by the [responsible party] and the intention of the [responsible party] to process the personal data'.[16]

Tricky area: On this interpretation, even using an operator in South Africa could trigger POPIA. That seems strange and impractical; for instance, does a foreign organisation have to register an information officer just because it uses an operator in South Africa? We are also cognisant of the fact that there is a presumption in South African law that legislation does not have extraterritorial effect.

What is clear, is that POPIA could have extraterritorial effect. When that will be the case must be determined per processing activity. This is not unusual; many data protection laws contain similar provisions. This means that organisations can be subject to several data protection laws at the same time. Until there is a global instrument to manage this, organisations will have to grapple with the complexities that are created by national data protection laws in 'a digital world that has few borders'.[17]

3.2.4.3 Some examples

The best way to explain these concepts is through some examples:

- A South African company processes the information of Namibian residents. In this instance POPIA will apply because the company is South African. It does not matter that the data subjects whose personal information is being processed are not South African.

[15] Article 29 Data Protection Working Party *Working document on determining the international application of EU data protection law to personal data processing on the Internet by non-EU based web sites* 9.

[16] Article 29 Data Protection Working Party *Working document on determining the international application of EU data protection law to personal data processing on the Internet by non-EU based web sites* 9.

[17] Elizabeth Denham 'Maintaining data flows for a digital world', available at https://ico.org.uk/about-the-ico/news-and-events/news-and-blogs/2021/01/maintaining-data-flows-for-a-digital-world/.

- A Nigerian company processes the personal information of South African residents, from records which are available on the internet. All of the processing takes place from Nigeria. In this case POPIA will not apply, because neither the company nor the means through which the information is processed is situated in South Africa.
- A company in the United States of America processes the personal information of South African residents which it collects by using a South African company (an 'operator'). In this case POPIA will apply to the operator and US company, because the means of collecting the personal information is situated in South Africa.
- A South African company uses servers in the United Kingdom to store the personal information of its customers. POPIA will apply, because the company is South African even though the means of storing the information is situated overseas.

Tricky area: This answer might change if the South African company is an 'operator' instead of a responsible party. The implications of being classified as an operator are discussed in chapter 4.

- A Zimbabwean company is sending the personal information of Zimbabwean citizens to Namibia via the internet which, during the transmission process, is routed through servers that are situated in South Africa. In this instance POPIA will not apply, because the responsible party is not a South African company and the personal information is just forwarded through South Africa and not processed here.

3.3 WHEN DOES POPIA NOT APPLY?

Some processing activities are completely excluded from the operation of POPIA. Other activities are excluded from one or more of the conditions for processing personal information.[18] We discuss each of these activities in more detail below.

[18] Section 4(2).

3.3.1 Personal and household activities

POPIA does not apply to processing personal information in purely personal or household activities.[19] The concept of a personal or household activity is not defined in POPIA. The exclusion will apply to the processing of personal information that is not in connection with a professional or commercial activity. For example, when an individual uses personal information to write to friends and family or take pictures for their own enjoyment, they are not subject to POPIA.

Tricky area: It is not always easy to determine where personal or household use begins and ends. The use of the word 'purely' suggests that if the information is also used for a commercial or professional purpose POPIA will apply. Here are two examples to illustrate this.

An individual installs a camera system at their family home for the purpose of protecting the property, health and life of the family who lives there. The system makes a video recording of the house and of people on the street outside the home (a public space). The recording is stored on a hard drive. Does this amount to processing for purely personal or household activities? Based on European case law, it might not qualify for this exclusion! To the extent that video surveillance covers a public space it may not be a purely personal or household activity and POPIA could apply.[20]

Many employers allow employees to use their personal devices for work. This is commonly known as 'bring your own device' or BYOD. Responsible parties must remain in control of personal information for which they are responsible, regardless of the ownership of the device used to carry out the processing. Control is challenging when employees use their personal devices. In an attempt to keep control many employers use tools like mobile device management or mobile application management to try and regain control. When using these tools an employer could inadvertently end up processing non-commercial information about the owner of the device and others who use it.

19 Section 6(1)*(a)*.

20 Judgment of the Court (Fourth Chamber) of 11 December 2014, Case C-212/13, *František Ryneš v Úrad pro ochranu osobních údaju*.

Similarly, employers must be careful when they monitor employees who are working from home. The ICO had the following to say on the topic: 'People expect that they can keep their personal lives private and that they are also entitled to a degree of privacy in the workplace.' The Article 29 Data Protection Working Party, published an opinion on data processing at work in 2017 in which it addressed the 'monitoring of home and remote working' in which they said that '[t]he key is addressing the risk posed by home and remote working in a proportionate, non-excessive manner'.[21]

3.3.2 De-identified/anonymised information

In order for POPIA to apply, the personal information needs to 'relate to' an identifiable individual or organisation.[22] This is confirmed in the exclusion contained in section 6(1)*(b)* which states that POPIA does not apply to information that has been de-identified to the extent that it cannot be re-identified again. There is also a definition of 'de-identify' which states that it means to delete all information that:

- identifies the data subject (e.g. their name)
- can be used or manipulated to identify the data subject; or
- can be linked to other information that identifies the data subject.[23]

This is where things get complicated. De-identification is very difficult to achieve, and the methods by which it can be undone (i.e. re-identified), increasingly sophisticated. For instance, data scientists have demonstrated that 87% of all Americans can be identified if you have their birth date, gender and zip code. [24] So, the legislature added that in order to meet a sufficient standard of de-identification there must be no 'reasonably foreseeable' method to re-identify the data subject.[25]

The wording of the definition is close to recital 26[26] of the EU GDPR which states that 'to determine whether a natural person is identifiable, account should be taken of all the means reasonably likely to be used'

21 Article 29 Data Protection Working Party *Opinion 2/2017 on Data Processing at Work*, available at https://ec.europa.eu/newsroom/article29/item-detail.cfm?item_id=610169.

22 The definition of 'personal information' in section 1.

23 The definition of 'de-identify' in section 1.

24 Latanya Sweeney 'Only you, your doctor, and many others may know' (September 2018) *Journal of Technology Science*, available at https://techscience.org/a/2015092903/.

25 The definition of 'de-identify' in section 1.

26 Recitals are not legally binding in the same way as the articles of the EU GDPR, but they can be used to interpret ambiguous provisions.

by the responsible party or another person to re-identify the data subject. The recital also states that responsible parties can determine what is 'reasonably likely' by taking into account 'all objective factors, such as the cost of and the amount of time required for identification, taking into consideration the available technology at the time of the processing and technological developments'.[27]

Tricky area: The definition of 'de-identify' includes that there must be no reasonably foreseeable method to re-identify the data subject. This leaves a bit of wriggle room in the event that new, unforeseeable, methods are developed. Section 6(1)*(b)* is written in more absolute terms – de-identified information, is information which 'cannot' be re-identified. That is an almost impossibly high bar. Consider that it might be objectively impossible to re-identify the information in 2021 but it might become possible to re-identify the personal information in 2024. This would mean that the information was correctly excluded from the scope of POPIA in 2021 but has to be reconsidered in 2024 as it is now within the scope of POPIA.

How would the responsible party determine whether information has been de-identified to an adequate level? A responsible party must consider what other information is out there, who it is available to and whether it is likely to be used in a re-identification process. The other information could be information available to certain organisations, to certain members of the public, or information that is available to everyone. The risk of re-identification will increase as data linkage techniques and computer processing power develop, and as more information becomes publicly available.[28] This, in conjunction with the requirement introduced in section 6(1)*(b)*, suggests that responsible parties should regularly re-evaluate whether the de-identification methods they used are still acceptable.

[27] Also see Article 29 Data Protection Working Party *Opinion 4/2007 on the concept of personal data*, available at https://ec.europa.eu/justice/article-29/documentation/opinion-recommendation/files/2007/wp136_en.pdf.

[28] ICO *Anonymisation: Managing Data Protection Risk Code of Practice* 18, available at https://ico.org.uk/media/for-organisations/documents/1061/anonymisation-code.pdf. Also see Article 29 Data Protection Working Party *Opinion 05/2014 on Anonymisation Techniques*, available at https://ec.europa.eu/justice/article-29/documentation/opinion-recommendation/files/2014/wp216_en.pdf.

Where de-identification is not an option, organisations should consider whether it is possible to mask or pseudonymise the personal information. Pseudonymisation is defined in the EU GDPR as 'the processing of personal data in such a manner that the personal data can no longer be attributed to a specific data subject without the use of additional information, provided that such additional information is kept separately and is subject to technical and organisational measures to ensure that the personal data are not attributed to an identified or identifiable natural person'.[29] Pseudonymisation is considered to be a very effective example of a 'technical and organisational measure' to protect personal information by default.[30] Why is it so effective? Masked personal information is useless to a person who wants to access it without additional information (e.g. a decryption key) – so twice the mischief is required. There are a whole host of techniques that can be used to pseudonymise personal information as set out in the European Union Agency for Cybersecurity's 'Pseudonymisation techniques and best practices'.[31]

De-identification and pseudonymisation are two different techniques:

Pseudonymisation	De-identification
Masks any identifying information	Destroys all identifying information
The process is reversible	The process cannot be reversed
POPIA still applies	POPIA no longer applies

29 Article 4(5) of the EU GDPR.

30 It is considered so effective that it is mentioned as an example in article 25(1) of the EU GDPR. It is not mentioned in POPIA, but will undoubtedly be given a similar status by information security management specialists. We discuss this (once more with feeling) in chapter 5 paragraph 5.5.2 in the context of information security management. Pseudonymisation can also be used to comply with the requirement of minimality, which is discussed in chapter 9.

31 3 December 2019, available at https://www.enisa.europa.eu/publications/pseudonymisation-techniques-and-best-practices. Also see Article 29 Data Protection Working Party 'Opinion 05/2014 on Anonymisation Techniques' 20, available at https://ec.europa.eu/justice/article-29/documentation/opinion-recommendation/files/2014/wp216_en.pdf and EDPS Introduction to the Hash Function as a Personal Data Pseudonymisation Technique, available at https://edps.europa.eu/sites/edp/files/publication/19-10-30_aepd-edps_paper_hash_final_en.pdf.

3.3.3 Certain functions of public bodies

POPIA applies equally to processing activities undertaken by public bodies. A public body is: [32]

- a national or provincial department (such as the justice and correctional services department or the department of housing in the Western Cape province); or
- a municipality or local government
- any institution which gets its mandate from the South African Constitution (such as the public protector) or from a provincial constitution (in health, education, agriculture, housing, environmental protection, and development planning); or
- an organisation that exercises a public function in terms of legislation (such as the short-term insurance Ombud or the Information Regulator which is created by POPIA).

Key point: An easy way to find out if an organisation thinks of themselves as a 'public body' is to look at the relevant organisation's PAIA manual.[33] PAIA separates out its responsibilities between public bodies (Part 2), which publish the PAIA manual in terms of section 14, and private bodies (Part 3), which publish the PAIA manual in terms of section 51. Be a little careful though. It is possible that they have not published their PAIA manual or they have made a mistake, but this tip is a quick and easy way to answer the question.

However, POPIA does not apply to a public body when:

- The processing of personal information relates to national security. National security includes the identification of financing used for terrorist and related activities or the defence of public safety.[34]

---

[32] See the definition of 'public body' in section 1 of POPIA. See further Francis Cronje & Eddie Laubscher *PAIA: What You Need to Know* (2016) at Addendum K for a useful list of information officers of public bodies in South Africa.

[33] Promotion of Access to Information Act 2 of 2000 (PAIA). The definition of 'public body' in PAIA is the same as the definition in POPIA.

[34] Section 6(1)*(c)*(i).

- The public body is involved in preventing, detecting, investigating or proving offences, prosecuting offenders, executing criminal sentences or providing security measures. This includes activities to identify the proceeds of unlawful activities and the combating of money laundering activities. This means that many of the processing activities undertaken by law enforcement will be excluded.[35]

Key point: This exclusion only applies to the extent that adequate safeguards have been established in legislation to protect the personal information used in these activities. As POPIA is so new not many pieces of legislation have sufficient safeguards to protect personal information which means that they will still fall inside the ambit of POPIA until they do have these safeguards. This problem is well illustrated by the *Amabhungane* case, which we discuss in chapter 4 paragraph 4.4.2.2.

Also see the more limited exemption in respect of certain functions which is discussed in paragraph 3.3.8 below.

3.3.4 The Cabinet and its committees or the Executive Council of a province

POPIA does not apply to the processing of personal information by the Cabinet of South Africa and its committees. The Cabinet consists of the President, the Deputy President and ministers. Similarly POPIA does not apply to the activities of the Executive Councils of the provinces.[36]

3.3.5 The judicial functions of a court

POPIA does not apply to the processing of personal information relating to the judicial functions of courts.[37]

---

35 Section 6(1)*(c)*(ii).

36 Section 6(1)*(d)*.

37 Section 6(1)*(e)*. The section refers to courts as defined in section 166 of the Constitution. This includes the Constitutional Court, the Supreme Court of Appeal, the High Courts, the Magistrates' Courts and any other court established or recognised in terms of an Act of Parliament.

Tricky area: The question here is what will be considered a 'judicial function of a court'? Does it include the publication of personal details in pleadings, and sometimes in the *Government Gazette*? PAIA contains a similar exclusion in section 12, which provides that PAIA 'does not apply to a record … relating to the judicial functions of … a court'. One of the questions here is whether the publication of the names and personal information of litigants during court proceedings falls within the application of POPIA? In *Februarie v Eskom Finance Company* (3196/19) [2019] ZAWCHC 145 (28 August 2019) the applicants argued that the publication of their personal information (full name, identity numbers and cell phone numbers) in a notice of sale in execution which was published in the *Government Gazette*, infringed their right to privacy. They alleged that it led to 'great public humiliation, degradation and tarnished and destroyed their reputation and embarrassed them'. The judge in this case found that the magistrates' courts rules justified the publication of a defendant's first names, residence or place of business, occupation and employment address of defendants.[38] The identity numbers were required to identify the property and the particulars of sale in an execution against immovable property.[39] Sharing cell phone numbers was justified because 'simple and expedited contact with the debtor can only be in the best interests of the debtor'.[40] This case was decided pre-POPIA. Would the answer change post-POPIA despite the exclusion of judicial functions? We think it might. It is likely that the exclusions will be given a very restricted interpretation and that practices such as the publication of personal information in court processes will have to be measured against the principles in POPIA to ensure that there is a legal basis for processing of personal information.

3.3.6 Journalistic, literary and artistic purposes

POPIA does not apply to personal information which is processed solely for the purpose of journalistic, literary or artistic expression. The exclusion will only apply if it is justified, in the particular case, to limit the right to privacy in favour of the right to freedom of expression.[41]

Chapter 3

38 Paragraphs 23 and 24.

39 Paragraphs 25 to 27.

40 Paragraph 28.

41 Section 7(1).

The balancing of competing constitutional rights is not new in South African law. Courts have in the past considered questions such as whether the publication of pseudonyms would have rendered the publication less authentic, the sensitivity of the personal information, the impact which the disclosure will have on the data subject (e.g. whether they will be stigmatised) and whether the disclosure of personal information serves a compelling public interest.[42]

Examples of what would be considered in the public interest are discussed in section 37(2) in the context of exemptions granted by the Information Regulator (discussed in paragraph 3.3.7 below). They include 'historical, statistical or research activity' and 'the interest in freedom of expression'.

Tricky area: What is included in journalistic, literary or artistic expression? In South African case law, someone is classified as a 'media defendant' when they are 'professionals involved in the distribution of information for commercial gain'.[43] Broader definitions have been adopted in Europe, which begs the question whether so-called 'citizen journalists' will fall under this exception. For instance, the European Court of Justice found that journalistic expression could include a YouTube video posted by someone who is not considered to be a journalist, provided that the sole purpose of the recording and publication of the video was the public disclosure of information, opinions or ideas.[44]

'Literary or artistic expression' is also not defined in POPIA. 'Literary expression' is an extremely broad term if one considers that the definition of literature is 'written works, especially those considered of superior or lasting artistic merit' or 'books and writings published on a particular subject' or 'leaflets and other printed matter used to advertise products or give advice'. Similarly an artistic expression can be any expression 'having or revealing natural creative skill'.[45]

---

42 See *NM v Smith* 2007 (5) SA 250 (CC) for an extensive discussion of the common law and constitutional law principles at play here.

43 See *NM v Smith* 2007 (5) SA 250 (CC) paragraph 98.

44 Case C-345/17 Request for preliminary ruling from the Augstāka tiesta, 14 February 2019, available at https://eur-lex.europa.eu/legal-content/EN/TXT/?uri=CELEX%3A62017CJ0345.

45 Oxford Languages.

The exclusion is extended in the case of publications for journalistic purposes if the publication is subject to a code of ethics, as long as the code provides adequate safeguards for the protection of personal information.[46] Here the public interest in the protection of personal information of data subjects must be weighed against the right to the free flow of information and the freedom of expression. If there is a dispute as to whether the safeguards are adequate or not, the following factors may be considered:

- the special importance of the public interest in freedom of expression
- domestic and international standards when balancing the right to privacy with the right to information
- the need to secure the integrity of personal information
- domestic and international standards of professional integrity for journalists; and
- any self-regulation in the profession.[47]

The South African Press Council's *Code of Ethics and Conduct for South African Print and Online Media* contains extensive provisions on privacy and POPIA:[48]

> '4. **Protection of Personal Information**
>
> The media shall:
>
> 4.1 take reasonable steps to ensure that the personal information under their control is protected from misuse, loss, and unauthorized access;
>
> 4.2 ensure that the personal information they gather is accurate, reasonably complete and up to date;
>
> 4.3 take steps to verify the accuracy of their information and, if necessary, amend it where a person requests a correction to be made to his or her personal information;
>
> 4.4 only disclose sufficient personal information to identify the person being reported on as some information, such as addresses, may enable others to intrude on their privacy and safety; and
>
> 4.5 inform the affected person(s) and take reasonable steps to mitigate any prejudicial effects where it is reasonably suspected that an unauthorized person may have obtained access to personal information held by the media.'

Whether these safeguards will be seen as adequate, only time will tell.

46 Section 7(2).

47 Section 7(3).

48 Paragraphs 3 and 4 of the *Code of Ethics and Conduct for South African Print and Online Media*, available at https://www.presscouncil.org.za/ContentPage?code=PRESSCODE.

3.3.7 Exemptions by the Information Regulator

A responsible party can apply for an exemption from the conditions that apply to the processing of personal information.[49] The Information Regulator will grant the exemption if:

- the public interest in processing the personal information substantially outweighs the infringement of the data subject's privacy;[50] or
- the processing involves a clear benefit to the data subject or a third party that outweighs the infringement of their privacy.[51]

'Public interest' is not defined in POPIA, but section 37(2) lists the following 'public interests':

- national security
- the prevention, detection and prosecution of offences
- important economic and financial interests of a public body
- fostering compliance with legislation that promotes:
  - the public interests mentioned in the prevention, detection and prosecution of offences
  - or the economic and financial interests of a public body
- historical, statistical or research activity;[52] or
- freedom of expression.

Tricky area: The processing activities that are associated with some of these 'public interests' are already fully or partially exempted from POPIA. For instance, POPIA already does not apply to public bodies that process personal information for purposes of national security, as long as satisfactory safeguards have already been established in legislation. It would not be necessary for such a public body to apply for any further exemption, provided that adequate safeguards already exist in legislation.

3.3.8 Exemptions for certain functions

The processing of personal information for the purpose of performing certain functions is exempt from certain sections of POPIA to the extent

49 Section 37. The Information Regulator has published a Guidance Note on Exemptions from the conditions for Lawful Processing of Personal Information in terms of Section 37 and 38 available at https://justice.gov.za/inforeg/docs/InfoRegSA-GuidanceNote-PPI-LawfulProcessing-202106.pdf and an Exemption Application Form available at https://justice.gov.za/inforeg/docs/forms/InfoRegSA-GuidanceNote-PPI-LawfulProcessing-ExemptionApplication-eForm-202106.pdf

50 Section 37(1)*(a)*.

51 Section 37(1)*(b)*.

52 We discuss the meaning of 'historical, statistical or research purpose' in chapter 2 paragraph 2.6.7.

that the application of those provisions to the personal information would be likely to prejudice the proper discharge of that function.[53]

This exemption applies to the functions of a public body or to functions conferred on any person in terms of the law and which are performed with the aim to protect members of the public against:

- financial loss due to dishonesty, malpractice or other seriously improper conduct by, or the unfitness or incompetence of, persons concerned in the provision of banking, insurance, investment or other financial services or in the management of bodies corporate; or
- dishonesty, malpractice or other serious improper conduct by, or the unfitness or incompetence of, persons authorised to carry on any profession or other activity.[54]

This exemption seems to be primarily aimed at regulators in the financial services industry (such as the Financial Sector Conduct Authority) and regulatory bodies such as the Legal Practice Council or the Allied Health Professions Council of South Africa.

This is not a total exemption from POPIA. Only some requirements are excluded:

Requirements that are excluded	Why it matters
The data subject does not have the right to object to processing where the responsible party is relying on the legal justifications that: • the processing protects a legitimate interest of the data subject • the processing is necessary for pursuing the legitimate interests of the responsible party or a third party; or • the processing is necessary for the proper performance of a public law duty by a public body.[55]	There are six legal justifications for the processing of personal information.[56] Data subjects have a right to object 'on reasonable grounds relating to his, her or its particular situation' depending on which legal justifications the responsible body is relying. This exclusion takes that right to object away, which means that data subjects will have less control over the processing of their personal information by regulators in the financial services industry and other 'professions'.

➥

[53] Section 38(1).

[54] Section 38(2).

[55] Section 11(3) and (4).

[56] These are discussed in chapter 6.

Requirements that are excluded	Why it matters
These responsible parties do not have to collect the information directly from the data subject.[57]	POPIA creates a default rule that personal information must be collected directly from the data subject, with certain exceptions.[58] This exclusion gives regulators in the financial services industry and other 'professions' the freedom to collect personal information from other sources.
These responsible parties do not have to comply with the requirement that 'further processing' must be compatible with the purpose for which the personal information was collected.[59]	Further processing (or 'secondary use') of personal information is discussed in chapter 12. There are certain requirements which responsible parties must meet if they want to use personal information for a purpose other than for what it was collected. This exclusion gives these regulators in the financial services industry and other 'professions' more leeway to use the personal information that was collected for another reason in their investigations into misconduct.
These responsible parties do not have to make the normal notifications to data subjects.[60]	Investigations into misconduct often require a bit of stealth and that is frustrated if you notify the data subject that you are investigating them. This exclusion exempts these regulators from notification duties.[61]

Key point: The exemption is not absolute. These responsible parties must motivate exactly why complying with these requirements 'would be likely to prejudice the proper discharge' of their functions.

[57] Section 12.

[58] This is discussed in chapter 10.

[59] Section 15.

[60] Section 18.

[61] Notification is discussed in chapter 11.

3.4 WHEN DID POPIA COME INTO EFFECT?

POPIA was signed into law on 19 November 2013. However, section 115 of the legislation provided that POPIA would only 'commence' on a date determined by the President by proclamation in the *Government Gazette*.

Section 1 (definitions), Part A of Chapter 5 (establishment of the Information Regulator) and sections 112 (Regulations), and 113 (procedures for making Regulations) commenced on 11 April 2014.[62] This was done to ensure that the Information Regulator could start preparing for the enforcement of the legislation. The members of the Information Regulator were appointed from 1 December 2016.[63]

The rest of POPIA commenced on 1 July 2020 with three exceptions:[64]

- POPIA amended the Public Protector Act,[65] the Promotion of Access to Information Act (PAIA),[66] the Electronic Communications and Transactions Act,[67] and the National Credit Act[68] from 30 June 2021.[69]
- The functions of the Human Rights Commission in terms of PAIA passed to the Information Regulator on 30 June 2021.[70]
- Section 58(2), which provides that responsible parties must stop processing personal information if an application for prior authorisation is pending, is in force from 1 February 2022.[71]

Key point: Section 114(1) of POPIA provides that '[a]ll processing of personal information must within one year after the commencement of this section be made to conform with this Act'. Given that section 114 commenced on 1 July 2020, this means that organisations had to comply by 30 June 2021.

The SA Law Reform Commission considered whether a grandfathering clause should be included in POPIA. A grandfathering clause is an exception that allows an old rule to continue to apply to some existing situations, when a

62 Proc R 25 of 2014 in *GG* 37544 of 11 April 2014.

63 The powers of the Information Regulator are discussed in chapter 19.

64 Proc R 21 of 2020 in GG 43461 of 22 June 2020.

65 Act 23 of 1994.

66 Act 2 of 2000.

67 Act 25 of 2002.

68 Act 34 of 2005.

69 Section 110 and Proc R 21 of 2020 in *GG* 43461 of 22 June 2020.

70 Section 114 (4).

71 Section 114(3). Prior authorisation is discussed in chapter 8.

new rule will apply to all future situations. The Commission decided that a grandfathering clause should not be included because responsible parties can solve problems with pre-legislation personal information practices by the gradual implementation of privacy principles. The Commission also noted that section 114 provided sufficient transitional arrangements, and that responsible parties have had enough time to introduce good business practices in their organisations. The Commission made this statement in 2009, when the Bill had been in development for five years.[72] One can only imagine what the Commission's response would be if an organisation had not made any effort to comply by 2021!

3.5 DOES POPIA APPLY RETROSPECTIVELY?

3.5.1 The unfairness test

In general, South African legislation does not apply to events that occurred before the legislation was in force unless it is clear in the legislation that it should apply to past events. This is referred to as the presumption against retrospectivity and it is important in the context of POPIA, because many of the processing activities that are now subject to the legislation may have started long before the effective date.[73]

> **Tricky area:** Can the Information Regulator hold a responsible party responsible for non-compliance with POPIA that would require time travel to fix? For instance, a responsible party cannot be held responsible for not keeping a record of all third parties who had access to personal information before POPIA came into full effect. Similarly, can a responsible party be held responsible for non-compliance with section 12 if the information was collected before 30 June 2021?

Our courts have distinguished between two types of 'retrospectivity': strong and weak retrospectivity. The concept of 'strong' versus 'weak' retrospectivity were explained as follows in the case of *Pienaar Brothers (Pty) Ltd v Commissioner, South African Revenue Service*:[74]

> 'In the context of retrospectivity of legislation, it was pointed out that South African case law distinguishes between retrospectivity of legislation in the "weak" and "strong" sense. A statutory provision is retrospective in the weak sense if it prospectively effects, or changes the consequences

---

[72] SA Law Reform Commission Project 124 on Privacy and Data Protection (2009 Report) 71.

[73] This is because of the very broad definition of 'processing'. Just storing information qualifies as processing. We discuss the definition in paragraph 3.2.1.2.

[74] 2017 (6) SA 435 (GP).

> for the future of, pre-existing transactions and matters. An enactment is retrospective in the strong sense if the provision is deemed to have been in force from an earlier date than that on which it was in fact enacted.'[75]

In *National Director of Public Prosecutions v Carolus*,[76] the presiding judge quoted Canadian precedent – which explains 'strong retrospectivity' and 'weak retrospectivity' in relation to the concept of a 'retroactive statute':

> 'A retroactive statute is one that operates as of a time prior to its enactment. A retrospective statute is one that operates for the future only. It is prospective, but it imposes new results in respect of a past event. A retroactive statute operates backwards. A retrospective statute operates forwards, but it looks backwards in that it attaches new consequences for the future to an event that took place before the statute was enacted. A retroactive statute changes the law from what it was; a retrospective changes the law from what it otherwise would be with respect to a prior event.'[77]

The presumption against legislation applying with retrospective effect applies in cases of both 'strong' and 'weak' retrospectivity.[78] The 'basis of the presumption is "elementary considerations of fairness (which) dictate that individuals should have an opportunity to know what the law is and to confirm their conduct accordingly"'.[79]

In the case of *Bareki NO v Gencor Ltd*,[80] the court had to consider whether certain sections of the National Environmental Management Act 107 of 1998 (NEMA) applied to acts of pollution and degradation that took place before 29 January 1999 (when NEMA came into force).[81] The court came to the conclusion that in order to determine whether the legislature intended POPIA[82] to create new obligations or duties in regard to events that took place before POPIA came into operation, the courts must apply 'the test of unfairness' in order to find the true intention of the legislature.[83] The test works as follows:

- Does the legislation attach new consequences for the future of an event which took place before the legislation was enacted? Put differently, does the legislation create new obligations or impose new duties in regard to events already past?

Chapter 3

75 *Pienaar Brothers (Pty) Ltd v Commissioner, South African Revenue Service* at paragraph 16.

76 1999 (2) SACR 607 (SCA).

77 *National Director of Public Prosecutions v Carolus* at paragraph 34.

78 *National Director of Public Prosecutions v Carolus* at paragraph 36.

79 *Bareki NO v Gencor Ltd* 2006 (1) SA 432 (T) 439.

80 2006 (1) SA 432 (T).

81 Yes, we are comparing responsible parties to polluters. Back in 2006 Clive Humby, a British data scientist, said 'data is the new oil', so the polluter analogy was not our idea. We discuss how much we hate the analogy in chapter 10 paragraph 10.5.2.

82 We just substituted POPIA for NEMA. We are drunk with power.

83 *Bareki NO v Gencor Ltd* 439.

Tricky area: POPIA applies to information which was collected before the legislation came into effect. Consider this example: A company purchases contact information from a data broker for purposes of direct marketing in 2020. In 2020, there was no regulation preventing either the company from purchasing or the data broker from selling the information. Section 12 of POPIA now provides that personal information must be collected directly from the data subject, unless one of the exceptions apply.[84] Does this mean that the company cannot continue to use the database it purchased; even though it complies with the rest of POPIA?

- If the answer to the first question is yes: Was the legislation enacted with the intention of attaching consequences or creating new obligations in respect of events which took place before the legislation came into operation? In answering this question, the Information Regulator will have to ask whether there would be unfairness or encroachment upon the rule of law to anyone, if the legislation in question was applied with retrospective effect.[85] This is determined by looking at the nature of the duty or obligation that is created and the circumstances under which it arises.

Key point: POPIA has fairness built in. Let's continue to use compliance with section 12 where collection took place before 1 July 2021 as an example. Unlike in the *Bareki* case, the liability which is created in respect of non-compliance with section 12 is not strict. It provides that compliance is not necessary if it is not 'reasonably practicable in the circumstances of the case'.[86] In cases where the obligation in POPIA is strict, a responsible party could argue that retrospective application of the requirement would be unfair.

- If there is unfairness or encroachment upon the rule of law, was it intended by the legislature?

---

84 Section 12 is discussed in chapter 10.

85 Why must the Information Regulator answer this question and not the responsible party? There is a presumption against retrospectivity and so the party alleging that POPIA must apply retrospectively must rebut the presumption that it is unfair.

86 We discuss this in chapter 10 paragraph 10.4.8. If the collection took place before POPIA came into force, the responsible party could argue compliance is not 'reasonably practicable' given that a responsible party cannot go back in time to the point of collection. If that argument is not successful, a responsible party could argue in the alternative that applying POPIA retrospectively is unfair.

Tricky area: Sometime the legislature makes its intent known by expressly stating that legislation will operate retroactively. In those instances, the unfairness was intentional. Section 114(1) of POPIA states that 'all processing of personal information must within one year after the commencement of this section be made to conform with this Act'. If anything, this statement confirms that POPIA does not look backwards, but that ongoing processing activities after 1 July 2021 must comply. There is no clear intent here.

3.5.2 Requirements of POPIA that require time travel

So what is the conclusion then? Some provisions in POPIA are ongoing, like the requirement that all processing must have a legal basis[87] and that the responsible party must secure the integrity and confidentiality of personal information;[88] they can be discharged in respect of ongoing processing activities that started before 1 July 2021. There are other obligations that must be discharged at certain points in a processing activity. For example, the rule that information can only be collected from the data subject directly or that the data subject must be notified at collection. If collection took place before 1 July 2021, it may be possible for responsible parties to rely on the presumption that POPIA does not apply retrospectively.

Based on the rules discussed above, there are some examples of requirements in POPIA which we do not think will apply to processing activities that took place before 1 July 2021:[89]

87 See chapters 6 and 7.

88 See chapter 5.

89 This list is not exhaustive. Exhausting, maybe.

The requirement	If [a responsible party] could turn back time, if [a responsible party] could find a way…[90]
Personal information must be collected from the data subject directly, unless one of the exceptions apply.[91]	We do not think that it is necessary to rely on an argument that POPIA does not apply retrospectively, because section 12(2)*(f)* provides that the responsible party does not have to comply if 'compliance is not reasonably practicable in the circumstances of the particular case'. Last time we checked, not even Cher could turn back time. If that argument is not successful, a responsible party could argue in the alternative that applying POPIA retrospectively is unfair. Responsible parties can continue to use databases obtained from third-party sources before POPIA came into effect, as long as they comply with the rest of POPIA.[92]
Personal information must be collected for a specific, explicitly defined and lawful purpose.[93]	Responsible parties were under no obligation to specifically define the purposes for which they collected personal information before POPIA came into effect. In many instances, the original purpose for which personal information was collected will be lost in the mists of time. As long as the responsible party has a specific, explicitly defined and lawful purpose for retaining the information post-1 July 2021, the responsible party cannot be held responsible for not knowing why it was collected in the first place.

➡

90 Cher 'If I Could Turn Back Time' *Heart of Stone* (1989).

91 Section 12 is discussed in chapter 10.

92 Even after 1 July 2021, POPIA does not prohibit collection of personal information from third-party sources. We discuss this thorny issue in chapter 13 paragraph 13.6.1.

93 Section 13 is discussed in chapter 6 paragraph 6.2.

The requirement	If [a responsible party] could turn back time, if [a responsible party] could find a way...
	Tricky area: There are a number of sections in POPIA which presuppose that a responsible party knows the original purpose for the collection of the personal information. For instance, a responsible party cannot assess whether 'further processing' of personal information is allowed, without knowing the purpose for which it is collected. Similarly, it will be difficult for responsible parties to gauge whether they are required to apply for prior authorisation for the further processing of unique identifiers for purposes of linking personal information.[94] While we do not think that a responsible party can be held liable for not explicitly defining the purpose at the time of collection if collection took place before 1 July 2021, not having documented the purpose for collection may make life difficult if the responsible party ever wants to prove that the processing it is doing is not further processing.[95]

[94] Further processing is discussed in chapter 12. Prior authorisation for certain uses of unique identifiers is discussed in chapter 8 paragraph 8.2.1.

[95] The legal justifications for 'further processing' in section 15 are different to the legal justifications in section 11.

The requirement	If [a responsible party] could turn back time, if [a responsible party] could find a way...
Section 18(1) contains a list of disclosures responsible parties must make 'before the information is collected' (in cases where the information is collected directly from the data subject) or 'as soon as reasonably practicable after it was collected' (in cases where information is obtained from third parties).[96]	On 1 July 2021, our inboxes were flooded with privacy notices. Presumably, responsible parties did this to ensure that they comply with section 18, even though the information was collected a long time ago. Section 18(2)'s requirement that this should have been done before collection was not complied with, because there was no bend in the space-time continuum. To hold a responsible party responsible for not notifying data subjects at the time would be unfair as it was not a requirement back then. Luckily, we do not think that it is necessary to rely on an argument that POPIA does not apply retrospectively, because section 18(4)*(e)* provides that the responsible party does not have to comply if 'compliance is not reasonably practicable in the circumstances of the particular case'. If that argument is not successful, a responsible party could argue in the alternative that applying POPIA retrospectively is unfair.
Responsible parties are required to secure the integrity and confidentiality of personal information. Responsible parties are also required to notify the Information Regulator of any security compromises as soon as reasonably possible after there are 'reasonable grounds to believe that the personal information of a data subject has been accessed or acquired by any unauthorised person'.[97]	Data breaches are discovered long after the data breach actually occurs. According to IBM, the average time it took to identify breaches in 2020 was 228 days. Can a responsible party be held responsible in terms of POPIA for a data breach which took place before 1 July 2021? The Information Regulator will probably argue that the breach is ongoing, but based on the *Bareki* case, we would argue that this type of retrospective effect was not intended by the legislature. However, if the responsible party becomes aware of the breach after 1 July 2021 and does not notify the Information Regulator within a reasonable time, the conclusion might be different.

➡

96 Section 18(2). Notification is discussed in detail in chapter 11.

97 Section 19(1) and section 22(1). This is discussed in chapter 5.

The requirement	If [a responsible party] could turn back time, if [a responsible party] could find a way…
Data subjects have several new rights in terms of POPIA, including the right to request a record or description about the identity of all third parties, or categories of third parties, who have, or have had, access to the personal information.[98]	Can a responsible party be faulted if it did not maintain a meticulous record of which third parties had access to what personal information prior to 1 July 2021? We think not.

3.6 PRACTICAL ADVICE

3.6.1 Identify your processing activities

POPIA compliance is assessed at a processing activity level. A processing activity is a collection of related tasks aimed at a specific outcome (e.g. onboarding a new customer or employee) during which personal information is created, collected, used, shared, transformed, stored or destroyed. [99] The first step towards becoming compliant is to identify all of the processing activities in an organisation. Ideally these business processes should be documented.[100]

3.6.2 Classify personal information

The second step is to identify which of the business processes involve personal information. POPIA introduces the need to classify all personal information. This is done by identifying all of the 'information assets' that are used in a process and determining whether that information asset contains personal information. An information asset is a body of information that is organised and managed as a unit. Examples include a database (whether it is an Excel spreadsheet or an information management system), a folder in which all information relating to a topic is kept in a centrally accessible location or physical records kept in a filing cabinet or filing room. Whenever personal information

98 Section 23(1)*(a)*.

99 Remember all the verbs in the definition of 'processing'? They were: collect, receive, record, organise, collate, store, update, modify, retrieve, alter, consult, use, disseminate (transmit, distribute or make available), merge, link, restrict, degrade, erase or destroy.

100 The role of standardisation in POPIA compliance is discussed in chapter 1 paragraph 1.2.3. Creating a record of processing activities (called a ROPA in other jurisdictions) is also part of documenting processing activities. This was discussed in chapter 1 paragraph 1.4.

'is entered into a record' by or for a responsible party, an information asset is created. The concept of an 'information asset' is central to information security management.[101]

Personal information is not the only type of information which organisations must manage. While identifying personal information, organisations may as well classify other types of information. This is referred to as 'information classification', which is another central concept in information security management. It is a process during which organisations assess the data that they hold and the level of protection it should be given.

Organisations usually classify information in terms of confidentiality but we recommend that they should add classifications of personal information for POPIA compliance. Here is an example of different classes of information:

- public information
- private information
- confidential information
- personal information; and
- special personal information.

Organisations can follow the guidelines set out in ISO/IEC 27001[102] which include the objective of information classification to ensure that information receives an appropriate level of protection in accordance with its importance to the organisation.[103]

3.6.3 The test for when POPIA applies in a nutshell

First identify each processing activity and then determine whether POPIA applies for each business activity. Once an organisation has listed all of the activities that involve information assets that contain personal information, only two questions remain to determine whether POPIA will apply:

- Is the responsible party by who (or for whom) the (personal) information asset was created domiciled in South Africa? **OR**
- If the responsible party is domiciled overseas, is any part of the business process taking place in South Africa?

[101] Information security management is discussed in chapter 5.

[102] ISO/IEC 27000 International Standard on Information technology – Security techniques – Information security management systems – Requirements.

[103] Information security management is discussed in chapter 5.

4 Who is accountable for POPIA compliance

4.1 WHAT TO EXPECT IN THIS CHAPTER

A friend of ours who works in an internal audit department made a joke once.[1] She said that the goal of compliance is to move from a state of unconscious incompetence to conscious incompetence. We find that organisations have compliance failures, not because they took a calculated risk, but because they were not aware that they were taking a risk in the first place. In the POPIA context, this often happens because an organisation is not aware that it is 'accountable'. This is what this chapter is about.

These days, personal information is almost never processed by just one organisation at a time. It is a hallmark of digital transformation that processing is happening in vast networks of related and unrelated organisations, each responsible for differing aspects of processing. The purpose of the principle of 'accountability' is to determine which amongst these organisations will ultimately be held accountable if the processing activity does not comply with POPIA. It is the responsible party's responsibility to ensure compliance with POPIA, maintain a record of processing activities[2] and co-operate with the Information Regulator if something goes wrong. It is the responsible party that could ultimately be faced with an enforcement notice, an administrative fine or civil liability.[3]

In this chapter we discuss the following:

- The role of 'accountability': A quick overview of who is accountable
- When to determine accountability
- How to identify operators and what they are accountable for
- Identifying co-responsible parties
- How to distinguish employees from responsible parties and operators
- Some practical examples of how to apply the definitions

1 Yes, people who work in internal audit can make jokes. We found it hard to believe at first, too.

2 Section 17 of POPIA. The 'documentation' requirement is discussed in chapter 1 paragraph 1.4.

3 Section 90 (information notices), section 95 (enforcement notices), section 99 (civil remedies), section 103(1) (failure to comply with information and enforcement notices) and section 109 (administrative fines) are the provisions in POPIA through which responsible parties are held accountable. All of these sections stipulate that the enforcement action is taken against the 'responsible party'. Refer to chapter 19 for more about enforcement.

4.2 THE ROLE OF 'ACCOUNTABILITY': A QUICK OVERVIEW OF WHO IS ACCOUNTABLE

Once you have determined that POPIA applies,[4] the next step is to determine which organisation must ensure that POPIA is complied with.[5] Sounds simple enough, but it rarely is.

Where there are multiple organisations taking part in the same processing activity, personal information is usually being shared between them. In chapter 13 we will discuss how to share personal information between different organisations in a POPIA-compliant way. This chapter is about how to determine which organisation(s) are accountable for POPIA compliance.

POPIA creates categories of organisations that determine who is accountable for what:

4.2.1 The responsible party

A responsible party is a public body, private body or any other person 'which, alone or in conjunction with others, determines the purpose of and means for processing personal information'.[6] 'Person' is defined as either a natural or a juristic person. For the most part, we refer to 'organisations' in this book, but these organisations can be big, small, public, private, incorporated or sole proprietors.

The definition of 'responsible party' has two elements:

- Who determines the purpose of the processing activity (why personal information is processed)?

  AND

- Who determines the means for the processing activity (how personal information is processed)?

The responsible party must ensure that POPIA is complied with before and during the processing of personal information.[7]

Section 90 (information notices), section 95 (enforcement notices), section 99 (civil remedies), section 103(1) (failure to comply with information and enforcement notices) and section 109 (administrative fines) are the provisions in POPIA through which responsible parties

Chapter 4

---

4 This is discussed in chapter 3.

5 This chapter is not about the accountability of individuals within organisations. Different roles and responsibilities in respect of POPIA compliance are discussed in chapter 1 paragraph 1.3.

6 Section 1.

7 Section 8. Remember that 'processing' includes the act of storing the personal information: see chapter 3.

are held accountable. All of these sections stipulate that the enforcement action is taken against the 'responsible party'.

The responsible party will be accountable even if the non-compliance is caused by another organisation which is processing the personal information on its behalf. The SA Law Reform Commission explained the rationale behind this decision as follows:

> '[S]ince the data processing activities are carried out for the benefit of the responsible parties (data controllers) the controllers should be accountable ... for complying with privacy protection rules and should not be relieved of this accountability merely because data processors are carrying out the processing activities on their behalf.'[8]

4.2.2 Co-responsible parties

Although they are not mentioned by name the definition of 'responsible party' caters for the possibility of multiple parties working together to form a single responsible party. Two (or more) responsible parties are co-responsible parties if they take joint decisions about the purposes and means of processing.[9]

Tricky area: Apart from acknowledging that joint or co-responsible parties are possible, POPIA does not impose additional requirements when this is the case, and provides no guidance on how liability will be apportioned should there be non-compliance with POPIA. All of the sections that deal with enforcement refer to the responsible party (singular). This was the same in the EU Data Protection Directive in 1995. The commentary under the EU GDPR, while useful for identifying when co-responsible parties exist, should be treated with care as the EU GDPR imposes new requirements on joint controllers and includes provisions on how liability should be apportioned.[10] The commentary on the EU GDPR can be treated as 'best practice', but not as requirements under POPIA.

So, we have to rely on old commentary on the EU Data Protection Directive to fill this gap in POPIA.

---

8 SA Law Reform Commission Project 124 on Privacy and Data Protection (2009 Report) from 166.

9 The definition of 'responsible party' in section 1.

10 Recital 79, article 4(7) and article 26 of the EU GDPR.

The Article 29 Data Protection Working Party had the following to say back in the day: 'Joint and several liability for all parties involved should be considered as a means of eliminating uncertainties and therefore assumed only in so far as an alternative, clear and equally effective allocation of obligations and responsibilities has not been established by the parties involved or does not clearly stem from factual circumstances.'[11] We would argue that holding co-responsible parties jointly and severally liable would be in 'harmony with international standards'.[12]

If co-responsible parties are held jointly and severally liable, the Information Regulator may hold any of the co-responsible parties liable for the full administrative fine or to take civil action against them. It would then be for the co-responsible parties to pursue claims against each other in terms of their contract or the common law.

4.2.3 Operators

An operator is a person:

- who processes personal information,
- for the responsible party,
- in terms of a contract or mandate,
- without coming under the direct authority of the responsible party.[13]

---

11 Article 29 Data Protection Working Party *Opinion 1/2010 on the concepts of 'controller' and 'processor'*, 24, available at https://ec.europa.eu/justice/article-29/documentation/opinion-recommendation/files/2010/wp169_en.pdf.

12 See chapter 2 paragraph 2.4 for when it is appropriate to consider international guidelines and foreign law.

13 The definition of 'operator' in section 1.

Tricky area: Operators are not accountable to the Information Regulator, but are accountable to the responsible party.[14] We base this statement on the fact that most of the provisions in POPIA refer to the 'responsible party'.[15] The extent of the accountability of the operator for data protection then depends on the contractual arrangements between the operator and the responsible party. An operator may also face civil liability from data subjects based on the common law, but not for an infringement of POPIA.

If you think this seems unfair, you are not alone. The failure to provide for direct operator liability has left a loophole in POPIA. This was one of the issues with the EU Data Protection Directive which was addressed in the EU GDPR. Article 82 now makes it clear that data processors can be held liable directly under certain circumstances.[16]

4.2.4 Sub-operators

Sub-operators are operators who have been appointed by operators themselves in terms of a mandate from the responsible party.

'Sub-operator' is not a term you will find in POPIA but it is a useful definition to show that this operator is actually being instructed by an operator itself. In theory it would be possible for there to be an unlimited number of sub-operators who would each take instructions from the operator with authority over them. In practice it is difficult to know how a responsible party could be exercising oversight and ensuring accountability over the sub-operators if their number becomes too large and their relationship with the responsible party becomes too distant.

---

14 Section 90 (information notices), section 95 (enforcement notices), section 99 (civil remedies), section 103(1) (failure to comply with information and enforcement notices) and section 109 (administrative fines) all refer to the 'responsible party'.

15 Full disclosure, there are specialists who disagree with us. They argue that section 4(1) of POPIA lists the 'conditions for the lawful processing of personal information by *or for* a responsible party' (our emphasis). We think that section 4(1) is eclipsed by the fact that section 8 states that '***the responsible party*** must ensure that the conditions set out in this Chapter, and all the measures that give effect to such conditions, are complied with' (our emphasis). Almost all of the sections in chapter 3 explicitly refer to the responsible party. Operators are only mentioned in sections 20 and 21.

16 As POPIA matures in South Africa we anticipate that there will be various amendments to the Act. One of the amendments we expect is direct operator liability in certain circumstances.

4.3 WHEN TO DETERMINE ACCOUNTABILITY

Accountability for POPIA starts when the responsible party determines why and how personal information will be processed (in other words, when the processing is being planned) as well as during the processing.[17] Put differently, the accountable organisation must ensure that POPIA is complied with throughout the information life cycle, which is set out below:

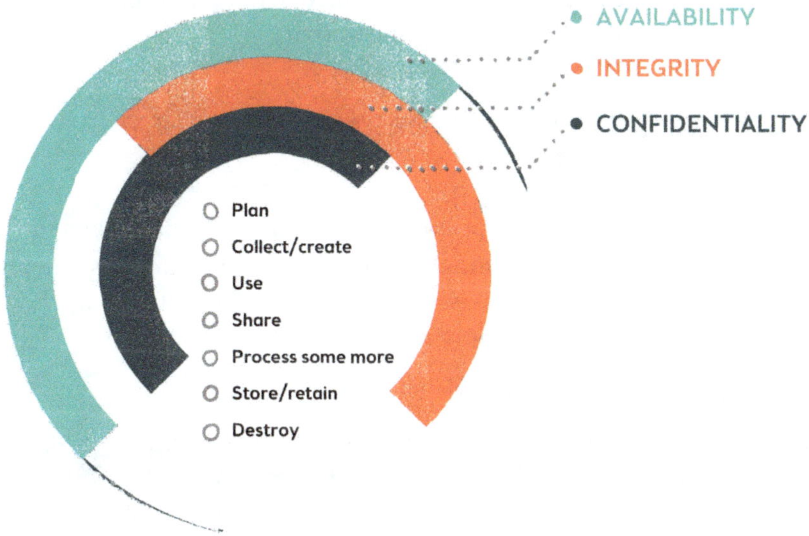

** This image depicts how POPIA creates new requirements for each stage of the personal information life cycle. The outside layers are the 'CIA triad', which is a layer of information security. We place this on the outside of the life cycle as information security must be maintained by the responsibility throughout the life cycle.*[18]

Whether an organisation is a responsible party or not, is determined per processing activity. It is quite possible for one organisation to be an operator for some processes while at the same time being a responsible party for other processes. In fact, it is quite likely that most companies will occupy the role of responsible party, operator, co-responsible party and sub-operator at the same time in respect of different processing activities. But they will only ever occupy a single role for a processing activity.

Key point: You need to identify the process before you can identify the role each party plays in that process. This is essential so that you can know who is accountable.

---

17 Section 8.

18 Information security is discussed in chapter 5.

Failing to accurately identify who the responsible party is for each processing activity, is probably the biggest mistake an organisation can make. After all, the first step towards discharging a responsibility is to realise that it is yours to discharge. In the remainder of this chapter, we will discuss:

- how to accurately identify responsible parties, co-responsible parties, operators, sub-operators and employees; and
- strategies to manage compliance where multiple organisations are involved in a processing activity.

4.4 HOW TO IDENTIFY OPERATORS AND WHAT THEY ARE ACCOUNTABLE FOR

4.4.1 How to distinguish responsible parties from operators

Once you have determined that an organisation is involved in a processing activity, it is time to determine whether they are a responsible party or an operator.

Here are some factors to consider:[19]

Responsible Party	Operator
They benefit from, or have an interest in, the processing activity. They make decisions about the data subject as part of the processing (for example whether to give the data subject a loan or not). The processing activity in question is typical of an organisation in their industry and usually includes data protection and privacy responsibilities. The processing impacts on their relationship with their employees, customers or suppliers. They determine how the processing is going to take place on their own. They have outsourced the processing activity to another organisation.	They process personal information for another organisation's purposes according to its documented instructions. Another party monitors their processing activities to ensure that they comply with instructions and terms of a contract. They do not pursue their own purpose in the processing other than their own business interest to provide services. They were contracted to carry out specific activities by someone who in turn has been contracted to process personal information on another party's behalf and on that party's documented instructions (they are a sub-operator).

19 European Data Protection Board *Guidelines 07/2020 on the concepts of controller and processor in the EU GDPR* 47, available at https://edpb.europa.eu/sites/edpb/files/consultation/edpb_guidelines_202007_controllerprocessor_en.pdf.

Here is a flowchart which can be used to distinguish the responsible party from the operator: [20]

**This image was adapted from the work by the European Data Protection Board's Guidelines 07/2020 on the Concepts of Controller and Processor in the EU GDPR. All hail the EDPB.*

4.4.2 The implications of using an operator (from the perspective of a responsible party)

Once an organisation has determined that it is a responsible party in a process, it should identify any operators involved in the process. If there is an operator involved in the process, then the immediate next step is to establish whether there is an agreement in place between the responsible party and the operator which governs that relationship. We have made recommendations for all of the aspects which should be

---

[20] European Data Protection Board *Guidelines 07/2020 on the concepts of controller and processor in the EU GDPR* 46, available at https://edpb.europa.eu/sites/edpb/files/consultation/edpb_guidelines_202007_controllerprocessor_en.pdf.

addressed in agreements between responsible parties and operators in paragraph 4.8.1.3. In this section we discuss the minimum requirements as prescribed by POPIA.[21]

Key point: These requirements are not formal requirements for the validity of the agreement between a responsible party and an operator. They are substantive requirements relating to the obligations that must be recorded in an agreement before a responsible party is allowed to make use of an operator.

Having an agreement with an operator is not the only requirement that POPIA imposes when operators are used. There are other obligations placed on the operator in sections 20 and 21(2). They will also be discussed in this section.

4.4.2.1 The minimum requirements for operator agreements

Section 21(1) provides that:

- there must be a written agreement between the responsible party and the operator,
- in terms of which the responsible party 'ensures' that the operator establishes and maintains the security measures referred to in section 19.[22]

This is the only obligation which must be recorded in a written agreement with the operator.[23] Section 1 of POPIA provides that 'writing' includes a 'data message' as set out in section 12 of the Electronic Communications and Transactions Act 25 of 2002. There is no requirement for a 'signature' within POPIA in respect of operator agreements.[24]

---

21 The minimum requirements are contained in sections 19 to 21. They relate to information security management which is discussed in chapter 5.

22 The security measures contemplated in section 19 are discussed in chapter 5.

23 There is no other specific reference to 'written' or 'in writing' in sections 20 and 21(2) which suggests that the omission of the word 'written' in these sections is intentional. In contrast the EU is crystal clear that the whole contract between a data controller and data processor must be in writing. See article 28 of the EU GDPR. See further at paragraph 101 of the European Data Protection Board *Guidelines 07/2020 on the concepts of controller and processor in the EU GDPR* 31.

24 POPIA Regulations specifically require a 'signature' in several forms (most notably for the purposes of form 4 which deals with direct marketing consent (see chapter 16) and go so far as to include a reference to both 'writing' and 'signature' in the definitions section of the POPIA Regulations (section 1). The definitions to the POPIA Regulations define 'signature' as an ordinary electronic signature in terms of the Electronic Communications and Transactions Act 25 of 2002.

4.4.2.2 The other requirements in sections 20 and 21 (authorisation and confidentiality)

The other requirements in sections 20 and 21 are that:

- **The operator must only process the (personal) information with the knowledge or the authorisation of the responsible party:**[25] As can be seen by the word 'or', POPIA seems to require mere knowledge by the responsible party rather than the responsible party's active permission (authorisation). This appears to run contrary to the whole principle that the operator processes personal information at the behest of the responsible party (as defined in section 1 of POPIA), but as things stand this is the requirement.

Key point: The purposes for which operators are processing personal information on behalf of a responsible party should be set out clearly in an agreement with the operator. Responsible parties should clarify what type of authorisation operators must obtain before processing personal information for other purposes.

- **The operator must treat personal information which comes to their knowledge as confidential:**[26] 'Confidentiality' is part of the CIA triad which is used in information security management.[27] It refers to the duty to ensure that information is only accessed by authorised users. These users could be internal users (people who work for the operator) or external users (third parties with whom the information is shared).

Key point: The agreement with the operator should be explicit about what measures the operator must put in place to ensure the confidentiality of the personal information.

- **The operator must not disclose the personal information:**[28] We are not sure what this obligation adds to the duty to keep the information confidential. It presumably refers to disclosing the personal information to 'third parties'.

25 Section 20*(a)*.

26 Section 20*(b)*.

27 This is discussed in chapter 5 paragraph 5.4.

28 Section 20*(b)*.

Key point: The agreement with the operator should be explicit about when the personal information can be disclosed and responsible parties should consider imposing an obligation on the operator to obtain authorisation before the information is disclosed.

These obligations are subject to several exemptions.

An operator can disregard these obligations if processing personal information is 'required by law'. This is a very broad exception. The source of this obligation can be the Constitution, common law, customary law, legislation or court decisions. However, the 'law' itself must not be 'materially consistent with an object, or specific provision' of POPIA. Put differently, the law itself must be POPIA compliant and the invasion of the data subjects' privacy must be justifiable.[29]

For example, where the operator is an internet service provider (ISP) it can be compelled by an 'interception direction' in terms of the Regulation of Interception of Communications and Provision of Communication-related Information Act (RICA) to intercept and channel the responsible party's communications to South Africa's Interception Centre.[30] The operator is obliged to not only channel the communications (which inevitably include personal information) to the Interception Centre, but it is also obliged not to tell the responsible party that its communications are being intercepted.[31]

An operator can also disregard these obligations 'in the course of the proper performance of their duties'.

Tricky area: We think that the exception should be interpreted to relate to the operator's 'duties' in terms of the mandate with that responsible party. If this is not the case, the exception could lead to operators processing personal information provided by responsible parties for their own (commercial) purposes. This would render the requirements in section 20*(a)* and *(b)* all but meaningless. Responsible parties should address this ambiguity explicitly in their contracts with operators by stating explicitly what the personal information provided to the operator can be used for and when the operator requires authorisation to process the information for other purposes.

29 This is discussed in chapter 2 paragraph 2.7.

30 In terms of sections 16–18 of the Regulation of Interception of Communications and Provision of Communication-related Information Act 70 of 2002 (RICA).

31 See sections 16(7), 17(6), 18(3)*(a)*, 19(6), 20(6), 21(6) and 22(7) of RICA. Or don't.

4.4.2.3 The operator must notify the responsible party of security compromises

The operator must notify the responsible party 'immediately where there are reasonable grounds to believe that the personal information of a data subject has been accessed or acquired by any unauthorised person'.[32] 'Security compromises' are discussed in chapter 5 paragraph 5.6.

It is important to note that section 21(2) obliges the operator to inform the responsible party 'immediately' of a security compromise while the responsible party needs to notify the Information Regulator and data subject 'as soon as reasonably possible'.[33] Note that the operator does not have any duty to report the security compromise to the Information Regulator.

Tricky area: The difference between 'immediately' and 'as soon as reasonably possible' is difficult to quantify and will depend on each case. Certainly, an operator does not seem to have much discretion as to how quickly it must notify the responsible party.

It is also important to consider how 'reasonable grounds to believe' will be interpreted. What if a security compromise affects several responsible parties (where a party is an operator to many responsible parties) and it is not obvious which of the responsible parties/data subject records were affected? Most operators would be loath to notify all the responsible parties of a potential security compromise only to find out later that several of the responsible parties that were notified were in fact unaffected by the security compromise. Where exactly the line is drawn as to what 'reasonable grounds' are is dealt with in chapter 5 paragraph 5.6.1.

32 Section 21(2).

33 It is even more nuanced than that as section 22 allows the responsible party not to notify the data subject where the notification would impede a criminal investigation.

4.4.2.4 What are the consequences of non-compliance for an operator?

> **Tricky area:** As discussed in paragraph 4.2, the Information Regulator cannot hold operators directly accountable for non-compliance with POPIA, because the enforcement provisions all refer to the 'responsible party'. It is therefore not clear what the consequences will be for an operator who does not comply with sections 20 and 21(2). It is advisable for responsible parties to include these obligations in their written agreements with operators to ensure some measure of accountability. We discuss the role of contracts in the management of compliance between different organisations involved in the same processing activity in paragraph 4.8.1 below.

What is clear is that the (minimum) written agreement explicitly required by POPIA is inadequate to fully protect responsible parties' interests and to mitigate the risks inherent in using operators to process personal information on their behalf. We have included other provisions which we believe should be included in these contracts in paragraph 4.8.1 below.

4.4.3 The implications of being an operator (from the perspective of an operator)

This book is written largely from the perspective of responsible parties (sorry operators). But that doesn't mean that operators can sit back and relax. Operators should consider the risks of not complying with POPIA proactively. The approach operators should take is summarised well by Dolly Parton: 'I know who I am, I know what I can and can't do. I know what I will and won't do. I know what I'm capable of and I don't agree to do things that I don't think I can pull off.'

The risks for operators are best illustrated by considering the (real life) example where a bank discovered a data breach with a third-party service provider while running an internal system audit and monitoring its procedures. The bank took action immediately by destroying all customer information in the service provider's possession, and the service provider's systems were disconnected from the internet to quarantine the breach. This means that the service provider couldn't continue to provide services to its other clients. The service provider was also named in the bank's press releases. Twelve months after the breach was reported the first hit on Google for the service provider's name is the press release from the bank about the breach. This level of reputational harm sinks businesses.

4.4.4 Using sub-operators

Sometimes, operators will want to use other organisations to process personal information on their behalf. We refer to an operator of an operator as a sub-operator. POPIA does not have any provisions relating to sub-operators, except that section 20*(b)* provides that operators must not 'disclose' personal information shared with them. However, as we saw above, there is quite a bit of uncertainty regarding the interpretation of section 20 and the exemptions that are available to operators. Article 28(2) of the EU GDPR is more explicit. It provides: 'The processor shall not engage another processor without prior specific or general written authorisation of the controller. In the case of general written authorisation, the processor shall inform the controller of any intended changes concerning the addition or replacement of other processors, thereby giving the controller the opportunity to object to such changes.'

Key point: Responsible parties should be explicit in their agreements with operators about the use of sub-operators.

4.5 IDENTIFYING CO-RESPONSIBLE PARTIES

4.5.1 How to identify co-responsible parties

If organisations that are participating in the same processing activity are not in a responsible party–operator relationship, they may be co-responsible parties. This will be the case if they jointly determine the purposes and means of a processing activity.

Key point: We expect litigation in the future where a co-responsible party will try to argue that they are merely an operator in order to escape liability, so the distinction is very important. The key is to determine whether there was 'joint participation in the determination of purpose and means'. This can take place through a common decision (deciding together) or through 'converging decisions'. A decision will be a converging decision if 'the processing would not be possible without both parties' participation in the sense that the processing by each party is inseparable, i.e. inextricably linked'.[34] This type of decision-making does not happen with an operator, as the responsible party is processing the personal information for its own purpose.

[34] European Data Protection Board *Guidelines 07/2020 on the concepts of controller and processor in the EU GDPR* 19, available at https://edpb.europa.eu/sites/edpb/files/consultation/edpb_guidelines_202007_controllerprocessor_en.pdf.

The flowchart below can help you identify whether you are a co-responsible party:[35]

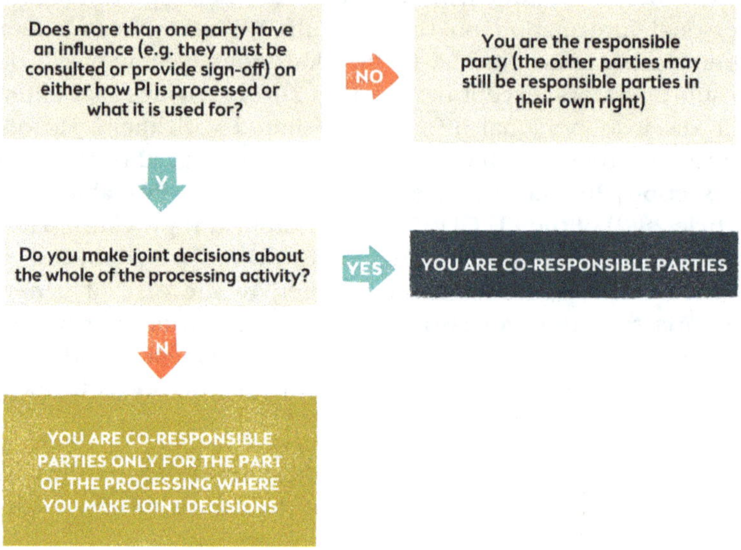

**This image was adapted from the work by the European Data Protection Board's Guidelines 07/2020 on the Concepts of Controller and Processor in the EU GDPR. To the EDPB we say 'Shall I compare thee to a summer's day...'*[36]

4.5.2 The implications of being co-responsible parties

In contrast to the requirements for operator agreements, there is no section in POPIA which prescribes what a contract between co-responsible parties must contain. This is consistent with the EU GDPR.[37] That said, the European Data Protection Board recommends that joint controllers conclude a comprehensive agreement. We argue in paragraph 4.2.2 that the Information Regulator may hold co-responsible parties jointly and severally liable unless the co-responsible parties agree to an 'alternative, clear and equally effective allocation of obligations and responsibilities'. So, co-responsible parties should have an agreement in place.

We have included the provisions which we believe should be included in these contracts in paragraph 4.8.1 below.

---

35 European Data Protection Board *Guidelines 07/2020 on the concepts of controller and processor in the EU GDPR* 48, available at https://edpb.europa.eu/sites/edpb/files/consultation/edpb_guidelines_202007_controllerprocessor_en.pdf.

36 William Shakespeare for 'you're the bomb!'

37 European Data Protection Board *Guidelines 07/2020 on the concepts of controller and processor in the EU GDPR* 22 at 4, available at https://edpb.europa.eu/sites/edpb/files/consultation/edpb_guidelines_202007_controllerprocessor_en.pdf.

4.6 HOW TO DISTINGUISH EMPLOYEES FROM RESPONSIBLE PARTIES AND OPERATORS

In addition to being responsible for the actions of operators and jointly responsible as co-responsible parties, a responsible party will also be vicariously liable for the actions of their employees.[38]

Key point: It might come as a shock as the responsible party would suddenly be vicariously liable for a person's actions when the responsible party did not think they were an employee.[39] As a result, it is essential to know who is an employee as opposed to another responsible party or operator.

Many companies prefer to contract with sub-contractors (either in the form of an operator or another responsible party) in order to avoid the onerous requirements of the Labour Relations Act (LRA),[40] the Basic Conditions of Employment Act (BCEA)[41] and a phalanx of tax and skills development legislation.[42] The practice of contracting with persons who are 'contractors' in theory, but are really employees became so widespread that in 2002 a presumption was created that a person was an employee (irrespective of what the contract said) if one or more of seven factors were present. These factors are:[43]

- '(T)he manner in which the person works is subject to the control or direction of another person;[44]
- the person's hours of work are subject to the control or direction of another person;
- in the case of a person who works for an organisation, the person is a part of that organisation;
- the person has worked for that other person for an average of at least 40 hours per month over the last three months;

Chapter 4

38 Provided that the actions of the employees are within the course and scope of their employment. See *K v Minister of Safety and Security* 2005 (6) SA 419 (CC) paragraph 24.

39 Provided that the actions of the employees are within the course and scope of their employment. See *K v Minister of Safety and Security* 2005 (6) SA 419 (CC) paragraph 24.

40 Act 66 of 1995.

41 Act 75 of 1997.

42 Such as the Income Tax Act 58 of 1962, Skills Development Levies Act 9 of 1999, Unemployment Insurance Contributions Act 4 of 2002, Tax Administration Act 28 of 2011, Employment Tax Incentive Act 26 of 2013, Companies Act 71 of 2008, and the Medical Schemes Act 131 of 1998.

43 Section 83A of the BCEA and section 200A in the LRA.

44 POPIA also incorporates some of the first factors in the definition of an operator in section 1 which provides that a person cannot be an operator if they come under the 'direct authority of [the responsible] party'.

- the person is economically dependent on the other person for whom that person works or renders services;
- the person is provided with tools of trade or work equipment by the other person; or
- the person only works for or renders services to one person.'[45]

If even just one of these factors is present, then the person is considered an employee and the responsible party will be vicariously liable for their actions. Surprise![46]

4.7 ACCOUNTABILITY BINGO!

This is a long section, and we could have made it longer. There are thousands of variations on how organisations are processing personal information together. In fact, collaboration between different organisations is at the heart of digital transformation and innovation.

> **Key point:** The definitions in the EU GDPR of 'data controller' (responsible party) and 'data processor' (operator) are so similar that it is safe to beg, borrow and steal from the commentary on the EU GDPR. Many of these examples were borrowed from the European Data Protection Board's (European Data Protection Board's) *Guidelines 07/2020 on the concepts of controller and processor in the EU GDPR* and adapted slightly for the South African context.

We refer to this as Accountability Bingo. Watch out for the bored game![47]

---

[45] Section 83A(1)*(a)*–*(g)* of the BCEA.

[46] If you don't like surprises, make sure that these factors do not apply to your contractors.

[47] That is not a typo.

Example	Who is accountable?
Public bodies The Department of Social Development pays social grants to citizens who qualify. The Department needs personal information about social grant holders to make the payments. The Department uses FTP (Pty) Ltd to process these payments on its behalf.	The Department of Social Development is the responsible party. In this case legislation gives the Department control over the processing activity. FTP (Pty) Ltd is an operator as long as they only use the personal information of the social grant holders to process payments. If they decide, say, to sell the personal information to insurance companies so they can send direct marketing to the data subjects, they are the responsible party in respect of this unrelated processing activity and they are accountable.[48]
Law firms BRB (Pty) Ltd hires a law firm to represent it in a dispute. In order to do this, the law firm processes personal information relating to the dispute. The law firm decides what information to use and how to use it. BRB (Pty) Ltd does not provide the law firm with any instructions on how to process the personal information.	This is what the European Data Protection Board says about this set of facts: 'This mandate however is not specifically targeted to personal data processing. The law firm acts with a significant degree of independence, for example in deciding what information to use and how to use it, and there are no instructions from the client company regarding the personal data processing. The processing that the law firm carries out in order to fulfil the task as legal representative for the company is therefore linked to the functional role of the law firm so that it is to be regarded as the controller for this processing.'[49] Would the answer change if the law firm was doing debt collection on behalf of BRB (Pty) Ltd? If the law firm receives detailed instructions on how to collect the debt and performs functions that BRB (Pty) Ltd could have performed themselves, like calling the delinquent customers, tracking and tracing them and sending statements, they may be classified as an operator.

➥

Chapter 4

[48] European Data Protection Board *Guidelines 07/2020 on the concepts of controller and processor in the EU GDPR* 11, available at https://edpb.europa.eu/sites/edpb/files/consultation/edpb_guidelines_202007_controllerprocessor_en.pdf. This was also the facts in *Black Sash Trust v Minister of Social Development* 2017 (3) SA 335 (CC).

[49] European Data Protection Board *Guidelines 07/2020 on the concepts of controller and processor in the EU GDPR* 12, available at https://edpb.europa.eu/sites/edpb/files/consultation/edpb_guidelines_202007_controllerprocessor_en.pdf.

Example	Who is accountable?
Payroll processing and banking FOMO (Pty) Ltd hires FTFY (Pty) Ltd to administer the payment of salaries to its employees. FOMO (Pty) Ltd tells FTFY (Pty) Ltd who to pay, what amounts, by when and into what bank account. FTFY (Pty) Ltd decides what software to use, what information security measures are in place and which employees work on the FOMO (Pty) Ltd account. FOMO (Pty) Ltd banks with WTF Bank. WTF Bank processes the payments to FOMO (Pty) Ltd's employees.	FOMO (Pty) Ltd is the responsible party. FTFY (Pty) Ltd is an operator. The decisions that they make about the means of processing (how the processing is done) are 'non-essential'.[50] WTF Bank is a responsible party, because: • it makes all of the decisions that are essential to performing the function of the bank; and • FOMO (Pty) Ltd has no control over WTF Bank's processes.[51]
Accounting services FOMO (Pty) Ltd also hires accountants to audit their books. In order to do this the accountants are given access to financial transactions that include personal information. The accountants are subject to legislation and detailed industry standards about how to conduct such an audit. FOMO (Pty) Ltd does not give the accountants any detailed instructions.	If the accountants get no instructions from FOMO (Pty) Ltd and are carrying out their statuary duties in accordance with the laws that regulate their profession, they are the responsible party. Statutory auditors will be seen as responsible parties, because they have to be independent and determine their own actions. If FOMO (Pty) Ltd was outsourcing some of the tasks which are part of its own accounting procedures (e.g. capturing transactions, doing reconciliations), the accountants will be an operator. Generally, when a service provider has to follow procedures which have been developed by their clients, these will be seen as detailed instructions, and the service provider will be an operator.[52]

[50] European Data Protection Board *Guidelines 07/2020 on the concepts of controller and processor in the EU GDPR* 14, available at https://edpb.europa.eu/sites/edpb/files/consultation/edpb_guidelines_202007_controllerprocessor_en.pdf.

[51] European Data Protection Board *Guidelines 07/2020 on the concepts of controller and processor in the EU GDPR* 14, available at https://edpb.europa.eu/sites/edpb/files/consultation/edpb_guidelines_202007_controllerprocessor_en.pdf.

[52] Accountancy Europe *GDPR: Implications for Auditors*, available at https://www.accountancyeurope.eu/publications/gdpr-implications-for-auditors/.

Example	Who is accountable?
Hosting services (and clouds) GTG (Pty) Ltd uses a customer relationship management system provided by IDC (Pty) Ltd. As part of the service, the personal information of GTG (PTY) Ltd's customers is stored (hosted) by IDC (Pty) Ltd. IDC (Pty) Ltd states in its (very long, size 6 font, riddled with Latin) contract[53] that it is just an operator, and not responsible for ensuring that the processing activities of GTG (Pty) Ltd are compliant with POPIA. It does concede that it will employ reasonable measures to safeguard the personal information against unauthorised access. However, there is an exclusion of liability which limits any claim against IDC (Pty) Ltd to the amount GTG (Pty) Ltd paid it.	IDC (Pty) Ltd is the operator and GTG (Pty) Ltd is the responsible party. This means that even if IDC (Pty) Ltd suffered a data breach, the Information Regulator and data subjects would have to pursue the matter against GTG (Pty) Ltd. **Key point:** GTG would then have to recoup its losses against the much better resourced IDC (Pty) Ltd and will probably lose because of an (hidden) exclusion of liability. May the odds be ever in your favour.

53 Software terms of service are widely held as the worst of the worst when it comes to fine print. Neil Gaiman and Terry Pratchett write: 'Along with the standard computer warranty agreement which said that if the machine 1) didn't work, 2) didn't do what the expensive advertisements said, 3) electrocuted the immediate neighborhood, 4) and in fact failed entirely to be inside the expensive box when you opened it, this was expressly, absolutely, implicitly and in no event the fault or responsibility of the manufacturer, that the purchaser should consider himself lucky to be allowed to give his money to the manufacturer, and that any attempt to treat what had just been paid for as the purchaser's own property would result in the attentions of serious men with menacing briefcases and very thin watches. Crowley had been extremely impressed with the warranties offered by the computer industry, and had in fact sent a bundle Below to the department that drew up the Immortal Soul agreements, with a yellow memo form attached just saying: "Learn, guys ..."' Neil Gaiman and Terry Pratchett, *Good Omens* (1990).

Example	Who is accountable?
Market research ICYMI (Pty) Ltd is a market research company. YOMO (Pty) Ltd wants ICYMI (Pty) Ltd to test its new website using a focus group. YOMO tells ICYMI what questions to ask. ICYMI (Pty) Ltd only gives YOMO (Pty) Ltd statistical information and does not share the personal information of participants with YOMO (Pty) Ltd.	YOMO (Pty) Ltd is the responsible party, because it provided detailed instructions on what personal information to collect and how the personal information must be processed. ICYMI (Pty) Ltd is an operator.[54] What is important about this example is that YOMO is responsible for what ICYMI does with the personal information even though it does not ever see or possess it!
Travel agents and travel service providers A travel agency provides personal information of a customer to an airline and a hotel to make reservations as part of a travel package. They confirm the reservation and the travel agent sends the travel documents to its customer.	The travel agent, airline and hotel are responsible parties. They are each carrying out their own activities independently and are each responsible parties in their own right. They are not co-responsible parties. If they were to set up an online platform for the common purpose of marketing and selling package travel deals, they would be co-responsible parties, because now they have shared 'means'.[55] They will still be independent responsible parties for processing activities that happen outside of the platform.
Joint research project Several universities decide to take part in a joint research project. One of the universities has a state of the art research data management platform. The universities decide to make use of this platform to store the research data they collect.	The universities are co-responsible parties, because they determined the purpose for the processing and decided together to store and disclose personal information on this platform.[56] In their information sharing agreement, they may stipulate how they will ensure compliance and who is responsible for specific aspects of POPIA. For instance, they may decide that the university who provides the platform is responsible for securing the personal information it stores.

➥

[54] European Data Protection Board *Guidelines 07/2020 on the concepts of controller and processor in the EU GDPR* 16, available at https://edpb.europa.eu/sites/edpb/files/consultation/edpb_guidelines_202007_controllerprocessor_en.pdf.

[55] European Data Protection Board *Guidelines 07/2020 on the concepts of controller and processor in the EU GDPR* 20, available at https://edpb.europa.eu/sites/edpb/files/consultation/edpb_guidelines_202007_controllerprocessor_en.pdf.

[56] European Data Protection Board *Guidelines 07/2020 on the concepts of controller and processor in the EU GDPR* 21, available at https://edpb.europa.eu/sites/edpb/files/consultation/edpb_guidelines_202007_controllerprocessor_en.pdf.

Example	Who is accountable?
Processing within a group of companies LMAO Group is made up of several separate financial service providers (FSPs) selling several different financial services products. They have a shared customer relationship management system, but each entity is responsible to market and sell their own products. Each FSP only has access to the personal information of their own customers. This was done to ensure that the different FSPs comply with the confidentiality requirements in financial services legislation. Their customers are not aware that there are different entities in the LMAO Group, because they are trading under one brand.	Each FSP is a responsible party. In this case, they share infrastructure in the form of a system, but each organisation only captures the personal information of their own prospects and clients and they process this personal information for their own purposes only. They cannot even access the personal information of one another's clients.[57] This answer might change depending on how integrated the entities are. For instance, many groups of companies have shared marketing, sales, human resources, information technology and management. They would be co-responsible parties who are working together with a joint purpose for many of the groups' processing activities. Some groups of companies may want to argue that they must be regarded as a single responsible party (co-responsible parties) for purposes of POPIA. Sometimes the argument may succeed; the facts will determine whether they truly are co-responsible parties. See paragraph 4.5.1 above.

➥

57 European Data Protection Board *Guidelines 07/2020 on the concepts of controller and processor in the EU GDPR* 22, available at https://edpb.europa.eu/sites/edpb/files/consultation/edpb_guidelines_202007_controllerprocessor_en.pdf.

Example	Who is accountable?
	There may of course be other reasons why companies in a group want to share personal information. In instances where they are acting as each other's operators, little justification is usually needed.[58] However, when the sharing of personal information is happening for purposes of cross-selling, enhanced customer profiling or other purposes that go beyond the purpose for which a responsible party collected it, it will usually amount to further processing (or 'secondary use'). Further processing will often require further steps to be taken by a responsible party before it will comply with POPIA (e.g. obtaining consent). Further processing is discussed in chapter 12. Sharing personal information within a group of organisations is discussed in chapter 13 paragraph 13.6.2.
Recruitment database ADIH (Pty) Ltd asks a recruitment agency to help it find suitable candidates for a position that has recently opened up. The recruitment agency has a look in its own extensive database of CVs and looks at the CVs received by ADIH (Pty) Ltd. ADIH (Pty) Ltd agrees that the CVs which they submit to the recruitment agency can be included in the agency's database.	They are co-responsible parties, because they jointly participate in the processing activity with the purpose of finding suitable candidates. This is what the European Data Protection Board refers to as 'converging decisions': (a) The recruitment agency decided to create and manage the database of CVs it receives, and (b) ADIH (Pty) Ltd decided to enrich the agency's database with the CVs it receives directly.[59] However: • The recruitment agency is the responsible party when it manages its database. • ADIH (Pty) Ltd is the responsible party in any subsequent hiring processes.

58 This is assuming that the processing activity which is being outsourced, or in this case 'insourced', is lawful. Having a legal justification for processing is discussed in chapter 6.

59 European Data Protection *Board Guidelines 07/2020 on the concepts of controller and processor in the EU GDPR* 22, available at https://edpb.europa.eu/sites/edpb/files/consultation/edpb_guidelines_202007_controllerprocessor_en.pdf.

Example	Who is accountable?
An operator goes rogue AFK (Pty) Ltd sends its clients' newsletters to databases provided to AFK by its clients. AFK (Pty) Ltd describes itself as an operator in its client terms. AFK (Pty) Ltd decides to create its own, combined database from its clients' databases which it uses to provide information enrichment and cleaning services.	AFK (Pty) Ltd may have been an operator when it was just sending bulk email on its clients' behalf. However, when AFK (Pty) Ltd decided to use its clients' databases for other purposes, AFK (Pty) Ltd became a responsible party for this new processing activity. In addition, this decision by AFK may well amount to a breach of its contract with its clients and of section 20 of POPIA, if AFK does not have its clients' permission to use the personal information for their own purposes.
Business process outsourcing CM (Pty) Ltd outsources its client support to BRB (Pty) Ltd which provides a call centre for this purpose. BRB (Pty) Ltd has to have access to CM (Pty) Ltd's customer database. BRB can only access the database in order to render the client support services and cannot process the personal information in the database for any other purpose.	BRB (Pty) Ltd is an operator.

Many of the organisations in the examples above may want to rethink their products, services or even their business model in order to change their status as responsible party, co-responsible party or operator if the cost of compliance with POPIA becomes prohibitive. It is important to ensure that the change is genuine, given that this is a factual enquiry.

Key point: Parties to an agreement cannot agree who the responsible party is; that is a factual question. While the agreement will give rise to a cause of action between the parties to the contract, a responsible party cannot to escape the ire of the Information Regulator. As the European Data Protection Board put it '[i]t is not possible either to become a [responsible party] or to escape [responsible party] obligations simply by shaping the contract in a certain way where the factual circumstances say something else'.[60]

---

60 European Data Protection Board *Guidelines 07/2020 on the concepts of controller and processor in the EU GDPR* 12, available at https://edpb.europa.eu/sites/edpb/files/consultation/edpb_guidelines_202007_controllerprocessor_en.pdf.

This is not to say that managing compliance between the different parties to a processing activity in an agreement is not a prudent idea. In the next section we will discuss the following ways of managing POPIA compliance where multiple organisations are involved in a processing activity:

- contracts
- binding corporate rules; and
- auditing third parties.

While these strategies may not change who is going to be held liable by the Information Regulator, they will assist in ensuring that organisations are aware of their respective responsibilities and that they manage information risk pro-actively. At least in theory. If these strategies do not prevent non-compliance from occurring, at least they will assist in apportioning blame (and liability) after the POPIA strikes the fan.

4.8 PRACTICAL ADVICE

4.8.1 Managing compliance between organisations through contracts

4.8.1.1 The role of contracts in determining accountability between different organisations

While contracts cannot change which organisation is the responsible party,[61] they can facilitate the process of correctly identifying the responsible party. The European Data Protection Board summarised this function of contracts as follows:

> 'Even if a contract is silent as to who is the controller, it may contain sufficient elements to infer who exercises a decision-making role with respect to the purposes and means of the processing. It may also be that the contract contains an explicit statement as to the identity of the controller. If there is no reason to doubt that this accurately reflects the reality, there is nothing against following the terms of the contract.'

This means that clearly setting out the roles and responsibilities of the parties in relation to POPIA compliance does have some value in identifying the responsible party, as long as the facts bear it out.

A carefully negotiated and drafted agreement can assist the different organisations involved in the processing activity to:

61 See paragraph 4.7 above.

- understand and appropriately allocate POPIA obligations; and
- agree on mechanisms to monitor and measure compliance with their contractual obligations.

This is a pre-emptive function in the sense that the contract prevents non-compliance that results from misunderstandings and provides the parties with a mechanism to detect and address non-compliance.

The reactive function of a contract is to manage liability when things do go wrong. Parties can do this by including:

- indemnities to apportion liability in the event of a data breach or fine; and
- a process to ensure rapid and effective data breach response.

Key point: Not all costs related to data breaches can be managed contractually. For instance, data breaches lead to significant reputational harm which often cannot be made good by an indemnity. See the discussion of the cost of data breaches in chapter 5 paragraph 5.6. In addition, contracts are an inherently weak reactive control, because of the cost of pursuing legal action and the risk that the party on the other side does not have the means to pay an award. Taking a proactive approach to managing obligations and preventing non-compliance is a far sounder strategy.

4.8.1.2 The role of contract management in POPIA compliance

Contract management is essential when it comes to POPIA compliance. Poor contract management can result in:

- inefficiency
- unfavourable contracts
- fraud
- failure to identify risks and their likelihood
- failure to continue with compliance with laws and contractual obligations throughout the contract life cycle
- administrative fines and other enforcement actions (see chapter 19)
- breach of contract

- litigation costs; and
- broken relationships.[62]

In this paragraph we consider the role of the different stages in contract life cycle management in POPIA compliance.

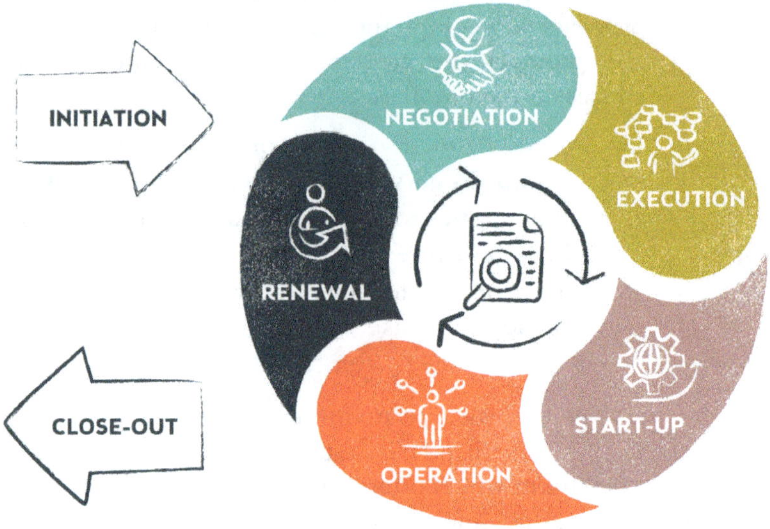

This image was adapted from an image created by Contract Now (powered by Gatekeeper).[63]

Phase	How it helps with POPIA compliance
Initiation	All contracts start with a business need. At this initiation stage, it is important to clearly document the need(s) and to assess whether the contract will involve the processing of personal information. If personal information is involved then perform a personal information impact assessment (PIIA) to identify POPIA requirements and data protection and privacy risks. This ensures that data protection and privacy is part of the proposal and the due diligence of a new service provider or sub-contractor.

➡

[62] *Importance of Contract Management*, available at https://ppp-certification.com/ppp-certification-guide/3-importance-contract-management. See further https://www.gatekeeperhq.com for useful guides on contract management.

[63] Shannon Greaney's blog 'What is contract management?' ContractNow, available at https://www.contractnow.com/blog/what-is-contract-management

Phase	How it helps with POPIA compliance
Negotiation	During this phase, ensure that the contract accurately reflects the respective POPIA obligations. Negotiations often take place between the lawyers, with little regard for the realities of the day-to-day operational requirements of the parties, and the lawyers are not involved in the other stages of the contract life cycle (we do not blame you, lawyers can be annoying). However, this disconnect can lead to breaches of contract, POPIA non-compliance and costly litigation. Ensure that drafts are shared with legal, business, and technical teams, and all other stakeholders to ensure that they are realistic. See chapter 20 paragraph 20.2.3 where we discuss how to identify and manage stakeholders. It is useful to have POPIA templates and negotiation playbooks to standardise contract wording and to ensure consistent negotiation, but be careful, because it must still accurately record the idiosyncrasies of the relationship, the purposes for which personal information will be shared and processed and reflect the findings of the PIIA which was performed. Ensure that the organisation keeps a meticulous record of negotiations, particularly if they include decisions about how POPIA obligations will be discharged and what safeguards will be put in place. If the organisation has to compromise and accept less than favourable terms (it happens; tech giants do not negotiate), prepare a contract risk register to record and manage POPIA risks that are created by the contract.
Execution	Make sure that the contract is formally approved, not only by the person signing it, but also by everybody else who will be involved in carrying out the organisation's responsibilities. This ensures that everybody in the organisation is aware of its POPIA obligations and is comfortable that they are achievable.
Start-up	Once a contract has been signed, do not let it gather dust in a folder somewhere. Ensure that POPIA requirements are embedded in the relevant business processes and agree with clients, service providers and sub-contractors on how compliance with POPIA obligations will be tracked. Make sure that everybody working with the client, service provider or sub-contractor is fully aware of and understands the organisation's obligations and make sure that clients, service providers and sub-contractors do the same. Keep the contract risk register up to date by adding any new risks. Consider whether there are any measures that can mitigate these risks.

Phase	How it helps with POPIA compliance
Operation	Contracts should be living documents, but rarely are. Contracts may need to change during their duration for various reasons ranging from shifts in business needs, to improvements in technology and changes to regulations. In order to stay POPIA compliant, the contract must keep up with reality. During this phase, monitor for these changes and ensure that the contract is kept up to date. Track whether the organisation, its clients, service providers and sub-contractors are keeping up their end of the bargain by doing periodic assessments. If something is wrong or new risks are uncovered then record this in the contract risk register and agree on what remedial action to take. Use this opportunity to keep data flow maps, and records of processing activities that document how personal information is shared, up to date.[64] Remember that a data subject has the right to 'information about the identity of all third parties, or categories of third parties, who have, or have had access to the information'.[65]
Renewal	There should always be a written agreement in place if personal information is being shared. This means that it is important to know when a contract is going to lapse. When a contract is up for renewal, it is also an opportunity to check that the contract is still relevant, that it is up to date and that it contains an accurate reflection of everybody's POPIA obligations.
Close-out	When a contract comes to an end, it is important to agree on what is going to happen to the personal information that was shared and used during the life of the contract. This ensures that the personal information remains protected and that an accurate record of how the personal information was processed is kept.

4.8.1.3 Checklists for contracts

In this paragraph we provide checklists which can be used to:

- draft POPIA agreements
- review POPIA agreements that were drafted by the other party; and
- update or renegotiate operator agreements.

---

[64] Documenting POPIA compliance by using data flow maps is discussed in chapter 1 paragraph 1.4.

[65] Section 23(1)*(b)*. This is discussed in chapter 18 paragraph 18.3.2.

CHECKLIST FOR AGREEMENTS BETWEEN RESPONSIBLE PARTIES AND OPERATORS		
Topic	**Description**	**POPIA section**
Audit	What right to audit exists, how does it get exercised, what happens if the audit finds non-compliance and who pays for the audit?	n/a[66]
Confidentiality	What information is confidential and under what conditions can it be disclosed?	sections 20*(b)* and 21(1)[67]
Legal basis	What consents must be obtained by the operator (if any)? Must the operator give the data subjects a right to object and process those objections?	section 11(1)[68]
Cross-border transfer	When can personal information be transferred to another country and what kind of permission is required?	section 72[69]
Data subject rights	In what way must the operator assist with data subject requests?	sections 23 to 25[70]
Retention and deletion	What records of the processing activity must the operator maintain? What strategy must be used to delete personal information, how to delete personal information, and when to return it?	section 14[71]
Documentation	What is expected to be documented, how it is checked and updated.	section 17[72]
Information officers	Who are the information officer(s) and how can they be contacted?	section 8, regulation 4[73]
Applicable law and conflict of laws	Confirmation of the country's law that applies. In the event of a conflict which law prevails?	section 72[74]

66 See paragraph 4.8.3 below on audits.

67 See paragraph 4.4.2 above and chapter 5 paragraph 5.4.2.

68 See chapter 6.

69 See chapter 14.

70 See chapter 18.

71 See chapter 17.

72 Documenting processing and compliance is discussed in chapter 1 paragraph 1.4.

73 See chapter 1 paragraph 1.3.5 for the roles and responsibilities of the information officer.

74 See chapter 14.

CHECKLIST FOR AGREEMENTS BETWEEN RESPONSIBLE PARTIES AND OPERATORS		
Topic	**Description**	**POPIA section**
Liability	Who pays for what if a data subject sues the responsible party or the operator, or the responsible party get fined by the Information Regulator, as well as liability for legal costs? Keep all the different 'costs' of data breaches in mind. We discuss this in chapter 5 paragraph 5.6.5.	n/a[75]
Notification	What notifications are provided to data subjects and who does it?	section 18[76]
Policies and processes	Whether they are binding and how they will be communicated and updated.	section 8[77]
Purpose	Personal information only to be used for purposes authorised by the responsible party.	section 20[78]
Quality	How to ensure that personal information remains accurate and who is responsible to ensure accuracy?	section 16[79]
Security	What security measures will be implemented? How will security risks be assessed and security measures be updated? What security breaches are, how to respond to them, and how to report them.	sections 19 to 22[80]
Special personal information	Restriction on use of special personal information and on children's information.	sections 26 to 35[81]

➡

[75] See paragraph 4.2 above for who will be responsible in terms of POPIA. Who is who, will determine the scope of the potential liability that needs to be managed in the contract.

[76] See chapter 11.

[77] Policies and processes are discussed in general in chapter 20 paragraph 20.2.5. In some operator agreements, the responsible party binds the operator to the responsible party's policies and to pre-approved processes.

[78] Operators are used for performing processing for specific purposes on behalf of the responsible party. Those purposes should be recorded in the contract. See paragraph 4.4.2.1 above.

[79] Information quality is discussed in chapter 9 paragraph 9.5.

[80] Information security management is discussed in chapter 5.

[81] Special personal information is discussed in chapter 7.

CHECKLIST FOR AGREEMENTS BETWEEN RESPONSIBLE PARTIES AND OPERATORS		
Topic	**Description**	**POPIA section**
Sub-operators	Whether they are allowed and if so, under what conditions.	sections 8, 20 and 21[82]

What if it is not a responsible party – operator relationship? Here is a checklist for information sharing agreements between co-responsible parties:

CHECKLIST FOR AGREEMENTS BETWEEN CO-RESPONSIBLE PARTIES		
Topic	**Description**	**POPIA section**
Notification	Who must notify the data subject when collecting personal information (publish a privacy notice)?	section 18[83]
Purpose	Who determines the purpose of processing?	section 13[84]
Collection	Who ensures that only the minimum personal information is collected (usually the party that determines what personal information is collected, e.g. the party who creates the application form) and that the information is coming from a lawful source?	sections 10 and 12[85]
Quality	Who ensures that the information is accurate and kept up to date?	section 16[86]
Retention and deletion	What record of the processing activity must the co-responsible parties maintain? What strategy must be used to delete personal information, how to delete personal information, and when to return it?	section 14[87]

➡

Chapter 4

82 Sub-operators are discussed in paragraph 4.2.4 above.

83 See chapter 10.

84 Purpose specification is discussed in chapter 6 paragraph 6.2. Co-responsible parties process personal information for a joint purpose(s). Those purposes should be recorded in the contract. See paragraph 4.5.2 above.

85 Minimality is discussed in chapter 9, and the collection or creation of personal information is discussed in chapter 10.

86 Information quality is discussed in chapter 9 paragraph 9.5.

87 See chapter 17.

CHECKLIST FOR AGREEMENTS BETWEEN CO-RESPONSIBLE PARTIES		
Topic	**Description**	**POPIA section**
Legal basis	Who determines the legal basis for processing and what is the legal basis?	section 11[88]
Security	Agree on the security measures that each co-responsible party must implement.	section 19[89]
Personal information impact assessment	Who will perform the personal information impact assessment for each processing activity?	regulation 4(1)*(b)*[90]
Operators	Who decides which operators to use and the content of operator agreements?	section 21[91]
Cross-border transfer	Who is responsible for compliance with the requirements for transborder information flows?	section 72[92]
Consent	Who is responsible for obtaining and managing consent when it is required for a specific processing activity (e.g. direct marketing, transborder information flows, processing the personal information of children etc.)?	There are 12 possible consents: sections 11(1)*(a)*, 12(2)*(b)*, 14(1)*(d)*, 14(7), 15(3), 18(4)*(a)*, 27(1)*(a)*, 28(3), 31(2), 69(1)*(a)*, 72(1)*(b)*, and 106(1).[93]
Security compromises	What is the process that must be followed in case of a personal information security compromise?	sections 21 and 22[94]
Data subject requests	Who will respond to data subject requests? What support must the other party provide?	section 23 to 25[95]

88 See chapter 6.

89 Information security management is discussed in chapter 5.

90 Personal information impact assessments are discussed in chapter 20 paragraph 20.3.

91 Operators are discussed in paragraph 4.4 above.

92 See chapter 14.

93 Consent is discussed in chapter 2 paragraph 2.6.6.

94 See chapter 5 paragraph 5.6.

95 See chapter 18.

CHECKLIST FOR AGREEMENTS BETWEEN CO-RESPONSIBLE PARTIES		
Topic	**Description**	**POPIA section**
Information officers	Who are the information officer(s) and how do you contact them? Who is the point of contact for the Information Regulator?	section 8, regulation 4[96]
Further processing	Who will ensure that personal information will not be processed for a new purpose that is incompatible with the purpose for collection?	section 15[97]
Documentation	What is expected to be documented, and how is it checked and updated?	section 17[98]
Audit	What right to audit exists, how does it get exercised, what happens if the audit finds non-compliance and who pays for the audit?	n/a[99]

4.8.2 Managing compliance in 'groups of undertakings' through binding corporate rules

A contract between the parties is not the only way their relationship can be managed. POPIA provides that responsible parties can use binding corporate rules (BCRs) to govern multiple organisations which are taking part in the same processing activities to enable them to transfer personal information to foreign countries.[100] However, BCRs are also a useful way of addressing other aspects of POPIA compliance. It is also possible to make corporate rules binding on an independent organisation (not part of a group) through a contract.

What are BCRs? They include policies, standards, practices and procedures that bind a 'group of undertakings'.[101] A 'group of undertakings' is defined in section 72 as a controlling undertaking and its controlled undertakings. The group will be comprised of responsible parties (either independent or co-responsible) and operators. If a responsible party develops policies that are persuasive rather than binding then they would not be BCRs for purposes of transborder transfers.[102]

Chapter 4

96 See chapter 1 paragraph 1.3.5 for the responsibilities of the information officer.

97 Further processing is discussed in chapter 12.

98 Documenting compliance is discussed in chapter 1 paragraph 1.4.

99 See paragraph 4.8.3 below on audits.

100 Section 72 of POPIA allows for binding corporate rules to govern cross-border transfers of personal information, but is not referred to elsewhere in relation to – for example – operator agreements.

101 Section 72(2) requires that the binding corporate rules are 'adhered to'.

102 This is certainly the EU's position (see https://ec.europa.eu/info/law/law-topic/data-protection/international-dimension-data-protection/binding-corporate-rules-bcr_en) but it follows that this would also be true for POPIA as a result of the wording of section 72(2).

Groups of organisations have a few options open to them. They can:

- govern data protection centrally through a set of binding corporate rules
- take a decentralised approach where each organisation is responsible for its own policies and compliance; or
- follow a hybrid model where there are centralised principles or standards, but where each entity remains responsible for its own implementation of the principles or standards and can apply for approval to deviate from certain principles if the implementation is too onerous (e.g. due to less onerous local privacy laws or commercial realities).

Tricky area: Corporate binding rules can be blunt tools that can lead to over-compliance in countries with more relaxed regulations. Over-compliance leads to unnecessary costs and may prevent the subsidiary from being able to compete. This can be resolved by creating an exception mechanism to cater for departures from the international standard.

4.8.3 Managing accountability through third-party risk management

4.8.3.1 What is third-party risk management

Responsible parties must manage third parties involved in processing personal information to remain compliant with POPIA. Third-party risk management involves the vetting and auditing of external parties such as partners, vendors, contractors and consultants.

POPIA does not explicitly require that responsible parties vet or audit third parties with whom they share processing responsibilities. However, the following gives some uncomfortable food for thought: According to Deloitte's *Third-party Risk Management (TPRM) Global Survey 2020,* 84% of respondents reported that their organisation had suffered a third-party incident in the last three years.[103] In IBM's annual *Cost of a Data Breach Report 2020,* third-party breaches accounted for 16% of malicious breaches and third-party breaches cost organisations USD207 411 more than the average cost of a data breach.[104]

103 Survey available at https://www2.deloitte.com/content/dam/Deloitte/uk/Documents/risk/deloitte-uk-third-party-risk-management-global-survey-2020.pdf.

104 Report available at https://www.capita.com/sites/g/files/nginej146/files/2020-08/Ponemon-Global-Cost-of-Data-Breach-Study-2020.pdf.

It is therefore not surprising that the EU GDPR introduced mandatory co-operation by processors in auditing activities in article 28(3)*(h)*.

However, is it really practical to do full GDPR or POPIA audits of all data processors or operators?[105] This then begs the question: Who should you audit and what should you audit?

4.8.3.2 Who to audit: A risk-based approach

The scope of an audit will depend on many factors including the audit cost and capacity (can you spare the employees who will be needed to assist with the audit?). Here, a risk-based approach is essential.[106] Some other factors to consider when determining who to audit are:

- Business continuity: Is the service essential to the business operations of the organisation?
- Contract size: What is the expected annual financial contract amount of the third-party service?
- Geographical location: Will all parts of the service be performed domestically?
- Difficulty of replacement: How difficult would it be to replace this service with an alternative if something goes wrong?
- Volume of records: What is the expected annual volume of records that will be accessed, processed, stored or transmitted by this third party?
- Regulatory requirements: Is any part of the third-party service being provided subject to any regulatory or compliance requirements?
- Access to sensitive data: Does this third party store, process, or transmit personal information as part of this service?
- Cloud computing: As a part of this service, will any of our data be stored in the cloud?

[105] See for example the 2012 opinion by the EU Data Protection Supervisor that identifies this need at paragraph 170–176, available at https://edps.europa.eu/sites/edp/files/publication/12-03-07_edps_reform_package_en.pdf.

[106] Throughout this book, we advocate for a risk-based approach. Our clamouring reaches its crescendo in chapter 20 paragraph 20.3.1.

- Access to technical infrastructure: As a part of this service, will the third party have access to the organisation's IT network or technical infrastructure?
- Outsourcing of services: Will any part of the service be outsourced as part of this agreement?[107]

4.8.3.3 What to audit

Perhaps a good place to start is with the ICO's approach to auditing data controllers.[108] This occurs when data controllers voluntarily request that the ICO conduct a data protection audit of their organisation and a high-level overview of the result is published on the ICO website.[109]

These are the auditing areas and evidence that the ICO looks at, adapted for the South African context. A word of warning, we are going to get ahead of ourselves, because we have not yet discussed some of the topics that may be audited.

Audit areas	The evidence that the ICO looks for
Data protection governance[110]	What policies and procedures are in place? Put differently, is there a (POPIA) 'compliance framework'?[111] What governance structures are in place to monitor the implementation of policies and procedures? What measures are in place to ensure compliance? Does the organisation perform regular audits? Does the organisation maintain a risk register? Does the organisation perform personal information impact assessments?

➡

[107] Process Unity 'How to spot your riskiest vendors: Managing inherent risk in third-party risk programs', available at https://www.processunity.com/inherent-risk-third-party-risk.

[108] 'Auditing data protection: A guide to ICO data protection audits', available at https://ico.org.uk/media/1533/auditing_data_protection.pdf.

[109] There are other websites that offer free vendor assessment toolkits and even publish the results. Our favourite is Educause's Higher Education Community Vendor Assessment Toolkit, available at https://library.educause.edu/resources/2020/4/higher-education-community-vendor-assessment-toolkit Vendors can share their assessments on their Community Broker Index (https://www.ren-isac.net/hecvat/cbi.html) to streamline procurement processes.

[110] POPIA 'governance' is discussed in chapters 1 and 20.

[111] We discuss all of the policies an organisation should have in place in chapter 20 paragraph 20.2.5.

Audit areas	The evidence that the ICO looks for
Training and awareness[112]	Are all employees made aware of their data protection responsibilities? Does roles-based training take place for the information officer, deputy information officer, management and other employees with data protection responsibilities? Is induction training done with new employees or where employees are promoted to new roles? Is refresher training performed at appropriate intervals? Is a record of training maintained?
Security of personal information[113]	Are adequate information security policies, procedures and standards in place? Do they cover the following aspects of information security: • information risk management • roles and responsibilities for information security • human resources security • asset management • access control • cryptography • physical and environmental security • operations security • communications security • systems, acquisition, development and maintenance • third-party management • information security incident management • information security aspects of business continuity management; and • information security aspects of compliance (the three lines of defence model)?[114] Does roles-based training on information security take place?

112 Change management is discussed in chapter 20.

113 Information security is discussed in chapter 5.

114 We discuss compliance management in chapter 1 paragraph 1.2.2.

Audit areas	The evidence that the ICO looks for
Personal information impact assessments (PIIAs)[115]	Is there a policy that determines when PIIAs must take place? Is there an adequate procedure on how they must be conducted? Does the organisation keep a record of all PIIAs? Does the organisation maintain a register of all risks identified during PIIAs? Are the risks identified during PIIAs managed by the organisation? Does the organisation maintain and monitor a register of all actions or projects undertaken to mitigate the risks identified during PIIAs? Does the organisation audit and review the PIIA process from time to time?
Personal information sharing[116]	Is there a policy and process in place to ensure that a PIIA is performed before personal information is shared? Are the appropriate contracts concluded before personal information is shared? Does the organisation maintain a register of what personal information was shared with whom and why?
Records management[117]	Are records management policies and procedures in place? Are roles and responsibilities in respect of records management clear? Does roles-based training on records management take place? Have all information assets been identified and have records retention rules been defined in respect of those assets? Are there clear rules on the secure destruction of personal information? Does the organisation perform regular audits of compliance with records management policies and procedures?

[115] PIIAs are discussed in chapter 20 paragraph 20.3.

[116] Sharing of personal information is discussed in chapter 13.

[117] Records management is discussed in chapter 17.

Audit areas	The evidence that the ICO looks for
Data subject and PAIA requests[118]	Are there adequate procedures in place to process requests? Does the organisation maintain a record (log) of data subject requests? Are there measures in place to ensure that personal information is de-identified (when appropriate) before it is released to someone other than the data subject? Does the organisation have a complaints procedure in place? Are these complaints reviewed and are the findings of any reviews implemented?

[118] Data subject requests are discussed in chapter 18.

5 Information security management

5.1 WHAT TO EXPECT IN THIS CHAPTER

We are not information security experts. We are not ashamed of it.[1] We probably have this in common with most information officers, deputy information officers, compliance officers and attorneys. Over the years, we realised that we are a bit like tourists in Paris who cannot speak French; in order to enjoy the trip, you need to learn just enough French to order something at a restaurant. That is why we refer to this chapter as learning to speak some G(r)eek. You will not know enough to implement an information security management system, but you will know enough to see when something is missing.

In this chapter we discuss the following:

- POPIA is not an IT project or (just) about cybersecurity
- Who is responsible for information security?
- What responsible parties must protect personal information against
- What does POPIA require of responsible parties?
- When the POPIA strikes the fan

5.2 POPIA IS NOT AN IT PROJECT OR (JUST) ABOUT CYBERSECURITY

5.2.1 POPIA is a people problem (not an IT one)

One of the most common, and most harmful, mistakes we see people make is to assume that POPIA is only an information technology (IT) problem. We discussed this and the proper role of IT in chapter 1 paragraph 1.2.5, but it bears repeating.

Key point: Just because an organisation has got an IT security policy, does not mean it can assume that the scope of that policy is sufficient to ensure compliance with section 19. POPIA applies to personal information regardless of the format in which it is being stored,[2] while IT security policies are often limited to digital information housed in certain systems. We discuss the scope and policy statements required to achieve that in chapter 20 paragraph 20.2.5.

In addition, not all information security risks are resolved by technology (or technology alone). Adrian Sanabria, a security analyst, once remarked: 'The security problems we're now facing can't be fixed

---

1 As Dr McCoy from Star Trek would say: 'Damnit Jim, I'm a lawyer not an information security expert!'

2 Remember the definition of a 'record'? We discuss it in chapter 3 paragraph 3.2.2.

with products alone. We can't fix them with more security analysts any more than a retailer could fix shoplifting by assigning a security guard to watch every shopper as they wander around the store.'

POPIA echoes this sentiment by prescribing that responsible parties must take 'appropriate, reasonable technical *and organisational* measures' to protect personal information. These organisational measures include policies, processes, controls, plans, assessments, contracts, training (more training) and monitoring.[3] This is why we say that POPIA (and even more so, information security) is a team sport:

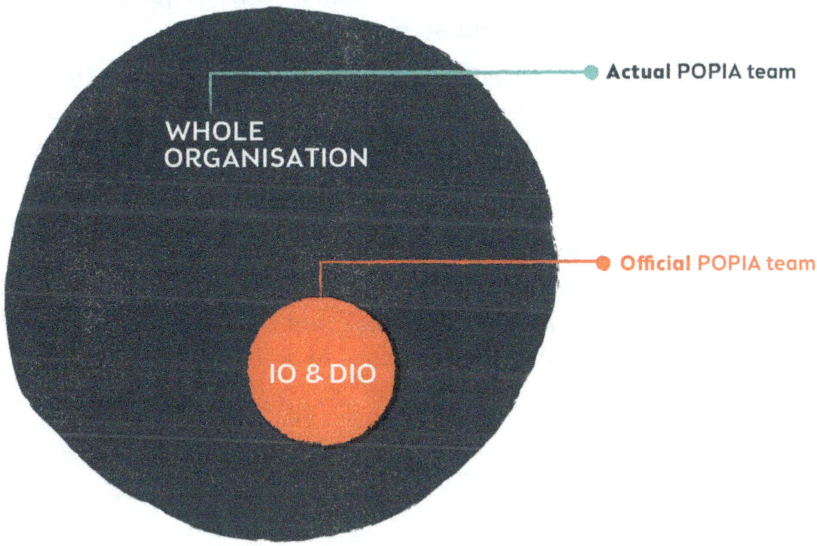

However, IT does have an important role to play. As we discuss POPIA's requirements in relation to information security, it will become clear that responsible parties cannot demonstrate that they are acting reasonably, if they do not take advancements in technology into account. In the EU GDPR, this requirement is explicit in article 32(1) which requires responsible parties to take the 'state of the art' into account when implementing appropriate technical and organisational

[3] We view (well-drafted) policies as an indispensable part of a compliance framework. We discuss them in chapter 20 paragraph 20.2.5. While policies are not explicitly required in POPIA, they are one of the factors the Information Regulator will take into account when determining the size of the administrative fine against a responsible party who is guilty of an offence (see chapter 19 paragraph 19.10.3). Section 109(3)*(g)* provides that the Information Regulator must consider 'any failure to carry out a risk assessment or a failure to operate good policies, procedures and practices to protect personal information'. The European Data Protection Board also lists policies as an example of appropriate organisational measures (European Data Protection Board *Guidelines 4/2019 on Article 25 Data Protection by Design and by Default* 8, available at https://edpb.europa.eu/sites/default/files/files/file1/edpb_guidelines_201904_dataprotection_by_design_and_by_default_v2.0_en.pdf.)

measures.[4] One of the functions of IT ought to be to provide advice on technology investments[5] that enable POPIA compliance, and to ensure that the responsible party keeps up to date with technological advancements. We discuss the role of IT in chapter 1 paragraph 1.2.5.

5.2.2 Why POPIA is about so much more than cybersecurity

Over the years, data protection has become synonymous with cybersecurity. Cybersecurity 'is the practice of defending computers, servers, mobile devices, electronic systems, networks, and data from malicious attacks'.[6] Here is why what POPIA requires in respect of 'security measures' is about so much more:

- Cybersecurity focuses on the defence of technology and electronic information,[7] and POPIA applies to all personal information, regardless of the format in which it is stored – so it applies to both electronic and physical information.
- Not all security risks are a result of cyberattacks. Quite often personal information can be lost, destroyed or accessed by the wrong people as a result of negligence or mistakes instead of malicious attacks. POPIA also requires that responsible parties consider these scenarios and so it is wider than the concept of 'cybersecurity'.

5.3 WHO IS RESPONSIBLE FOR INFORMATION SECURITY?

5.3.1 Under whose 'control' is the personal information?

Section 19 provides that a responsible party must 'secure … the personal information in its possession or under its control'.[8] This is slightly different to the test for accountability which we discussed in chapter 4 which assigns accountability to the party who determines the purposes and means for processing personal information.

4 Article 32(1).

5 E.g. the software, hardware and communications technology (ways to connect by telephone and internet) you buy or use.

6 See https://www.kaspersky.com/resource-center/definitions/what-is-cyber-security.

7 This is why it is sometimes called 'information technology security' or 'electronic information security'.

8 Section 19(1).

Tricky area: Is it possible for the accountability in section 19 to be assigned to a different responsible party than the one(s) who is generally accountable in terms of section 8? We think so. For instance, a group of responsible parties may be processing personal information together as co-responsible parties. The co-responsible party who has possession of or control over the personal information may be responsible on its own for the security of the personal information. It is also possible to be a responsible party without even having access to, much less control over, the personal information in question. We included an example of this in the Accountability Bingo in chapter 4 paragraph 4.7.

5.3.2 The accountability of operators

As we discussed in chapter 4,[9] the Information Regulator cannot hold operators directly accountable for non-compliance with POPIA, because the enforcement provisions all refer to the 'responsible party'. But, is section 19 different? It still refers to the responsible party ...

Tricky area: Will the Information Regulator hold the responsible party accountable for the operator's non-compliance with section 19? If the personal information is in the possession of the operator, the answer to this question will depend on whether one can say that the information is still under the control of the responsible party. It may well be that the responsible party does 'control' the personal information, because of the contract the responsible party must conclude with the operator. However, consider that often the operator does retain some discretion over how the personal information is processed. See the discussion of section 20 in chapter 4 paragraph 4.4.2.

If the Information Regulator can hold the responsible party accountable for the actions of its operator, this does not mean that the offending operator will get away scot-free; quite the contrary. As discussed in chapter 4 paragraph 4.3.3 the impact of a breach can be disastrous for operators as their clients may hold them contractually liable and will probably also cancel their agreements with the operator in droves.

9 Paragraph 4.2.3.

5.3.3 Managing third parties

All of this underscores the necessity for risk management through contracts and contract management, binding corporate rules (policies, standards, practices and procedures between 'groups of undertakings') and third-party risk management (vetting and auditing). These strategies are discussed in chapter 4 paragraph 4.8.3.

5.4 WHAT RESPONSIBLE PARTIES MUST PROTECT PERSONAL INFORMATION AGAINST

5.4.1 What POPIA says

POPIA conjures the image of a guy sitting in a dark basement, hacking away at the CIA mainframe. This is a rather limited view of all of the threats information must be protected against. Section 19 of POPIA is not just about cybersecurity. The section provides that the responsible party must protect personal information against:

- loss
- damage
- unauthorised destruction
- unlawful access; and
- unlawful processing.

Add to that, that section 16 provides that a responsible party must take reasonably practicable steps to ensure that the personal information they have is complete, accurate, not misleading and updated where necessary. Quality issues will often also be security issues (and vice versa).[10]

Here are just a few examples of things that go bump in the night:

Tricky area: We are about to speak some serious geek.[11] We believe all information officers and deputy information officers should learn enough of this strange language to hold their own in a conversation. Luckily there are some fantastic glossaries out there.[12] We recommend that you spend some time trawling through them.

[10] Information quality is discussed in chapter 9.

[11] Before you get too indignant about this, just remember that compliance and legal folk also regularly subject IT to legalese with little or no explanation. Consider this payback.

[12] See Cybercrime Magazine 'The Motherlist Glossary of Cybersecurity and Cybercrime Definitions', available at https://cybersecurityventures.com/cybersecurity-glossary/. Wikipedia will also do.

- Employee/human error. This includes misconfiguration, misdelivery and publishing errors.[13] Show us someone who hasn't sent an email to the wrong person at least once and we'll refund whatever you paid for this book.[14]
- Malicious insiders. Revenge or financial gain can be powerful motivators. This happens when people who have access to systems and information use that information with malicious intent.
- Malware. Password dumpers are the most common among malware varieties. Emails associated with phishing and direct installs that require credentials are the other top performers. Ransomware is also a common malware breach variety.[15]
- Data loss. Sometimes organisations just lose data. Data loss prevention is a part of business continuity management and is comprised of sets of practices and tools that prevent (amongst other things) accidental data destruction.[16]
- Hacking. Hacking includes those using stolen or brute-forced credentials, those exploiting vulnerabilities, and attacks using backdoors and Command and Control functionality. More than 80% of these breaches involve brute force or the use of lost or stolen credentials.[17] This is a form of unlawful access.
- Social engineering. Social engineering is a confidence trick where you convince someone who has access to the personal information that they ought to give the personal information (or access to the personal information) to you as you are entitled to have it. This is how Verizon describes it: 'If action types were people, you would probably give Hacking, Malware and Error a wide berth because they just sound like they would be less friendly. But Social sounds as though it would be much more happy-go-lucky. More likely to house-sit for you, invite you to play bunko and include you in the neighbourhood barbeques. You'd be wrong though. Social comes with a devious attitude and a "take me to your manager" haircut.' The top two types of social engineering are phishing and pretexting.[18]

---

13 According to the IBM *Cost of a Data Breach Report 2020* (30) human error accounted for 23% of the root causes of data breaches.

14 Not really. Just trying to prove a point here.

15 Verizon 2020 Data Breach Investigations Report 15, available at https://enterprise.verizon.com/en-gb/resources/reports/dbir/. This report is equal parts hilarious and terrifying. If you enjoy a rollercoaster of emotions, read it.

16 See Gilad David Maayan 'Seven reasons why data loss prevention is necessary for business', available at https://www.dataversity.net/seven-reasons-why-data-loss-prevention-is-necessary-for-business/.

17 Verizon 2020 Data Breach Investigations Report 19, available at https://enterprise.verizon.com/en-gb/resources/reports/dbir/.

18 Verizon 2020 Data Breach Investigations Report 24, available at https://enterprise.verizon.com/en-gb/resources/reports/dbir/.

Key point: Humans and their behaviour sit at the heart of many information security threats. It is important to understand the cognitive science that explores why it is that we are so vulnerable. In *Thinking about Thinking: Exploring bias in cybersecurity with insights from cognitive science*, Dr Margaret Cunningham points out that: 'by improving our understanding of biases, it becomes easier to identify and mitigate the impact of flawed reasoning and decision-making conventions. Our efforts to build harmony between the best characteristics of humans and the best characteristics of technology to tackle cybersecurity challenges depend on understanding and overcoming bias.'[19] For instance, in social engineering, attackers take advantage of people by putting them in a hot state by either making them very excited (you have just inherited R5 million) or anxious (I know you have been visiting a porn site). Their minds then become clouded by emotion and they struggle to make rational decisions and practice self-control. We also need to understand that people do not naturally feel and understand socially constructed concepts like exchanging information on the internet (for instance). As Dr Jessica Barker puts it: 'Although we generally perceive fear as an emotion, it is actually a social construct: for people to be scared of a tiger, in the first instance they have to understand what a tiger is and to comprehend the danger it poses to them.'[20] This underscores the importance of training which we discuss in chapter 20 paragraph 20.5.

- Physical theft. An oldie but a goodie. Who hasn't had their mobile phone or laptop stolen? No-one? Thought so. Sometimes physical files get stolen from filing cabinets, boots of cars, briefcases or dumpsters. Don't forget that POPIA applies to these security compromises too! Diving in dumpsters for personal information is how a lot of identity theft starts.[21]

---

19 Dr Margaret Cunningham *Thinking about Thinking: Exploring bias in cybersecurity with insights from cognitive science* 3, available at https://www.forcepoint.com/resources/reports/thinking-about-thinking-exploring-bias-cybersecurity-insights-cognitive-science. Also see Dr Margaret Cunningham *Exploring the Gray Space of Cybersecurity with Insights from Cognitive Science*, available at https://www.forcepoint.com/resources/reports/exploring-gray-space-cybersecurity-insights-cognitive-science.

20 Jessica Barker 'Oh, behave! What information security can learn from behavioural economics' *Tripwire*, available at https://www.tripwire.com/state-of-security/security-awareness/oh-behave-what-information-security-can-learn-from-behavioural-economics/.

21 Preparing for a life of crime? Read how it is done in Stephen Mihm 'Dumpster-Diving for Your Identity' New York Times, available at https://www.nytimes.com/2003/12/21/magazine/dumpster-diving-for-your-identity.html

- Unlawful processing. This happens when a responsible party, operator or third party uses personal information without a legal justification.[22] This also often happens when a responsible party uses personal information it collected for one purpose, for another, incompatible purpose without doing a compatibility assessment.[23]

5.4.2 Introducing the CIA triad

The ISO 27000 standard defines information security as '[t]he preservation of confidentiality, integrity, and availability of information'.[24] Let's unpack the different elements of this definition and link them to POPIA:

[22] Having a lawful basis for processing is discussed in chapter 6.

[23] Further processing is discussed in chapter 12. Compatibility assessments are discussed in paragraph 12.4.

[24] We discuss standards in paragraph 5.5.3 below. The reason why we like ISO in particular, is because their standards get developed by a panel of experts within a technical committee. When a draft is ready, all ISO members are asked to comment and vote. In their own words: 'ISO's role is similar to that of a conductor, while the orchestra is made up of independent technical experts nominated by our members.' A bit pretentious, but it makes sense. We would change it to 'ISO's role is similar to that of a DJ at an alternative rock nightclub (say, The Doors in Johannesburg). The technical experts are all in the mosh pit, head banging, sweating, pushing and getting each other's hair in their mouths.' The other reason we are fans of ISO, is because they have published the first international standard for privacy information management, ISO/IEC 27701 (see IAPP 'ISO publishes first International Standards for privacy information management, available at https://iapp.org/news/a/iso-publishes-first-international-standards-for-privacy-information-management/ and IT Governance 'ISO 27701: The international standard for privacy information management', available at https://www.itgovernance.co.uk/iso-27701).

ISO element	What POPIA says
Confidentiality: Information is not made available or disclosed to unauthorised individuals, entities and processes. A breach of confidentiality happens when an unauthorised person can read and could take advantage of having access to the personal information.[25]	A responsible party must take measures to prevent the unlawful access to or processing of personal information. Unlawful access happens when people who should not have access to personal information are given access due to an error or oversight, or if they gain access by nefarious means.[26] An operator or anyone processing personal information on behalf of a responsible party or operator, must treat personal information which comes to their knowledge as confidential and must not disclose it.[27]
Integrity: Safeguarding the accuracy and completeness of information assets. For example, integrity is breached if an unauthorised person makes changes to information.	A responsible party must take measures to prevent damage to personal information.[28] A responsible party must take reasonably practicable steps to ensure that the personal information is complete, accurate, not misleading and updated where necessary. What is necessary will depend on the purpose for which the personal information is collected or further processed.[29] Data subjects have the right to request a responsible party to correct any personal information that is inaccurate, out of date, incomplete or misleading.[30] When a data subject contests the accuracy of their personal information held by a responsible party, the responsible party must restrict the processing of that information while the responsible party verifies the accuracy of the information.[31]

➡

25 The point here is not that they do take advantage of it, but rather that they COULD take advantage of it. It is still a breach of confidentiality if an unauthorised person sees the confidential information even if that person is completely trustworthy and will not use the confidential information (it is just that the impact and risk of the security breach is much lower because the person is trustworthy).

26 Section 19(1)*(b)*.

27 Section 20*(b)*.

28 Section 19(1)*(a)*.

29 Section 16. We discuss information quality in chapter 9. Before the shouting starts, we know data integrity and data quality are not the same thing.

30 Section 24(1).

31 Section 14(6).

ISO element	What POPIA says
Availability: Information being accessible and usable upon demand by an authorised user. A breach of availability happens when authorised users are denied access to information.	A responsible party must take measures to prevent the loss or unauthorised destruction of personal information.[32] Availability of information is usually addressed by business continuity management and disaster recovery plans.
And POPIA adds privacy: ISO 27701 'bolts privacy processing controls onto ISO 27001'. ISO 27701 'relates to the way an organisation collects personal data and prevents unauthorised use or disclosure'.[33]	All of POPIA deal with aspects of privacy, but section 19 specifically adds unlawful processing of personal information to the CIA triad.[34]
Information: This includes information held electronically (usually referred to as cybersecurity), physically (security of physical information includes locks on doors and filing cabinets), and knowledge (e.g. how to retain or access the knowledge that a person has when they leave the organisation).[35]	**Key point:** As you will see in chapter 20 paragraph 20.2.5, we separate information security management from privacy when we develop policies. Why do we do that? Not because POPIA says so, but because POPIA (only) applies to personal information. We believe that an information security management policy should apply to all information (not just personal information), because there may be other types of information even more worthy of protection than personal information (e.g. an organisation's intellectual property).

[32] Section 19(1)*(a)*.

[33] IT Governance 'An introduction to ISO 27701: The international standard for data privacy', available at https://www.itgovernance.eu/blog/en/iso-27701-the-new-international-standard-for-data-privacy.

[34] Section 19(1)*(b)*.

[35] See https://www.isms.online/iso-27001/information-security-risk-management-explained/.

The confidentiality, integrity and availability legs of the definition are often referred to as the CIA triad. All three of them are required for information security.

* *We are not information security experts. Except when we drink wine, then we are experts in everything.*[36]

5.5 WHAT DOES POPIA REQUIRE OF RESPONSIBLE PARTIES?

5.5.1 (Information) risk management and something about Winnie the Pooh

Our favourite risk management quote is from Winnie the Pooh:

> '"Supposing a tree fell down, Pooh, when we were underneath it?"
>
> "Supposing it didn't," said Pooh after careful thought. Piglet was comforted by this.'

A bit closer to home: 'One of the main [POPIA risks] is to think they don't exist. The other is to try and treat all potential risks. Fix the basics, protect first what matters for your business and be ready to react properly to pertinent threats. Think data, but also business services integrity, awareness, customer experience, compliance, and reputation.'[37]

Both of these quotes illustrate that a risk-based approach is vital to ensure that an organisation deploys its resources where it matters most. Section 19(2) requires the responsible party to take reasonable measures to:

---

36 In the words of Tyrion Lannister: 'That's what I do. I drink and I know things.'

37 Stephane Nappo, Global Chief Information Security Officer, 2018 Global CISO of the year.

- identify risks to personal information in its possession or under its control
- establish and maintain appropriate safeguards against the risks identified
- regularly verify that the safeguards are properly implemented; and
- regularly update safeguards in response to new risks or deficiencies in safeguards.

This is risk management 101. In a picture:

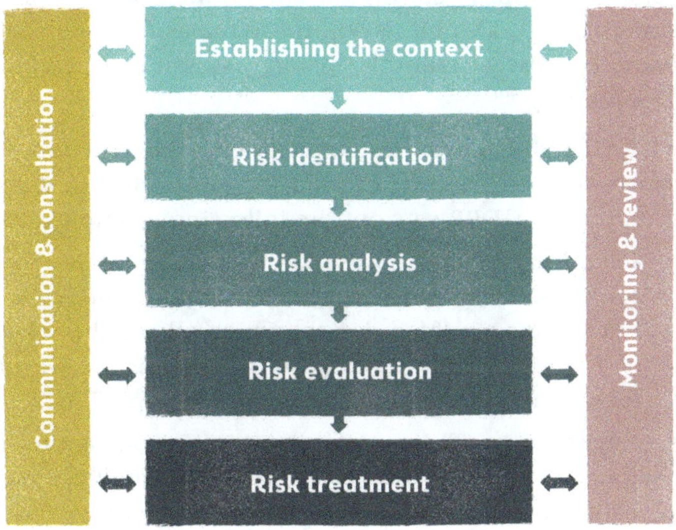

The ISO 31000 Risk Management Guidelines say that the risk management process should be an integral part of management and decision-making, and integrated into the structure, operations and processes of an organisation.[38]

The SA Law Reform Commission acknowledged that organisations fail to manage information security risks because:

- they do not appreciate the gravity of the risk
- some organisations don't have the expertise to assess key risk factors and to devise ways of mitigating risks; and
- some organisations fail to devote or co-ordinate adequate resources to address the risk.[39]

Chapter 5

[38] ISO 31000 (2018) Risk Management Guideline 9.

[39] SA Law Reform Commission Project 124 on Privacy and Data Protection (2009 Report) 267.

If a responsible party doesn't already have an established risk management structure, POPIA forces them to put one in place. Information officers and deputy information officers will also need basic risk management skills.

We discuss the risk-based approach to POPIA and 'personal information impact assessments' in chapter 20 paragraph 20.3.

5.5.2 Reasonable technical and organisational measures

POPIA prescribes that responsible parties must take 'appropriate, reasonable technical and organisational measures' to protect personal information. At a high level, these measures include technology, policies, processes, controls, plans, assessments, contracts, training and monitoring.[40]

The EU GDPR also requires 'appropriate technical and organisational measures to ensure a level of security appropriate to the risk'.[41] Useful as ever, the EU GDPR sets out the following examples:

- **Pseudonymisation:** Pseudonymisation is a technique that removes information in a dataset that identifies a data subject, but retains a related dataset which allows the responsible party to re-identify the information if it needs to. We discussed this technique in detail in chapter 3 paragraph 3.3.2.
- **Encryption:** This is the process of using an algorithm to transform information to make it unreadable, except to people with the decryption key. Extensive encryption can vastly reduce the impact of a data breach.[42]
- **Ensuring the ongoing confidentiality, integrity and availability and resilience of processing systems and services:** This just confirms the CIA triad which we discussed in paragraph 5.4.2 above.

---

40 We view (well-drafted) policies as an indispensable part of a compliance framework. We discuss them in chapter 20 paragraph 20.2.5. While policies are not explicitly required in POPIA, it is one of the factors the Information Regulator will take into account when determining the size of the administrative fine against a responsible party who is guilty of an offence (see chapter 19 paragraph 19.10.3). Section 109(3)*(g)* provides that the Information Regulator must consider 'any failure to carry out a risk assessment or a failure to operate good policies, procedures and practices to protect personal information'. The European Data Protection Board also lists policies as an example of appropriate organisational measures (European Data Protection Board *Guidelines 4/2019 on Article 25 Data Protection by Design and by Default* 8, available at https://edpb.europa.eu/sites/default/files/files/file1/edpb_guidelines_201904_dataprotection_by_design_and_by_default_v2.0_en.pdf.)

41 Article 32(1).

42 IBM *Cost of a Data Breach Report 2020*, 42, available at https://www.ibm.com/security/digital-assets/cost-data-breach-report/#/.

- **The ability to restore availability and access in the event of a physical or technical incident:** This refers to business continuity management and disaster recovery planning. Business continuity is also responsible for a significant reduction in the cost of data breaches as it minimises down-time.[43]
- **A process of regularly testing, assessing and evaluating the effectiveness of technical and organisational measures:** This is a reference to information risk management. Testing in this context includes red team testing, vulnerability testing, penetration testing and all manner of other Hollywood-sounding things.[44]

Key point: But what on Earth will be appropriate and reasonable? We discuss the concept of reasonableness and what is 'reasonably practicable' extensively in chapter 2 paragraphs 2.6.1 and 2.6.2. The ICO says that what is 'appropriate' will depend on the risks presented by the processing and 'the state of the art and costs of implementation, as well as the nature, scope, context and purpose' of the processing. We would add the severity and likelihood of the risks. There is no 'one size fits all' solution and no definitive checklist.[45] Or there are too many.

43 IBM *Cost of a Data Breach Report 2020*, 42, available at https://www.ibm.com/security/digital-assets/cost-data-breach-report/#/.

44 IBM *Cost of a Data Breach Report 2020* 42, available at https://www.ibm.com/security/digital-assets/cost-data-breach-report/#/. Red team testing is when you artificially separate a team from the remainder of your organisation and get them to pretend that they are hackers in order to assess whether you have security vulnerabilities. Penetration testing is to see whether someone without proper authorisation can bypass existing security controls meant to keep unauthorised people out. Vulnerability testing is seeing who in your organisation cries first.

45 ICO *Security Outcomes*, available at https://ico.org.uk/for-organisations/security-outcomes/#appropriate. Take ownership of your own security so that it is – in your view – reasonable security. If you can afford the time and cost, get IT and physical security experts to check if they agree with you.

Here are the four outcomes (aims) that the ICO has set to get responsible parties started:

Outcome	Just get on with it
Manage security risk	**Governance:** Responsible parties must have appropriate privacy protection and information security policies and processes in place. The information officer is accountable to put a POPIA compliance framework in place.[46] **Risk management:** Responsible parties identify, assess and understand security risks to personal information and the systems that process the information.[47] Information security risk management is a requirement in terms of section 19(2). **Asset management:** Responsible parties must understand and document the personal information processed and the purposes for which it is processed. Section 17 requires the documentation of all personal information processing activities. **Third-party management:** Responsible parties must understand and manage the security risks related to using operators, and ensure that operators implement appropriate security measures.[48]

➥

46 Regulation 4(1)*(a)* of the POPIA Regulations.

47 Here is some handy guidance on risk management for cybersecurity: https://www.ncsc.gov.uk/collection/risk-management-collection/essential-topics/introduction-risk-management-cybersecurity-guidance.

48 Section 21(1). We discuss third-party management in chapter 4.

Outcome	Just get on with it
Protect personal information against cyber-attacks	**Service protection policies and processes:** Responsible parties must define, implement, communicate and enforce appropriate policies and processes that determine their approach to securing systems that process personal information. They should also consider implementing controls set out in generally accepted frameworks (discussed in the next section). **Identity and access control:** Responsible parties must understand, document and manage access to personal information and systems that process personal information. They should implement authentication measures such as two-factor authentication.[49] **Data security:** Responsible parties must implement technical controls, such as encryption, to prevent unauthorised or unlawful processing of personal information. **System security:** Responsible parties must implement measures to protect systems, technologies and digital services that process personal information from cyberattacks. Examples include: encrypting personal information at rest on devices and when transmitted electronically, actively managing software vulnerabilities, managing end user devices etc.[50] **Staff awareness and training:** Responsible parties must give their staff appropriate support to help them manage personal information securely.[51]
Detect security incidents	**Security monitoring:** Responsible parties must monitor the status of systems processing personal information and monitor user access to personal information.[52]

➡

49 See the General Access Control Guidance for Cloud Systems published by NIST, available at https://www.nist.gov/publications/general-access-control-guidance-cloud-systems.

50 The ICO published a guide on 'Protecting personal data in online services: learning from the mistakes of others' describing eight frequently arising computer security issues in an online environment, together with a summary on how to guard against these issues. See https://ico.org.uk/media/for-organisations/documents/1042221/protecting-personal-data-in-online-services-learning-from-the-mistakes-of-others.pdf. The OWASP Top 10 presents the most critical security risks to web applications: https://owasp.org/www-project-top-ten/. The European Union Agency for cybersecurity published guidelines on the security of personal data processing specifically aimed at SMEs, available at https://www.enisa.europa.eu/publications/guidelines-for-smes-on-the-security-of-personal-data-processing.

51 See the NIST aids and materials to raise employees' awareness about the importance of security: https://www.nist.gov/itl/smallbusinesscyber/guidance-topic/employee-awareness.

52 For more information on monitoring, go to https://www.ncsc.gov.uk/collection/10-steps-to-cyber-security/the-10-steps/monitoring.

Outcome	Just get on with it
Minimise the impact	**Response and recovery planning:** Responsible parties must have a tested incident response plan.[53] **Improvements:** When a breach occurs, responsible parties must take steps to understand the root cause and take appropriate remediating action.

5.5.3 Generally accepted information security practices and procedures

Section 19(3) says that a 'responsible party must have due regard to generally accepted information security practices and procedures which may apply to it generally or be required in terms of a specific industry or professional rules and regulations'.

Luckily there are loads of frameworks, guides and standards out there. If you think this book is complicated, you ain't seen nothing yet:

- ITIL: The Information Technology Infrastructure Library[54]
- ISO/IEC 20000: The IT service management standard[55]
- ISO/IEC 27000: Standards for an information security management system[56]
- COBIT (Control Objectives for Information and Related Technologies): An IT management framework developed by ISACA to help organisations develop, organise and implement information management and governance strategies[57]
- CMMI (Capability Maturity Model Integration): This one helps with process improvement[58]
- The Open Group Architecture Framework (TOGAF): This one helps to align IT goals with overall business goals[59]

53 For more information on incident management, see https://www.ncsc.gov.uk/collection/10-steps-to-cyber-security/the-10-steps/incident-management, and the NIST guidance on responding to a cyber incident: https://www.nist.gov/itl/smallbusinesscyber/responding-cyber-incident.

54 This article in IT Governance explains ITIL (kind of): https://ico.org.uk/media/for-organisations/documents/1570/it_asset_disposal_for_organisations.pdf.

55 See https://www.iso.org/standard/70636.html.

56 See https://www.iso.org/isoiec-27001-information-security.html.

57 This article explains COBIT: https://www.cio.com/article/3243684/what-is-cobit-a-framework-for-alignment-and-governance.html.

58 This article explains CMMI: https://www.cio.com/article/2437864/process-improvement-capability-maturity-model-integration-cmmi-definition-and-solutions.html.

59 This article explains TOGAF: https://www.cio.com/article/3251707/what-is-togaf-an-enterprise-architecture-methodology-for-business.html.

- The US National Institute of Standards and Technology (NIST) Cybersecurity Framework: This framework consists of standards, guidelines and best practices to manage cybersecurity risk[60]
- OECD Recommendations: Digital Security Risk Management for Economic and Social Prosperity[61] and the OECD Recommendation on Digital Security of Critical Activities;[62] and
- The SANS Institute's 20 Critical Security Controls.[63]

Key point: Just be careful, some of these standards are drafted for IT, whereas information security management is not (just) an IT problem. Your information security management policy should not be 'owned' by IT. We discuss the role of IT in chapter 1 paragraph 1.2.5 and information security management policies in chapter 20 paragraph 20.2.5.

5.6 WHEN THE POPIA STRIKES THE FAN

Organisations should expect to be targeted and breached. As Robert Mueller III once remarked: 'There are only two types of companies: Those that have been hacked and those that will be hacked.'[64] Section 22 deals with security compromises and when they must be reported to the Information Regulator and the affected data subjects. We look at these requirements in detail below.

However, it is also critically important to understand the other implications of 'data breaches' and the havoc they can wreak on an organisation.

5.6.1 What is a 'security compromise'

Not all non-compliance with section 19 qualify as a security compromise in terms of section 22. A breach is only a 'security compromise' if 'there are reasonable grounds to believe that the personal information of a data subject has been accessed or acquired by any unauthorised person'. The important elements of the definition of 'security compromise' in POPIA are as follows:

- there must be 'reasonable grounds to believe'

60 See https://www.nist.gov/cyberframework.

61 See https://www.oecd.org/sti/ieconomy/digital-security-risk-management.pdf.

62 See https://legalinstruments.oecd.org/en/instruments/OECD-LEGAL-0456.

63 See https://www.sans.org/critical-security-controls.

64 Yes, that Robert Mueller III, former Director of the FBI.

Tricky area: What does 'reasonable grounds to believe' mean? It is not enough that it is possible that an unauthorised person could have accessed or acquired the personal information. There has to be some evidence to back up the belief.

- that the information was 'accessed' or 'acquired'
- by any unauthorised person.

Tricky area: Who is this 'unauthorised person'? Does this person have to be a third party or can it be an employee of the responsible party? A responsible party should give certain employees access to personal information depending on whether their role requires it. This should be governed by the responsible party's access control policies and procedures. Is non-compliance with an internal access control policy that results in an unauthorised employee of the responsible party getting access to the personal information a notifiable 'security compromise'? We do not think that it is.

The definition of 'security compromise' is a narrow definition; not all infringements of section 19 (or the rest of POPIA for that matter), will be considered 'security compromises'. Instead security compromises appear to be limited to confidentiality breaches; i.e. where there is unauthorised disclosure of or access to personal information. So, while integrity and availability breaches may fall foul of POPIA, the responsible party does not have to notify the Information Regulator about these types of security breaches.

In another sense, the definition is quite broad. Only one data subject's personal information had to be compromised for the breach to qualify as a 'security incident'. Article 33(1) of the EU GDPR states that a responsible party does not have to notify the supervisory authority if 'the personal data breach is unlikely to result in a risk to the rights and freedoms of natural persons'. POPIA does not contain this provision which means that even low (or no risk) security compromises must be brought to the attention of the Information Regulator. We will keep the Information Regulator in our thoughts.

Key point: What is in a name? Well, it is important that a responsible party labels events as this will determine what processes must be followed and whether the process involves notifying the Information Regulator. Here are some categories to consider:

- **Events**: Something happened. It could be bad, or not.
- **Security incidents**: An event that compromises the confidentiality, integrity or availability of any information asset (not necessarily personal information).
- **Privacy incidents**: There has been unlawful processing of personal information, but the Information Regulator does not have to be notified.
- **A data breach or 'security compromise' as POPIA calls it**: '[T]here are reasonable grounds to believe that the personal information of a data subject has been accessed or acquired by any unauthorised person.' In this case, the Information Regulator must be notified.

5.6.2 Notifying the Information Regulator

A responsible party must notify the Information Regulator as soon as reasonably possible after discovery of a security compromise. In deciding when to notify the Information Regulator the responsible party may take the legitimate needs of law enforcement, or any measures reasonably necessary to determine the scope of the compromise and to restore the integrity of their information system, into account.[65]

When is 'as soon as reasonably possible'? POPIA does not prescribe a specific period within which the Information Regulator must be notified. In the absence of a prescribed period, it is useful to look at similar reporting requirements in other legislation:

Chapter 5

65 Section 22(1) and 22(2).

Laws	Whooshing deadlines[66]
Cybercrimes Act[67]	Electronic communications service providers and financial institutions that are aware or become aware that their electronic communications service or electronic communications network is involved in the commission of any category or class of offences in terms of the Act must report the offence to the SAPS 'without undue delay and, where feasible, **not later than 72 hours** after having become aware of the offence'.[68]
South African Reserve Bank Prudential Authority Directive 2/19: Reporting of material information technology and/or cyber incidents	Banks must notify the Prudential Authority as soon as practically possible but **not later than one day**, following the discovery of a material IT and/or cyber incident.[69] The bank must also submit a root cause and impact analysis report within 14 days from the date of notification.[70]
EU GDPR: Article 33	Controllers must notify the supervisory authority of a personal data breach **no later than 72 hours** after becoming aware of the breach, unless the personal data breach is unlikely to result in a risk to the rights and freedoms of natural persons. If the notification is not made within 72 hours it must be accompanied by reasons for the delay.[71]
Kenya Data Protection Act	Data controllers have an obligation to notify the Data Protection Commissioner of any breaches **within 72 hours** of becoming aware of a breach. If the controller fails to notify the Commissioner within 72 hours, they must provide reasons for the delay.[72]

➡

66 Here's a Douglas Adams quote that felt all too familiar as we were writing this book: 'I love deadlines. I like the whooshing sound they make as they fly by.'

67 Act 19 of 2020.

68 Section 54(1)*(a)* of the Cybercrimes Act.

69 Paragraph 2.1.4 of the directive, available at https://www.resbank.co.za/en/home/publications/publication-detail-pages/prudential-authority/pa-deposit-takers/banks-directives/2019/9487.

70 Paragraph 2.1.6 of the directive.

71 Article 33 of the EU GDPR.

72 Section 43(1)–(2) of the Data Protection Act, 2019.

Laws	Whooshing deadlines
Mauritius Data Protection Act	A controller must without undue delay and, where feasible, **not later than 72 hours** after having become aware of it, notify the personal data breach to the Commissioner. If the controller fails to notify the Commissioner within 72 hours, they must provide reasons for the delay.[73]

Key point: Based on what we see in other SA legislation and in other jurisdictions, it seems like 72 hours is considered a reasonable time to delay notifying the Information Regulator, but not much longer unless a responsible party has valid reasons. '72 hours' also makes an appearance in POPIA, in section 90(5) which allows the Information Regulator to issue an urgent information notice which requires a response from the responsible party within 72 hours.[74]

5.6.3 Notifying data subjects

A responsible party must usually also notify all affected data subjects about a security compromise as soon as reasonably possible, unless the responsible party cannot establish the identity of the data subject.[75] Notification to data subjects may be delayed if 'a public body responsible for the prevention, detection or investigation of offences or the Regulator determines that notification will impede a criminal investigation by the public body concerned'.[76]

[73] Section 25(1)–(2) of the Data Protection Act 2017.

[74] To put this in perspective we researched what else one can do with 72 hours: Watch all but the last episode of Game of Thrones (which is the best way to watch it), read 2160 pages, digest a steak, travel one-way to the moon, plant radishes and watch them sprout, bake a batch of croissants or take 69 120 breaths.

[75] Section 22(1)*(b)*.

[76] Section 22(3).

Key point: When will the SAPS or the Information Regulator want an organisation to delay reporting the security breach to data subjects? The most obvious answer to this is when the security breach is continuing (i.e. it hasn't been fixed yet) and notification of the data subjects could give rise to more people exploiting the security breach. Another answer could be where the SAPS wants to conduct a sting operation to catch the perpetrators. All this means that you should prepare your communication to the data subjects but do not send it unless the SAPS and the Information Regulator approve your communication.

The notification to data subjects must include 'sufficient information to allow the data subject to take protective measures against potential consequences of the compromise, including:

- a description of the possible consequences of the security compromise;
- a description of the measures that the responsible party will take or has taken to address the security compromise;
- a recommendation on what data subjects can do to mitigate the possible adverse effects of the security compromise; and
- if known to the responsible party, the identity of the unauthorised person who may have accessed or acquired the personal information.'[77]

The notification to the data subject must be in writing and communicated in at least one of the following ways:

- mailed to last known physical or postal address
- emailed to last known email address
- placed in a prominent position of the responsible party's website
- published in the news media; or
- as may be directed by the Regulator.

5.6.4 Washing dirty laundry (publicising compromises to integrity and confidentiality)

The Regulator may direct a responsible party to publicise any compromise to the integrity and confidentiality of personal information if the Regulator believes that publicity would protect an affected data subject.[78]

---

77 Section 22(5).

78 Section 22(6).

But what does this mean? In theory the Information Regulator could instruct a responsible party to publish a notification of the security compromise in the Sunday newspapers, and on social media sites. If the reputational damage of the actual security compromise itself does not sink a business, this just might!

Tricky area: Here the legislature did not use 'security compromise' but rather 'any compromise to the integrity and confidentiality of personal information'. It is wider. Does this mean that even if it is not a notifiable incident the Regulator can make a responsible party publicise? We do not think so. If an organisation is not required to notify the Information Regulator, then surely the Regulator cannot direct them to publicise it?

5.6.5 Other consequences (and costs!) of a data breach

Key point: The Information Regulator cannot automatically fine a responsible party if there is a security compromise.

We discuss the enforcement of POPIA in chapter 19. It is important to note that non-compliance with section 19 is not an offence in terms of POPIA; which means that the Information Regulator cannot necessarily fine the responsible party.[79] It is an 'interference with the protection of personal information' in terms of section 73. This triggers an investigation (and information notices) that may culminate in an enforcement notice. The enforcement notice will include a directive to 'take specified steps within a period specified in the notice, or to refrain from taking such steps' or 'to stop processing personal information specified in the notice, or to stop processing personal information for a purpose or in a manner specified in the notice within a period specified in the notice'.[80] The responsible party can appeal the notice within 30 days or must comply with it.[81] Non-compliance with an enforcement notice is an offence.[82] When this happens, the responsible party may be fined or there will be a criminal investigation.[83]

Chapter 5

79 Section 107.

80 Section 95(1).

81 Section 97(1).

82 Section 103(1).

83 Section 109.

In addition to a fine, a responsible party may also be exposed to civil liability in terms of section 99. This is discussed in chapter 19, but suffice it to say that this civil liability is also not strict. In other words, data subject is not entitled to compensation just because there was a security compromise.

However, liability in terms of POPIA is not the only harm which responsible parties will be exposed to. Every year, IBM publishes its *Cost of a Data Breach Report*. In 2020, the average cost of a data breach was USD3.86 million.[84] It is divided into four categories:[85]

- **Detection and escalation:** Forensic auditing, investigations, assessments, audits, crisis management, communications to executives and boards.
- **Notification:** Notifying data subjects (emails, letters, outbound calls or general notices), communicating with the Information Regulator, legal advice (to determine the POPIA impact and content of notifications and communication with the Information Regulator) and other outside advice.
- **Ex-post[86] response:** Helpdesk and other inbound communication channels, credit monitoring and identity protection services, issuing new accounts or credit cards, legal expenditures (including class action law suits and legal costs), product discounts and regulator fines.
- **Lost business:** Business disruption and revenue losses from system downtime, cost of lost customers and acquiring new customers, loss of reputation and diminished goodwill.

In data breaches, size does matter. 'Mega breaches', where more than 100,000 records are compromised, tend to be more than 100 times costlier than the average breach.

We would add the following to these categories:

- **The cost of remedying the root cause of the breach:** As we discussed above, responsible parties can expect to receive information and enforcement notices. An enforcement notice may force organisations to halt processing or to make costly changes to their business practices.

---

84 Another way to quantify the cost is per customer record. For each record the cost was USD150.

85 IBM *Cost of a Data Breach Report 2020* 7, available at https://www.ibm.com/security/data-breach.

86 Surely not a real word, we thought. It turns out it means 'after the fact' (https://www.investopedia.com/terms/e/expost.asp).

- **The human cost:** Data breaches create a lot of stress and burnout among staff and it is not unusual for information officers, security officers and even chief executive officers to step down from their roles.[87]

Key point: It is important to properly quantify the impact of a data breach on an organisation. A failure to appreciate the consequences could lead to an organisation underestimating the risk and not planning properly.

5.6.6 Incident management

There are a number of factors that can lower the cost of a data breach:

- incident response testing
- business continuity planning
- forming an incident response team
- artificial intelligence (AI) platforms (that can detect new threats and anomalies without human intervention)
- red team testing
- employee training
- extensive encryption
- security analytics
- threat intelligence sharing
- involvement from the board of directors
- cyber insurance
- DevSecOps[88]
- vulnerability testing
- data loss prevention; and
- appointing a Chief Information Security Officer.

Tricky area: More geek, we know! Here, information officers and deputy information officers should know enough about incident response management to know when the organisation is not prepared.

[87] For a good example of this see Sooraj Shah 'On the inside of a hacking catastrophe' *BBC*, available at https://www.bbc.com/news/business-49823935.

[88] Short for development, security, and operations – automates the integration of security at every phase of the software development life cycle, from initial design through integration, testing, deployment, and software delivery. See https://www.ibm.com/cloud/learn/devsecops.

Incident response preparedness saves companies the most money at an average of USD2 million. This is what IBM had to say about it:[89]

> 'Organisations in the study who have formed incident response (IR) teams and tested their incident response plans reduced the average total cost of a data breach by $2 million, compared to organisations without IR teams that had not tested any IR plans. The mantra "train like you fight and fight like you train" means developing and testing incident response play books to help optimize your business' ability to respond quickly and effectively to attacks.'

More about incident response in paragraph 5.7.2 below.

5.7 PRACTICAL ADVICE

5.7.1 The Equifax breach: section 19 in action

Equifax, an American credit bureau, suffered a major data breach in 2017. The data that was compromised included account information of Equifax's credit services such as data subjects' names, addresses, dates of birth, usernames, passwords (in plaintext), secret questions and answers (in plain text), credit card numbers (obscured) and some payment amounts. The compromised personal information was held in plaintext files despite Equifax's Cryptography Standard specifically requiring that passwords were to be stored in encrypted, hashed, masked, tokenised or other approved forms. The file contained 'live' data and was created for testing purposes. Contrary to Equifax's applicable data handling standard the file was not encrypted. The attack exploited a vulnerability in a framework that Equifax used in its customer-facing online disputes portal. It was a known vulnerability and Equifax's key personnel responsible for installations were notified one day prior to the attack, but did not patch the vulnerability. A total of 146 million individuals in the US and 15 million unique records of UK individuals were compromised in the attack. Equifax was found to be in breach of various principles of the UK Data Protection Act, including principle 7 which requires that 'appropriate technical and organisational measures shall be taken against unauthorised or unlawful processing of personal data and against accidental loss or destruction of, or damage to, personal data'.

---

89 IBM *Cost of a Data Breach Report 2020* 68, available at https://www.ibm.com/security/data-breach.

Key point: Principle 7 of the UK Data Protection Act is similar enough to POPIA that we can treat the findings against Equifax as a cautionary tale.

These are some of the reasons why the ICO found Equifax to be in breach of principle 7:

- Equifax Ltd (data controller) did not undertake adequate risk assessments of security arrangements put in place by Equifax Inc (data processor) before transferring data to it or following the transfer.
- The data protection agreement(s) between Equifax Ltd and Equifax Inc. was inadequate because it failed to provide appropriate safeguards including security requirements, and failed to incorporate the required standard contractual clauses.
- Equifax Ltd failed to carry out appropriate audits and checks of Equifax Inc to ensure it complied with the relevant security requirements, despite having a contractual right to do so.
- Equifax Ltd failed to ensure that Equifax Inc took adequate security measures, including the following:
    - encryption was inadequate
    - user passwords were not adequately protected
    - known IT vulnerabilities were not addressed
    - software was not up to date
    - not undertaking sufficient system scans
    - inappropriate network segregation
    - ineffective access control
    - storing passwords in plaintext within files accessible by staff
    - allowing an expired certificate in an SSL decryptor which prevented traffic from being properly checked by its Intrusion Prevention System
    - continued storing without legal basis; and
    - Equifax Inc delayed notifying Equifax Ltd of the breach by more than a month.

The ICO considered the state of technological development, the cost of implementing any measures, the nature of the relevant personal data and the harm that might ensue from its misuse and found that Equifax Ltd contravened principle 7 in the case of each of the inadequacies listed above.[90]

[90] See https://ico.org.uk/media/action-weve-taken/mpns/2259808/equifax-ltd-mpn-20180919.pdf.

Multiple class action claims were instituted against Equifax in the US. In an earnings release of May 2019 Equifax Inc revealed that since the incident, they had incurred a total of USD1 352 billion of costs related to the incident, incremental technology and data security costs, and an accrual for losses associated with legal proceedings and investigations related to the incident.[91] In February 2020 Equifax was reported to say that the breach has cost them USD2 billion thus far.[92]

Key point: At the time of the breach, Equifax had USD125 million cybersecurity insurance coverage. Ouch.

5.7.2 Sonofabreach! (incident management)

Incident response is incredibly important. The ICO has created a checklist (which we adapted slightly):[93]

Let's do this!	Okay, how?
Detecting, managing and recording incidents and breaches	• The organisation has trained its staff to recognise different types of incidents. • A dedicated person on the incident response team manages incidents. They know who they are and have simulated some incidents to ensure that the team has the skills to be effective; including technical, legal, crisis management and communication skills. Pick someone with a light case of megalomania and call them the Breach Tsar; they will take to it like a fish to water. • Staff knows how to report and escalate incidents quickly. • Procedures and systems for reporting incidents are in place and have been tested. • The organisation has an incident response plan. The plan has been tested and the organisation monitors whether it is followed.

➡

91 See https://otp.tools.investis.com/clients/us/equifax/SEC/sec-show.aspx?FilingId=13419350&Cik=0000033185&Type=PDF&hasPdf=1.

92 See https://www.bizjournals.com/atlanta/news/2020/02/13/equifax-says-data-breach-has-cost-it-nearly-2.html.

93 Available at https://ico.org.uk/for-organisations/accountability-framework/breach-response-and-monitoring/.

Let's do this!	Okay, how?
Detecting, managing and recording incidents and breaches (continue)	• The incident response team centrally logs and documents incidents (actual ones and near misses. • The log includes: ▪ the facts of the breach ▪ its root causes ▪ what personal information was affected ▪ the effects of the breach ▪ technical and legal advice received; and ▪ all actions taken during the incident response and why they were (or were not) taken.
Assessing and reporting	• The organisation has transparent and easy to find procedures in place to assess the likelihood and severity of risks to individuals and organisations as a result of the incident. The relevant staff have been trained on how to conduct a risk assessment. • There is a procedure in place that must be followed to determine whether the incident is a notifiable security compromise, to notify the Information Regulator within a reasonable time, what the notification should contain and who should approve it. • The organisation has a procedure for responding to information notices, warrants and enforcement notices issued by the Information Regulator.
Notification and publicity	• The organisation has a crisis communication plan in place and a crisis communication specialist on the incident response team. The plan includes details around what inbound and outbound communication channels will be used. The employees involved in this process have been trained on the plan. • There is a process in place to determine what notification and publicity is required in terms of POPIA and what that communication should contain. • There is a process in place to ensure clear, plain language communication to affected data subjects. This process includes the review and sign-off process. • There is a plan in place to determine what advice data subjects will be given to protect themselves and the measures the organisation will put in place to support them (e.g. free fraud monitoring).

Let's do this!	Okay, how?
Reviewing and monitoring	• The organisation analyses incidents to prevent recurrence. • The type, volume and cost of incidents is monitored and the organisation analyses trends. • Governance types review the trends.
Internal audit programme	• The organisation monitors its own compliance and regularly tests the effectiveness of the controls it has in place. • Staff adherence to policies and procedures is checked regularly. • The internal audit function is independent from the rest of the business. • There is a central audit plan in place that includes planned audits of privacy and information security compliance. • Audit reports are produced to document the findings and action is taken to address them.
External audit	• The organisation uses externally provided self-assessment tools to provide assurance on privacy and information security compliance. • The organisation also employs the service of external auditors. • The findings of internal and external audits are documented and action is taken to address the findings.
Performance and compliance information	• The organisation measures data subject access requests by volume of requests and the percentage completed within a reasonable time. • The organisation measures the completion of privacy and information security training. • The organisation measures information security, including the number of incidents.

6 Processing must be for a lawful purpose

6.1 WHAT TO EXPECT IN THIS CHAPTER

In this chapter we discuss how to answer the question 'is this thing I want to do with personal information legal?' POPIA provides a closed list of legal justifications, and one of them must apply for a processing activity to be legal.[1]

There are three different sets of justifications:

- Ordinary personal information (section 11)
- 'Special personal information' (section 26 to 33) ; and
- Children's personal information (section 34 and 35).

In chapter 7 we discuss the legal justifications for processing special personal information and children's personal information.

[1] Section 11(1).

The responsible party must have a legal justification for each piece of personal information used in an activity, otherwise the organisation is using personal information illegally. This is why we refer to sections 11, 26 to 35 as the heart of POPIA.

Key point: Organisations are often not aware of all the personal information in their possession and the purposes for which the personal information is used. We jokingly refer to this as a state of unconscious incompetence. An essential step in becoming POPIA compliant is to compile a comprehensive list of what personal information the organisation has; why the personal information was collected initially; and all of the purposes for which the personal information is used currently. This process is often referred to as 'data discovery' and includes finding what personal information an organisation has, cataloguing it and classifying it. Data discovery is used to build a 'data processing inventory' which is a repository of all the processing activities an organisation performs. This repository will be filled with data flow maps.[2] In other jurisdictions this is sometimes referred to as a record of processing activities. This is a massive undertaking, and while it is considered an essential step, it can be done over time. Organisations certainly should not wait for this task to be completed before they start managing POPIA risks which they are already aware of! This is called analysis paralysis – a real problem with its own Wikipedia page which is defined as 'an individual or group process when overanalysing or overthinking a situation can cause forward motion or decision-making to become "paralysed", meaning that no solution or course of action is decided upon'.[3] We encountered this problem frequently while we were writing this book.

As you can probably gather, considering the legal justification for processing is not a simple question. We tried to draw a picture of it, and it came out like this:[4]

2 We discuss documenting POPIA compliance in chapter 1 paragraph 1.4.

3 Available at https://en.wikipedia.org/wiki/Analysis_paralysis.

4 No, a chameleon did not just vomit on the page. This is a visual representation of section 4(2)–(5) of POPIA. Don't shoot the messengers.

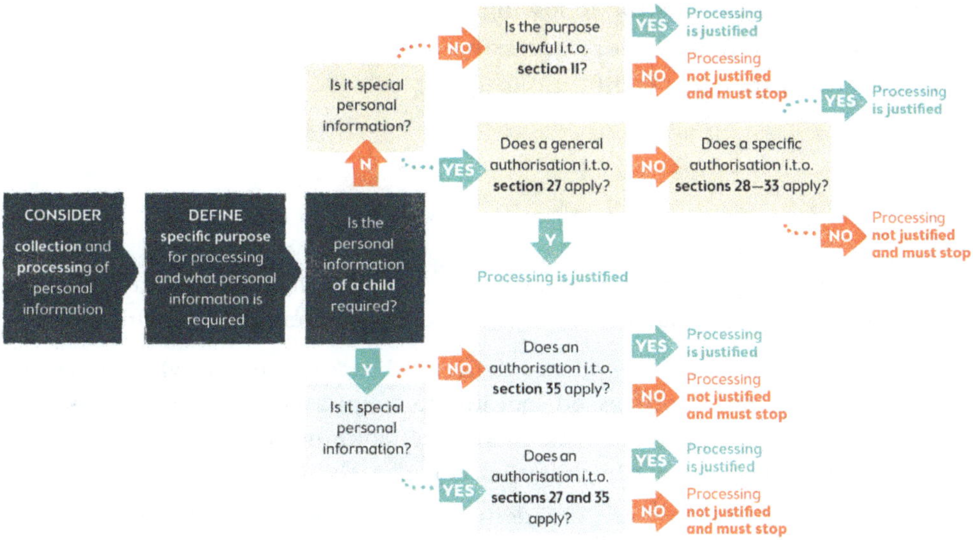

Our suggestion is to read through this chapter and chapter 7 and come back to this picture. That probably won't help, but it is worth a shot. Then, you should go and read section 4(2) to (5). This will lead to loud cursing which will make you feel better for a bit. Then listen to Metallica's 'Nothing Else Matters'. 'So close, no matter how far...'[5]

Key point: We realise that we have not really dealt with what special personal information is yet. How rude. We will do that in chapter 7 paragraph 7.2. For now, you need to know that special personal information is personal information concerning religious or philosophical beliefs, race or ethnic origin, trade union membership, political persuasion, health or sex life, biometric information and information concerning criminal behaviour (that relates to the alleged commission of an offence or any proceedings related to an alleged offence).[6] POPIA prohibits the processing of 'special personal information'. Processing will only be authorised if one of the general or specific authorisations for processing special personal information applies. We also have not dealt with children's personal information yet, but it is illegal to process the personal information of children without complying with section 35. That is discussed in chapter 7 paragraph 7.5.

5 We are of the view that an organisation either has to comply with section 11 (for 'ordinary' personal information) OR with section 27; never both. If the personal information concerns a child, section 35 will apply. If the responsible party is procesing special personal information of a child, both section 27 and 35 applies.

6 Section 26.

In this chapter we discuss the following:

- Defining the purpose for processing
- Do any of the legal justifications apply?

6.2 DEFINING THE PURPOSE FOR PROCESSING

6.2.1 The importance of 'purpose' in POPIA compliance

POPIA expressly requires that personal information may only be collected for a purpose(s) that is specific and explicitly defined.[7]

The importance of explicitly defining the purposes for which personal information is processed cannot be emphasised enough. These are some of the problems that will be encountered if the purpose(s) for which the personal information is processed is not known:

- If purposes are not defined it may be impossible to establish who the responsible party is.[8] Being explicit about the purpose for which personal information is processed when organisations are processing information together promotes certainty and accountability. This is why the purposes for collecting personal information must be specified prior to, or at least no later than, when the collection occurs.
- Knowing the purpose is a prerequisite for applying other data quality requirements. For instance adequacy, relevance, accuracy and proportionality are all determined in relation to a specific purpose.[9]
- It will be impossible to determine the appropriate period to retain the personal information if the purpose for which the personal information is collected is not known.
- The notification duties prescribed by POPIA cannot be met if the purpose is not specified.[10]
- The lawfulness of processing personal information cannot be assessed without knowing what the purpose of the processing activity is.[11]

---

7 Section 13(1).

8 See chapter 4.

9 See chapter 9.

10 See chapter 11.

11 See the rest of this chapter.

Key point: Throughout this chapter, we refer to purpose, singular. The same personal information can be collected for more than one purpose. Each separate purpose should be specified in enough detail to assess whether collection of personal information for this purpose is lawful.

6.2.2 The purpose for processing must be specific and explicitly defined

Any purpose must be sufficiently defined to enable the implementation of any safeguards and duties in POPIA, and to limit the scope of the processing. This means that a purpose specification such as 'personal information is used for business purposes' is not good enough. Failing to document the purposes for which personal information is processed with sufficient specificity and before collection, may mean that any notifications and consents that the organisation had to make or obtain are invalid.

Key point: As is the case with many requirements in POPIA the rule of thumb should be: 'Will the customer/employee/supplier be surprised to learn what their personal information is used for?' If the answer is 'yes' it means that the description of the purpose is not specific enough.

The fact that the purpose must be 'explicitly defined', means that the responsible party must document and demonstrate that it has specified the purposes of all the personal information that it processes in an unambiguous and clear manner.

6.3 DO ANY OF THE LEGAL JUSTIFICATIONS APPLY?

Once a specific purpose for processing personal information has been defined, the next question is whether the processing of personal information for that purpose is lawful. Put differently, the processing of each piece of personal information must be justified. There are six legal justifications:[12]

- processing is necessary to carry out actions to conclude or perform in terms of a contract
- processing complies with an obligation imposed by law on the responsible party

12 Section 11(1).

- processing protects a legitimate interest of the data subject
- processing is necessary for the proper performance of a public law duty by a public body
- processing is necessary for pursuing the legitimate interests of the responsible party or of a third party to whom the information is supplied; or
- the data subject, or a competent person on behalf of a child, consents to processing.

If the processing of special personal information or the personal information of a child is required to fulfil the purpose, the justifications listed here do not apply, but rather the authorisations discussed in chapter 7.

Key point: Some of you might have noticed that we changed the order in which the legal justifications are listed in section 11(1). This is because consent should not be first among the legal justifications; it is the last resort and should only be used if none of the other justifications are present. We have already made this point in chapter 2 paragraph 2.6.6 and will make it again as over-using (and abusing) consent is one of the biggest mistakes responsible parties make.

We will now discuss each of the legal justifications in further detail.

6.3.1 Necessary to conclude or perform in terms of a contract

If a processing activity is necessary to conclude or perform in terms of a contract with the data subject, the processing activity is considered lawful.[13]

Responsible parties can rely on this justification if:

- they have a contract with a data subject and they need to process the data subject's personal information to comply with their responsibilities in terms of the contract
- they have a contract with a data subject and they need to process the data subject's personal information so that they can comply with any counter-obligations in the contract, for instance if they process payment details; or

[13] Section 11(1)*(b)*.

- they don't have a contract with the data subject yet, but the data subject asked them to take a step towards an agreement, for instance providing a quote, and the responsible parties need to process the data subject's personal information to take this step.[14]

When determining what is 'necessary' to conclude or perform in terms of a contract, a fact-based assessment must be made of the processing to determine whether the processing is necessary for the objective pursued by the contract. The responsible party must also consider whether there are realistic, less intrusive alternatives to achieve the objective. If such alternatives exist, the processing is not necessary.[15]

This justification cannot be relied on where the processing is not genuinely necessary for the performance of the contract, but rather unilaterally imposed on the data subject by the responsible party by writing the processing into the contract. This is especially relevant for digital contracts where the data subject has no power to negotiate conditions about advertising, payments or the use of cookies. The responsible party must justify the necessity of the processing activity with regards to the fundamental and mutually understood purpose of the contract.[16] For instance, activities such as advertising and the use of cookies are not seen as 'necessary' for the performance of a contract. To assess whether this justification applies, ask these questions:

- What is the nature of the goods or service being provided to the data subject?
- What is the fundamental object (substance) of the contract?
- What are the essential elements of the contract?
- What are the perspectives and expectations of the parties to the contract?

---

14 The ICO's Guide to the EU GDPR, available at https://ico.org.uk/for-organisations/guide-to-data-protection/guide-to-the-general-data-protection-regulation-gdpr/lawful-basis-for-processing/contract/.

15 This is known as the principle of minimality which we discuss in chapter 8. The European Data Protection Board *Guidelines 2/2019 on the processing of personal data under Article 6(1)(b) EU GDPR in the context of the provision of online services to data subjects Version 2.0* at 8, available at https://edpb.europa.eu/sites/edpb/files/files/file1/edpb_guidelines-art_6-1-b-adopted_after_public_consultation_en.pdf.

16 The European Data Protection Board *Guidelines 2/2019 on the processing of personal data under Article 6(1)(b) EU GDPR in the context of the provision of online services to data subjects Version 2.0* at 9, available at https://edpb.europa.eu/sites/edpb/files/files/file1/edpb_guidelines-art_6-1-b-adopted_after_public_consultation_en.pdf.

Key point: Responsible parties cannot rely on this legal basis just because they recorded all of the purposes for which they would use personal information in their terms and conditions. Guidance under the Data Protection Directive and EU GDPR states that '[i]t is important to determine the exact rationale of the contract, i.e. its substance and fundamental objective, as it is against that it will be tested whether the data processing is necessary for its performance'. Equally, a responsible party can rely on a purpose that is not recorded in the contract.[17]

Responsible parties cannot rely on this justification if the responsible party takes pre-contractual steps on its own initiative.[18] In other words, the data subject has to take the first step. This prevents responsible parties from using this justification to prescreen data subjects for products or services and then sending marketing to them based on this justification.

6.3.2 To comply with any obligation imposed by law on the responsible party

If the law requires that a processing activity take place, and the law is compatible with POPIA, then it is lawful.[19] The source of this obligation can be the Constitution, common law, customary law, legislation or court decisions.

This justification will apply to the processing of most employee information. For instance the Employment Equity Act 55 of 1998, the Labour Relations Act 66 of 1995 and the Basic Conditions of Employment Act 75 of 1997 provide justification for the processing of a lot of employee information, some of which is special personal information. The Financial Intelligence Centre Act 38 of 2001 is another example of legislation which requires the processing of personal information.

---

17 The European Data Protection Board *Guidelines 2/2019 on the processing of personal data under Article 6(1)(b) EU GDPR in the context of the provision of online services to data subjects Version 2.0* at 10, available at https://edpb.europa.eu/sites/edpb/files/files/file1/edpb_guidelines-art_6-1-b-adopted_after_public_consultation_en.pdf.

18 The ICO's Guide to the EU GDPR, available at https://ico.org.uk/for-organisations/guide-to-data-protection/guide-to-the-general-data-protection-regulation-gdpr/lawful-basis-for-processing/contract/.

19 Section 11(1)*(c)*. Unless the legislation itself contradicts POPIA.

Key point: Responsible parties must be accurate when determining whether this legal basis applies. For example, it is best practice to document the exact provision of the legislation that requires the processing activity. Responsible parties must also guard against doing more than what the legislation requires. As with reliance on a contract as the legal basis for processing, the processing must be 'necessary'.[20] POPIA may well force responsible parties to assess the way in which they comply with other pieces of legislation to ensure that they only perform the 'necessary' processing and do not fall foul of the minimality requirement. Put simply, attorneys and compliance officers must rein in their natural inclination to over-comply!

The legal provision itself and the way in which it is enforced must also be POPIA compliant. For instance, the processing prescribed must be necessary to fulfil the purpose of the legal provision and it must be the least invasive way to achieve that purpose. This means POPIA will force government and other public bodies to re-evaluate the legislation from which they derive their mandates and how they enforce that legislation. If their methods lead to excessive processing of personal information when measured against the purpose of the legislation, they will be in breach of POPIA.

Tricky area: What happens if a responsible party is compelled by the government or another public body to do more processing than is required by the legislation in question? This will often place a responsible party between a rock and a hard place. Where a responsible party believes that the required processing activity is excessive, the responsible party should request that the Information Regulator assesses whether processing required by the government is compliant with POPIA.[21] When performing this assessment, the Information Regulator should consider (a) whether the legislation in question is consistent with POPIA, and (b) if it is, whether the government or public body's interpretation of the legislation and the requirements that are being imposed are adequate, relevant and not excessive.[22]

---

[20] Unlike section 11(1)*(b)*, section 11(1)*(c)* does not refer to necessity explicitly. However, as discussed in chapter 9, the principle of minimality requires a constant assessment of whether processing is 'necessary' to fulfil the purpose of the processing activity.

[21] Sections 40(1)*(b)*(vi) and 89.

[22] Section 10. The principle of minimality is addressed in chapter 9.

6.3.3 To protect the legitimate interest of the data subject

If the processing protects the legitimate interest of the data subject it will be lawful.[23]

Key point: Be careful when relying on the interpretation of the EU GDPR regarding this legal basis. The corresponding justification in the EU GDPR has slightly different wording. It provides a lawful basis for processing where processing is necessary in order to protect the 'vital interests' of the data subject or of another natural person.[24] It is clear from recital 46 of the EU GDPR that 'vital interests' cover only interests essential for the life of the data subject. Another difference between POPIA and the EU GDPR is that anyone's vital interests can provide a basis for processing in terms of the EU GDPR, not just those of the data subjects themselves. Lastly, according to recital 46, the justification is only available in the EU GDPR if the data subject is incapable of giving consent; which is not the case in POPIA. In POPIA, the 'legitimate interest' of the data subject could be wider than instances of life and death. In order to rely on section 11(1)*(d)*, responsible parties must document that they considered what the impact of the processing would be on the data subject. This exercise forms part of performing a legitimate interest assessment. This was discussed in chapter 2 paragraph 2.6.3.

Consider this example: A responsible party has personal information which could save a data subject from a potentially dangerous situation, for instance a natural disaster. Is the responsible party allowed to disclose this information in order to save the data subject from harm? It is likely that safety and the prevention of harm are legitimate interests and that the processing is therefore justified.[25]

When a responsible party relies on this justification, the data subject can object to the processing activity at any time on reasonable grounds relating to their situation.[26]

---

23 Section 11(1)*(d)*.

24 Article 6(1)*(d)*.

25 The use of 'legitimate interest' as a legal justification and how to perform a 'legitimate interest assessment' is discussed in chapter 2 paragraph 2.6.3.

26 Section 11(3)*(a)*. We discuss this right of the data subject in chapter 18.

This justification may not be appropriate for large-scale, planned processing activities.[27] It is more likely to be the appropriate justification for unusual processing activities involving single or small numbers of records. However, this justification may apply on a large scale where a responsible party is processing personal information on humanitarian grounds such as monitoring epidemics.

Tricky area: In many cases the protection of legitimate interests arises in the context of personal information regarding the data subject's health or safety. Health information is considered special personal information, and responsible parties cannot rely on the legitimate interest of the data subject to process it as it is not listed as a justification in section 27(1). However, section 32 provides for exceptions to the general prohibition on processing health information and must be kept in mind.[28] For instance, health information can obviously be processed by healthcare providers. Responsible parties should avoid processing health information to protect a data subject's health and safety when possible. For instance, getting emergency assistance for a data subject in distress can be done by a responsible party (who isn't a healthcare provider) without entering health information into a record. In those cases, this legal justification may still apply.

6.3.4 The performance of a public law duty by a public body

If the processing is necessary for the performance of a public law duty by a public body it will be justified. Public law regulates the relationship between the state and individuals. 'Public body' is defined in section 1 of POPIA.

27 ICO 'Vital interests', available at https://ico.org.uk/for-organisations/guide-to-data-protection/guide-to-the-general-data-protection-regulation-gdpr/lawful-basis-for-processing/vital-interests/. So, this conclusion was made in the context of the EU GDPR where the scope of the justification is narrower in that it only relates to 'vital' interests.

28 See chapter 7 paragraphs 7.2.5 and 7.2.6.

Key point: Many people are under the mistaken belief that POPIA does not apply to government. Remember that a number of public law duties, particularly those related to public safety and the investigation and prosecution of criminal activity, have been excluded from the scope of POPIA.[29] However, the majority of public law duties are still within the scope of the Act. The provision of basic services like electricity and water is a good example. The processing activities conducted by the state and some parastatals in order to provide these services are justified on this basis.

Whether the processing activity is 'necessary' must be measured against the exact reason for the public function.[30]

When a responsible party relies on this justification, the data subject can object to the processing activity at any time on reasonable grounds relating to their situation.[31]

Key point: If a public body does not want data subjects to have the right to object to the processing, that body should not rely on this justification. Instead, the public body should assess whether the processing activity is necessary to ensure that the public body complies with an obligation imposed on it by law.[32] If there is no current law that justifies the processing, the public body should consider lobbying Parliament to introduce such a law.

6.3.5 To pursue the legitimate interests of the responsible party or a third party to whom the information is supplied

The processing of personal information is justified if the activity is necessary for pursuing the legitimate interest of the responsible party, or of a third party to whom the information is supplied.[33] The responsible party's interest in the processing must be distinguished from the purpose of the processing activity. The purpose is the

---

29 See chapter 3 paragraph 3.3.3.

30 See the discussion in paragraph 6.2 above, as well as the discussion in chapter 2 paragraph 2.7 of what to do when government or public bodies require more processing of personal information than their mandate allows.

31 Section 11(3)*(a)*. We discuss this right of the data subject in chapter 18 paragraph 18.6.

32 Section 11(1)*(c)*.

33 Section 11(1)*(f)*.

specific reason why the personal information is processed, whereas the responsible party's interest in the processing activity is the broader stake that it has in the processing or the benefit that it might derive from the processing activity.

The use of 'legitimate interest' as a legal justification and how to perform a 'legitimate interest assessment' are discussed in chapter 2 paragraph 2.6.3.

When a responsible party relies on this justification, the data subject can object to the processing activity at any time on reasonable grounds relating to their situation.[34]

6.3.6 If the data subject has consented

If the data subject, or a competent person where the data subject is a child, consents to the processing, then the processing of personal information is justified.[35]

The requirements for valid consent are discussed in detail in chapter 2 paragraph 2.6.6. Here is a reminder. In order to be valid, consent must be a:

- voluntary,
- specific,
- informed,
- expression of will.

Key point: Suffice it to say here that the overwhelming majority of consents we see in practice will not be valid. The main culprit is that very few consents are voluntary and many cannot be withdrawn at all or cannot be withdrawn without detriment to the data subject. They are bundled with terms and conditions and state something to the effect of 'by accepting these terms you consent to the processing of your personal information'; the data subject cannot accept the terms and withhold consent, which means that it is not voluntary. Consent must be given through a clear, unambiguous, affirmative act. Silence or inactivity cannot be taken as consent, which is why the use of pre-ticked opt-in boxes is not allowed.

---

[34] Section 11(3)*(a)*. We discuss this right of the data subject in chapter 18 paragraph 18.6.

[35] Section 11(1)*(a)*.

> To avoid ambiguity, the action of giving consent must also be distinct from other actions such as agreeing to a contract.[36] That consent is also not specific enough (the second culprit) – to be valid the consent must relate to a specific processing activity or purpose. A blanket consent to the processing of personal information will never be valid.[37] The third culprit is legalese. The data subject must be given information about the consent before they make their decision. The consent must be drafted in clear, plain language[38] and for this the responsible party must take the kind of audience the consent is aimed at into account.[39]

Consent should always be a last resort. Here is why:

- Asking for consent is inefficient: Responsible parties who can rely on a contract or law to justify their processing activities can go ahead with the processing in question. Data subjects cannot even object. This means that responsible parties do not have to build processes and systems that can handle data subjects that withheld consent or objected. Even if a responsible party relies on one of the legitimate interest justifications, it can go ahead with the processing (unless it receives a valid objection). The vast majority of data subjects will not object.
- Consent is difficult to get right, and if you get it wrong, the consequences are dire: As we see time and time again, creating a valid consent is easier said than done. If a consent is declared invalid, the processing activity in question is unlawful.
- Consents are expensive to maintain: The onus is on the responsible party to prove that it obtained a valid consent, when it was provided, the information that was provided to the data subject at the time and that there was an affirmative expression of will. The responsible party will also have to develop processes and systems that can process the withdrawal of consent and ensure that processing stops when the data subject withdraws.[40]

---

36 European Data Protection Board *Guidelines 05/2020 on consent under Regulation 2016/679* 18.

37 European Data Protection Board *Guidelines 05/2020 on consent under Regulation 2016/679* 14.

38 Yes, we believe that consents must be in plain language. Even though POPIA does not require it expressly, the Consumer Protection Act 68 of 2008 will apply to any notifications made in terms of POPIA. We explain why in chapter 11. It is also the right thing to do.

39 European Data Protection Board *Guidelines 05/2020 on consent under Regulation 2016/679* 16. For a comprehensive guide on how to obtain valid consent, see chapter 2 paragraph 2.6.6.

40 Chapter 18 paragraph 18.5.

For instance, many responsible parties struggle to process withdrawals centrally throughout the organisation, resulting in processing continuing after consent has been withdrawn.

Key point: A data subject has the absolute right to withdraw consent. This is discussed in chapter 18 paragraph 18.5. This underscores that it is never appropriate to rely on consent in instances where the processing is compulsory and the responsible party cannot give them the ongoing power to decide whether their personal information can be processed or not.

6.4 PRACTICAL ADVICE

Responsible parties must document their decision about which lawful basis they are relying on for each processing activity and ensure that their reasoning can be justified.[41] This should be a section in the organisation's personal information impact assessments.[42] POPIA does not require it,[43] but it is also a good idea to record the legal justification a responsible party is relying on in its privacy notices.[44]

Here are examples of the type of information responsible parties should have at hand regarding the legal justification or authority they are relying on: [45]

Legal justification	A checklist[45]
When relying on a contract	When relying on this justification the organisation must ensure that: • the specific obligation in the contract or pre-contractual step on which it is relying is identified • the processing is necessary to comply with the contractual obligation or to perform the pre-contractual step • there is not a less invasive way to comply with the contractual obligation or perform the pre-contractual step; and • the decision to rely on this justification is documented.

➡

[41] Section 17.

[42] Personal information impact assessments are discussed in chapter 20 paragraph 20.3.

[43] This is an obligation in terms of the EU GDPR. See article 13(1)*(c)*.

[44] The obligation to notify and privacy notices are discussed in chapter 11.

[45] We have the ICO to thank for these checklists. They can be found here: https://ico.org.uk/for-organisations/guide-to-data-protection/guide-to-the-general-data-protection-regulation-gdpr/lawful-basis-for-processing/.

Legal justification	A checklist
When relying on an obligation imposed by law	When relying on this justification the organisation must ensure that:[46] • the specific legal provision on which it is relying is identified[47] • the processing is necessary to comply with the legal obligation[48] • there is not a less invasive way to comply with the legal obligation;[49] and • the decision to rely on this justification is documented.
	Tricky area: (more like a landmine, actually): If you feel that a public body or the legislation itself infringes the data subject's privacy to an unjustifiable degree, but you are compelled to perform the processing, write to the Information Regulator.

[46] ICO *Guide to the General Data Protection Regulation (EU GDPR)* 69. Section 11(1)*(c)* of POPIA is very similar to article 6(1)*(c)* of the EU GDPR. It is therefore appropriate to take guidance from the commentary on the EU GDPR.

[47] This can be done either by reference to the legal provision itself (e.g. legislation) or to 'an appropriate source of advice or guidance that sets it out clearly'. For instance, if a government department advises the organisation that the processing is required, the organisation is entitled to assume that the requirement set by the department is required by law.

[48] Section 9*(b)* read with section 10. The requirement of 'minimality' is discussed in chapter 9. Over compliance by, for instance, processing more personal information than is necessary, is a contravention of POPIA.

[49] For instance, if the object of the legal requirement can be met by processing de-identified personal information, the information should be de-identified.

Legal justification	A checklist
When relying in the legitimate interest of the data subject	When relying on this justification the organisation must ensure that: • the specific legitimate interest on which it is relying is identified • the processing is necessary to protect the legitimate interest • there is not a less invasive way to protect the legitimate interest • the decision to rely on this justification is documented • data subjects can object to the processing activity; and • it can stop processing the data subject's personal information if an objection is received. **Key point: Ensure that you have a system in place to deal with objections and document the criteria you will take into account to determine whether objections are reasonable.**
When relying in the legitimate interest of the data subject	When relying on this justification the organisation must ensure that: • the specific public law duty on which it is relying is identified • the processing is necessary to perform the public law duty • there is not a less invasive way to perform the public law duty • the decision to rely on this justification is documented • data subjects can object to the processing activity; and • it can stop processing the data subject's personal information if an objection is received.

➥

Legal justification	A checklist
When relying on the legitimate interest of the responsible party or of a third party	When relying on this justification the organisation must ensure that: • the specific legitimate interest on which it is relying is identified[50] • a legitimate interest assessment is conducted and will be repeated • the processing is necessary to pursue the legitimate interest • there is not a less invasive way to pursue the legitimate interest • all appropriate safeguards are put in place • the decision to rely on this justification and the outcome of the legitimate interest assessment is documented • data subjects can object to the processing activity; and • it can stop processing the data subject's personal information if an objection is received.

[50] The legitimate interest must not be vague or speculative. It requires 'a real and present interest, something that corresponds with current activities or benefits that are expected in the very near future'. Article 29 Data Protection Working Party *Legitimate Interests* 24.

Legal justification	A checklist
When relying on consent	When requesting consent the organisation must ensure that:[51] • consent is the most appropriate justification[52] • the consent is prominent and separate from any contract which may apply • the consent is in an opt-in format and no pre-ticked boxes or other type of default consent was used • the consent is drafted in clear, plain language • the consent contains specific information about the processing activity to which it relates, including:[53] ▪ the organisation's identity ▪ the identity of any third parties who will be relying on the consent[54] ▪ the purpose of each of the processing activities covered by the consent ▪ what type of personal information will be collected and used ▪ the existence of the right to withdraw consent ▪ information about the use of the data for automated decision-making;[55] and ▪ information about any transborder transfers of personal information • the data subject can consent separately for different purposes and types of processing • the consent informs data subjects that they are entitled to withdraw consent and the process they must follow to do so • the organisation has ensured that data subjects can refuse consent without detriment; and • the consent is not a precondition of a service or product.

➥

51 ICO *EU GDPR Guide* 60.

52 European Data Protection Board *Guidelines 05/2020 on consent under Regulation 2016/679.*

53 The transparency requirement is discussed in further detail in chapter 11. This information does not necessarily have to be in the consent itself (e.g. in an SMS); it can be in a privacy notice referenced in the consent.

54 Article 29 Data Protection Working Party *Consent* 13.

55 See chapter 18.

Legal justification	A checklist
	The organisation must keep a record of:[56] • when and how consent was obtained; and • exactly what the data subject was told at the time. The organisation must manage consents by:[57] • regularly reviewing consents to check that the purposes and processing activity have not changed • having processes in place to refresh consent at appropriate intervals[58] • considering using privacy dashboards or other preference-management tools • making it easy for individuals to withdraw their consent at any time, and publicise how to do so • acting on withdrawals of consent as soon as possible; and • not penalising individuals who wish to withdraw consent.

Key point: The ICO developed a fantastic lawful basis interactive guidance tool.[59] Go and play around with it; the wording of article 6 of the EU GDPR and section 11 of POPIA is similar enough.

[56] ICO *EU GDPR Guide* 61.

[57] ICO *EU GDPR Guide* 61.

[58] There is no time limit for consent. How long it will last will depend on the context. If the processing activities change or evolve significantly, the original consent may no longer be valid. In addition, it is considered best practice to 'refresh' consent at appropriate intervals. Article 29 Data Protection Working Party *Consent* 21.

[59] Google it.

7 Special personal information and children's personal information

7.1 WHAT TO EXPECT IN THIS CHAPTER

Chapter 6 deals with the legal justifications that are available to organisations when they are processing personal information. Those are listed in section 11 of the Act. However, they do not always apply:

- When the personal information being processed is 'special personal information', a different set of justifications applies. These are called authorisations and they can be found in sections 27 to 34.
- If a child's personal information is being processed, section 35 lists the authorisations that must apply.

Key point: If this is confusing to you, you are not alone. Go back to the diagram at the beginning of chapter 6; it will definitely make it worse. The most important point is that if the organisation is processing special personal information or a child's personal information, different justifications apply. Then you know when to call the cavalry.

In this chapter we discuss the following:

- Identifying special personal information
- When will the processing of special personal information be authorised?
- Specific authorisations for certain types of special personal information
- Processing the personal information of children

7.2 IDENTIFYING SPECIAL PERSONAL INFORMATION

The definition of 'personal information' was discussed in chapter 3 paragraph 3.2.1. POPIA creates a category of personal information called 'special personal information' and prescribes different requirements that must be met for the processing of special personal information to be 'authorised' (i.e. lawful).

Key point: This means that responsible parties must also determine what special personal information they have, because different legal justifications will apply to it. However, it would be a mistake to assume that special personal information requires a higher duty of care because it is inherently more sensitive that other types of personal information.[1] Sensitivity is a function of the degree of harm a breach of the confidentiality, integrity or availability of personal information can cause to an organisation or the data subject. There are types of personal information which are not 'special', but are undoubtedly sensitive due to the consequences of the information falling into the wrong (unauthorised) hands, e.g. ID numbers, banking details, physical address. And yes, in a sense, all personal information is sensitive.

The first step is understanding what qualifies as special personal information. It is information 'concerning' a data subject's:

- religious or philosophical beliefs
- race or ethnic origin
- trade union membership
- political persuasion
- health
- sex life

1 The SA Law Reform Commission did refer to this list as 'sensitive information', but described sensitive information as being 'concerned with confidential aspects of information of a personal kind' (SA Law Reform Commission Project 124 on Privacy and Data Protection (2009 Report) 19).

- biometric information; or
- criminal behaviour of a data subject relating to the alleged commission of an offence or proceedings relating to an alleged offence.

Key point: Many organisations accidentally collect information that qualifies as special personal information. For instance, an organisation may want to know whether a person has any special dietary requirements. Instead of asking that, the organisation asks what religion the person belongs to. When you encounter special personal information in an organisation, always first ask whether the organisation really requires the special personal information. In this respect, less truly is more. Before we discuss the legal justifications that must be present for the processing of special personal information to be lawful, we will look at what these different categories of special personal information might include.

7.2.1 Religious and philosophical beliefs

This is any personal information which could identify a person's religious and philosophical beliefs. This could range from information about a person's membership to organisations to questions relating to a person's dietary requirements.

7.2.1.1 What is a religious belief?

For a belief to constitute a religious belief (to do or abstain from something in the name of a religion) for the purposes of being protected under the right to freedom of religion under South African law, certain requirements have to be met.[2] These include: the belief must be central to that religion, the person holding this belief must be genuine in practising their religion and the belief and the person's observance of this belief must be considered essential in that they hold a clear purpose.[3] However, it is important to note that whether a belief is mandatory or voluntary in terms of the religion is irrelevant for the purposes of determining whether it is a

[2] M McGregor 'Employees' right to freedom of religion versus employers' commercial interests: A balancing act in favour of religious diversity: A decade of cases: Analyses' (2013) 25 (2) *SA Merc LJ* 223 at 241–243.

[3] M McGregor 'Employees' right to freedom of religion versus employers' commercial interests: A balancing act in favour of religious diversity: A decade of cases: Analyses' (2013) 25 (2) *SA Merc LJ* 223 at 241–243.

valid religious belief worthy of legal protection.[4] Examples of religious beliefs recognised by courts in South Africa (but not necessarily considered justified under the constitutional right to freedom of religion, or considered unfair discrimination on the grounds of religion under equality and labour laws) include that using cannabis is a central tenet of Rastafarianism,[5] and that wearing a nose-stud is a religious practice in the Hindu religion.[6]

7.2.1.2 What is a philosophical belief?

South African law does not have legal precedent for the definition of a 'philosophical belief'. However, there is a significant amount of case law in the UK around the definition of a 'philosophical belief' in terms of the UK's Equality Act[7] (this act serves a similar purpose to the Employment Equity Act[8] and the Promotion of Equality and Prevention of Unfair Discrimination Act).[9] Under UK law, in order for a belief to constitute a 'philosophical belief' (and therefore be worthy of legal protection), the belief:

- must be genuinely held
- must be belief about weighty and substantial aspect of human life and behaviour
- must be convincing, serious, cohesive and important
- must be worthy of respect in a democratic society, not be incompatible with human dignity and not conflict with the fundamental rights of others; and
- must be more than just an opinion or viewpoint based on the present state of information available.[10]

Examples of recognised philosophical beliefs under UK law include anti-fox hunting views, climate change, Scottish independence and ethical veganism.[11]

---

4 *MEC for Education, KwaZulu-Natal v Pillay* 2008 (1) SA 474 (CC) at 498A–B paragraph 67.

5 *Prince v President, Cape Law Society* 2002 (2) SA 794 (CC).

6 *MEC for Education, KwaZulu-Natal v Pillay* 2008 (1) SA 474 (CC) at 495H-496A paragraph 60.

7 of 2010.

8 Act 55 of 1998.

9 Act 4 of 2000.

10 *Grainger Plc & Ors v. Nicholson* [2009] UKEAT 0219_09_0311 (3 November 2009) at paragraph 24.

11 Littler 'UK: What constitutes a protected philosophical belief?', available at https://www.littler.com/publication-press/publication/uk-what-constitutes-protected-philosophical-belief.

7.2.2 Race or ethnic origin

7.2.2.1 What is a person's race?

Race can be defined as a social construct referring to group of people who share distinct and similar physical characteristics.[12] For example, race is often used to define a person by their skin colour, as well as other physical, social, and biological attributes.[13] South Africa does not have a legal definition for 'race' – but the 2011 census refers to 'population groups' – where respondents had the option to choose between 'Black African', 'Coloured', 'Indian or Asian', 'White' and 'Other'.[14] This is in line with the different categories referred to in both the Broad-based Black Economic Empowerment Act[15] and the Employment Equity Act[16], for employment equity and empowerment targeting purposes.[17]

7.2.2.2 What is a person's ethnic origin?

Ethnic origin or ethnicity can be defined as 'shared cultural practices, perspectives, and distinctions that set apart one group of people from another'.[18] The most common characteristics which distinguish a different ethnic group or background are ancestry, territorial possession, language, forms of dress, a sense of history and religion. South Africa does not have a legal definition for 'ethnic origin'. But, for example in the 2011 census, respondents were asked to pick the two languages most commonly spoken in their household.[19]

---

12 SA History 'Race and ethnicity,' available at https://www.sahistory.org.za/article/race-and-ethnicity-south-africa

13 The Oprah Magazine 'So, What's the Difference Between Race and Ethnicity?', available at https://www.oprahmag.com/life/a28787295/race-vs-ethnicity-difference/. Yes, Oprah Magazine.

14 Stats SA 'Census 2011', available at http://www.statssa.gov.za/?page_id=3852.

15 Act 53 of 2003.

16 Act 55 of 1998.

17 These Acts define 'black people' as 'a generic term which means Africans, Coloureds and Indians'. This definition has also been widened to include 'Chinese people' as a result of the judgment held in *Chinese Association of South Africa v Minister of Labour* (59251/2007) [2008] ZAGPHC 174 (18 June 2008).

18 SA History 'race and ethnicity,' available at https://www.sahistory.org.za/article/race-and-ethnicity-south-africa

19 Stats SA 'Census 2011', available at http://www.statssa.gov.za/?page_id=3852

7.2.3 Trade union membership

The Labour Relations Act[20] defines a trade union as 'an association of employees whose principal purpose is to regulate relations between employees and employers, including any employers' organisation'.[21] A data subject's membership of a trade union is considered special personal information under POPIA.

7.2.4 Political persuasion

Political persuasion can be defined as belief or a set of beliefs in relation to government or public affairs.[22] In this context, the term 'political persuasion' is synonymous with 'a political opinion'.[23]

'Political persuasion' is not limited to information relating to membership within a political party. It could include information such as a person's voting record, whether they have ever had an interaction with a political party and political views expressed on social media.

7.2.5 Health or sex life

7.2.5.1 Information concerning health

POPIA does not define health information. In the EU GDPR 'data concerning health' is defined as 'personal data related to the physical or mental health of a natural person, including the provision of health care services, which reveal information about his or her health status'.[24]

South Africa's National Health Act[25] does not include a formal definition for any term such as 'health record' or 'medical record'. However, 'health research' is defined as 'any research which contributes to knowledge of (a) the biological, clinical, psychological or social processes in human beings; (b) improved methods for the provision of health services; (c) human pathology; (d) the causes of disease; (e) the effects of the environment on the human body; (f) the development of new application of pharmaceuticals, medicines and related substances; and the (g) the development of new applications of health technology'.[26]

---

[20] Act 66 of 1995.

[21] Section 213 of the Labour Relations Act.

[22] Lexico, available at https://www.lexico.com/definition/persuasion

[23] See section 6 of the Employment Equity Act and article 9(1) of the EU GDPR.

[24] Article 4(15).

[25] Act 61 of 2003.

[26] Section 1.

Tricky area: Will the Information Regulator adopt a narrow or wide definition of personal information concerning a data subject's health? A narrow definition would include personal information generated in a health care or medical environment. A broader definition could also extend to information relating to 'social processes' or behavioural information. Many aspects of human behaviour such as information concerning a person's religious or philosophical beliefs is special personal information, but is probably not health information. This question is significant, given that different legal justifications apply to different types of special personal information.

The Health Professions Council of South Africa (HPCSA)' Guidelines on Patient Records' includes a definition for 'health record'. The HPCSA defines a 'health record' as:

> 'Any relevant record made by a health care practitioner at the time of or subsequent to a consultation and / or examination or the application of health management. A health record contains the information about the health of an identifiable individual recorded by a health care professional, either personally or at his or her direction.'[27]

Examples given of 'health records' include:[28]

> '2.1.1 Hand-written contemporaneous notes taken by the health care practitioner.
>
> 2.1.2 Notes taken by previous practitioners attending health care or other health care practitioners, including a typed patient discharge summary or summaries.
>
> 2.1.3 Referral letters to and from other health care practitioners.
>
> 2.1.4 Laboratory reports and other laboratory evidence such as histology sections; cytology slides and printouts from automated analysers, X-ray films and reports, ECG races, etc.
>
> 2.1.5 Audiovisual records such as photographs, videos and tape-recordings.
>
> 2.1.6 Clinical research forms and clinical trial data.
>
> 2.1.7 Other forms completed during the health interaction such as insurance forms, disability assessments and documentation of injury on duty.
>
> 2.1.8 Death certificates and autopsy reports.'

27 Section 1 of the HPCSA's Guidelines on Patient Records.

28 Section 2.

In terms of the EU GDPR,[29] health information has a wide definition to include information about an individual's past, current or future health status. It not only covers specific details of medical conditions, tests or treatment, but includes any related data which reveals anything about the state of someone's health.[30] Examples given of health information include: any information on injury, disease, disability or disease risk, including medical history, medical opinions, diagnosis and clinical treatment; medical examination data, test results, data from medical devices, or data from fitness trackers; information collected from the individual when they register for health services or access treatment; and any appointment details, reminders and invoices which tell you something about the health status of the individual.[31]

The European Data Protection Supervisor (EDPS)[32] has stated that health information also includes 'administrative documents that include personal data relating to the health status of a person. Amongst those documents are medical certificates (e.g. documents certifying medical aptitude for work), forms concerning sick leave or the reimbursement of medical expenses'.[33]

7.2.5.2 Information concerning a data subject's sex life

Information concerning a data subject's sex life includes information about a person's sexual activity, relationships or sexual orientation or sexual proclivities.

---

29 Recital 35 of the EU GDPR.

30 ICO 'What is special category data?', available at https://ico.org.uk/for-organisations/guide-to-data-protection/guide-to-the-general-data-protection-regulation-gdpr/special-category-data/what-is-special-category-data/.

31 ICO 'What is special category data?', available at https://ico.org.uk/for-organisations/guide-to-data-protection/guide-to-the-general-data-protection-regulation-gdpr/special-category-data/what-is-special-category-data/.

32 The EDPS is the EU's independent data protection authority, which has the general mission to monitor and ensure the protection of personal data and privacy when EU institutions and bodies process the personal information of individuals.

33 EDPS 'Guidelines on the processing of health data in the workplace by EU institutions and bodies' at 2, available at https://edps.europa.eu/sites/edp/files/publication/09-09-28_guidelines_healthdata_atwork_en.pdf.

7.2.6 Inherited characteristics

This is a form of health information, but additional requirements apply to it over and above those that apply to information regarding health and sex life generally.[34] POPIA does not define what information relating to inherited characteristics is.

The EU GDPR defines genetic data as:[35]

> 'personal data relating to the inherited or acquired genetic characteristics of a natural person which give unique information about the physiology or the health of that natural person and which result, in particular, from an analysis of a biological sample from the natural person in question.'

7.2.7 Biometric information

'Biometrics' is defined in section 1 as 'a technique of personal identification that is based on physical, physiological or behavioural characterisation including blood typing, fingerprinting, DNA analysis, retinal scanning and voice recognition'.[36] This is helpful, but still leaves the question of what 'personal information concerning ... biometric information' means.[37] For instance, does this definition mean that all photographs of people are 'biometric information', because they could be used in facial recognition?

Biometric data is defined in article 4(14) of the EU GDPR as 'personal data resulting from specific technical processing relating to the physical, physiological or behavioural characteristics of a natural person, which allow or confirm the unique identification of that natural person, such as facial images or dactyloscopic data'. So, there needs to be some technical processing before it is considered biometric data. A video or a photograph of a person on its own is not considered biometric data.[38] We are of the view that POPIA should be interpreted in the same way.

Obviously biometric information is only relevant for individuals[39] since juristic persons like companies do not have these characteristics.

---

34 Section 32(5).

35 Article 4(13) of the EU GDPR.

36 New forms of biometrics are being thought up all the time. For instance, smell recognition is now a thing. Not kidding. Odour biometrics is a thing. Google it.

37 Yes, an odd bit of drafting.

38 European Data Protection Board Guidelines 3/2019 on processing of personal data through video devices, available at https://edpb.europa.eu/our-work-tools/public-consultations/2019/guidelines-32019-processing-personal-data-through-video_en.

39 A sidenote for the lawyers. We have stopped using 'natural person' when we mean individual. A participant in a focus group once thought that a 'natural person' is someone who does not wear makeup.

7.2.8 Criminal behaviour

'Criminal behaviour' means allegations of criminal behaviour, not actual criminal convictions. Information relating to criminal convictions are not special personal information.[40]

The Criminal Procedure Act[41] defines an offence as 'an act or omission punishable by law'.[42] Therefore criminal behaviour information only relates to act or omissions punishable by the law of South Africa, i.e. statutory or common-law offences.[43] For example, information relating to an individual not complying with an employer's code of conduct would not fall into this category of special personal information, as this conduct would not meet the definition of 'an act or omission punishable by law'.

7.3 WHEN WILL THE PROCESSING OF SPECIAL PERSONAL INFORMATION BE AUTHORISED?

Key point: The default position is that special personal information may not be processed.

However, section 27 contains a list of general 'authorisations' when the processing of special personal information is allowed, and sections 28 to 33 contain additional authorisations which are specific to the type of special personal information. In other words, if an organisation is processing special personal information, the processing must be 'authorised' by section 27 or one of the specific authorisations in sections 28 to 33.

Once it is established that an exception to the prohibition on the processing of special personal information applies, the processing is justified, but it is still subject to all of the conditions of lawful processing.

40 It is personal information though. This means that it must be justified in terms of section 11.

41 Act 51 of 1977.

42 Section 1 'Definitions' of the Criminal Procedure Act.

43 See wider definition.

Key point: Processing of special personal information cannot be authorised based on the justifications in section 11. For instance, this means that processing of special personal information aimed at protecting the legitimate interest of the data subject, the responsible party or a third party will not be authorised. The processing must be authorised in terms of section 27 (or one of the specific authorisations we are about to discuss).

7.3.1 Data subjects have consented

The requirements for valid consent and the limitations of this justification are discussed in chapter 2 paragraph 2.6.6.

Tricky area: Section 11(3)*(b)* states that a data subject may withdraw consent provided in terms of section 11(1)*(a)* at any time. The right to withdraw consent is not mentioned in section 27(1)*(a)*. However, we are of the view that data subjects also have the right to withdraw other consents due to the requirement, that consent must be voluntary.[44] Can the responsible party just refuse to continue to process the data subject's personal information, because they withhold consent to process special personal information? We do not think so. Data subjects must be free to withdraw consent without undue effort and without any detrimental effects such as an increase in cost, a cessation of services or a decrease in service levels.[45]

7.3.2 The processing is necessary for the establishment, exercise or defence of a right or obligation in law

This is a very wide exception. The wording was based on the wording of the corresponding section in the EU Data Directive. It states that:

> 'Paragraph 1 shall not apply where: the processing relates to data which are manifestly made public by the data subject or is necessary for the establishment, exercise or defence of legal claims.'

---

44 Section 1 of POPIA.

45 European Data Protection Board *Guidelines 05/2020 on Consent under Regulation 2016/679* 13, available at https://edpb.europa.eu/sites/edpb/files/files/file1/edpb_guidelines_202005_consent_en.pdf.

We are of the view that this refers to any recognised legal right (e.g. right to access to health care services, a claim of money owed, property rights, a contractual claim, etc.) a data subject may have in terms of South African law.

7.3.3 The processing is necessary to comply with an obligation of international public law

For example, in order to return a kidnapped person to their home country.

Public international law has three main sources: customary international law; treaties and conventions; and soft law (guidelines and non-binding judgments).[46] South Africa's Constitution[47] recognises international customary law as law in South Africa unless it is inconsistent with the Constitution[48] or local legislation. South Africa is bound by international treaties once a treaty is approved by the National Assembly and the National Council of Provinces.[49] Section 39 of the Constitution requires that courts and other legal bodies must consider public international law when interpreting the Bill of Rights.

Key point: Don't confuse this authorisation with the justification in section 11(1)*(e)* which provides that personal information may be processed if 'processing is necessary for the proper performance of a public law duty by a public body'. The authorisation for processing special personal information is not only available to public bodies, but to any responsible party that has obligations in terms of international public law. In addition, in order to process special personal information under this justification, it has to be an international public law duty.

7.3.4 The processing is for historical, statistical or research purposes

We discuss the definition of 'historical, statistical or research purposes' in chapter 2 paragraph 2.6.7.[50]

---

46 Section 27 'The role of international law in South African health law and policy-making' at 131, available at https://section27.org.za/wp-content/uploads/2010/04/Chapter5.pdf.

47 The Constitution of the Republic of South Africa, 1996.

48 Section 232 of the Constitution.

49 Section 231 of the Constitution.

50 Spoiler alert, POPIA does not define it, but we hit it with our best shot.

To rely on this authorisation the responsible party must provide sufficient guarantees that the individual privacy of the data subject is not adversely affected, AND EITHER

- processing is necessary to serve a public interest; OR
- it appears to be impossible or would involve disproportionate effort[51] to ask for consent.

Tricky area: What is 'sufficient guarantees'? This phrase is used in the EU GDPR in the context of processors (operators).[52] Examples of what might provide sufficient guarantees in terms of the EU GDPR are adherence to an approved code of conduct or an approved certification mechanism.

In addition, what is processing in the public interest? As discussed in chapter 2 paragraph 2.5, there is a public interest in:

- freedom of expression
- national security
- the prevention, detection and prosecution of offences
- public health and safety
- research; and
- important economic and financial interests of a public body.

The processing activities that are associated with some of these 'public interests' are already fully or partially exempted from POPIA. For instance, POPIA already does not apply to public bodies that process personal information for purposes of national security, as long as adequate safeguards have already been established in legislation.[53]

7.3.5 The special personal information was deliberately made public by the data subject

There are two requirements here. The special personal information must have been (1) deliberately made public (2) by the data subject. These requirements can be difficult to satisfy. They are discussed in detail in chapter 10 paragraph 10.4.2.

---

51 We discuss what 'disproportionate effort' means in chapter 10 paragraph 10.4.8.

52 Recital 81 and article 28(1), (4) and (5) of the EU GDPR.

53 See section 6(1)*(c)*. The exclusions are discussed in chapter 3 paragraph 3.3.

7.3.6 The Information Regulator has authorised the processing of special personal information

This would have been done on application from the responsible party. The Information Regulator may only grant this authorisation if:

- the processing is in the public interest; and
- appropriate safeguards have been put in place to protect the personal information.[54]

The Information Regulator has published a Guidance Note on Processing of Special Personal Information[55] and an Application Form for Authorisation to Process Special Personal Information.[56] The guide explains the process that a responsible party must follow to apply for authorisation, and provides some explanation of what may be accepted as 'public interest' and 'appropriate safeguards' in this context.

7.3.7 It is necessary to provide proper medical treatment or health care

It may be necessary to supplement information about the data subject's health in order for a medical professional, healthcare institution or facility or for social services to provide proper treatment or care.[57] We list this authorisation here, because even though it relates to the processing of health information, it authorises the use of any other types of special personal information.

7.3.8 The processing is carried out by bodies charged by law with applying criminal law

It may be necessary to supplement information about the data subject's criminal behaviour or biometric information if the processing is carried out by bodies charged by law with applying criminal law, by responsible parties who have obtained that information legally or by an employer who is processing the information (as long as they comply with labour legislation).[58] We list this authorisation here, because even though it relates to the processing of criminal behaviour or biometric information, it authorises the use of any other types of special personal information.

---

54 Section 27(2).

55 Available at https://justice.gov.za/inforeg/docs/InfoRegSA-GuidanceNote-Processing-SpecialPersonalInformation-20210628.pdf.

56 Available at https://www.justice.gov.za/inforeg/docs/forms/InfoRegSA-Form-Application%20form%20for%20authorisation%20to%20process%20Personal%20Information%20of%20Children-eForm-2021.pdf

57 Section 32(4).

58 Section 33(3).

Keep in mind that certain functions of public bodies such as national security and those of the Department of Justice and the police are excluded from the application of POPIA under certain circumstances.[59]

7.3.9 Specific authorisations for certain types of special personal information

But wait, there's more![60]

If none of the general authorisations discussed above apply, the processing of the special personal information will be illegal unless the specific authorisation for that type of special personal information applies. They are discussed in the next part of this chapter.

7.4 SPECIFIC AUTHORISATIONS FOR CERTAIN TYPES OF SPECIAL PERSONAL INFORMATION

7.4.1 Religious or philosophical beliefs

There are specific authorisations for the processing of information concerning or philosophical beliefs depending on the type of organisation doing the processing.

7.4.1.1 Spiritual or religious organisations

The prohibition on processing personal information relating to the religious or philosophical beliefs of a data subject does not apply to 'spiritual or religious organisations, or independent sections of those organisations', for instance churches. [61] This exception only applies if the data subject is a member of the organisation, or if the processing activity is necessary to achieve the aims and principles of the organisation.[62]

59 See the discussion in chapter 3.

60 Of course there is, it is POPIA. The gift that keeps on giving. Section 27(1)*(f)*.

61 Section 28(1)*(a)*.

62 Section 28(1)*(a)*(i) and (ii).

Key point: Note the 'or' in the previous statement.[63] The special personal information of non-members of a religious organisation can also be processed as long as the processing is necessary to achieve the organisation's aims and principles. For example, this could authorise activities relating to recruitment of new members. However, recruitment activities may be seen as direct marketing.[64]

This authorisation extends to information about the 'religion or philosophy of life' of the family members of the data subject if the organisation maintains regular contact with them in connection with its aim and the family members have not objected in writing to the processing.[65] This objection does not have to be made 'on reasonable grounds relating to his, her or its particular situation' as is the case with objections in section 11(3).[66] In other words, it appears that family members of the data subject have the absolute right to withhold the information. This means that relying on this authorisation is not appropriate in cases where providing the information is not voluntary.

Tricky area: We are not sure why the family members are not just data subjects in their own right; in other words, why they are not treated in the same way as non-members. Section 28(2) also refers to 'philosophy of life' instead of 'philosophical beliefs'.

7.4.1.2 Institutions founded on religious or philosophical principles

Institutions founded on religious or philosophical principles (e.g. a religious school or other organisation with a religious 'ethos')[67] can process information about

63 You have got to love the difference that a conjunction can make. We are big fans of these tiny words, except for the 'bastard conjunction', and/or (*Conitto v Fuerst Bros. & Co. Ltd.*, 1944 A. C. 75). We are not Andorians.

64 Direct marketing is discussed in chapter 16. One could argue that a church does not supply a service, but the definition of 'service' in section 1 of the Consumer Protection Act 68 of 2008 (which is where the definition of direct marketing is from), is very wide. In any event, if the church is requesting the person to make a donation, the communication will be seen as direct marketing.

65 Section 28(2). Another important conjunction – note the 'and'. Both requirements have to be met for this authorisation to apply.

66 We discuss the data subject's right to object in chapter 18 paragraph 18.6.

67 Section 28(1)*(b)*.

religious or philosophical beliefs. 'Institutions founded on religious or philosophical principles' can process the religious and philosophical beliefs of their members, employees or other data subjects if it is necessary to achieve their aims and principles.

Tricky area: It is not altogether clear what the difference is between a 'spiritual or religious organisation' and an 'institution founded on religious or philosophical principles'. It matters, because the authorisation for the latter type of organisation is broader.

7.4.1.3 Other institutions

Other institutions can process this type of personal information if 'the processing is necessary to protect the spiritual welfare of the data subjects, unless they have indicated that they object to the processing'. For instance, an organisation may want to know whether people require Halaal or Kosher meals in order to meet their needs. This will be authorised as long as the data subjects can object to providing the information. This objection does not have to be 'on reasonable grounds relating to his, her or its particular situation' as is the case with objections in section 11(3).[68] In other words, it appears that the data subject has the absolute right to withhold the information. This means that relying on this authorisation is not appropriate in cases where providing the information is not voluntary.

Key point: However, always consider whether you can obtain the information you need without recording the religion of the data subject or whether you can ask the question in a more neutral way. For instance, do not ask 'Are you Jewish?' when you are enquiring about dietary requirements. Rather ask 'Do you have any dietary requirements?' If you want to know whether a person requires the use of a prayer room, ask 'Do you require a prayer room?' instead of asking 'Are you Muslim?'

[68] We discuss the data subject's right to object in chapter 18 paragraph 18.6.

7.4.1.4 The sharing of personal information concerning religious or philosophical beliefs

Responsible parties may only share personal information concerning religious or philosophical beliefs with third parties if the data subject consented[69] or if one of the general authorisations in section 27 applies to that sharing activity.[70]

7.4.2 Race or ethnic origin

Processing information relating to race or ethnic origin is authorised if the responsible party complies with these two requirements:

- Processing information relating to race or ethnicity is essential to identify the data subject[71] – this authorisation only applies where it is 'essential for that purpose'. In other words, if there is a way to identify the person without referring to their race, the authorisation does not apply.
- Processing information relating to race or ethnicity is required to comply with legislation and other measures designed to 'protect or advance persons, or categories of persons, disadvantaged by unfair discrimination'.[72] The second leg of the exception is a reference to legislation such as the Broad-based Black Economic Empowerment Act 53 of 2003, B-BBEE Codes of Good Practice as well as the Employment Equity Act 55 of 1998. These pieces of legislation are examples of laws that justify the collection of racial information of suppliers, employees and customers.

Key point: Responsible parties must ensure that they do not over-comply with the legislation as this will be a breach of the principle of 'minimality'.[73] For instance, we often see organisations collect the race of employees over and over, despite the fact that they already have the information. Re-collecting information you already have will almost always be a breach of the principle of minimal processing.

69 Section 28(3).

70 We discuss the general authorisations in paragraph 7.3 above.

71 Section 29*(a)*.

72 Section 29*(b)*.

73 Discussed in chapter 9.

In addition, many organisations want to collect information about the race or ethnic origin of their customers or employees for statistical purposes. If the statistics do not have to be in an identifiable format, so the best way to do this is anonymously. If the statistics have to be identifiable, obtaining consent in terms of section 27(1)*(a)* is the appropriate authorisation, unless the research is in the public interest and it is impossible to obtain consent.[74]

7.4.3 Trade union membership

A trade union (or the trade union federation to which the trade union belongs) can process the trade union membership of its own members if the processing is necessary to achieve the trade union's (or trade union federation's) aims. The trade union or trade union federation is not permitted to share this personal information with third parties without the data subject's consent[75] unless one of the general authorisations in section 27 applies to that sharing activity.[76]

7.4.4 Political persuasion

Institutions founded on political principles may process the personal information relating to a data subject's political persuasion under these circumstances:

Of its members, employees or other persons belonging to the institution[77]	If it is 'necessary to achieve the aims or principles of the institution'.
Other data subjects[78]	If the processing of the data subject's political persuasion is necessary for the purposes of: • forming a political party • participating in activities of a political nature, recruiting members or canvassing for supporters or voters for an election or referendum; or • campaigning for a political party or cause.

[74] Section 27(1)*(d)*. The consent would have to comply with all the requirements for a valid consent, which were discussed in chapter 2 paragraph 2.6.6.

[75] Section 30(2). See the discussions of consent in chapter 2 paragraph 2.6.6.

[76] We discuss the general authorisations in paragraph 7.3 above.

[77] Section 31(1)*(a)*.

[78] Section 31(1)*(b)*.

The institution is not allowed to share this personal information with third parties without the consent of the data subject unless one of the general exceptions in section 27 applies.[79]

The Information Regulator has published a guidance note on the processing of personal information of a voter by a political party in terms of POPIA.[80] Here are the highlights:

- The guidance note confirms that political parties are responsible parties in terms of POPIA and must therefore comply with the conditions for the lawful processing of personal information of voters.
- It then states that a political party may only process information that it reasonably needs after obtaining consent directly from a voter.

Key point: We disagree with this statement. There are other justifications available to political parties in terms of sections 27 and 31 (and section 11 for personal information which is not special) which would be more appropriate than consent.[81] For example the political party can process voters' special personal information to comply with an obligation imposed by law,[82] or to achieve its aims or principles.[83] See chapter 19 paragraph 19.4 for a discussion on the legal status of guidance notes.

- The guidance then deals with the processing of the political persuasion of voters and confirms the authorisation discussed above. It goes on to say: '(s)ection 31 is an exception to the prohibition on the processing of a voter's political persuasion. A political party must still comply with the conditions for the lawful processing of personal information mentioned above when processing the political persuasion of a voter. This means that a political party may not bombard voters with messages without first obtaining a voter's consent to process his or her other personal information (such as a telephone number or an e-mail address).' Although we certainly agree with the sentiment of this statement, we believe that it is misleading as it again relies too much on consent. If the messages are not direct

[79] Section 31(2). We discuss the general authorisations in paragraph 7.3 above.

[80] Available at https://www.justice.gov.za/inforeg/docs/InfoRegSA-GuidanceNote-PPI-PolParties.pdf.

[81] See our tirade about only using consent as the last resort in chapter 2 paragraph 2.6.6.

[82] Section 27(1)*(b)*.

[83] Section 31(1)*(a)*.

marketing, using a voter's contact details to send them messages that are necessary for the political party to function, consent will not be required.[84]

- Voters may object against the political party's processing of their personal information at any time. The political party must stop the processing if the voter objects. It is important to note that the voter has a right to object if the political party justifies processing the voter's personal information based on the voter's consent, to protect the data subject's legitimate interest, and if processing is necessary for pursuing the legitimate interests of the political party. The data subject does not have a right to object if the political party is processing the information for performance of a contract or when it complies with an obligation imposed by law.[85]
- Campaigning or canvassing does not fall within the definition of direct marketing, but requesting a donation does.[86]

Tricky area: In South Africa, in order for a message to be considered direct marketing, the responsible party must be promoting a product or service, or soliciting donations. Promoting a political party does not clearly fall within that definition; one would have to argue that the political party provides a service to its members. The definition of 'service' can be found in section 1 the Consumer Protection Act 68 of 2008, which contains the same definition of 'direct marketing' as POPIA.

7.4.5 Health or sex life

Tricky area: We are not sure why health and sex life are grouped together, but they are.

There are a number of responsible parties who have to be able to process personal information relating to a person's health or sex life. This is reflected in the following authorisation to the general prohibition of the processing of special personal information:[87]

---

84 The political party could rely on section 11(1)*(b)* or *(f)* to justify using the contact details of its members because contact details are not special personal information. Section 11 was discussed in chapter 6 paragraph 6.3.

85 Section 11(3). The right to object is discussed in chapter 18 paragraph 18.6.

86 See chapter 16.

87 Section 32(1).

Type of responsible party	What they are authorised to do
Medical professionals, healthcare institutions or social services[88]	If the processing of information about the data subject's health or sex life is necessary for the proper treatment of the data subject or for administrative purposes, it is authorised.
Insurance companies, medical schemes, medical scheme administrators and managed healthcare organisations[89]	These organisations can process the personal information relating to health or sex life if it is necessary for: • the assessment of the risk to be 'insured' by the insurance company or medical scheme
	Tricky area: The data subject can object to this processing,[90] but presumably the insurance company or medical scheme can then refuse coverage as long as they can prove they must obtain the personal information to provide their services and that the use of the personal information does not contravene South Africa's equality legislation. However, in that case they would be authorised under section 27, so this right to object is a bit strange. • the performance of an insurance or medical scheme agreement; or • the enforcement of any contractual rights and obligations.

[88] Section 32(1)*(a)*.

[89] Section 32(1)*(b)*.

[90] Section 21(1)*(b)*(i).

Type of responsible party	What they are authorised to do
Schools[91]	If it is necessary to provide special support or make special arrangements for the pupil in question the processing of personal information relating to health or sex life is authorised. The processing of a child's personal information is subject to additional requirements.[92]
Any responsible party who manages the care of a child[93]	If it is necessary in order to carry out its lawful functions, the processing of information relating to health or sex life is authorised. The processing of a child's personal information is subject to additional requirements.[94]
Any public body responsible for prison sentences or detention measures[95]	If it is necessary for the implementation of prison sentences or detention measures, the processing of information relating to health or sex life is authorised.
Administrative bodies, pension funds, employers, 'or institutions working for them'[96]	If it is necessary for: • the implementation of legislation, pension regulations or collective agreements that create rights that are dependent on the data subject's health or sex life; or • the reintegration of, or support for, workers or persons who are entitled to benefits in relation to their sickness or work incapacity, the processing of information relating to health or sex life is authorised.

Even if the processing of information relating to health or sex life is authorised, the information may only be processed if the responsible party is subject to a duty of confidentiality.[97] This duty can arise from:

- rules that attach to the office, employment or profession of the responsible party (e.g. doctor-patient confidentiality); or
- an agreement between the responsible party and the data subject.

91 Section 32(1)*(c)*. POPIA does not define 'school'. We are of the view that it should apply to early childhood development centres, universities and other tertiary institutions or any institution that provides education. It should apply to private and public institutions.

92 Discussed in paragraph 7.5 below.

93 Section 32(1)*(d)*.

94 Discussed in paragraph 7.5 below.

95 Section 32(1)*(e)*.

96 Section 32(1)*(f)*.

97 Section 32(2).

Tricky area: Responsible parties will often have policies in place that state that personal information is 'confidential'. Will this count as a rule that attaches to the office, employment or profession of the responsible party?

If neither is the case,[98] the responsible party must still treat information relating to health or sex life as confidential, unless the responsible party is sharing the information with an organisation which is authorised to process such information in terms of section 32(1) (discussed above) and communicating the information is:

- required by law; or
- necessary for the performance of their duties.

7.4.6 Inherited characteristics

There are additional requirements that apply to the processing of inherited characteristics (e.g. genetic traits) by responsible parties who rely on this authorisation. This type of health information can only be processed if one of the following conditions applies:

A serious medical interest prevails.[99]	**Tricky area:** The legislation does not say whose medical interest has to prevail – in other words, it does not necessarily need to be the data subject's medical interest; it can be a public health interest.

[98] Section 32(3). This is a strange section, because if the responsible party is not subject to an 'obligation of confidentiality', the processing of health information is prohibited in terms of section 32(2). So, is it prohibited, or is it permitted as long as you treat the information as confidential? We do not know, but the moral of the story is that health information must be treated as confidential.

[99] Section 32(5)*(a)*.

The processing is necessary for historical, statistical or research activity.[100]	Keep in mind that processing of information relating to inherited characteristics for historical, statistical or research purposes will be authorised under section 27(1)*(d)*,[101] as long as it serves a public interest, it would have been impossible or have taken a disproportionate effort[102] to obtain consent and there are sufficient guarantees[103] to ensure that the privacy of the data subject is not disproportionately affected. If an organisation wants to process information concerning inherited characteristics, but it cannot rely on the authorisation in 27(1)*(d)* for some reason, it may be able to rely on section 32(1).

Tricky area: The processing of information relating to a person's health or sex life is complex and controversial. The Information Regulator has called for submissions to develop a specific regulation for the processing of health information. At the time of writing this, these regulations have not been published.

7.4.7 Criminal behaviour or biometric information

Tricky area: We do not know why criminal behaviour and biometric information are grouped together. When the SA Law Reform Commission published the updated version of the POPI Bill in 2009 after extensive consultation, biometric information was not yet included as a type of special personal information. There is no indication in the wording of the act that this authorisation relates only to the use of biometric information in the context of criminal behaviour, so we have to assume that it covers all uses of biometric information.

Personal information relating to criminal behaviour or biometric information can be processed by:

- 'bodies charged by law with applying criminal law'; or

---

[100] Section 32(5)*(b)*. We discuss the meaning of 'historical, statistical or research purposes' in chapter 2 paragraph 2.6.7.

[101] Discussed in paragraph 7.2.6 above.

[102] We discuss what 'disproportionate effort' means in chapter 10 paragraph 10.4.8.

[103] See our discussion of 'sufficient guarantees' in paragraph 7.3 above.

Key point: Also remember that public bodies that are processing personal information for the purpose of preventing, detecting, investigating or prosecuting crime are not subject to POPIA at all.[104]

- responsible parties who have obtained the personal information 'in accordance with the law'.[105]

Tricky area: The second authorisation is extremely broad. On the face of it, it could mean that responsible parties can process information relating to criminal behaviour or biometric information, as long as they obtained it legally. That would render this authorisation so broad as to undo the protections provided by POPIA in other sections. The other alternative is to interpret it to mean that the responsible party must have a legal duty to process information relating to criminal behaviour or biometric information. In other words, it is prohibited unless the law specifically authorises it. This interpretation is also strange, because the use of personal information is already lawful if it 'complies with an obligation imposed by law' as long as adequate safeguards have been established in legislation for the protection of the personal information.[106]

Employers must also comply with labour legislation when processing the personal information relating to criminal behaviour and biometric information of an employee.[107] At present labour legislation does not say anything specific on the topic, but this may change in future.

Key point: The processing of information on criminal behaviour or on unlawful or objectionable conduct on behalf of third parties is subject to prior authorisation from the Information Regulator.[108]

---

104 Section 6(1)*(c)*(ii). See chapter 3.

105 Section 33(1).

106 Section 11(1)*(c)* and section 27(1)*(b)*.

107 Section 33(2).

108 Section 57(1)*(b)*. Prior authorisation is discussed in chapter 8.

Responsible parties may also process any other type of special personal information if it is necessary to supplement the information on criminal behaviour or biometric information permitted under this authorisation.[109]

Tricky area: The use of facial recognition technology is a hot topic across the globe mainly because of its controversial use by law enforcement. The European Data Protection Board warns that: 'Researchers report that software used for facial identification, recognition, or analysis performs differently based on the age, gender, and ethnicity of the person it's identifying. Algorithms would perform based on different demographics, thus, bias in facial recognition threatens to reinforce the prejudices of society.'[110] Many jurisdictions and even some service providers, have banned the use of facial recognition technology due to concerns about racial bias, abuse, and because its use remains largely unregulated.[111]

7.5 PROCESSING THE PERSONAL INFORMATION OF CHILDREN

Once you have run the gauntlet of determining whether you have authority to process special personal information,[112] there might be one last obstacle in your way. If you are processing the personal information (special or not) of children, you have to (also) comply with sections 34 and 35.[113]

The SA Law Reform Commission had this to say about protecting the personal information of children:

> 'The inherent vulnerability of children coupled with the vast amount of personal information being collected already, seems to motivate special treatment. Online networking throws up two additional issues for consideration. The first is young people choosing to disclose information about themselves. Secondly, is the ability of third parties to post, alter or remove personal information about one another. Children should therefore first of all be protected against their own immaturity and, secondly, against malicious third parties.'[114]

---

109 Section 33(3).

110 European Data Protection Board *Guidelines 3/19 on processing of personal data through video devices* 4, available at https://edpb.europa.eu/sites/edpb/files/consultation/edpb_guidelines_201903_videosurveillance.pdf.

111 See https://www.bbc.com/news/business-52989128, https://www.nytimes.com/2019/05/14/us/facial-recognition-ban-san-francisco.html and https://www.bbc.com/news/technology-51148501.

112 See paragraph 7.2 above.

113 Why both? Section 4(5) states that the processing of special personal information of a child must comply with both sections 27 and 35.

114 SA Law Reform Commission Project 124 on Privacy and Data Protection (2009 Report) 295.

7.5.1 Who is considered a child?

A child is defined in POPIA as any natural person under the age of 18 years who is not legally competent to take any action or decision for themselves without assistance of a competent person.[115]

Key point: If the child is under the age of 18, but is legally competent to take the action or decision involved in the processing activity, the responsible party will not have to comply with section 35. This will be the case if the child is emancipated, or to specific activities where children are given the right to make decisions on their own behalf. There are many pieces of legislation that allow children under the age of 18 to act independently of their parents or guardians. For instance, under certain circumstances a child who is 12 or older may consent to medical treatment.[116] In addition, in terms of the common law, a child under the age of 18 can enter into a contract without the assistance of a parent or guardian as long as the child only acquires rights and no obligations in terms of that contract.[117] In these situations, section 35 of POPIA will not apply, and the child will be treated in the same way as an adult data subject. This means that responsible parties should first determine whether a data subject under the age of 18 is competent in respect of that processing activity.

POPIA does not explicitly require that a responsible party must verify the age of data subjects. However, it will be incumbent on the responsible party to show that the conditions for the lawful processing of personal information have been met.[118] Given that different requirements apply depending on the age of the data subject, it is implicitly required that responsible parties verify the age of data subjects whose personal information they are processing, particularly where products or services are targeting children. The measures implemented by responsible parties must be proportionate to the nature and risks of the processing activities. Age verification should not lead to excessive processing of personal information and the mechanism chosen to verify the personal information of the data subject must involve a risk assessment for the proposed processing.[119]

115 See the definition of 'child' in section 1 of POPIA.

116 Section 129 of the Children's Act 38 of 2005.

117 This is a common-law principle. See *Edelstein v Edelstein NO* 1952 (3) SA 1 (A).

118 Section 8.

119 European Data Protection Board *Guidelines 05/2020 on consent under Regulation 2016/679* 28.

7.5.2 When will the processing of the personal information of children be authorised?

Key point: The default position is that the personal information of children may not be processed.

Responsible parties are only authorised to process the personal information of children if any of the following authorisations apply:

A competent person consents to the processing on the child's behalf.	**Tricky area:** POPIA defines a 'competent person' as 'any person who is legally competent to consent to any action or decision being taken in respect of any matter concerning a child'.[120] In other words, a competent person would be a person who has parental responsibilities in respect of the child. The Children's Act gives parental responsibilities to a parent and a legal guardian, and states that a parent or legal guardian must assist or represent a child in administrative, contractual, and other legal matters.[121] If a child has more than one guardian, either guardian can provide consent without the permission of the other (in most instances).[122] As the High Court of South Africa is the upper guardian of all children, it can step in and appoint a legal guardian for children who do not have parents or a legal guardian and in some cases make the decision.[123] This consent must also comply with the requirements for valid consent.[124] The formulation of this provision also explicitly refers to the fact that the consent must be obtained prior to processing.

[120] Section 1.

[121] Section 18(3)*(b)* of the Children's Act 38 of 2005.

[122] Section 18(5) of the Children's Act 38 of 2005.

[123] Section 45(4) of the Children's Act 38 of 2005.

[124] Discussed in chapter 2 paragraph 2.6.6.

	Key point: What happens once the child attains majority? We believe that if a responsible party was relying on consent by a competent person, the responsible party must obtain the consent of the child once they attain majority. Just another way in which adulting sucks.
The processing is necessary for the establishment, exercise or defence of a right or obligation in law.	This authorisation is discussed in paragraph 7.3.2 above.
The processing is necessary to comply with an obligation of international public law.	This authorisation is discussed in paragraph 7.3.3 above.
The processing is for historical, statistical or research purposes.[125]	This authorisation is discussed in paragraph 7.3.4 above.
The child's personal information was deliberately made public by the child with the consent of a competent person.	There are three requirements here. The child's personal information must have been (1) deliberately made public (2) by the data subject (3) with the consent of a competent person for this justification to apply. Be careful to ensure that it was the data subject (rather than someone else) who made the personal information public.[126] **Tricky area:** The most challenging part of this authorisation is determining whether a parent or guardian consented to the disclosure of information by the child.

➡

125 Section 35(1)*(d)*. We discuss the meaning of 'historical, statistical or research purposes' in chapter 2 paragraph 2.6.7.

126 We discuss this in chapter 10 paragraph 10.4.2.

The Information Regulator has authorised the processing of the personal information of children on application from the responsible party.	This authorisation is discussed in paragraph 7.3.6 above. However, this section goes further than its equivalent in section 27. It provides a list of the type of conditions the Information Regulator may impose.[127]

If the personal information of children is going to be transferred to a recipient in another country an adequate level of protection must be provided for the processing of personal information.[128] This protection may be provided by the law that the recipient is subject to, binding corporate rules or a binding agreement with the recipient.[129] If adequate protection is not provided, prior authorisation must be obtained from the Information Regulator.[130]

Tricky area: The definition of 'child' is not the same in all countries (for example in Lesotho the age of majority is 21 and in the EU the age at which a child can consent on their own behalf is between 13 and 16 years). Note that it does not matter if the child is a South African citizen or not, as POPIA applies to foreign data subjects too if their personal information is processed in South Africa. This means that it does not matter that the age of majority in other countries can be quite different from South Africa; if POPIA applies, all persons under 18 will be children, and those who are 18 and older will not be subject to the requirements of section 34. Conversely, if the processing is happening in another country, South African children may not have the same protection in a country with a lower age of majority. This will cause some difficulties when the processing activity is not limited to South Africans or if it has a transborder component.

---

127 Section 35(3). It is interesting that the same was not done in respect of special personal information in section 27(3). The Information Regulator has published an Application form for Authorisation to process Personal Information of Children available at https://justice.gov.za/inforeg/docs/forms/InfoRegSA-Form-Application%20form%20for%20authorisation%20to%20process%20Personal%20Information%20of%20Children-eForm-2021.pdf.

128 We discuss the requirements for adequate protection in chapter 14 paragraph 14.2.3.1.

129 See chapter 14.

130 Section 57(1)*(d)*. Prior authorisation is discussed in chapter 8.

7.5.3 When will the processing of the special personal information of a child be justified?

Section 4(5) provides that the 'processing of the special personal information of a child is prohibited in terms of sections 26 and 34, unless the provisions of sections 27 and 35 are applicable'. This means that one of the authorisations for processing special personal information AND an authorisation for processing the personal information of a child must apply.

7.6 PRACTICAL ADVICE

7.6.1 Document the legal justification

Responsible parties must document their decision about which legal justification they are relying on for each processing activity and ensure that their reasoning can be justified.[131] This should be a section in the organisation's personal information impact assessments, which should include assessing whether a process involves the use of special personal information.[132] Due to the complexity of these authorisations, it is a good idea to obtain legal advice, particularly if processing special personal information is central to what a organisation does.

As with non-special personal information, POPIA does not require it,[133] but it is also a good idea to record the legal justification a responsible party is relying on in its privacy notice.[134]

7.6.2 Learn from other jurisdictions

As we pointed out above, South Africa's provisions on the processing of the personal information of children are fairly unique. However, that does not mean that we cannot learn from the approach taken by other jurisdictions and the best practices adopted there. In fact, we should.[135]

---

131 Section 17.

132 Personal information impact assessments are discussed in chapter 20 paragraph 20.3.

133 This is an obligation in terms of the EU GDPR. See article 13(1)*(c)*.

134 The obligation to notify and privacy notices are discussed in chapter 11.

135 Considering international guidelines and foreign law was discussed in chapter 2 paragraph 2.4.

Key point: The ICO has published *Age Appropriate Design: A Code of Practice for Online Services.*[136] It is a must-read for organisations whose products or services have children as a target audience, and the recommendations can be implemented outside of the online services environment. As always, be mindful of the differences between UK privacy laws and POPIA, but they are certainly similar enough for this code to be useful.

[136] The code can be found here: https://ico.org.uk/for-organisations/guide-to-data-protection/key-data-protection-themes/age-appropriate-design-a-code-of-practice-for-online-services/.

8

When the Information Regulator must be approached for prior authorisation

Chapter 8

8.1 WHAT TO EXPECT IN THIS CHAPTER

There are some instances where a responsible party has to obtain authorisation from the Information Regulator before processing personal information.

What fresh hell is this? Prior authorisation? There are certain high-risk or large-scale forms of processing that require prior authorisation. This is also referred to as 'prior checking' (under the Data Protection Directive) or 'prior consultation' under the EU GDPR. It is described by the SA Law Reform Commission as 'the strictest form of control over processing operations'.[1]

In this chapter we discuss the following:

- When is prior authorisation required?
- How must the responsible party obtain prior authorisation?
- No prior authorisation is required by industries governed by a code of conduct
- Consequences of not obtaining prior authorisation

8.2 WHEN IS PRIOR AUTHORISATION REQUIRED?

In this section we discuss the instances when the responsible party must obtain authorisation from the Information Regulator before processing personal information.

> **Tricky area:** This must happen before processing starts.[2] It is called 'prior' authorisation after all. But, what about processing that started before POPIA became effective? The transitional arrangements state that 'section 58(2) does not apply to processing … which is taking place on the date of commencement of this Act, until the Regulator determines otherwise by notice in *Gazette* (sic)'.[3] At the date of publication, section 58(2) was going to commence on 1 February 2022.[4]

---

1 See article 20(1) of the Data Protection Directive and article 36(1) of the EU GDPR. Also see SA Law Reform Commission Project 124 on Privacy and Data Protection (2009 Report) 534.

2 Section 57(1).

3 Section 114(3).

4 See the amended notice available at https://www.justice.gov.za/inforeg/docs/InfoRegSA-Notice-Sec58-2-20210618.pdf.

> We interpret this to mean that organisations who are engaged in these activities will have to apply even if the processing started before POPIA's commencement date (1 July 2020), but they do not have to stop processing while they wait for authorisation to be granted until section 58(2) kicks in on 1 February 2022.[5] We discuss the process for applying for prior authorisation and the effect of section 58(2) in paragraph 8.3.

The requirement for prior authorisation is a way for the Information Regulator to have oversight and control over certain high risk processing activities. The concept of prior authorisation in POPIA was borrowed from the system of 'prior checking' by national information authorities with respect to processing operations that are likely to present specific risks to the rights and freedoms of data subjects established by the EU Data Protection Directive.[6] The Directive refers to operations that are likely to pose specific risks 'by virtue of their nature, their scope or their purposes, such as excluding individuals from a right, benefit or contract, or by virtue of the specific use of new technologies'.[7]

8.2.1 Processing unique identifiers to link personal information

In terms of section 57(1)*(a)* prior authorisation is required:

- If unique identifiers are used in the processing activity
- to link information held by multiple responsible parties; and
- if the linking activity constitutes further processing which is incompatible with the original purpose for which the unique identifier was collected or created. We discuss further processing in detail in chapter 12.

---

5 Proc R 21 of 2020 in *GG* 43461 of 22 June 2020. There is a common misconception that POPIA 'commenced' on 1 July 2021. The wording of the proclamation and section 115 refers to 30 June 2020 as the commencement date in respect of most of the sections. The fact that organisations had a year to become compliant did not delay the commencement of the legislation.

6 Article 20(1) of the EU Data Protection Directive. SA Law Reform Commission Project 124 on Privacy and Data Protection (2009 Report) 534.

7 Recital 53. Examples of activities that require(d) prior checks in EU member states include the processing of sensitive information, processing for the purpose of credit referencing, processing involving interconnections between different databases, processing by staff recruitment agencies, keeping legal information systems, and recording of information obtained through a responsible party's own observations if the data subject is not informed of this.

8.2.1.1 What are unique identifiers?

A unique identifier is a code or a number that a responsible party uses to identify a data subject in its operations,[8] for example a client code or a student number that uniquely identifies a data subject in relation to a specific responsible party. Responsible parties often create their own unique identifiers for customers for security and operational reasons.

> **Tricky area:** There has been some robust debate between the co-authors about whether ID numbers and company registration numbers are 'unique identifiers' given that they are not generated by a specific responsible party, but by the government. The 'ID numbers are unique identifiers' faction wore the others down. In addition, account numbers which are issued by responsible parties will also qualify as unique identifiers.[9] The Information Regulator is of the view that unique identifiers include 'bank account numbers or any account number; policy number; identity number; employee number; student number; telephone or cell phone number; or reference number'.[10]

The Information Regulator is also tasked with monitoring the use of unique identifiers of data subjects generally and reporting to Parliament on its findings. The report may include recommendations to Parliament to take legislative or administrative action to give better protection to the personal information of data subjects.[11]

Do not panic, not all processing of unique identifiers is subject to prior authorisation. It is only required in respect of any planned processing of unique identifiers of data subjects:

---

8 Section 1.

9 'Account numbers' are defined in section 105(5). Certain unlawful acts relating to account numbers are offences in terms of sections 105 and 106. This is discussed in detail in chapter 19 paragraph 19.10.2.

10 See the Information Regulator's *Guidance note on applications for prior authorisation*, available at https://www.justice.gov.za/inforeg/docs/InfoRegSA-GuidanceNote-PriorAuthorisation-20210311.pdf For a discussion on the legal status of guidance notes see chapter 19 paragraph 19.4.

11 Section 40(1)*(b)*(vii).

- to link the information with another responsible party's information; and
- this was not the purpose that the unique identifier was collected or created for.[12]

8.2.1.2 What does 'linking' mean?

Tricky area: What does 'with the aim of linking the information together with information processed by other responsible parties' mean? We think a new dataset has to be created. In order for the prior authorisation requirement to apply, the linked personal information (the 'new', linked dataset) must be available to both responsible parties. In other words, it is not enough if responsible party A shares personal information with responsible party B and responsible party B links it using a unique identifier; responsible party B must also share the linked dataset with responsible party A. In order for the prior authorisation requirement to apply, the new, linked dataset must be processed by both responsible party A and B.

8.2.1.3 Must the linking constitute further processing?

Section 57(1)*(a)* applies if the linking activity is not the purpose 'for which the identifier was specifically intended at collection'. This means that the linking activity must constitute further processing.

Tricky area: Some of the writers believe that if the further processing is compatible with the purpose of collection in terms of section 15(2) or 15(3), the processing does not constitute further processing and prior authorisation is not required. Others believe that the wording of section 57(1)(a) which states 'for a purpose other than the one for which the identifier was specifically intended at collection' does not require a compatibility assessment. It is a factual question of whether the purpose is 'new'. Each interpretation comes with its own risks and a responsible party should get legal advice before deciding on which peg to hang their POPIA hat.

12 Section 57(1)*(a)*. This could also constitute an 'information matching programme'. We discuss this in chapter 13 paragraph 13.5. However, all linking is not necessarily an information matching programme.

8.2.2 Processing criminal behaviour or unlawful or objectionable conduct on behalf of third parties

A responsible party must obtain the prior authorisation of the Information Regulator to process information about criminal behaviour or about unlawful or objectionable conduct on behalf of third parties.[13]

Key point: Responsible parties do not need prior authorisation to process information about criminal behaviour or about unlawful or objectionable conduct if they are not doing so on behalf of third parties.[14] However, criminal behaviour is special personal information and so there are additional requirements for lawful processing.[15]

Consider these examples:

Example	Does the responsible party need prior authorisation?
An industry association decides to compile a registry of all employees who have been dismissed by the members of the industry association. Members can check whether job applicants appear on this list. In other words, it is a 'black list'.	Yes, the industry association must apply for prior authorisation.
A verification agency compiles a list of all individuals who have criminal records. Prospective employers can submit the names and ID numbers of job applicants to the verification agency to check against this list.	Yes, the verification agency must apply for prior authorisation. The employer does not have to apply. They are processing the information for their own purposes.

13 Section 57(1)*(b)*.

14 'Third party' is not defined in POPIA, but we are of the view that the definition in article 4(10) of the EU GDPR is sensible. It provides that a "third party" means a natural or legal person, public authority, agency or body other than the data subject, controller, processor and person who, under the direct authority of the controller or processor, [is] authorised to process personal data'.

15 Section 26 read with sections 27 and 33. See chapter 7.

Example	Does the responsible party need prior authorisation?
SAPS offers a service where an individual can apply for a Police Clearance Certificate which states whether or not any criminal convictions have been reported against them.	No. The information is not being processed on behalf of a third party, but on behalf of the data subjects.[16]

Certain types of information relating to criminal behaviour are special personal information.[17] The wording of section 57(1)*(b)* is a bit different. Here are the two side-by-side:

Criminal behaviour as special personal information	Criminal behaviour for purposes of prior authorisation
Personal information concerning 'the criminal behaviour of a data subject to the extent that such information relates to— (i) the alleged commission by a data subject of any offence; or (ii) any proceedings in respect of any offence allegedly committed by a data subject or the disposal of such proceedings.'[18]	'[I]nformation on criminal behaviour or on unlawful or objectionable conduct.'[19]

Tricky area: We do not believe that the more limited definition for purposes of determining what type of information is 'special personal information' can be applied to 'criminal behaviour' in the context of prior authorisation. 'Unlawful conduct' is not necessarily criminal and 'objectionable conduct' is an even wider concept. For instance, objectionable conduct can be any conduct that leads to a negative inference being drawn about a person without there having to be a whiff of unlawful behaviour. While criminal convictions are not considered special personal information, it is hard to deny that they are information about 'unlawful conduct'.

16 The authors were not unanimous on this conclusion. The conclusion is based on the assumption that 'third party' does not include the data subject itself. 'Third party' is not defined in POPIA, but we are of the view that the definition in article 4(10) of the EU GDPR is sensible. It provides that a "third party" means a natural or legal person, public authority, agency or body other than the data subject, controller, processor and person who, under the direct authority of the controller or processor, are authorised to process personal data'.

17 See chapter 7 paragraph 7.2.8.

18 Section 26*(b)*.

19 Section 57(1)*(b)*.

8.2.3 Processing personal information for the purpose of credit reporting

A responsible party must obtain prior authorisation from the Information Regulator to process personal information to do credit reporting.[20] What constitutes 'credit reporting'? It is not defined in POPIA, the National Credit Act or the Code of Conduct that has been developed by the Credit Bureau Association.[21] It is defined in the Information Regulator's *Guidance note on applications for prior authorisation* as 'the processing of personal payment history, lending, and credit worthiness of a data subject by creating a credit report based on that information, and lenders or credit providers use credit reports along with other personal information to determine a data subject's creditworthiness'.[22]

Tricky area: It is not clear whether the requirement only applies to credit reports generated by credit bureaus as contemplated in the National Credit Act. We think that only responsible parties that compile the credit reports and provide them to others would have to apply for prior authorisation; in other words, credit bureaus that are registered in terms of section 43 of the National Credit Act.[23] Credit bureaus are now subject to both POPIA and the NCA.[24]

8.2.4 Transferring special personal information or a child's personal information to foreign countries

A responsible party must obtain prior authorisation from the Information Regulator to transfer special personal information or the personal information of children to a third party in a foreign country

---

20 Section 57(1)*(c)*.

21 This code was in the process of being accredited. All codes of conduct can be accessed here: https://www.justice.gov.za/inforeg/docs6-coc.html.

22 See the Information Regulator's *Guidance note on applications for prior authorisation*, available at https://www.justice.gov.za/inforeg/docs/InfoRegSA-GuidanceNote-PriorAuthorisation-20210311.pdf For a discussion on the legal status of guidance notes see chapter 19 paragraph 19.4.

23 Credit bureaus are regulated by the National Credit Act, which is enforced by the National Credit Regulator and the National Consumer Tribunal. Credit bureaus are authorised to compile credit reports in terms of the National Credit Act. Credit bureaus may collect information from financial institutions, non-bank lenders, telecommunication companies, courts, insurance companies, the Department of Home Affairs, the Companies and Intellectual Property Commission and other sources to compile credit reports. Section 70(2)*(g)* read with regulation 18 of the National Credit Act 34 of 2005.

24 We discuss the rules that apply when POPIA applies to activities that are already regulated by legislation in chapter 2 paragraph 2.7.

that does not provide adequate protection for the processing of personal information.[25]

POPIA imposes requirements on all transfers of personal information across borders in section 72. This is discussed in detail in chapter 14.

Here are the steps you must follow to determine whether prior authorisation is required for the transfer of special personal information or the information of a child:

Step	Explanation
Is the responsible party transferring: • special personal information,[26] or • personal information of children[27] to a third party in a foreign country?	**Key point:** The transfer of information across borders can take many forms. Sometimes the information will actually be sent to an organisation located in another country. In other instances, responsible parties might grant access to the information to the organisation – in other words, the information is 'at rest'; it does not leave the responsible party's systems. Both of these scenarios can be considered a transfer of information across borders.[28]

25 Section 57(1)*(d)*.

26 See chapter 7 paragraph 7.2 for a discussion on what constitutes special personal information.

27 See chapter 7 paragraph 7.5.1 for a discussion on the definition of 'child'. Remember that a person under the age of 18 may still be competent in respect of the processing activity in question, which means that they are not considered a child.

28 This is discussed in chapter 14 paragraph 14.2.1.

Step	Explanation
Is the third party subject to protections that provide 'an adequate level of protection'?	In terms of section 72(1)*(a)*, a responsible party can transfer personal information to a 'third party who is in a foreign country' as long as the third party is subject to a law, binding corporate rules or binding agreement which provides protection that is substantially similar to the protection provided in POPIA, and that requires similar protection for the further sharing of the personal information with third parties.[29] Establishing whether law, binding corporate rules or binding agreement provides for 'an adequate level of protection' is not easy. When compared to POPIA, other data protection laws will have some provisions that are stricter and others that provide weaker protections. In the EU, this exercise is referred to as 'adequacy decisions'.[30] We discuss this in chapter 14 paragraph 14.2.3.1. **Key point:** In terms of section 72(1)*(a)*, the adequate level of protection can be established in terms of a law, binding corporate rules or binding agreement. If at the end of the assessment, the responsible party comes to the conclusion that the law, binding corporate rules or binding agreement of the third party in the foreign country is not adequate, the responsible party must apply for prior authorisation. In addition, a responsible party will have to obtain consent for the transmission of the special personal information (section 72(1)*(b)*) or rely on any of the other exceptions in section 72(1)*(c)* to *(e)*.

[29] This is discussed in chapter 14 paragraph 14.2.3.1.

[30] Visit this page to see which countries have been the lucky recipients of adequacy decisions: https://ec.europa.eu/info/sites/info/files/research_and_innovation/law_and_regulations/documents/adequacy-japan-factsheet_en_2019_1.pdf.

8.2.5 Other processing activities that carry a particular risk for the legitimate interest of the data subject

The Information Regulator may identify other processing activities that carry a particular risk for the legitimate interest of the data subject and make prior authorisation a requirement. The Regulator may do this by law or by regulation.[31]

8.3 HOW MUST THE RESPONSIBLE PARTY OBTAIN PRIOR AUTHORISATION?

Section 58 prescribes the procedural rules relating to the way in which the Information Regulator will deal with requests for prior authorisation:

- The responsible party must notify the Information Regulator if any of the processing activities discussed above are planned.[32]
- The Information Regulator must inform the responsible party within four weeks of receiving the notification whether it will conduct a more detailed investigation.

> **Tricky area:** POPIA does not explicitly state this, but it appears that if the Regulator does not want to conduct a detailed investigation, the responsible party can continue with the contemplated processing activity. In other words, the Information Regulator cannot deny prior authorisation without conducting a detailed investigation.

- If the Information Regulator decides that it wants to conduct a more detailed investigation it must indicate the period within which it plans to conduct the investigation in the notification. This period must not exceed 13 weeks.
- Once the Information Regulator has conducted the detailed investigation, it must issue a statement on the lawfulness of the processing. This statement has the status of an enforcement notice.[33]

---

[31] The Information Regulator does not have the power to make legislation. We assume that this would have to happen in the form of a regulation or that the Information Regulator would lobby Parliament to make or amend a law. Section 57(2) is not listed in section 112 as a topic on which the Regulator can make regulations.

[32] The Information Regulator includes an Application Form for Prior Authorisation in its Guidance Note on Application for Prior Authorisation available at https://justice.gov.za/inforeg/docs/InfoRegSA-GuidanceNote-PriorAuthorisation-20210311.pdf.

[33] Enforcement notices are discussed in chapter 19 paragraph 19.6.8.3.

> **Key point:** We can hear the collective moaning of sceptics about how this is going to slow down commerce. The drafters thought of that and included section 58(7) which states that if the Information Regulator misses any of the deadlines, the responsible party can continue with the processing activity. Put differently, the responsible party 'may presume a decision in its favour' and continue with its processing. Peachy.

An organisation only has to apply for prior authorisation once, and not 'each time that personal information is received or processed'. However, if the processing departs from what was authorised by the Information Regulator, the organisation has to re-apply. We think.[34]

8.4 NO PRIOR AUTHORISATION IS REQUIRED BY INDUSTRIES GOVERNED BY A CODE OF CONDUCT

If the responsible party is subject to a code of conduct issued in terms of chapter 7 of POPIA, prior authorisation is not required.[35] Codes of conduct are discussed in chapter 19 paragraph 19.5. Let the Codes of Conduct roll!

8.5 CONSEQUENCES OF NOT OBTAINING PRIOR AUTHORISATION

A failure to:

- request prior authorisation when it is required; or
- comply with the rules regarding how prior authorisation must be requested

is a criminal offence.[36] The penalties and fines that can result are discussed in chapter 19.

8.6 PRACTICAL ADVICE

8.6.1 Identify and evaluate existing processing activities that require prior authorisation (even if they started before commencement)

As we mentioned in paragraph 8.2, even processing that commenced before the commencement date is subject to prior authorisation.

It is therefore advisable for responsible parties to identify all existing processing activities to determine whether they may require (prior)

[34] See for yourself in section 57(4).

[35] Section 57(3).

[36] Section 59.

authorisation. The second step would be to evaluate how integral that processing activity is to the organisation's activities. This will determine the impact it will have on the organisation should the Information Regulator refuse prior authorisation in future.

Sectors that routinely engage in activities that are subject to prior authorisation could also consider accrediting a code of conduct. Codes of conduct are discussed in chapter 19 paragraph 19.5.

8.6.2 Ensure that processing that will require prior authorisation is identified early

The worst outcome is if an organisation were to invest resources in a processing activity only to find out later that it requires prior authorisation and that authorisation is refused.

It is essential to put processes in place that will assist organisations to identify plans that may lead to processing that requires prior authorisation as early in the planning phase as possible. We discuss personal information impact assessments (PIIAs) in chapter 20 paragraph 20.3. A PIIA should always be triggered if an organisation plans a new processing activity. The assessment should include questions aimed at identifying when prior authorisation might be required.

8.6.3 Document applications carefully

The responsible party must be able to prove that they notified the Information Regulator of their plans to process personal information in any of the circumstances that require prior authorisation. The evidence is very important in instances where the responsible party received no response from the Information Regulator within four weeks of the notification, and the responsible party has to prove that the four weeks have passed.

Similarly, the responsible party must keep any notice received from the Information Regulator that further investigation was required, to prove the deadline by which the Information Regulator must make their decision after the investigation. The responsible party must keep any notice received from the Information Regulator approving the planned processing activity as evidence of compliance.

9

Minimality and information quality

9.1 WHAT TO EXPECT IN THIS CHAPTER

Minimality. The state or quality of being minimal.[1] It is the smallest of the principles, weighing in at only 22 words, but it punches above its weight. It is also the reason why reviewing forms and other ways in which personal information is collected should be very high on any organisation's POPIA agenda.

---

1 Merriam Webster.

The principle of minimality and the requirement that responsible parties must take reasonable steps to ensure that the personal information is of a satisfactory quality are very similar and the same techniques are applied to achieve compliance.[2]

In this chapter we discuss the following:

- The role of minimality in data protection: the 'less is more' principle
- The relationship between minimality, information quality, information security and records management
- Unpacking minimality
- How long is a piece of string: The quality standard required by POPIA

9.2 THE ROLE OF MINIMALITY IN DATA PROTECTION: THE 'LESS IS MORE' PRINCIPLE

The principle of minimality states that a responsible party can only process personal information if the personal information is adequate, relevant, and not excessive considering the purpose of the processing activity.[3]

All processing of personal information must be done reasonably,[4] and to determine what is reasonable, the principle of minimality is considered.[5] We discussed reasonableness at length in chapter 2,[6] but it bears repeating that it involves an assessment of necessity and proportionality.[7] The ICO lists the following two main considerations:[8]

- Will the processing that you plan to do achieve your purpose for processing the personal information?[9]
- Is there any other reasonable way to achieve the same result?

---

2 Information quality is discussed in paragraph 9.5.

3 Section 10.

4 Section 9*(b)*.

5 Section 10.

6 Paragraph 2.6.1.

7 Article 29 Data Protection Working Party *Guidelines on Data Protection Impact Assessment (DPIA)*, Annexure A, available at https://ec.europa.eu/newsroom/article29/item-detail.cfm?item_id=611236; European Data Protection Supervisor 'EDPS Guidelines on assessing the proportionality of measures that limit the fundamental rights to privacy and to the protection of personal data', available at https://edps.europa.eu/sites/edp/files/publication/19-12-19_edps_proportionality_guidelines_en.pdf.

8 ICO 'How do we do a DPIA?', available at https://ico.org.uk/for-organisations/guide-to-data-protection/guide-to-the-general-data-protection-regulation-gdpr/data-protection-impact-assessments-dpias/how-do-we-do-a-dpia/#how9. See step 4.

9 You will see that the principle that personal information must only be collected for a 'specific, explicitly defined and lawful purpose' is at the heart of POPIA compliance. This is discussed in chapter 6.

Key point: The principle of minimality requires that personal information must be adequate for the purpose, and that the personal information must be relevant and limited to what is necessary. In the European Union, this crucial principal is called 'data minimisation'. We find it is best described by the mantra 'less is more'. This is probably the single most important rule of thumb in data protection, but it is also a good rule to apply if an organisation wants to be more efficient and cost effective. The phrase was made famous by the German-America architect Mies van der Rohe. We like how the author Tracy Chevalier (Girl With a Pearl Earring) refers to it as 'cutting the flab'. She might as well have been talking about processing activities. See Joe Fassler 'Why the Phrase "Less Is More" Means So Much to Tracy Chevalier' The Atlantic, available at https://www.theatlantic.com/entertainment/archive/2013/01/why-the-phrase-less-is-more-means-so-much-to-tracy-chevalier/267399/. In a sense, data protection is about reducing an organisation's personal information footprint, but increasing the usefulness of that personal information. After all, 'size doesn't matter, fast data is better than big data'.[10]

The minimality requirement is intrinsically linked to the requirements that personal information:

- may only be collected for a specific purpose[11]
- must be complete, accurate, not misleading and kept up to date;[12] and
- may only be retained for a limited time.[13]

Without a clear, documented purpose, a responsible party will be unable to determine the minimum amount of personal information to fulfil that purpose, that the information is accurate, or for how long the personal information should be retained.

[10] Hilary Mason.

[11] Section 13.

[12] Section 16.

[13] Section 14.

9.3 THE RELATIONSHIP BETWEEN MINIMALITY, INFORMATION QUALITY, INFORMATION SECURITY AND RECORDS MANAGEMENT

9.3.1 Two peas in a pod: Minimality and quality

The principle of minimality and the requirement that responsible parties must take reasonable steps to ensure that the personal information is of a satisfactory quality are very similar. Here they are side-by-side:

Minimality	Information quality[14]
'Personal information may only be processed if, given the purpose for which it is processed, it is adequate, relevant and not excessive.'	'A responsible party must take reasonably practicable steps to ensure that the personal information is complete, accurate, not misleading and updated where necessary.' AND '[T]he responsible party must have regard to the purpose for which personal information is collected or further processed.'

This is the definition that is given for 'data quality' in the Data Management Body of Knowledge (DMBOK): '[T]he planning, implementation, and control of activities that apply quality management techniques to data, in order to assure it is fit for consumption and meet the needs of data consumers.'[15] Information that is not fit for purpose will also fall foul of the principle of minimality.

Key point: The same techniques applied to improve the quality of personal information will often also include trimming the excess.

9.3.2 Information quality and information security

As we discussed in chapter 5 paragraph 5.4.2, integrity is one leg of the CIA triad. Data integrity and data quality are not the same. This is how they are different:[16]

---

14 Section 16.

15 Available at https://www.dataversity.net/what-is-data-quality/. See the discussion of data governance principles in chapter 1 paragraph 1.2.4.

16 Muhammed Raza 'Data integrity vs data quality: An introduction', available at https://www.bmc.com/blogs/data-integrity-vs-data-quality/.

Data quality	Data integrity
'The characteristics that determine the reliability of information to serve an intended purpose including planning, decision making and operations.'	'The characteristics that determine the reliability of the information in terms of its physical and logical validity. Data integrity is based on parameters such as accuracy, validity and consistency of the data across its lifecycle. It is the absence of unintended change to the information between two successive updates or modification to data records.'

Key point: So, they say, that data integrity is a subset of data quality. While this distinction is enormously important for people who dabble in the dark arts of data science and data governance geeks, compliance folk just need to understand that both of them are important.

9.3.3 The tension between minimality and records management

The minimality requirement often seems at odds with records retention requirements. A responsible party must be clear about the purpose for which personal information is collected and retained, as it could affect what information is adequate, relevant, accurate and complete. For example, if personal information has changed it does not mean that a historical record is inaccurate or no longer relevant. It must just be clear that it is a historical record. If a data subject moves house from Gqeberha to Pretoria, a record saying that she currently lives in Gqeberha will be inaccurate. However, a record saying that she lived in Gqeberha on a certain past date remains accurate. The responsible party will have to determine if it has a legitimate purpose for retaining the historical record.

Another example of where the accuracy and minimality requirements must be considered together is when a doctor records a medical opinion about possible diagnoses. An initial diagnosis, even though it may later be proven incorrect, should stay on a patient's record. The record is not inaccurate, because it accurately reflects the doctor's opinion at the time. Also, the doctor's initial diagnosis may assist those treating the patient later. This information is required to comply with the adequacy element of the minimality requirement.[17]

[17] ICO *Guide to the General Data Protection Regulation*, Principle (d): Accuracy, available at https://ico.org.uk/for-organisations/guide-to-data-protection/guide-to-the-general-data-protection-regulation-gdpr/principles/accuracy/.

9.4 UNPACKING MINIMALITY

In the remainder of this chapter we will discuss the elements of section 10, which provides that personal information must

- be adequate,
- be relevant, and
- must not be excessive.

9.4.1 Personal information must be adequate

Information is adequate if it is of acceptable quality or quantity – information will be inadequate if it is incomplete, out of date, or inaccurate. If a processing activity does not achieve the purpose it was designed for, it is likely that the personal information is inadequate and the processing must be stopped. In some circumstances it may be necessary for a responsible party to collect additional personal information to that originally anticipated to fulfil their purpose.

9.4.2 Personal information must be relevant

The information must be relevant to the purpose for which it is collected or used. This requirement refers to the fact that the personal information collected must be appropriately connected to the purpose for which the information is being processed. If the personal information is not needed to achieve the purpose, the responsible party does not have the right to retain the information because it is not relevant. We discuss when records can be retained in chapter 17.

Consider this example: An online retailer records telephone conversations between customers and the retailer's customer service consultants for employee training purposes. The full telephone conversations, including customers' payment card details, are stored permanently for this purpose. The person in charge of employee training listens to only one recording per customer service consultant per week. Keeping full and permanent recordings of all customer calls is excessive for employee training purposes and also introduces a huge security risk which should not have been allowed.[18]

Sometimes personal information may have been relevant when it was collected but is no longer relevant because it is dated. For instance, the fact that a person was declared bankrupt 15 years ago, is no longer relevant when a responsible party wants to assess a person's ability

---

[18] *French Data Protection Authority (CNIL) fines Spartoo* (5 August 2020), available at https://www.cnil.fr/fr/spartoo-sanction-de-250-000-euros-et-injonction-sous-astreinte-de-se-conformer-au-rgpd.

to work with money. This is referred to as 'the right to be forgotten', which was recognised for the first time in the *Google Spain* case.[19] This right is not expressly included in POPIA, but it is implied given that the wording of POPIA is the same as the wording in the Data Protection Directive, which inspired the European Court of Justice to recognise the right to be forgotten.

Key point: Does a data subject have the 'right to be forgotten' in terms of POPIA? The right to be forgotten is explicitly included in article 17 of the EU GDPR, but this right was first afforded to a data subject in the *Google Spain* case. The *Google Spain* case was decided on Directive 95/46/EC of the European Parliament and the Council of 24 October 1995, the predecessor to the EU GDPR. The court found that the controller must take every reasonable step to ensure that data which do not meet these requirements are erased or rectified.[20] The court noted that personal data may become inadequate, irrelevant or excessive over time.[21] The court found that the data subject had the right to be de-linked from information which has become inadequate, irrelevant or excessive in relation to the purpose of the processing activity. The Article 29 Data Protection Working Party published a guideline on the implementation of the *Google Spain* case (keep in mind that this predates the EU GDPR). The guideline says that a fair balance must be found between an individual's fundamental rights to privacy and data protection, and the economic interests of Google, and the rights of internet users to have access to information through the search engine. The outcome may depend on the sensitivity of the information and the interest of the public to have access to that information. The interest of the public will be significantly higher if the data subject plays a role in public life.[22]

19 *Google Spain SL and Google Inc. v Agencia Española de Protección de Datos (AEPD) and Mario Costeja González* C-131/12.

20 *Google Spain* paragraph 72.

21 *Google Spain* paragraph 93.

22 Article 29 Data Protection Working Party 'Guidelines on the implementation of the Court of Justice of the European Union judgment on "Google Spain and Inc v. Agencia Española de Protección de Datos (AEPD) and Mario Costeja González" C-131/12', available at https://ec.europa.eu/justice/article-29/documentation/opinion-recommendation/files/2014/wp225_en.pdf.

We believe that a similar interpretation could be followed by the Information Regulator and South African courts. South African data subjects have the right to request that a responsible party deletes personal information that has become 'inaccurate, irrelevant, excessive, out of date, incomplete, misleading or obtained unlawfully'.[23] Sure sounds like a right to be forgotten to us.

9.4.3 Personal information must not be excessive

Responsible parties must not collect more personal information than what is needed to fulfil the purpose for which they are collecting it. Consider this example: a debt collection agency is contracted to find a debtor. The agency finds several individuals with a similar name as the debtor. The agency makes further enquiries until they identify the debtor. The agency should delete most of the personal information of the individuals who were discounted, and keep only the minimum information to confirm why the person was removed from the search. It is appropriate to keep this information to ensure that these individuals are not contacted again regarding this debt.[24]

Collecting personal information just in case it may be used in future is unacceptable, however, a responsible party may collect the personal information needed for a foreseeable event that may occur. Consider this example: an employer collects the details of the blood groups of some of its employees who do hazardous work. This information is needed in case of an accident, even though an accident may never happen.[25] What and how much personal information is adequate may differ from one case to another. For instance, it may be reasonable for an employer to collect the blood type of employees who do hazardous work, but not that of office workers.[26]

---

23 Data subject rights are discussed in chapter 18.

24 ICO Guide to the UK General Data Protection Regulation, Principle (c): Data minimisation, available at https://ico.org.uk/for-organisations/guide-to-data-protection/guide-to-the-general-data-protection-regulation-gdpr/principles/data-minimisation/.

25 ICO Guide to the UK General Data Protection Regulation, Principle (c): Data minimisation, available at https://ico.org.uk/for-organisations/guide-to-data-protection/guide-to-the-general-data-protection-regulation-gdpr/principles/data-minimisation/.

26 ICO Guide to the UK General Data Protection Regulation, Principle (c): Data minimisation, available at https://ico.org.uk/for-organisations/guide-to-data-protection/guide-to-the-general-data-protection-regulation-gdpr/principles/data-minimisation/.

9.5 HOW LONG IS A PIECE OF STRING: THE QUALITY STANDARD REQUIRED BY POPIA

Section 16 requires that a responsible party take 'reasonably practicable' steps to ensure that personal information is complete, accurate, not misleading and updated where necessary.

Let's look at each of these requirements:

- **Completeness:** A record can be accurate, but incomplete. This is very important when it comes to personal information that is used to decide whether a person qualifies for a product or service, or if there is a legal consequence for the data subject, such as being offered employment. Missing information can be very harmful.
- **Accuracy:** This refers to the correctness of a record; is it true? Common mistakes are not updating contact details, which may lead to a failure to deliver products or services. Whether personal information is accurate will depend on the purpose for which it is used. For instance, a data subject's address may have changed, but their previous address may be kept on record for purposes of proof or as an historical record.
- **Not misleading:** Inaccurate or outdated personal information can easily be misleading. If, for instance, a person's financial record is not updated or accurate, a misleading impression of their financial status is created which can have dire implications for the data subject. It is sometimes difficult to determine if a record should be kept if something was a mistake. A data subject may not want their payment record to be tarnished by an incorrectly allocated penalty, but the responsible party may need to keep the record of the penalty, and its reversal, for accounting purposes. It is acceptable to keep records of mistakes, as long as those records are not misleading about the facts.[27]
- **Updated when necessary:** If a mistake or inaccuracy comes to the attention of a responsible party, steps should be taken to rectify it. If it is important for a data subject's information to remain current, for instance if it is used often or in important decisions, it must be kept up to date. In some instances it will not be necessary for a responsible party to proactively keep a data subject's information up to date. For instance, if a data subject places a single order from an online retailer, the retailer will collect and use the data subject's address to deliver the order. Until the data subject places another order, there is no reason for the retailer to take proactive steps to keep the data subject's address up to date. Only when the data subject places another order will the retailer confirm the accuracy of the address they have on record with the data subject.

[27] See https://ico.org.uk/for-organisations/guide-to-data-protection/guide-to-the-general-data-protection-regulation-gdpr/principles/accuracy/.

What does 'reasonably practicable steps' and 'where necessary' mean in the context of section 16? POPIA does not provide guidance on this question apart from the risk-based approach prescribed in section 19(2) that we discussed earlier in this chapter. We would argue that what is reasonably practicable should be considered against the following factors:

- The risk posed to data subjects if their information is out of date. This will often be determined by the type of personal information involved, the number of data subjects impacted and the likelihood of substantial damage or distress.[28]
- The availability of technical or other measures to ensure the quality of information. For instance, a responsible party could allow data subjects to update their online profile information directly.
- The cost of compliance for the responsible party. In some instances, the cost of compliance may be prohibitive or excessive compared to the risk posed to data subjects.

9.6 PRACTICAL ADVICE

9.6.1 How de-identification can help compliance with the minimality requirement

A practical way to comply with the minimality requirement is to de-identify information for certain purposes.[29] If it is not necessary to know the identity of a data subject to fulfil the purpose of processing, the responsible party should rather use de-identified information. For example, a medical aid is required to protect the identities and health information of its members, but may also want to publish statistics about health care in South Africa. De-identifying the information used in the statistical report helps the medical aid to comply with the requirements of POPIA whilst enabling the medical aid to make valuable information available to the public.[30]

De-identification is recommended for the publication of statistical information. The fact that a responsible party may have access to all the personal information from which statistical information is derived, does not prevent it from processing the information in such a way that it becomes information from which a data subject can no longer be identified. But the reader of the statistics must not be able to use the statistics or link it to other information to determine to whom the information relates. If converting the underlying personal information

28 These factors are all relevant when determining an appropriate fine in terms of section 109(3).

29 De-identification is discussed in chapter 3, paragraph 3.3.2.

30 ICO *Anonymisation: Managing Data Protection Risk Code of Practice* 12.

into statistics can achieve this, the responsible party can disclose information in statistical form because it will no longer be personal information, and POPIA will not apply to the published statistics.[31] However, research has demonstrated that de-identified information can be re-identified more often than one would expect. For instance, academic research has found that when the location of a person is updated hourly, only four spatio-temporal data points are necessary to identify 95% of individuals. Two spatio-temporal data points would identify 50% of individuals.[32]

If there is any uncertainty as to whether information has been sufficiently de-identified, the responsible party should consider the potential harm to data subjects if the information is ever re-identified, taking into account the nature of the information, the context in which it was disclosed, and who it is about. In borderline cases where the consequences of re-identification could be significant, the responsible party should rather ask the data subject's consent and limit disclosure.[33]

9.6.2 Minimality vs. big data

Big data analytics is becoming more and more prevalent. Big data means high-volume, high-velocity, and high-variety information assets that demand cost-effective, innovative forms of information processing for enhanced insight and decision-making.[34] Big data, machine learning and AI are becoming part of business as usual for many organisations. Some of the qualities of big data analytics are:

- the use of algorithms
- the opacity of the processing
- the tendency to collect 'all the data'
- the repurposing of data; and
- the use of new types of data.[35]

---

31 *R (Department of Health) v Information Commissioner* [2011] EWHC 1430 (Admin) paragraphs 51 and 55.

32 YA de Montjoye, CA Hidalgo, M Verleysen and VD Blondel 'Unique in the crowd: The privacy bounds of human mobility' (25 March 2013) 3 *Scientific Reports*, Article Number: 1379 (https://www.nature.com/articles/srep01376).

33 ICO *Anonymisation: Managing data protection risk code of practice* 20.

34 Gartner IT Glossary Big Data, available at https://www.gartner.com/en/information-technology/glossary/big-data.

35 ICO *Discussion paper on Big data, artificial intelligence, machine learning and data protection* (Version 2.2 20170904) 9.

It is not difficult to see why privacy and big data analytics seems incompatible. Although there are many proven benefits of big data analytics, it can have intrusive effects on data subjects. In order to ensure that it meets POPIA requirements the responsible party must perform a detailed personal information impact assessment (PIIA) before embarking on big data analysis. PIIAs are discussed in chapter 20 paragraph 20.3. Responsible parties should also consider whether they require prior authorisation as generating big data usually involves the linking of information between different responsible parties by using 'unique identifiers'.[36]

9.6.3 Responsible parties should review their forms

The way in which organisations ask for information is important and should be reviewed with POPIA compliance in mind.[37] One of the principles of 'privacy by design' is that privacy should be 'embedded' into (form) design. This means that a personal information impact assessment should be carried out on the form and the purposes for which personal information is being collected. This will ensure that the responsible party doesn't collect unnecessary or irrelevant information. We discuss collection in the next chapter.

Here are some suggestions on how organisations can design POPIA-compliant forms that make life easier for them and the person completing the form:

Does the organisation really need the form?	Does the organisation not already have this information? If the organisation already has the information, it should not collect it again.
Does the form's title describe the form's purpose?	The title should give a clear indication of what the form is used for. 'Form 224b-A' doesn't help the data subject, but 'Death benefit application form' does.
Does the organisation need every piece of information on the form?	Organisations should consider each field on the form and make sure that it is really necessary for their purpose. For instance, if the form already asks for an ID number, it is not necessary to also ask for a person's date of birth.

➡

[36] This is discussed in chapter 8. We deal with sharing of personal information in chapter 12, which includes information matching.

[37] We think that 'privacy by form design' should be a thing.

What does the organisation use each piece of information for?	List all the purposes and create a data flow map.[38] This step is also necessary for creating a privacy notice.[39]
Will it be clear to the data subject why the information is required?	If the reason is not obvious, it should be explained on the form. Forms should also refer to the organisation's privacy notice which should contain detailed information on all purposes for processing personal information.
Does the form clearly indicate compulsory and optional fields?	The effect of not providing optional information must be explained.[40]
Does the form collect the personal information of a child?	Ensure that sections 34 and 35 are complied with.[41] In most cases the responsible party will need the consent of the parent or guardian.
Does the form collect special personal information?	Ensure that sections 26 to 33 are complied with.[42]

9.6.4 Understanding the consequences of not complying with the minimality requirement

As with the other requirements for the legal processing of personal information, a responsible party's compliance may be assessed by the Information Regulator.[43] We discuss enforcement in chapter 19.

Having unnecessary information may not sound like a big deal, but the information commissioners in Europe take non-compliance with the equivalent data minimisation principle in the EU GDPR very seriously.[44] For instance, the Berlin Commissioner for Data Protection and Freedom of Information recently imposed a fine of EUR14.5 million on a real estate company for using an archiving system that did not enable them to remove data that was no longer required. The fine was so high because the Berlin Commissioner found that the real estate company deliberately created the data archive in question and processed the affected data inappropriately over a long time. A mitigating factor that was considered by the Berlin Commissioner when determining the fine was that the company did not misuse access to the inadmissibly

38 We discuss data flow maps in chapter 1 paragraph 1.4.

39 We discuss notification in chapter 11.

40 We discuss this requirement in chapter 11 paragraph 11.3.

41 We discuss the justifications for processing the personal information of children in chapter 7.

42 We discuss the justifications for processing special personal information in chapter 7.

43 Section 40(1)*(b)*(vi).

44 Article 5*(c)*.

stored data.[45] This example illustrates that responsible parties could be fined just for having unnecessary information or information that is no longer relevant, even if the information is not used. Perhaps even more importantly, it leads to enormous wasted cost. The responsible party must safeguard unused personal information, keep it updated, and pay for the storage of the information.

9.6.5 How to achieve information quality

9.6.5.1 The Information Commissioner's Office does it again

Here are the 'expectations' of the ICO when it comes to information quality:[46]

- conduct regular information quality reviews
- make staff aware of quality issues that are detected during the reviews to prevent history from repeating itself
- 'weed' records containing personal information to reduce the risk of inaccuracies and excessive retention
- ensure that it is clear where the personal information came from
- carefully consider challenges to the accuracy of the information; and
- consider whether it is necessary to update the information periodically (e.g. by prompting customers to check that their personal information is still up to date).

Key point: This does not mean that a responsible party should change the course of history.[47] There is often a legitimate reason to maintain a record of changes to personal information.[48] As long as it is clear which version of the personal information is correct and mistakes are labelled as mistakes, it is actually recommended that responsible parties maintain an audit trail of corrections and updates.

---

45 European Data Protection Board 'Berlin Commissioner for Data Protection imposes fine on real estate company', available at https://edpb.europa.eu/news/national-news/2019/berlin-commissioner-data-protection-imposes-fine-real-estate-company_en.

46 See the checklist available at https://ico.org.uk/for-organisations/accountability-framework/records-management-and-security/#quality and the extensive guidance on data accuracy, available at https://ico.org.uk/for-organisations/guide-to-data-protection/guide-to-the-general-data-protection-regulation-gdpr/principles/accuracy/.

47 Only hobbits can do that.

48 For POPIA's principles relating to records management, see chapter 17.

9.6.5.2 Some musings on reference and master data management

We discussed data management in chapter 1 paragraph 1.2.4. Without good data management, compliance with the information quality requirement becomes virtually impossible.

The SA Law Reform Commission considered that certain factors make complying with section 16 difficult. For instance, information may be saved in different formats and in different mediums and it may be difficult to migrate information from one medium to another. The cost of compliance for the responsible party was also considered. The SA Law Reform Commission final recommendation was that:[49]

> 'Even though there may be cost implications for business, it is envisaged that this principle would encourage good record information management, which is an excellent principle to work towards. It reaffirms the idea that the data protection legislation should be seen as the implementation of ordinary, good business practice.'

This is where POPIA programmes can deliver business value. In *From Privacy to Profit: Achieving Positive Returns on Privacy Investments*, CISCO reports that 72% of companies achieved operational efficiency through their privacy controls and that on average, for every dollar spent on privacy, organisations receive USD2.70 in benefits.[50] This is achieved through practising good data management. For instance, reference and master data management play a significant role when it comes to improving efficiency. One of the authorities on master data management is Scott Taylor and we cannot explain this better than he does:[51]

> 'Data transformation journeys usually follow a three-phase path, says Scott. "Most enterprises start in a legacy state of multiple silos," he says. Supply chain, procurement, sales, marketing and finance for example – are all worlds unto themselves.'

---

49 SA Law Reform Commission Project 124 on Privacy and Data Protection (2009 Report) 227–228.

50 CISCO *From Privacy to Profit: Achieving Positive Returns on Privacy Investments*, available at https://www.cisco.com/c/dam/global/en_uk/products/collateral/security/2020-data-privacy-cybersecurity-series-jan-2020.pdf.

51 Cory Comer 'Beyond silo-breaking: Building a trusted data ecosystem with Scott Taylor' *Ratelinx*, available at https://www.ratelinx.com/resources/beyond-silo-breaking-building-a-trusted-data-ecosystem-with-scott-taylor/.

Does that sound familiar? Many organisations function in this legacy state characterised by separate systems, disparate data, differing definitions for concepts such as 'customer', a lack of standards, significant operational barriers and an inability to scale. What else is impossible (or difficult)? Ensuring data integrity, data quality, good records management and responding to data subject requests quickly and effectively.[52]

> 'In the second stage, the organisation becomes focused on their relationships, incorporating 360-degree solutions for suppliers and vendors. "They've made that leap from legacy state to an integrated enterprise," Scott says.'[53]

This is what Scott refers to as an integrated enterprise. In this state an organisation has a 360-degree view of its customers, employees and vendors; also known as a 'golden record' or 'common version of the truth'. The quality of the information is managed centrally and the organisation can start leveraging technology like machine learning and artificial intelligence that are dependent on high quality data. Questions like 'what personal information do you have about me?' and 'who did you share it with?' become easy to answer.

> 'That sets the stage for the third step: The company becomes part of an ecosystem of partners, vendors, suppliers, and service providers. But that network requires trust, and trust depends on accuracy. "In many cases, business dealings based on personal feelings and good faith can sour quickly if the data supporting that relationship is inaccurate," Scott warns. A master data strategy is integral to successfully support operations in the ecosystem. "Using the same standard data and definitions, or links to the same data standard and definitions, across verticals and markets provides the basis for seamless integration," says Scott. "Leveraging common data and syndicated processes between external parties enables the interoperability in a trust network to scale."'

No, POPIA does not prevent this type of trust network from forming between combinations of independent responsible parties, co-responsible parties and operators, but it does require that the management of the flow of information must comply with POPIA. We discuss information sharing in chapter 13.

---

52 We discuss records management in chapter 17 and data subject rights in chapter 18.

53 Cory Comer 'Beyond silo-breaking: Building a trusted data ecosystem with Scott Taylor' *Ratelinx*, available at https://www.ratelinx.com/resources/beyond-silo-breaking-building-a-trusted-data-ecosystem-with-scott-taylor/.

10 Collecting and creating personal information

10.1 WHAT TO EXPECT IN THIS CHAPTER

'I see personal information. All the time. I see it everywhere.'[1]

This chapter focuses on the different sources of personal information and includes personal information that is 'generated' by an organisation. Just because responsible parties see the personal information everywhere, does not mean they can use it.

Key point: POPIA contains stricter rules on data collection than the EU GDPR. So, Google the answers at your own risk.

In this chapter we discuss the following:

- Overview of collection
- Collecting personal information from the data subject directly (the default rule)
- When collecting personal information from other sources will be justified
- Creating or generating personal information
- Some typical case studies

10.2 OVERVIEW OF COLLECTION

Before assessing their collection practices, organisations should already know the answers to these questions:

- whether POPIA applies[2]
- who the responsible party is and if there are any operators involved[3]
- planned security measures[4]
- what the personal information will be used for (i.e. the purpose for processing)[5]
- whether prior authorisation is needed to collect the personal information (and if so, whether an application for prior authorisation has been made);[6] and

---

1 Ok, so M Night Shyamalan has not made a movie about POPIA, yet, but one can dream. We are available.

2 Chapter 3.

3 Chapter 4.

4 Chapter 5.

5 Chapter 6.

6 Chapter 8.

- the bare minimum amount of personal information required to accomplish the purpose(s).[7]

If an organisation can answer these questions then it is ready to consider where it is going to collect the personal information from.

Key point: It is a common mistake to only think of personal information which the responsible party collects from data subjects or other sources. This overlooks the considerable amount of personal information that organisations generate about data subjects. For instance, responsible parties generate transactional data (who bought what, when), social media giants help data subjects to publish and share their views and preferences, applications may collect location data and map who data subjects come into contact with, hospitals generate clinical data, and, increasingly, responsible parties are analysing all of this personal information to make judgments and predictions about data subjects. Not only does POPIA also apply to this 'generated' personal information, these activities are the battleground of the future.[8]

10.3 COLLECTING PERSONAL INFORMATION FROM THE DATA SUBJECT DIRECTLY (THE DEFAULT RULE)

The default rule in section 12(1) of POPIA is that responsible parties must always collect personal information directly from the data subject.[9] As always, this default rule is subject to several exceptions which we will discuss in paragraph 10.4.

There are several reasons for this rule:

- When personal information is collected from the data subject, the data subject is usually aware of the collection and has (some) control over what information is provided.[10]
- The data subject will in most cases be the most reliable source of information. In other words, the responsible party is entitled to assume that the personal information is correct.[11]

Chapter 10

---

7 Chapter 9.

8 Does this statement pique your interest? Read Soshana Zuboff *The Age of Surveillance Capitalism: The Fight for a Human Future at the New Frontier of Power* (2019). If you are not into reading, watch *The Great Hack* or *Social Dilemma*.

9 Section 12(1).

10 We wrote about the myth of control in chapter 2 paragraph 2.6.4.

11 Information quality is discussed in chapter 9.

Sometimes people confuse section 11 (the lawfulness of the processing of the personal information) with section 12 (the lawfulness of the source of the personal information). These are two distinct concepts and need to be addressed separately. As we observed above, responsible parties should already have considered the lawfulness of the processing of the personal information[12] However, even if the responsible party has a legal justification in terms of section 11 (or sections 27 to 33 for special personal information, and section 35 if there are children involved), they might still be prevented by section 12 from collecting the personal information from their desired source.

Key point: Be careful about confusing the legal justification for the use of the personal information for (section 11), with whether you are allowed to collect it from that source (section 12)! The assessment of whether personal information was collected from an appropriate source is in addition to determining whether the responsible party has a legal justification for processing the personal information in terms of section 11. Think of it like a two-step dance move.[13]

The good news is that if a responsible party collects all its personal information directly from the data subject, then that is the end of this chapter. In practice, however, this rarely happens as most often there is a combination of collecting personal information from the data subject, collecting personal information about the data subject from third parties, and the internal generation of new personal information.

Consider, for example, the following situation: An attorney meets a new client, Mr Sithole, for the first time and collects some personal information during the meeting about a traffic accident. The attorney then obtains additional information about the client from Mr Sithole's website and from a credit bureau to authenticate the client. Thereafter the attorney collects information about Mr Sithole from a witness to the accident and comes to the conclusion that Mr Sithole probably committed a criminal offence by leaving the scene of the accident. In this example there are five separate points of collection:

---

12 See chapter 6.

13 It really is quite a bit like the two-step. Consider this explanation in Wikipedia: 'A two-step consists of two steps in approximately the same direction onto the same foot, separated by a joining or uniting step with the other foot. For example, a right two-step forward is a forward step onto the right foot, a closing step with the left foot, and a forward step onto the right foot. The closing step may be done directly beside the other foot, or obliquely beside, or even crossed, as long as the closing foot does not go past the other foot.' Available at https://en.wikipedia.org/wiki/Two-step_(dance_move).

- Mr Sithole (data subject)
- Mr Sithole's website (publicly available personal information)
- the credit bureau (third party)
- the witness (third party); and
- the conclusion made by attorney based on the evidence (internal generation of personal information).

Are any of these collection practices illegal, because they do not comply with the default rule? No. There are numerous exceptions to this rule. We anticipate that many of these exceptions will become hotly debated topics between lawyers in the years to come, because they are quite ambiguous. In the rest of this chapter, we will attempt to shed some light on how they might be interpreted. In this endeavour, we borrowed from, New Zealand. South Africa's rules and exceptions on collection are very similar to principle 2 in both New Zealand's Privacy Act of 1993[14] and its recently (1 December 2020) updated Privacy Act of 2020.[15] The Privacy Commissioner's website provides helpful insight into personal information collection.[16]

10.4 WHEN COLLECTING PERSONAL INFORMATION FROM OTHER SOURCES WILL BE JUSTIFIED

10.4.1 Personal information in or derived from a public record

The first exception to the rule is if the personal information is either in or derived from a public record. A public record is a record that:

- is accessible in the public domain; and
- is in the possession of or under the control of a public body (but not necessarily created by the public body).[17]

[14] Available at https://www.legislation.govt.nz/act/public/1993/0028/latest/DLM297053.html.

[15] Available at https://www.legislation.govt.nz/act/public/2020/0031/latest/LMS23223.html.

[16] Available at https://privacy.org.nz.

[17] See the definition of 'public record' in section 1 of POPIA.

> **Tricky area:** When is a record 'accessible in the public domain'? For instance, must access be unfettered, or will records that are available for a fee still be seen as accessible in the public domain? What if there is no fee, but you need to register an account? We are of the view that if there is any impediment (e.g. a paywall or a data wall) to the accessibility of the information it is not accessible in the public domain. However, this view may not be correct. In New Zealand for instance 'publicly available information' means personal information published in a publication '(including a register, list, or roll of data) in printed or electronic form that is, or will be, generally available to members of the public free of charge or on payment of a fee'.[18] POPIA is not explicit in this regard and we think that the Information Regulator will take an interpretation that limits the scope of the exception in favour of the privacy of the data subject.

A public body is:

- a national or provincial department (such as the justice and correctional services department or the department of housing in the Western Cape province), or
- a municipality or local government, or
- any institution which gets its mandate from the South African Constitution (such as the public protector) or from a provincial constitution (in health, education, agriculture, housing, environmental protection, and development planning), or
- an organisation that exercises a public function in terms of legislation (such as the short-term insurance Ombud or the Information Regulator which is created by POPIA).

The definition of a public body is quite wide, and includes provisional government, municipalities and any institution that gets its mandate from the South African Constitution and from legislation. In order to rely on this exception, a responsible party will have to confirm whether the organisation administrating the public record qualifies as a public body.

---

18 Section 7 (Interpretation), available at https://www.legislation.govt.nz/act/public/2020/0031/latest/LMS23312.html. This position is confirmed in Case note 100413 [2007] NZ PrivCmr 20, available at https://privacy.org.nz/publications/case-notes-and-court-decisions/case-note-100413-2007-nz-privcmr-20-google-search-reveals-personal-information-on-law-firm-website/.

Key point: An easy way to find out if an organisation thinks of itself as a 'public body' is to look at the relevant organisation's PAIA manual.[19] PAIA separates out its responsibilities between public bodies (Part 2), which publish the PAIA manual in terms of section 14, and private bodies (Part 3), which publish the PAIA manual in terms of section 51. Be a little careful though. It is possible that they have not published their PAIA manual or that they make a mistake, but this tip is a quick and easy way to answer the question.

POPIA's exceptions relating to 'public records' administered by 'public bodies' is not an easy exception to rely on, due to the complex definitions. If a responsible party is incorrect in their interpretation, they may not be able to retain and use the personal information they collected. New Zealand changed its approach in its 2020 Privacy Act to allow personal information to be collected from a third-party source when the agency (responsible party) 'believes, on reasonable grounds, that the information is publicly available information', and this seems to be a much simpler mechanism.[20]

Key point: Responsible parties sometimes mistakenly believe that they can process personal information for any reason if it is derived from a public record. This is a misunderstanding of section 12 of POPIA. All section 12(2)*(a)* allows a responsible party to do is to collect the personal information from a public record rather than directly from the data subject – every other POPIA requirement still applies (particularly section 11)!

10.4.2 Personal information which the data subject deliberately made public

The next exception to the 'collect directly from the data subject' rule is where the data subject has deliberately made the personal information public.[21] There is a temptation to focus solely on the internet as a place where personal information is deliberately made public, but

19 Promotion of Access to Information Act 2 of 2000 (PAIA). The definition of 'public body' in PAIA is the same as the definition in POPIA.

20 Principle 2(2)(d), available at https://www.legislation.govt.nz/act/public/2020/0031/latest/LMS23342.html. Originally, New Zealand's 1993 Privacy Act contained an entire section dealing with 'public registers' which was very similar to POPIA's approach towards 'public records' of 'public bodies'.

21 Section 12(2)*(a)* of POPIA.

other examples of personal information deliberately made public – like estate agents' telephone numbers on 'for sale' signs – are included in this exception.

The primary concern here is how to establish whether the data subject intended to make the personal information public and what 'public' means? Consider the following examples:

Personal information collection event	Challenge
Anakin Skywalker attends a conference and pictures of him are published on the event organiser's website.	How does a responsible party know if Anakin Skywalker had a hand in the publication of his picture (i.e. was it 'deliberate')? If the event organiser published the photograph, does that qualify as being deliberately made public 'by the data subject'?
Leia Organa is getting married and puts her details on a publicly available wedding registry.	What happens if the wedding registry is protected by a password, or only people with the right hyperlink are able to access the registry? What exactly does 'public' mean?
The Empire successfully tenders for a contract with a retailer and the retailer publishes the personal information of the successful tenderer on its publicly accessible website.	The retailer required that the details of The Empire would be published and The Empire agreed to this in order to submit its tender. Does this qualify as deliberately made public 'by the data subject'?
Han Solo makes his contact details publicly available on his website but starts getting so much spam that he removes his contact details from his website. However this information is still available in historical records of his website as stored by Google.	This is a situation where at one point the personal information was deliberately made public by the data subject, but it has since been removed from the website and would not be accessible had it not been for Google's historical records. Can a responsible party still get the personal information from Google's historical records? What if the responsible party got the contact information from the website when it was originally made public but this information has now been removed?

Some light can be shed on the term 'deliberately' in section 12 of POPIA by comparing it with article 9(2)(e) of the EU GDPR.[22]

Section 12(1)(a) of POPIA	GDPR article 9(2)(e)
'It is not necessary to comply with subsection (1) if— *(a)* the information is contained in or derived from a public record or has **deliberately been made public** by the data subject;'	'[P]rocessing relates to personal data which are **manifestly made public by the data subject**.'

What is the difference between deliberately and manifestly? 'Manifestly' is defined as 'in a way that is clear or obvious to the eye or mind'.[23] At first glance, it appears that this is less strict than 'deliberately'. The European Data Protection Board has provided that the context or surrounding circumstances should indicate that the data subject intended to make the personal information public.[24] It also states that the bar is quite high before publicly accessible personal information can be considered to be 'manifestly made public' and consider it to be similar to an 'unmistakably deliberate act'.[25] Dove and Chen have proposed a three step test to see whether the personal information is manifestly made public: [26]

- 'The processing activity is directly connected to those personal data which have been manifestly made public by the data subject;
- There is evidence of a deliberate, affirmative act by the data subject themself to make their data available, and the data are public such that any hypothetical interested member of the public could access them; and

Chapter 10

22 Article 9 of the GDPR is the equivalent of section 27 of POPIA. Article 9(2)*(e)* provides that the processing of special personal information is not prohibited if the processing relates to personal data which are manifestly made public by the data subject.

23 Oxford Languages, available at https://www.google.com/search?q=manifestly+definition&rlz=1C5CHFA_enZA912ZA912&oq=mani fest ly+def init ion.

24 'Guidelines 8/2020 on the targeting of social media users', 2 September 2020, available at https://edpb.europa.eu/sites/edpb/files/consultation/edpb_guidelines_202008_onthetargetingofsocialmediausers_en.pdf.

25 See E Dove & J Chen 'What does it mean for a data subject to make their personal data "manifestly public"? An analysis of GDPR Article 9(2)(e)', 2020, available at https://papers.ssrn.com/sol3/papers.cfm?abstract_id=3699572.

26 See E Dove & J Chen 'What does it mean for a data subject to make their personal data "manifestly public"? An analysis of GDPR Article 9(2)(e)', 2020, available at https://papers.ssrn.com/sol3/papers.cfm?abstract_id=3699572.

- The data have been made manifestly public by the data subject themself (i.e. directly made public by them), or the data subject has given a clear indication to an intermediary to make their data public (i.e. indirectly made public by them).'[27]

Tricky area: It appears that the responsible party would need to prove that the data subject deliberately made the personal information public. This is obviously very difficult for the responsible party as the evidence to prove this is often in the data subject's possession.

Turning to the question of whether the personal information is 'public' or not, as we saw in paragraph 10.4.1, this too is not as easy to define as it first appears. Consider for example personal information that is deliberately made available by Obi-Wan Kenobi on his Facebook page. If this Facebook page is not protected in any way then it certainly is 'public' but if Obi-Wan Kenobi has restricted access to the page to only his friends then there is a good argument that this is no longer 'public' information. In other words, responsible parties can only 'scrape' personal information from public-facing social media accounts.[28] As a general rule, it is probably a good idea to avoid collecting personal information if there is any protection mechanism to prohibit the public having access to the personal information.

Key point: Many organisations justify scraping the internet by saying 'well, the information is already public'. This does not hold water, because the internet is not a public record unless the site in question is administered by a public body. The responsible party would have to prove that the data subject deliberately made the personal information available on the internet. We discuss this in paragraph 10.4.1, but we hear it so often that it bears repeating.

---

27 See E Dove & J Chen 'What does it mean for a data subject to make their personal data "manifestly public"? An analysis of GDPR Article 9(2)(e)', 2020, available at https://papers.ssrn.com/sol3/papers.cfm?abstract_id=3699572.

28 Using scraping to collect personal information from websites and applications is often a violation of their terms. See Facebook 'How we combat scraping', available at https://about.fb.com/news/2021/04/how-we-combat-scraping/. Web-scraping is also discussed in paragraph 10.6.1.

10.4.3 Consent to collection of personal information from third parties

It is possible for a responsible party to ask the data subject to consent to the collection of personal information from a third party.[29]

However, relying on consent to collect personal information from sources other than the data subject is not without its challenges. Consider this example: A potential lessee (data subject) approaches an estate agency (responsible party) to rent a house and the estate agency asks the data subject to consent to obtain a reference from their previous landlord.

As we discussed previously,[30] any consent in terms of POPIA must be:

- specific (in this case specifically consenting to personal information being obtained from a third party)

Key point: New Zealand's privacy commissioner notes that a broad consent to collect personal information from 'other sources' in the context of a rental agreement is not acceptable.[31] Given POPIA's definition of consent, this may be the case in South Africa too. This means that responsible parties may have to list which third parties they get information from in order for the consent to be specific enough. In any event, responsible parties are required to disclose where they get personal information from (if not the data subject).[32]

- informed (the estate agency will use the personal information to consider the data subject's rental offer)
- voluntary (if consent is not given then that will not necessarily result in the rental offer being declined); and

29 Section 12(2)*(b)* of POPIA.

30 See chapter 2 paragraph 2.6.6.

31 New Zealand Privacy Commissioner 'Privacy Act guidance for landlords and tenants', available at https://privacy.org.nz/publications/guidance-resources/privacy-act-guidance-for-landlords-and-tenants/.

32 Notification and what needs to be in a privacy notice is discussed in chapter 11 paragraph 11.3.

Tricky area: Section 11(3)*(b)* states that a data subject may withdraw consent provided in terms of section 11(1)*(a)* at any time. The right to withdraw consent is not mentioned in section 12(2)*(b)*. However, we are of the view that data subjects also have the right to withdraw other consents due to the requirement that consent must be voluntary.[33] Can the responsible party just refuse to continue to process the data subject's personal information, because they withhold consent to collect information from a third party? Data subjects must be free to withdraw consent without undue effort and without any detrimental effects such as an increase in cost, a cessation of services or a decrease in service levels.[34]

- an expression of will (either a signature or some form of positive act that signifies that the data subject consented to this).[35]

Tricky area: In many scenarios, it will be unpalatable to responsible parties that the data subject's consent must be voluntary and that they cannot be penalised for withholding consent. What this means is that responsible parties should avoid relying on this exception at all costs.[36] Often, as is the case with our landlord (above), responsible parties will be able to rely on many of the other exceptions such as 'to maintain the legitimate interest of the responsible party' or that 'compliance would prejudice a lawful purpose of the collection'.

10.4.4 No prejudice to the legitimate interest of the data subject

If a responsible party can demonstrate that collecting the personal information from another source does not prejudice a legitimate interest of the data subject, they can go ahead with the collection. Given that collecting personal information from a 'third party' is inherently intrusive and will almost always erode a data subject's interest in privacy, this exception is very limited.

---

33 Section 1 of POPIA.

34 European Data Protection Board *Guidelines 05/2020 on Consent under Regulation 2016/679* 13, available at https://edpb.europa.eu/sites/edpb/files/files/file1/edpb_guidelines_202005_consent_en.pdf.

35 A useful guideline for landlords is provided by New Zealand's privacy commissioner at https://privacy.org.nz/publications/guidance-resources/privacy-act-guidance-for-landlords-and-tenants/.

36 This is also the position when the responsible party has to determine which legal justification applies. See chapter 6 paragraph 6.3.6.

The New Zealand Privacy Act also allows for an exception to the direct collection duty if the collection does 'not prejudice the interests of the individual concerned'.[37] Consider this New Zealand case: [38] The New Zealand Ministry of Education started an investigation into complaints that the children in a childcare centre were given medication without the consent of their parents and that the childcare centre had allowed children with infectious diseases to attend school. The Ministry obtained a copy of a register of medication administered to children from the childcare centre. The parents then complained and asked why the information was not obtained with parental consent? In this matter New Zealand's Privacy Commissioner approved the collection of the personal information directly from the child care centre justifying it by stating that '[i]n view of serious allegations about the running of the centre, it appeared that the interests of the complainants' daughter were being protected rather than prejudiced' or – put differently – there was no prejudice to the legitimate interests of the data subjects (the children).

Tricky area: While this exception is reminiscent of the legal justification in section 11(1)*(d)* that the processing is for a legitimate interest of the data subject, the two are not identical.[39] While the legal justification requires that the responsible party must show a positive impact, the exception to the direct collection rule requires that the responsible party shows that there was not a negative impact. Should responsible parties still do a legitimate interest assessment? It certainly could not hurt for responsible parties to document that they considered what the impact of the processing would be on the data subject. But perhaps, in this case, the countervailing interests of the responsible party will not carry any weight if there is a negative impact on the data subject? This exercise forms part of performing a legitimate interest assessment. This was discussed in chapter 2 paragraph 2.6.3.

---

37 See principle 2(2) of the Privacy Act, available at https://www.legislation.govt.nz/act/public/2020/0031/latest/whole.html#LMS23376.

38 Case Note 4339 [2001] NZPrivCmr 2, available at https://privacy.org.nz/publications/case-notes-and-court-decisions/case-note-4339-2001-nzprivcmr-2-parents-question-why-ministry-of-education-collected-information-from-medication-register/.

39 Section 11(1)*(d)* is discussed in chapter 6 paragraph 6.3.3.

10.4.5 Collection from third-party sources required for law and order

A responsible party is entitled to collect personal information from a third-party source if this is necessary for the following purposes:

- 'to avoid prejudice to the maintenance of law by any public body' which includes the 'prevention, detection, investigation, prosecution and punishment of offences'[40]
- protecting the interest of 'national security'[41]
- complying with 'an obligation imposed by law'
- to enforce legislation concerning the collection of revenue as defined in section 1 of the South African Revenue Service Act;[42] or
- conducting 'proceedings in any court or tribunal that have commenced or are reasonably contemplated'.[43]

Tricky area: Interestingly there is no indication in section 12(2)*(d)*(iii) that the courts or tribunals need to be South African courts or tribunals. In contrast, the exception from the application of POPIA as found in section 6(1)*(e)* makes it clear that the courts that enjoy a blanket exemption from POPIA are only South African courts.[44] From this we can assume that not only local courts but also foreign courts and tribunals will enjoy an exemption from having to collect personal information directly from the data subject. Of course, there are other considerations aside from collecting personal information directly from the data subject which these courts and tribunals would have to consider, which would potentially include cross-border transfer of personal information,[45] so be careful about assuming that foreign courts and tribunals are entitled to a free-for-all.

The most important word to consider in subsection (2)*(d)* is the word 'necessary'. In chapter 6 paragraph 6.3.1 we first considered the concept of 'necessary' and the questions set out there can be amended to apply to collection from third parties as well, namely:

---

40 Section 12(2)*(d)*(i).

41 Section 12(2)*(d)*(iv).

42 Section 12(2)*(d)*(ii).

43 Section 12(2)*(d)*(iii).

44 Section 6(1)*(e)* of POPIA refers to 'a court referred to in s 166 of the South African Constitution' which naturally only refers to the establishment of South African courts. See https://www.justice.gov.za/legislation/constitution/SAConstitution-web-eng.pdf for a full list of these courts.

45 See chapter 14.

- What is the fundamental purpose(s) of the processing activity?
- Is there a way to achieve these fundamental purpose(s) without collecting this personal information from a source other than the data subject?

Information privacy principle 2(2)(e) of New Zealand's Privacy Act of 2020 is almost identical to POPIA's section 12(2)*(d)* and also includes the word 'necessary'. New Zealand's Privacy Commissioner makes the following observation: 'You don't need to be able to demonstrate that it was absolutely necessary for you to collect the information – that is, that you had no other option. However, you need to be able to explain clearly why it was reasonable to collect it for these purposes. If you can carry out your purposes easily and effectively without the information, it will be much harder to show that you really needed it.'[46]

Tricky area: A responsible party should ask whether POPIA applies to these activities at all as – as we saw in the exclusions in chapter 3 paragraph 3.3 – *some* public bodies are exempted from the whole of POPIA. However if you take a closer look at section 6(1)*(c)* of POPIA you will notice that this exception only applies, 'to the extent that adequate safeguards have been established in legislation for the protection of personal information'. By implication then, section 12(2)*(d)*(i) and (iv) assumes that adequate safeguards have **not** been established in the legislation but nonetheless still allows the collection of personal information from third parties if it is necessary and collected by a public body dealing with criminal offences or in the interests of national security.[47]

10.4.6 Collection from third party necessary to maintain the legitimate interests of the responsible party or a third party

POPIA allows a responsible party to collect personal information from a third party 'to maintain the legitimate interests of the responsible party or of a third party to whom the information is supplied'.[48] As with the 'legitimate interest' of the data subject above, determining the 'legitimate interest(s)' of the responsible party and the third party will be the product of a three-step balancing act.[49]

---

46 New Zealand Privacy Commissioner 'How do I know if collection is necessary?', available at https://privacy.org.nz/tools/knowledge-base/view/270?t=247732_339677.

47 Section 12(2)*(d)*(i).

48 Section 12(2)*(d)*(v).

49 Legitimate interest assessments are discussed in detail in chapter 2 paragraph 2.6.3.

The EU GDPR recital lists the following examples as 'legitimate interests' of a responsible party:

- processing for direct marketing purposes[50] (and the cheering begins, but keep reading ...)
- processing to prevent fraud[51]
- processing for internal administration purposes[52]
- processing for security reasons;[53] and
- processing to report criminal activity.[54]

All of these interests may justify the collection of information from other sources. However, identifying the interest is not the end of the road. The responsible party or third party will also have to show that obtaining the information from another source was necessary and that the impact on the data subject does not outweigh the responsible party or third party's interests.

Key point: Be careful not to conflate whether the collection of personal information from another source is lawful, with whether the processing itself is lawful. For instance, if a responsible party is collecting information from another source for the purpose of unsolicited electronic direct marketing, the responsible party still needs data subject consent for the 'purpose' of direct marketing regardless of whether the collection from another source is legal. Refer to chapter 16 for more about direct marketing.

10.4.7 Collection from the data subject prejudices a lawful purpose of collection

In chapter 6 we discussed determining and documenting:

- the purpose for which personal information is processed; and
- the legal justification for the processing activity (is the processing lawful).

This exception provides that a responsible party can collect personal information from another source, if collecting it from the data subject directly will undermine the lawful purpose for which the personal

50 Recital 47 of the EU GDPR.

51 Recital 47 of the EU GDPR.

52 Recital 48 of the EU GDPR.

53 Recital 49 of the EU GDPR.

54 Recital 50 of the EU GDPR.

information is required. This will often be the case where a law imposes a duty on the responsible party and requesting the information directly from the data subject could compromise that purpose (for example the data subject may lie to the responsible party).

Consider the following examples:

- An auditor has various duties towards the shareholders of the company that has employed him. These duties would include investigating any irregularity including an irregularity that while not illegal, is contrary to internal company policy. The employees at the company are unlikely to be honest with the auditor about their own misconduct. Hence, South African law allows for the concept of whistle-blowers.
- A credit provider is obliged to request a credit bureau report for a consumer (data subject) in terms of regulation 23A of the National Credit Act 34 of 2005. Although a part of this regulation has been successfully challenged on various grounds[55] it does require that bank statements and proof of income be obtained and that the credit provider take 'practical steps to validate gross income' of the consumer,[56] and regulation 23A(12) requires that the 'consumer's credit profile held by a registered credit bureau' must be considered. This is a clear indication that a third-party source must be used where the data subject is motivated to fib – in this case the data subject would downplay their monthly expenses or inflate their income in order to get a loan.
- This exception could be used to justify activities such as checking the references, degrees and criminal convictions of job applicants to ensure a fair recruitment process.

10.4.8 Compliance is not 'reasonably practicable'

A responsible party does not have to collect the personal information from the data subject if this is not 'reasonably practicable in the circumstances of the particular case'. We dealt with the concept of 'reasonably practicable' in chapter 2[57] as it occurs so many times within POPIA, and it is worth referring back to this chapter when you consider this exception.

55 See *Truworths Ltd v Minister of Trade and Industry* 2018 (3) SA 558 (WCC), which is apparently being appealed.

56 Regulation 23A(4).

57 Paragraph 2.6.2.

The concept of 'reasonably practicable' can be equated with the EU concept of 'disproportionate effort' as found in article 14(5)*(b)* of the EU GDPR.[58] While the concept of 'disproportionate effort' is still not entirely clear, we can be guided by a recent Polish decision.[59] In this case a company collected information from public sources and had to consider how to inform the data subjects that it had their personal information. It decided that sending individual emails to the data subjects would be too expensive, so instead it published the fact that it had information about the data subjects on its website. The court of first instance had to decide whether the company's argument that sending individual emails out at great cost would involve 'disproportionate effort'. The court ruled that simply publishing the details on the website was unacceptable and that individual notifications were required and as a result fined the company 220 000 Euros (about R4 million). The company appealed the matter and the appeal court partially overturned the decision for technical reasons.[60] However the key part of the appeal decision related to the question of what 'disproportionate effort' really means. The appeal court found that where compliance with the EU GDPR is required then it can only be deviated from if compliance is 'virtually impossible'.

Turning to New Zealand's Privacy Act of 2020, information privacy principle 2(2)*(f)* is identical to POPIA's section 12(2)*(f)*.[61] See the case mentioned in paragraph 10.4.1 above,[62] where the Ministry of Education obtaining a registry of medication from a child care centre was cited as an example of where it was not 'reasonably practicable' to obtain the medication list from the child as the child was too young, nor from the parents as the parents could only confirm the medication but could not confirm that the medication was actually being administered by the child care centre.[63]

---

[58] We realise that the context is slightly different. Article 14 is about the duty to notify when information was collected from sources other than the data subject. However, we think that the underlying principle is similar.

[59] Polish President of the Personal Data Protection Office on 15 March 2019, Case no: ZSPR.421.3.2018. Available at https://uodo.gov.pl/decyzje/ZSPR.421.3.2018. See also Ewa Kacperek and Weronika Wolosiuk 'First fine imposed by the Polish DPA under the EU GDPR', available at https://www.engage.hoganlovells.com/knowledgeservices/news/first-fine-imposed-by-the-polish-dpa-under-the-gdpr.

[60] See Joanna Tomaszewska 'Polish court overturns DPA's first GDPR fine' IAPP, available at https://iapp.org/news/a/polish-court-overturns-dpas-first-gdpr-fine/.

[61] See New Zealand's Privacy Act 2020, available at https://www.legislation.govt.nz/act/public/2020/0031/latest/LMS23342.html.

[62] Case Note 4339 [2001] NZPrivCmr 2; see paragraph 10.4.1 above.

[63] Case Note 4339 [2001] NZPrivCmr 2, available at https://privacy.org.nz/publications/case-notes-and-court-decisions/case-note-4339-2001-nzprivcmr-2-parents-question-why-ministry-of-education-collected-information-from-medication-register/.

It is likely that our courts will follow the approach of the EU GDPR by requiring that collection from the data subject must be 'virtually impossible' before a responsible party can rely on the exception of collection not being 'reasonably practicable'.

Tricky area: Sometimes responsible parties collect personal information from other sources, because the data subject does not have the information in question about themselves. For instance, marketers could ask us to tell them all of the locations we visited on- and offline, what our likes and dislikes are, what ads we clicked on and which emails or SMSes we opened, but on a good day we cannot remember what we had for breakfast. In these circumstances, they could argue that it is not reasonably practicable to ask a data subject to track and profile themselves.

Of course, this does not mean that they have a legal justification to track and profile; they still have to comply with section 11.

What about ongoing processing activities where collection took place before 1 July 2021? We discuss the presumption against retrospective application of POPIA in chapter 3 paragraph 3.5. Last time we checked, time travel was not yet 'reasonably practicable'. In all seriousness, the presumption against retrospective application may well mean that responsible parties who compiled databases in the past from sources other than the data subject, may continue to use those databases as long as they have a legal justification for the processing activity and they comply with the rest of POPIA.

Chapter 10

10.4.9 Exemption in respect of certain functions

If an organisation performs any of the functions in section 38 of POPIA, it does not have to comply with section 12.

Key point: This exemption only applies to public bodies[64] or to other organisations who must perform these functions 'in terms of the law'.[65] It also only applies to the extent that the function is 'performed with the view to protecting members of the public'. Therefore, the exemption would apply to regulators and statutory industry associations.

64 See the definition of 'public body' in section 1.

65 Section 38(2).

The 'relevant functions' are functions that protect members of the public against:

- financial loss due to dishonesty, malpractice or other seriously improper conduct by, or the unfitness or incompetence of, persons providing banking, insurance, investment or other financial services or the management of bodies corporate; or
- dishonesty, malpractice or other seriously improper conduct by, or the unfitness or incompetence of, persons authorised to carry on any profession or other activity.

Tricky area: What does 'performed with the view to protecting members of the public' mean? For one thing, the exemption will not apply to functions performed by a responsible party to protect itself. For instance, it will certainly cover the Financial Sector Conduct Authority when it polices compliance with the fit and proper requirements imposed on intermediaries in terms of the Financial Advisory and Intermediary Services Act (FAIS).[66] However, will it cover the collection of personal information about intermediaries from other sources so the FSCA can sell that information? Given that exemptions will be interpreted narrowly, the FSCA will only be covered for activities that are necessary for enforcing FAIS. The minute an activity is performed for purposes other than enforcing FAIS, the exemption will no longer apply.

10.5 CREATING OR GENERATING PERSONAL INFORMATION

10.5.1 What is internally generated personal information?

While responsible parties may know where they collect personal information from, one of the most common 'blind spots' for an organisation is the personal information it generates internally (in other words, it did not collect it from anyone, including the data subject). Examples of this are the search history which Google has, a data subject's shopping behaviour, or a data subject's driving patterns which are uploaded to a car insurance company. This information is clearly 'personal information' as it relates to an identifiable data subject, but quite often the data subjects themselves could not give this personal information to a responsible party as they themselves are unaware of it. Decisions or deductions made from the personal

[66] Act 37 of 2002.

information are also themselves part of the 'personal information' of the data subject.[67]

Tricky area: When personal information is created by a responsible party, we do not believe that section 12 applies, because it is not 'collected'. However, if we are wrong and section 12 does apply, the responsible party could rely on section 12(2)*(f)* given that it is not reasonably practicable to 'collect' the information from the data subject. Another (somewhat creepy) argument could be that the responsible party is collecting the personal information from the data subject by observing or surveilling the data subject.

Consider the example of Jon Snow applying for a loan. Here are the different streams of personal information involved in the credit provider's loan approval processes:

Jon Snow provides personal information to the credit provider, such as his ID number, address, income and expenses, and FICA documentation.	The personal information is sourced from the data subject directly. The credit provider is complying with section 12 of POPIA.
The credit provider verifies the information and requests further information from a credit bureau, including a credit profile of Jon Snow.	The credit provider is using the credit bureau to verify information and to obtain a credit profile. The credit bureau sources this information from other credit providers, public records and other sources. The credit provider is obtaining information from a source other than the data subject and must therefore determine whether any of the exceptions in section 12(2) apply. If none of them apply, this collection method is illegal. As we discussed above, a credit provider is required by the National Credit Act (NCA) to perform an affordability assessment. As long as the information it receives from the credit bureau is related to compliance with the NCA and there is no over-collection, the credit provider can rely on section 12(2)*(e)*.[68] The credit provider could also potentially rely on section 12(2)*(d)*(v).[69]

67 See chapter 3 paragraph 3.2 for a detailed discussion of what constitutes personal information. See chapter 15 for a discussion on profiling and automated decision-making.

68 This was discussed in paragraph 10.4.7.

69 This was discussed in paragraph 10.4.6.

<table>
<tr>
<td></td>
<td>Tricky area: Data broking and credit bureaus have always been a hotly debated topic in privacy circles. This will be discussed in chapter 13.</td>
</tr>
<tr>
<td>The credit provider takes the information provided by Jon Snow and the credit bureau and applies its own algorithm to the information in order to generate a risk profile of Jon Snow.

This risk profile is used by the credit provider to make a decision about whether to grant a loan or not, the amount of the loan and other commercial terms.</td>
<td>Through analysis, the credit provider has created new personal information about Jon Snow (the risk profile) to make a series of decisions. The outcome of those decisions (whether to grant a loan and on what terms) is personal information relating to Jon Snow. This new information about Jon Snow is not 'collected', it is created and therefore section 12 may not apply.

Key point: While section 12 may not apply, the rest of POPIA will. So, it is essential to ensure that responsible parties are aware of internally generated personal information and that it forms part of their POPIA Programme.

If the decisions are 'automated' section 71 of POPIA will apply, because these decisions have legal consequences for Jon Snow which will affect him to a substantial degree and which are based on a profile created about his credit worthiness. Automated decision-making is discussed in chapter 15.</td>
</tr>
</table>

While section 12 might not apply, it is crucial to consider the rest of POPIA when personal information is generated by an organisation. This information is often incredibly comprehensive and sensitive. In fact, in some instances large corporations know more about us than we know about ourselves. Consider for a moment that Cambridge Analytica, the firm investigated in the documentary *The Great Hack* claimed to have 5 000 data points on over 220 million Americans and used that information to change the way in which Americans voted. The following statement by Christopher Wylie, the whistle-blower at the heart of the scandal, to the journalist who exposed Cambridge Analytica, Carole Cadwalladr:[70] 'I think that, yes, this was a grossly unethical experiment. You are playing with the psychology of an entire nation without their consent or awareness. And not only, like, are you playing with the psychology of an entire nation. You are playing with the psychology of an entire nation in the context of the democratic process.'

Given the amount of influence this 'generated' personal information gives organisations and the resources they expend to create proprietary algorithms to create it, it is not surprising that a fight is brewing for ownership and control over this information. That is what the next section is about.

10.5.2 Ownership of personal information generated by organisations

Before POPIA, personal information was considered to be an asset which could be sold and exploited as the organisation wished. POPIA changes this by inserting various restrictions on the 'assets' of the organisation and so POPIA has indirectly restricted the intellectual property rights of organisations over 'assets' that use personal information.[71]

The importance of this change should not be underestimated. These days, information is often more valuable than physical property. Therefore it is important to know who owns information. Many see data as the 'new oil'. Clive Humby, a British mathematician, first used the phrase in 2006 as follows:

> 'Data is the new oil. It's valuable, but unrefined it cannot really be used. It has to be changed into gas, plastic, chemicals, etc. to create a valuable entity that drives profitable activity; so data must be broken down, analyzed for it to have value.'[72]

Chapter 10

---

70 This excerpt is from Netflix's *The Great Hack*. See https://www.theguardian.com/uk-news/2019/jul/20/the-great-hack-cambridge-analytica-scandal-facebook-netflix.

71 We have witnessed borderline violent exchanges on LinkedIn on the question of who 'owns' personal information. We have no desire for death threats, but fortune favours the brave. For some deep thinking about this topic see https://royalsociety.org/-/media/policy/projects/data-governance/data-ownership-rights-and-controls-October-2018.pdf.

72 Concepta 'Refining the "new oil": The importance of putting data to work', available at https://www.conceptatech.com/blog/refining-new-oil-importance-putting-data-work.

Many commentators and institutions, including the World Economic Forum, disagree with this analogy.[73] Data and oil differ in a number of ways including that oil is a finite resource, whereas data is infinitely durable and can be re-used. Data becomes more useful as it is used and processed, whereas oil loses its energy with heat or light. But, similarly to oil, data gives power to those who control it. Unregulated data-mining by big organisations means that those organisations continue to grow in power, and the imbalance between organisations and individuals escalates. Laws, like POPIA, aim to give data subjects back some power over their own personal information, by limiting what organisations can do with the information and giving data subjects the right to access their personal information.

The ownership of personal information came to the fore in the case of *Discovery Ltd v Liberty Group Ltd*,[74] where it was common cause that a Vitality member's Vitality status does not form part of Discovery's confidential, proprietary information. Instead it is the members' personal information, and Vitality members are free to make it public, and to disclose it to Liberty. However, the underlying science, proprietary algorithms, data and modelling that underpin the Vitality programme, and which are used to determine members' Vitality status, are confidential information and proprietary to Discovery,[75] and protected by the Copyright Act.[76]

If you expand this reasoning to data brokers, there is a good argument that the actual datasets could only be sold with the data subject's consent as data subjects own their individual records. We discuss data brokers in chapter 13.

Tricky area: Do not confuse data protection rights associated with personal information of a data subject with the intellectual property rights that the responsible party may have. It is perfectly possible for the responsible party to have significant intellectual property rights in the deductions it makes based on a data subject's personal information while at the same time being forced to disclose these to a data subject on request.

73 Adam Schlosser (WEF) 'You may have heard data is the new oil. It's not', available at https://www.weforum.org/agenda/2018/01/data-is-not-the-new-oil/.

74 2020 (4) SA 160 (GJ).

75 *Discovery Ltd v Liberty Group Ltd* 2020 (4) SA 160 (GJ) paragraph 68.

76 Section 2 of the Copyright Act 98 of 1978.

Remember that it is also possible for a computer to generate personal information without there being any human intervention whatsoever. We consider profiling and automated decisions in more detail in chapter 15.

10.6 SOME TYPICAL CASE STUDIES

10.6.1 Web-scraping

The practice of 'web-scraping' or trawling through the internet is a popular method of collecting personal information, because it can be done by means of computer tools such as HTML parsing or Google Sheets.

At a high level when you scrape the internet there are other legal considerations to take into account other than POPIA, including the following:

- The scraping breaches the copyright of the owner.
- The scraping breaches the terms and conditions of the website.
- The scraping bypasses technical controls and so amounts to 'hacking'.[77]

A responsible party could argue that the personal information has been deliberately made public by the data subject (section 12(2)*(a)*). As we point out in paragraph 10.4.2 above a responsible party cannot simply assume that the data subject intended to make their personal information public; the responsible party has to prove it. This means that pure web-scraping without any further restrictions or parameters is almost certainly illegal. An example of a parameter or restriction is to only scrape websites where the responsible party has confirmed that the personal information is deliberately made public by the data subjects.

While the collection of the personal information by scraping information from public sources or from information deliberately made public is clearly possible in terms of section 12 of POPIA, the question then remains as to what the lawful purpose would be that the responsible web-scraper would use it for (see chapter 6 or chapter 7 if the personal information being collected is special personal information or the personal information of a child). The information serves no purpose if it can be collected but the responsible party does not have a legal justification for using it.

Chapter 10

---

77 See section 86 of the Electronic Communications and Transactions Act. See https://www.gov.za/sites/default/files/gcis_document/201409/a25-02.pdf. This is soon to be replaced in South Africa by the Cybercrimes Act 19 of 2020.

One of the most famous examples of 'screen scraping' is Clearview AI that managed to pull together a database of 3 billion images which it then plugged into its artificial intelligence engine to create one of the most comprehensive surveillance tools available. The US company has come to the attention of the European Parliament and it seems likely that this practice will be declared illegal by the EU.[78]

Tricky area: Scraping social media platforms is one of the reasons why you often see stories in the news about large data breaches involving LinkedIn, Facebook or other social media platforms.[79] This is a breach of the terms of use of the social media platforms, but is it also a breach of POPIA?[80] Not if the scraper can successfully argue that the collection falls within one of the exemptions we discussed above.

10.6.2 Cookies

Scraping the web is not the only way in which personal information is harvested off the internet. Cookies and similar tracking technologies are used to track data subjects when they browse the internet and to build data subjects' profiles over time, so their interests can be matched to the advertisements they are shown on different websites.[81] Behavioural advertising is driven by the data subject's personal information such as their browsing history, online transactions, purchase history and login information.[82] In the vast majority of cases online behavioural advertising involves the use of cookies, or similar tracking technologies.

---

78 See https://www.europarl.europa.eu/doceo/document/E-9-2020-000491_EN.html.

79 For example, see Business Insider 'Personal data of 1.3m Clubhouse users leaked online after LinkedIn and Facebook also suffered data breaches', available at https://www.businessinsider.co.za/clubhouse-data-leak-1-million-users-2021-4.

80 See Facebook 'How we combat scraping', available at https://about.fb.com/news/2021/04/how-we-combat-scraping/.

81 Article 29 Data Protection Working Party 'Opinion 2/2010 on online behavioral advertising', available at https://ec.europa.eu/justice/article-29/documentation/opinion-recommendation/files/2010/wp171_en.pdf.

82 ICO 'Direct marketing code of practice: Draft code for consultation' at 87 available at https://ico.org.uk/media/about-the-ico/consultations/2616882/direct-marketing-code-draft-guidance.pdf.

Tricky area: While we were writing this book the world was becoming a very hostile place for cookies. Privacy activists decided to take IAB Tech labs to court about real-time bidding, calling it an ongoing data breach.[83] The Apple iOS 14.5 update included an 'app tracking transparency feature' which requires applications to ask for consent before they can track users across other applications and websites.[84] The verdict? Not surprisingly, the vast majority of people do not want to be tracked.[85] And, Google announced the end of third-party cookies (at some point in the near future).[86] But just saying that cookies are evil, is an unnuanced view. As we have become accustomed to when thinking about POPIA, there are competing interests to be balanced here. In short, the price for having free access to all the information on the internet is our privacy. But, increasingly, this 'choice' is becoming intolerable:[87]

> 'It's difficult to conceive of the internet we know today – with information on every topic, in every language, at the fingertips of billions of people – without advertising as its economic foundation. But as our industry has strived to deliver relevant ads to consumers across the web, it has created a proliferation of individual user data across thousands of companies, typically gathered through third-party cookies. This has led to an erosion of trust: In fact, 72% of people feel that almost all of what they do online is being tracked by advertisers, technology firms and other companies, and 81% say that the potential risks they face because of data collection outweigh the benefits, according to a study by Pew Research Center. If digital advertising does not evolve to address the growing concerns people have about their privacy and how their personal identity is being used, we risk the future of the free and open web.'

Chapter 10

83 For information about the complaint, see the press release on the website of the Irish Council for Civil Liberties, available here: https://www.iccl.ie/rtb-june-2021/#press and Natasha Lomas 'Adtech "data breach" GDPR complaint is headed to court in EU' *Tech Crunch*, available at https://techcrunch.com/2021/06/16/adtech-data-breach-gdpr-complaint-is-headed-to-court-in-eu/.

84 For a nice explanation see Alex Hern 'Apple iOS 14.5 update includes "app tracking transparency" feature', *The Guardian*, available at https://www.theguardian.com/technology/2021/apr/27/apple-ios-145-update-includes-app-tracking-transparency-feature.

85 See the weekly numbers generated by Flurry (a division of Verizon), here: https://www.flurry.com/blog/ios-14-5-opt-in-rate-idfa-app-tracking-transparency-weekly/.

86 See Google's own explanation, available at https://blog.google/products/ads-commerce/a-more-privacy-first-web/.

87 See Google's own explanation, available at https://blog.google/products/ads-commerce/a-more-privacy-first-web/. Also see the results of a 2019 Amnesty International poll, which surveyed nearly 10 000 people across nine countries and showed that 71% of those surveyed worried about how tech companies (such as Google) collected and used their personal information (Amnesty International

So, it seems that cookies are on their way out, but in the meantime we need to answer the question, 'What does POPIA mean for third-party cookies?' That is what the remainder of this section is about.

10.6.2.1 Why are they called cookies?

Obviously, the most important thing to understand is why they are called cookies. It is short for 'magic cookie', which is a reference to fortune cookies[88] – 'a cookie with an embedded message'.[89]

10.6.2.2 What are cookies?

Back to basics. A cookie is a small text file that is downloaded onto 'terminal equipment' (e.g. a computer or smartphone) when the user accesses a website. It allows the website to recognise that user's device and store some information about the user's preferences or past actions.[90]

Cookies store user-specific information for a variety of purposes such as enabling the data subject to stay logged in to a website, to enable a website to recognise a data subject when they log in at a later date and storing the data subject's preferences, e.g. what language they prefer.[91] While cookies are used to make websites function better and enhance the 'user experience' through remembering preferences, the information they collect is often also used for marketing purposes. Some cookies store and transmit a data subject's personal information in an anonymised format, and some do not.

Key point: Many cookies will be relatively harmless from a privacy perspective. Let's not throw the cookies out with the bathwater!

'New poll reveals 7 in 10 people want governments to regulate Big Tech over personal data fears', available at https://www.amnesty.org/en/latest/news/2019/12/big-tech-privacy-poll-shows-people-worried/).

88 We were disappointed too.

89 For this and other interesting internet etymology see https://www.inlife.co.uk/why-are-cookies-called-cookies/.

90 The ICO 'Cookies and similar technologies' available at https://ico.org.uk/for-organisations/guide-to-pecr/cookies-and-similar-technologies/.

91 Rocketlawyer 'What are cookies?' https://www.rocketlawyer.com/gb/en/quick-guides/different-types-of-internet-cookies.

Here are some examples of types of cookies:

- **First-party cookies:** These cookies are stored by the website domain which the data subject is using directly. First-party cookies only track and store information about that data subject in relation to that website.[92] Sometimes they are temporary cookies which will store a data subject's information for as long as they are using the website – i.e. once the session is closed, these cookies get deleted. These 'session cookies' are often used by e-commerce websites to remember a data subject's activities there.[93] Session cookies can also be used by websites to provide security that is essential to comply with information security requirements for an online service the user has requested e.g. online banking.[94]
- **Second-party cookies:** This is not a thing.[95]
- **Third-party cookies:** These cookies are stored by a third party on the website which the data subject is using. For example, YouTube third-party cookies that are embedded on an e-commerce website. These cookies will then relay information about the data subject's activity on the e-commerce website to YouTube, so that YouTube can target advertisements and videos to the data subject that are in line with their preferences.[96] Third-party cookies are the ones used most heavily for online behavioural advertising, because these cookies track a data subject's activities across different websites and generate targeted ads

92 CookiePro Knowledgebase 'What's the Difference Between First and Third-Party Cookies' available at https://www.cookiepro.com/knowledge/whats-the-difference-between-first-and-third-party-cookies/.

93 CookiePro Knowledgebase 'What's the Difference Between First and Third-Party Cookies' available at https://www.cookiepro.com/knowledge/whats-the-difference-between-first-and-third-party-cookies/.

94 The ICO 'Cookies and similar technologies' available at https://ico.org.uk/for-organisations/guide-to-pecr/cookies-and-similar-technologies/.

95 Well, technically the second party is the data subject. Information provided by the data subject is sometimes referred to as 'zero-party data'. It is different from first-party data, which is information. that is collected as a customer interacts with a marketer on its website and other communication channels. With zero party data 'customers willingly give brands more insight into their preferences and future needs in exchange for a better and more personalised experience'. See Alex Leicester 'Third-party cookies have gone stale. First-party data is the new secret ingredient' *The Drum*, available at https://www.thedrum.com/profile/acquia/news/third-party-cookies-have-gone-stale-first-party-data-is-the-new-secret-ingredient.

96 CookiePro Knowledgebase 'What's the difference between first and third-party cookies', available at https://www.cookiepro.com/knowledge/whats-the-difference-between-first-and-third-party-cookies/.

based on that data subject's preferences. As a result, these cookies can contain significant amounts of personal information about the data subject's online activity, preferences, and location.[97]

10.6.2.3 Does POPIA even apply?

Is the information slurped up by cookies personal information? As with any other activity or process, POPIA only applies when you process personal information. Personal information includes any information relating to an identifiable person, and includes location information and online identifiers.[98] Online identifiers include IP addresses, cookie identifiers, radio frequency identification (RFID) tags, tracking pixels, device fingerprints, MAC addresses, advertising IDs and account handles.[99] These are the types of personal information that cookies collect. However, POPIA will only apply if the responsible party collects:[100]

- enough information to identify the data subject
- information that can be linked by a reasonably foreseeable method to other information that identifies the data subject; or
- information that can be used or manipulated by a reasonably foreseeable method to identify the data subject.

Recital 30 of the GDPR deals specifically with online identifiers and states that data subjects 'may be associated with online identifiers provided by their devices, applications, tools and protocols, such as internet protocol addresses, cookie identifiers or other identifiers such as radio frequency identification tags. This may leave traces which, when combined with unique identifiers and other information received by the servers, may be used to create profiles of the natural persons and identify them.'

Let's apply this test to dynamic internet protocol (IP) addresses. They are a set of numbers which changes for every

---

97 EU GDPR 'Cookies, the GDPR, and the ePrivacy Directive' available at https://gdpr.eu/cookies/.

98 The definition of personal information in section 1 of POPIA.

99 Recital 30 of the EU GDPR and the Guide to the UK GDPR, available at https://ico.org.uk/for-organisations/guide-to-data-protection/guide-to-the-general-data-protection-regulation-gdpr/what-is-personal-data/what-are-identifiers-and-related-factors/.

100 We discuss the application of POPIA in chapter 3.

session – hence the 'dynamic'. This IP address is randomly assigned to the user by their internet service provider (ISP) and so only the ISP would be able to reverse engineer this and see who they assigned it to at a particular date and time. In a 2016 judgment by the Court of Justice of the European Union it was held that dynamic IP addresses are personal data in the hands of a website operator if:

- there is another party (e.g. an ISP) that can link the dynamic IP address to the identity of a data subject; and
- the website operator has a 'legal means' of obtaining access to the information held by the ISP in order to identify the data subject.[101]

Key point: This test can be used to assess whether POPIA applies to the personal information collected by a cookie. It is an example of the test for whether personal information is 'identifiable' which we discussed in chapter 3.

10.6.2.4 How to justify using cookies to collect personal information

POPIA does not deal with cookies or similar technologies directly as it aims to be technology-neutral. Neither does the Electronic Communications and Transactions Act.[102] Therefore, the legal requirements for using cookies in a South African context are still uncertain. What is certain, is that if the cookies collect and process personal information in an identified or identifiable format, POPIA will apply.

How does section 12 apply to the use of cookies (and other tracking technology for that matter)? When a responsible party(s)[103] uses third-party cookies to collect personal information via another website, they are collecting personal information from a source other than the data subject

---

[101] Case 582/14 – *Patrick Breyer v Germany* available at https://curia.europa.eu/juris/document/document.jsf?text=&docid=184668&pageIndex=0&doclang=en.

[102] Act 25 of 2002.

[103] It is not always easy to tell who the responsible party is. Website owners will probably be surprised to learn that they might be co-responsible parties with Google and Facebook when they make use of their third-party cookies. We discuss accountability in chapter 4. Also see European Data Protection Board *Guidelines 8/2020 on the Targeting of Social Media Users*, 10ff, available at https://edpb.europa.eu/sites/default/files/consultation/edpb_guidelines_202008_onthetargetingofsocialmediausers_en.pdf.

themselves. Which of the exemptions to section 12(1) can be used to justify this? This will depend on the type of cookies we are talking about:

- First-party cookies: The owner of the website is collecting the information directly from the data subject.
- Third-party cookies: The owner of the website is collecting the information directly from the data subject, but is then sharing the personal information with a third party.[104] So, while the website owner is complying with section 12(1), the third party is not. Which one of the exemptions can be used to justify this? The only exemption that appears to apply here is that it is in the legitimate interest of the responsible party or a third party to whom the information is supplied.[105] This is discussed in paragraph 10.4.6.

Tricky area: The European Data Protection Board states that it does not consider legitimate interest as an appropriate legal basis for the processing of personal information in regard to cookies in their Guideline.[106] The reason given for this, is that here the use of cookies can involve the monitoring of individuals' behaviour across websites and locations using tracking technologies.[107]

---

104 As we discussed in paragraph 10.5.1 above, suggesting that personal information be collected through surveilling the data subject (as opposed to asking them) is a bit creepy.

105 Section 12(2)*(d)*(v).

106 European Data Protection Board 'Guidelines 8/2020 on the targeting of social media users' at paras 71–72 available at https://edpb.europa.eu/our-work-tools/public-consultations-art-704/2020/guidelines-082020-targeting-social-media-users_en.

107 European Data Protection Board 'Guidelines 8/2020 on the targeting of social media users' at paras 71–72 available at https://edpb.europa.eu/our-work-tools/public-consultations-art-704/2020/guidelines-082020-targeting-social-media-users_en.

This is considered too invasive on the data subject's right to privacy to be justified on the grounds of legitimate interest of the responsible party for processing.[108] Of course, the European Data Protection Board was talking about the legal justification for using the information gathered by the third-party cookie for targeting data subjects, and not whether the indirect collection is justified. Remember that the EU GDPR does not have the equivalent of section 12. In addition, the use of cookies in the EU is regulated by the ePrivacy Directive (for now).[109] In other words, the regulations that apply to cookies in the EU is stricter than POPIA.

Bear in mind that even if the responsible party is justified in collecting personal information about a data subject using third-party cookies, they must still have a legal justification for using that personal information or sharing that information with third parties. Aaaand in come the ubiquitous cookie banners.[110]

[108] European Data Protection Board 'Guidelines 8/2020 on the targeting of social media users' at paras 71–72 available at https://edpb.europa.eu/our-work-tools/public-consultations-art-704/2020/guidelines-082020-targeting-social-media-users_en.

[109] Directive 2002/58/EC of the European Parliament and of the Council of 12 July 2002 concerning the processing of personal data and the protection of privacy in the electronic communications sector (Directive on privacy and electronic communications), available at https://eur-lex.europa.eu/legal-content/EN/TXT/PDF/?uri=CELEX:32002L0058&from=EN. The ePrivacy Directive was supposed to have been replaced by the ePrivacy Regulation, but at the time of publication negotiations were still ongoing. The Proposal for a Regulation of the European Parliament and of the Council concerning the respect for private life and the protection of personal data in electronic communications and repealing Directive 2002/58/EC (Regulation on Privacy and Electronic Communication), is available at https://eur-lex.europa.eu/legal-content/EN/TXT/?uri=CELEX%3A52017PC0010.

[110] Remember our hatred of privacy notices (see chapter 2 paragraph 2.6.4)? We feel even more strongly about cookie banners. For a fun discussion on consent fatigue see Milovan Jovicic 'UX blindspot: Cookie diabetes and consent fatigue' *UX Collective*, available at https://uxdesign.cc/ux-blindspot-cookie-diabetes-and-consent-fatigue-d53220292a0a. We discussed dark patterns and how people are not really in control of their (privacy) decisions in chapter 2 paragraph 2.6.5.

Tricky area: Does POPIA require that the data subject must consent to the use of cookies on a website before browsing? POPIA does not say anything about cookies; much less that responsible parties need consent to use them. Whether a responsible party needs consent or whether they can rely on 'legitimate interest' depends on the type of cookie, what personal information is harvested, who the information is shared with and what the personal information that is being harvested is going to be used for.[111] We discuss legal justification in chapters 6 and 7. If the personal information is going to be shared with third parties and used for a purpose other than what the personal information was collected for, the rules relating to further processing might apply and consent could be required.[112]

What is clear is that website owners will have to be transparent about what cookies are being used and what the personal information they are harvesting will be used for. Hiding this information in a website privacy notice or cookie notice without bringing it to the attention of the data subject will probably not be enough if the cookies being used are significant, so cookie banners are here to stay.[113] Notification is discussed in chapter 11.

10.7 PRACTICAL ADVICE

10.7.1 Map! Map! Map!

At a high level each responsible party should have a written record which shows:

- all the collection points of personal information (data subject, third party, internal)

[111] The trend with regard to tracking technology is towards consent. See European Data Protection Board 'Guidelines 8/2020 on the targeting of social media users' 20ff, available at https://edpb.europa.eu/our-work-tools/public-consultations-art-704/2020/guidelines-082020-targeting-social-media-users_en. Just be careful, while POPIA and the EU GDPR may be similar, South Africa does not have the equivalent of the ePrivacy Directive.

[112] Further processing is discussed in chapter 12.

[113] But we probably still will not read them. Who has the time?

Key point: A responsible party that does not know the source of the personal information will find it difficult to demonstrate compliance with section 12. In addition, a data subject is entitled to information about where a responsible party got their personal information from (but there are some exceptions to this rule).[114]

- where personal information is not collected directly from the data subject, the exception(s) the responsible party relies on to collect the personal information from another source
- a record of any assessment that was performed to establish which exception applies (i.e. a personal information impact assessment); and
- a record of all of the decisions made by the responsible party and the information that the decision-makers took into account (e.g. that collecting information directly from the data subject was not 'reasonably practicable').

It is not always easy to identify the ingress points of personal information, particularly if the responsible party has not mapped all its processes. It could be useful to associate metadata with personal information when it is collected. In essence this means that as personal information moves around the organisation it remains associated with a number of different POPIA 'records', which include where it came from, its purpose, any consent provided, when it would be due to be deleted and so forth.

Key point: Data flow mapping and retaining metadata as a means of documenting compliance is discussed in chapter 1 paragraph 1.4. It is also discussed as part of performing personal information assessments in chapter 20 paragraph 20.3.

10.7.2 What to do about cookies

As always, the first step is to move away from unconscious incompetence to conscious incompetence. All too many information officers and deputy information officers do not even know what cookies their organisation is using, much less what they are used for.

[114] Section 18(1)*(a)*. This is discussed in chapter 11.

Once you have identified which cookies are in use, determine whether the responsible party is actually using the personal information they collect and what they are using it for. Remember the principle of minimality?[115] If the personal information is not used, the cookie should be removed and the personal information purged.

Key point: There are some very useful guidelines out there on how to use cookies in a compliant way. We particularly like the ICO's *Guidance on the Use of Cookies and Similar Technologies*.[116] However, tread carefully. The European rules on cookies are stricter (or at least more specific) than POPIA.

115 See chapter 9.

116 Available at https://ico.org.uk/for-organisations/guide-to-pecr/guidance-on-the-use-of-cookies-and-similar-technologies/how-do-we-comply-with-the-cookie-rules/.

11

Notification to data subjects

11.1 WHAT TO EXPECT IN THIS CHAPTER

When we discuss the principles of openness and transparency, we are always reminded of this quote by Douglas Adams: 'Let us prepare to grapple with the ineffable itself, and see if we may not eff it after all.'[1] Or, in the words of the SA Law Reform Commission: '[E]ven the most comprehensive measures for protecting information are worthless if the individual does not have [such] knowledge.'[2]

Tricky area: Before we start, we would like to come clean. We dream of a world without privacy notices. Why do we say that? We are extremely sceptical about privacy regulations that are predicated on the notion that data subjects will be more protected as long as there is transparency, and they are given back control over their personal information. We wrote about what we call the myth of control and choice in chapter 2 paragraph 2.6. Instead, we dream of a world where organisations behave ethically when it comes to privacy by default, even when no one is watching.

This chapter focuses on when and how responsible parties need to notify the data subject about the personal information they have and how they process it.

---

1 The full quote is 'Let's think the unthinkable, let's do the undoable. Let us prepare to grapple with the ineffable itself, and see if we may not eff it after all.' (Douglas Adams *Dirk Gently's Holistic Detective Agency* (1987)) 'Ineffable' is defined as 'too great or extreme to be expressed or described in words'. (Oxford Dictionaries) We cannot think of a better word to describe what some organisations do with personal information.

2 SA Law Reform Commission Project 124 on Privacy and Data Protection (2009 Report) paragraph 4.2.199.

In this chapter we discuss the following:

- About the condition of openness
- What do responsible parties need to disclose?
- When the notification should be made
- How the notification should happen
- Exceptions to the notification duty
- A comparison between POPIA and PAIA notification requirements
- Trust marks, privacy seals and POPIA certification

11.2 ABOUT THE CONDITION OF OPENNESS

One of the major themes of POPIA is the promotion of transparency. This is achieved through the condition of openness (sections 17 and 18), which require that data subjects must be informed when their personal information is collected. In addition, responsible parties are required to keep a record of all processing activities for which they are responsible.[3]

Section 17 of POPIA deals with a responsible party's duty to document all processing activities as required by sections 14 or 51 of PAIA, which in turn require that each responsible party publish a manual with a fair amount of information about all its processing 'operations'.[4] As you will see in paragraph 11.7 below, the notification duty in the PAIA manual (as amended by POPIA) and the notification duty in section 18 are sufficiently different for it to be impractical to only have a PAIA manual.

The majority of this chapter is focused on section 18 which sets out the what, how, when, why and who of notification.

[3] Determining who the 'responsible party' is, is discussed in chapter 4.

[4] See chapter 1 paragraph 1.4 for a more general overview of documenting compliance with POPIA.

11.3 WHAT DO RESPONSIBLE PARTIES NEED TO DISCLOSE?

11.3.1 The disclosures responsible parties must make

Here is a list of the disclosures which responsible parties must make:

What organisations must be transparent about	What this means
The information[5] being collected	This sounds easy. However, many organisations do not have a reliable record of what personal information they collect. Mapping data flows can be of assistance here, because it forces organisations to record what personal information is obtained from which sources.[6] A good place to start is to review all of the paper and electronic forms used to collect personal information. But that really is just the start. Most organisations also obtain personal information from sources other than the data subject and generate even more personal information about the data subject.[7]
The source from which information is collected	Not all information is collected from data subjects directly. We wrote about when it will be legal to collect information from other sources in chapter 10. What this requires is that organisations know and keep a record of the provenance of the personal information they have.

5 It is a bit strange that section 18 refers to 'information' and not 'personal information', but we would not read too much into it.

6 We mention data flow mapping for the first time in chapter 1 paragraph 1.4 as one of the ways in which compliance with POPIA can be documented.

7 The collection and creation of personal information was discussed in chapter 10.

What organisations must be transparent about	What this means
	Tricky area: Tracing and keeping track of the source of personal information will be new to many responsible parties. What if the responsible party does not know where the information came from? This could be the case if the responsible party used various sources to compile its dataset.[8] If it is truly impossible (not just difficult and time consuming), the responsible party could provide the data subject with general information describing the various sources.[9] We discuss the various exceptions to the notification obligation in paragraph 11.6 below.
The name and address of the responsible party	It is important to make an email address, telephone number and other channels available for data subjects to contact the responsible party if they need more information or if they want to exercise their rights. These rights are discussed in chapter 18. Identifying who the responsible party is, is discussed in chapter 4. Section 18(1)*(b)* does not require that the name and contact details of the information officer must be disclosed. However, this is a requirement in PAIA.[10]

8 This possibility is mentioned specifically in recital 61 of the EU GDPR.

9 Guidelines on Transparency under Regulation 2016/679 (wp260rev.01) 29 paragraph 60, available at https://ec.europa.eu/newsroom/article29/item-detail.cfm?item_id=622227.

10 The Promotion of Access to Information Act 2 of 2000 as amended by POPIA requires the details of the information officer of a public body (section 14(1)*(a)*(ii)) and the 'head' of a private body which is the information officer (section 51(1)*(a)*(i)) to be included in an organisation's PAIA manual. The identity and role of the information officer is discussed in chapter 1 paragraph 1.3.5.

What organisations must be transparent about	What this means
	Of course, data subjects should not have a direct line to the information officer; this email address or telephone number can be manned by other employees. However, the information officer is responsible for seeing to it that the responsible party has an adequate 'system to process requests'.[11] This is discussed in chapter 18.
The purpose(s) for which the information is being collected	Purpose specification was discussed in chapter 6 paragraph 6.2. The purpose must be specific and explicitly defined.[12] This means that the purpose cannot be vague, e.g. 'for commercial purposes'.
Whether the supply of the personal information by that data subject is voluntary or mandatory	Typically, the personal information that is mandatory on an online form is designated with a * to show that it must be filled in. In this context 'mandatory' means not only as required by law but also if the process cannot continue without that field of personal information being filled in. For instance, a credit provider may refuse to accept an application for a loan if a specific piece of personal information (such as how long the data subject has been employed) is essential information to its internal loan application calculations. Even when it is voluntary for the data subject to provide the information, the organisation must still have a purpose for collecting the personal information. For example, the voluntary personal information could be used for statistical purposes or for additional services or functionality. Often personal information that is voluntarily provided enhances the user's experience of the website and allows for personalisation of services (such as suggesting which movies they are more likely to enjoy).

➡

11 Regulation 4(1)*(d)* of the POPIA Regulations.

12 Section 13(1).

What organisations must be transparent about	What this means
	Tricky area: Responsible parties must always adhere to the principle of minimality; they cannot collect personal information that is not required for a specified purpose. This means that responsible parties cannot collect personal information (on a voluntary or mandatory basis) 'just in case we need it in future'.[13]
The consequences of failure to provide the information	The consequences of providing (or not providing) the personal information must be spelled out.[14] For instance, if not providing voluntary personal information will limit the services the responsible party renders in some way, data subjects must be made aware of that. Logically the failure to provide the mandatory personal information should make it impossible to proceed with the processing activity (which is why the personal information is 'mandatory').
Any law authorising or requiring the collection of the information	Compiling a compliance universe[15] for a responsible party is essential, not just to comply with this section, but also to determine when there is a legal basis for processing personal information and to determine for how long personal information must be retained.[16]

13 The principle of minimality is discussed in chapter 9.

14 Section 18(1)*(d)*.

15 See the definition of 'compliance universe' in the Compliance Institute of South Africa's Generally Accepted Compliance Practice (GACP) Framework. We discussed compiling a compliance universe (sometimes referred to as a regulatory compliance universe) in chapter 1 paragraph 1.2.2.

16 See chapters 1, 6 and 17 for more about this.

What organisations must be transparent about	What this means
	There is some similarity between the requirements of section 18(1)*(f)* of POPIA and the PAIA manual as the PAIA manual requires that responsible parties describe all the records that are available in terms of other legislation.[17]
The fact that the responsible party intends to transfer the information to another country or international organisation and the level of protection afforded to the information by that third country or international organisation.[18]	How specific must the notification be? Does the responsible party name all the countries they send personal information to, and what happens when those countries change? The Article 29 Data Protection Working Party's guidelines on transparency in the context of the EU GDPR recommend that the disclosure should be as meaningful as possible, 'this will generally mean that the third countries will be named'.[19] The next question is how to disclose the 'level of protection' afforded by that country or international organisation. Is this just the responsible party's opinion on their data protection laws? It is best practice for responsible parties to disclose whether that country has a data protection law and where to access it, where to find the international organisation's privacy notice and any agreement that the third party has agreed to, to respect data protection rights.[20]

➡

17 The Promotion of Access to Information Act 2 of 2000 as amended by POPIA in section 51(1)*(b)*(iii)) for private bodies. Curiously this same requirement is absent from section 14, but in practice this information is included in the PAIA manual for public bodies. For example, see the Department of Home Affairs PAIA manual at http://www.dha.gov.za/index.php/about-us/home-affairs-today/36-paia/148-paia-manual.

18 Transborder information flows are discussed in chapter 14.

19 Guidelines on Transparency under Regulation 2016/679 (wp260rev.01) 38, available at https://ec.europa.eu/newsroom/article29/item-detail.cfm?item_id=622227. Transborder information flows are discussed in chapter 14.

20 Guidelines on Transparency under Regulation 2016/679 (wp260rev.01) 38, available at https://ec.europa.eu/newsroom/article29/item-detail.cfm?item_id=622227. Transborder information flows is discussed in chapter 14.

What organisations must be transparent about	What this means
A general description allowing a preliminary assessment of the suitability of the information security measures to be implemented by the responsible party to ensure the confidentiality, integrity and availability of the information which is to be processed.	**Key point:** You will not find this in section 18(1) of POPIA. That is because it was introduced in an amendment to sections 14(2)*(v)* and 51(2)*(v)* of PAIA.[21] Organisations' responsibilities in respect of information security management and the role of confidentiality, integrity and availability are discussed in chapter 5.

➥

[21] Schedule to POPIA.

What organisations must be transparent about	What this means
	Tricky area: This notification obligation requires that responsible parties disclose some of the steps they will take to manage information security. The question is how far must they go? The formulation of the subsection indicates that enough information must be given that data subjects or other requesters[22] can do a 'preliminary assessment of the suitability' of the information security measures. Given that most organisations consider the technical and operational measures they take to secure information confidential (with good reason),[23] most will be loath to publish specifics that would allow for any meaningful assessment. Having said that, organisations could consider disclosing the generally accepted information security practices that they adhere to, or any information security accreditations they may hold.

22 Remember that this subsection appears in PAIA where requesters are not necessarily data subjects.

23 For one thing, disclosing specifics regarding security 'posture' would compromise that security. For another, stating that an organisation is 'secure' is like waving a red flag in front of a hacker. And, unlike bulls, hackers are not colour blind.

11.3.2 Further information that may be disclosed

Tricky area: Section 18(1)*(a)* to *(g)* contains notifications which organisations must make. Section 18(1)*(h)* then contains the instruction that the responsible party must also provide 'any further information, such as ... which is necessary, having regard to the specific circumstances in which the information is or is not to be processed, to enable processing in respect of the data subject to be reasonable'. This second list is therefore not always required.[24] The test for whether more disclosures are required – such as the ones in the second list – is based on reasonableness.[25] A good rule of thumb is that data subjects should never be surprised about what personal information responsible parties have about them or what the personal information is being used for.

Here are the pieces of 'further information' listed in section 18(1)*(h)*.

What organisations may* also have to be transparent about[26]	What this means
Recipient or category of recipients	'Recipient' could be given a narrow or wide definition: • Narrow: All recipients outside of the responsible party; i.e. third parties. • Wide: It could also refer to 'internal' recipients; i.e. employees of the responsible party.

➡

Chapter 11

[24] The EU GDPR also split the list of disclosures into two lists, but the wording is different. The second list starts with the instruction that the responsible party 'shall ... provide the data subject with the following further information necessary to ensure fair and transparent processing'. See article 13(2). The Article 29 Data Protection Working Party said the following on this topic: '[T]here is no difference between the status of the information to be provided under sub-article 1 and 2 of Articles 13 and 14 respectively. All of the information across these sub-articles is of equal importance and must be provided to the data subject.' Guidelines on Transparency under Regulation 2016/679 (wp260rev.01) at 14 paragraph 23, available at https://ec.europa.eu/newsroom/article29/item-detail.cfm?item_id=622227.

[25] Reasonableness in the context of POPIA is discussed in chapter 2 paragraph 2.6.1.

[26] Keep reminding yourself that these disclosures will not always be required.

What organisations may* also have to be transparent about	What this means
	In the EU GDPR 'recipient' is defined as 'a natural or legal person, public authority, agency or another body, to which the personal data are disclosed, *whether a third party or not'* (our emphasis).[27] Third party is also defined in the EU GDPR. The gist of this definition is that in order to be considered a third party, the third party must not be under the direct authority of the responsible party.[28] **Tricky area: Unfortunately, POPIA does not contain a definition of 'recipient'. It is conceivable that there may be instances where it will be 'reasonable' to disclose who the 'internal recipients' of the information are.**
	In addition, the subsection does not prescribe whether data subjects have to be notified of each recipient who will receive their personal information by name or whether it is sufficient to refer to recipients in more generic terms (e.g. 'your personal information may be sent to third parties who assist us with marketing communications'). The fact that the subsection refers to a 'category of recipients' suggests that a generic reference will be enough. However, section 23(1)*(b)* provides that the data subject has the right to request the identity of all third parties or categories of third parties who have had access to the personal information.[29]

27 Article 4(9).

28 Article 4(10).

29 Data subject rights are discussed in chapter 18.

What organisations may* also have to be transparent about	What this means
	Tricky area: It is not clear under what circumstances a responsible party may be required to disclose the actual identity of all third parties who had access to personal information. Having said that, responsible parties should maintain a detailed record of all internal and external parties who had access in order to satisfy the information security management requirements in POPIA.[30] In addition, the principle of accountability dictates that a responsible party must have contracts in place with all operators who have access to personal information.[31] We are of the view that publishing the identity of all internal and external parties who had access will not be practical. However, a full record should be available in the event that a data subject or the Information Regulator requests them.

[30] Information security management is discussed in chapter 5.

[31] This is discussed in chapter 4 paragraph 4.4.

What organisations may* also have to be transparent about	What this means
	Here are some instances where we do believe specific recipients must be listed: • When personal information is being processed by co-responsible parties, all of the responsible parties must be disclosed. Section 18(1)*(b)* refers to 'responsible party' (singular). However, the definition of responsible party clearly contemplates that there may be multiple responsible parties acting with a common purpose.[32] All responsible parties should be listed in the privacy notice. • When personal information will be shared with an independent responsible party to process it for their own purposes. We think that if a responsible party is going to share personal information with another, independent responsible party, this should be specified in the privacy notice and this other responsible party should be identified. This will often be the case in groups of organisations that have a shared database.

➡

[32] Co-responsible parties are discussed in chapter 4 paragraph 4.5.

What organisations may* also have to be transparent about	What this means
	Tricky area: When organisations sell personal information (referred to as data brokers), should data subjects be notified who the information will be sold to? This is often the most challenging data protection requirement for data brokers. It is also possible that the seller, buyer or both may need the consent of the data subject. At the very least, data subjects will have the right to object, but to exercise this right, they have to know that their information is being sold, who it is being sold to and for what purpose. Data broking is discussed in some detail in chapter 13. • Any instance where the data subject would be surprised to learn that their information is being shared with another organisation.

➥

What organisations may* also have to be transparent about	What this means
Nature or category of the information	**Tricky area: It is not clear under which circumstances a responsible party would need to indicate the nature or category of the information, given that the responsible party has to list the personal information that it collects or generates.** In the EU GDPR and its predecessor, the Data Protection Directive, the nature or category of the information is only disclosed to data subjects where the personal information was not obtained directly from the data subject.[33] In other words, but for the notification, the data subject would not know what information was being collected. We would argue that section 18(1)*(f)* of POPIA should also be interpreted along these lines.
Existence of data subject rights	Data subject rights are discussed in chapter 18. Even though this is not a mandatory disclosure, we are of the view that responsible parties should notify data subjects of their rights and how to exercise them.
The contact details of the Information Regulator	The contact details of the Information Regulator will probably change more often than this book is updated. Refer to their website at https://www.justice.gov.za/inforeg/ for the most up-to-date contact details. Once again, it is not clear why this is not a mandatory disclosure. We see no harm in always including the Information Regulator's contact details in a privacy notice.

[33] Article 11(1)*(c)* of the Data Protection Directive.

11.3.3 A comparison between GDPR and POPIA notification requirements

The EU has an entire working paper on how to deal with transparency (or openness) as found in articles 13 and 14 of the EU GDPR.[34] The exact list of notification requirements is found in the Annex to the working paper and follows a broadly similar approach to section 18 of POPIA. There is, however, one structural difference which is that the EU has a different notification duty depending on whether the personal information was collected from the data subject (article 13) or from a third party (article 14). POPIA makes no such distinction. This distinction was also made in the EU GDPR's predecessor, the Data Protection Directive.[35]

Here are the notification duties that the EU GDPR contains which is not in POPIA:

Legal basis for processing	The EU GDPR requires that the responsible party must disclose the legal basis for processing.[36] The EU GDPR is referring to the legal justifications which we discussed in chapter 6 paragraph 6.3. POPIA does not require the responsible party to disclose this. However, it is prudent for a responsible party to keep a careful record of which legal justification applies (and how it arrived at that view) as the Information Regulator may request that information. Privacy notices are a handy place to keep this record.[37] In addition, it will be difficult to identify when a data subject will have a right to object to the processing (and notify them of that right) if the legal justification is not identified in the notice.[38]

➡

[34] Available at https://ec.europa.eu/newsroom/article29/item-detail.cfm?item_id=622227.

[35] Articles 10 and 11.

[36] Article 13(1)*(c)*.

[37] The use of privacy notices as a method of documenting compliance is discussed in chapter 1 paragraph 1.4.

[38] Section 11(3) lists the legal justifications which are subject to a right to object. This is discussed in chapter 18 paragraph 18.6.

Legitimate interests of a responsible party or third party	The EU GDPR requires that a data controller (responsible party) must disclose if it is relying on its own legitimate interests, or that of a third party as a legal justification.[39] As discussed in chapter 2 paragraph 2.6.3, when relying on a 'legitimate interest' to justify processing personal information, we believe that responsible parties should complete a legitimate interest assessment. We are not suggesting that the entire assessment should be provided to data subjects (although some controllers do that), but listing what the interest is that the responsible party or third party is relying on. Not doing so will make it impossible for data subjects to make an informed decision about whether they want to object to the processing.[40]
Storage period	The EU GDPR requires that the storage period of the personal information is disclosed.[41] This forces the data controller to actually think about and implement its retention and destruction policies and complements data subjects' right to request the deletion of information that is not subject to a retention period.[42] There is no similar requirement in POPIA, but the responsible party should inform data subjects of their right to request the deletion of information.
Automated decision-making	In terms of the EU GDPR, data subjects must be informed if they are subject to automated decision-making.[43] Section 18 of POPIA does not include this requirement, but there are disclosure requirements in section 71 which regulates automated decision-making. In addition, data subjects must be given an opportunity to make representations about the outcome of the decision and must be provided with sufficient information to enable them to make these representations.[44]

39 Article 13(1)*(d)* or 14(2)*(b)* of the EU GDPR.

40 Data subjects have the right to object to processing which is justified on the basis of legitimate interests (section 11(3)*(a)*). The right to object is discussed chapter 18 paragraph 18.6.

41 Article 13(2)*(a)* and 14(2)*(a)* of the EU GDPR. While POPIA does require that the responsible party knows the storage period of the personal information, there is no specific requirement that the storage period of the personal information be disclosed.

42 Section 24(1)*(b)*. Data subject rights are discussed in chapter 18. Records management is discussed in chapter 17.

43 Article 13(2)*(f)* and 14(2)*(g)*. This omission from section 18 of POPIA is curious, as the data subject has important rights relating to automated decision-making as we discuss more fully in chapter 15.

44 Section 71(3).

While responsible parties may not be legally obliged by POPIA to provide the above information, they may choose to supply it either to make their organisation compliant with both POPIA and the EU GDPR, or simply as a means to document compliance.

11.3.4 The word 'consent' should not appear in the privacy notice

A guaranteed way to get our blood boiling is to include a blanket consent to privacy practices within a privacy notice. Something like, 'by using our services you consent to our processing of your personal information' is legal nonsense. This is because there is no possibility that this could ever be considered to be consent, as it is:

- not specific
- not voluntary
- probably not informed; and
- not a clear expression of will.

Despite this we still frequently see this phrase in privacy notices.

Key point: First determine if you must get consent and then decide how you will ensure that the data subject intentionally provides specific, voluntary and informed consent.[45] These consents should be separated out from your privacy notice which is intended to inform, rather than to gather a response. It should also never be 'bundled' with the responsible party's terms and conditions.

11.4 WHEN THE NOTIFICATION SHOULD BE MADE

11.4.1 When personal information is collected directly from the data subject

The general principle is that the notification cannot take place after the fact; the data subject must be informed before the personal information is collected.[46] More often than not, the most practical time to provide the prescribed notifications is at the point of collection. Make sure that any forms contain the appropriate disclosures or a reference to a privacy notice!

---

45 Paragraph 2.6.6.

46 Section 18(2)*(a)*.

Key point: There is no need to state the obvious. We will discuss using plain language in a moment (see paragraph 11.5.4), but suffice it to say that conciseness is crucial. It is therefore not surprising that section 18(3)*(a)* states that there is no need to notify the data subject if they are already aware of the information in the privacy notice. Of course, the responsible party will have to be in a position to prove that the data subject was already aware.

11.4.2 When personal information is being collected from other sources

In cases where the personal information is collected from another source the data subject must preferably be notified before collection takes place[47] or, if that is not possible, 'as soon as reasonably practicable after it has been collected'.[48] The meaning of reasonable practicality was discussed in chapter 2 paragraph 2.6.2. It is a pity that POPIA did not provide more specific guidelines in this regard. However, the EU GDPR provides that the notifications must be made:[49]

- within a reasonable time after collection, 'but at the latest within one month, having regard to the specific circumstances in which the personal data are processed'
- 'at the latest at the time of the first communication' with the data subject (if the personal data will be used to communicate with the data subject); or
- before the personal information is shared with any 'recipient'.[50]

Tricky area: Even though POPIA is silent on what would qualify as 'as soon as reasonably practicable', the standard set by the EU GDPR is a useful indication of 'best practice'. Responsible parties should carefully document their decision-making process when they determine when data subjects will be notified and be ready to defend their decision about when to notify.

---

47 See chapter 10.

48 Section 18(2)*(b)*.

49 Article 14(3).

50 A 'recipient' is defined as 'a natural or legal person, public authority, agency or another body, to which the personal data are disclosed, whether a third party or not'. Article 4(9).

11.4.3 When more information is collected from the data subject

Do responsible parties need to re-notify the data subject every time they collect more information from the data subject? POPIA provides some relief from constant notifications in the form of section 18(3), which states that the responsible party does not need to re-notify if both of the following requirements are met:

The personal information is the same, or 'information of the same kind'	It is reasonable to assume that 'information of the same kind' can refer to categories of personal information (for example, contact information or health-related personal information).
The purpose(s) remains the same	Do the purposes have to remain exactly the same? The safe answer would be to re-notify if there has been any change, no matter how inconsequential. However, we do not believe that bombarding data subjects with information necessarily provides them with better protection. In fact, they start suffering from information overload.[51] **Tricky area:** We believe that the test for compatibility of a 'new' purpose with the original purpose can be used as a guideline here. 'Further processing' (where the purposes for which personal information is processed changes), is discussed in chapter 12. Suffice it to say that if the changed purpose is inconsistent with the original purpose for which the information was collected, the data subject will have to be notified again. However, note that if the new processing purpose does not comply with section 15(2) or (3), it cannot take place. No amount of transparency will remedy that.

[51] We discussed this in chapter 2 paragraphs 2.6.1 and 2.6.2.

11.4.4 When processing activities change

What if a responsible party makes changes to their processing activities? POPIA does not explicitly refer to updates to privacy notices, apart from what we discussed in paragraph 11.4.3. However, it stands to reason that if one has a duty to provide certain information to data subjects, they should receive a notification if any of that information changes. However, does this rule apply for every change? Here are some factors to consider when determining whether an update is necessary: [52]

- Is there an impact on data subjects? For instance, do they need the new information to exercise any data subject rights?
- Would the change be unexpected or surprising to data subjects?

Here are instances where the Article 29 Data Protection Working Party (commenting on the EU GDPR) believes that changes to a privacy notice must be communicated:

- changes in the processing purpose
- when the responsible party changes (or another (co-)responsible party is added)
- changes in how data subjects can exercise their rights; and [53]
- changes to the nature of the processing (e.g. adding a category of recipients or sending the personal information to another country).[54]

The changes should be communicated to the data subjects before the change takes place, in an effective and explicit manner so as to ensure that they do not miss it and have time to consider the implications and exercise their rights.

Key point: We often see privacy notices that include statements to the effect that data subjects should regularly check the privacy notice for updates, effectively attempting to make awareness of the changes a data subject problem. According to the Article 29 Data Protection Working Party, this approach is unacceptable.[55]

---

52 Guidelines on Transparency under Regulation 2016/679 (wp260rev.01) 16 paragraph 29, available at https://ec.europa.eu/newsroom/article29/item-detail.cfm?item_id=622227.

53 Guidelines on Transparency under Regulation 2016/679 (wp260rev.01) 17 paragraph 29, available at https://ec.europa.eu/newsroom/article29/item-detail.cfm?item_id=622227.

54 Guidelines on Transparency under Regulation 2016/679 (wp260rev.01) 17 paragraph 30, available at https://ec.europa.eu/newsroom/article29/item-detail.cfm?item_id=622227.

55 Guidelines on Transparency under Regulation 2016/679 (wp260rev.01) 17 paragraph 29, available at https://ec.europa.eu/newsroom/article29/item-detail.cfm?item_id=622227.

11.5 HOW THE NOTIFICATION SHOULD HAPPEN

11.5.1 'Reasonably practicable steps'

POPIA requires that responsible parties must take 'reasonably practicable steps' to 'ensure that the data subject is aware of' all of the required information. We dealt with the concept of 'reasonably practicable' in chapter 2 paragraph 2.6.2.

In the EU, responsible parties must take 'appropriate measures' to provide the required information.[56] When determining what is appropriate, responsible parties should take the circumstances of the collection and processing into account to determine the appropriate format of the information and how it will be delivered. The Article 29 Data Protection Working Party goes so far as to recommend that responsible parties 'trial different modalities by way of user testing' to get feedback from data subjects.[57]

In the remainder of this section we will investigate the form these 'reasonably practicable' steps must take by discussing:

- the role of the privacy notice
- the plain language requirement; and
- methods of making data subjects aware.

11.5.2 The role of the 'privacy notice'

The traditional method of notifying data subjects is through a so-called 'privacy policy' but data protection terms have moved on since then and the tendency is now to refer to them as 'privacy notices'. We prefer 'privacy notice', because people confuse a privacy policy with an internal privacy policy aimed at achieving POPIA compliance in an organisation. Privacy notices are often public documents and are necessary to comply with POPIA's notification requirements. Privacy notices can either take the form of a single document which data subjects are referred to or data subjects can be given the applicable 'ad hoc' notices as and when the personal information is collected in, for instance, an application form. The latter method (which could be referred to as a 'just in time' privacy notice) is more effective as it does not require any additional steps by the data subject in order to gain access to the notification and only the relevant information is provided to the data subject at the time that they need it.[58]

---

56 Article 12(1) of the EU GDPR.

57 Guidelines on Transparency under Regulation 2016/679 (wp260rev.01) 14 paragraph 25, available at https://ec.europa.eu/newsroom/article29/item-detail.cfm?item_id=622227.

58 Guidelines on Transparency under Regulation 2016/679 (wp260rev.01) 41 paragraph 39, available at https://ec.europa.eu/newsroom/article29/item-detail.cfm?item_id=622227.

11.5.3 One privacy notice to rule them all ...[59]

Should a responsible party have one comprehensive privacy notice or several different privacy notices? POPIA is not prescriptive in this regard. However, it is an extremely important question and the answer hinges on what the most effective and user-friendly approach will be. An approach which leads to the data subject having to actively search for the information relevant to their situation may land responsible parties in hot water.[60]

Key point: There is no provision in POPIA that states that responsible parties must have one privacy notice. We always create separate privacy notices for different 'categories' of data subjects. Examples of categories are clients, prospective clients, employees, applicants for employment, and vendors (suppliers or service providers). Our primary reason for this is to make it easy for data subjects to find the information relevant to them. Another reason is that in terms of PAIA, responsible parties are required to list all of the categories of data subjects whose personal information is processed. We discuss this in paragraph 11.7.

Come to think of it, there is no rule in POPIA that states that responsible parties must have a privacy notice. It can be a privacy video, a privacy song, a privacy smoke signal, a privacy carrier pigeon, a privacy fish called Fernando ...[61]

Current trends in privacy notifications lean towards taking a layered approach where privacy notices are 'used to link to the various categories of information which must be provided to the data subject, rather than displaying all such information in a single notice'.[62] However, be sure not to split it up so much that data subjects have to click[63] several times to get to the important information. The information that is most pertinent to a data subject (use the 'would it be surprising test') should be in the first layer.

---

59 ... and in the darkness bind them. Naturally.

60 See the discussion of the *Google France* case in paragraph 11.5.4 below.

61 Fernando is real and is also the best teacher on what should be in a privacy notice. Find him here: https://www.august.com.au/privacy-policy/.

62 Guidelines on Transparency under Regulation 2016/679 (wp260rev.01), at 19 paragraph 35, available at https://ec.europa.eu/newsroom/article29/item-detail.cfm?item_id=622227.

63 The layered approach can work in a non-digital environment. See Guidelines on Transparency under Regulation 2016/679 (wp260rev.01), at 20 paragraph 38, available at https://ec.europa.eu/newsroom/article29/item-detail.cfm?item_id=622227.

The second important trend is towards 'just-in-time' notifications where 'specific "privacy information" [is provided] in an ad hoc manner, as and when it is most relevant for the data subject to read'. In other words, short privacy statements are provided at various points throughout the process of personal information collection.[64]

11.5.4 The plain language requirement

Unlike the Consumer Protection Act (CPA)[65] and the National Credit Act[66] there is no express requirement in POPIA that notifications should be in plain language. Of course, one could argue that it is inherent in the requirement that the responsible parties take 'reasonably practicable steps' and, as discussed in chapter 2,[67] if the responsible party is relying on consent, it has to be an 'informed' consent which we believe includes a requirement that it must be in plain language.

While the requirement for plain language is not contained within POPIA, there is a good argument that it will often be required, because of section 22 of the Consumer Protection Act which states:

> '22. (1) The producer of a notice, document or visual representation that is **required**, in terms of this Act **or any other law**, to be produced, **provided or displayed to a consumer** must produce, provide or display that notice, document or visual representation–
>
> *(a)* in the form prescribed in terms of this Act or any other legislation, if any, for that notice, document or visual representation; or
>
> *(b)* **in plain language, if no form has been prescribed** for that notice, document or visual representation.' (our emphasis)

Given that POPIA prescribes that data subjects must be notified of the information listed in section 18, section 22 of the CPA is triggered in cases where the data subject falls within the definition of 'consumer' in the CPA.[68]

Chapter 11

64 For examples see Guidelines on Transparency under Regulation 2016/679 (wp260rev.01) 21 paragraph 39, available at https://ec.europa.eu/newsroom/article29/item-detail.cfm?item_id=622227.

65 Section 22 of the Consumer Protection Act 68 of 2008.

66 Section 64 of the National Credit Act 34 of 2005.

67 Paragraph 2.6.6.

68 See section 1 of the CPA.

Tricky area: The Consumer Protection Act only applies to 'consumers' as defined in section 1. It is a complex definition, with several qualifications.[69] In short, the definition of 'consumer' and the definition of 'data subject' do not align.[70] For instance, while the definition will include most individuals, only small juristic persons will qualify as consumers. The CPA includes a very complex financial threshold of an asset value of or annual turnover of under R2 million (at the time of publication) to determine which entities qualify for protection.[71] In addition, if an industry or type of transaction has been exempted from the operation of the CPA (e.g. financial services), the plain language requirement will not apply.

It is unfortunate that POPIA did not explicitly introduce a plain language requirement when communicating to all data subjects. While the CPA provides some relief, this seems to lead to the absurd situation that whether a data subject will also be a consumer or not will depend on:

- what industry the responsible party operates in
- whether an individual is a customer or an employee; and
- the annual turnover or asset value of a juristic person at any given time.

This not only erodes the level of protection provided to data subjects, but also creates a complicated double standard which will be difficult for responsible parties to manage.

In case you are wondering whether people care about transparency, they do. CISCO does an annual consumer privacy survey. Here are two interesting statistics from 2020:[72]

- 29% of consumers are described as privacy actives. These are people who not only care about privacy, but are also willing to act to protect it and have already switched brands due to data practices.

---

69 De Stadler & Du Plessis 'Section 5' in *Commentary on the Consumer Protection Act* (2016) at 5-14 to 5-15.

70 For a discussion on the scope of POPIA, see chapter 3.

71 De Stadler & Du Plessis 'Section 5' in *Commentary on the Consumer Protection Act* (2016) at 5-14 to 5-15.

72 The 2020 survey is available at https://www.cisco.com/c/dam/en_us/about/doing_business/trust-center/docs/cisco-consumer-privacy-infographic-2020.pdf.

- 48% of consumers do not feel they can adequately protect their privacy. 79% of those say that this is because they 'can't figure out what companies are doing with data'.

Here is another interesting statistic that should guide our thinking around transparency. According to a survey done by Accenture in 2018, '83% of consumers are willing to share their data to enable a personalized experience as long as businesses are transparent about how they are going to use it and that customers have control over it'.[73]

Key point: Organisations should commit to transparency enabled by plain language, not because that is what POPIA requires, but because it makes good business sense.

In the EU it is recognised that using plain language is an integral part of ensuring transparency. Consider the following aspects of transparency as found in article 12(1) of the EU GDPR when it deals with notification. Notification must:

- be concise, transparent, intelligible and easily accessible
- use clear and plain language; and
- take special precautions to be in plain language when providing information to children.[74]

Key point: For guidelines on how these requirements are interpreted see the EU's Guidelines on Transparency under Regulation 2016/679.[74]

In case transparency still sounds like a 'nice to have', the stakes could not be higher as illustrated by a decision by the Council of State in France against Google LLC in June 2020.[75] In this matter two associations – supported by more than 10 000 people – complained that Google had no legal basis to process their personal data. On investigation it was found that essential information, such as the purpose of the processing and the period of storage of the personal data, was distributed over

73 Available at https://www.accenture.com/_acnmedia/PDF-77/Accenture-Pulse-Survey.pdf.

74 wp260rev.01, available at https://ec.europa.eu/newsroom/article29/item-detail.cfm?item_id=622227 from 6.

75 Délibération no SAN-2019-001 du 21 Janvier 2019 Délibération de la formation restreinte no SAN – 2019-001 du 21 Janvier 2019 Prononçant une sanction pécuniaire à l'encontre de la société GOOGLE LLC. Decision available at https://www.cnil.fr/en/cnils-restricted-committee-imposes-financial-penalty-50-million-euros-against-google-llc.

several documents which required that the data subject click or link to each document, often requiring five to six steps. The investigation also found that the information that actually was provided was neither clear nor comprehensive but rather was generically and vaguely worded. Ultimately Google was fined 50 million Euros (almost R1 billion).

11.5.5 How to 'ensure' that the data subject 'is aware'

Will an inconspicuous link to a privacy notice at the bottom of an organisation's website be enough to comply with section 18? Probably not. The reason behind this is that section 18(1) of POPIA requires that the responsible party must take 'reasonably practicable' steps to 'ensure' that the data subject is 'aware' of the information the responsible party must disclose. Often this information is communicated by means of a privacy notice, but there is no reason why other methods cannot be employed as well.

Different types of disclosures are discussed by the Article 29 Data Protection Working Party:[76]

Environment	Methods of notification
Hard copy/ paper environment	For example when entering into contracts by postal means: written explanations, leaflets, information in contractual documentation, cartoons, infographics or flowcharts.
Telephonic environment	Oral explanations by a real person to allow interaction and questions to be answered or automated or pre-recorded information with options to hear further, more detailed information.
Screenless smart technology/ IoT[77] environment such as Wi-Fi tracking analytics	Icons, QR codes,[78] voice alerts, written details incorporated into paper set-up instructions, videos incorporated into digital set-up instructions, written information on the smart device, messages sent by SMS or email, visible boards containing the information, public signage or public information campaigns.

➡

76 wp260rev.01 at 21 paragraph 40, available at https://ec.europa.eu/newsroom/article29/item-detail.cfm?item_id=622227.

77 Internet of Things (such as smart fridges that are connected to the internet and have the ability to warn you that you need milk).

78 Quick Response codes are a type of barcode that can be scanned by a device.

Environment	Methods of notification
Person-to-person environment	Such as responding to opinion polls, registering in person for a service, oral explanations or written explanations provided in hard or soft copy format.
'Real-life' environment with CCTV/ drone recording	Visible boards containing the information, public signage, public information campaigns or newspaper/ media notices.

11.6 EXCEPTIONS TO THE NOTIFICATION DUTY

Section 18(4) provides several exceptions to the responsible party's notification duty.

Key point: Although it is not clear from section 18, a responsible party needs to consider whether an exception applies to each of the processing activity it uses personal information for. If an exception applies to just one processing activity then the responsible party still needs to make the appropriate notifications for the remainder of its activities.

11.6.1 Consent not to notify

It is possible for a responsible party to ask the data subject to consent to not being notified.[79]

Tricky area: Wait, what? At first glance, consent not to notify seems an odd type of consent as – by implication – you need to have notified the data subject that you intend not to notify them. An example of this type of consent would be where a hospital is using the personal information of a patient to find an organ donor match. The hospital would be sending the personal information to different recipients and may be sending it overseas to several jurisdictions and so it could ask for patient consent to not need to notify them every time it sends their personal information to a new country.[80]

Chapter 11

[79] Section 18(4)*(a)* of POPIA.

[80] Section 18(1)*(g)* requires this notification. Transborder information flows are also discussed in chapter 14.

However, relying on consent not to notify has its challenges. So, in our example above, the data subject must be able to say 'no' and the hospital would have to notify the data subject. This means that consent cannot be used in instances where it is not possible for the responsible party to notify.

As we discussed previously,[81] any consent in terms of POPIA must be:

- specific (in this case specifically consenting to not being notified every time personal information is being sent to another country)
- informed (the consent should explain the risk of not being notified)
- voluntary (if consent is not given then the hospital must continue with its search, but must notify the data subject every time that search results in the personal information being sent to another country); and

Tricky area: Section 11(3)*(b)* states that a data subject may withdraw consent provided in terms of section 11(1)*(a)* at any time. The right to withdraw consent is not mentioned in section 18(4)*(a)*. However, we are of the view that data subjects also have the right to withdraw other consents due to the requirement that consent must be voluntary.[82] Can the responsible party just refuse to continue to process the data subject's personal information, because they withhold consent not to notify? Data subjects must be free to withdraw consent without undue effort and without any detrimental effects such as an increase in cost, a cessation of services or a decrease in service levels.[83] In many scenarios, it will be unpalatable to responsible parties that the data subject's consent must be voluntary and that they cannot be penalised for withholding consent. What this means is that responsible parties should avoid relying on this exception at all costs.[84] For instance, consent cannot be used in instances where it is not possible for the responsible party to notify.

- an expression of will (either a signature or some form of positive act that signifies that the data subject consented to this).

---

81 See chapter 2 paragraph 2.6.6.

82 Section 1 of POPIA.

83 European Data Protection Board *Guidelines 05/2020 on Consent under Regulation 2016/679* 13, available at https://edpb.europa.eu/sites/edpb/files/files/file1/edpb_guidelines_202005_consent_en.pdf.

84 This is also the position when the responsible party has to determine which legal justification applies. See chapter 6 paragraph 6.3.6.

Key point: The consent not to notify cannot be buried in terms and conditions. It needs to be an independent expression of will.[85]

11.6.2 No prejudice to the legitimate interest of the data subject

If a responsible party can demonstrate that not notifying the data subject does not prejudice the legitimate interest of the data subject 'as set out in terms of this Act', they can go ahead with the processing without notification. Given that processing personal information without notifying the data subject is inherently intrusive and will almost always erode a data subject's interest in privacy, this exception is very limited.

An example which comes to mind is where notification does not happen, because it is an emergency situation (e.g. a data subject has been injured and the responsible party shares personal information with medical professionals) and the responsible party is processing personal information to protect the data subject's health or safety. See the discussion of the similar exemption to the direct collection rule which we discuss in chapter 10 paragraph 10.4.4.

11.6.3 Not notifying the data subject is required for law and order

A responsible party does not have to notify a data subject if this is necessary for the following purposes:

- 'to avoid prejudice to the maintenance of law by any public body' which includes the 'prevention, detection, investigation, prosecution and punishment of offences'[86]
- protecting the interest of 'national security'[87]
- complying with 'an obligation imposed by law' or to enforce legislation concerning the collection of revenue as defined in section 1 of the South African Revenue Service Act';[88] or
- conducting 'proceedings in any court or tribunal that have commenced or are reasonably contemplated'.[89]

Chapter 11

85 This, and the other requirements for a valid consent is discussed in chapter 2 paragraph 2.6.6.

86 Section 18(4)*(c)*(i).

87 Section 18(4)*(c)*(iv).

88 Section 18(4)*(d)*(ii).

89 Section 18(4)*(c)*(iii).

Tricky area: Interestingly there is no indication in section 18(4)*(c)*(iii) that the courts or tribunals need to be South African courts or tribunals. In contrast, the exception from the application of POPIA as found in section 6(1)*(e)* makes it clear that the courts that enjoy a blanket exemption from POPIA are only South African courts.[90] From this we can assume that not only local courts, but also foreign courts and tribunals will enjoy an exemption from having to notify the data subject. Of course, there are other considerations aside from notifying the data subject which these courts and tribunals would have to consider, which would potentially include cross-border transfer of personal information,[91] so be careful about assuming that foreign courts and tribunals are entitled to a free-for-all.

The most important word to consider in subsection (4)*(c)* is the word 'necessary'. In chapter 6 paragraph 6.3.1 we first considered the concept of 'necessary' and the questions set out there can be amended to apply to notifying as well, namely:

- What is the fundamental purpose(s) of the processing activity?
- Is there a way to achieve the fundamental purpose and still notify the data subject?

Tricky area: A responsible party should ask whether POPIA applies to some of these activities at all, because – as we saw in the exclusions in chapter 3 paragraph 3.3 – *some* public bodies are exempted from the whole of POPIA. However, if you take a closer look at section 6(1)*(c)* of POPIA you will notice that this exception only applies 'to the extent that adequate safeguards have been established in legislation for the protection of personal information'. By implication then, section 18(4)*(c)*(i) and (iv) assumes that adequate safeguards have not been established in the legislation but nonetheless still allows for an exception from the notification duty if it is necessary and collected by a public body dealing with criminal offences or in the interests of national security.[92]

[90] Section 6(1)*(e)* of POPIA refers to 'a court referred to in s 166 of the South African Constitution' which naturally only refers to the establishment of South African courts. See https://www.justice.gov.za/legislation/constitution/SAConstitution-web-eng.pdf for a full list of these courts.

[91] See chapter 14.

[92] Section 18(4)*(c)*(i) and (iv).

11.6.4 Notifying the data subject prejudices a lawful purpose of collection

In chapter 6 we discussed determining and documenting:

- the purpose for which personal information is processed; and
- the legal justification for the processing activity (is the processing lawful).

This exception provides that a responsible party does not have to notify the data subject, if the notification will undermine the lawful purpose for which the personal information is required.[93] This will often be the case where a law imposes a duty on the responsible party and notifying the data subject could compromise that purpose.

Consider the following example: Take the obligation on a bank to report money laundering.[94] As an accountable institution a bank is required to report suspicious transactions and it would undermine the purpose of the legislation if the parties associated with that transaction would get notification that they were under investigation. In fact, it is an offence to disclose the Suspicious Transaction Report (STR) to the person about whom the STR relates.[95]

11.6.5 Compliance is not 'reasonably practicable'

A responsible party does not have to notify the data subject if this is not 'reasonably practicable in the circumstances of the particular case'.[96] We dealt with the concept of 'reasonably practicable' in chapter 2[97] as it occurs so many times within POPIA, and it is worth referring back to this chapter again when you consider this exception.

Article 14(5) of the GDPR provides a similar exception when 'the provision of such information proves impossible or would involve a disproportionate effort'. Here are some examples which the Article 29 Data Protection Working Party used to demonstrate impossibility:

- Where the responsible party 'has no means to directly contact the data subject'.[98]

Chapter 11

93 Section 18(4)*(d)*.

94 Financial Intelligence Centre Act 38 of 2001 (FICA).

95 See section 53 of FICA.

96 This echoes section 18(1) which states that responsible parties must take reasonably practicable steps to make the data subjects aware.

97 Paragraph 2.6.2.

98 Article 29 Data Protection Working Party *Guidelines on Transparency under Regulation 2016/679* 29, available at https://ec.europa.eu/newsroom/article29/items/622227/en.

- Where the responsible party cannot provide information about the origin of the personal information, because 'different pieces of personal data relating to the same data subject cannot be attributed to a particular source'. However 'the mere fact that a database comprising the personal data of multiple data subjects has been compiled by a data controller using more than one source is not enough to lift this requirement if it is possible (although time consuming or burdensome) to identify the source from which the personal data of individual data subjects was derived'.[99]

Key point: Be extremely careful when relying on commentary on article 13 and 14 of the EU GDPR when interpreting section 18(4)*(e)*. The wording is quite different. For instance, the 'disproportionate effort' exemption only applies when personal information is not collected from the data subject directly. This is not the case in POPIA.

The Guidelines suggest that the responsible party should perform a 'balancing exercise to assess the effort involved for the [responsible party] to provide the information of the data subject against the impact and effects on the data subject if he or she was not provided with the information'.[100]

While the concept of 'disproportionate effort' is unclear, we can be guided by a recent Polish decision where the meaning was considered.[101] In this case a company collected information from public sources and had to consider how to inform the data subjects that it had their personal information. It decided that sending individual emails to the data subjects would be too expensive, so instead it published the fact that it had information about the data subjects on its website. The court of first instance had to decide whether the company's argument that sending individual emails out at great cost would involve 'disproportionate effort'. The court ruled that simply publishing the details on the website was unacceptable and that individual

99 Article 29 Data Protection Working Party *Guidelines on Transparency under Regulation 2016/679* 29, available at https://ec.europa.eu/newsroom/article29/items/622227/en.

100 Paragraph 64.

101 Polish President of the Personal Data Protection Office on 15 March 2019, Case no: ZSPR.421.3.2018. Available at https://uodo.gov.pl/decyzje/ZSPR.421.3.2018. See also Ewa Kacperek and Weronika Wolosiuk 'First fine imposed by the Polish DPA under the EU GDPR', available at https://www.engage.hoganlovells.com/knowledgeservices/news/first-fine-imposed-by-the-polish-dpa-under-the-gdpr.

notifications were required and as a result fined the company 220 000 Euros (about R4 million). The company appealed the matter and the appeal court partially overturned the decision for technical reasons.[102] However the key part of the appeal decision related to the question of what 'disproportionate effort' really means. The appeal court found that where compliance with the EU GDPR is required then it can only be deviated from if compliance is 'virtually impossible'.

In another example a credit bureau relied on the argument that it would take disproportionate effort to notify data subjects of the use of their credit reference information for direct marketing purposes during an investigation by the UK ICO. After stating that the exemption must be narrowly construed, the ICO stated that: [103]

> 'The mere fact that there are large numbers of data subjects cannot in itself be a determinative factor against the proportionality of notification: otherwise controllers are given a perverse incentive to accumulate data about as many individuals as possible, in order to support their case on proportionality and hence reduce the burden of notification.
>
> It is recognised that compliance with [section 18] may be costly to Experian (although it is not accepted that all of the sums proposed need to be incurred at the level set out by Experian in its representations, or indeed at all). However, the cost will inevitably be high if viewed in isolation; this is because it is the cost of catching up on an accumulation of many years during which there has been a failure to give notifications.[104] It cannot be right that a controller can fail over many years to give notifications to data subjects, and then rely on the cost of rectifying that failure as providing a justification for taking no further action; such an approach likewise creates a perverse incentive for a data controller to fail to comply with its [section 18] obligations over a prolonged period.
>
> The Commissioner also has regard to the fact that in the context of this processing, it is inherently likely that Experian has relevant contact details for the data subjects, since without such contact details, the processing for marketing purposes would be ineffectual.'

Chapter 11

[102] https://orzeczenia.nsa.gov.pl/doc/30EDD316DA. See also Joanna Tomaszewska 'Polish court overturns DPA's first GDPR fine' IAPP, available at https://iapp.org/news/a/polish-court-overturns-dpas-first-gdpr-fine/.

[103] See the ICO's enforcement notice against Experian paragraph 51, available at https://ico.org.uk/media/2618467/experian-limited-enforcement-report.pdf.

[104] Remember that at this point Europe already had decades of data protection regulation. We are not of the view that the duty to notify is retrospective. We discussed this in chapter 3 paragraph 3.5.

Key point: We would quote all of this enforcement notice if we could. The credit bureau was given nine months to provide adequate information. In answer to complaints about the financial costs the ICO pointed out that 'it is, however, the cost of lawful processing, and results from Experian's own choices as to how it conducts its business'.[105]

On balance it would seem likely that our courts will follow the approach of the EU GDPR by requiring that notification to the data subject must be 'virtually impossible' before a responsible party can rely on the exception that notification is not 'reasonably practicable'.

11.6.6 The information will not be used in a form in which the data subject will be identified

This exception is a curious one, because POPIA does not apply at all where the information has been de-identified.[106] We discussed de-identification in chapter 3 paragraph 3.3.2.

Tricky area: If personal information has been successfully de-identified (no small feat), POPIA does not apply and naturally, there would be no obligation to notify data subjects. For this exception to make any sense, what is referred to in this subsection would have to be something less than de-identification. We believe that what is referred to here is pseudonymisation,[107] where personal information is used in such a way that the personal information cannot be attributed to a specific data subject without the use of additional information.[108]

If our conclusion in the tricky area block above is correct, in order for this exception to apply, the additional information (e.g. the decryption key) which can be used to re-identify the data subject must be:

- stored separately from the pseudonymised information; and
- protected by technical and operational measures against unauthorised re-identification.[109]

---

105 Paragraph 87.

106 Section 18(4)*(f)*.

107 We discussed pseudonymisation in chapter 3 paragraph 3.3.2.

108 Article 4(5) of the EU GDPR.

109 Article 4(5) of the EU GDPR.

The scope of the exception is also limited. It would only apply to the processing activities where the personal information being used has already been pseudonymised. In order to be in a position to do so, a responsible party would have had to collect the information in an identifiable format. Until the information is pseudonymised, the notification duty would still apply.

Consider this example: WTF (Pty) Ltd shares pseudonymised information about its clients with IDK (Pty) Ltd to train an algorithm on how to perform predictive analytics. WTF (Pty) Ltd would need to notify its clients of everything it does with their information, except for sharing it with IDK (Pty) Ltd, unless one of the other exceptions to the notification obligation applies. This notification would include stating that WTF (Pty) Ltd pseudonymises the information and for what purpose that pseudonymised information will be used.[110] IDK (Pty) Ltd never receives the information in an identifiable format. While POPIA still applies, because the information can be re-identified,[111] IDK (Pty) Ltd does not have to notify the data subjects of its processing activities.

11.6.7 Exemption in respect of information that will be used for historical, statistical or research purposes

We discussed what is included in historical, statistical or research purposes in chapter 2 paragraph 2.6.7.

Key point: The wording of this exemption is broad with no qualifications. In the EU it is qualified by requiring that notification must require disproportionate effort. We expect that the Information Regulator will limit this exemption by taking a narrow interpretation of what type of processing is included under 'historical, statistical or research purposes'.

110 This is because the act of pseudonymising the information falls within the definition of 'processing'. See chapter 3 paragraph 3.2.

111 Consider the definition of de-identification carefully. It is not about whether IDK (Pty) Ltd can re-identify the information (in our example it cannot). It is about whether anybody could re-identify it. This is discussed in chapter 3 paragraph 3.3.2.

11.6.8 Exemption in respect of certain functions

If an organisation performs any of the functions as set out in section 38 of POPIA, it does not have to comply with the notification obligation.

Key point: This exemption only applies to public bodies[112] or to other organisations who must perform these functions 'in terms of the law'.[113] It also only applies to the extent that the function is 'performed with the view to protecting members of the public'. Therefore, the exemption would apply to regulators and statutory industry associations.

The 'relevant functions' are functions that protect members of the public against:

- financial loss due to dishonesty, malpractice or other seriously improper conduct by, or the unfitness or incompetence of, persons providing banking, insurance, investment or other financial services or the management of bodies corporate; or
- dishonesty, malpractice or other seriously improper conduct by, or the unfitness or incompetence of, persons authorised to carry on any profession or other activity.

Tricky area: What does 'performed with the view to protecting members of the public' mean? For one thing, the exemption will not apply to functions performed by a responsible party to protect itself. For instance, it will certainly cover the Financial Sector Conduct Authority when it polices compliance with the fit and proper requirements imposed on intermediaries in terms of the Financial Advisory and Intermediary Services Act (FAIS).[114] However, will it cover a financial services provider when its human resources department uses the same information in its recruitment process for purposes of deciding between candidates for employment? Given that exemptions will be interpreted narrowly, the financial service provider will only be covered for activities that are necessary for its own compliance with FAIS. The minute an activity is performed for purposes other than complying with FAIS, the exemption will no longer apply.

112 See the definition of 'public body' in section 1.

113 Section 38(2).

114 Act 37 of 2002.

11.7 A COMPARISON BETWEEN POPIA AND PAIA NOTIFICATION REQUIREMENTS

In 2009, the SA Law Reform Commission noted that: 'Provision has, therefore, been made for notification in terms of both acts (POPIA and PAIA) to be done simultaneously, should the responsible party so prefer'.[115] In essence the SA Law Reform Commission believed that you could comply with both sections 14 and 51 of PAIA and section 18 of POPIA in a single document which would presumably be the responsible party's PAIA manual.

Key point: As we were finalising this book, the Information Regulator published a guide on how to use the Promotion of Access to Information Act and it also released PAIA manual templates for public and private bodies.[116]

Sections 14 and 51 of PAIA were amended by POPIA and require that the manual referred to in PAIA must contain the following information in relation to POPIA:[117]

- the purposes of processing[118]
- a description of the categories of data subjects

Key point: Listing the categories of data subjects is not a requirement in terms of section 18 of POPIA. Typical examples of categories of data subjects are clients, prospective clients, employees, prospective employees, and vendors (suppliers or service providers).

In order to provide concise and relevant information to data subjects, we believe that it is appropriate to create a privacy notice per category of data subject as discussed in paragraph 11.5.3 above. This is quite different from PAIA which only requires a single PAIA manual which is used for all audiences.

- a description of the information or categories of information relating to the different categories of data subjects

Chapter 11

[115] SA Law Reform Commission Project 124 on Privacy and Data Protection (2009 Report) paragraph 4.2.222.

[116] These documents can be accessed at https://www.justice.gov.za/inforeg/docs.html.

[117] Sections 14(1)*(c)* and 51(1)*(c)* of PAIA (as amended).

[118] Section 18(1)*(c)* also requires that the purpose for processing must be disclosed.

Key point: POPIA is stricter. It requires that responsible parties must notify data subjects of the 'information being collected', and does not allow for 'categories of information' to be listed instead. Given that section 2(2)*(a)* of POPIA provides that it will apply in cases where other legislation provides weaker protection,[119] we believe that responsible parties must comply with section 18.

- the recipients or categories of recipients to whom personal information may be supplied[120]
- planned transborder flows of personal information; and

Key point: This requirement in PAIA is similar, but a great deal less detailed, than section 18(1)*(g)* of POPIA. The more specific provision should apply. This is discussed in paragraph 11.4.1.

- a general description of the information security measures implemented to ensure the confidentiality, integrity and availability of the information.

Key point: This notification does not appear anywhere in POPIA. This is why we added it to the mandatory notifications we discussed in paragraph 11.4.1.

The remainder of sections 14 and 51 also require a host of notifications that are not relevant for POPIA purposes. This is because PAIA applies to all types of information, not just personal information.

Key point: Consider reading Francis Cronje and Eddie Laubscher's *PAIA: What You Need to Know* (2016) – which integrates PAIA and POPIA. This is a useful publication to have on hand when comparing these two pieces of legislation or when preparing a PAIA manual.[121]

---

119 How to address conflicts between POPIA and other legislation is discussed in chapter 2 paragraph 2.7.

120 This is also listed in section 18(1)*(h)*(i) as part of the list of information which the responsible party must provide if it is 'necessary, having regard to the specific circumstances in which the information is or is not to be processed, to enable processing in respect of the data subject to be reasonable'.

121 As is inevitable when writing a book, a mistake crept in on page 88. Both public and private bodies must provide a general description in their manual allowing a preliminary assessment of the suitability of the information security measures to be implemented by it to ensure the confidentiality, integrity and availability of the information which is to be processed.

This then leaves the question of whether it is a good idea to combine an organisation's PAIA manual and privacy notice(s). We believe that it is not, because meaningful compliance with the disclosure duties of POPIA requires that the information provided to data subjects must be concise and relevant to them.[122] PAIA manuals contain a lot of information that is not relevant to data subjects. On this basis alone, the different types of information should be clearly separated.

11.8 TRUST MARKS, PRIVACY SEALS AND POPIA CERTIFICATION

As we discussed above,[123] transparency is not just about ensuring that data subjects can exercise their rights effectively; it is also about trust. Data subjects are willing to share personal information with responsible parties they can trust, and many are willing to walk away if that trust is broken. It is not surprising, from a commercial perspective, that organisations want to 'certify' themselves as POPIA compliant.

The EU Data Protection Directive of 1995[124] dealt with the concept of a privacy seal, trust marks or certification. While the SA Law Reform Commission did consider privacy seals it noted that 'current (privacy) seal programmes have not, however, inspired great confidence'.[125] As a result POPIA does not set out a framework for the Information Regulator to certify that a responsible party complies with POPIA and provide a 'privacy seal'.

Key point: There have been attempts by privacy consultants and vendors to sell a 'POPIA compliant' mark or seal in South Africa. The Information Regulator does not currently provide a certification or seal of this nature and no structure currently exists for it to do so. Any trust mark, seal or certification is, at best, the opinion of the organisation selling it rather than a formal certification.

122 See our discussion about how notification should take place in paragraph 11.5 above.

123 Paragraph 11.5.4.

124 Available at https://eur-lex.europa.eu/legal-content/EN/TXT/?uri=CELEX%3A31995L0046.

125 SA Law Reform Commission Project 124 on Privacy and Data Protection (2009 Report). It would seem that the concern was that providing such a certification would compromise the independence of the regulatory body and invite corruption (see footnote 117 of the SA Law Reform Commission Project 124 on Privacy and Data Protection (2009 Report)).

While there is currently no structure in POPIA to accredit existing privacy seals or trust marks,[126] this does not mean that they would not be useful as a means to notify data subjects that the responsible party complies with POPIA. Notably the international position on trust marks and certification has matured and now the EU GDPR[127] allows for the Data Protection Authorities (DPAs) to issue trust marks or certificates. The EU has set out criteria for certification.[128]

Key point: It seems likely that the next version of POPIA may well support a certification programme similar to the EU GDPR's programme.

11.9 PRACTICAL ADVICE

11.9.1 Wait until you are ready

Many organisations want to start their POPIA compliance efforts with a privacy notice. While it is understandable,[129] it is a little misguided. An organisation is ready to draft its privacy notice(s) if it can answer these questions:

- Who is the responsible party(s)?[130]
- Who are the different categories of data subjects that must be notified?[131]
- What personal information is being collected? Is any of the personal information special personal information?[132]
- What are the sources of the personal information?[133]

[126] An example of a South African trust mark is Privyseal: http://privyseal.co.za.

[127] Article 42 of the EU GDPR.

[128] Available at https://edpb.europa.eu/our-work-tools/our-documents/guidelines/guidelines-12018-certification-and-identifying_en, published on 4 June 2019. See further the ICO advisory on certification, available at https://ico.org.uk/for-organisations/guide-to-data-protection/guide-to-the-general-data-protection-regulation-gdpr/accountability-and-governance/certification/.

[129] Privacy notices are probably the one thing about POPIA that most people understand. It is also something that makes organisations look POPIA compliant, but often that compliance is skin deep.

[130] Identifying the responsible party is discussed in chapter 4.

[131] Having a privacy notice per 'category' of data subject is discussed in paragraph 11.5.3.

[132] The definition of 'personal information' is discussed in chapter 3 paragraph 3.2.1 and special personal information is discussed in chapter 7 paragraph 7.2.

[133] Collecting personal information from sources other than the data subject is discussed in chapter 10.

- Was providing the personal information voluntary or mandatory and what are the implications of not providing the information?[134]
- What are the purposes for which the personal information will be used?[135]
- What are the legal justifications the responsible party is relying on?[136]
- With whom will the information be shared?[137]
- Will the information be sent out of South Africa? To which countries will it be sent? What level of protection will the information have?[138]
- How will the information be secured?[139]
- What rights do data subjects have and how must they exercise these rights?[140]
- For how long will the information be retained?[141]
- When will data subjects be notified?[142]
- How will data subjects be notified?[143]
- How will data subjects be notified of updates to the privacy notice?[144]

134 This is discussed in paragraph 11.3.1.

135 Purpose specification is discussed in chapter 6 paragraph 6.2.

136 This notification is not strictly required, but we discussed why it would be prudent to include it in paragraph 11.3.1 above.

137 Sharing personal information between different organisations is discussed in chapter 13. This notification is discussed in paragraph 11.3.2 above.

138 Transborder information flows are discussed in chapter 14.

139 This requirement is discussed in paragraph 11.3.1 above. Information security management is discussed in chapter 5.

140 Data subject rights are discussed in chapter 18.

141 Records management is discussed in chapter 17.

142 The timing of the notification is discussed in paragraph 11.4 above.

143 The form of the notification is discussed in paragraph 11.5 above.

144 Updating privacy notices is discussed in paragraph 11.4.4 above.

Key point: Organisations are usually only ready to draft their privacy notice(s) after mapping their personal information collection and processing activities (often referred to as data flow maps)[145] and conducting personal information impact assessments[146] on these processing activities.

11.9.2 Beg, borrow and steal

POPIA does not provide much direct guidance on the format of privacy notices but there is a highly useful guide provided by the ICO on what information about data protection should be provided,[147] as well as a free privacy notice template[148] and a checklist of what to consider,[149] which is a good place to start. It provides examples of good (and bad) privacy notices.

Key point: If you are feeling insecure about drafting your privacy notice, try looking at other organisations' privacy notices and reading the EU's Guidelines on Transparency under Regulation 2016/679.[150]

Having said that, be careful, because each organisation is different and we have seen many copy-and-paste mistakes in privacy notices.

11.9.3 Remember who the privacy notice is for

The most important aspect of plain language is that responsible parties must take the target audience (also referred to as a market segment) into account.[151] This means that information officers should work closely with specialists who can provide a profile of the typical data

---

145 We referred to data flow maps in chapter 1 paragraph 1.4.

146 Personal information impact assessments are discussed in chapter 20 paragraph 20.3.

147 Available at https://ico.org.uk/for-organisations/guide-to-data-protection/guide-to-the-general-data-protection-regulation-gdpr/the-right-to-be-informed/what-privacy-information-should-we-provide/.

148 Available at https://ico.org.uk/for-organisations/make-your-own-privacy-notice/. See also https://iapp.org//media/pdf/resource_center/Data%20Protection%20Policy%20Model%202013.pdf for a template.

149 Available at https://ico.org.uk/for-organisations/guide-to-data-protection/guide-to-the-general-data-protection-regulation-gdpr/individual-rights/right-to-be-informed/.

150 wp260rev.01, available at https://ec.europa.eu/newsroom/article29/item-detail.cfm?item_id=622227.

151 Plain language was discussed in paragraph 11.5.4 above. It was also discussed in the context of informed consent in chapter 2 paragraph 2.6.4.

subject for whom the privacy notice is intended.[152] These specialists could be hiding in an organisation's marketing, human resources or communications departments. Befriend them.

Key point: Legalese is death to transparency. Yes, lawyers, we are talking to you.

Privacy notices are also an opportunity to appeal to new market segments. Read the annual CISCO consumer privacy survey.[153] In 2020, 29% of respondents identified as 'privacy actives'. A privacy active is a person who cares about privacy, is willing to act to protect it and has already switched brands due to their privacy practices. What this means is that there is an entire market segment that is motivated by privacy concerns, and so if a responsible party can demonstrate that it respects data subjects' privacy and personal information it has the ability to tap into that market.[154]

This is done by:

- getting feedback from the privacy actives and finding out what they think
- engaging with the privacy actives on how to do it better
- shortening and simplifying privacy notices so that people can read them in no more than two minutes, and being clear on what they get in return for their personal information; and
- creating a transparency strategy that is able to adjust to the dynamic privacy landscape.[155]

[152] This is also prescribed in the definition of plain language in section 1 of the Consumer Protection Act 68 of 2008.

[153] Available at https://www.cisco.com/c/dam/en_us/about/doing_business/trust-center/docs/cisco-consumer-privacy-infographic-2020.pdf.

[154] Thomas C Redman and Robert M Waitman 'Do you care about privacy as much as your customers do?' *Harvard Business Review*, available at https://hbr.org/2020/01/do-you-care-about-privacy-as-much-as-your-customers-do.

[155] Thomas C Redman and Robert M Waitman 'Do you care about privacy as much as your customers do?' *Harvard Business Review*, available at https://hbr.org/2020/01/do-you-care-about-privacy-as-much-as-your-customers-do.

12 Further processing of personal information (secondary use)

12.1 WHAT TO EXPECT IN THIS CHAPTER

As we saw in previous chapters, the purpose for which personal information is collected is key to almost all aspects of POPIA compliance.[1] But what if an organisation wants to process personal information for a new purpose? After all, using personal information for new purposes, or finding new methods of processing personal information, lies at the heart of innovation and digital transformation.

Shifting purposes may introduce new privacy risks. So it is not surprising that the fourth condition for the lawful processing of personal information is the 'further processing limitation'.[2] Further processing happens when a responsible party uses personal information for a purpose other than the purpose for which the information was originally collected. This will only be acceptable if the further processing is still compatible with the original purpose.

In this chapter we discuss the following:

- Why a further processing limitation?
- The role of the concept of compatibility in POPIA
- Assessing general compatibility with the original purpose
- When processing for a new purpose is automatically justified
- Further processing of personal information created by the responsible party
- Consequences of incompatibility

12.2 WHY A FURTHER PROCESSING LIMITATION?

If one wants to understand the way in which the world is changing, it is interesting to look at trends in employment. Every year, the World Economic Forum conducts a *Future of Jobs Survey*.[3] In 2020, these were the top 20 jobs that are in increasing demand across industries:[4]

1 We discussed the purposes and justifications for processing personal information in chapter 6.

2 Section 15.

3 Available at https://www.weforum.org/reports/the-future-of-jobs-report-2020. We also noticed that Mechanics and Machinery Repairers are in both columns. We don't know why, but didn't want the facts to get in the way of a good story.

4 At 30 of the survey report.

	INCREASING DEMAND		DECREASING DEMAND
1	Data Analysts and Scientists	1	Data Entry Clerks
2	AI and Machine Learning Specialists	2	Administrative and Executive Secretaries
3	Big Data Specialists	3	Accounting, Bookkeeping and Payroll Clerks
4	Digital Marketing and Strategy Specialists	4	Accountants and Auditors
5	Process Automation Specialists	5	Assembly and Factory Workers
6	Business Development Professionals	6	Business Services and Administration Managers
7	Digital Transformation Specialists	7	Client Information and Customer Service Workers
8	Information Security Analysts	8	General and Operations Managers
9	Software and Applications Developers	9	Mechanics and Machinery Repairers
10	Internet of Things Specialists	10	Material-Recording and Stock-Keeping Clerks
11	Project Managers	11	Financial Analysts
12	Business Services and Administration Managers	12	Postal Service Clerks
13	Database and Network Professionals	13	Sales Rep., Wholesale and Manuf., Tech. and Sci.Products
14	Robotics Engineers	14	Relationship Managers
15	Strategic Advisors	15	Bank Tellers and Related Clerks
16	Management and Organisation Analysts	16	Door-To-Door Sales, News and Street Vendors
17	FinTech Engineers	17	Electronics and Telecoms Installers and Repairers
18	Mechanics and Machinery Repairers	18	Human Resources Specialists
19	Organisational Development Specialists	19	Training and Development Specialists
20	Risk Management Specialists	20	Construction Labourers

By our calculation, there are only two roles for which there is increased demand that do not have much to do with the processing of personal information.[5] What does this tell us? It confirms the exponential increase in the speed and breadth of technological innovation – and that innovation is fuelled by (personal) data.

There are three laws of technology that explain this rapid growth:[6]

- Moore's Law: Transistors per chip will double every two years. Translated from the original Geek this means that computing power will double in capacity every two years.
- Koomey's Law: The energy it takes to generate this computing power is halved every 18 months.
- Kryder's Law: The amount of data you can store in a space will double every two years. Put differently, the cost of storage will halve every 18 months.

[5] Have fun connecting the dots and then considering a career change.

[6] For an explanation (and criticism) of these technology laws see Angus Hervey 'Moore's Law is probably dead', available at https://medium.com/future-crunch/moore-s-law-isn-t-the-only-technology-law-it-may-not-even-be-the-most-important-1964581dc0ab.

Put in human terms: '[a]n executive moving from graduation to management over 20 years will face technology 500,000 times more powerful than the day they started work'.[7]

Interesting, but what has this got to do with POPIA? With computing power increasing and the cost of computing and storing data decreasing exponentially, it is becoming easier, faster and cheaper for organisations to process more and more personal information. With all of this change and innovation, it stands to reason that the purposes for which an organisation collects and uses personal information today, might not be the same purposes for which that personal information will be used tomorrow. When the purpose for which personal information is used changes, it is referred to as 'further processing'.[8] The purpose of section 15 of POPIA is to ensure that data subjects still enjoy the same level of protection when things change.

Tricky area: We hear people criticise POPIA (or any regulatory compliance really) as being death to innovation. In 2020 CISCO surveyed 2 500 professionals in 13 countries for its study 'From Privacy to Profit: Achieving Positive Returns on Privacy Investments'.[9] Spoiler alert: 71% the organisations surveyed indicated that their privacy programmes enabled agility and innovation. That was just one of the findings that led to the over-arching finding that for every dollar spent on privacy, these organisations saw a return on investment of USD2.70. Well worth a read for anybody who has to convince the powers that be to invest in privacy!

---

7 Tony Crabb 'The pace of technological change', available at https://www.australianpropertyjournal.com.au/2018/10/18/the-pace-of-technological-change/.

8 There is no definition for 'further processing' in POPIA. The SA Law Reform Commission stated that further processing includes both the use and disclosure of information (SA Law Reform Commission Project 124 on Privacy and Data Protection (2009 Report) 221). Further processing is described as follows in recital 50 of the EU GDPR: 'The processing of personal data for purposes other than those for which the personal data were initially collected …' In other jurisdictions, the purpose for which the personal information was collected is referred to as primary use, and the 'new' purpose is referred to as further processing (or 'secondary use'). For a detailed discussion of where section 15 came from, see the SA Law Reform Commission Project 124 on Privacy and Data Protection (2005 Discussion Paper) from 40 paragraph 4.2.79.

9 Available at https://www.cisco.com/c/dam/global/en_uk/products/collateral/security/2020-data-privacy-cybersecurity-series-jan-2020.pdf.

12.3 THE ROLE OF THE CONCEPT OF COMPATIBILITY IN POPIA

The key question is whether the further processing requires a further legal justification. In a sense, section 15 is a companion to section 11(1), which was discussed in chapter 6 paragraph 6.3. This is what we mean:

- If an organisation is collecting personal information for the first time, the organisation has to have a legal justification for each purpose for which the personal information will be processed. The list of the six possible legal justifications is in section 11.
- If an organisation wants to process personal information it already has for a new purpose, the organisation has to comply with section 15.

Section 15 asks one question: Is the new purpose 'in accordance with or compatible with' the purpose for which the personal information was collected?

> **Key point:** The crucial point in time for determining the original purpose is when the personal information is collected. Personal information can be collected from the data subject, or, under certain circumstances, from other sources. We discuss this in chapter 10.

If it is not compatible, the new processing activity is unlawful.[10] In order to demonstrate compatibility, the new purpose behind the further processing must either:

- be generally compatible in terms of section 15(2); or
- meet the criteria of one of the specific legal justifications in section 15(3).

> **Key point:** What is the relationship between section 15(2) and section 15(3)? Does a responsible party have to comply with both, or only one of the two? According to the SA Law Reform Commission, section 15(2) gives the guidelines on how to determine if a purpose is compatible and section 15(3) provides a number of exceptions – circumstances in which further processing will be regarded as compatible with the original purpose of collection. This means that a responsible party has to comply with either section 15(2) or section 15(3).

10 We discuss the consequences of incompatibility in paragraph 12.7.

12.4 ASSESSING GENERAL COMPATIBILITY WITH THE ORIGINAL PURPOSE

Key point: When considering the intent behind the concept of compatibility, it is useful to consider the commentary of the Article 29 Data Protection Working Party on 'purpose limitation',[11] which was the equivalent of section 15 under the Data Protection Directive that preceded the EU GDPR. Tread carefully though, because the wording of article 6(1)*(b)* is very different to section 15.[12]

Here are some of the observations the Article 29 Data Protection Working Party made on assessing compatibility:[13]

- Just because a purpose is different, does not mean that it is incompatible. This needs to be assessed on a case-by-case basis and the approach has to be flexible.
- The assessment has to take any changes to 'the expectations of society – or of the data subjects themselves – ... about what additional use the data would be put to' into account. This takes into account the possibility that the responsible party and data subjects could not foresee all of the purposes for which personal information would be useful at the time of collection.
- The assessment should not be a formalistic comparison of the disclosed original purpose for collection and the new processing activity. It should be a 'substantive assessment [that] will go beyond formal statements to identify both the new and the original purpose, considering the way they are (or should be) understood, depending on the context and other factors'.

Further processing is always a matter of degree:

- In some cases, the compatibility of the original and the new purpose will be obvious. Consider this example: A customer signs up for a wine of the month club. After the initial collection of the customer's delivery address and payment details, the information is used each month to process payment and to deliver the wine. These activities are obviously compatible with the original purpose for the collection and no further analysis is required.

---

11 Available at https://ec.europa.eu/justice/article-29/documentation/opinion-recommendation/files/2013/wp203_en.pdf.

12 For a detailed discussion of where section 15 came from, see the SA Law Reform Commission Project 124 on Privacy and Data Protection (2009 Report) 206 paragraph 4.2.135.

13 Article 29 Data Protection Working Party *Opinion 03/2013 on purpose limitation* (2 April 2013) 21, available at https://ec.europa.eu/justice/article-29/documentation/opinion-recommendation/files/2013/wp203_en.pdf.

- In many cases, the answer is not obvious and further analysis is needed. There may be a connection between the original purpose and the new purpose, but the purposes do not match completely. Consider this example: The wine of the month club wants to use the customer's email address to offer the customer a discount voucher for a wine tasting event.[14] The club cannot assume that the new purpose is compatible with the original purpose and must do a further detailed analysis and consider the factors listed in section 15(2).
- Sometimes a new purpose is obviously incompatible with the original purpose. The new purpose will be incompatible if the new activity is unexpected, inappropriate or objectionable. Consider this example: The wine of the month club sells the data subject's information to an insurance company. The insurance company intends to contact the data subject to market its insurance products. Obviously, the data subject won't expect that the wine of the month club will sell their information, and this activity will be objectionable to the reasonable person. The new purpose in this example is not compatible with the original purpose for collection; or at least not without consent.[15]

Key point: Even before POPIA, the concept of limiting the processing of personal information for new and unexpected purposes has been considered by our courts. In the case of *Black Sash Trust v Minister of Social Development*[16] the Constitutional Court determined that the South African Social Security Agency (SASSA) is under a duty to protect the personal information of the beneficiaries of grants from the government. The order was for SASSA to include terms in their contract with the company that processed payments on their behalf for adequate safeguards to ensure that:

- the personal information processed during payment remains private and that it may not be used for any purposes other than paying grants or a purpose sanctioned by the Minister in terms of the Social Assistance Act; and
- no contracting party may contact beneficiaries for direct marketing purposes.

➡

Chapter 12

14 This example came to one of the authors in a dream. She's still waiting for this dream to come true.

15 Apparently, rampant further processing is the one exception to the Tyrion Lannister rule which states that 'everything's better with some wine in the belly'. See Laura Reilly 'Tyrion Lannister's 12 best boozy quotes'. Available at https://www.thrillist.com/culture/best-tyrion-lannister-quotes.

16 2017 (3) SA 335 (CC).

A word of caution about this case: It was decided before POPIA came into effect and the judgment does not reference POPIA, much less 'further processing'. As we have seen, there may be scenarios where this type of further processing could take place.

Section 15(2) lists the factors that must be taken into account when considering compatibility. We will analyse these factors in the remainder of this section.

Key point: To assess the compatibility of a new processing activity, the responsible party has to identify the original purpose for collecting the personal information and the proposed purpose for processing.[17] This is another reason why documenting the purpose is so important. It is equally important that responsible parties should document the assessment performed to ensure that new purposes are compatible. We will discuss this in paragraph 12.8 below.

12.4.1 The relationship between the original purpose and the new purpose

It is perhaps stating the obvious, but the relationship between the purpose of the intended further processing and the purpose for which the personal information was collected must be assessed.[18] The focus should be on the substance of the relationship between the purposes of collection and the purposes of the new processing activity and not (just) what the original disclosed purposes were.[19]

Key point: If the new purpose was implied in the original purpose (e.g. it was a logical next step), it will be compatible. It may even be compatible where the link is more tenuous, for instance if the different stakeholders (including data subjects) commonly understood that the further processing would take place. We are back to our old rule of thumb: Will the data subject be surprised to learn that the further processing is taking place?

---

17 Article 29 Data Protection Working Party *Opinion 03/2013 on purpose limitation*, 21, available at https://ec.europa.eu/justice/article-29/documentation/opinion-recommendation/files/2013/wp203_en.pdf.

18 Section 15(2)*(a)*.

19 Article 29 Data Protection Working Party *Opinion 03/2013 on purpose limitation* (2 April 2013) 21, available at https://ec.europa.eu/justice/article-29/documentation/opinion-recommendation/files/2013/wp203_en.pdf.

12.4.2 The nature of the information concerned

The nature of the personal information involved in the new processing activity should also be considered.[20] The responsible party must evaluate whether the new purpose requires the processing of sensitive personal information, for example, special personal information or the personal information of a child. Because sensitive personal information justifies higher levels of protection, the test for compatibility with the original purpose will be stricter.[21]

Key point: Always remember to take the principle of minimality into account. If there is a way to perform the further processing without using sensitive personal information, that is what the responsible party must do. This is an independent enquiry from assessing compatibility and was discussed in chapter 9.

12.4.3 The consequences of the further processing on the data subject

Here, the consequences (both negative and positive) for the data subject are examined in order to gauge compatibility.[22] If the new purpose would have a large or very negative impact on the data subject, it is unlikely that it is compatible. The responsible party must also consider whether there is an alternative method available to achieve its objectives. The new purpose will be less likely to be compatible if less invasive methods are available.[23]

Here are some of the types of impacts that the Article 29 Data Protection Working Party lists under this factor:[24]

- Does the further processing involve potential decisions or actions by third parties?
- Can the further processing lead to exclusion or discrimination?

20 Section 15(2)*(b)*.

21 Article 29 Data Protection Working Party *Opinion 03/2013 on purpose limitation* 25, available at https://ec.europa.eu/justice/article-29/documentation/opinion-recommendation/files/2013/wp203_en.pdf.

22 Section 15(2)*(c)*.

23 Article 29 Data Protection Working Party *Opinion 03/2013 on purpose limitation* 26, available at https://ec.europa.eu/justice/article-29/documentation/opinion-recommendation/files/2013/wp203_en.pdf.

24 Article 29 Data Protection Working Party *Opinion 03/2013 on purpose limitation* 25, available at https://ec.europa.eu/justice/article-29/documentation/opinion-recommendation/files/2013/wp203_en.pdf.

- What is the emotional impact of the further processing on data subjects? For example, will they be irritated or experience fear or distress at losing control over their personal information or will they feel that their privacy has been compromised?
- Will the further processing involve another responsible party?
- Will the further processing lead to the personal information being publicised or made available to a large number of people?
- Will large amounts of personal information be processed or combined with other personal information (e.g. profiling data subjects)?
- Are there less intrusive means to achieve the new purpose?

12.4.4 The manner in which the personal information was collected

The circumstances surrounding the collection of the personal information are relevant to assessing compatibility.[25] As much as we have said that the notifications made to the data subjects at the time of collection should not be the only factor, it, and the other circumstances surrounding the collection of the information, are relevant, because they inform the reasonable expectations of the data subject.

Key point: The more unexpected or surprising the new processing activity is, the more likely it is that the new purpose would be incompatible with the original purpose. The Article 29 Data Protection Working Party asks 'what a reasonable person in the data subject's situation would expect his or her data to be used for based on the context of the collection'.[26] So, manage those expectations!

12.4.5 Any contractual rights between the data subject and the responsible party

The nature of the relationship between the data subject and the responsible party has an impact on the potential compatibility of a new processing activity.[27] POPIA focuses on the contract between the parties as the dominant indicator of the nature of this relationship. If further processing is required to perform the responsible party's

---

25 Section 15(2)*(d)*.

26 Article 29 Data Protection Working Party *Opinion 03/2013 on purpose limitation* 24, available at https://ec.europa.eu/justice/article-29/documentation/opinion-recommendation/files/2013/wp203_en.pdf.

27 Section 15(2)*(d)*.

obligations in terms of a contract, it is likely that the processing will be compatible.

The Article 29 Data Protection Working Party looks further than the contract. Here are some additional factors relating to the nature of the relationship that they consider:[28]

- customary and generally expected practice in the context
- the balance of power between the data subject and the responsible party (e.g. was the data subject obliged to provide the personal information to the responsible party)
- the bargaining power of the data subject (e.g. how easy is it for the data subject to terminate the contract with the responsible party and find an alternative service provider or employer); and
- if the data subject consented to the original purpose, how voluntary was that consent and was it specific and informed.

Key point: The key questions remains whether the contractual obligations (or other factors relating to the nature of the relationship) give rise to 'reasonable expectations of stricter confidentiality and stricter limitations on further use. In general, the more specific and restrictive the context of collection, the more limitations there are likely to be on further use. Here again, it is necessary to take account of the factual context rather than simply rely on text in small print.'[29]

12.5 WHEN PROCESSING FOR A NEW PURPOSE IS AUTOMATICALLY JUSTIFIED

Our story does not end here. Section 15(3) contains a list of instances when further processing will automatically be compatible.[30] The first step is to get past the double negative 'personal information is not incompatible with' to realise that further processing will automatically be compatible (and therefore justified) in the instances discussed in the remainder of this section.[31]

[28] Article 29 Data Protection Working Party *Opinion 03/2013 on purpose limitation* 24, available at https://ec.europa.eu/justice/article-29/documentation/opinion-recommendation/files/2013/wp203_en.pdf.

[29] Article 29 Data Protection Working Party *Opinion 03/2013 on purpose limitation* 25, available at https://ec.europa.eu/justice/article-29/documentation/opinion-recommendation/files/2013/wp203_en.pdf.

[30] The SA Law Reform Commission states: 'A number of exceptions are, furthermore, included that indicate circumstances in which the further processing will not be regarded as incompatible with the original purpose of collection.' This quote can be found in the SA Law Reform Commission Project 124 on Privacy and Data Protection (2009 Report) paragraph 4.2.175.

[31] Section 15(3). You will find this double negative in the EU GDPR. According to the Article 29 Data Protection Working Party it would appear that this was done to give more flexibility with regard to future use. We think it was force of (lawyer) habit.

12.5.1 The data subject consented

It is possible for a responsible party to ask the data subject to consent to the further processing.[32]

Key point: This is a new consent which is obtained before the further processing commences.[33] The consent must comply with all of the requirements for a valid consent which were discussed in chapter 2 paragraph 2.6.6. We also discussed the consent as a legal justification for processing in chapter 6.

However, relying on consent for further processing is not without its challenges. The data subject must be able to say 'no' and the responsible party must continue with the original processing activities, without doing the further processing. This means that consent cannot be used in instances where it is not possible for the responsible party to continue its relationship with the data subject without doing the further processing.

As we discussed previously,[34] any consent in terms of POPIA must be:

- specific (a blanket consent to 'further processing' at the time of collection will not be valid)
- informed (the consent should perhaps explain the impact (negative and positive) of the further processing)
- voluntary (if consent is not given then the responsible party must continue with the original processing activities, without doing the further processing); and
- an expression of will (either a signature or some form of positive act that signifies that the data subject consented to this).

32 Section 15(3)*(a)*.

33 ICO *Guide to the General Data Protection Regulation,* available at https://ico.org.uk/for-organisations/guide-to-data-protection/guide-to-the-general-data-protection-regulation-gdpr/principles/purpose-limitation/.

34 See chapter 2 paragraph 2.6.6.

Tricky area: In many scenarios, it will be unpalatable to responsible parties that the data subject's consent must be voluntary and that they cannot be penalised for withholding consent. What this means is that responsible parties should avoid relying on this justification at all cost. For instance, consent cannot be used in instances where it is not possible for the responsible party to avoid the further processing.

12.5.2 The personal information is available in or derived from a public record

If the personal information is available or derived from a public record, any further processing that uses that personal information will be compatible.[35]

Key point: A 'public record' is a record that is accessible in the public domain and which is in the possession of or under the control of a public body, whether or not it was created by that public body. This definition and the misconceptions around what it means are discussed in chapter 10 paragraph 10.4.1. Suffice it to state that POPIA's exceptions relating to 'public records' administered by 'public bodies' are not easy exceptions to rely on, due to the complex definitions. If a responsible party is incorrect in their interpretation, they may not be able to continue with the further processing.

Many organisations justify scraping the internet by saying 'well, the information is already public'. This does not hold water, because the internet is not a public record unless the site in question is administered by a public body.

12.5.3 The personal information was deliberately made public by the data subject

The primary concern here is how to establish whether the data subject intended to make the personal information public and what 'public' means? This is discussed in detail in chapter 10 paragraph 10.4.2, but suffice it to say that the bar is very high and it will be difficult for responsible parties to prove that the information was made public by the data subject, deliberately.

[35] Section 15(3)*(b)*.

12.5.4 The further processing is required for law and order

Further processing of personal information will be justified if it is necessary for the following purposes:

- 'to avoid prejudice to the maintenance of law by any public body' which includes the 'prevention, detection, investigation, prosecution and punishment of offences'[36]
- protecting the interest of 'national security'[37]
- complying with 'an obligation imposed by law' or to enforce legislation concerning the collection of revenue as defined in section 1 of the South African Revenue Service Act';[38] or
- conducting 'proceedings in any court or tribunal that have commenced or are reasonably contemplated'.[39]

Tricky area: Interestingly there is no indication in section 18(4)*(c)*(iii) that the courts or tribunals need to be South African courts or tribunals. In contrast, the exception from the application of POPIA as found in section 6(1)*(e)* makes it clear that the courts that enjoy a blanket exemption from POPIA are only South African courts.[40] From this we can assume that not only local courts but also foreign courts and tribunals will have the right to do further processing. Of course, there are other considerations aside from further processing which these courts and tribunals would have to consider, which would potentially include cross-border transfer of personal information,[41] so be careful about assuming that foreign courts and tribunals are entitled to a free-for-all.

The most important word to consider in subsection (3)*(c)* is the word 'necessary'. In chapter 6 paragraph 6.3.1, we first considered the concept of 'necessary' and the questions set out there can be amended to apply to further processing as well, namely:

- What is the fundamental purpose(s) of the further processing activity?
- Is there a way to achieve these fundamental purpose(s) without further processing?

---

36 Section 15(3)*(c)*(i).

37 Section 15(3)*(c)*(iv).

38 Section 15(3)*(c)*(ii).

39 Section 15(3)*(c)*(iii).

40 Section 6(1)*(e)* of POPIA refers to 'a court referred to in s 166 of the South African Constitution' which naturally only refers to the establishment of South African courts. See https://www.justice.gov.za/legislation/constitution/SAConstitution-web-eng.pdf for a full list of these courts.

41 See chapter 14.

Tricky area: A responsible party should ask whether POPIA applies to these activities at all as – as we saw in the exclusions in chapter 3 paragraph 3.3 – *some* public bodies are exempted from the whole of POPIA. However, if you take a closer look at section 6(1)*(c)* of POPIA you will notice that this exception only applies, 'to the extent that adequate safeguards have been established in legislation for the protection of personal information'. By implication then, section 15(3)*(c)*(i) and (iv) assumes that adequate safeguards have **not** been established in the legislation but nonetheless still allows for a general justification of further processing if it is necessary and collected by a public body dealing with criminal offences or in the interests of national security.[42]

12.5.5 Preventing or mitigating a serious or imminent threat to health and safety

Further processing will be allowed if it is aimed at preventing or mitigating a serious or imminent threat to:

- public health or safety; or
- the life or health of the data subject or another individual.[43]

This justification of further processing is reminiscent of article 6(1)*(d)* of the EU GDPR which provides that the processing of personal information will be lawful if it is 'necessary in order to protect the vital interests of the data subject or of another person'.[44] This article in the EU GDPR does not pertain to further processing, but the underlying considerations are the same. Recital 46 provides that '[s]ome types of processing may service both important grounds of public interest and the vital interests of the data subject as for instance when processing is necessary for humanitarian purposes, including for monitoring epidemics and their spread or in situations of humanitarian emergencies, in particular in situations of natural and man-made disasters'. This justification for further processing will apply to public bodies as well as other organisations (e.g. any employer might be put in the position where they have to rely on this justification for further processing).

[42] Section 18(4)*(c)*(i) and (iv) of POPIA.

[43] Section 15(3)*(d)*.

[44] This was discussed in chapter 6 paragraph 6.3.3. That discussion was more limited, because section 11(1)*(d)* only relates to individual data subjects and not the public.

This ground for allowing further processing seemed almost prescient when we were drafting this book. The global response to the COVID-19 pandemic tested privacy regulators on an unprecedented level and set off a flurry of guidelines.[45] The response of privacy regulators and civil society is an excellent illustration of the limitations of this justification for further processing. The guidelines and safeguards suggested by privacy regulators can be grouped in the following topics:[46]

- **Lawfulness:** In the context of the pandemic, regulators pointed out that the interventions must be provided for by law and justified by legitimate public health objectives. They pointed out that interventions must be proportionate and that governments must be transparent.
- **Time-bound:** The new powers given to governments and the private sector must be temporary. When the crisis ends, the powers must lapse. For example, the pandemic must not be an excuse for indefinite surveillance.
- **Purpose limitation:** The use of personal information should be limited to combating the pandemic. For instance, governments and the private sector should not commercialise the personal information.
- **Address risks to marginalised populations:** Marginalised populations should not be discriminated against by using datasets that do not reflect their realities.
- **Limit sharing:** The sharing of personal information used to combat the pandemic should be controlled through data sharing agreements, due diligence, sunset clauses, and the personal information should be firewalled from other business and commercial interests.
- **There must be oversight:** Individuals should be able to challenge the use of their personal information.
- **Meaningful participation:** All relevant stakeholders should be empowered through free, active and meaningful participation in shaping policies.

It does not have to be your privacy or your life.

---

45 See the International Association of Privacy Professionals' COVID-19 Guidance and Resources page, available at https://iapp.org/resources/topics/covid-19-guidance-and-resources/.

46 See Human Rights Watch 'Joint Civil Society Statement: States use of digital surveillance technologies to fight pandemic must respect human rights', available at https://www.hrw.org/news/2020/04/02/joint-civil-society-statement-states-use-digital-surveillance-technologies-fight.

12.5.6 Historical, statistical or research purposes

Further processing will be justified if the personal information is used for historical, statistical, or research purposes[47] and the responsible party ensures that the:

- personal information is not used for any other purposes; and
- the results will not be published in an identifiable form.[48]

12.5.7 The Information Regulator has granted an exemption

Further processing can be justified by the Information Regulator by granting an exemption to a responsible party.[49] This was discussed in chapter 3 paragraph 3.3.7.

12.5.8 Exemption in respect of certain functions

If an organisation performs any of the functions in section 38 of POPIA, it can do further processing.

Key point: This exemption only applies to public bodies[50] or to other organisations who must perform these functions 'in terms of the law'.[51] It also only applies to the extent that the function is 'performed with the view to protecting members of the public'.

The 'relevant functions' are functions that protect members of the public against:

- financial loss due to dishonesty, malpractice or other seriously improper conduct by, or the unfitness or incompetence of, persons providing banking, insurance, investment or other financial services or the management of bodies corporate; or
- dishonesty, malpractice or other seriously improper conduct by, or the unfitness or incompetence of, persons authorised to carry on any profession or other activity.

[47] We discuss the meaning of 'historical, statistical or research purposes in chapter 2 paragraph 2.6.7.

[48] Section 15(3)*(e)*.

[49] Section 37.

[50] See the definition of 'public body' in section 1.

[51] Section 38(2).

Tricky area: What does 'performed with the view to protecting members of the public' mean? For one thing, the exemption will not apply to functions performed by a responsible party to protect itself. For instance, it will certainly cover the Financial Sector Conduct Authority when it polices compliance with the fit and proper requirements imposed on intermediaries in terms of the Financial Advisory and Intermediary Services Act (FAIS).[52] However, will it cover a financial services provider when its human resources department uses the same information in its recruitment process for purposes of deciding between candidates for employment? Given that justifications will be interpreted narrowly, the financial service provider will only be covered for activities that are necessary for its own compliance with FAIS. The minute an activity is performed for purposes other than complying with FAIS, the justification will no longer apply.

12.6 FURTHER PROCESSING OF PERSONAL INFORMATION CREATED BY THE RESPONSIBLE PARTY

Responsible parties often create personal information about their customers, employees or even members of the public. Consider this in the context of an 'online bookstore'.[53] The bookstore collects a data subject's personal information when she creates an account and every time she makes a purchase. The bookstore creates an algorithm that uses the records of past purchases to create a profile of the data subject. The bookstore uses the profile (created personal information) to recommend books to the data subject when she next visits their website. This is a new purpose and the bookstore will have to consider whether the further processing is compatible with the original purpose of collection or creation.

Tricky area: If this is the first time the bookstore is doing predictive analytics and they are using the personal information of existing customers, it is further processing and must comply with section 15. Of course, in respect of all new customers, predictive analytics is now one of the purposes for which the personal information is created, and the 'online bookstore' needs to comply with section 11.

---

52 Act 37 of 2002.

53 These are air quotes. When we say 'online bookstore', we mean Amazon.

12.7 CONSEQUENCES OF INCOMPATIBILITY

What if the further processing is not compatible with the original purpose for collecting personal information? It is clear that proceeding with the further processing despite the incompatibility would be a contravention of POPIA, but what are the alternatives open to responsible parties? If a last-ditch attempt at getting consent fails (or consent is not a viable option),[54] is that the end of the road? Or can a responsible party restart the process, pretend that it is going to collect the personal information afresh and rely on one of the legal justifications in section 11?[55]

Tricky area: The Article 29 Data Protection Working Party had the following to say when commenting on the Data Protection Directive:[56] '[T]he data controller cannot simply consider the further processing as a new processing activity disconnected from the previous one and circumvent this prohibition by using one of the legal grounds in Article 7 [POPIA's section 11] to legitimise the processing. As explained above, the requirements under Article 6 [which contains POPIA's section 15(1)] and Article 7 [section 11] are cumulative: both must be met simultaneously. Legalising an otherwise incompatible processing activity simply by changing the terms of a contract with the data subject, or by identifying an additional legitimate interest of the controller, would go against the spirit of the purpose limitation principle and remove its substance.' We agree. There was even an attempt to change this in the EU GDPR, but ultimately, the approach stayed the same.

Before we get burnt at the stake, a quick reminder: This does not mean that personal information can never be processed for a new purpose. It just means that a change of purpose can only happen if it is compatible with the original purpose. This entire chapter has been aimed at showing when this will be the case.

[54] See paragraph 12.5.1 above where we explain why consent should be the last resort, if it is possible at all.

[55] Section 11 is discussed in chapter 6.

[56] Article 29 Data Protection Working Party *Opinion 03/2013 on purpose limitation* 36, available at https://ec.europa.eu/justice/article-29/documentation/opinion-recommendation/files/2013/wp203_en.pdf. Admittedly, POPIA's wording is different, but the underlying premise of the Working Party's statement still holds true.

12.8 PRACTICAL ADVICE

The key to staying POPIA compliant is to perform and document compatibility assessments when the purpose(s) for which an organisation processes personal information shifts. Yes, yes, another assessment!

The aim is to ensure that the new purpose for which you want to use the personal information is either compatible under section 15(2) or falls within one of the specific justifications listed in section 15(3). Compatibility is not the only aspect of the new processing activity which should be assessed. Responsible parties should conduct a full personal information impact assessment (PIIA). As we mention in chapter 20,[57] where we discuss PIIAs, they should be done when processing takes place for a new purpose. Instead of assessing which of the legal justifications in section 11 applies, this type of PIIA will contain a compatibility assessment.

[57] Paragraph 20.3.

13 Assessing sharing personal information between organisations

13.1 WHAT TO EXPECT IN THIS CHAPTER

The sharing of personal information between organisations is one of the most controversial topics within privacy. As is often the case in this book, there are competing interests at work. On the one hand, giving data subjects control over their personal information requires that they also have a say in who should have access to their personal information. Data subjects care deeply about who their information is shared with. Even in cases where they are comfortable disclosing their personal information directly to an organisation, they become uncomfortable if that information is shared with third parties without their knowledge. They are also deeply disturbed when these organisations make inferences about them.[1] This is not surprising – no one likes it when they are talked about behind their backs. These concerns can become so severe that data subjects will move away from an organisation in droves.[2]

On the other hand, sharing personal information leads to many economic and social benefits. In her foreword to the ICO's *Data Sharing Code of Practice*, Elizabeth Denham (the Information Commissioner) said:

> 'Utilising the data we collectively hold and allowing it to be maximized properly will have economic benefits. Data sharing that engenders trust in how personal data is being used is a driver of innovation, competition, economic growth and greater choice for consumers and citizens. This is also true in the sphere of public service delivery where efficient sharing of data can improve insights, outcomes and increase options for recipients.'[3]

---

1 Leslie K Jona, Tami Kim and Kate Barasz 'Ads that don't overstep' *Harvard Business Review*, available at https://hbr.org/2018/01/ads-that-dont-overstep.

2 CISCO *Consumer Privacy Survey: The growing imperative of getting data privacy right*, available at https://www.cisco.com/c/dam/global/en_uk/products/collateral/security/cybersecurity-series-2019-cps.pdf. Also see the commentary on the report by Thomas C Redman and Rober M Waitman 'Do you care about privacy as much as your customers do?' *Harvard Business Review*, available at https://hbr.org/2020/01/do-you-care-about-privacy-as-much-as-your-customers-do. In their 2020 Consumer Privacy Survey, CISCO focused on privacy perceptions during the COVID-19 pandemic and found that the top two concerns with sharing personal information during the pandemic are that the personal information will be used for unrelated purposes, and that it will be shared too broadly. An infographic of the 2020 report is available at https://www.cisco.com/c/dam/global/en_uk/products/collateral/security/2020-data-privacy-cybersecurity-series-jan-2020.pdf.

3 Elizabeth Denham is one of our favourite Elizabeths. She was appointed the UK Information Commissioner in July 2016.

Key point: This chapter serves two purposes. Yes, it is about POPIA's impact on the sharing of personal information between organisations, but it is also an illustration of how all of the principles we have addressed thus far come together when assessing a process. In this case, the process of sharing personal information between organisations.

In this chapter we discuss the following:

- What do we mean by 'sharing'?
- What does POPIA say about sharing?
- How do the principles in POPIA apply to sharing?
- Information matching programmes
- Some typical sharing case studies

13.2 WHAT DO WE MEAN BY 'SHARING'?

When we refer to the sharing of personal information in this chapter, we are referring to the transfer of personal information from one organisation to another. It can either be the sharing of one record or millions of records. The 'transfer' of the personal information can also be passive – that is when the personal information stays where it is (i.e. it is not transmitted),[4] but another organisation is given access to it by whatever means.

Key point: Organisations will often declare that they do not share personal information with any third party, but on closer examination, they have given access to that information to individuals from other organisations. This qualifies as sharing. Organisations also sometimes decide to 'pool' personal information in a single database. We also consider this to be sharing.

This chapter does *not* deal with:

- Sharing of personal information with employees of the responsible party: The management of access to personal information within an organisation is often referred to as access control. This is an important part of information security management, which is discussed in chapter 5.

4 This is referred to as giving access to personal information 'at rest'.

- Sharing between a responsible party and an operator: That was dealt with in chapter 4 paragraph 4.4. Why do we not deal with it in this chapter? When information is shared with an operator, the operator essentially becomes an extension of the responsible party and piggybacks on whatever legal justification the responsible party has for processing the personal information. In this chapter, we are concerned with sharing between responsible parties.

Key point: This chapter does not cover sharing between responsible parties and their operators. That is covered in chapter 4 paragraph 4.4.

13.3 WHAT DOES POPIA SAY ABOUT SHARING?

POPIA says very little about sharing specifically.[5] Instead, the principles in POPIA must be applied to the sharing activity to ensure that it is POPIA compliant (just like any other form of processing).

Key point: One of the most pervasive myths about POPIA is that it prevents the sharing of personal information between organisations without the data subject's consent. This is categorically untrue. We will spend the rest of the chapter convincing you of this. Having said that, there are certain sharing practices such as data brokering, lead generation and other activities involving the commercialisation of personal information that will either need to be significantly constrained or they will need valid consent to be lawful.[6]

13.4 HOW DO THE PRINCIPLES IN POPIA APPLY TO SHARING?

In this section we will discuss how the different principles in POPIA apply to the sharing of information, by going through a series of questions. These are also the questions information officers, their deputies and advisers should ask themselves when assessing a sharing activity.

We have not repeated the detailed analysis of the principles, but have included cross-references and applied them to sharing activities.

[5] There are some requirements that apply when responsible parties share information with operators (discussed in sections 20 and 21), certain types of sharing and linking information that require prior authorisation from the Regulator (section 57) and rules that apply when personal information is shared across borders (section 72). All of these aspects will be discussed in this chapter.

[6] See chapter 2 paragraph 2.6.6 on the requirements for consent.

13.4.1 What personal information is being shared?

Before considering whether sharing of information is POPIA compliant, it is vital to get a very firm grip on exactly what information is being shared between the responsible parties. This is often referred to as data flow mapping.[7] The most important information to document for the purposes of assessing whether the sharing activity is POPIA compliant is:

- Exactly what personal information (field by field) is being shared? In what format will the personal information be shared? This is sometimes referred to as a 'data specification'. If this is not documented, it will be impossible to determine compliance with POPIA.
- Who is the personal information being shared with? Sharing activities can get quite complex, and it is vital to ensure that all of the players are identified.
- How is the information being transmitted or how is access granted? Personal information is vulnerable when it is 'in transit'. Ensuring that the confidentiality and integrity of the personal information is protected should be a high priority.[8] In order to evaluate the security of the personal information being shared, it is important to record how the information will be transmitted.

It is also important to determine whether any of the personal information being shared is special personal information or the personal information of children. As we saw in chapter 7, the legal justifications available for the processing of special personal information and children's personal information are different.

13.4.2 What is the purpose for sharing the personal information?

It is important to have a clear understanding as to why the information is being shared. Sometimes, the personal information is collected for a purpose that involves sharing it with another organisation. For instance, lead generators gather personal information with the express purpose of sharing it with marketers.

In other cases, the personal information is collected for one purpose (e.g. to process an application for a credit card) and then later shared with third parties for a different purpose (e.g. sharing the information

[7] This is discussed as in chapter 1 paragraph 1.4 and again as an integral part of personal information impact assessments (PIIAs) in chapter 20 paragraph 20.3.

[8] Information security management is discussed in chapter 5. The aspect of information security management that deals with the sharing of information is often called 'third-party risk management'. This was also discussed in chapter 4.

of the unsuccessful credit card applicants with payday loan providers for direct marketing purposes).[9] We discussed the importance of defining the purpose(s) for which personal information was collected in chapter 6 paragraph 6.2. In the context of sharing, it is crucial to dig up this original purpose(s) for which the personal information was collected. If the responsible party does not know why the personal information in its possession was collected in the first place, even the continued processing of that personal information (not just sharing it with other responsible parties), will be extremely problematic.[10]

The purpose of the sharing activity and its relationship with the original purpose for which the information was collected will be used to determine whether there is an appropriate legal justification for sharing the information. This is discussed in paragraph 13.4.6 below.

13.4.3 Who is accountable to ensure that the sharing activity complies with POPIA?

When there is only one responsible party, accountability is simple. However, sharing activities always have at least two sides. In order to determine who is accountable, you have to determine who the 'responsible party' is. This was discussed in detail in chapter 4. For the purposes of this chapter, there are two possible scenarios:[11]

- The organisations who are participating in the sharing activity are each independent responsible parties. This will be the case where each organisation independently determined the purpose and means of the sharing activity. They will each be responsible for their own processing activities.
- The organisations jointly determined the purpose and means of the sharing activity. Here, POPIA is not clear on how liability will be apportioned. Commentary under the EU Data Protection Directive states that unless the co-responsible parties or the factual circumstances indicate otherwise, the liability will be joint and several.[12]

9 This is actually an extremely tricky example. Section 74(6)*(b)*(ii) of the National Credit Act provides that customers must be provided with the option to be excluded from any 'marketing or customer list that may be sold or distributed by the credit provider, other than as required by this Act'. Could one ever argue that the National Credit Act requires that credit provider must sell or distribute information for purposes of direct marketing? Probably not.

10 E.g. without determining the original purpose(s) it is impossible to determine whether the purpose of the sharing activity is 'compatible' with an original purpose.

11 This chapter does not apply to the sharing of information between responsible parties and operators. That is covered in chapter 4 paragraph 4.4.

12 See the full discussion in chapter 4 paragraph 4.5.

Key point: A gentle reminder. This chapter does not cover sharing between responsible parties and their operators. That is covered in chapter 4 paragraph 4.4.

When accountability is not clear, the parties involved should come to a written agreement about who will be responsible for which aspects of POPIA compliance.[13] You know what they say about assumption? It is the mother of all POPIA non-compliance.

Key point: It is not good enough for parties to simply 'warrant that they are POPIA compliant'. The agreement should contain specific provisions on who will be performing tasks such as notifying data subjects of the sharing activity, who will obtain consent (if it is required) and how consent will be maintained, who is responsible for the accuracy of the information etc. We included a checklist for agreements between responsible parties in chapter 4 paragraph 4.8.1.3.

13.4.4 Does the responsible party(s) need prior authorisation?

The responsible party will need to apply for prior authorisation from the Information Regulator if the information sharing activity involves any of the following activities:

- processing unique identifiers to link personal information between the responsible purpose (if that was not the purpose for which the unique identifiers were collected for)
- processing criminal behaviour or unlawful or objectionable conduct on behalf of third parties
- processing personal information for the purposes of credit reporting (credit bureaus)
- transferring special personal information or the personal information of children to foreign countries without adequate protection; or
- any other processing activities that the Information Regulator identifies as carrying a particular risk for the legitimate interest of data subjects.

All of these activities and applying for prior authorisation are discussed in chapter 8.

[13] There is no requirement in POPIA that co-responsible parties must conclude an agreement before sharing personal information with each other. Section 21(1) provides that when information is shared with an operator, a written agreement must be concluded. This was discussed in chapter 4 paragraph 4.8.

13.4.5 Is personal information being shared across borders?

Transborder information flows are discussed in chapter 14. For purposes of this chapter, it is important to remember that if the sharing is happening across borders, there are added requirements.

13.4.6 Does the responsible party(s) have a legal justification for sharing?

As we discussed in chapters 6 and 7, all processing activities must have a legal justification. When personal information is being shared between responsible parties, each of them must have a legal justification for sharing or receiving the personal information. In instances where they are working towards a shared purpose (co-responsible parties), the same legal justification will apply to both responsible parties. If the responsible parties involved in the sharing activity each have their own purpose in mind for the personal information, each responsible party must have a legal justification for the processing.

There are two sets of legal justifications that could apply to sharing activities:

- If sharing was contemplated at collection section 11(1) contains the list for ordinary personal information, sections 27 or 28 to 33 for special personal information or section 35 for the personal information of children.
- If the sharing is so-called 'further processing' you had better hope that section 15(2) and (3) has got you covered.

Key point: 'Further processing' is when a responsible party uses personal information for a purpose other than the purpose for which it was collected. While further processing is legally possible, it must meet the requirements in section 15. Section 15 was discussed in chapter 12. In many instances, sharing activities will be considered further processing. In fact, when one reads the SA Law Reform Commission Project 124 on Privacy and Data Protection 2005 Discussion Paper[14] and the SA Law Reform Commission Project 124 on Privacy and Data Protection 2009 Report,[15] it appears that they thought that sharing is always considered further processing.[16] This is not the case. It is quite possible that even when collecting the personal information for the first time the responsible party(s) already intended to share the personal information.

13.4.6.1 Sharing was already contemplated at the time of collection

Key point: When it comes to assessing sharing practices, the devil truly is in the detail. We have attempted to provide examples for each legal justification. However, there may be specific circumstances that can change our conclusions.

If the responsible party(s) collect information with a purpose in mind that includes sharing the personal information with another responsible party or a co-responsible party, section 11(1) will apply in respect of 'ordinary personal information'. This means that one of the following legal justifications must be present:

- **Sharing the information is necessary to carry out actions to conclude or perform in terms of a contract:**[17] For example, a customer buys a product on an e-commerce platform and the platform passes the information on to the relevant supplier to fulfil the order.

[14] SA Law Reform Commission Project 124 on Privacy and Data Protection (2005 Discussion Paper) from paragraph 4.2.93.

[15] SA Law Reform Commission Project 124 on Privacy and Data Protection (2009 Report) from paragraph 4.2.158.

[16] SA Law Reform Commission Project 124 on Privacy and Data Protection (2009 Report) see paragraph 4.1.174.

[17] Section 11(1)*(b)*. The requirements for this legal justification are discussed in chapter 6 paragraph 6.3.1.

- **Sharing the information complies with an obligation imposed by law on the responsible party:**[18] For example, credit providers must share personal information with credit bureaus in terms of the National Credit Act 34 of 2005.[19]
- **Sharing the information protects a legitimate interest of the data subject:**[20] For example, a data subject suffers a medical emergency at work. The employer shares critical personal information about the data subject with the medical professionals attending to the employee. In POPIA, the 'legitimate interest' of the data subject could be wider than instances of life and death. In order to rely on section 11(1)*(d)* or this section, responsible parties must document that they considered what the impact of the processing would be on the data subject. This exercise forms part of performing a legitimate interest assessment. This was discussed in chapter 2 paragraph 2.6.3.
- **Sharing is necessary for the proper performance of a public law duty by a public body:**[21] For example, the National Consumer Commission is investigating product recall. The NCC asks retailers of the products to give them the information of consumers who purchased it in order to conduct an investigation.
- **Sharing is necessary for pursuing the legitimate interests of the responsible party or of a third party to whom the information is supplied:**[22] For example, much of modern marketing is built on collecting and sharing massive amounts of personal information about data subjects. Legitimate interest is often the legal justification which responsible parties rely on to share personal information for lead generation (i.e. profiling, pre-vetting or screening of

---

18 Section 11(1)*(c)*. The requirements for this legal justification are discussed in chapter 6 paragraph 6.3.2.

19 Section 69.

20 Section 11(1)*(d)*. The requirements for this legal justification are discussed in chapter 6 paragraph 6.3.3. For a general discussion on the concept of 'legitimate interest', see chapter 2 paragraph 2.6.3.

21 Section 11(1)*(e)*. The requirements for this legal justification are discussed in chapter 6 paragraph 6.3.4.

22 Section 11(1)*(f)*. The requirements for this legal justification are discussed in chapter 6 paragraph 6.3.5. For a general discussion on the concept of 'legitimate interest', see chapter 2 paragraph 2.6.3.

suitable prospects). Of course, whether the practice will 'pass' a legitimate interest assessment depends on the circumstances.[23] In addition, once they have decided who to contact, the direct marketer will have to comply with section 69 of POPIA.[24]

- **The data subject has consented to the sharing:**[25] For example, when the data subject purchases a car, the dealer asks the data subject if they would like to be contacted by an insurer. The data subject agrees and the dealer sends the data subject's contact details to the insurer.

Key point: We see many consents for the sharing of personal information hidden in terms and conditions. Such a consent will not be valid, as it is often not voluntary; in other words, the data subject cannot withhold consent *and* accept the terms and conditions.[26] It is also inappropriate to use consent as a legal justification if sharing the information is mandatory.

If the responsible party is relying on a legitimate interest (its own, that of the data subject or that of a third party) or on the fact that the sharing is necessary for the proper performance of a public law duty, the data subject will have the right to object to the processing on reasonable grounds related to the data subject's particular situation.[27] The responsible party must be able to stop sharing if it receives a valid objection. If it can't stop sharing (for operational or technical reasons) then it needs to either change its business process or see if another justification applies.

[23] We discuss this in paragraph 13.6.1 below.

[24] Direct marketing is discussed in chapter 16.

[25] Section 11(1)*(a)*. The requirements for this legal justification are discussed in chapter 6 paragraph 6.3.6. For a general discussion on the concept of 'consent', see chapter 2 paragraph 2.6.6.

[26] We refer to this as a fit-in-or-eff-off consent. How rude. For a general discussion on the concept of 'consent', see chapter 2 paragraph 2.6.6.

[27] The right to object and other data subject rights are discussed in chapter 18 paragraph 18.6.

Key point: If the sharing activity involves special personal information, a different set of legal justifications apply. Similarly, processing the personal information of children is subject to a separate set of rules. This was discussed in detail in chapter 7. It is crucial to take this into account, as the justifications are not the same. For instance, 'legitimate interest' is not recognised as a legal justification for the processing of special personal information or the personal information of children.

13.4.6.2 Sharing was not contemplated at the time of collection

This is referred to as 'further processing', which was discussed in chapter 12. Note that while the justifications are different for different types of personal information at the point of collection, section 15 applies to further processing of ordinary personal information, special personal information and the personal information of children.

Key point: If the sharing activity was not something which the responsible party contemplated when the personal information was collected, section 15 (which governs further processing) will apply instead of section 11(1) (ordinary personal information), sections 27 or 28 to 33 (special personal information), or section 35 (personal information of children). If you are trying to comply with both, you are doing it wrong!

The cardinal rule is that the sharing activity must still be 'compatible' with the original purpose. Section 15(2) lists the following 'factors' which must be considered when determining whether the sharing activity is compatible with the original purpose for which the information was collected:[28]

- **The relationship between the original purpose and the sharing activity:** If the sharing activity is a logical next step and the data subjects would expect the sharing to take place, the sharing activity may be compatible. Further processing (and sharing) often takes place when new technology or other innovations are introduced.

[28] Section 15(2). For a general discussion see chapter 12 paragraph 12.4.

- **The nature of the personal information concerned:** If special personal information or the personal information of children is involved, it will be harder to motivate why the sharing activity is compatible.
- **The consequences of the further processing on the data subject:** The negative and positive consequences of the sharing activity on the data subjects must be considered. See chapter 12 paragraph 12.4.3 for a list of the types of impacts that are considered in the EU.
- **The manner in which the personal information was collected:** Was there anything in the privacy notice or other notifications made to the data subject at the time of collection that suggested that sharing may take place? Anything that would have influenced the data subjects' expectations regarding the sharing of information will be taken into account.
- **Any contractual rights between the data subject and the responsible party:** If the contractual obligations (and other factors relating to the nature of the relationship) give rise to 'reasonable expectations of stricter confidentiality and stricter limitations on further use' it is less likely sharing will be compatible. Here again, it is necessary to take account of the factual context rather than simply relying on text in small print.[29]

If, after considering these factors, the conclusion is that the sharing activity is incompatible with the original purpose, all hope is not lost. There are some exceptions to the rule that the further processing must be compatible:[30]

- **The data subject consented to the sharing activity:** Of course, this consent must comply with POPIA's requirements for valid consent. Usually, the stumbling block in sharing activities is that the consent has to be voluntary. Consent in the context of further processing is discussed in chapter 12 paragraph 12.5.1.

---

29 Article 29 Data Protection Working Party *Opinion 03/2013 on purpose limitation* 25, available at https://ec.europa.eu/justice/article-29/documentation/opinion-recommendation/files/2013/wp203_en.pdf.

30 They are discussed in full in chapter 12 paragraph 12.5.

- **The personal information is available in or derived from a public record:** This is a popular justification in the data brokering industry. A data broker is a company that sells personal information.[31] The problem that data brokers face is that the definition of a public record is very narrow. For instance, it does not include information generally published on the internet. See the discussion of the definition of 'public record' in chapter 10 paragraph 10.4.1.
- **The personal information has deliberately been made public by the data subject:** Many organisations justify scraping the internet by saying 'well, the information is already public'. This justification is also not as simple as it looks. If you are using a web crawler[32] to index personal information on the internet, how do you know that that personal information was put on the internet by the data subject (on purpose). They key (and challenge) is being able to demonstrate that the data subject made it public and that it was deliberate. See the discussion in chapter 10 paragraph 10.4.2.
- **Further processing is necessary for certain forms of crime prevention, national security, collection of revenue by SARS, and court proceedings:** These justifications are very specific and narrow and should be treated with care. See the discussion in chapter 12 paragraph 12.5.4.
- **Preventing or mitigating a serious or imminent threat to public health or safety or the life or health of a data subject:** This will apply to further processing in emergency situations. In general, sharing information with (for instance) medical staff would be a justifiable instance of further processing.[33]
- **Historical, statistical or research purposes:** Further processing will be justified if the personal information is used for historical, statistical, or

---

31 We have included a case study relating to data brokering in paragraph 13.6.1.

32 Sorry for speaking Geek. A crawler is a program that browses the internet in order to create an index of information. They are sometimes referred to as spiders or bots.

33 See the discussion in chapter 12 paragraph 12.5.5.

research purposes[34] and the responsible party ensures that the personal information is not used for any other purposes and the results will not be published in an identifiable form.[35]

- **The Information Regulator has granted an exemption:** Further processing can be justified by the Information Regulator by granting an exemption to a responsible party.[36] This was discussed in chapter 3 paragraph 3.3.7.
- **Exemption in respect of certain functions:** Public bodies or other organisations who in terms of the law must protect members of the public against financial loss due to dishonesty, malpractice or other seriously improper conduct in regulated industries or by people in certain professions who are allowed to perform further processing.[37]

Key point: If none of the exceptions applies, and the sharing activity is incompatible with the original purpose for which the personal information was collected, the sharing cannot take place. See the detailed discussion of the consequences of incompatibility in chapter 12 paragraph 12.7.

13.4.7 Does the responsible party receiving the personal information fall within one of the exemptions to the direct collection rule?

In general, responsible parties should avoid 'invisible processing'. Invisible processing is 'when you obtain personal [information] from somewhere other than directly from the [data subject] themselves, and you don't provide them with the privacy information required by [section 18]. The processing is "invisible" because the [data subject] is unaware that you are collecting and using the personal [information], even if you publish a privacy notice on your website.'[38]

[34] We discuss the meaning of 'historical, statistical or research purposes in chapter 2 paragraph 2.6.7.

[35] See the discussion in chapter 3 paragraph 3.3.2.

[36] Section 37.

[37] See the discussion in chapter 12 paragraph 12.5.8.

[38] UK ICO 'What does "invisible processing" mean?', available at https://ico.org.uk/for-organisations/guide-to-data-protection/guide-to-the-general-data-protection-regulation-gdpr/data-protection-impact-assessments-dpias/when-do-we-need-to-do-a-dpia/#when10.

Key point: POPIA takes a very stern view of collecting personal information from sources other than the data subject. POPIA is stricter than the EU GDPR, because it explicitly states that personal information must be collected from the data subject directly, unless one of the exceptions applies.[39]

This means that when a responsible party is on the receiving end of a sharing activity, one of the following exceptions *must* apply for the sharing activity to be POPIA compliant:

Key point: Please read chapter 10 paragraph 10.4 where these exceptions are discussed in detail.

- The personal information is in or derived from a public record.
- The data subject made the personal information public deliberately.
- The data subject has consented to the collection of personal information from third parties.
- The collection of the information from third parties does not prejudice the legitimate interest of the data subject.
- Collecting the personal information from a third party is necessary for certain forms of crime prevention, national security, legal obligations, collection of revenue by SARS and court proceedings.
- Collecting personal information from another source is necessary to maintain the legitimate interest of the responsible party (receiving the information) or of a third party.
- Collecting the personal information directly from the data subject would prejudice a lawful purpose of collection.
- Compliance with the direct collection rule is not reasonably practicable.
- Collecting the personal information from another source is necessary to protect members of the public against financial loss due to dishonesty, malpractice or other seriously improper conduct in regulated industries or by people in certain professions.[40]

---

39 POPIA borrowed this approach from the New Zealand Privacy Act of 1993, available at https://www.legislation.govt.nz/act/public/1993/0028/latest/DLM297053.html. It has since been replaced by the Privacy Act of 2020 which still contains similar provisions.

40 This exemption is discussed in chapter 10 paragraph 10.4.9.

13.4.8 Has the responsible party(s) met the notification requirements?

We discussed notification in detail in chapter 11. When it comes to sharing activities, the duty to notify data subjects is very important. It enables data subjects to exercise some control over the use of their personal information and gives them the opportunity to exercise any rights they might have.[41]

13.4.8.1 Is the notification specific enough?

The question is how specific the notification regarding the sharing activity must be? For instance, section 18(1)*(b)*(i) suggests that informing the data subject of a 'category of recipients' rather than the actual recipient will be good enough.[42] We discussed this requirement in chapter 11 paragraph 11.3.2.

Tricky area: It is not clear under what circumstances a responsible party may be required to disclose the actual identity of all third parties who had access to personal information. Having said that, responsible parties should maintain a detailed record of all internal and external parties who had access in order to satisfy the information security management requirements in POPIA.[43] We are of the view that publishing the identity of all internal and external parties who had access will not be practical. However, a full record should be available in the event that a data subject or the Information Regulator requests it.

However, here are some instances where we do believe specific recipients must be listed:

- **When personal information is being processed by co-responsible parties.** In this case all of the responsible parties must be disclosed. Section 18(1)*(b)* refers to 'responsible party' (singular). However, the definition of 'responsible party' clearly contemplates that there may be multiple responsible parties acting

[41] We are very sceptical of this notion that data subjects will protect themselves if only they are given control and some rights. We discuss this scepticism in chapter 2 paragraph 2.6.4.

[42] Section 23(1)*(b)* also provides that data subjects have the right to request 'a record or a description of the personal information about the data subject held by the responsible party, including information about the identity of all third parties, or categories of third parties, who have, or have had, access to the information'. Data subject rights are discussed in chapter 18.

[43] Information security management is discussed in chapter 5.

with a common purpose.[44] All responsible parties should be listed in the privacy notice.

- **When personal information will be shared with an independent responsible party to process it for their own purposes.** We believe that if a responsible party is going to share personal information with another, independent responsible party, this should be specified in the privacy notice and this other responsible party should be identified. This will often be the case in groups of organisations that have a shared database.
- **Any instance where the data subject would be surprised to learn that their information is being shared with another organisation.**

Tricky area: When organisations sell personal information (referred to as data brokers), data subjects should be notified about who the information will be sold to. This is often the most challenging data protection requirement for data brokers. The seller, buyer or both may also need the consent of the data subject. At the very least, data subjects will have the right to object, but to exercise this right, they have to know that their information is being sold, who it is being sold to and for what purpose. We discuss data brokering in paragraph 13.6.1 below.

13.4.8.2 When will notification take place?

The general principle is that the notification cannot take place after the fact; the data subject must be informed before the personal information is shared. There are three times where notification should take place depending on the circumstances:[45]

- Notification can take place at the time the personal information is collected.
- When the personal information of the data subject is collected from sources other than the data subject, the notification must take place as soon as reasonably practicable after the information was collected.

---

[44] Co-responsible parties are discussed in chapter 11 paragraph 11.4.

[45] This requirement is discussed in chapter 11 paragraph 11.4.

- If the sharing activity is 'further processing' (i.e. the responsible party did not contemplate the sharing activity at the time of collection), the data subject should be notified, even though POPIA does not state this explicitly (unless one of the exemptions to the notification duty applies).[46]

13.4.8.3 Who must make the notification?

Where the parties to the sharing activity are co-responsible parties, working towards a shared purpose, the notification should be 'joint'. When the parties are independent responsible parties, each party has a notification duty to discharge.

From a practical perspective, the responsible party who discloses the personal information will be the party to notify the data subjects, because notification must take place before the sharing activity takes place, and the responsible party on the receiving end will not yet have the personal information of the data subjects.

Key point: Responsible parties should agree on who will take care of the notification to ensure that it happens.

13.4.8.4 Do any of the exceptions to the notification duty apply?

Of course, there are several exceptions to the notification duty:[47]

- **The data subject gave consent not to be notified of sharing:** This consent has to meet all of the requirements for valid consent.[48] Usually, the problem is that the consent is not voluntary, because the responsible party cannot notify the data subject. This means that responsible parties should not rely on consent if notifying data subjects of the sharing activity is impossible. That is one of the exceptions discussed below.

---

46 See the discussion in chapter 11 paragraph 11.4.4.

47 See chapter 11 paragraph 11.6.

48 Section 18(4)*(a)*. The requirements for valid consent are discussed in chapter 2 paragraph 2.6.6.

- **Not notifying the data subject of the sharing activity does not prejudice the legitimate interest of the data subject:**[49] This exception can be used in emergencies, when the responsible party is sharing personal information to safeguard the data subject's health or safety. In POPIA, the 'legitimate interest' of the data subject could be wider than instances of life and death. In order to rely on section 11(1)*(d)* or this section, responsible parties must document that they considered what the impact of the processing would be on the data subject. This exercise forms part of performing a legitimate interest assessment. This was discussed in chapter 2 paragraph 2.6.3.
- **Not notifying the data subject of the sharing activity is required for law and order:** This refers to the collection of justifications relating to crime prevention, national security, the collection of revenue by SARS and court proceedings. These justifications are very specific and narrow and should be treated with care. See the discussion in chapter 11 paragraph 11.6.3.
- **If the data subject is notified, it would prejudice a lawful purpose of collection:** This will often be the case where a law imposing a duty on the responsible party notifying the data subject could compromise that purpose (for example the data subject may lie to the responsible party).
- **Compliance is not reasonably practicable:** We dealt with the concept of 'reasonably practicable' in chapter 2[50] as it occurs so many times within POPIA, and it is worth referring back to this chapter again when you consider this exception. The concept of 'reasonably practicable' can be equated with the concept of 'disproportionate effort' as found in article 14 of the EU GDPR. This was discussed in chapter 11 paragraph 11.6.5.
- **The information will not be used in a form in which the data subject is identified:** If personal information has been successfully de-identified

49 Section 18(4)*(b)*. See the discussion in chapter 11 paragraph 11.6.2.

50 Paragraph 2.6.2.

(no small feat), POPIA does not apply[51] and naturally, there would be no obligation to notify data subjects when sharing de-identified information (it is no longer 'personal information'). For this exception to make any sense, what is referred to in this subsection would have to be something less than de-identification. We believe that what is referred to here is pseudonymisation,[52] where personal information is used in such a way that the personal information cannot be attributed to a specific data subject without the use of additional information.[53] The scope of the exception is also limited. It would only apply to the processing activities where the personal information being used had already been pseudonymised. In order to be in a position to do so, a responsible party would have had to collect the information in an identifiable form. Until the information is pseudonymised, the notification duty would still apply.

- **The information being shared will be used for historical, statistical or research purposes:** See the discussion in chapter 2 paragraph 2.6.7 about what activities fall within these categories.
- If the sharing of personal information is necessary to protect members of the public against financial loss due to dishonesty, malpractice or other seriously improper conduct in regulated industries or by people in certain professions and it is being done by a regulator or a statutory industry assocation, notification might not be required.[54]

13.4.9 Does the sharing activity comply with the principle of minimal processing?

The principle of minimality states that a responsible party can only process personal information if the personal information is adequate, relevant, and not excessive considering the purpose of the processing activity.[55]

---

51 See chapter chapter 3 paragraph 3.3.2.

52 We discussed pseudonymisation in chapter 3 paragraph 3.3.2 and again in chapter 5 paragraph 5.5.2.

53 Article 4(5) of the EU GDPR.

54 This exemption is discussed in chapter 11 paragraph 11.6.8.

55 Section 10.

In the context of information sharing activities, it is important for responsible parties to consider the following questions before the sharing activity takes place:

- Is it possible to achieve the same purpose without sharing the personal information?
- Could the purpose be fulfilled with de-identified personal information?
- If personal information has to be shared, is the minimum amount of personal information being shared?

Consider this example: A photography studio specialises in graduation photos and has made an arrangement with a university to give a discount to its students, in exchange for access to the university's database of graduands to market their services. The university should ask itself a series of questions:

- **What is the purpose of sharing the personal information?** To make students aware of the discount.
- **Is there a way of achieving this purpose without sharing the personal information of students with the photography studio?** Yes, there is. The university could make use of its usual communication channels for graduands to inform them of the deal. Of course, depending on the way in which the information is provided, it may constitute direct marketing on behalf of a third party, but many universities already have POPIA compliant ways to inform students of promotions. If the university does not want to do 'direct marketing', it can advertise the deal on notice boards (for instance).
- **If the University does decide to share the information and it meets all of the other requirements discussed in this chapter, is it sharing the minimum amount of information?** In order to fulfil this purpose, all the photography studio needs is a list of email addresses of students who will be graduating. For instance, it does not need the students' student numbers, ID numbers or to know what degrees are being conferred in order to send direct marketing relating to the promotion. It can collect further information about students when they take the photography studio up on the deal. And it certainly does not need the personal information of students who are not graduating.

Key point: It should be clear that evaluating the purpose for the sharing activity is crucial for determining whether it is POPIA compliant. If the responsible party doing the sharing does not know why the receiving party wants the information, it is not possible to determine whether all POPIA requirements are met.

13.4.10 Does the sharing activity comply with information security management principles?

POPIA's requirements on information security management are discussed in chapter 5. Third-party risk management involves the vetting and auditing of external parties such as partners, vendors, contractors and consultants. When independent responsible parties or co-responsible parties share information with each other, they must apply the principles of third-party risk management to ensure that the personal information remains protected. These principles are discussed in chapter 4 paragraph 4.9. We will not discuss the vetting and auditing process here. Instead, we want to discuss aspects of information security management specific to sharing, which should be addressed by the responsible party(s).

Key point: We are not information security management experts. Treat what we say with caution as this is a very technical field. The purpose of this section is to teach you enough G(r)eek to know when something has not been discussed by the responsible parties or has not been adequately addressed in the agreement between them.

13.4.10.1 Is the personal information protected against unlawful access and processing?

Section 19(1)*(a)* provides that personal information must be protected against unlawful access and unlawful processing. As discussed in chapter 5, responsible parties must ensure that the personal information 'in its possession or under its control' is protected against unlawful access or processing.

Here are just two specific risks involving sharing that can lead to unlawful access or processing:

- **Criminals will often impersonate a trusted third party in order to dupe a responsible party into sharing personal information with them.** When sharing personal information with each other, responsible parties must ensure that they employ high levels of authentication to guard personal information against this risk.[56]
- **Personal information is also vulnerable while it is being transferred.** Just think how many times you have accidentally sent an email to the incorrect person? Now imagine if there was an Excel spreadsheet with the personal information of 22 000 people attached to that email.[57] This will be considered a 'security compromise' in terms of POPIA.[58] In order to guard personal information against this risk and the risk that the information is intercepted, responsible parties must ensure that they use secure methods of sharing personal information such as secure file transfer protocols, secure mail servers, encrypted file storage retrieval that requires password access and investing in secure file transfer solutions. Avoid sending personal information in plain text emails!

13.4.10.2 Have reasonable steps been taken to ensure that the personal information is complete, accurate, not misleading and updated when necessary?

Section 16 of POPIA requires that responsible parties must take steps to ensure that information is complete, accurate, not misleading and updated when necessary. In information security management, this is referred to as the 'integrity' of the personal information.

Often, to achieve the purpose for which the information is being shared, it is essential that the information must be of a high quality. In addition to not being fit for the purpose the organisation(s) wants to achieve, poor information quality can also lead to security breaches. Consider this example:

---

56 This type of deception can be the result of a phishing attack, malware or good old social engineering. If you don't know what these are, Google is your friend.

57 True story.

58 The consequences of security compromises are discussed in chapter 5 paragraph 5.6.

A bank sends the customer's credit card statement to the incorrect email address. That credit card statement contains personal information about the customer, which has now been disclosed to an unauthorised third party. This example is useful also to illustrate that you don't need to have a malicious party (like a hacker) to have a security compromise.

When personal information is shared, it is important to consider the following to ensure that responsible parties comply with section 16:

- **Have the parties sharing the information agreed on what personal information will be shared?** This sounds deceptively simple, but information quality issues are often caused in sharing activities (for instance) if responsible parties have different names for different types of personal information. For instance, some organisations interpret the gender field as 'male or female', while others call that field 'sex'.[59]
- **Have they agreed on the format or configuration of the information?** Different organisations may have different ways of writing cell phone numbers or the date. Sometimes it will be the answer options that will differ. For instance, different organisations may have different options for race. These types of issues can also lead to integration problems and errors.
- **Has the responsible party who is receiving the information from a third party created rules it will apply when deciding to integrate the new information with the information it already has?** Consider this example: A data subject likes receiving newsletters from her alma mater at her Gmail address instead of her work address. The university decides to enrich its database and replaces her Gmail address with her work address; undoing a valid instruction from her. If her Gmail address were no longer accurate, it would have been a different story.

[59] 'Sex' is the correct way to ask a person whether they are male or female. The answer you get most often when you use it in a form is 'yes please'.

Key point: Deciding on what information will be shared and the format of that information is often referred to as a 'data specification'. The rules about when to update existing records with new information are often referred to as 'data integration rules'. Sharing information, and then deciding how the information will be used, takes planning!

The integrity of information can also be compromised through 'transfer errors'. That is when unintended alterations are made or the personal information is compromised (corrupted) while it is transferred from one device to another. This can be caused by human error (e.g. misreading or mistyping personal information) and computer-induced transcription errors (e.g. software bugs). Responsible parties should take steps to validate information that has been shared and measures to detect integrity problems.

One of the most challenging aspects of POPIA is how to keep personal information up to date. Every time personal information is shared with a third party, a copy of that personal information is created. Responsible parties should consider how the shared information will be kept up to date. We discussed a discipline called master data management in chapter 9 paragraph 9.6.5.

Key point: The integrity of personal information is important when that personal information will be used to make important decisions about a data subject (e.g. whether to grant a loan or not). Consider the example of a data subject who is denied a mortgage due to a judgment which has been incorrectly associated with the data subject's credit record. If that decision is automated (there is no human intervention), data subjects have the right to information about how the decision was made and to make representations. This is discussed in chapter 15. Data subjects also have the more general right to request the correction or deletion of their personal information. This is discussed in chapter 18.

13.4.11 Can the responsible party(s) honour data subject rights?

Data subject rights are discussed in full in chapter 18. When information is being shared between responsible parties, they have to ensure that they can co-ordinate their responses to data subject requests.

The following data subject requests are relevant when there is personal information sharing:

- The right to access to information 'about the identity of all third parties, or categories of third parties who have, or have had, access to their personal information'.[60]

Tricky area: It is not clear how specific the responsible party's response must be. This is discussed in chapter 18 paragraph 18.3.2, but suffice it to say that it is not clear whether the data subject can insist on the actual identities of all of the third parties.

- The right to request that a responsible party corrects or deletes their personal information that is inaccurate, irrelevant, excessive, out of date, incomplete, misleading, or obtained unlawfully.[61]

Key point: If personal information is shared without a legal basis, the data subject will have the right to demand the deletion of that information.

- The right to withdraw consent. If the consent of the data subject is used to justify the sharing activity,[62] the responsible party must allow data subjects to withdraw their consent, in which case the sharing activity must stop.[63] This right to withdraw consent is absolute; in other words, there are no grounds on which the responsible party can reject the withdrawal.
- The right to object to the processing. If the responsible parties are relying on the legitimate interests of the data subject, the responsible party or a third party or on the fact that the processing is necessary for the proper performance of a public law duty by a public body,[64] the data subject will have the right to object 'on reasonable grounds relating to his, her or its particular situation'.[65]

---

[60] Section 23(1)*(b)*. This is discussed in chapter 18 paragraph 18.3.

[61] Section 24(1)*(a)*. This is discussed in chapter 18 paragraph 18.4.

[62] Legal justification for sharing activities was discussed in paragraph 13.4.6 above.

[63] Section 11(3)*(b)* states that a data subject may withdraw consent provided in terms of section 11(1)*(a)* at any time. Of course, consent features in many other sections of POPIA. See chapter 2 paragraph 2.6.6 for a full list. We are of the view that data subjects also have the right to withdraw these other consents due to the requirement (in section 1) that consent must be voluntary.

[64] Section 11(1)*(d)* to *(f)*.

[65] Section 11(3)*(a)*. The right to object is discussed in chapter 18 paragraph 18.6.

13.5 INFORMATION MATCHING PROGRAMMES

13.5.1 What are information matching programmes?

POPIA deals specifically with a processing activity referred to as 'information matching programmes'. This is defined as 'the comparison, whether manually or by means of any electronic or other device, of any document that contains personal information about ten or more data subjects with one or more documents that contain personal information of ten or more data subjects, for the purpose of producing or verifying information that may be used for the purpose of taking any action in regard to an identifiable data subject'.[66]

Are credit bureaus, data brokers and verification agencies in the business of running information matching programmes? This is an important question, because when this service is performed on documents that contain personal information about ten or more data subjects and the information produced will be used to 'take any action' with regard to an identifiable data subject, additional requirements may apply.

13.5.2 POPIA's approach to information matching programmes

Tricky area: Information matching programmes occupy a strange position in POPIA. They are clearly important and present a high risk to the individual privacy of data subjects, but there are no specific rules that apply to these 'programmes'. It seems like the concept was imported from New Zealand. For a fascinating discussion on information matching programmes, see the New Zealand Law Reform Commission's *Review of the Privacy Act 1993*.[67]

Of course, these programmes must comply with all of the principles in POPIA.

13.5.2.1 Information matching programmes provided for in legislation

Information matching programmes are often prescribed by legislation. Section 40(1)*(b)*(ix)*(bb)*[68] provides that the Information Regulator must monitor and enforce compliance

[66] See the definition of 'information matching programme' in section 1.

[67] Available at https://www.lawcom.govt.nz/sites/default/files/projectAvailableFormats/NZLC%20R123.pdf.

[68] No, Elizabeth's cat did not walk across her keyboard, this is the actual reference. We triple checked.

with POPIA by examining any proposed legislation that makes provision for the sharing of personal information between responsible parties that might be used for the purpose of an information matching programme. When considering such legislation, the Information Regulator must consider whether:[69]

- the objective of the programme relates to a matter of significant public importance
- the programme will result in significant and quantifiable monetary savings or other comparable benefits to society
- there is another way of achieving the monetary savings or other benefits to society
- the public interest of allowing the programme outweighs the interest in complying with POPIA; and
- the scale of the programme is excessive given the number of responsible parties or operators involved or the amount of detail about data subjects that will be matched.

This section is consistent with the assessment which must be performed in terms of section 36(1) of the Constitution when legislation limits a constitutional right such as the right to privacy.[70]

13.5.2.2 Information matching provided for in codes of conduct

Section 60(4)*(a)* of POPIA provides that any code of conduct accredited in terms of POPIA[71] 'must also specify appropriate measures ... for information matching programmes if such programmes are used within a specific sector'. Although the Information Regulator has released a guideline on codes of conduct, it does not provide much assistance in setting out what 'appropriate measures' might be for information matching programmes.[72]

[69] Section 44(2).

[70] This was discussed in chapter 2 paragraph 2.6.1.

[71] Codes of conduct are discussed in chapter 19.

[72] Guidelines to Develop Code of Conduct, 15 February 2021, issued under the Protection of Personal Information Act 4 of 2013 (POPIA), available at https://www.justice.gov.za/inforeg/docs.html.

13.5.2.3 Information matching involving unique identifiers

Information matching programmes always makes use of 'unique identifiers' to link and combine personal information of a data subject from different sources. The definition of a unique identifier is 'any identifier that is assigned to a data subject and is used by a responsible party for the purposes of the operations of that responsible party and that uniquely identifies that data subject in relation to that responsible party'.[73] If an information matching programme also makes use of 'unique identifiers', the responsible party(s) may have to apply for prior authorisation from the Information Regulator.[74] This was discussed in chapter 8.

If the unique identifiers are account numbers which were issued by (a) a financial institution, or (b) another institution that enables data subjects to access their own or joint funds or credit facilities, there are specific offences that apply for contraventions of POPIA.[75]

Key point: Account numbers must be shared and used with extreme care! A contravention of POPIA that involves 'account numbers' may attract a fine or imprisonment of ten years (or both!) for the responsible party if the contravention is serious, persistent or will likely cause substantial damage or distress to the data subject.[76] The responsible party will be able to defend itself by showing that it took reasonable steps to prevent the contravention.[77]

This is relevant in the context of sharing, because it highlights that both the responsible party who shares account numbers and the responsible party who receives them need to have consensus about exactly what the account numbers will be used for.

73 See the definition of 'unique identifier' in section 1.

74 Section 57(1)*(a)*(ii).

75 See the definition of 'account number' in section 105(5).

76 Section 105 read with section 107*(a)*.

77 Section 105(3)*(b)* and section 105(5).

13.5.2.4 Information matching used in automated decisions

Information matching programmes are often used to produce or verify the personal information used in automated decision-making. For a decision to be automated it must:[78]

- be based solely on automated processing aimed at providing a profile of the data subject's performance at work, credit worthiness, reliability, location, health, personal preferences or conduct; and
- result in legal consequences for the data subject *or* must affect the data subject to a substantial degree.

The additional requirements prescribed for automated decision-making are discussed in chapter 15 paragraph 15.3.

13.6 SOME TYPICAL SHARING CASE STUDIES

The purpose of this section is to discuss certain typical sharing activities and to highlight which POPIA principles may be problematic. We will use the topics discussed in the previous paragraphs as a checklist to evaluate the different sharing activities.

13.6.1 Buying and selling information (data brokering) for marketing purposes

Data brokers have been called 'privacy deathstars'.[79] In 2018, Privacy International filed complaints[80] against seven data brokers which resulted in enforcement action by the ICO against Experian, Equifax and TransUnion.[81] These data brokers were selling personal information to third parties to use for profiling and direct marketing.[82]

---

78 Section 71.

79 Thank you, *Financial Times*.

80 The complaints are available at https://privacyinternational.org/advocacy/2426/our-complaints-against-acxiom-criteo-equifax-experian-oracle-quantcast-tapad. The complaints contain a treasure trove of research and analysis on data broking and its impact on society.

81 ICO 'Investigation into data protection compliance in the direct marketing data broking sector' (October 2020), available at https://ico.org.uk/media/action-weve-taken/2618470/investigation-into-data-protection-compliance-in-the-direct-marketing-data-broking-sector.pdf.

82 Direct marketing is discussed in detail in chapter 16.

Consider this example: A data broker collects information about individuals from various sources including court records, the internet (through cookies and scraping), social media, the voter's roll, the deeds registry, credit bureaus and campaigns the data broker runs on behalf of its clients. All-in-all the data broker has 3 000 data points on each individual. This information is used to profile individuals by linking them to 'demographic, socio-economic and behavioural characteristics'.[83] Marketers can access this information in order to identify leads to who they intend to send unsolicited electronic direct marketing.

Let us apply the checklist (with a sprinkling of the findings of the ICO):

- **What personal information is being shared?** Is any of the personal information special personal information?[84] In our example, the data broker shares up to 3 000 data points on each individual. These datasets may include special personal information.
- **What is the purpose for sharing the personal information?**[85] In our example, the information is being sold to a marketer to allow them to have more insight into consumer behaviour and to target specific individuals through various forms of direct marketing.
- **Who is accountable to ensure that the sharing activity complies with POPIA?**[86] Could it be argued that the data broker is an operator of the marketer (a responsible party)? It will depend on the nature of the service provided by the data broker. In this example, when the data broker builds its vast database, it is the responsible party as it is not doing it on the instruction of the marketer. Of course, the marketer is also a responsible party in its own right. This is therefore a case of two independent responsible parties.
- **Does the responsible party(s) need prior authorisation?**[87] Data brokers make use of unique identifiers to link personal information being processed by other responsible parties. If using the unique identifiers for this purpose was not the original purpose for which the identifier was collected, the data broker may have to apply for prior authorisation.[88] Some data brokers

[83] Profiling and automated decisions are discussed in chapter 15.

[84] Special personal information is discussed in chapter 7.

[85] The purpose specification requirement is discussed in chapter 6 paragraph 6.2.

[86] This is discussed in paragraph 13.4.3 above. Accountability is discussed in detail in chapter 4.

[87] The activities which require prior authorisation were discussed in detail in chapter 8.

[88] Section 57(1)*(a)*.

are also credit bureaus and will be processing information for credit reporting. This also requires prior authorisation unless they are subject to an approved code of conduct.[89]

- **Is the personal information being shared across borders?**[90] POPIA's provisions on transborder information flows[91] will be triggered if the data broker shares the personal information with marketers who are located outside South Africa.
- **Does the responsible party(s) have a legal justification for sharing?**[92] This is where the rubber hits the road. If the personal information was collected specifically for the purposes of selling it, the data broker must have a legal justification in terms of section 11(1) to sell the information.[93] From the ICO report it is clear that the data brokers were either relying on legitimate interest or on consent. In respect of legitimate interest the ICO found that the legitimate interest assessment performed by the data brokers was not properly weighted; they were not giving enough 'weight to the fact that they were processing a large amount of personal data in highly targeted ways, profiling individuals, along with significant issues of non-transparency'.[94] Note that the ICO did not say that the data brokers could not rely on legitimate interest, just that they did not do a proper assessment. If the legitimate interest assessment does not favour the interests of the data broker, the processing must stop. The ICO also found that the consents which were used by some of the data brokers were not informed nor specific.[95] Lastly, the ICO found that the data brokers cannot switch from using consent

89 Section 57(1)*(c)*. Section 57(3) provides that a responsible party that is governed by an approved code of conduct will not require prior authorisation. See Guidelines to Develop Code of Conduct, 15 February 2021, issued under the Protection of Personal Information Act 4 of 2013 (POPIA), available at https://www.justice.gov.za/inforeg/docs/coc/InfoRegSA-Guidelines-DevelopCodeOfConduct-22Feb2021.pdf. A code of conduct for credit bureaus was in development at the date of publication.

90 This is discussed in chapter 14.

91 Section 72.

92 This is discussed in paragraph 13.4.6. The legal justifications are discussed in chapter 6.

93 Section 11 is discussed in chapter 6. It the data broker is also selling special personal information, a legal justification from section 27 or 28 to 33 must apply (see chapter 7). If there is information of children, they must comply with section 35 (also in chapter 7).

94 Page 32 of the ICO Enforcement Notice against Experian, available at https://ico.org.uk/media/action-weve-taken/enforcement-notices/2618467/experian-limited-enforcement-report.pdf.

95 Page 32 of the ICO Enforcement Notice against Experian, available at https://ico.org.uk/media/action-weve-taken/enforcement-notices/2618467/experian-limited-enforcement-report.pdf. The requirements for valid consent in terms of POPIA are similar to the EU GDPR and are discussed in chapter 2 paragraph 2.6.6.

as a basis, to relying on legitimate interest.[96] In the enforcement notice, they were asked to delete the information processed under the invalid consents.

Tricky area: Where sharing was not part of the original purpose for collecting the information, the requirements of further processing must be met.[97] In the cases the ICO investigated, these data brokers were also credit bureaus and were holding personal information for 'credit referencing purposes'. Even though the data brokers were not selling the credit data, this personal information was being used to screen individuals for direct marketers based on their financial status. The ICO found that, '[the credit bureaus] did not make clear to individuals that they would use the credit data for direct marketing purposes and did not obtain their consent'.

In South Africa, credit bureaus obtain 'consumer credit information' in terms of the National Credit Act 34 of 2005 (the NCA).[98] This means that credit bureaus in South Africa may be in a weaker position than those in the United Kingdom.[99] The NCA places restrictions on what credit bureaus can do with 'confidential information'. The NCA states that they must protect the confidentiality of that information and that they must use it 'only for a purpose permitted or required in terms of [the NCA], other national or applicable provincial legislation'. They are also only allowed to report or release the information to the consumer or prospective consumer or to 'another person' if the NCA or other legislation requires it, if the consumer or prospective consumer instructed them to release the information or if there is an order of a court or the National Credit Tribunal.[100] Section 70(2)*(g)* goes a bit further and states that a credit bureau can issue a report to a person 'for a prescribed purpose or a purpose contemplated in [the NCA]'. Regulation 18 of the NCA contains a list of additional 'prescribed purposes':

> '*(a)* an investigation into fraud, corruption or theft, provided that the South African Police Service or any other statutory enforcement agency conducts such an investigation;

---

[96] Page 34 of the ICO Enforcement Notice against Experian, available at https://ico.org.uk/media/action-weve-taken/enforcement-notices/2618467/experian-limited-enforcement-report.pdf.

[97] This is discussed in paragraph 13.4.6.2 above. Further processing is discussed in detail in chapter 12.

[98] See sections 68 to 70 of the NCA.

[99] Not only does POPIA include section 12 (which the EU GDPR does not), but they also have to contend with the NCA.

[100] Section 68(1).

(b) fraud detection and fraud prevention services;

(c) considering a candidate for employment in a position that requires trust and honesty and entails the handling of cash or finances;

(d) an assessment of the debtors book of a business for the purposes of:

(i) the sale of the business or debtors book of that business;

(ii) any other transaction that is dependent upon determining the value of the business or the debtors book of that business;

(e) setting a limit of service provision in respect of any continuous service;

(f) assessing an application for insurance;

(g) verifying qualifications and employment;

(h) obtaining consumer information to distribute unclaimed funds, including pension funds and insurance claims;

(i) tracing of a consumer by a credit provider in respect of a credit agreement entered into between the consumer and the credit provider;

(j) developing a credit scoring system by a credit provider or credit bureau.'

If the person requesting the report needs it for the purposes listed in sub-regulation (4)*(c)* or *(e)* to *(g)*, the person making the request must get the consumer's consent.

So is profiling or pre-vetting prospective customers one of the prescribed or required purposes of the NCA? The reference to prospective customers suggests that pre-vetting or profiling when it relates to prospective customers for credit products may be required or contemplated in terms of the NCA.[101] In addition, credit providers are required to assess prospective customers to ensure that the credit provider does not enter into reckless credit agreements.[102] It would therefore be justified as an obligation that is imposed by law on the responsible party.[103] However, this argument does not extend to pre-vetting or profiling for non-credit products. In those instances, the NCA's prohibition on the release of 'confidential information' kicks in.

What is confidential information as defined in the NCA? According to section 1 of the NCA it is 'personal information that belongs to a person and is not generally available or known to others'. This is strange given that the definition of 'personal information' in POPIA does not require that the information must not be 'generally available or known to others'. This means that credit bureaus could argue that they can sell personal information for purposes of direct marketing if that personal information is already available or known to others! Or does it? Credit bureaus will still have to show that selling personal information to direct marketers is compatible with the original

101 See section 68(1)*(a)* read with section 70(2)*(g)* of the NCA.

102 Section 80(1) and 81(3) of the NCA read with regulation 23A.

103 Section 11(1)*(c)* of POPIA. This is discussed in chapter 6 paragraph 6.3.2.

purpose for which it was collected.[104] Due to the intrusive nature of data brokering, it is unlikely that the Information Regulator will find that this further processing is generally compatible in terms of section 15(2). This means that they must comply with one of the justifications in section 15(3).[105] These legal justifications are very limited. The credit bureaus will have to show that the personal information was derived from a 'public record' or has deliberately been made public by the data subject'.[106] This justification is much narrower than allowing the sharing of information that is 'generally available or known to others'. If they cannot meet the requirements of section 15(3)*(b)*, we believe that they have no option but to obtain consent to sell the information.

Key point: The EU GDPR is different to POPIA when it comes to further processing[107] and, to a lesser degree, lawfulness. In addition, the UK does not have an equivalent to the NCA. So, tread carefully when evaluating the ICO's findings. It is also important to note that the ICO report was specifically considering the sale of personal information for direct marketing and screening (or profiling) purposes. The outcome may well be different when the information is being sold for another purpose such as data enrichment or cleaning.

- **Is the minimum amount of personal information being shared to achieve the purpose for sharing?**[108] Only the information required to achieve the purpose for which it is being shared should be shared. If a data broker is providing its customers with more data than they need to fulfil the purpose for which they are purchasing it, both the data broker and the marketer may be falling foul of the minimal processing rule.
- **Does the responsible party receiving the personal information (in this example, the marketer) fall within one of the exemptions to the direct collection rule?**[109] Responsible parties

[104] Section 15.

[105] Further processing is discussed in chapter 12.

[106] Section 15(3)*(b)*. The meanings of these phrases are discussed in chapter 10 paragraphs 10.4.1 and 10.4.2.

[107] Article 5(1)*(b)* of the EU GDPR deals with purpose limitation.

[108] This is discussed in paragraph 13.4.9. The principle of minimal processing is discussed in detail in chapter 9.

[109] This is discussed in paragraph 13.4.7 above. The exceptions to the direct collection rule are discussed in detail in chapter 10 paragraph 10.4.

who make use of data brokers must consider whether they fall into one of the exceptions to the direct collection rule. The most common exemption used in this context is that the information is 'contained in or derived from a public record' or that the personal information 'has deliberately been made public by the data subject'.[110] As we discussed in chapter 10 paragraph 10.4.1 and paragraph 10.4.2, the scope of these two exemptions is more limited than people (and data brokers) think. It is unlikely to be true of all 3 000 data points in our example. Consent from the data subject to collect their information from a data broker is also an attractive option. Kidding, it rarely is, because the data broker probably is not in contact with the data subject (the processing is hidden), the marketer does not know who the data subject is before the collection has already taken place and both would probably be concerned that the data subject would politely (or impolitely) decline. As always, that consent must be a voluntary, informed and specific expression of will.[111] What about the exception that collecting the personal information from a data broker is in the legitimate interest of the marketer?[112] Maybe, but it is also possible that the intrusive nature of the processing might outweigh the marketer's interest in ultra-targeted marketing; in order to rely on this exemption the responsible party should perform a well-weighted legitimate interest assessment.[113] At this point we can hear marketers wail, 'but it is impossible to do this any other way!'. We agree, we barely know 3 000 things about ourselves which we could share. As it happens the last exemption to the direct collection rule is that 'compliance is not reasonably practicable in the circumstances of the particular case'.[114] The data subject is not in a position to provide the information, because they do not know themselves as well as the data broker knows them. However, as you will see in the next bullet, the ICO rejected a similar argument in the context of a failure to notify data subjects. We think it is likely that it would suffer the same fate in this context – responsible parties simply cannot say that compliance is impossible due to the sheer volume of the personal information they have about us!

---

110 Section 12(2)*(a)*.

111 Section 12(2)*(b)*. The requirements for valid consent in terms of POPIA are discussed in chapter 2 paragraph 2.6.6.

112 Section 12(2)*(d)*(v).

113 Legitimate interest assessments are discussed in chapter 2 paragraph 2.6.3.

114 Section 12(2)*(f)*. This is discussed in detail in chapter 10 paragraph 10.4.8.

Tricky area: In this example, the data broker will also have to justify why it is entitled to collect personal information from so many sources other than the data subject. The ICO did not address this issue, because the EU GDPR does not contain a 'collect from the data subject' rule as set out in section 12 of POPIA. In this regard the data broker and the marketer will be faced with much the same difficulties.

- **Has the responsible party(s) met the notification requirements?**[115] Notification and transparency was a key issue in the ICO report.[116] The data brokers in the ICO investigation were engaging in 'invisible processing', where the data subject does not have a direct relationship with the data brokers and is not aware that the broker is collecting and using their personal information. The EU GDPR and POPIA require that data subjects must be notified of the processing of their personal information as soon as reasonably practicable after the information is collected.[117] The data brokers argued that the data subjects have already been notified in the privacy notices of the responsible parties who provide the personal information to the data brokers. However, the ICO found that the privacy notices 'of third parties did not clearly draw attention to the processing of the [data brokers] for these purposes. Individuals would only discover it was happening if they reviewed the third party's policies and followed links within those policies.'[118] The data brokers also argued that directly notifying the data subjects would involve 'disproportionate effort' due to the large volume of personal information they process.[119] The ICO rejected this argument and pointed out that '[v]ery large numbers of individuals cannot be the deciding factor against it being proportional to notify people about the processing in these circumstances. Otherwise this would give controllers a perverse incentive to gather as much data as possible in order to reduce the burden on them

---

115 This is discussed in paragraph 13.4.8 above. Notification is discussed in detail in chapter 11.

116 ICO Enforcement Notice against Experian, available at https://ico.org.uk/media/action-weve-taken/enforcement-notices/2618467/experian-limited-enforcement-report.pdf.

117 See the discussion of section 18 in chapter 11.

118 Page 28.

119 POPIA includes a similar exemption to the notification duty in section 18(4)*(e)*. This is discussed in chapter 11 paragraph 11.6.5.

to notify them.'[120] The ICO concluded that data brokers must provide direct notifications to all individuals for whom they hold personal information.[121] In short, the privacy information was not sufficiently prominent and did not 'sufficiently explain how the data was collected, what sources were used, how it was processed, or how it was sold'.

- **Does the sharing activity comply with information security management principles?**[122] The South African Experian data breach in 2020 was a good example of information security concerns in the context of the sharing of information. In this case, the South African arm of Experian, per their FAQ about the breach 'was the victim of fraud in which the perpetrator, pretending to be a legitimate client, made a fraudulent data inquiry'. They added that they 'have introduced additional authentication controls to prevent this type of incident from occurring again'.[123]
- **Can the responsible party(s) honour data subject rights?**[124] For instance, if a data subject objects to the processing (if either the data broker or the marketer is relying on legitimate interest as a legal justification) or withdraws consent, or wants to know from the data broker 'information about the identity of all third parties ... who have, or have had, access to the information', will the data broker be able to respect these rights? In addition, pre-vetting is also a form of automated decision-making. That is when a profile about a person's creditworthiness, reliability, location, health, personal preferences or conduct is used to make an automated decision about a data subject. If this results in legal consequences or affects the data subject to a substantial degree, the data broker must also comply with section 71.[125] One can argue about whether pre-vetting and profiling has legal consequences or a substantial impact,[126] but if it has, the data

---

120 Page 29.

121 This was also the conclusion of the Article 29 Data Protection Working Party *Guidelines on Automated Individual Decision-making and Profiling for the Purposes of Regulation 2016/679* 16, available at https://ec.europa.eu/newsroom/article29/item-detail.cfm?item_id=612053.

122 This is discussed in paragraph 13.4.10 above. Information security management is discussed in detail in chapter 5.

123 The FAQ is available at https://www.experian.co.za/fraudulent-data-incident/faqs.

124 This is discussed in paragraph 13.4.11 above. Data subject rights are discussed in detail in chapter 18.

125 Section 71(1). Automated decision-making is discussed in chapter 15.

126 The European Data Protection Board has debated this exact question and concluded that the effects of profiling in the marketing context could be substantial depending on the particular case. We discuss this in chapter 15 paragraph 15.2.2.2.

subject has the right to be informed about the underlying logic and to make representations.[127] So, automated decision-making without transparency will not be allowed.[128]

Key point: Are we saying that data brokers are on their way out? Probably not, but POPIA will be even more challenging than the EU GDPR, due to the direct collection rule. We are also witnessing a move away from these third-party databases due to the fact that the very customers marketers are trying to reach hate being talked about behind their backs. Instead, there is a new focus on building authentic, direct relationships with customers through 'earned data'. That is personal information that customers 'volunteer in order to improve their experience, with full understanding of how it's to be used, and as part of a genuine value exchange'.[129] We are sure that the data brokering industry will answer our concerns with: '[We] find your lack of faith disturbing.'[130]

13.6.2 Sharing information within a group of companies

During the drafting of POPIA one of the major banks submitted that a group of companies should be able to share information across subsidiaries or affiliates, across brands, divisions and product areas for the purposes of cross-selling (where a lead is passed on from one subsidiary to another) and marketing.[131] Direct marketing is discussed in chapter 16. This is a practice which we often see in the financial services sector, where it is not unusual to see a group of companies who are selling all manner of financial services.

Here are some typical reasons why groups of companies want to share or pool personal information:

- it is more cost-effective to have joint information management infrastructure (e.g. they use the same system)

---

127 Section 71(3). This is discussed in chapter 15.

128 As you know by now, we are deeply, deeply cynical about the ability of transparency and data subject rights to safeguard privacy. We discussed this in chapter 2 paragraph 2.6.4.

129 World Federation of Advertisers *Data Ethics: The Rise of Mortality in Technology*, available at https://wfanet.org/leadership/data-ethics-report. The quote is from David Eldrigde '74% of CMOs say "data ethics" will be more important to their role in the next five years' *3radical*, available at https://3radical.com/blog/74-of-cmos-say-data-ethics-will-be-more-important-to-their-role-in-the-next-five-years/.

130 Darth Vader, *Star Wars Episode IV: A New Hope*.

131 SA Law Reform Commission Project 124 on Privacy and Data Protection (2009 Report) 260.

- the subsidiaries provide services to each other
- they want to generate insights (business intelligence) from the pooled personal information to improve their products or services; or
- the subsidiaries want to cross-sell their products or services to each other's clients.

Consider the following example: Explore Ltd is a group of companies that sell banking services, medical aid, retirement annuities, long-term insurance products (e.g. life insurance), vehicle insurance and run a comprehensive loyalty programme. If a data subject signs up for the medical aid and the loyalty programme, can that data subject's information be shared between the medical aid and the insurer in the group for direct marketing purposes?

Let's apply the checklist:

- **What personal information is being shared?** Is any of the personal information special personal information?[132] In order to manage compliance, it is important for groups of companies to map exactly what personal information is flowing where in the group.
- **What is the purpose for sharing the personal information?**[133] In other words, determine why information is being shared between subsidiaries. Without identifying the purpose(s) for sharing, compliance with the rest of the requirements of POPIA is impossible.
- **Who is accountable to ensure that the sharing activity complies with POPIA?** Sometimes, personal information is being shared between subsidiaries because they have a joint purpose. They will be co-responsible parties.[134] In other instances, subsidiaries are performing services to each other. For instance, one subsidiary may be the responsible party, but another subsidiary may be acting as their operator. Determining the nature of the relationship is crucial, because it determines who is responsible for POPIA compliance. The relationship should be documented in agreements between the subsidiaries.

---

132 Special personal information is discussed in chapter 7.

133 The purpose specification requirement is discussed in chapter 6 paragraph 6.2.

134 This is discussed in paragraph 13.4.3 above. Accountability is discussed in detail in chapter 4.

- **Does the responsible party(s) need prior authorisation?** For instance, if the subsidiaries are sharing unique identifiers with the aim of linking the information held about a data subject across a group, prior authorisation may be required.[135]
- **Is the personal information being shared across borders?** If the group is multinational, transborder information flows must be considered.[136] POPIA's provisions on transborder information flows[137] will be triggered if a South African subsidiary is sharing personal information with a subsidiary located in another country. If the personal information is flowing in the other direction (from an overseas subsidiary to a South African subsidiary), the question is whether the South African subsidiary might not be subject to another data protection law (e.g. the EU GDPR). It is not unusual for a multinational group of companies to be subject to multiple data protection laws. This can lead to a devilish level of complexity. Multinationals often opt to resolve this through binding corporate rules or information sharing agreements.
- **Does the responsible party(s) have a legal justification for sharing?**[138] The typical legal justifications that may apply within a group of companies are that the sharing is necessary to conclude or perform a contract with the data subject, the processing is in the legitimate interest of the group (in which case the data subject could object) or that the data subject consented to the personal information being shared within the group.[139] Where sharing was not part of the original purpose for collecting the information, the requirements of further processing must be met.[140] If the companies are providing services to one another (i.e. one is an operator), an additional legal justification for the sharing is not required, because the operator is processing the personal information on behalf of the responsible party.
- **Is the minimum amount of personal information being shared to achieve the purpose for sharing?**[141] Only the information required to achieve the purpose for which it is being shared should be shared. Where the group of companies have

135 The activities which require prior authorisation are discussed in detail in chapter 8.

136 This is discussed in chapter 14.

137 Section 72.

138 This is discussed in paragraph 13.4.6 above. The legal justifications are discussed in chapter 6.

139 While consent is often used, it is rarely appropriate. See chapter 2 paragraph 2.6.6.

140 This is discussed in paragraph 13.4.6.2 above. Further processing is discussed in detail in chapter 12.

141 This is discussed in paragraph 13.4.9 above. The principle of minimal processing is discussed in detail in chapter 9.

joint information management infrastructure (e.g. they use the same system), they should limit access to the information to those subsidiaries who require it. This will not only ensure compliance with the principle of minimality, but it will also improve compliance with POPIA's information security requirements.[142]

- **Does the responsible party receiving the personal information fall within one of the exemptions to the direct collection rule?**[143] When information is collected by a group of companies from the outset, one could argue that all of the subsidiaries in the group are collecting the information directly from the data subjects. In other instances, the subsidiaries with whom the personal information is being shared who are responsible parties (as opposed to operators)[144] will have to consider whether they fall into one of the exceptions to the direct collection rule. Consent from the data subject and the legitimate interest of the responsible party are commonly used exceptions.
- **Has the responsible party(s) met the notification requirements?**[145] It is entirely possible for a group of companies to have a joint privacy notice, particularly where they are co-responsible parties with a shared purpose. All of the different legal entities should be named in the privacy notice.
- **Does the sharing activity comply with information security management principles?**[146] Groups that process personal information together must pay attention to limiting access to the information to those entities and individuals who require access to fulfil their roles. Another challenge is managing the integrity of the information. For instance, how do entities in a group ensure that if personal information is updated by one entity, that update is made across the whole group? To achieve this, groups must invest in master data management.[147]

---

142 Information security management is discussed in chapter 5. Access control is an important part of information security management.

143 This is discussed in paragraph 13.4.7 above. The exceptions to the direct collection rule are discussed in detail in chapter 10 paragraph 10.4.

144 Operators do not have to comply with the direct collection rule. Operators are discussed in chapter 4 paragraph 4.4.

145 This is discussed in paragraph 13.4.8 above. Notification is discussed in detail in chapter 11.

146 This is discussed in paragraph 13.4.10 above. Information security management is discussed in detail in chapter 5.

147 Managing information quality is discussed in paragraph 13.4.10.2 above. Master data management is discussed in chapter 9 paragraph 9.6.5.

- **Can the responsible party(s) honour data subject rights?**[148] For instance, if a data subject asks for access to the personal information the group has about him or her, or objects to the processing, does the group have procedures in place to ensure that the data subject's rights are honoured across all of the entities in the group? This will often require an investment in master data management.[149]

Key point: POPIA does not prevent information sharing between different entities in a group, but it does increase the compliance burden. POPIA provides an opportunity to document the data flows between entities in a group, and to put policies, procedures and standards in place to make sure that sharing happens in a POPIA compliant way. It is not all doom, gloom and new red tape. Performing these tasks will also place groups of companies on a path towards efficiency, superior data quality and digital transformation.

13.6.3 Verifying information through credit bureaus and verification agencies

Organisations often make use of credit bureaus and verification agencies to do various background checks or to verify the information provided by data subjects. For example:

- Employers verify that prospective employees have the degrees they say they have and that they do not have a criminal history.
- Accountable institutions use verification agencies to 'know their customer' and perform customer due diligences to comply with the Financial Intelligence Centre Act 38 of 2001.
- Responsible parties often use tracing agents (and credit bureaus) to confirm addresses for data subjects who owe them money.
- Responsible parties use the services of data brokers to 'clean' their databases.

---

148 This is discussed in paragraph 13.4.11 above. Data subject rights are discussed in detail in chapter 18.

149 Managing information quality is discussed in paragraph 13.4.10.2 above. Master data management is discussed in chapter 9 paragraph 9.6.5.

Key point: In this paragraph, we are not talking about buying information from a data broker (we discussed that in paragraph 13.6.1). This paragraph is about verifying information the responsible party already has.

Let us apply the checklist:

- **What personal information is being shared?** Is any of the personal information special personal information?[150] In order to manage compliance, it is important for responsible parties to map which personal information they verify, what sources they use to verify information and what the rules are that apply when the personal information they already have is updated during the verification process.
- **What is the purpose for sharing the personal information?**[151] In this example, information is being shared in order to verify the information the responsible party already has. If the purpose were to 'enrich' or supplement the personal information the outcome of this checklist would be different. For a discussion on the rules that apply when a responsible party purchases information it does not already have, see paragraph 13.6.1 above.
- **Who is accountable to ensure that the sharing activity complies with POPIA?**[152] Could it be argued that the verification agency is an operator of the responsible party? They certainly act on the instruction of the responsible party when they are asked to verify the personal information of specific data subjects. However, like data brokers (in fact, they often are data brokers) some verification agencies do this by building vast databases. In other words, they do not only collect the personal information of a data subject when asked to do so by the responsible party. So, in many instances they will be an independent responsible party.
- Does the responsible party(s) need prior authorisation?[153] Verification agencies make use of unique identifiers to link personal information being processed by other responsible parties. If this was not the original purpose for which the

150 Special personal information is discussed in chapter 7.

151 The purpose specification requirement is discussed in chapter 6 paragraph 6.2.

152 This is discussed in paragraph 13.4.3 above. Accountability is discussed in detail in chapter 4.

153 The activities which require prior authorisation are discussed in detail in chapter 8.

identifier was collected, the verification agency may have to apply for prior authorisation.[154] If a verification agency processes information on criminal behaviour or unlawful or objectionable conduct on behalf of third parties, the verification agency may have to apply for prior authorisation.[155]

- **Is the personal information being shared across borders?**[156] POPIA's provisions on transborder information flows[157] will be triggered if the verification agency has clients in another country.
- **Does the responsible party(s) have a legal justification for sharing?**[158] The typical legal justification that may apply when information is verified by using a source other than the data subject is that the responsible party is subject to an obligation imposed by law to verify the information.[159] This is a very strong form of justification, because the data subject does not have the right to object. For instance, FICA requires that an accountable institution must verify the identity of prospective customers to screen them against various sanctions lists.[160] Always remember that the use of an external verification agency must be 'necessary' for compliance; over-compliance will not be justifiable.

Tricky area: POPIA provides that responsible parties must use 'reasonably practicable steps' to ensure that the personal information it uses is accurate.[161] We would argue that using a verification agency may be a 'reasonably practicable step', particularly when the data subject may be incentivised to provide false information (e.g. inflating their qualifications when they apply for a job) and where the responsible party is going to base an important decision on the personal information.

---

[154] Section 57(1)*(a)*. But remember that section 57(3) provides that a responsible party that is governed by an approved code of conduct will not require prior authorisation. See Guidelines to develop Code of Conduct, 15 Feb 2021, issued under the Protection of Personal Information Act 4 of 2013 (POPIA), available at https://www.justice.gov.za/inforeg/docs/coc/InfoRegSA-Guidelines-DevelopCodeOfConduct-22Feb2021.pdf.

[155] Section 57(1)*(b)*. This is discussed in chapter 8.

[156] This is discussed in chapter 14.

[157] Section 72.

[158] This is discussed in paragraph 13.4.6 above. The legal justifications are discussed in chapter 6.

[159] Section 11(1)*(c)*. This is discussed in detail in chapter 6 paragraph 6.3.2.

[160] The Financial Intelligence Centre specifically lists 'screening tools' as a method of managing risk. See FIC *Guidance Note on the Implementation of Various Aspects of the Financial Intelligence Centre Act 38 of 2001*, available at https://www.fic.gov.za/Documents/171002_FIC%20Guidance%20Note%2007.pdf.

[161] Section 16. This is discussed in chapter 9 paragraph 9.5.

Responsible parties could also rely on their legitimate interest to justify the processing,[162] but then the data subject will have the right to object.[163] If a responsible party relies on consent to verify, the consent has to be a voluntary, informed and specific expression of will. A data subject has to be able to withhold or withdraw consent and the processing must continue; it cannot be 'consent, or else'.[164]

- **Is the minimum amount of personal information being shared to achieve the purpose for sharing?**[165] Only the information required to verify the personal information should be shared.
- **Does the responsible party receiving the personal information fall within one of the exemptions to the direct collection rule?**[166] When information is collected from a verification agency, the responsible party has to consider whether the sharing falls within one of the exemptions to the direct collection rule. Commonly, responsible parties argue that the information is 'contained in or derived from a public record' or that the personal information 'has deliberately been made public by the data subject'.[167] As we discussed in chapter 10 paragraph 10.4.1 and paragraph 10.4.2, the scope of these two exemptions are more limited than people think. Responsible parties can also rely on the exemption to the direct collection rule when 'compliance would prejudice the lawful purpose of the collection'.[168] For instance, if a responsible party is verifying information about a customer who is suspected of money laundering, the responsible party would not want to alert the customer by asking them directly. Consent from the data subject to collect their information from a verification agency is also an attractive option, if the responsible party already knows who the data subject is. As always, that consent must be a voluntary, informed and specific expression of will.[169] This is particularly relevant for credit bureaus who can lower the credit score of a

162 Section 11(1)*(f)*. This is discussed in detail in chapter 6 paragraph 6.3.5.

163 Section 11(3). The right to object is discussed in chapter 18 paragraph 18.6.

164 The requirement for valid consent is discussed in chapter 2 paragraph 2.6.6.

165 This is discussed in paragraph 13.4.9. The principle of minimal processing is discussed in detail in chapter 9.

166 This is discussed in paragraph 13.4.7. The exceptions to the direct collection rule are discussed in detail in chapter 10 paragraph 10.4.

167 Section 12(2)*(a)*.

168 Section 12(2)*(e)*.

169 Section 12(2)*(b)*. The requirements for valid consent in terms of POPIA are discussed in chapter 2 paragraph 2.6.6.

consumer that has too many requests. This is a good example of what the data subject should be 'informed' about. Collecting the personal information from a verification agency could also be in the legitimate interest of the responsible party.[170] The last relevant exemption to the direct collection rule is that 'compliance is not reasonably practicable in the circumstances of the particular case'.[171] This may be the case where the responsible party is trying to verify the data subjects' contact details.

- **Has the responsible party(s) met the notification requirements?**[172] Generally, responsible parties should notify data subjects if their information will be obtained from another source. There may be instances where the responsible party does not want to do this; if notifying the data subject would 'prejudice a lawful purpose of the collection',[173] the responsible party does not have to notify. For instance, if a responsible party is verifying information about a customer who is suspected of money laundering, the responsible party would not want to alert the customer by notifying them.
- **Does the sharing activity comply with information security management principles?**[174] How reliable is the verification agency? The predominant concern when using verification agencies to clean personal information is to ensure that the activity does not introduce new data integrity issues.[175] Data integrity issues can be introduced if the information provided by the verification agency is incorrect or if something goes wrong during the process of updating the information, e.g. transcription errors, where the incorrect information is associated with a data subject.
- **Can the responsible party(s) honour data subject rights?**[176] For instance, if a data subject asks where the information was obtained, will the responsible party be able to answer? In order to answer, the responsible party will have to maintain a record of its verification activities.

---

170 Section 12(2)*(d)*(v).

171 Section 12(2)*(f)*.

172 This is discussed in paragraph 13.4.8. Notification is discussed in detail in chapter 11.

173 Section 18(4)*(d)*. The exemptions to the notification duty are discussed in detail in chapter 11 paragraph 11.6.

174 This is discussed in paragraph 13.4.10 above. Information security management is discussed in detail in chapter 5.

175 Managing information quality is discussed in paragraph 13.4.10.2 above. Master data management is discussed in chapter 1 paragraph 1.4.2.4.

176 This is discussed in paragraph 13.4.11 above. Data subject rights are discussed in detail in chapter 18.

13.7 PRACTICAL ADVICE

13.7.1 A sharing checklist

In order to determine whether a specific instance of sharing of information is POPIA compliant, we ask the following questions:

- What personal information is being shared?
- What is the purpose for sharing the personal information?
- Who is accountable to ensure that the sharing activity complies with POPIA?
- Does the responsible party(s) need prior authorisation?
- Is the personal information being shared across borders?
- Does the responsible party(s) have a legal justification for sharing?
- Is the minimum amount of personal information being shared to achieve the purpose for sharing?
- Does the responsible party receiving the personal information fall within one of the exemptions to the direct collection rule?
- Has the responsible party(s) met the notification requirements?
- Does the sharing activity comply with information security management principles?
- Can the responsible party(s) honour data subject rights?

The trick is to ensure that the checklist is applied every time information is shared with the responsible party or where the responsible party shares information with others. In practice, we incorporate this in the third-party risk management process.

13.7.2 Third-party risk management

Third-party risk management ought to be a significant part of any POPIA Programme. It starts with identifying sharing activities, both where information flows into the organisation and when it flows out. Documenting and evaluating all sharing activities forms part of third-party risk management. We gave practical advice on how to approach third-party risk management in chapter 4 paragraph 4.8.3.

14

Transborder information flows and extra-territorial application

14.1 WHAT TO EXPECT IN THIS CHAPTER

In this chapter we discuss one of the most confounding questions in data protection. How can national data protection laws regulate information flows that cross jurisdictions in a flash? The issue was eloquently summarised during the United Nations Conference on Trade and Development:[1]

> 'In the global information economy, personal data have become the fuel driving much of current online activity. Every day, vast amounts of information are transmitted, stored and collected across the globe enabled by massive improvements in computing and communication power. Some broadband packages of today are 36,000 times faster than what dial-up internet connections could offer when the first internet browser was introduced two decades ago.'

We are certainly glad about the faster internet connections, but the effortless sharing of personal information across borders has introduced a devilish level of complexity when it comes to complying with data protection regulations. With the advent of cloud computing, even simple questions like 'where is the personal information stored?' have become tough to answer.

---

1 United Nations Conference on Trade and Development 'Data protection regulations and international data flows: Implications for trade and development' (2016) 2, available at https://www.tralac.org/images/docs/9500/data-protection-regulations-and-international-data-flows-implications-for-trade-and-development-unctad-april-2016.pdf.

The SA Law Reform Commission had the following to say about this issue in 2009:[2]

> '[T]he ease with which electronic data flows across borders leads to a concern that information protection laws could be circumvented by simply transferring personal information to other countries, where the national law of the country of origin does not apply. This information could then be processed in those countries, frequently called "information havens", without any limitations.'

There are three types of provisions that are used in data protection regulations to try and address this issue:

Transborder information flow provisions	These provisions impose requirements on responsible parties who transfer personal information to third parties in foreign countries. Section 72 of POPIA is an example of this.
Adequacy decisions	This is when a country's information regulator assesses the data protection laws in a foreign country and declares that they are adequate. POPIA does not have such a provision, but the Information Regulator can provide advice on issues such as 'adequacy'.[3] Section 57(1)*(d)* does provide that the Regulator must be approached for prior authorisation when a responsible party wants to transfer special personal information or a child's personal information to a foreign organisation.[4] However, this is only the case where the foreign organisation is not subject to 'an adequate level of protection'. Granting prior authorisation in those circumstances is not the same as an adequacy decision in respect of that country; if the protection in the country was adequate, the need for prior authorisation would not arise.
Extra-territorial application	These provisions extend the application of a data protection regulation to organisations that are normally outside their jurisdiction. POPIA does this (albeit to a limited degree) in section 3(1)*(b)*(ii).

POPIA also requires that responsible parties must be transparent about transborder information flows. That's nice.[5]

2 SA Law Reform Commission Project 124 on Privacy and Data Protection (2009 Report) 401.

3 The Information Regulator has been doing this in the form of 'guidance notes'. The status of guidance notes is discussed in chapter 19 paragraph 19.4.

4 This is discussed in chapter 8 paragraph 8.2.4.

5 We are not fans of regulation that is based on the assumption that data subjects will be able to protect themselves as long as they know how their personal information will be processed. We

In this chapter we discuss the following:

- Transborder information flows
- Extra-territorial application of data protection laws
- Disclosing transborder information flows

14.2 TRANSBORDER INFORMATION FLOWS

14.2.1 When does section 72 apply?

Section 72 applies when a responsible party in South Africa transfers personal information to a third party who is in a foreign country.[6] There are three elements to consider here:

- Is the information flowing out of South Africa?
- What does 'transfer' mean?
- When will the recipient be considered a 'third party'?

Key point: Section 72 is incredibly restrictive. Make sure that you are really 'transferring' personal information to a 'third party' in a foreign country!

14.2.1.1 Is the information flowing out of South Africa?

For section 72 to apply, personal information has to be flowing out of South Africa. Organisations often forget this and apply section 72 unnecessarily. For instance, section 72 is not triggered if a European organisation uses a South African organisation as an operator.[7] But, as usual, we cannot just leave it there ...

When information is flowing from another country to South Africa, the transborder information flow provisions of the country where the personal information is coming from may apply. In some instances, this can have the result that a South African organisation has to comply with foreign legislation in order to receive the information.

discuss this in depth in chapter 2 paragraph 2.6.4. It is particularly true in this context – it is not like the average data subject is a privacy law expert who is able to compare the strength of regulations in different countries. Most privacy law experts cannot even do that.

6 Section 72(1).

7 However, if a foreign organisation uses an operator in South Africa, that foreign organisation may be subject to POPIA. That is because section 3(1)*(b)*(ii) provides that POPIA can apply to a foreign organisation not domiciled (resident) in South Africa if it uses 'means' in South Africa to process personal information. The application of POPIA is discussed in chapter 3.

Key point: This obligation is often contractual; in other words, the South African organisation does not fall under the jurisdiction of a foreign regulator, but the responsible party sending the personal information to the South African organisation is forcing them to comply. While breaching a contract of this nature gives rise to financial and legal risk, it is not because the South African organisation can get a fine from a foreign regulator. It is because the South African organisation might lose a client and get sued!

14.2.1.2 What does transfer mean?

POPIA does not define the term 'transfer'. The ICO defines a 'transfer' as 'an intentional sending of personal data to another party or making the data accessible by it, where neither sender nor recipient is a data subject'.[8] The South African Law Reform Commission also weighed in and made the following observations:[9]

- The ordinary meaning of the word is 'transmission from one place, person, etc. to another'.
- The test is whether the information has been 'sent' to a recipient in another country.
- Transmitting the information is not the same as 'the transit of information through a country'. They explain that '[i]f personal information is, for e.g., transferred from country A to country B via a server in country C and no access to or manipulation of the information happens in country C, then the transfer is only to country B'.
- If information is placed on a website which is accessible from other countries, the transfer will only take place when the information is actually accessed by someone from another country.

---

8 ICO *International Transfers after the UK Exit from the EU Implementation Period*, available at https://ico.org.uk/for-organisations/guide-to-data-protection/guide-to-the-general-data-protection-regulation-gdpr/international-transfers-after-uk-exit/.

9 SA Law Reform Commission Project 124 on Privacy and Data Protection (2009 Report) 402.

Key point: The SA Law Reform Commission does not quite come out and say it,[10] but a transfer of information can be passive. That means that the personal information could be staying in South Africa, but if it is made accessible to a third party in a foreign country, section 72 will apply.[11]

14.2.1.3 When will the recipient be considered a third party?

When will the recipient be considered a 'third party'? The term is not defined in POPIA, but it was defined in the Data Protection Directive, which POPIA was based on.[12] The gist of this definition is that in order to be considered a third party, the third party must not be under the direct authority of the responsible party.[13] The ICO states that the 'receiver' must be 'legally distinct' from the responsible party making the transfer.[14]

14.2.1.4 Some examples of when section 72 applies

Here are some examples:[15]

A South African company uses a centralised human resource system in the Unites States which is provided by its parent company. The South African company shares employee information with the parent company.	Section 72 applies, even though the companies are in the same group.

➡

10 We think that when they refer to a 'website' which is accessible to third parties in foreign countries, the website may be hosted in South Africa.

11 ICO *International Transfers after the UK Exit from the EU Implementation Period*, available at https://ico.org.uk/for-organisations/guide-to-data-protection/guide-to-the-general-data-protection-regulation-gdpr/international-transfers-after-uk-exit/.

12 We discuss this in chapter 11 paragraph 11.3.2 in the context of notifying the data subject that their personal information will be shared with a third party.

13 Article 2*(f)* of the Data Protection Directive. The definition was retained in article 4(10) of the EU GDPR.

14 ICO *International Transfers after the UK Exit from the EU Implementation Period*, available at https://ico.org.uk/for-organisations/guide-to-data-protection/guide-to-the-general-data-protection-regulation-gdpr/international-transfers-after-uk-exit/.

15 ICO *International Transfers after the UK Exit from the EU Implementation Period*, available at https://ico.org.uk/for-organisations/guide-to-data-protection/guide-to-the-general-data-protection-regulation-gdpr/international-transfers-after-uk-exit/. We adapted the examples for the South African context.

A South African company sells holidays in Australia. The South African company sends the personal information of South African customers who have bought the holidays to the hotels they have chosen in order to secure their bookings.	Section 72 applies, because the information is transferred to a third party in a foreign country.
A South African company transfers personal information to another company in South Africa via a server in the UK. There is no intention that the personal information will be accessed or manipulated while it is in the UK.	Section 72 does not apply, because the personal information is just being transmitted through the UK.
A South African company has employees who work from Nigeria. In order to do their work, they need access to the personal information of the company's customers. Sometimes they access this information remotely on the South African company's systems and servers which are located in South Africa.	Section 72 does not apply, because the recipients are employed by the South African company. **Key point: Employees are not third parties.**
A South African company uses Google Drive (or Microsoft, Dropbox, Amazon or any cloud service provider) as its main platform for collaboration. Some of the information used on these platforms is personal information. These services generally allow you to select a region in which the information will be stored.	Section 72 will apply if the South African company selected servers outside of South Africa, because the cloud service provider has access to the information in a foreign country. If the South African company selected that the information must be hosted locally, the question will be whether the cloud service provider can access the information from a foreign country. If it can only be accessed by a South Africa subsidiary of the cloud service provider, section 72 might not apply.

	Key point: The cloud service provider is an operator of the South African company; however, they are still a 'third party' for purposes of section 72. Even though they act on a mandate from the South African responsible party, they are not under the authority of the South African responsible party.
A South African company makes use of an operator to capture personal information which was collected using editable pdf forms. The operator is located in South Africa, but makes use of cloud services to store the information the responsible party provides to it. The servers are located in Amsterdam. The responsible party did not ask where the information would be stored and is unaware that it will be transferred to Amsterdam.	It is not the responsible party making the transfer, but the operator.[16] **Tricky area:** Section 72 expressly refers to transfers by responsible parties. However, section 20 provides that operators must not disclose personal information 'unless required ... in the course of the proper performance of their duties'. We would argue that the operator in this example is in breach of section 20*(b)*, but as we discussed in chapter 4 paragraph 4.4.2, this is all but clear. Responsible parties who are making use of operators should always determine who the operator will share the personal information with and whether the personal information will be transferred to another country to ensure compliance with section 72.

[16] How to identify an 'operator' and the implications of being one is discussed in chapter 4 paragraph 4.4.

A South African company makes use of a cloud service provider to store personal information of its customers. The cloud service provider's servers are located in the United States, but the service provider makes use of a zero knowledge encryption standard. This means that the cloud service provider cannot decrypt the information themselves, because only the South African company (and a separate encryption provider) has the decryption key.	Zero knowledge encryption protocol is a very effective way to section 72-proof cloud storage.[17] Because the cloud service provider cannot access the information, section 72 does not apply.

14.2.2 The default rule is that the personal information stays put

The default rule is that personal information should not be transferred to a third party in a foreign country unless one of the exemptions in section 72(2) applies.

14.2.3 When can personal information be transferred to another country?

Section 72(1) contains several exemptions to the default rule that personal information must not be transferred to a third party in a foreign country. Because they are exemptions, they should be interpreted restrictively.

14.2.3.1 There is an adequate level of protection

Personal information can be transferred to another country if the third party who is receiving the information is subject to:[18]

- a law
- binding corporate rules; or
- a binding agreement

which provides an adequate level of protection. It is very tempting to answer the question 'what is adequate?' with a resounding 'how long is a piece of string?' Luckily, (a) POPIA does provide some guidance, and (b) other countries have been using adequacy decisions for quite some time.

Protection will be considered adequate if the law, rules or agreement:

17 There are companies that offer this service. We will not name them; this is not an infomercial.

18 Section 72(1).

- is 'effective'
- upholds principles for reasonable processing of personal information that are 'substantially similar' to the principles in POPIA; and
- includes provisions about the further transfer to another third party in a foreign country that are 'substantially similar' to section 72.

Tricky area: Who makes this determination? Article 45 of the EU GDPR caters for transfers on the basis of an 'adequacy decision' which is made by the European Commission. POPIA does not give the Information Regulator similar powers. This means that it is each responsible party who must make this decision. A daunting task. POPIA does give the Information Regulator wide-ranging powers to make public statements 'in relation to any matter affecting the protection of the personal information of … a class of data subjects' or even to provide advice to public or private bodies on their obligations in terms of POPIA.[19] If guidance on these matters is not forthcoming, the uncertainty will probably drive responsible parties towards data localisation, where responsible parties opt to store information within the boundaries of South Africa. Sounds grand, but it can be costly and have a chilling effect on investment as global organisations will avoid South Africa.[20] Here is an extract from the World Economic Forum's white paper *A Roadmap for Cross-border Data Flows: Future-Proofing Readiness and Cooperation in the New Data Economy*:[21]

19 Section 40(1)*(a)*(ii) and (v).

20 See Ardent 'Storage wars: The pros and cons of data localisation/nationalisation', available at https://ardentprivacy.ai/data-security-blog/storage-wars-the-pros-and-cons-of-data-localization-nationalization/.

21 World Economic Forum *A Roadmap for Cross-Border Data Flows: Future-Proofing Readiness and Cooperation in the New Data Economy*, available at https://www3.weforum.org/docs/WEF_A_Roadmap_for_Cross_Border_Data_Flows_2020.pdf.

'When unjustified, data localization requirements can prove highly problematic. As well as driving up the cost of cloud computing, upon which SMEs are highly reliant, it becomes difficult to achieve access to high-quality data at scale, upon which technological development relies – and from there, problems quickly amplify. We see associated economic consequences when companies need to create and maintain multiple data centres in different jurisdictions, at great cost in both monetary and environmental terms. Furthermore, companies relying upon such services may find they avoid certain markets altogether due to the increased cost of doing business there. This then has further knock-on effects for the attractiveness of regions when it comes to investment of capital and retention of talent, with data localization restrictions acting as digital walls between countries.'

The SA Law Reform Commission states that the adequacy analysis has two basic elements:

- Are the eight conditions for the lawful processing of personal information present?
- Is the data protection law effectively enforced?

Key point: The Article 29 Data Protection Working Party *Adequacy Referential* (2018)[22] gives a useful glimpse into how this assessment should be done, but always keep the differences between POPIA and the EU GDPR in mind! To see the assessment in action, see the European Commission's decision in January 2019 to designate Japan as a secure country after Japan implemented supplementary rules applicable only to personal information from the EU.[23] The long-awaited adequacy decision in favour of the United Kingdom post-Brexit is also interesting, primarily because it is the first adequacy decision with a 'sunset clause'.[24]

The adequate rules can be in any of the following sources:

- a law
- binding corporate rules; or
- a binding agreement.

[22] Available at https://ec.europa.eu/newsroom/article29/item-detail.cfm?item_id=614108.

[23] Available at https://ec.europa.eu/info/sites/info/files/research_and_innovation/law_and_regulations/documents/adequacy-japan-factsheet_en_2019_1.pdf.

[24] See the European Commission's press release, available at https://ec.europa.eu/commission/presscorner/detail/en/ip_21_3183.

Many countries have data protection laws and they are quite diverse.[25] The first challenge is to know whether a country has a law, and the second is comparing it to POPIA. Comparing legislation is a labour intensive (and tedious!) task fraught with problems; it presupposes that the person doing the comparing is both proficient in POPIA and the law (and legal system) that he or she is comparing it to. We do not anticipate seeing many legal professionals with the confidence to assert that a foreign data protection law is 'substantially similar' to POPIA without confirmation from the Information Regulator.

If the transfer is taking place within a 'group of undertakings', developing a set of 'binding corporate rules' may be a more comfortable avenue to follow. Both of these phrases are defined, which limits this option to transfers which take place within a group structure and which are governed by a set of 'personal information processing policies'. We discuss this mechanism in chapter 4 paragraph 4.8.2.

Key point: We have seen many group data protection policies, but often they are not effectively implemented and compliance with them is not monitored by the group (e.g. by a compliance function and by internal audit). As we discuss in chapter 20 paragraph 20.2.6, policy implementation is not complete until compliance with the policy is measured and non-compliance is routinely addressed.

A binding agreement between the organisations is a third option.[26] In effect, the agreement would force the organisation who is receiving the information to comply with POPIA or with the 'personal information processing policies' of the responsible party who is transmitting the personal information. Here too the enforcement of the contract is going to be key. We discuss regulating compliance through contracts in chapter 4 paragraph 4.8.

[25] For a useful source see DLA Piper *Data Protection Laws of the World*, available at https://www.dlapiperdataprotection.com/. Also see the IAPP *Resource Centre* which lists other comparative guides.

[26] This option is available whether the transfer is taking place outside of a 'group of undertakings' or not.

14.2.3.2 The data subject consents to the transfer

The responsible party can transfer the personal information to a third party in a foreign country if the data subject consents to the transfer.[27]

This consent must comply with the definition of consent in section 1 of POPIA. These requirements are discussed in chapter 2 paragraph 2.6.6.

Tricky area: Section 11(3)*(b)* states that a data subject may withdraw consent provided in terms of section 11(1)*(a)* at any time. The right to withdraw consent is not mentioned in section 72. However, we believe that data subjects also have the right to withdraw these other consents due to the requirement that consent must be voluntary.[28] Can the responsible party just refuse to continue to process the data subject's personal information, because they withhold consent to transfer the information? Data subjects must be free to withdraw consent without undue effort and without any detrimental effects such as an increase in cost, a cessation of services or a decrease in service levels.[29]

This means that consent cannot be used in instances where it is not possible for the responsible party to avoid transferring the personal information of that data subject to a foreign country. In other words, there must be an alternative method of processing the personal information that does not include transferring the information. As the European Data Protection Board has pointed out, 'consent might prove not to be a feasible long-term solution for transfers to third countries'.[30]

---

27 Section 72(1)*(b)*.

28 Section 1 of POPIA.

29 European Data Protection Board *Guidelines 05/2020 on Consent under Regulation 2016/679* 13, available at https://edpb.europa.eu/sites/edpb/files/files/file1/edpb_guidelines_202005_consent_en.pdf.

30 European Data Protection Board *Guidelines 2/2018 on Derogations of Article 49 under Regulation 2016/679* 8, available at https://edpb.europa.eu/sites/edpb/files/files/file1/edpb_guidelines_2_2018_derogations_en.pdf.

Key point: Article 49(1)*(a)* of the EU GDPR also contains this exception. The European Data Protection Board provided guidelines for consent in this context.[31] While these guidelines are helpful as a source of 'best practice', it is important to note that the EU GDPR is stricter than POPIA when it comes to transborder transmission. For instance, the data subject must have been 'informed of the possible risks of such transfers for the data subject' and consent can only be used 'if the transfer is not repetitive, concerns only a limited number of data subjects, is necessary for the purpose of compelling legitimate interests pursued by the controller which are not overridden by the interests or rights and freedoms of the data subject, and the controller has assessed all the circumstances surrounding the data transfer and has on the basis of that assessment provided suitable safeguards with regard to the protection of personal data'.

14.2.3.3 The transfer is necessary for the performance of a contract or to implement pre-contractual measures

Section 72(1)*(c)* contains two further exceptions. Personal information can be transferred to a third party in a foreign country if it is necessary:

- for the performance of a contract between the data subject and the responsible party; or
- to implement pre-contractual measures taken in response to the data subject's request.

Key point: For this exemption to apply, the data subject has to trigger the pre-contractual measures; not the responsible party.

Here are some examples:

- A travel agent transfers personal information of a traveller to a hotel in a foreign country to book the traveller's stay.[32]

---

[31] European Data Protection Board *Guidelines 2/2018 on Derogations of Article 49 under Regulation 2016/679* 6, available at https://edpb.europa.eu/sites/edpb/files/files/file1/edpb_guidelines_2_2018_derogations_en.pdf.

[32] European Data Protection Board *Guidelines 2/2018 on Derogations of Article 49 under Regulation 2016/679* 9, available at https://edpb.europa.eu/sites/edpb/files/files/file1/edpb_guidelines_2_2018_derogations_en.pdf.

- A bank in South Africa transfers personal information to a foreign bank to execute a client's request to make a payment.[33]

These exceptions should be interpreted in a similar way to the legal justification that personal information may be processed if the processing is necessary to carry out actions for the performance or conclusion of a contract. The limitations of that justification were discussed in chapter 6 paragraph 6.3.1.

Key point: When determining what is 'necessary' to conclude or perform in terms of a contract, a fact-based assessment must be made of the processing and it must be determined that the transfer is necessary for the objective pursued by the contract. The responsible party must also consider whether there are realistic, less intrusive alternatives to achieve the objective. In other words, can the responsible party perform in terms of the contract without transferring the personal information? If alternatives exist, the processing is not necessary.[34]

Article 49(1)*(b)* of the EU GDPR also contains this exception. This is what the European Data Protection Board guidelines have to say about the 'necessity test':[35]

- This exception cannot be used for transfer of additional information that is not 'necessary'.
- It requires a 'close and substantial connection between the data transfer and the purposes of the contract'.

---

33 European Data Protection Board *Guidelines 2/2018 on Derogations of Article 49 under Regulation 2016/679* 9, available at https://edpb.europa.eu/sites/edpb/files/files/file1/edpb_guidelines_2_2018_derogations_en.pdf.

34 This is known as the principle of minimality, which we discuss in chapter 9. The European Data Protection Board *Guidelines 2/2019 on the processing of personal data under Article 6(1)(b) GDPR in the context of the provision of online services to data subjects Version 2.0* 8, available at https://edpb.europa.eu/sites/edpb/files/files/file1/edpb_guidelines-art_6-1-b-adopted_after_public_consultation_en.pdf.

35 European Data Protection Board *Guidelines 2/2018 on Derogations of Article 49 under Regulation 2016/679* 8, available at https://edpb.europa.eu/sites/edpb/files/files/file1/edpb_guidelines_2_2018_derogations_en.pdf.

Key point: The European Data Protection Board states that '[t]his derogation cannot be used for example when a corporate group has, for business purposes, centralised its payroll and human resources management functions for all its staff in a third country as there is no direct and objective link between the performance of the employment contract and such transfer'. One of the other exemptions (e.g. adequate safeguards in binding corporate rules) would be more appropriate.

- This exception can only be used when the transfer is occasional. This is an additional requirement which POPIA does not contain, but we are of the view that when the transmission happens regularly, safeguards such as requiring adequate protections in binding corporate rules or an agreement with the foreign third party would be more appropriate.

14.2.3.4 The transfer is necessary for the performance of a contract between the responsible party and a third party 'in the interest of the data subject'

The previous exception applies where there is a direct contractual relationship (or a potential contractual relationship) between the responsible party (in South Africa) and the data subject. In section 72(1)*(d)*, the exemption relates to a transmission of personal information which is necessary for the conclusion or performance of a contract between the responsible party and the third party in the foreign country. In order for the exemption to apply, the contract between the responsible party and the third party needs to be 'concluded in the interest of the data subject'.

Article 49(1)*(c)* of the EU GDPR also contains this exception. The requirements of necessity and that the transfer must be occasional also apply here. This is what the European Data Protection Board guidelines have to say about the 'necessity test' in this context:[36]

[36] European Data Protection Board *Guidelines 2/2018 on Derogations of Article 49 under Regulation 2016/679* 10, available at https://edpb.europa.eu/sites/edpb/files/files/file1/edpb_guidelines_2_2018_derogations_en.pdf.

> 'Where an organisation has, for business purposes, outsourced activities such as payroll management to service providers outside the EU, this derogation will not provide a basis for data transfers for such purposes, since no close and substantial link between the transfer and a contract concluded in the data subject's interest can be established even if the end purpose of the transfer is the management of the pay of the employee.'

It would be more appropriate to include adequate safeguards in an agreement with the third party in those instances.

14.2.3.5 The transfer is for the benefit of the data subject and it was not reasonably practicable to obtain consent (and if it were, the data subject would likely have given consent)

Section 72(1)*(e)* provides that personal information can be transmitted to a third party in a foreign country if:

- the transfer is for the benefit of the data subject
- it is not reasonably practicable to obtain consent; and
- if it were possible to obtain consent, the data subject 'would be likely to give it'.

Article 49(1)*(f)* of the EU GDPR provides that information may be transmitted to a foreign country if it is 'necessary in order to protect the vital interests of the data subject or of other persons, where the data subject is physically or legally incapable of giving consent'. This is clearly very different to section 72(1)*(e)*, which is much broader. However, the examples given by the European Data Protection Board would also qualify for an exemption under section 72(1)*(e)*:[37]

- A South African is injured while vacationing in a foreign country and is unconscious and in need of urgent medical attention. His South African insurance company is asked to share personal information with the foreign hospital.[38]
- During a natural disaster in another country, the South African government is asked to share personal information of all South Africans known to be in that country with a foreign government for purposes of the rescue and retrieval operations.

---

[37] European Data Protection Board *Guidelines 2/2018 on Derogations of Article 49 under Regulation 2016/679* 12, available at https://edpb.europa.eu/sites/edpb/files/files/file1/edpb_guidelines_2_2018_derogations_en.pdf.

[38] Note that if the information being transferred is health information, prior authorisation from the Information Regulator might be required!

14.3 EXTRA-TERRITORIAL APPLICATION OF DATA PROTECTION LAWS

A South African company may fall under the jurisdiction of a foreign regulator due to the nature of its business. For instance, the EU GDPR can apply to a South African company, if it is:[39]

- 'established' in the European Union ('established' means 'the effective and real exercise of activity through stable arrangements')[40]

Key point: South African organisations often think they are subject to the EU GDPR, because they are making use of an operator who is processing information on their behalf and who is located in the EU. A non-EU organisation will not become subject to the EU GDPR simply because it uses an operator in the EU.[41]

- offering goods or services to data subjects who are physically located in the EU; or[42]

Key point: Apart from 'just get consent', the most common foul-up we see lawyers make is 'if you process the personal information of EU citizens you are subject to the EU GDPR'. Nope. Even selling goods or service to the occasional individual who is physically located in the EU will not be enough. In order for the EU GDPR to be triggered 'it must be apparent that the controller or processor envisages offering services to data subjects in one or more member states'.[43]

---

39 The horror. See article 3(1) and (2).

40 Article 3(1) and recital 22. Also see European Data Protection Board *Guideline 3/2018 on the territorial scope of the EU GDPR (Article 3)*, available at https://edpb.europa.eu/our-work-tools/our-documents/riktlinjer/guidelines-32018-territorial-scope-gdpr-article-3-version_en.

41 European Data Protection Board *Guideline 3/2018 on the territorial scope of the EU GDPR (Article 3)* 12.

42 Article 3(2)*(a)*.

43 Recital 23. The recital goes on to say that '[w]hereas the mere accessibility of the controller's, processor's or an intermediary's website in the Union, or of an email address or of other contact details, or the use of a language generally used in the third country where the controller is established, is insufficient to ascertain such intention, factors such as the use of a language or a currency generally used in one or more Member States with the possibility of ordering goods and services in that other language, or the mentioning of customers or users who are in the Union, may make it apparent that the controller envisages offering goods or services to data subjects in the Union'. Hellish sentence. For a more digestible interpretation, see European Data Protection Board *Guideline 3/2018 on the territorial scope of the EU GDPR (Article 3)* from 14.

- monitoring behaviour of data subjects as long as that behaviour takes place in the EU.[44]

Key point: If a South African organisation monitors the behaviour of data subjects while they are in the EU through behavioural advertising, geo-localisation activities (particularly for marketing purposes), online tracking through cookies or other tracking techniques that identify data subjects, personalised health analytics services, CCTV, market surveys, behavioural research, etc., the EU GDPR may apply to that processing activity. But, the data subjects must be identifiable!

We focused on the EU GDPR, but there are other data protection regulations that contain extra-territorial provisions:

- POPIA

Key point: Section 3(1)*(b)*(ii) provides that POPIA can apply to a foreign organisation which is not domiciled (resident) in South Africa if it uses 'means' in South Africa to process personal information. This means that if a foreign organisation uses an operator or co-responsible party in South Africa, that foreign organisation may be subject to POPIA. The extra-territorial application of POPIA is discussed in chapter 3 paragraph 3.2.4.

- Canada
- Singapore
- Bahrain
- China
- Australia
- New Zealand
- Brazil
- Kenya
- California (not a country)
- Quitting now, but you get the point.

44 Article 3(2)*(b)* and recital 24.

14.4 DISCLOSING TRANSBORDER INFORMATION FLOWS

Transparency and the mandatory notifications which responsible parties must make are discussed in chapter 11 paragraph 11.3.

One of these disclosures is the following:[45]

The fact that the responsible party intends to transfer the information to a third country or international organisation and the level of protection afforded to the information by that third country or international organisation.	How specific must the responsible party be? Does the responsible party name all the countries it sends personal information to, and what happens when those countries change? The Article 29 Data Protection Working Party's guidelines on transparency in the context of the EU GDPR recommend that the disclosure should be as meaningful as possible, 'this will generally mean that the third countries will be named'.[46] The next question is how to disclose the 'level of protection' afforded by that country or international organisation. Is this just the responsible party's opinion on the data protection laws? It is best practice for responsible parties to disclose whether that country has a data protection law and where to access it, where to find the international organisation's privacy notice and any contractual agreement that the third party has agreed to, to respect data protection rights.[47]

This disclosure duty has also been included in the Promotion of Access to Information Act (PAIA) in sections 14(1)*(c)* and 51(1)*(c)* (as amended by POPIA). The requirement in PAIA is similar, but a great deal less detailed, than section 18(1)*(g)* of POPIA. The more specific provision should apply.[48]

45 Section 18(1)*(g)*.

46 Guidelines on Transparency under Regulation 2016/679 (wp260rev.01) 38, available at https://ec.europa.eu/newsroom/article29/item-detail.cfm?item_id=622227.

47 Guidelines on Transparency under Regulation 2016/679 (wp260rev.01) 38, available at https://ec.europa.eu/newsroom/article29/item-detail.cfm?item_id=622227.

48 The relationship between POPIA and PAIA is discussed in chapter 11 paragraph 11.7.

14.5 PRACTICAL ADVICE

The first step for responsible parties is to understand international flows of personal information. When conducting third-party risk management, confirming whether personal information is being transmitted to another country is a vital part of the assessment. This is discussed in chapter 4 paragraph 4.8.3. Responsible parties must document and keep a record of when information flows across borders.

It is equally important to determine whether information is flowing into South Africa (just not for purposes of determining whether section 72 applies). In these cases, it is quite likely that the organisation has signed a contract or agreed to be bound by policies due to the transborder provisions of the country where the personal information is coming from. Here, proper contract management is crucial to ensure that the organisation complies with the contract.[49]

Lastly, organisations that process the personal information of data subjects who are not located in South Africa or processes personal information in another country should determine whether they are subject to any other country's data protection laws. We have come across organisations that are subject to as many as 54 different data protection laws. How are we supposed to identify and keep track of all of these privacy laws? It is difficult. A good start is to subscribe to the newsletters and services of institutions like the International Association of Privacy Professionals.[50] There are also privacy technology providers that provide products that are 'privacy information managers' designed to 'provide organisations with extensive and often automated information on the latest privacy laws around the world'.[51]

---

49 We discuss contract management in chapter 4 paragraph 4.8.1.2.

50 See www.iapp.org.

51 IAPP *Annual Privacy Tech Vendor Report*, available at https://iapp.org/resources/article/privacy-tech-vendor-report/.

15

Profiling, automated decision-making and 1984

Chapter 15

15.1 WHAT TO EXPECT IN THIS CHAPTER

> 'The telescreen received and transmitted simultaneously. Any sound that Winston made, above the level of a very low whisper, would be picked up by it; moreover ... he could be seen as well as heard. There was of course no way of knowing whether you were being watched at any given moment ... It was conceivable that they watched everybody at the same time.'[1]

---

1 George Orwell *1984* 2.

The world has gotten 1984-level creepy. Yes, we believe that 'creepy' should formally be adopted in the privacy law lexicon to describe that feeling we get when an advertisement about Lego Death Stars is following us around the internet, or we are seeing too many articles about cholesterol even though we have not told anybody that ours is high or we think our phone is listening to us, because we just told someone that we like those new Bart Simpson Vans and now they are everywhere.[2]

But perhaps the word 'creepy' is too trivial to describe what is happening and the impact it will have on society in the years to come. Consider this chilling bit of dialogue from Netflix's *The Great Hack*:

> 'Carole Cadwalladr:[3] And people had no idea that their data was being taken in this way?
>
> Christopher Wylie:[4] No.
>
> Carole: And you didn't stop and think, "actually, this is people's personal information and we're taking it, and we're using it in ways that they don't understand."
>
> Christopher: No. Throughout history you have examples of grossly unethical experiments.
>
> Carole: Is that what this was?
>
> Christopher: I think that, yes, this was a grossly unethical experiment. You are playing with the psychology of an entire nation without their consent or awareness. And not only, like, are you playing with the psychology of an entire nation. You are playing with the psychology of an entire nation in the context of the democratic process.'

The Cambridge Analytica tale is an example of a phenomenon which is referred to as 'surveillance capitalism'. It refers to a process where personal information becomes a commodity which is harvested from various sources such as social media platforms, the internet, public records, credit bureaus and other sources of 'big data'. This form of capitalism is often explained as follows: 'If you are not paying for it, you're not the customer; you're the product being sold.' Interestingly, the quote was not originally about Facebook, or Google, it was first used in 1973 about television.[5] The phrase 'surveillance capitalism' was coined by Shoshana Zuboff in *The Age of Surveillance Capitalism: The Fight for a Human Future at the New Frontier of Power*:

> 'Surveillance capitalism unilaterally claims human experience as free raw material for translation into behavioural data.'

---

2 True stories. According to *Merriam Webster* the definition of 'creepy' is 'producing a nervous shivery apprehension'.

3 The journalist who exposed the Cambridge Analytica (and Facebook) scandal.

4 The whistle-blower.

5 Bill Oremus 'Are you really the product?' *Slate*, available at https://slate.com/technology/2018/04/are-you-really-facebooks-product-the-history-of-a-dangerous-idea.html.

Surveillance capitalism is characterised by the collection of massive amounts of personal information (online and offline) which is then used to create a very detailed 'profile' of the data subject. These profiles are then used to make automated decisions about data subjects by applying algorithms to these large datasets. Sounds like this should be regulated, right? In comes data protection regulation (with a sprinkling of competition law, but that is the subject of another book). While all of the principles in POPIA are aimed at regulating profiling and automated decision-making as examples of 'processing activities', section 71 takes a bold shot at regulating it, by outlawing it. But, in true POPIA fashion, also by not outlawing it.

In this chapter we discuss the following:

- What are profiling and automated decision-making?
- When automated decisions are allowed
- How the other principles in POPIA apply to profiling and automated decisions

15.2 WHAT ARE PROFILING AND AUTOMATED DECISION-MAKING?

Section 71 gives data subjects the right not to be subject to a decision which results in legal consequences for them, or which affects them to a substantial degree, if the decision is based solely on the automated processing of personal information intended to profile the data subject. As usual, there are exceptions to this rule which we will discuss in paragraph 15.3 below.[6]

But first, how does POPIA define profiling and automated decision-making?

15.2.1 What is profiling?

Before section 71 will apply, there must be 'automated processing' of personal information to provide a 'profile'. POPIA does not define 'profiling' or 'automated processing', but it defines 'automated means' as 'any equipment capable of operating automatically in response to instructions given for the purpose of processing information'.[7] 'Profiling' and 'automated processing' are used together in sections 5(1)*(g)* and 71(1) in a way that shows that not only must the processing of the personal information be 'automated' but it must lead to a 'profile' of a person being created.

---

6 Death by a thousand exceptions. That is POPIA for you.

7 Section 3(4).

Key point: Although POPIA does not define profiling, article 4(4) of the EU GDPR defines 'profiling' as 'any form of automated processing of personal data consisting of the use of personal data to evaluate certain personal aspects relating to a natural person, in particular to analyse or predict aspects concerning that natural person's performance at work, economic situation, health, personal preferences, interests, reliability, behaviour, location or movements'. Of course, POPIA also applies to organisations and not just natural persons. Apart from that, South African responsible parties can learn from this definition.

Section 71(1) of POPIA includes a list of examples that would be considered as 'profiling' including profiles created to assess the data subject's 'performance at work, or his, her or its credit worthiness, reliability, location, health, personal preferences or conduct'.

The SA Law Reform Commission described profiling (or information matching) as a situation 'where information which relates to an individual is structured in such a way that it can begin to answer questions about that person, so as to put his or her private behaviour under surveillance' in their report.[8] They continued to say that a profiling process has two main components:

- profile generation: the process of inferring a profile; and
- profile application: the process of treating persons/entities in light of this profile.[9]

'Treating' refers to making a decision about the data subject based on the profile. In order for section 71 to apply, the profile must be applied by making an automated decision about the data subject. In addition to being 'automated' this decision cannot be a trivial decision; it must have legal consequences or affect the data subject to a substantial degree.

15.2.2 What are automated decisions with legal consequences or a substantial effect

15.2.2.1 Decisions based solely on automated processing

If the automated decision is 'based solely on the basis of the automated processing of personal information' the ban in section 71 will apply. The decision also needs to be automated.

---

8 SA Law Reform Commission Project 124 on Privacy and Data Protection (2009 Report) 367.

9 SA Law Reform Commission Project 124 on Privacy and Data Protection (2009 Report) 368.

The ICO has described solely automated decision-making as processing where there is 'no human involvement'.[10]

Tricky area: Companies that use call centres often argue that there is a 'person' who speaks to the data subject on the telephone and so the decision is not based 'solely' on automated decision-making. The test here is to ask whether that call centre agent has any discretion regarding decisions involving the data subject, or whether the agent is required to simply inform the data subject of the decision they read on their computer screen. If they simply inform the data subject of the computer's decision then there is no discretion and this is automated decision-making for purposes of section 71.[11]

15.2.2.2 Legal consequences or a substantial effect

The automated decision must have legal consequences or a substantial effect on the data subject before section 71 will be triggered. Usually, 'legal consequences' refers to decisions to enter into a contract or not (e.g. processing applications for services or employment) or decisions that may subject the data subject to legal action (e.g. flagging objectionable or criminal behaviour).

Even if there are no legal consequences, section 71 will still be triggered if the decision has substantial consequences for a data subject. What is 'significant' or 'substantial' may vary from person to person depending on their unique circumstances. The Article 29 Data Protection Working Party wrote guidelines on automated decision-making and profiling which give an indication of what might be considered substantial or significant by the Information Regulator. The guideline provides examples of automated decisions that are 'significant' for a data subject. It includes decisions that:

- have a prolonged or permanent impact
- affect the behaviour and choices of data subjects
- lead to discrimination or exclusion of individuals

---

10 ICO *Direct Marketing Code of Practice: Draft Code for Consultation* at 58, available at https://ico.org.uk/media/about-the-ico/consultations/2616882/direct-marketing-code-draft-guidance.pdf.

11 Pages 20–21 of the *Guidelines on Automated Individual Decision-making and Profiling for the Purposes of Regulation 2016/679*, available at https://ec.europa.eu/newsroom/article29/item-detail.cfm?item_id=612053.

- affect their financial circumstances (e.g. their eligibility for credit)
- affect their access to health care
- deny someone an employment opportunity or put them at a serious disadvantage; and
- affect their access to education (e.g. university admission).[12]

It is also useful to consider what AI systems are classified as high risk in the EU *Proposal for a Regulation on Artificial Intelligence.*[13] Some of them are listed in paragraph 15.5.2. These systems have been classified as high risk because 'in the light of their intended purpose, they pose a high risk of harm to the health and safety or the fundamental rights of persons, taking into account both the severity of the possible harm and its probability of occurrence'.[14] We are of the view that automated decisions made by these AI systems will also be 'significant' for purposes of section 71.

Tricky area: An example of an automated decision is where an organisation uses the personal information of its customers to create profiles which help it identify those customers who may qualify for additional products (pre-vetting), but does this type of automated decision have legal or substantial consequences for the data subject?[15] This is what the ICO says:[16]

> 'Whilst the majority of direct marketing based on solely automated profiling is unlikely to have a legal or 'similarly significant effect', there could be situations where it does for example:

➡

---

[12] Article 29 Data Protection Working Party *Guidelines on Automated individual decision-making and Profiling for the purposes of Regulation 2016/679* 21 to 22, available at https://ec.europa.eu/newsroom/article29/item-detail.cfm?item_id=612053.

[13] 'A proposal for a regulation of the European Parliament and of the Council laying down harmonized rules on artificial intelligence (Artificial Intelligence Act) and amending certain Union legislative acts, available at https://eur-lex.europa.eu/resource.html?uri=cellar:e0649735-a372-11eb-9585-01aa75ed71a1.0001.02/DOC_1&format=PDF.

[14] Recital 32.

[15] We discuss profiling or pre-vetting prospective customers using third-party databases in chapter 13 paragraph 13.6.1.

[16] ICO *Direct Marketing Code of Practice: Draft Code for Consultation* 59, available at https://ico.org.uk/media/for-organisations/documents/2021/2619043/direct-marketing-code-draft-guidance-122020.pdf.

- profiling to target vulnerable groups or children;
- targeting individuals known to be in financial difficulty with marketing about high interest loans;
- targeting known problem gamblers with adverts for betting websites; or
- using profiling to effectively "price-out" individuals of owning a particular product by giving them a much higher price than other people.'

The Article 29 Data Protection Working Party is of the view that the following 'characteristics' may result in the conclusion that an automated decision to present targeted advertising based on profiling may have a significant effect:[17]

- how intrusive the profiling is (e.g. are individuals tracked across different websites, devices and services)
- the expectations and wishes of the individuals who are being profiled
- the way in which the marketing is delivered; and
- whether the data subject's vulnerabilities are targeted.

If the type of pre-vetting or profiling rises to the level of automated decision-making, then it must comply with section 71(2), otherwise the responsible party must stop doing it.

Direct marketing is subject to additional rules which are discussed in chapter 16.

[17] Article 29 Data Protection Working Party *Guidelines on Automated Individual Decision-making and Profiling for the Purposes of Regulation 2016/679* 21 to 22, available at https://ec.europa.eu/newsroom/article29/item-detail.cfm?item_id=612053.

15.2.3 Some examples

Here are some examples of profiling and automated decisions and our thoughts on whether the profiling is subject to section 71.

Example of profiling and automated decisions	Does section 71 apply?
'Some insurers offer insurance rates and services based on an individual's driving behaviour. Elements taken into account in these cases could include the distance travelled, the time spent driving and the journey undertaken as well as predictions based on other data collected by the sensors in a (smart) car. The data collected is used for profiling to identify bad driving behaviour (such as fast acceleration, sudden braking and speeding). This information can be cross-referenced with other sources (for example the weather, traffic, type of road) to better understand the driver's behaviour.'[18]	Yes, the profiling has legal consequences for the data subject as it affects their insurance premium.
'As part of their recruitment process, an organisation decides to interview certain people based entirely on the results achieved in an online aptitude test.'[19]	The ICO came to the conclusion that automated decisions that determine whether a person will be considered for a job do have a significant effect on a data subject. We agree.

➡

18 Article 29 Data Protection Working Party *Guidelines on Automated Individual Decision-making and Profiling for the Purposes of Regulation 2016/679* 10, available at https://ec.europa.eu/newsroom/article29/item-detail.cfm?item_id=612053.

19 ICO *What Does the UK GDPR Say About Automated Decision-making*, available at https://ico.org.uk/for-organisations/guide-to-data-protection/guide-to-the-general-data-protection-regulation-gdpr/automated-decision-making-and-profiling/what-does-the-uk-gdpr-say-about-automated-decision-making-and-profiling/#id3.

Example of profiling and automated decisions	Does section 71 apply?
Many retailers do profiling. A famous example is Target who 'has figured its way into your womb, to figure out whether you have a baby on the way long before you need to start buying diapers'.[20] The *New York Times* talked to Target statistician, Andrew Pole:[21] '[Pole] ran test after test, analyzing the data, and before long some useful patterns emerged. Lotions, for example. Lots of people buy lotion, but one of Pole's colleagues noticed that women on the baby registry were buying larger quantities of unscented lotion around the beginning of their second trimester. Another analyst noticed that sometime in the first 20 weeks, pregnant women loaded up on supplements like calcium, magnesium and zinc. Many shoppers purchase soap and cotton balls, but when someone suddenly starts buying lots of scent-free soap and extra-big bags of cotton balls, in addition to hand sanitizers and washcloths, it signals they could be getting close to their delivery date. As Pole's computers crawled through the data, he was able to identify about 25 products that, when analyzed together, allowed him to assign each shopper a "pregnancy prediction" score. More important, he could also estimate her due date to within a small window, so Target could send coupons timed to very specific stages of her pregnancy.' What could possibly go wrong? Note the title to the *Forbes* article: 'How Target figured out a teen girl was pregnant before her father did.'	If we apply the Article 29 Data Protection Working Party factors discussed above,[22] this profiling may be considered so intrusive that it has a substantial effect on data subjects, but it is borderline.

➥

Chapter 15

20 Kashmir Hill 'How target figured out a teen girl was pregnant before her father did' *Forbes*, available at https://www.forbes.com/sites/kashmirhill/2012/02/16/how-target-figured-out-a-teen-girl-was-pregnant-before-her-father-did/?sh=5d3527386668.

21 Charles Duhig 'How companies learn your secrets' *The New York Times Magazine*, available at https://www.nytimes.com/2012/02/19/magazine/shopping-habits.html?pagewanted=1&_r=1&hp.

22 See paragraph 15.2.2.2.

Example of profiling and automated decisions	Does section 71 apply?
'A data broker sells consumer profiles to financial companies without consumer permission or knowledge of the underlying data. The profiles define consumer into categories (carrying titles such as "Rural and Barely Making It," "Ethnic Second-City Strugglers," "Tough Start: Young Single Parents") or "score" them, focusing on consumers' financial vulnerability. The financial companies offer these consumers payday loans and other "non-traditional" financial services (high-cost loans and other financially risky products).'[23]	Section 71 applies, because this profiling has a substantial effect on the data subjects; their financial vulnerability is targeted. Also, 'Ethnic Second-City Strugglers'? What the frak?
'An individual applies for a loan online. The website uses algorithms and automated credit searching to provide an immediate yes/no decision on the application.'[24]	Section 71 applies, because the decision has a legal effect on the data subject.
'Take the example from Kenya, where the M-Pesa mobile money transfer services have been widely used, but also are a generator of data. This has been one source of data for fintech start-ups like Tala and Branch, who use it to provide lending. But they also take a broad range of data from the borrower's smartphone, including location, call records, and SMS messages. This results in them making decisions based on factors like how often a customer calls their mother – based on call records on the phone and the contents of SMSes. Tala analysed the data provided by M-Pesa for purposes of "alternative credit scoring" and found that people who make regular calls to family are 4% more likely to repay their loan. To do this analysis they need to know who your family is: from the content of text messages that call someone "mama", and the pattern of calls.'[25]	This definitely feels creepy due to the intrusive nature of the collection and the unexpected uses that the personal information is being put to. In addition, when this type of profiling is used in credit scoring for purposes of vetting of credit applications, the automated decision will have a legal effect on the data subject. Section 71 will apply.

➡

23 Article 29 Data Protection Working Party *Guidelines on Automated Individual Decision-making and Profiling for the Purposes of Regulation 2016/679* 10, available at https://ec.europa.eu/newsroom/article29/item-detail.cfm?item_id=612053.

24 ICO *What Does the UK GDPR Say About Automated Decision-making*, available at https://ico.org.uk/for-organisations/guide-to-data-protection/guide-to-the-general-data-protection-regulation-gdpr/automated-decision-making-and-profiling/what-does-the-uk-gdpr-say-about-automated-decision-making-and-profiling/#id3.

25 Privacy International *Fintech: Privacy and Identity in the New Data-Intensive Financial Sector*, available at https://privacyinternational.org/sites/default/files/2017-12/Fintech%20report.pdf.

Example of profiling and automated decisions	Does section 71 apply?
'Some mobile applications provide location services allowing the user to find nearby restaurants offering discounts. However, the data collected is also used to build a profile on the data subject for marketing purposes – to identify their food preferences, or lifestyle in general. The data subject expects their data will be used to find restaurants, but not to receive adverts for pizza delivery just because the app has identified that they arrive home late.'[26]	Section 71 might not apply, because receiving marketing (or not receiving marketing) for restaurants does not have a legal impact on the data subject and probably does not rise to the level of a substantial effect.

Key point: Even if the profiling is not subject to section 71, the rest of POPIA will still apply. We discuss the implications of other sections in paragraph 15.4.

15.3 WHEN AUTOMATED DECISIONS ARE ALLOWED

Okay, so section 71 applies. What now? The default rule is that the automated decision-making is banned. However, all is not lost.

The data subject has a right not to be subject to an automated decision unless the decision:

- is taken in connection with the conclusion or execution of a contract; and:
    - the request of the data subject in terms of the contract has been met; or
    - appropriate measures have been taken to protect the data subject's legitimate interests; or
- is governed by a law or code of conduct in which appropriate measures are specified for protecting the legitimate interests of data subjects.[27]

Again with the double negatives. What this means is that if these requirements are met, automated decisions are allowed.

We discuss these exceptions in more detail below.

---

[26] Article 29 Data Protection Working Party *Guidelines on Automated Individual Decision-making and Profiling for the Purposes of Regulation 2016/679* 11, available at https://ec.europa.eu/newsroom/article29/item-detail.cfm?item_id=612053.

[27] Section 71(2).

15.3.1 Automated decisions in connection with the conclusion or execution of a contract

It is permissible to make automated decisions based on profiling 'in connection with the conclusion or the execution of a contract' as long as certain requirements are met.[28]

Tricky area: Sometimes responsible parties will use profiles to pre-screen potential customers before they are targeted for direct marketing. As discussed in paragraph 15.2.2.2, these automated decisions may be subject to section 71 if they affect the data subject to a substantial degree. If it does not, the pre-screening does not qualify as automated decision-making, the prohibition in section 71 will not apply and the processing activity can continue as long as the responsible party complies with the rest of POPIA.[29] But let's assume that it does have a substantial effect. How closely must the profiling be related to the conclusion of the contract in order to qualify for this exemption to the prohibition of automated decision-making? The Article 29 Data Protection Working Party thought that the automated screening of job applicants' CVs in order to arrive at a short list of candidates, was sufficiently close to be considered part of entering into a contract.[30] Pre-screening of prospective customers for targeted marketing is not quite as closely connected to the conclusion of the contract. However, using an algorithm to process applications is quite clearly connected to the conclusion of the contract.

A common example of where this exemption will apply is where a data subject applies for a loan online. A credit provider would be entitled to make a decision based on the profile it created of the data subject without any human intervention. If the loan application was approved the decision is allowed under POPIA. But if the application is not approved, the credit provider must have also taken appropriate measures to protect the data subject's legitimate interests for the decision to be allowed. The responsible party must take the following 'appropriate measures':[31]

---

28 Section 71(2)*(a)*.

29 The impact of the rest of POPIA on profiling (with or without automated decisions) is discussed in paragraph 15.4.

30 Article 29 Data Protection Working Party *Guidelines on Automated Individual Decision-making and Profiling for the Purposes of Regulation 2016/679* 23, available at https://ec.europa.eu/newsroom/article29/item-detail.cfm?item_id=612053.

31 Section 71(3).

- the data subject must be given the opportunity to make representations about the decision; and
- the responsible party must provide the data subject with sufficient information about the underlying logic of the automated processing of the information to allow them to make representations.

What does 'sufficient information regarding the underlying logic' mean? This can become difficult when the decision is not being made by a regular algorithm that uses predetermined 'if this, then that' logic. Artificial intelligence learns the decision-making logic by ingesting training data which gives rise to the interesting, but horrifying, 'black box problem'. That is when we humans have no idea how the AI-based tool made the decision; we cannot see what the artificial neural network learnt or how it analyses the personal information it is fed; we can only see the result. This of course leads to various ethical concerns, because AI can make mistakes and suffer from bias. This can have serious consequences when the tools are used by the police, doctors, banks, insurance companies and advertisers.[32] This is why there is a big emphasis on the 'right to explanation'.

The Article 29 Working Party provides some guidance on what will be considered sufficient:[33]

- The information must be meaningful, but not a complex explanation of algorithms used or the full algorithm.
- The information should 'be sufficiently comprehensive for the data subject to understand the reasons for the decision'.
- The examples of specific information that is required include 'the main characteristics considered in reaching the decision, the source of the information and the relevance'.
- In terms of the GDPR,[34] it is also required to explain the significance of and the effect that the automated decision-making might have on the data subject.

They also point out that '[c]omplexity is no excuse for failing to provide information to the data subject. Recital 58 states that the principle of transparency is "of particular relevance in situations where the

---

32 See Think Automation 'The AI black box problem', available at https://www.thinkautomation.com/bots-and-ai/the-ai-black-box-problem/. They cut through the geek nicely.

33 Article 29 Data Protection Working Party *Guidelines on Automated Individual Decision-making and Profiling for the Purposes of Regulation 2016/679* 25, available at https://ec.europa.eu/newsroom/article29/item-detail.cfm?item_id=612053.

34 Article 13(2)*(f)* and 14(2)*(g)*.

proliferation of actors and the technological complexity of practice makes it difficult for the data subject to know and understand whether, by who and for what purpose personal data relating to him are being collected, such as in the case of online advertising."' Notification is discussed in chapter 11.

The 'appropriate measures' listed in section 71(3) are not the only safeguards that a responsible party could put in place. They are the minimum requirements if the automated decision is made in 'connection with the conclusion or execution of a contract'. The wording in the EU GDPR around automated decision-making and profiling is somewhat different to the wording in POPIA. But the concept of 'suitable safeguards' is similar to 'appropriate measures' in POPIA, so we can look to the EU GDPR when interpreting this concept in POPIA.[35] Recital 71 of the EU GDPR states that suitable safeguards include 'specific information to the data subject and the right to obtain human intervention, to express his or her point of view, to obtain an explanation of the decision reached after such assessment and to challenge the decision'. It continues to state that:

> 'in order to ensure fair and transparent processing in respect of the data subject, taking into account the specific circumstances and context in which the personal data are processed, the controller should use appropriate mathematical or statistical procedures for the profiling, implement technical and organisational measures appropriate to ensure, in particular, that factors which result in inaccuracies in personal data are corrected and the risk of errors is minimised, secure personal data in a manner that takes account of the potential risks involved for the interests and rights of the data subject and that prevents, inter alia, discriminatory effects on natural persons on the basis of racial or ethnic origin, political opinion, religion or beliefs, trade union membership, genetic or health status or sexual orientation, or that result in measures having such an effect. Automated decision-making and profiling based on special categories of personal data should be allowed only under specific conditions.'

For further examples of appropriate safeguards, see the recommendations section of the Article 29 Data Protection Working Group *Guidelines on Automated Individual Decision-making and Profiling.*

---

[35] See our discussion on interpretation in chapter 2.

Key point: It is a pity that this 'right of explanation' is only given in respect of automated processing in the context of 'the conclusion or execution of a contract' and then only if the attempt to contract was unsuccessful. It should be granted in all automated decisions that might result in legal consequences or which affect data subjects to a substantial degree. It is generally accepted as part of the ethical principles that should govern artificial intelligence and machine learning. They are discussed in paragraph 15.5.

15.3.2 Automated decisions that are governed by a law or code of conduct

Automated decisions are also permissible where there is a law or code of conduct in which 'appropriate measures are taken to safeguard the legitimate interests of data subjects'.[36]

Here is an existing example of a South African law that introduced measures to safeguard the legitimate interests of data subjects. The Financial Services Conduct Authority included fit and proper requirements for intermediaries who give automated advice.[37] 'Automated advice' is defined as 'the furnishing of advice through an electronic medium that uses algorithms and technology without the direct involvement of a natural person'. We discuss the details of the framework they have proposed in paragraph 15.5.3.

Key point: Who has to determine whether the requirements the FSCA introduced are satisfactory? Presumably it is up to the responsible party to determine whether it complied with POPIA, even if there are other laws in place. It would also be possible for the FSCA to engage with the Information Regulator on behalf of the financial services industry.

Presumably, the codes of conduct referred to in this subsection can also refer to POPIA codes of conduct accredited in terms of section 61.[38] In the Guidelines to Develop Codes of Conduct the Information Regulator incorporates the requirement that a code of conduct must specify 'appropriate measures' for information matching

36 Section 71(2)*(b)*.

37 Section 37 of Board Notice 194 of 2017, Determination of fit and proper requirements for financial services providers (2017), *GG* 41321 of 15 December 2017.

38 We discuss codes of conduct in chapter 19 paragraph 19.5.

programmes and for protecting the legitimate interests of data subjects in so far as automated decision-making is concerned.[39] The Regulator does not, however, give any indication of what these appropriate measures should be.

The 'appropriate measures' that we discussed in the previous section only relates to automated decisions in connection with a contract. However, we imagine that appropriate measures in a law or code of conduct could also include giving the data subject the opportunity to make representations and that the responsible party must provide sufficient information. Other measures may also be appropriate depending on the purpose of processing and the effect the decision has on the data subject.

15.4 HOW THE OTHER PRINCIPLES IN POPIA APPLY TO PROFILING AND AUTOMATED DECISIONS

Key point: When responsible parties engage in profiling and automated decisions, section 71 is not the only section they have to worry about; even if they clear the section 71 hurdle, the rest of POPIA still applies. As we have seen, there are also instances where profiling and automated decisions will not be subject to section 71, because they do not have legal consequences for or a significant effect on data subjects.

Here are some of the questions profilers will have to consider:

- **What personal information is being used?**[40] There are two issues to consider here. Vast amounts of personal information are used to create the profile and the profiling activity will also create further personal information about the data subject (e.g. the data subject's 'score'). Consider the famous Target debacle where a father discovered that his teenage daughter was pregnant, because Target successfully predicted that she was pregnant by profiling her shopping behaviour and sent her coupons for baby products.[41] One of the challenges of governing these prediction

---

39 'Notice Relating to Amended Guidelines to Develop Codes of Conduct in Terms of Chapter 7 of The Protection of Personal Information Act of 2013', 12, available at https://justice.gov.za/inforeg/legal/InfoRegSA-Guidelines-Invite-20191205.pdf.

40 See the definition of personal information in chapter 3 paragraph 3.2.1.1. Identifying special personal information is discussed in chapter 7 paragraph 7.2.

41 The poor father contacted Target thinking that they were encouraging her to become pregnant by sending coupons. He had to call back later to apologise and said: 'It turns out there's been

engines, is that executives do not understand how they work, what data is used in the process and the risks posed to data subjects by inherent biases in the datasets used to 'train' the algorithms. This problem is reflected in many of The Responsible Machine Learning Principles.[42] They are discussed in paragraph 15.5.1. Information officers must ensure that they understand what personal information is being used and created.

Key point: The profile can also create special or sensitive personal information. Here is a very scary paragraph from the Article 29 Data Protection Working Party:

> 'One study combined Facebook "likes" with limited survey information and found that researchers accurately predicted a male user's sexual orientation 88% of the time; a user's ethnic origin 95% of the time; and whether a user was Christian or Muslim 82% of the time.'[43]

- **What is the purpose of the profiling:**[44] In order to ensure that there is a legal basis for profiling activities, responsible parties must ensure that they have documented the original purpose for which the personal information that is used in the profiling. This will enable them to determine whether the profiling is still compatible with the original purpose for which the information was collected. This will have an impact on what legal justifications should be applied and whether the responsible party needs prior authorisation from the Information Regulator.[45]
- **Who is accountable to ensure that the profiling complies with POPIA?** Profiling often involves the sharing of big datasets between organisations or the use of artificial intelligence and machine learning platforms. It is important for these organisations to determine whether they are independent responsible parties, co-responsible parties or operators. This is discussed in chapter 4.

---

some activities in my house I haven't been completely aware of. She's due in August. I owe you an apology.' Kashmir Hill 'How target figured out a teen girl was pregnant before her father did *Forbes*, available at https://www.forbes.com/sites/kashmirhill/2012/02/16/how-target-figured-out-a-teen-girl-was-pregnant-before-her-father-did/?sh=5d3527386668.

42 The Institute for Ethical AI & Machine Learning is a UK research centre. The Machine Learning Principles are a practical framework put together by domain experts to provide guidance for technologists to develop machine learning systems. The principles are available at https://ethical.institute/principles.html.

43 Article 29 Data Protection Working Party *Guidelines on Automated Individual Decision-making and Profiling for the Purposes of Regulation 2016/679* 15, available at https://ec.europa.eu/newsroom/article29/item-detail.cfm?item_id=612053.

44 Purpose specification is discussed in chapter 6 paragraph 6.2. Further processing is discussed in chapter 12.

45 Prior authorisation is discussed in chapter 8.

- **Does the responsible party(s) need prior authorisation?** Prior authorisation is discussed in chapter 8. Many profiling activities will involve the linking of information held by different responsible parties, using unique identifiers for a purpose other than that for which the identifier was collected. Some profiling activities may also involve credit reporting or the processing of criminal or objectionable conduct on behalf of third parties. If any of these activities are involved, the responsible party will have to apply for prior authorisation from the Information Regulator (unless the activity is governed by a code of conduct).
- **Does the responsible party(s) have a legal justification for the profiling?** If the profiling is compatible with the original purpose for which the personal information is collected, the responsible party has to determine whether any of the justifications in section 11 (ordinary personal information), personal information of children (section 35) or section 27 or 28 to 33 (special personal information) applies.[46] The legal justification for processing will often be that it is in the legitimate interest of the responsible party, in which case the data subject will have the right to object.[47] If the profiling is further processing, responsible parties have to comply with section 15 and may need consent if the processing is not compatible with the original purpose for which the personal information was collected and if none of the other exceptions in section 15(3) apply.[48]
- **Does the responsible party comply with the direct collection rule?** When a responsible party collects personal information from another source (which is often the case in profiling activities), the responsible party must determine whether one of the exceptions to the direct collection rule applies. The direct collection rule (and the exceptions) are discussed in chapter 10 and the sharing of personal information between different organisations is discussed in chapter 13. Often responsible parties will try to argue that the indirect collection of the personal information is justified because it is in their legitimate interest or because collecting the information from the data subject is not practical (the data subject simply does not know these things about themselves). We discussed these arguments in the context of data broking in chapter 13 paragraph 13.6.1.

---

46 These legal justifications are discussed in chapters 6 and 7. When processing special personal information of children, both section 27 or 28 to 33 (special personal information), and section 35 (personal information of children) applies.

47 Legitimate interest is discussed in chapter 2 paragraph 2.6.3 and chapter 6 paragraph 6.3.5. For a discussion of all of the legal justifications and how they may (or may not) apply to profiling, see Article 29 Data Protection Working Party *Guidelines on Automated Individual Decision-making and Profiling for the Purposes of Regulation 2016/679* 12ff, available at https://ec.europa.eu/newsroom/article29/item-detail.cfm?item_id=612053.

48 Further processing is discussed in chapter 12. See the discussion of profiling and further processing in Article 29 Data Protection Working Party *Guidelines on Automated Individual Decision-making and Profiling for the Purposes of Regulation 2016/679* 11, available at https://ec.europa.eu/newsroom/article29/item-detail.cfm?item_id=612053.

- **Has the responsible party met the notification requirements?**[49] Whether section 71 applies or not, profilers must 'explain clearly and simply to individuals how the profiling or automated decision-making works and any rights that the data subject might have.[50] We discuss the notification duty in the context of data brokers who create profiles that are then shared with other companies in chapter 13 paragraph 13.6.1; it seems that both the data broker and the company will have notification duties to ensure that no 'hidden processing' takes place. It is often the notification duty that causes the most headaches for profilers.
- **Does the profiling comply with the principle of minimal processing?**[51] There is an inherent tension between the principle of minimality (less is more) and the concept of profiling and the 'big data' it relies on. We wrote about this struggle in chapter 9 paragraph 9.6.2. The Article 29 Data Protection Working Party states that when profiling, responsible parties 'should be able to clearly explain and justify the need to collect and hold personal data, or consider using aggregated, anonymised or (when this provides sufficient protection) pseudonymised data for profiling.'[52] Good advice.
- **Is the personal information used in the profiling and the automated decisions made based on the profile accurate?** There is a saying in data science 'garbage in, garbage out'. If the information used to build the profile is not 'complete, accurate, not misleading and updated where necessary',[53] the automated decisions are going to be incorrect or biased. The Responsible Machine Learning Principles[54] address this issue by requiring that responsible parties must 'understand the consequences of incorrect predictions, especially when automating critical processes that can have significant impact in human lives (e.g. justice, health, transport, etc.)' and provides that 'human-in-the-loop' review processes should be involved in the design. Fraud detection evaluation is mentioned as one of the areas in which the results of automated decisions should be verified from time to time to mitigate the harm that can flow from 'false positives'. Sometimes, the incorrect decisions do not flow from incorrect personal information, but from biased information ('misleading' would be the POPIA term).

---

49 Notification duties are discussed in chapter 11.

50 Article 29 Data Protection Working Party *Guidelines on Automated Individual Decision-making and Profiling for the Purposes of Regulation 2016/679* 16, available at https://ec.europa.eu/newsroom/article29/item-detail.cfm?item_id=612053.

51 The principle of minimality is discussed in chapter 9.

52 Article 29 Data Protection Working Party *Guidelines on Automated Individual Decision-making and Profiling for the Purposes of Regulation 2016/679* 16, available at https://ec.europa.eu/newsroom/article29/item-detail.cfm?item_id=612053.

53 This wording is taken from section 16 of POPIA. We discuss section 16 in chapter 9 paragraph 9.5.

54 They are discussed in paragraph 15.5.1. They are available at https://ethical.institute/principles.html.

The Responsible Machine Learning Principles[55] address this issue by requiring that responsible parties must not only 'embed ethics directly into the algorithms themselves', but must also 'focus on building processes and methods to identify and document the inherent bias in the data, features and inference results, and subsequently the implications of this bias'.

- **Does the profiling comply with information security management principles?** Due to the sheer volume of personal information that is collected, used and created in profiling activities, it opens the door to so-called mega-breaches.[56] It is therefore not surprising that one of The Responsible Machine Learning Principles[57] relates to data risk awareness.
- **Can the responsible party honour data subject rights?** Data subject rights are discussed in chapter 18. Responsible parties who make use of profiling must have processes in place to process requests by the data subject for access to all of the information the responsible party has of them, should prepare to process objections and should think about what will happen if a data subject challenges the accuracy or relevance of the information (and by extension the validity of any automated decisions that were made).

15.5 PRACTICAL ADVICE

Technology moves fast. Let's face it making and implementing laws is slow work, it took about 16 years for POPIA to get from a glint in the eye of the SA Law Reform Commission in 2005 to being fully enforceable in 2021. The World Economic Forum summarises the new challenges faced by law-makers as we enter the Fourth Industrial Revolution:[58]

> 'Given the Fourth Industrial Revolution's extraordinarily fast technological and social change, relying only on government legislation and incentives to ensure the right outcomes is ill-advised. These are likely to be out-of-date or redundant by the time they are implemented.'

That is lovely, but where does it leave us?

In chapter 2, we discussed POPIA as an example of principles-based legislation. We said that 'the strength of principle-based regulation lies in its flexibility and ability to respond to new issues without needing to amend the legislation.'[59] The

---

55 They are discussed in paragraph 15.5.1. They are available at https://ethical.institute/principles.html.

56 We discuss information security and breaches in chapter 5.

57 They are discussed in paragraph 15.5.1. They are available at https://ethical.institute/principles.html.

58 World Economic Forum *Values and the Fourth Industrial Revolution: Connecting the Dots Between Value, Values, Profit and Purpose*, available at https://www.weforum.org/whitepapers/values-and-the-fourth-industrial-revolution-connecting-the-dots-between-value-values-profit-and-purpose.

59 See paragraph 2.2.

SA Law Reform Commission pointed out that in principles-based regulation the ethics and culture of organisations will play an important role in compliance.

Still vague. What does ethics even mean? We think it means, doing the right thing even when no one is looking, but to give it meaning, let's look at some of the frameworks much cleverer (and probably more ethical) people have developed.

15.5.1 The Responsible Machine Learning Principles

The Institute for Ethical AI and Machine Learning is a research institution.[60] The Machine Learning Principles 'are a practical framework put together by domain experts. Their objective is to provide guidance for technologists to develop machine learning systems responsibly.' We have substituted 'technologists' with 'responsible party'. In order to design truly POPIA compliant systems, responsible parties should adopt these principles in their policies and standards.

The Responsible Machine Learning Principles[61]	What do they mean?
Human augmentation	Responsible parties must 'commit to assess the impact of incorrect predictions and, when reasonable, design systems with human-in-the-loop review processes'. As discussed in paragraph 15.3.1, providing the option for human intervention is considered one of the 'appropriate measures to protect the data subject's legitimate interest'.

➥

60 See their website at https://ethical.institute/index.html#phases.

61 They are available at https://ethical.institute/principles.html. Also see the Microsoft AI Principles, available at https://www.microsoft.com/en-us/ai/responsible-ai?activetab=pivot1%3aprimaryr6.

The Responsible Machine Learning Principles	What do they mean?
Bias evaluation	Responsible parties must 'commit to continuously develop processes that allow [the responsible party] to understand, document and monitor bias in development and production'. One of the safeguards that responsible parties should put in place is to monitor for bias in its automated decision-making. This is discussed in paragraph 15.3.1.
Explainability by justification	It is important that machine learning models be transparent and explainable. The risk is always that technologists and the responsible parties who employ them do not understand how the model works themselves! Without it the model becomes a 'black box'. To combat this, POPIA introduces a 'right of explanation' in section 71(3)*(b)*. We discuss this in paragraph 15.3.1. The point is that if the responsible party does not understand how the underlying logic of the automated processing works, it will not be able to comply with section 71(3)*(b)* and the processing will be prohibited.
Reproducible operations	Related to the inability of AI to 'show its work' is the inability to produce the same results using the same AI method. The emphasis here is on documenting or abstracting data, configurations, environments and computational steps. Without this machine learning systems cannot diagnose or respond effectively when something goes wrong. In other words, the system is unreliable.
Displacement strategy	We were not worried about the robots taking over, until we researched ethics in AI. Then you start seeing ominous articles like 'Robots Aren't Taking Over the World (Yet) – Artificial Plus Human Intelligence Is Still the Best Combo'.[62] This principle requires that organisations 'look beyond the technology' at the impact it will have on individuals through change strategies and transition plans.

➡

[62] Thank you, Forbes. Available at https://www.forbes.com/sites/forbestechcouncil/2021/04/28/robots-arent-taking-over-the-world-yet---artificial-plus-human-intelligence-is-still-the-best-combo/.

The Responsible Machine Learning Principles	What do they mean?
Practical accuracy	Organisations must develop metrics to understand the accuracy and performance of the model and to understand the implications of different types of errors. Ensuring the accuracy of the decisions produced by the machine learning system is also part of the responsible party's duty to ensure the quality of the personal information it uses.[63]
Trust by privacy	This principle requires that organisations use privacy by design when they design machine learning models to ensure that they build trust. Organisations should consider whether they are exposing unexpected (often new) personal information and what the potential privacy implications are. The Cambridge Analytica scandal is listed as an example of how AI experiments can go wrong![64]
Data risk awareness	Organisations must ensure that information security management principles are taken into account when machine learning systems are developed. Information security management is discussed in chapter 5.

15.5.2 A risk-based approach: The EU proposal for AI regulation

The European Union has published *A Proposal for a Regulation on Artificial Intelligence*.[65]

Key point: So what? It is useful to understand the way which the wind is blowing when organisations consider making investments into these technologies. In addition, the proposed Regulation provides guidance on what type of AI systems pose an inherently high risk to fundamental human rights (such as privacy). We can apply this in the process of determining whether automated decisions affect data subjects substantially.[66]

63 Section 16 of POPIA. The duty to ensure the quality of personal information is discussed in chapter 9.

64 We started this chapter with a quote from *The Great Hack*. We have come full circle.

65 'A proposal for a Regulation of the European Parliament and of the Council laying down harmonized rules on artificial intelligence (Artificial Intelligence Act) and amending certain Union legislative acts', available at https://eur-lex.europa.eu/resource.html?uri=cellar:e0649735-a372-11eb-9585-01aa75ed71a1.0001.02/DOC_1&format=PDF. Also see the ICO's response to the proposed Regulation available at https://ico.org.uk/media/about-the-ico/consultation-responses/2620291/ico-response-eu-artificial-intelligence-act-20210728.pdf.

66 We discussed this in paragraph 15.2.2.2.

Some artificial intelligence practices are prohibited.[67] For instance, AI systems that deploy 'subliminal techniques beyond a person's consciousness in order to materially distort a person's behaviour in a manner that causes or is likely to cause that person or another person physical or psychological harm' are prohibited. There are also restrictions on AI systems that exploit vulnerabilities of groups due to their age or disability and restrictions on AI systems used by public bodies to determine trustworthiness and the use of 'real-time remote biometric identification systems'.

Other AI systems are classified as high-risk, for example AI systems intended to be used for:[68]

- 'real-time' or 'post' remote biometric identification of individuals
- determining access or assigning natural persons to educational and vocational training institutions
- assessing students in educational and vocational training institutions and for assessing participants in tests commonly required for admission to educational institutions
- recruitment or selection of individuals, screening or filtering applications and evaluating candidates
- making decisions on promotion and termination of employees or monitoring and evaluating employees
- assessing the eligibility of individuals for public assistance benefits and services
- assessing the creditworthiness of individuals or to establish their credit score
- prioritising emergency first response services (e.g. firefighters or medical assistance)
- assessments by law enforcement of the risk of an individual offending or reoffending or the risk for potential victims of criminal offences
- polygraphs and similar tools or to detect the emotional state of individuals for purposes of law enforcement; or for
- other law enforcement related purposes such as detecting deep fakes, evaluating the reliability of evidence or the use of profiling to predict crimes or criminality.

---

67 Article 5(1).

68 See Annex III to the Regulation, available at https://eur-lex.europa.eu/resource.html?uri=cellar:e0649735-a372-11eb-9585-01aa75ed71a1.0001.02/DOC_2&format=PDF.

If an AI system is classified as high-risk, a host of governance obligations kick in, including:

- establishing, implementing, documenting and maintaining a risk management system[69]
- ensuring that training, validation and testing data are subject to appropriate data management and governance practices to ensure that the datasets are 'relevant, representative, free of errors and complete'[70]
- maintaining technical documentation and record-keeping[71]
- ensuring that they are 'sufficiently transparent to enable users [responsible parties] to interpret the system's output'[72]
- including appropriate human oversight to prevent or minimise the risks to health, safety or other fundamental rights (such as privacy);[73] and
- achieving an appropriate level of accuracy, robustness and cybersecurity.[74]

Key point: These AI systems would also have to comply with the EU GDPR.

The European Data Protection Board and the European Data Protection Supervisor (EDPS) issued a Joint Opinion 5/2021 on the proposed Regulation. The Opinion is critical of the proposed Regulation in several respects. The two that are interesting (and reflect general criticism of the proposed Regulation)[75] are the following:[76]

---

69 Article 9.

70 Article 10.

71 Article 11 and 12.

72 Article 13.

73 Article 14.

74 Article 15.

75 Natasha Lomas 'UK's ICO warns over "Big Data" surveillance threat of live facial recognition in public' *Tech Crunch*, available at https://techcrunch.com/2021/06/18/uks-ico-warns-over-big-data-surveillance-threat-of-live-facial-recognition-in-public/ and Justin Sherman 'Dumbed down AI rhetoric harms everyone' *Wired*, available at https://www.wired.com/story/dumbed-down-ai-rhetoric-harms-everyone/.

76 European Data Protection Board and EDPS *Joint Opinion 5/2021* 2, available at https://edpb.europa.eu/system/files/2021-06/edpb-edps_joint_opinion_ai_regulation_en.pdf.

- 'Social scoring' should not just be prohibited when done by public authorities. The European Data Protection Board and EDPS point out that 'private companies such as social media and cloud service providers can process vast amounts of personal data and conduct social scoring.' Can't imagine who they might be thinking of …
- They are also calling for a 'general ban on any use of AI for an automated recognition of human features in publicly accessible spaces – such as of faces but also of gait, fingerprints, DNA, voice, keystrokes and other biometric or behavioural signals – in any context.' They take an equally dim view of AI that uses biometrics to categorise individuals into clusters and AI that infers emotions as 'highly undesirable'.

15.5.3 A South African framework: Regulating robo-advisers in the financial services industry

Did you know, that the Financial Services Conduct Authority included fit and proper requirements for intermediaries who give automated advice?[77] 'Automated advice' is defined as 'the furnishing of advice through an electronic medium that uses algorithms and technology without the direct involvement of a natural person'. It is a good blueprint for how systems that do profiling and automated decisions should be governed and what could constitute 'appropriate measures' for purposes of section 71(2)*(b)*.[78]

Here is the blueprint (tip: you can substitute 'advice' for automated decisions):

Human resource requirement	The financial service provider (FSP) that provides the advice must have adequate and appropriate 'human resources' to: • understand the technology and algorithms, the methodology and assumptions embedded in the algorithms • understand the preferences or biases that exist in the algorithms • understand the risk and rules underpinning the algorithms • identify the risks to clients; and • monitor and review the automated advice to ensure the quality and suitability of the advice and that the advice complies with the law.

➡

77 Section 38 of Board Notice 194 of 2017, *Determination of Fit and Proper Requirements for Financial Services Providers* (2017), *GG* 41321 of 15 December 2017.

78 This was discussed in paragraph 15.3.1.

Policies and procedures	The FSP must establish, implement and maintain adequate policies and procedures to: • monitor, review and test the algorithms and the advice (or automated decisions) they generate • monitor, review and test the filters implemented to ensure that clients for whom the automated advice is not suitable are filtered out; and • set out the level of human review that will be undertaken.
Monitoring and testing	The FSP must: • have appropriate system design documentation that sets out the purpose, scope and design of the algorithms and filters • have a documented test strategy that explains the scope of testing, including test plans, test cases, test results, defect resolution and final test results • have appropriate processes for managing any changes to the algorithm and filters that include having security arrangements in place to monitor and prevent unauthorised access to the algorithms • be able to control, monitor and reconstruct any changes to algorithms or filters • review and update algorithms whenever there are factors that may affect their relevance • have controls and processes in place to suspend the use of the algorithm if errors are detected; and • be able to frequently monitor and supervise the performance of the algorithms and filters.
Technology	The FSP must have the technological resources to: • maintain client records and data integrity • protect confidential and other information; and • meet current and anticipated operational needs.

15.5.4 What now?

Information officers should ensure that organisations assess the potential deployment of AI or machine learning systems carefully to ensure that they can be deployed in a POPIA-compliant way. However, as we pointed out at the beginning of this chapter, the law will probably struggle to keep up with the pace of technological development and information officers will come under pressure to get out of the way.

This is why information officers should not just consider what is legally allowed, but should also take ethical considerations into account. As Dumbledore would say: 'Dark and difficult times lie ahead. Soon we must all face the choice between what is right and what is easy.'[79]

[79] From Harry Potter and the Goblet of Fire (2005).

16 Direct marketing

16.1 WHAT TO EXPECT WHEN YOU ARE EXPECTING TO SPAM

When you read this chapter you should play the 'Spam song' from the 'Spam' episode of Monty Python's Flying Circus in the background. 'Lovely spam, wonderful spam, spam, spam ....'[1]

Joking aside, in Dan Solove's *Taxonomy of Privacy*, one category of harm which data subjects suffer when their privacy is infringed is 'invasion', which includes 'invasive acts that disturb one's tranquillity or solitude'[2] or more simply 'the right to be let alone'.[3] The SA Law Reform Commission contextualised the regulation of direct marketing as follows:

> 'However, with the rise of the Internet and electronic commerce, there is a growing concern in modern society over the unlimited harvesting and uncontrolled trading of personal information, the creation of vast information bases of personal profiles, aggressive advertising, increasing use of unfair practices and serious breaches of privacy.'[4]

It would be tempting to decry all direct marketing as evil, but the fact of the matter is that direct marketing plays an important part in the economy if it is carried out responsibly.[5] During the drafting process, it was also acknowledged that direct marketing regulation has to balance the right of responsible parties to communicate effectively with the public and data subjects' right to privacy.[6]

Here is a mind map of how POPIA impacts direct marketing activities:

1 Electronic marketing is often called 'spam'. For those of you who have ever wondered why, the term is derived from the Monty Python's Flying Circus spam sketch.

2 Professor Solove's *Taxonomy of Privacy* was adapted from Daniel J Solove *Understanding Privacy* (2008) and is available at https://www.privacysecurityacademy.com/wp-content/uploads/2018/02/Handout-Foundations-and-Themes-Professor-Soloves-Taxonomy-of-Privacy-01.pdf.

3 See S Warren and L Brandeis, 'The right to privacy' (1890) 4 *Harvard Law Review* 193 at 193.

4 SA Law Reform Commission Project 124 on Privacy and Data Protection (2009 Report) 355.

5 SA Law Reform Commission Project 124 on Privacy and Data Protection (2009 Report) 360.

6 The Constitutional rights to freedom of expression (section 16), freedom of trade, occupation and profession (section 22) and the right to access to information (section 32) were mentioned in the SA Law Reform Commission Project 124 on Privacy and Data Protection (2009 Report) 361.

In this chapter we discuss the following:

- What is direct marketing?
- What is electronic communication and why does it matter?
- Unsolicited direct marketing
- Electronic direct marketing to data subjects who are already customers
- Unsubscribing from direct marketing (and getting out of roach motels)
- Sending direct marketing on behalf of someone else
- What about other legislation that applies to direct marketing?

16.2 WHAT IS DIRECT MARKETING?

This is how POPIA defines direct marketing: '[D]irect marketing means to approach a data subject, either in person or by mail or electronic communication, for the direct or indirect purpose of – *(a)* Promoting or offering to supply, in the ordinary course of business, any goods or services to the data subject; or *(b)* Requesting the data subject to make a donation of any kind for any reason.'[7]

To qualify as direct marketing in terms of POPIA, the marketing message must:

- be directed at a particular data subject and not at the public in general as with advertising; and

> **Key point:** Always remember that the definition of 'data subject' includes juristic persons.[8] This means that POPIA will also apply to business-to-business marketing.

- have the 'direct or indirect' purpose of promoting or offering goods or services for supply or to request a donation.

> **Key point:** Section 69 will apply to donations solicited through electronic communications. This will have an impact on the ability of charities and non-profit organisations to obtain donations.

Not all communications with data subjects will constitute 'direct marketing'. Routine client service messages do not qualify as direct marketing. Neither POPIA, nor the EU's GDPR and ePrivacy Directive, define exactly what type

---

7 See the definition of 'direct marketing' in section 1 of POPIA.

8 See the definition of 'data subject' read with the definition of 'person' in section 1 of POPIA.

of communications constitute 'a service message'.[9] However, the ICO (the UK's information regulator) has given guidance as to what the difference is between routine service messages and direct marketing messages in their 2019 ruling against EE Limited.[10] Here, EE Limited was fined £100 000 for sending over 2.5 million direct marketing messages to its customers without consent.[11] EE Limited's defence was that these messages were 'service messages', and so the company did not require their customers' consent to send these 'service messages'. In the ICO's ruling against EE Limited the Information Regulator held that:

> 'These were marketing messages which promoted the company's products and services. The direct marketing guidance is clear: if a message that contains customer service information also includes promotional material to buy extra products or services, it is no longer a service message and electronic marketing rules apply.'[12]

The ICO also provides more guidance for organisations to determine the difference between 'direct marketing messages' and 'service messages' in its 'Direct marketing: Code of practice, Information Commissioner's Office Draft code for consultation' (which was issued in 2020). Here the ICO states that a service message, 'is a way of describing a communication sent to an individual for administrative or customer service purposes'.[13] Examples of service messages given include reminding a customer how to contact the organisation in case of a problem, checking that a customer's details are correct, or updating a customer on any changes in an organisation's terms and conditions.[14] The ICO states that care must be taken in terms of the phrasing, tone and context to ensure that a routine service message does not become a direct marketing message. If a message actively encourages a customer to start using a specific service, take up a special offer or upgrade, for example, then this message is most likely

---

9 ICO 'Direct marketing: code of practice, Information Commissioner's Office Draft code for consultation' 19, available at https://ico.org.uk/about-the-ico/ico-and-stakeholder-consultations/ico-consultation-on-the-draft-direct-marketing-code-of-practice/.

10 ICO 'ICO fines telecoms company EE Limited for sending unlawful text messages', available at https://ico.org.uk/about-the-ico/news-and-events/news-and-blogs/2019/06/ico-fines-telecoms-company-ee-limited-for-sending-unlawful-text-messages/.

11 ICO 'ICO fines telecoms company EE Limited for sending unlawful text messages', available at https://ico.org.uk/about-the-ico/news-and-events/news-and-blogs/2019/06/ico-fines-telecoms-company-ee-limited-for-sending-unlawful-text-messages/.

12 ICO 'ICO fines telecoms company EE Limited for sending unlawful text messages', available at https://ico.org.uk/about-the-ico/news-and-events/news-and-blogs/2019/06/ico-fines-telecoms-company-ee-limited-for-sending-unlawful-text-messages/.

13 ICO 'Direct marketing: Code of practice, Information Commissioner's Office Draft code for consultation' 19, available at https://ico.org.uk/about-the-ico/ico-and-stakeholder-consultations/ico-consultation-on-the-draft-direct-marketing-code-of-practice/.

14 ICO 'Direct marketing: Code of practice, Information Commissioner's Office Draft code for consultation' 19, available at https://ico.org.uk/about-the-ico/ico-and-stakeholder-consultations/ico-consultation-on-the-draft-direct-marketing-code-of-practice/.

'direct marketing'.[15] If we follow a similar interpretation, the direct marketing sections of POPIA will then apply to this communication.

Key point: All communications to customers should be clearly classified as either direct marketing or service messages. It is a contravention of POPIA to combine the two if the responsible party does not have the recipient's consent to send direct marketing, as the recipient is forced to accept the marketing if they want to receive service messages.[16] It is even worse if those service messages are required by law (e.g., a monthly statement for a credit card).

But what if the marketing message is the service? Consider the example of a loyalty programme or a subscription service where the data subject has signed up to receive information about deals.

The ICO has acknowledged that receiving direct marketing messaging can, in some circumstances, be a 'core service' of a contract and is necessary for delivering that service, e.g. in the case of a loyalty programme. The ICO says:

> 'There may be occasions when making direct marketing a condition of service is necessary for that service. For example, a retail loyalty scheme that is operated purely for the purposes of sending people marketing offers, is likely to be able to show that the direct marketing is necessary for that service. But you need to be upfront and clear about this purpose and ensure that the consent[17] individuals provide when signing up meets the GDPR standard.'[18]

The ICO has also considered this issue of direct marketing being a condition of service for a loyalty programme in relation to the Privacy and Electronic Communications Regulations (PECR). The PECR is the UK's version of the ePrivacy Directive and contains very similar provisions to section 69 of POPIA in relation to the requirements for sending consumers electronic direct marketing. The ICO stated:

---

15 ICO 'Direct marketing: Code of practice, Information Commissioner's Office Draft code for consultation' 19, available at https://ico.org.uk/about-the-ico/ico-and-stakeholder-consultations/ico-consultation-on-the-draft-direct-marketing-code-of-practice/.

16 In the ICO's ruling against EE Limited, the ICO stated: 'Companies should be aware that texts and emails providing service information which also include a marketing or promotional element must comply with the relevant legislation or could face a fine up to £500,000.' See ICO 'ICO fines telecoms company EE Limited for sending unlawful text messages', available at https://ico.org.uk/about-the-ico/news-and-events/news-and-blogs/2019/06/ico-fines-telecoms-company-ee-limited-for-sending-unlawful-text-messages/.

17 We don't think that this means 'consent' in terms of consenting to direct marketing, but rather the data subject agreeing to the T&Cs of a contract for a loyalty programme where receiving direct marketing is a core service.

18 See ICO *Direct Marketing Code of Practice: Draft Code for Consultation* at 38, available at https://ico.org.uk/media/about-the-ico/consultations/2616882/direct-marketing-code-draft-guidance.pdf

> 'If you operate a loyalty scheme, you should make sure your customers understand what messages they will receive if they sign up. They are likely to expect a periodic update on how many points or vouchers they have earned. In our view, under the soft opt-in rule [their version of section 69(3) of POPIA], as long as you provide a clear opt-out when they sign up and in every subsequent message, you may also send them further electronic mail about other promotions unless they opt out.
>
> If you operate a joint loyalty scheme with other companies, you must make sure customers are fully aware of the nature of the scheme and range of the promotions you propose to send. In our view, under the soft opt-in rule [their version of section 69(3) of POPIA], as long as you do so and provide a clear opt-out when they sign up and in every message, the scheme may send electronic mail about incentives offered by any of the partners.
>
> However, if a participating company wants to send additional marketing messages outside the loyalty scheme, it must have the individual's clear consent to do so. If there are several partners in a loyalty scheme, you may therefore find it easier to provide specific opt-in boxes when people sign up.'[19]

16.3 WHAT IS ELECTRONIC COMMUNICATION AND WHY DOES IT MATTER?

POPIA covers direct marketing sent through the following channels:

- email
- SMS
- fax[20]
- automatic calling machines[21]
- push notifications
- direct messaging via social media
- advertising through social media platforms or display banners when a custom audience is targeted
- snail mail (including messages delivered by carrier pigeon, owl and raven)
- telemarketing; and
- any other channels that become available as technology evolves.

---

[19] See https://ico.org.uk/for-organisations/guide-to-pecr/electronic-and-telephone-marketing/using-marketing-lists/#loyaltyschemes.

[20] Yes, it still exists. We are told that fax marketing is a thing.

[21] Means a machine that is able to do automated calls without human intervention. See section 69(5) of POPIA.

Key point: The rules are not the same for all communication channels. Section 69 of POPIA, which contains the (in)famous strict consent requirements, only applies to 'electronic communications' which exclude channels such as telemarketing and snail mail. This does not mean that POPIA will not apply to telemarketing or snail mail. POPIA is 115 sections long and all that has happened is that you have excluded one section (section 69) but you still have 114 other sections to consider. We explain this in more detail in the rest of this chapter.

So, for marketers one of the most important definitions in POPIA is 'electronic communication'. If direct marketing is done 'by means of electronic communication', the consent requirements in section 69 will apply. In POPIA 'electronic communication' is defined as any text, voice, sound or image message sent over an electronic communications network which is stored in the network or in the recipient's terminal equipment until it is collected by the recipient'.[22] Section 69(1) provides that electronic communication includes automatic calling machines, facsimile machines, SMSes or email.

The definition of electronic communication has three elements:

- any text, voice, sound or image message,
- sent over an electronic communications network,[23]
- which is stored in the network or in the recipient's terminal equipment until it is collected by the recipient.

Key point: For section 69 to apply, all three elements of the definition of electronic communications must apply. For example, it is not enough that a message is sent over an electronic communications network; the marketing message must also be stored in the network until it is collected by the data subject.

22 See the definition of 'electronic communication' in section 1 of POPIA.

23 The Electronic Communications Act 36 of 2005 provides the following definition for 'electronic communications network' in section 1: 'any system of electronic communications facilities (excluding subscriber equipment), including without limitation— *(a)* satellite systems; *(b)* fixed systems (circuit- and packet-switched); *(c)* mobile systems; *(d)* fibre optic cables (undersea and land-based); *(e)* electricity cable systems (to the extent used for electronic communications services); and *(f)* other transmission systems, used for conveyance of electronic communications'.

Here is the short version of how this definition applies to different forms of direct marketing:

Electronic communication …so, section 69 applies.	**Not electronic communication*** *but remember the rest of POPIA applies!
Automatic calling machines	Telephone calls, whether transmitted through mobile networks, fixed networks or voice over internet protocols
Facsimile machines (OK Boomer)	Snail mail
SMS	Targeted social media marketing and behavioural advertising
Email	
Push notifications or in-app direct messages (e.g. a 'DM' on social media)	

Not satisfied? We are pretty confident. Here's why…

16.3.1 Electronic communication

There are a number of forms of electronic communication that are helpfully listed in section 69(1):

- Automatic calling machines
- Facsimile machines
- Email
- SMS

Automatic calling machines are specifically mentioned in section 69(1) as a form of electronic direct marketing. Section 69(5) refers to 'automated calling systems without human intervention'. This would not include automatic diallers that connect to a call centre agent but would include so-called robocalls where the data subject hears a recorded message. The reason why the stricter rules of section 69 apply, is because it is impossible for the data subject to opt out during the call as there is no simultaneous participation between the data subject and the marketer.[24]

[24] SA Law Reform Commission Project 124 on Privacy and Data Protection (2009 Report) 346.

Tricky area: The definition of 'electronic communication' requires that a message must be 'stored in the network or in the recipient's terminal equipment until it is collected by the recipient'. The definition of electronic communication in section 1 of POPIA was based on the definition of 'electronic mail' in the EU Directive on privacy and electronic communications.[25] The requirement that a message must be stored did not apply to 'automatic calling machines' in the Directive, but only to electronic mail. In POPIA, the requirement is included in the definition of electronic communication and 'automatic calling machines' are listed as an example of an electronic communication. This means that automatic calling machines would only be subject to section 69 if a message is left for the data subject to retrieve.

Facsimile machines are also listed by name in section 69(1). The *Mail and Guardian* eloquently asks 'Who the fax is still sending faxes?'[26] Wikipedia says that roughly 2% of marketers (in the United States) still use fax, mostly for business-to-business marketing.[27]

Lastly, SMS and email are also listed as electronic communications. No surprises there.

Of course, these are just examples. There are other communication methods that have emerged since POPIA was drafted back in 2009. For instance, push notifications or in-app direct messages (e.g. a 'DM' on social media).

The European Data Protection Board and the UK's ICO confirms that the marketing delivered via a direct in-app message (e.g. a direct message or 'DM' on Instagram or LinkedIn) or a push notification to the user constitutes 'electronic direct marketing'.[28] This is in keeping with the South African definition of 'electronic communication'.

---

25 Directive 2002/58/EC of the European Parliament and of the Council of 12 July 2002 concerning the processing of personal data and the protection of privacy in the electronic communications sector (Directive on privacy and electronic communications).

26 Mail & Guardian 'Who the fax is still sending faxes?', available at https://mg.co.za/article/2018-01-19-00-who-the-fax-is-still-sending-faxes/.

27 Wikipedia 'Direct Marketing', available at https://en.wikipedia.org/wiki/Direct_marketing#Broadcast_faxing.

28 ICO 'Direct marketing: Code of practice, Information Commissioner's Office Draft code for consultation' 16 and 90, available at https://ico.org.uk/about-the-ico/ico-and-stakeholder-consultations/ico-consultation-on-the-draft-direct-marketing-code-of-practice/. Given that POPIA's definition of 'electronic communication' is almost word-for-word identical to the ePrivacy Directive's definition of 'electronic mail', we think it is safe to apply the findings of the European Data Protection Board in a South African context as well.

16.3.2 NOT electronic communication

Direct marketing done via the telephone is not subject to section 69 regardless of whether the call is placed via a mobile network, fixed network or voice over internet protocols. This is because the marketing message is not stored in the network or in the recipient's terminal equipment until it is collected by the recipient. When there is simultaneous participation, such as a live telephone call, the marketing message is not retrieved by the data subject later.

When there is simultaneous participation, such as a live telephone call, the marketing message is not retrieved by the data subject later.

Key point: When POPIA was first signed into law, we were puzzled by the fact that section 69 does not apply to telemarketing; in fact, we assumed that it was a mistake. However, a close examination of the SA Law Reform Commission Project 124 on Privacy and Data Protection 2009 Report, reveals that it was a calculated decision based on a strategy of the Department of Trade and Industry to promote call centres within South Africa and to offer incentives to attract call centre business to South Africa[29] and the role of telemarketing in ensuring that vulnerable consumers have access to goods and services.[30] The SA Law Reform Commission recommended that 'a regulatory framework for direct marketing be promoted that will balance the rights of consumers not to be targeted unreasonably, with the right of business to communicate effectively with the public'.[31] The result was an opt-in regime for unsolicited electronic marketing which would operate alongside the opt-out regime in the Consumer Protection Act 68 of 2008 (CPA) for other forms of marketing.

29 SA Law Reform Commission Project 124 on Privacy and Data Protection (2009 Report) 35. Be sure to read footnote 102; it is very interesting.

30 SA Law Reform Commission Project 124 on Privacy and Data Protection (2009 Report) 360.

31 SA Law Reform Commission Project 124 on Privacy and Data Protection (2009 Report) 362. The Constitutional right to freedom of expression includes the freedom to 'impart information' (section 16(1)(c)(iv)). In addition, section 22 establishes the right to choose a trade, occupation or profession and section 32 establishes the right to access to information. The SA Law Reform Commission balanced these rights with the right to privacy and added that: 'it is important to note that it is widely recognised by political and economic commentators that economic growth is essential for the realisation of social and economic transformation in South Africa. Fair marketing practices designed to approach, inform and retain customers must accordingly be regarded as of critical importance to the growth of the South African economy.'

Marketing delivered via mail is not subject to section 69 of POPIA. When this marketing is directed at a 'consumer', the CPA will apply.

What about targeted social media marketing and behavioural advertising?

Social media platforms allow responsible parties to create an 'audience' out of the social media platform's users to display adverts to these users about the goods and services in question. Sometimes, the responsible party will send personal information it already has (e.g. email addresses) to the social media platform and they will match it to their users. This is often referred to as list-based targeting tools. In other instances, social media platforms will offer responsible parties the ability to build an audience based on desirable demographics or preferences. This is referred to as 'lookalike audiences'. Once the audience has been identified, advertising will be displayed to members of that audience.

Similarly, behavioural advertising allows marketers to display relevant advertising on websites. In this case, the audience is selected based on their web-browsing behaviour which is tracked through the use of cookies.

Does 'electronic communication' under POPIA include social media marketing where the marketing is not sent to the data subject, but rather displayed? The European Data Protection Board states that '[t]he use of the word "sent" implies the use of technological communication means that necessarily involve the conveyance of a communication, whereas most advertising on the web (through social media platforms or on websites) would not involve "sending" advertisements in the strict sense.'[32] In other words, this form of marketing does not fall within the definition of 'electronic communication', because the marketing is not 'sent' and a message is not 'stored in the network or in the recipient's terminal equipment until it is collected by the recipient'.

32 See Article 29 Data Protection Working Party 'Opinion 01/2017 on the Proposed Regulation for the ePrivacy Regulation (2002/58/EC)' at 20 to 21, available at https://ec.europa.eu/newsroom/article29/item-detail.cfm?item_id=610140. Also see European Data Protection Board 'Guidelines 8/2020 on the targeting of social media user' at paragraph 31, available at https://edpb.europa.eu/our-work-tools/public-consultations-art-704/2020/guidelines-082020-targeting-social-media-users_en on social media marketing and who is accountable.

16.3.3 Once more with feeling

Key point: To summarise, telemarketing, snail mail, some forms of social media marketing and behavioural advertising (e.g., facilitated by tracking cookies) are not considered 'electronic' and are not subject to section 69 of POPIA. This means that these forms of marketing must be justified in terms of section 11. Responsible parties could argue that marketing their products and services is in the 'legitimate interest of the responsible party'.[33] If a responsible party wants to rely on this legal basis, it must perform a legitimate interest assessment to ensure that the limitation of the right to privacy is justified.[34] When a responsible party relies on its legitimate interest to market, the data subject will have a right to object.[35] In addition, when the data subject is also a 'consumer', the right to unsubscribe from direct marketing in terms of the CPA will apply.

16.4 UNSOLICITED DIRECT MARKETING

Section 69(1) distinguishes between unsolicited direct marketing and direct marketing that is sent to a data subject that is a customer of the responsible party. Section 69(1)*(a)* provides that responsible parties can only send unsolicited direct marketing to data subjects if they have consented.

In this section we will discuss the following:

- when direct marketing is 'unsolicited'
- the requirements for a valid direct marketing consent (form 4); and
- how many times a data subject may be approached to obtain consent.

16.4.1 When is direct marketing 'unsolicited'

Direct marketing is unsolicited if it is sent to a data subject with whom the responsible party has no prior relationship. A good rule of thumb to apply is to ask 'does this data subject expect to hear from us?'

---

33 Article 29 Data Protection Working Party *Opinion 06/2014 on the Notion of Legitimate Interests of the Data Controller under Article 7 of Directive 95/46/EC.*

34 Legitimate interest assessments are discussed in chapter 2 paragraph 2.6.3.

35 The right to object is discussed in chapter 18.

Consider these scenarios:

Scenario	Unsolicited or solicited direct marketing?
A responsible party collects contact details from a source other than the data subject (e.g. by scraping the internet, from a public record or by purchasing a list from a list broker) and sends SMSes to all of the data subjects on the list.	This is unsolicited direct marketing. The responsible party will need to get opt-in consent for direct marketing first.[36] In addition, the responsible party will have to determine whether collecting the information from a source other than the data subject is compliant with section 12.[37]
A data subject signs up for a newsletter on the responsible party's website.	This is solicited direct marketing. The responsible party does not have to ask for consent before sending the newsletter.
A data subject starts filling in an online order form or application form for products or services. They never complete the form (for whatever reason). The responsible party uses the data subject's cell phone number to send them marketing via SMS.	This is unsolicited direct marketing. The responsible party will need to get consent for direct marketing first.[38] If the data subject completed the online order form or application form and became the 'customer' of the responsible party, the responsible party would not need consent, if the responsible party complies with section 69(3).[39] This is only the case where the data subject becomes a customer of the responsible party.
A responsible party obtains a list of names, ID numbers and cell phone numbers which it uses for direct marketing via the telephone.	This is a trick question! It is not electronic direct marketing at all, and section 69 does not apply. The responsible party has to consider whether they have a legal basis for using the personal information for telemarketing in terms of section 11.[40] In addition, the responsible party will have to determine whether collecting the information from a source other than the data subject is compliant with section 12.[41]

➡

[36] Section 69(1)*(a)* and Form 4 in the December 2018 POPIA Regulations. We discuss Form 4 in paragraph 16.4.2.

[37] This is discussed in chapter 10.

[38] Section 69(1)*(a)*.

[39] Section 69(1)*(b)* and (3) is discussed in paragraph 16.5.

[40] This is discussed in chapter 6. The responsible party would probably rely on the fact that marketing its products or services is in its legitimate interest and would have to do a legitimate interest assessment. Legitimate interest assessments are discussed in chapter 2 paragraph 2.6.3.

[41] This is discussed in chapter 10.

Scenario	Unsolicited or solicited direct marketing?
A responsible party shares the contact details of its customers with a third party who now markets its own products to these data subjects via email and SMS.	This is unsolicited direct marketing. The third party will need to get consent for direct marketing first.[42] The third party can either obtain consent itself, or the responsible party could obtain consent on the third party's behalf. This 'third-party consent' would have to comply with all of the requirements for a valid direct marketing consent, including the name of the third party.[43] A blanket consent 'to share personal information with third parties for direct marketing purposes' would not suffice. The responsible party has to consider whether they have a legal basis for sharing the personal information with the third party. If sharing the information was the original purpose for which the responsible party collected the information, it must rely on section 11.[44] If sharing the personal information was not the original intention, then the responsible party has to comply with section 15, because sharing it is further processing.[45] In addition, the third party will have to determine whether collecting the information from a source other than the data subject is compliant with section 12.[46]
A data subject asks the responsible party for more information on a product or a quote.	Another trick question! A quotation is not direct marketing. Even if it were, in this case it is solicited. The responsible party does not have to ask for consent before sending the information or quote.

➥

[42] Section 69(1)*(a)*.

[43] The requirements for a valid direct marketing consent are discussed in paragraph 16.4.2 below.

[44] This is discussed in chapter 6. The responsible party would probably rely on the fact that sharing the information for purposes of direct marketing is in the legitimate interest of the third party and would have to do a legitimate interest assessment. Legitimate interest assessments are discussed in chapter 2 paragraph 2.6.3.

[45] Further processing is discussed in chapter 12.

[46] This is discussed in chapter 10.

Scenario	Unsolicited or solicited direct marketing?
A responsible party sends a newsletter and SMSes to customers who have signed up for the responsible party's loyalty programme to tell them about new products and special offers for loyalty card members.	When a customer signs up or subscribes to a loyalty programme, the responsible party is contractually obliged to send the customer information which enables to the customer to take advantage of the loyalty programme (e.g. send them vouchers, information about special offers for loyalty members, instructions on how to redeem their points). We do not believe that these messages are direct marketing. If the data subject no longer wants to receive the benefits of the loyalty programme, they should terminate their membership. Even if it were direct marketing, it is solicited direct marketing and section 69(1)*(b)* and (3) will apply. No opt-in consent is required, unless the responsible party does not meet the requirements of section 69(3) which are discussed in paragraph 16.5.2.

16.4.2 The requirements for a valid direct marketing consent

Key point: What are the implications if the electronic direct marketing is unsolicited? The responsible party needs to obtain consent.[47] We have spoken about consent a lot in this book, but this time it is different. While the consent still has to be a voluntary, specific and informed expression of will,[48] section 69(1) has its own additional requirements.

Enter Form 4. In the POPIA Regulations, the Information Regulator has issued a form ('Form 4') which must be followed when consent is obtained from the data subject in these circumstances.[49] The bad news is that (despite being mercifully shorter than prior versions) the adopted version of Form 4 is a bit of a nightmare due to its length, the use of legalese and an utter disregard for user-experience principles.

---

47 Section 69(1)*(b)*.

48 For a discussion on how to obtain a valid consent in terms of POPIA, see chapter 2 paragraph 2.6.6.

49 Form 4 of the Regulations relating to the Protection of Personal Information, 2018 ('the POPIA Regulations') read with section 69(2)*(b)* of POPIA. As we were reading the final proofs of this edition the Information Regulator published draft amendments to Form 4 for comment (GN 45120, GoN 829). We considered the draft regulations – they did not change the conclusions we made in this chapter.

FORM 4

APPLICATION FOR THE CONSENT OF A DATA SUBJECT FOR THE PROCESSING OF PERSONAL INFORMATION FOR THE PURPOSE OF DIRECT MARKETING

IN TERMS OF SECTION 69(2) OF THE PROTECTION OF PERSONAL INFORMATION ACT, 2013 (ACT 4 OF 2013)

REGULATIONS RELATING TO THE PROTECTION OF PERSONAL INFORMATION, 2018

[Regulation 6]

TO: ....
....
....
(Name of data subject)

FROM: ....
....
Contact number(s): ....
Fax number: ....
E-mail address: ....
(Name, address and contact details of responsible party)

Full names and designation of person signing on behalf of responsible party:

....

....
Signature of designated person

Date: ....

PART B

I, ... *(full names of data subject)* hereby:

☐ **Give my consent.**

To receive direct marketing of goods or services to be marketed by means of electronic communication.

SPECIFY GOODS or SERVICES:

SPECIFY METHOD OF COMMUNICATION: FAX..
E - MAIL..
SMS:..
OTHERS – SPECIFY: ....

Signed at.. this day of......................20 ....

....
Signature of data subject

Key point: Do responsible parties have to use the form verbatim? No! The rationale for this answer is hidden. The definition of 'form' in the POPIA Regulations provides that the forms that are attached to the POPIA Regulations must be used 'or any form which is substantially similar to that form'.[50] To be considered substantially similar to Form 4, it does not have to use the exact wording or layout of Form 4, but your direct marketing consent form must comply with the essential elements of Form 4.

We have broken down Form 4 into its essential elements below which responsible parties must fulfil to have a valid consent under POPIA to send direct marketing by means of unsolicited electronic communications to data subjects:

- **Full name of the data subject who gives consent.** Form 4 requires the 'name of data subject' in Part A and the 'full name of data subject' in Part B. We know that many responsible parties in the past have only collected the email address or the cell phone number of the data subject. Additionally, we think this is breaching POPIA's own principle of minimality regarding personal information.[51] In our opinion, as long as the consent recorded is linked to the data subject via an email address, cell phone number or account name that distinctly identifies the data subject, this will comply with Form 4's requirements.
- **The signature of the data subject.** It can be signed in person or electronically.[52] Even though the form looks like it has to be completed as a hard copy, the definition of 'submit' in the POPIA Regulations includes electronic submissions. Mercifully, the signature does not have to be an advanced electronic signature.

50 Section 1 of the POPIA Regulations. As we were finalising this book, the Information Regulator published draft amendments to the December 2018 Regulations (GN 45120, GoN 829). The draft Regulations includes an amendment to regulation 6. It still states that the consent must be substantially similar to form 4, but added that consent can be asked in 'any manner that may be expedient, free of charge and reasonably accessible'. Given that the new regulations were still in draft form, we did not include them here. We had to draw the line somewhere.

51 Section 10 of POPIA.

52 Section 1 of the POPIA Regulations also includes a definition of 'signature' and 'submit'. 'Signature' includes an electronic signature as defined in the Electronic Communications and Transactions Act. 'Submit' includes submit by data message, electronic communication, registered post, electronic mail, facsimile and personal delivery. This means that a consent for direct marketing may now be signed and submitted electronically.

- **The date and location where consent is given.** As long as the data is captured by the responsibility in the back end, this is sufficient. Capturing the location where the consent was given is a curious requirement. We are of the view that requiring responsible parties to capture location data for the purpose of unsubscribing is a (very ironic) breach of the minimality principle of POPIA.[53]
- **The identity and contact information of the responsible party (the relevant organisation's details).** This is important. To meet the POPIA requirement that consent must be a 'voluntary, specific and informed expression of will',[54] the data subject needs to know the exact identity of the responsible party.[55]

Key point: If the responsible party wants to use this direct marketing consent for cross-selling with other entities within their group or other third parties, the responsible party must get additional consents from the data subject for each of these other entities or third parties. The consent must specifically list all the parties who can send direct marketing to the data subject.[56] Organisations cannot rely on vague third-party consents such as 'you consent to your personal information being shared with carefully selected third parties for direct marketing purposes'.[57] Note that the sharing of personal information for direct marketing purposes also has to comply with section 12, which is discussed in chapter 10.

- **The identity, contact information and signature of the person designated to act on behalf of the responsible party (usually the information officer or the deputy information officer).** This is a controversial requirement, because the Information Regulator seems to think that consent is an agreement that needs to be signed by both parties. Consent is not an agreement. For one thing, the data subject can withdraw it at any time.

[53] Minimality is discussed in chapter 9.

[54] See the definition of 'consent' in section 1 of POPIA. The definition of consent is discussed in chapter 2 paragraph 2.6.6.

[55] See chapter 2 paragraph 2.6.6.

[56] European Data Protection Board 'Guidelines 05/2020 on consent under Regulation 2016/679' at paragraph 65, available at https://edpb.europa.eu/sites/edpb/files/files/file1/edpb_guidelines_202005_consent_en.pdf.

[57] This type of consent was not considered adequate under the Data Protection Act of 1998 (the predecessor to the UK's local version of the EU GDPR) in the Bounty case. See https://ico.org.uk/about-the-ico/news-and-events/news-and-blogs/2019/04/bounty-uk-fined-400-000-for-sharing-personal-data-unlawfully/.

Framing consent as some kind of 'agreement', creates the impression that responsible parties can contract out of POPIA compliance; they cannot.[58] It is just a legal basis for processing. We suggest that the responsible party should keep a record of who approved the consent form used. Some organisations are putting a statement in their consent forms or their privacy notice, which says something to the effect that the information officer has approved the wording of all consents. We don't think it is necessary.

- **The responsible party must specify what goods or services they will be marketing to the data subject.** Consent must always be 'specific' and 'informed'.[59] When creating Form 4, the Information Regulator clearly felt that in this context, this means that the responsible party must describe the goods or services in sufficient enough detail so the specific purpose of the consent is clear.[60] But, how long is a piece of string? Must the responsible party list every product or service? Clearly this would not be practical. Instead, it should be clear to the data subject what category of goods or services will be marketed to them.[61] In addition, if it is clear from the context what type of goods or services will be marketed, we do not think that the consent needs to expressly reference the type of goods. The rule of thumb is that the data subject must not be surprised to receive direct marketing about a good or service. For example, if a data subject consented to receive direct marketing about 'groceries', they may be surprised to receive direct marketing about life insurance from the responsible party.
- **The responsible party must specify the electronic communication channels they will use.** In order for the consent to fulfil these requirements of being 'specific' and informed', the channel(s) which the responsible party will use must be specified.

Chapter 16

58 We often get asked for 'POPIA disclaimers'. The answer is always 'uhm, no'. Form 4 did not help put this baby to bed.

59 Consent is defined in POPIA as a 'voluntary, specific and informed expression of will'. See the definition of 'consent' in section 1 of POPIA.

60 See European Data Protection Board 'Guidelines 05/2020 on consent under Regulation 2016/679' at paragraph 57, available at https://edpb.europa.eu/sites/edpb/files/files/file1/edpb_guidelines_202005_consent_en.pdf.

61 See Article 29 Data Protection Working Party Opinion 5/2004 on unsolicited communications for marketing purposes under article 13 of Directive 2002/58/EC 5, available at https://ec.europa.eu/justice/article-29/documentation/opinion-recommendation/files/2004/wp90_en.pdf. What should those categories be? For inspiration, we look at the industry categories used by Statistics South Africa, available at http://www.statssa.gov.za/?page_id=4519 or the classes of goods recognised for purposes of registering a trademark (https://www.wipo.int/classifications/nice/en/). These ideas were revealed to us in a dream.

It is a bit strange that Form 4 does not require that the responsible party must provide information about how to unsubscribe given that this is a requirement in section 69(4)*(b)*. This should not be seen as a justification for the responsible party to omit the unsubscribe information! Instructions on how to unsubscribe must be provided to the data subject. We discuss this in paragraph 16.6.

Responsible parties must always consider the general consent requirements too. They are discussed in chapter 2 paragraph 2.6.6.

16.4.3 How many times may a customer be asked to consent to direct marketing?

There are also rules relating to how many times data subjects can be approached by responsible parties to ask for this consent in terms of section 69(1) of POPIA. Section 69(2)*(a)* of POPIA states:

> 'A responsible party may approach a data subject— (i) whose consent is required in terms of subsection (1)*(a)*; and (ii) who has not previously withheld such consent, only once in order to request the consent of that data subject.'

Sounds simple at first, but as always the devil is in the detail. What exactly do 'who has not previously withheld such consent' and 'only once' mean?

Key point: So, what does 'withheld' mean exactly in this context? A savvy responsible party may try to argue that if the data subject simply does not reply to a request for their consent in this context, the data subject is not actually 'withholding' their consent within the meaning of section 69(2)*(a)*. On the basis of this logic, the data subject can be contacted as many times as possible before the data subject actually says 'no, I will not give my consent to receive direct marketing from you'. The persistence of responsible parties was not underestimated by the drafters of POPIA. The SA Law Reform Commission states firmly (in relation to section 69(2)*(a)* of POPIA):

> 'In both opt-in and opt-out cases the business will be allowed to make contact with the data subject or consumer. However, with the opt-in position, if the data subject does not respond to the responsible party's invitation to make use of its direct marketing advances, the responsible party will not be able to contact the consumer for a second time. With the opt-out position the responsible party may keep on contacting the consumer until the consumer objects.'[62]

[62] SA Law Reform Commission Project 124 on Privacy and Data Protection (2009 Report) 353.

So, if the data subject does not respond to the first application (as Form 4 calls it) for direct marketing consent, the responsible party cannot contact that data subject again. Silence counts as 'withholding' consent.

But, given how specific a direct marketing consent must be to comply with Form 4, when will it simply be considered a new consent? Consider these examples:

(Exceedingly common) examples	Can the responsible party ask for consent 'again'? I.e. is it a new consent?
A responsible party asks for consent to market groceries via SMS. A couple of months later, the responsible party decides to launch an email newsletter.	Form 4 states that the responsible party must indicate which communication channel(s) will be used. However, these channels may change over time, even in respect of the same category of goods. Does this mean that once a responsible party has committed to a channel in Form 4, that can never change? Section 69(2)*(a)* undoubtedly means that a responsible party cannot send the same Form 4 request for consent to data subjects over and over again. If something essential,[63] like the communication channel, changes, the responsible party should be able to ask for consent again. **Tricky area: Is the communication channel essential? The authors could not reach consensus on this one.**
A responsible party asks for consent to market flights via SMS and email. That same responsible party launches a vehicle rental service and wants to market it via SMS and email.	Here, the product being marketed has changed. The fact that Form 4 requires that the category of goods must be specified, means that when the responsible party launches a new product or service, they should be able to ask for consent for that new product or service.

[63] We define 'essential' in this context as anything that is required by Form 4.

(Exceedingly common) examples	Can the responsible party ask for consent 'again'? I.e. is it a new consent?
Companies A, B and C are all subsidiaries in the same group of companies. They all operate under the same brand and most data subjects will not realise that they are separate companies until they go and read the group's privacy notice. They share a leads database with each other. Company A asks for consent to market its services as a medical scheme via email. Company B asks for consent from the same data subjects to market its gap cover to the same data subjects via SMS. Company C joined the group much later and markets life insurance to the same database via SMS.	The first question will always be whether they have a legal basis for sharing the database. This is discussed in chapter 13.[64] They can (and should!) ask for separate consents. They can do it on behalf of each other as long as the consent is specific enough.

Key point: Responsible parties should not use our interpretation of section 69(2)*(a)* read with Form 4 to circumvent the requirement that data subjects should only be approached once to ask for their consent. Our argument above is that if a responsible party's products or services, or the mechanism through which they deliver the marketing, changes after the data subject was first approached, they can ask for consent again as this is 'further processing' for a new (direct marketing) purpose.

Clearly, responsible parties should not be allowed to pester or harass data subjects. In an attempt to capture the 'spirit' of section 69(2)*(a)*, let's look at the definitions of 'pester' or 'harass':[65]

- Pester: 'trouble or annoy (someone) with frequent or persistent requests or interruptions'.
- Harass: 'subject to aggressive pressure or intimidation' or 'make repeated small-scale attacks on (an enemy)'.

The trick is not to treat a prospective customer like the enemy.[66]

64 The responsible party(s) would probably rely on the fact that sharing the information for purposes of direct marketing is in the legitimate interest of the third party (the rest of the group) and would have to do a legitimate interest assessment. Legitimate interest assessments are discussed in chapter 2 paragraph 2.6.3.

65 *Oxford Dictionary*, available at https://www.oed.com/.

66 In keeping with the war metaphor, in Dan Solove's *Taxonomy of Privacy*, one category of harm which data subjects suffer when their privacy is infringed is 'invasion' which includes 'invasive

16.5 ELECTRONIC DIRECT MARKETING TO DATA SUBJECTS WHO ARE ALREADY CUSTOMERS

POPIA allows for a more lenient approach when electronic direct marketing is sent to existing customers; there are instances where responsible parties will not need consent.[67] In the words of the SA Law Reform Commission this is in recognition of the 'strong view worldwide that some forms of direct marketing are, or have the capacity to be, more intrusive than others'. Unsolicited electronic communications are seen as very intrusive and should therefore be subject to opt-in requirements.

So, what if the data subject is a customer? Section 69(1)*(b)* provides that the personal information of a 'customer of the responsible party' may be processed for the purpose of direct marketing by means of electronic marketing, provided that the requirements in section 69(3) are met.

Key point: If the data subject is a customer of the responsible party and all of the requirements of section 69(3) are met, the responsible party does not need to use Form 4. Booyah![68]

In this section we will discuss:

- when a data subject will be considered a 'customer' of the responsible party; and
- the requirements of section 69(3).

16.5.1 When will a data subject be considered a customer?

In order for section 69(1)*(b)* to apply, the data subject has to be 'a customer of the responsible party'. POPIA does not define when a data subject will be considered a customer. Let's start with a no-brainer: A data subject who has concluded an agreement with a responsible party for the delivery of goods or services will be considered a customer.

---

acts that disturb one's tranquillity or solitude'. Professor Solove's *Taxonomy of Privacy* was adapted from Daniel J Solove *Understanding Privacy* (2008) and is available at https://www.privacysecurityacademy.com/wp-content/uploads/2018/02/Handout-Foundations-and-Themes-Professor-Soloves-Taxonomy-of-Privacy-01.pdf.

67 Section 69(3) of POPIA.

68 This word is either an expression of exuberance or triumph or refers to a stew or thick soup (originally spelled bouillon). Either meaning works in this context.

Tricky area: When is a customer, a customer? Consider these examples: A data subject starts to complete an application or order form on a website. For whatever reason, the data subject's session is interrupted before the application or order form is submitted. What if the data subject applied for a service, but did not qualify? Does a responsible party need the consent of these 'almost customers' before sending them direct marketing? Some co-authors argued that the requirement in section 69(3)*(a)* that the contact details of the data subject must have been obtained 'in the context of a sale of a product or service' suggests that something less than a successful transaction will suffice. In other words, even if the data subject tried (but failed) to transact with the responsible party, a Form 4 compliant consent is not required. The other authors argued that before section 69(3)*(a)* is even considered, the data subject must first be a customer; section 69(3)*(a)* is a requirement for how the contact details must be collected in order for section 69(1)*(b)* to apply. In addition, the ordinary meaning of 'customer' is 'one that purchases a commodity or service' as opposed to 'one who enquires about a commodity or service'.[69] However, the South African Law Reform Commission stated that marketing is unsolicited where 'there is no previous link between the marketer and the data subject'.[70]

The wording of section 69(1)*(b)* is very similar to article 13(2) of the EU Directive on Privacy and Electronic Communications[71] and is described as a 'soft opt-in'. Not all of the EU member states interpreted article 13 to mean that a completed transaction is required.[72]

Only the responsible party(s) who are a party to the transaction with the customer will be able to rely on the fact that the data subject is a customer.[73]

69 See https://www.merriam-webster.com/dictionary/customer.

70 This suggests that something less than a transaction may be sufficient.

71 Directive 2002/58/EC of the European Parliament and of the Council of 12 July 2002 concerning the processing of personal data and the protection of privacy in the electronic communications sector (Directive on privacy and electronic communications).

72 For a summary on how the Directive was implemented see Field Fisher 'Email marketing across Europe: National law requirements', available at https://res.cloudinary.com/fieldfisher/image/upload/v1585817516/PDFs/EU_e-marketing_requirements_updated_March_2020_g6jh2u.pdf.

73 Recital 41 of Directive 2002/58/EC.

16.5.2 The requirements of section 69(3)

If the data subject is a customer of the responsible party, the responsible party has to comply with the requirements of section 69(3) in order to avoid asking for consent using Form 4. In this section, we discuss the following requirements:

- the responsible party obtained the contact details of the data subject 'in the context of the sale of a product or service',
- the responsible party is marketing their 'own similar products or services', AND
- the data subject was given a reasonable opportunity(s) to object.

Key point: If a responsible party does not comply with all three of these requirements or cannot prove that they comply, section 69(3) does not apply. This means that the responsible party would have to obtain a consent that complies with Form 4. This is often referred to as 're-permissioning' or 're-consenting' an existing database. It is not something that marketers like doing, because low response rates will shrink the database substantially. Do not do it unless you absolutely have to! If you do have to, get advice on how to do it and speak to the creatives (not just the lawyers)[74] about how to do it. We are not the first country to go through this change, and there is a lot we can learn from how other marketers dealt with it.[75]

16.5.2.1 Contact details obtained 'in the context of the sale of a product or service'

As discussed above, the data subject must be a 'customer' of the responsible party, but there are diverging opinions about what this means. Whatever the case may be, section 69(3)*(a)* requires that the contact details must have been collected 'in the context of a sale' and not after the transaction was concluded. If a responsible party only collects the contact details at a later stage, for the purpose of direct marketing, the responsible party will need to obtain consent using Form 4.

Chapter 16

[74] As Dr McCoy from Star Trek would say: 'Damnit Jim, I'm a lawyer not a marketer!'

[75] Here is a good example of advice on how to plan for and do a re-permissioning campaign: https://econsultancy.com/gdpr-examples-repermissioning-emails-campaigns/. Not all of the campaigns will meet the POPIA standard, but they are good for some inspiration!

Could 'in the context of the sale of a product or service' mean that section 69(3) will apply if the contact details are obtained well before the sale of a product or service or must it have been obtained as part of the negotiations? We believe that if there was a transaction, it does not really matter when the contact details were first collected. The ICO writes extensively about the fact that the data subject must have already expressed an interest or that there must be active negotiations, but that is because the UK does not require that a transaction must have been concluded.[76] In other words, the meaning of 'in the context of a sale' will depend on whether a transaction is required before someone will be considered a 'customer'. We discuss this particularly tricky area in 16.5.1. Even if a transaction is not required, the data subject should at least have expressed an interest.

Tricky area: Must the responsible party obtain the information directly from the data subject for the requirement to be fulfilled? In the EU the requirement has been interpreted to mean that the contact details must be obtained directly from the data subject and not (for instance) from a list broker.[77] Be careful though! Article 13(2) of the EU Directive on Privacy and Electronic Communications[78] states that 'where a natural or legal person obtains *from its customers their electronic contact details for direct marketing*' while section 69(3)*(a)* is formulated 'if the responsible party obtained the contact details of the data subject in the context of the sale of a product or service'; POPIA does not state where the contact details must have been obtained from. Section 12 of POPIA contains a list of instances when it will be acceptable for responsible parties to collect information from sources other than the data subject. This is discussed in chapter 10 but the point here is that it is permissible, even for direct marketing purposes.

76 ICO *Direct Marketing* from paragraph 134, available at https://ico.org.uk/media/1555/direct-marketing-guidance.pdf.

77 ICO *Direct Marketing* paragraph 133, available at https://ico.org.uk/media/1555/direct-marketing-guidance.pdf.

78 Directive 2002/58/EC of the European Parliament and of the Council of 12 July 2002 concerning the processing of personal data and the protection of privacy in the electronic communications sector (Directive on privacy and electronic communications).

16.5.2.2 The responsible party's 'own similar products or services'

Section 69(3) only applies to direct marketing that is sent by the same responsible party who collected the contact details and has a relationship[79] with the data subject. In other words, section 69(3) cannot be used to justify direct marketing sent by (or for) another responsible party.

In addition, the products or services that the responsible party is marketing must be 'similar' to the products or services the data subject purchased. In other words, section 69(3) cannot be used as a justification to cross-sell products or services, even if the other (different) products or services are sold by the same responsible party. A consent that complies with Form 4 will have to be obtained for other products or services.

Tricky area: How similar is similar enough? The ordinary meaning of 'similar' is 'having a resemblance in appearance, character, or quantity, without being identical'.[80] For instance, if a data subject has purchased apples from the responsible party before (and this is how the responsible party obtained the data subject's contact details), under section 69(3) of POPIA it would be perfectly appropriate for the responsible party to send the data subject direct marketing about oranges. This is because these goods are in the same category (food). Life insurance or credit, on the other hand, is an entirely different type of product. If the responsible party wants to send this data subject direct marketing about life insurance or credit, the responsible party will need to get an additional consent from the data subject to do so. The line can get a whole lot blurrier when goods are 'kind of' related to each other. E.g., we said above that a travel company that markets flights can ask for consent again if they start renting out vehicles. If a data subject already booked a flight from that company, does it mean that the company can rely on section 69(3) to market vehicle rentals to that customer without first asking for consent? Both fall in the category of 'transport' and are often bought together, so we believe the answer is yes.[81]

---

79 Remember that we could not agree whether a transaction needed to be concluded or not. So, we opted to say 'relationship' here. An ambiguous term as some of us know from awkward moments in our personal lives. You know? When one person thinks they are going steady, and another person is still dating other people.

80 *Oxford Dictionary*, available at https://www.oed.com/.

81 See Article 29 Data Protection Working Party Opinion 5/2004 on unsolicited communications for marketing purposes under article 13 of Directive 2002/58/EC 5, available at https://ec.europa.eu/

The ICO considered this question and stated:[82]

> 'We consider that the key question here is whether the customer would reasonably expect messages about the product or service in question. This is likely to depend on the context – including the type of business and the category of product. For example, someone who has shopped at a supermarket might reasonably expect messages about a much wider range of goods than someone who has shopped at a specialist store for a specialist product. Consider this example: A customer buys groceries online from a large supermarket chain. Although they only bought bread and bananas on that occasion, they might reasonably expect emails about a wide range of products – including bread, fruit, and other groceries, but also books, DVDs, kitchen equipment and other everyday goods commonly sold in supermarkets. However, they are unlikely to expect emails about banking or insurance products sold under the supermarket brand. These products are not bought and sold in a similar context.'

Responsible parties should focus on managing the expectations of data subjects about what type of marketing they can expect to receive at the point of sale; data subjects who are not surprised about what they are going to receive will (probably) not complain.

16.5.2.3 Reasonable opportunity(s) to object

Section 69(3) will only apply if the data subject was given a reasonable opportunity to object to the use of his or her 'electronic details':

- at the time the information was collected; and
- on the occasion of each communication with the data subject for the purpose of marketing.

There are two aspects that are important here:

- the substance of the unsubscribe; and
- when it must be communicated to the data subject.

We discuss the form of the unsubscribe in paragraph 16.6 below. As for the timing, in order to rely on section 69(3), the responsible party will have to show that the data subject was informed and given an opportunity to object at collection and again every time they were contacted.

---

justice/article-29/documentation/opinion-recommendation/files/2004/wp90_en.pdf. What should those categories be? For inspiration, we look at the industry categories used by Statistics South Africa, available at http://www.statssa.gov.za/?page_id=4519 or the classes of goods recognised for purposes of registering a trademark (https://www.wipo.int/classifications/nice/en/). These ideas were revealed to us in a dream.

82 ICO *Direct Marketing* from paragraph 136, available at https://ico.org.uk/media/1555/direct-marketing-guidance.pdf.

Tricky area: What if the personal information was not collected from the data subject directly? As we discussed in paragraph 16.5.2.1 it is not a requirement that the contact details are obtained from the data subject directly for section 69(3) to apply. In cases where the information was collected from another source, we apply section 18(2)*(b)* which provides that where information was not collected from the data subject, notification can take place 'as soon as reasonably practicable after it has been collected'.[83] However, if notification of the right to unsubscribe did not take place at all (for whatever reason),[84] the responsible party cannot rely on section 69(3) and would have to ask for consent and comply with Form 4.

What this means is that the responsible party has to prove that this information was given to data subjects, even where collection took place decades ago! The reality for many direct marketers is that they will not be able to prove this. When this is the case, a pragmatic approach is called for – think very carefully before you re-consent. We return to this in paragraph 16.9.3.

16.6 UNSUBSCRIBING FROM DIRECT MARKETING (AND GETTING OUT OF ROACH MOTELS)

Data subjects have the right to 'unsubscribe' from direct marketing. It is referred to as the right to object, but most of us know this as unsubscribing.[85]

Key point: This not only applies to electronic direct marketing,[86] but also in respect of non-electronic forms of marketing.[87] For electronic direct marketing, the unsubscribe requirement is contained in section 69(3)*(c)*. For non-electronic marketing, section 11(3)*(b)*.[88]

83 This is discussed in chapter 11 paragraph 11.4.

84 Including acceptable reasons not to notify in terms of section 18(4).

85 This is not the only time when the data subject will have the right to object. See chapter 18 paragraph 18.6 for a discussion of the right to object. When it comes to unsubscribing from direct marketing (electronic or otherwise), the data subject does not have to have 'reasonable grounds relating to his, her or its particular situation'. That is because the data subject is relying on section 11(3)*(b)* and not section 11(3)*(a)*.

86 Section 69(4).

87 Section 11(3)*(b)*.

88 The fact that different sections apply to electronic versus non-electronic direct marketing is confirmed in section 5*(e)*.

Once a data subject has unsubscribed, the responsible party must stop sending direct marketing to that data subject. Internationally under the EU GDPR, many companies have been fined large sums by regulators for failing to process their unsubscribes properly. For example, in March 2020 a Romanian company was fined approximately EUR3 000 for sending a commercial message to just one customer who had already unsubscribed.[89] Additionally, in October 2019, a Greek telecommunications company was fined EUR200 000 for contacting a large number of customers via telemarketing when all these customers had specifically opted out of receiving telemarketing from them. The unsubscribes had not been processed properly due to technical issues.[90] These examples demonstrate how important it is to manage direct marketing unsubscribes properly for all forms of direct marketing, and the negative repercussions organisations can face if they do not.

Key point: While the Information Regulator may not fine a South African company without giving it an opportunity to fix its unsubscribe process,[91] a complaint for failing to honour an unsubscribe has other consequences. The cost and inconvenience of being investigated by the Information Regulator will be significant and once the Information Regulator starts investigating an organisation, there is no telling where the investigation could lead.

There are no general requirements in POPIA for the form the unsubscribe must take. However, when unsubscribes are being considered for purposes of section 69(3)*(c)*, the following requirements are listed:

- It must be free of charge.
- The opportunity to unsubscribe must be 'free of unnecessary formality'.

---

89 OneTrust DataGuidance 'Romania: ANSPDCP fines Dante International €3,000 for GDPR violation', available at https://www.dataguidance.com/news/romania-anspdcp-fines-dante-international-%E2%82%AC3000-gdpr-violation.

90 OneTrust DataGuidance 'Greece: HDPA fines telecom service provider for GDPR violations', available at https://www.dataguidance.com/news/greece-hdpa-fines-telecom-service-provider-gdpr-violations.

91 Responsible parties can only be fined for 'offences'. Not honouring an unsubscribe is undoubtedly a breach of POPIA, but for it to be an offence, the responsible party would first have to ignore an enforcement notice from the Information Regulator. This is discussed in chapter 19, paragraph 19.10.1.

Key point: We believe that these requirements should be viewed as 'best practice' for all unsubscribes, not just when compliance with section 69(3)*(c)* is being considered in respect of electronic direct marketing to 'customers'. In other words, we believe that these requirements should be applied to the withdrawal of consent by data subjects who are not (yet) customers and when considering compliance with section 11(3)*(b)* in respect of non-electronic direct marketing too, even though the requirements are not mentioned there. In any event, if the direct marketing is being sent to a consumer as defined in the Consumer Protection Act (CPA), section 11 of that act provides that a responsible party must 'implement appropriate procedures to facilitate the receipt of [unsubscribes] and must not charge the consumer a fee for unsubscribing'.[92] The reason why we would apply these requirements to all unsubscribes is to avoid the complexity of having to manage compliance with different sets of rules depending on the rather fine distinctions between section 69(3)*(c)*, section 11(3)*(b)* and section 11 of the CPA.

92 Section 11(4)*(a)* and 11(5) of the CPA.

Before you take our suggestion and over-comply, here are the three requirements compared:

Electronic direct marketing (section 69(3)(c) and 69(4))	Non-electronic direct marketing (section 11(3)(b)	Section 11 of the CPA
'Any communication for the purpose of direct marketing must contain *(a)* the details of the identity of the sender or the person on whose behalf the communication has been sent and *(b)* an address or other contact details to which the recipient may send a request that such communications cease.'[93] AND In terms of section 69(3)*(c)* the data subject must have been given a reasonable opportunity to object, free of charge and in a manner free of unnecessary formality'.	Section 11(3)*(b)* does not provide any further requirements. As we were finalising this book, the Information Regulator published draft amendments to the December 2018 Regulations (GN 45120, GoN 829). The draft Regulations includes new requirements for unsubscribing from non-electronic direct marketing in terms of section 11(3)(b). Given that the new regulations were still in draft form, we did not include them here. We had to draw the line somewhere.[94]	We discuss the provisions of the CPA in detail in paragraph 16.8.1. Section 11(1)*(b)* provides that '[t]he right of every person to privacy includes the right to … require another person to discontinue … any approach or communication to that person, if the approach or communication is primarily for the purpose of direct marketing'.

➡

[93] Section 69(4).

[94] The POPIA Regulations provide a prescribed form for objections in terms of section 11(3)(a) and that '[t]he responsible party, or a designated person, must render such reasonable assistance as is necessary, free of charge, to enable a data subject to complete Form 1', but this only applies to objections in terms of section 11(3)*(a)* and not for direct marketing 'objections' which are dealt with in section 11(3)*(b)*.

Electronic direct marketing (section 69(3)(c) and 69(4))	Non-electronic direct marketing (section 11(3)(b)	Section 11 of the CPA
		In addition, direct marketers are required to check whether consumers have registered a pre-emptive block on the national do not contact registry.[95] This right is hypothetical at the moment as such a registry has not been established yet.[96] Regulation 4(1)*(b)*(ii) also provides that the consumer must be given written confirmation that their unsubscribe has been received.

Chapter 16

In order to meet these different requirements, a responsible party would have to design an unsubscribe process that distinguishes between:

- data subjects to whom they haven't marketed before and existing customers
- electronic direct marketing and non-electronic marketing; and
- data subjects who are consumers and those who are not consumers.

This would make for a very complicated unsubscribe process which will be difficult to implement. Hence we suggest that all unsubscribes should be:

- free of charge
- free of any 'unnecessary formality'; and
- followed up with a confirmation of receipt.

The requirement that the unsubscribe must be free of charge is quite clear, albeit not always simple to execute. However, defining what would constitute 'unnecessary formality' is harder to quantify. Here are the guidelines provided by the ICO:[97]

95 Section 11(3) of the CPA.

96 The Direct Marketing Association of South Africa has such a registry. Membership to the DMASA is voluntary, but marketers who are also members of the DMASA must check for pre-emptive blocks before sending direct marketing.

97 ICO *Direct Marketing* paragraph 138, available at https://ico.org.uk/media/1555/direct-marketing-guidance.pdf.

- It must be simple to opt out.
- When first collecting the data subject's details it must be part of the same process (e.g. the form should contain a prominent opt-out box or staff should offer it when information is being collected 'in person').
- In subsequent communication, the data subject should be able to unsubscribe by replying to the message or by clicking on an unsubscribe link.
- If the marketing is taking place via SMS, the data subject should be able to unsubscribe by sending a stop message to a short code.

This brings us back to the impact design can have on privacy. We wrote about dark patterns and how data subjects can be nudged to make decisions that erode their privacy in chapter 2 paragraph 2.6.5. Increasingly, legislatures and regulators are paying attention to how design can deprive data subjects of their rights.[98] For a cautionary tale about making unsubscribing too difficult, see the complaints of the US Federal Trade Commission against Age of Learning.[99] The Federal Trade Commission described the implications of 'digital tricks and traps' as follows:[100]

> 'Typically, digital tricks and traps work in concert, and dark patterns often employ a wide array of both. Dark pattern tricks involve an online sleight of hand using visual misdirection, confusing language, hidden alternatives, or fake urgency to steer people toward or away from certain choices. This could include using buttons with the same style but different language, a checkbox with double negative language, disguised ads, or time pressure designed to dupe users into clicking, subscribing, consenting or buying.
>
> Dark patterns use technology and design to create a situation Brignull has described as a "roach motel,"[101] where it is easy to get in, but almost impossible to escape.'

There you have it. Do not be a roach motel.

---

98 Marketing 'tricks' such as negative option marketing have been seen as unfair business practices and were expressly prohibited in the CPA (section 31). In the US legislation has been introduced to make it unlawful for large online operators to 'design, modify, or manipulate a user interface with the purpose or substantial effect of obscuring, subverting, or impairing user autonomy, decision-making, or choice to obtain consent or user data'. It is called the Deceptive Experiences to Online Users Reduction Act. The California Consumer Privacy Act, rather ingeniously, provides that it can take no more steps to opt out than it took to opt in. See Sean Kellogg 'How US, EU approach regulating "dark patterns"', available at https://iapp.org/news/a/ongoing-dark-pattern-regulation/.

99 Available here: https://www.ftc.gov/system/files/documents/cases/1723086abcmousecomplaint.pdf.

100 This is a reference to Harry Brignull who registered darkpatterns.org, which names and shames organisations who have embraced the dark side of the force.

101 Roach motels lure cockroaches into a compartment in which they become trapped in a sticky substance. Sound familiar?

16.7 SENDING DIRECT MARKETING ON BEHALF OF SOMEONE ELSE

There are many businesses in South Africa that send direct marketing on behalf of other organisations. These services can be described as lead generation outsourcing. They are not just operators conducting direct marketing on behalf of a responsible party; they also help marketers by doing a combination of:

- **Data enrichment or appending:** Lead generators will use a combination of public records, scraping the internet, acquired 'lists', credit bureau information etc. to compile their own database which they then use to enrich their clients' data.
- **Profiling and pre-vetting:** POPIA refers to profiling in the context of 'automated decision-making' and describes it as 'the automated processing of personal information intended to provide a profile of such person including his or her performance at work, or his, her or its credit worthiness, reliability, location, health, personal preferences or conduct'.[102] Lead generators will use profiling techniques to select the most appropriate leads for their customers. This is discussed in detail in chapter 15 paragraph 15.2.
- **Affiliate marketing:** Affiliate marketers typically earn a commission for marketing another organisation's products or services. Affiliate marketers may or may not use direct marketing as a method of generating leads.
- **Data brokering:** Some lead generators will sell or rent lists to their customers. This is discussed in chapter 13 paragraph 13.6.1.
- **Sales prospecting:** Lead generators often prospect on behalf of their customers by communicating with data subjects to gauge their interest in particular products or 'deals'. This can be done through a variety of direct marketing channels such as cold-calling, SMS, or email. Once a lead has been 'warmed up' (i.e. the lead has expressed an interest in the product or service), the personal information of that lead is shared with the client.

> **Key point:** Where lead generators are sending direct marketing on behalf of a third party, section 69(4)*(a)* requires that the communication must contain 'details of the identity of the sender *or* the person on whose behalf the communication has been sent'.

[102] See section 71. This is very similar to the definition of profiling in article 4(4) of the EU GDPR. The general position is that profiling may not be used to make automated decisions about a data subject 'which results in legal consequences for him, her or it', unless appropriate measures are in place to protect the data subject's legitimate interests.

None of these services are prohibited in terms of POPIA, but they will be impacted. How they will be impacted will depend a lot on the context and exact combination of services a lead generator provides. It seems that lead generators may be responsible parties in their own right and will have to navigate section 11 (or section 69, if they are sending electronic direct marketing on behalf of responsible parties), section 12 and section 18 for parts of their services. In addition, their client (the party whose products or services are being marketed) will need to comply with POPIA and will look to the lead generator to confirm that their end of the lead generation process is compliant. We discussed some of these aspects in the case study on data brokers in chapter 13 paragraph 13.6.1.

16.8 WHAT ABOUT OTHER LEGISLATION THAT APPLIES TO DIRECT MARKETING

Since well before POPIA, direct marketing in South Africa has been regulated by several different pieces of legislation such as the Consumer Protection Act[103] (CPA), the Electronic Communications and Transactions Act[104] (ECTA), the General Code of Conduct for Authorised Financial Services Providers and Representatives[105] and the National Credit Act (NCA).[106] While POPIA repeals sections 45, 50 and 51 of ECTA[107] and section 68(2) of the NCA,[108] the remainder of these pieces of legislation have not been repealed by POPIA.[109] In terms of section 3(2) of POPIA, this means that in any given scenario, whichever legislation has conditions that are 'more extensive' will be the law that will prevail.[110]

While these different pieces of legislation have regulated direct marketing via specific channels (e.g. electronic communications) or in specific sectors (e.g. the credit industry), POPIA is now the umbrella legislation that applies to all direct

103 68 of 2008.

104 25 of 2002.

105 General Code of Conduct for Authorised Financial Services Providers and Representatives, 2002.

106 34 of 2005.

107 Section 45 dealt with 'unsolicited goods, services or communications'. It provided that the consumer must always have the right to cancel their subscription to a mailing list and has a right to the 'identifying particulars' of the source of the consumer's personal information. Sections 50 and 51 dealt with the 'scope of protection of personal information' and 'principles for electronically collecting personal information'. This means that for purposes of direct marketing, ECTA is no longer relevant.

108 Parts of the NCA will now be subject to POPIA's compliance procedures. They are section 68 (the right to confidential treatment), parts of section 70 (credit bureau information) and parts of section 72 (right to access and challenge credit records and information). Sections 74 to 77, which deal with credit marketing practices, are still in force.

109 See section 110 and the Schedule to POPIA.

110 Section 3(2)*(a)* of POPIA. The interpretation of POPIA in cases where other legislation also applies was discussed in chapter 2.

marketing irrespective of which channel it is done via or which sector it is done in. This means that responsible parties will have to navigate multiple pieces of legislation to divine the rules. If you think this seems complicated, then you would be right.

We have (rather arbitrarily) elected to discuss the CPA, NCA and the General Code of Conduct for Authorised Financial Services Providers and Representatives. The following questions will help you identify which of these pieces of legislation apply:

Question	Laws that apply
Is the data subject also a 'consumer' as defined by the Consumer Protection Act?[111]	POPIA and the CPA
Is the data subject also defined as a consumer in terms of the National Credit Act?[112]	POPIA, the NCA and (possibly) the CPA[113]
Is the responsible party governed by the General Code of Conduct for Authorised Financial Services Providers and Representatives? [114]	POPIA and the General Code of Conduct for Authorised Financial Services Providers and Representatives[115]

111 See the definition of 'consumer' in section 1 of the CPA. The definition is like a Russian nesting doll. To understand the definition of 'consumer' you must understand the definition of 'goods', 'services', 'service provider' and 'supplier'. To understand the definitions of 'service provider' and 'supplier' you must understand the definition of 'promote', 'supply' and 'market'. Lawyers, urgh. For some support see De Stadler & Du Plessis 'Section 5' in *Commentary on the Consumer Protection Act.*

112 See section 1 of the NCA.

113 Section 5(2)*(d)* of the CPA states that the CPA does not apply to 'any transaction which constitutes a credit agreement under the National Credit Act'. This exception does not appear to include the promotion of the credit service offering itself. Sections 74 to 77 of the NCA regulate marketing practices for credit providers, and overlap with the CPA's requirements for fair and responsible marketing. Section 2(9) of the CPA provides that in situations where the NCA and the CPA both apply, they must apply concurrently. In the event that the NCA and CPA are contradictory, the legislation which provides greater protection to consumers must apply. The NCA and CPA are largely complementary in relation to marketing, so these two pieces of legislation will apply concurrently. Credit providers must therefore comply with both the NCA's and the CPA's (and POPIA's) rules on direct marketing. The specific direct marketing rules for credit providers under the NCA are dealt with in more detail at paragraph 16.8.2. See De Stadler & Du Plessis 'Section 5' in *Commentary on the Consumer Protection Act* at 5-35.

114 Since the enactment of the Financial Services Laws General Amendment Act of 2013, the financial services sector (what we refer to as banks, insurers, pension funds, collective investment schemes etc. collectively) has been completely exempt from the CPA's direct marketing rules. See De Stadler & Du Plessis 'Section 5' in *Commentary on the Consumer Protection Act* at 5-11.

115 The financial services industry was exempted from the CPA.

Key point: The legislature has elected to create an extremely complex web of legislation. At first glance, the provisions in some of these laws and POPIA appear to be at odds with each other; for instance, the CPA is an opt-out regime while POPIA is a hybrid regime. Remember that in any given scenario, the legislation that is 'more extensive' will prevail.[116]

16.8.1 The Consumer Protection Act

Key point: The CPA will still apply to all direct marketing that is sent to 'consumers' as defined in that legislation. This means that it will apply concurrently with POPIA.

Under the CPA, these are the rules in relation to direct marketing:

- Direct marketing can only be done at certain times and on certain days as prescribed by the Minister.[117]
- A consumer has the right to a cooling-off period in relation to a transaction which resulted from direct marketing.[118]
- The consumer has the right to restrict unwanted direct marketing by demanding, during or within a reasonable time after the direct marketing communication, that the responsible party desist from initiating any further communication.[119] I.e. the consumer has the right to 'opt out' or unsubscribe from the direct marketing. No fee may be charged for this.[120]

---

116 Section 3(2)*(a)* of POPIA. The interpretation of POPIA in cases where other legislation also applies was discussed in chapter 2 paragraph 2.7.

117 Section 12 of the CPA. Regulation 1(2) 'Notice' of the Consumer Protection Act Regulations, 2011 states: 'For purposes of section 12(2) of the Act, the following are days, dates, public holidays or times of days when a supplier may not engage in any direct marketing directed to a consumer at home: *(a)* Sundays or public holidays contemplated in the Public Holidays Act, 1994 (Act No. 36 of 1994); *(b)* Saturdays before 09h00 and after 13h00; and *(c)* all other days between the hours of 20h00 and 08h00 the following day.'

118 Section 16 of the CPA.

119 Section 11(2) of the CPA.

120 Section 11(5) of the CPA.

Key point: The CPA established an opt-out regime. POPIA establishes an opt-in regime for direct marketing sent via electronic communications to data subjects who are not customers. This means that direct marketing to 'consumers' via telephone and other 'non-electronic' channels (see paragraph 16.3), will still be subject to the CPA's opt-out regime. A close examination of the SA Law Reform Commission Project 124 on Privacy and Data Protection 2009 Report, reveals that it was a calculated decision based on a strategy of the Department of Trade and Industry to promote call centres within South Africa and to offer incentives to attract call centre business to South Africa[121] and on the role of telemarketing in ensuring that vulnerable consumers have access to goods and services.[122]

- In the case of an approach other than in person, the consumer has the right to restrict unwanted direct marketing by pre-emptively blocking any approach or communication, if the approach or communication is primarily for the purpose of direct marketing.[123] No fee may be charged for this.[124]

121 SA Law Reform Commission Project 124 on Privacy and Data Protection (2009 Report) 357. Be sure to read footnote 102; it is very interesting.

122 SA Law Reform Commission Project 124 on Privacy and Data Protection (2009 Report) 360.

123 Sections 11(1), 11(2) and 11(3) of the CPA.

124 Section 11(5) of the CPA.

Tricky area: Section 11(3) of the CPA gave the National Consumer Commission (NCC) the power to 'establish, or recognise as authoritative, a registry in which any person may register a pre-emptive block, either generally or for specific purposes, against any communication that is primarily for the purpose of direct marketing'. The Direct Marketing Association of South Africa has a national opt-out database, but it has never been recognised as authoritative. If we assume that at some point the NCC is either going to establish or recognise a national opt-out registry, the question becomes how it will co-exist with section 69 of POPIA? It was after all the explicit intention that the principles in POPIA would 'operate alongside the Consumer Protection Bill provisions that provide for a statutory register which will provide additional protection to the consumers (data subjects) against unreasonable direct marketing practices'.[125] Perhaps the recognition of a national opt-out registry will mean that responsible parties will not be able to ask data subjects for consent to send direct marketing in terms of section 69(1)*(a)* if they are 'consumers' in terms of the CPA and they have registered a pre-emptive block. Will responsible parties be able to continue to send direct marketing to customers if the customer has registered a pre-emptive block? Probably not. Lots of perhapses and probablies here – hopefully the NCC and the Information Regulator will provide guidance.

- A responsible party must implement appropriate procedures to facilitate the receipt of unsubscribes from consumers.[126]
- A responsible party must not send any more direct marketing to consumers who have opted out of receiving direct marketing from the responsible party or to consumers who have pre-emptively blocked the responsible party.[127]

16.8.2 The National Credit Act

The NCA states that when a credit provider enters into a credit agreement with a consumer, the credit provider must provide consumers with the option to opt out of future direct marketing activities done by a variety of channels.[128] When entering into a credit agreement, a consumer must be given the opportunity to opt out of:

---

125 SA Law Reform Commission Project 124 on Privacy and Data Protection (2009 Report) 363.

126 Section 11(4*(a)* of the CPA.

127 Section 11(4)*(b)* of the CPA.

128 Section 74(6)*(b)* of the NCA.

- any telemarketing campaigns to be conducted by the credit provider or on behalf of the credit provider
- any marketing or customer list that may be sold or distributed by the credit provider other than as required by the NCA; and

Key point: Section 76(4)*(b)*(ii) provides that the distribution or sale of 'marketing or customer lists' by credit providers can take place if it is required by the NCA.[129] In all other instances, consumers must be given the opportunity to remove their names from any 'marketing or customer list' that the credit provider wants to sell or distribute. This implies that if the consumer has not opted out, credit providers are entitled to distribute or sell 'marketing or customer lists' for direct marketing purposes. POPIA also governs the selling and sharing of personal information. This was discussed in chapter 13. In order to legally sell marketing or customer lists, credit providers will have to have a legal basis for the sale in terms of POPIA. This will either be explicit, voluntary and informed consent or that the sale is in the legitimate interest of the responsible party or a third party (section 11(1)*(a)* or *(f)*.[130] If the buyer of the marketing or customer list wants to use the information for electronic direct marketing, they will need to comply with section 69 (and the rest of POPIA). We are of the view that POPIA is stricter than section 76(4)*(b)*(ii) and will therefore apply; simply providing an opt-out will not necessarily suffice.

- any mass distribution of email or SMS messages.[131]

[129] This appears consistent with section 11(1)*(c)* which states that personal information can be processed (including distribution or sale) if the 'processing complies with an obligation imposed by law'. Of course, this begs the question of what is 'required by the Act' or 'imposed by law'. Does it only apply to explicit requirements, or also implicit ones? For instance, section 3 of the NCA states that one of the purposes of the NCA is to promote a 'credit market that is accessible to all South Africans'. Could that be used to authorise the distribution of customer lists to market credit products to them?

[130] Section 11 is discussed in chapter 6.

[131] Section 74(6)*(b)*(i)-(iii) of the NCA.

Key point: Section 74(6)*(b)*(iii) of the NCA provides that the consumer has a right to opt out of mass distribution of email or SMS messages. This will apply to direct marketing messages sent via bulk email or SMS. Section 69(1) and (2) prescribes that a responsible party must have consent (opt-in) before sending electronic marketing; not an opt-out as this subsection of the NCA appears to prescribe. Given that section 69(1) and (2) is stricter than the NCA, POPIA will apply to electronic direct marketing.[132] Similarly, section 69(3) contains more requirements than section 74(6)*(b)*(iii) when it comes to sending electronic direct marketing to customers.

Lastly, the credit provider must also maintain a register of the consumer's choices and must not act contrary to the consumer's choice.[133]

16.8.3 The General Code of Conduct for Authorised Financial Service Providers and Representatives

The General Code of Conduct for Authorised Financial Services Providers and Representatives (Code) sets out the rules for direct marketing and advertising for financial service providers and their representatives. The Code was amended in 2020.[134] These amendments to the Code amended the definitions of advertising and direct marketing, and creates an opt-out system for 'unwanted direct advertising'.[135]

The Code defines 'direct marketing' as 'the rendering of financial services by way of telephone, internet, digital application platform, media insert, direct or electronic mail but excludes the publication of an advertisement'.[136]

This means that the definition of 'advertisement' is very important. The Code defines an 'advertisement' in relation to a provider as 'any written, printed, electronic or oral communication ... which is directed to ... any client on request, by any such person, which is intended merely to call attention to the marketing or promotion of financial

132 Conflicts between POPIA and other legislation were discussed in chapter 2 paragraph 2.6.7.

133 Section 74(7) of the NCA.

134 By GN 706 in *GG* 43474 of 26 June 2020, available at https://www.gov.za/sites/default/files/gcis_document/202006/43474gon706.pdf.

135 Section 14(9) of the amended General Code of Conduct for Authorised Financial Services Providers and Representatives.

136 Section 14(9) of the amended General Code of Conduct for Authorised Financial Services Providers and Representatives.

services offered by such person, and which does not purport to provide detailed information regarding any such financial services …'.[137] Never mind, TL;DR.[138] The definition is meant to distinguish direct marketing from advertisements aimed at the public, but which do not provide detailed information to a specific client regarding a specific financial service.

Tricky area: Is this definition of direct marketing consistent with POPIA's definition of direct marketing? According to the Code, you have to be rendering a financial service (e.g. furnishing advice).[139] The definition in POPIA is a great deal wider. It includes communications with the indirect purpose of promoting a financial product. Hold this thought.

The Code creates an opt-out system from 'unwanted direct advertising'.[140] It provides the following:

- Where a provider or any person acting on its behalf uses a telephone or mobile phone call, voice or text message or other electronic communication for an advertisement, it must allow the client during that call or within a reasonable time after receiving the message, the opportunity to demand that the provider or other person does not publish any further advertisements to the client through any of these mediums.
- A provider or any person acting on its behalf may not charge a client a fee or allow a service supplier to charge a client a fee for unsubscribing.[141]

---

137 The definition of 'advertisement' in section 1(1) of the amended General Code of Conduct for Authorised Financial Service Providers and Representatives.

138 Too Long; Didn't Read.

139 See the definition of 'financial services' in the Financial Advisory and Intermediary Services Act 37 of 2002. This leads you to the definition of 'financial service provider' which is defined as 'any person, other than a representative, who as a regular feature of the business of such person *(a)* furnishes advice; or *(b)* furnishes advice and renders any intermediary service; or *(c)* renders an intermediary service'. Now we should discuss the definition of 'intermediary service', but we do not want to. Another Russian nesting doll of an Act. Lawyers, urgh.

140 The description of 'direct advertising' is similar to 'direct marketing by means of electronic communications' in POPIA, but 'direct advertising' also includes telemarketing, which falls outside the ambit of 'electronic communication' in POPIA.

141 Section 14(9) of the amended General Code of Conduct for Authorised Financial Service Providers and Representatives.

Key point: Remember that in any given scenario, the legislation that is 'more extensive' will prevail.[142] This means that POPIA will apply in respect of electronic direct marketing. The Code's provisions will apply to telemarketing, but only to the extent that the financial service provider is 'furnishing advice'. If the marketing in question does not meet the more restricted definition of the Code, section 11(3)*(b)* will give the data subject the right to object to direct marketing (POPIA's version) via telephone in any event.

16.9 PRACTICAL ADVICE

16.9.1 Responsible parties must classify the messages they send and record the legal basis

Responsible parties should classify the messages they send, to ensure that they do not ask for consent or allow for unsubscribes when they do not need to. This was discussed in paragraph 16.2.

Once the responsible party has created the different classifications, they should record the legal basis they are relying on for each class of message. Responsible parties should take care to identify all direct marketing regulations to which they are subject when doing this exercise.

Here is an example:[143]

Type of message (and channel)	Legal basis	Can the data subject unsubscribe?
Invoices and statements (via email and mail).	Section 11(2)*(b)*: Sending invoices and statements are necessary for the performance of our services contract with the data subject.	No[144]

[142] Section 3(2)*(a)* of POPIA. The interpretation of POPIA in cases where other legislation also applies was discussed in chapter 2.

[143] This table is also a summary of POPIA's requirements when it comes to direct marketing. For purposes of this example we have assumed that only POPIA applies to this responsible party. The application of the CPA would not have made a material difference to the answers.

[144] Data subjects do not have a right to object when the responsible party can rely on section 11(1)*(b)* (conclusion or performance of a contract) or section 11(1)(c) (obligation imposed by law).

Type of message (and channel)	Legal basis	Can the data subject unsubscribe?
Service messages and instructions about how to access or use our services (via email, mail and SMS).	Section 11(2)*(b)*: Sending service messages and instructions about how to access or use our services are necessary for the performance of our services contract with the data subject.	No[145]
Messages relating to our loyalty programme to loyalty programme members (via email and SMS).	Section 11(2)*(b)*: Sending messages to loyalty members that enable them to take advantage of loyalty membership are necessary for the performance of our loyalty programme contract with the data subject.	No[146]
Messages marketing our loyalty programme to customers who are not loyalty programme members (via telephone call).	Section 11(2)*(f)*: It is in our legitimate interest to market our loyalty programme to our customers via telephone.[147]	Yes[148]
Messages marketing our loyalty programme to customers who are not loyalty programme members (via email and SMS).	Section 69(1)*(b)*: The data subject is already our customer and we have complied with section 69(3)*(a)* to *(c)*.	Yes[149]
Messages marketing new services to existing customers (via telephone).	Section 11(2)*(f)*: It is in our legitimate interest to market new services to our customers via telephone.[150]	Yes[151]

➡

[145] Data subjects do not have a right to object when the responsible party can rely on section 11(1)*(b)* (conclusion or performance of a contract) or section 11(1)*(c)* (obligation imposed by law).

[146] Data subjects do not have a right to object when the responsible party can rely on section 11(1)*(b)* (conclusion or performance of a contract) or section 11(1)*(c)* (obligation imposed by law).

[147] Ensure that the organisation has actually performed a legitimate interest assessment. This is discussed in chapter 6 paragraph 6.3.5 and chapter 2 paragraph 2.6.3.

[148] Data subjects have the right to object to non-electronic direct marketing in terms of section 11(3)*(b)*.

[149] Section 69(4)*(b)*.

[150] Ensure that the organisation has actually performed a legitimate interest assessment. This is discussed in chapter 6, paragraph 6.3.5 and chapter 2 paragraph 2.6.3.

[151] Section 11(3)*(b)*.

Type of message (and channel)	Legal basis	Can the data subject unsubscribe?
Messages marketing new services to existing customers that are similar to the services they have already signed up for (via email and SMS).	Section 69(1)*(b)*: The data subject is already our customer and we have complied with section 69(3)*(a)* to *(c)*.	Yes[152]
Messages marketing our services to data subjects (leads) who are not customers (telephone).	Section 11(2)*(f)*: It is in our legitimate interest to market new services to leads via telephone.[153]	Yes[154]
Messages marketing our services to data subjects (leads) who are not customers (via email and SMS).	Section 69(1)*(a)*: We ask for consent before we send marketing to leads via email and SMS.	Yes[155]
Messages marketing services to existing customers that are not similar to the services they have already signed up for (via telephone).	Section 11(2)*(f)*: It is in our legitimate interest to market our other (dissimilar) services to customers via telephone.[156]	Yes[157]
Messages marketing services to existing customers that are not similar to the services they have already signed up for (via email and SMS).	Section 69(1)*(a)*: We ask for consent before we send marketing about other (dissimilar) services to customers via email and SMS.	Yes[158]

➡

152 Section 69(4)*(b)*.

153 Ensure that the organisation has actually performed a legitimate interest assessment. This is discussed in chapter 6 paragraph 6.3.5 and chapter 2 paragraph 2.6.3.

154 Section 11(3)*(b)*.

155 Section 69(4)*(b)*.

156 Ensure that the organisation has actually performed a legitimate interest assessment. This is discussed in chapter 6 paragraph 6.3.5 and chapter 2 paragraph 2.6.3.

157 Data subjects have the right to object to non-electronic direct marketing in terms of section 11(3)*(b)*.

158 Section 69(4)*(b)*.

Type of message (and channel)	Legal basis	Can the data subject unsubscribe?
Messages marketing the services of other responsible parties, regardless of whether the data subject is an existing customer or not.	Section 69(1)*(a)*: We ask for consent on behalf of other responsible parties before we send their marketing to our customers or leads via email and SMS.	Yes[159]

This should be incorporated in a policy document or formally documented somewhere else.

16.9.2 Create template wording for direct marketing consents, unsubscribe messages and forms

Responsible parties should create templates or guidelines for:

- Direct marketing consents: They must comply with Form 4. These requirements were discussed in paragraph 16.4.2.
- Unsubscribes: There are no specific requirements for the wording, apart from the fact that the process must be easy to follow. This was discussed in paragraph 16.6.
- Application or order forms and privacy notices: Responsible parties must ensure that their application or order forms comply with section 69(3). This will ensure that the responsible party can rely on section 69(3) for future marketing of similar products.

16.9.3 What to do with your pre-POPIA database: A risk-based approach

Some of the bloodiest POPIA battles we have ever witnessed were between marketers and legal advisers. It is usually about their pre-POPIA database, and whether they need to be asked for an opt-in consent. The legal advisers want to go full Form 4, and the marketers know that they will lose most of their direct marketing database. There are good people on both sides.

So, what to do if you have a marketing database, but you are not sure whether you complied with section 69(3) all the time, or you can't prove that you did? We are a fan of a risk-based approach. We suggest an exercise where we consider the following questions:

---

159 Section 69(4)*(b)*.

- When last did you market to the database? Will they be surprised to hear from you? Worse yet, will they think 'Who is this?' or 'Where did they get my information?' A surprised data subject is one who is more likely to complain to the Information Regulator. But, if your database is used to hearing from you, the risk is lower.
- How many unsubscribes do you get? If people like receiving your marketing, they also are unlikely to complain. If, however, you have high unsubscribe rates on your database, you might already be annoying them.
- Do you have a fool-proof unsubscribe process (and have you tested it)? If a data subject doesn't want to hear from you, they will probably just unsubscribe. If they unsubscribe, but you do not process it and they hear from you again they will complain to the Information Regulator.
- How well is your database performing? What is your return on investment? How are those open-rates? How essential is direct marketing to your bottom line compared to other forms of marketing? No risk analysis is complete without knowing this. If you are not making money out of your direct marketing, why risk getting into trouble?

If your return on your direct marketing is great and your customers are loyal, maybe you can afford to take the risk. Give your legal adviser a biscuit or something though; they will find this hard to handle.

16.9.4 Audit unsubscribe processes

Responsible parties must ensure that their unsubscribe process works as it should. Nothing will irritate someone who is already irritated more than continuing to receive the messages that irritated them. Remember, do not be a roach motel!

17

Records management

17.1 WHAT TO EXPECT IN THIS CHAPTER

Our favourite author on records management is Marie Kondo.[1] Here are just three quotes that we believe are relevant for any discussion on records management:

> 'But when we really delve into the reasons for why we can't let something go, there are only two: an attachment to the past or a fear for the future.'

1 Yes, thát Marie Kondo.

and ...

> 'Visible mess helps distract us from the true source of the disorder.'

and finally ...

> 'Storage experts are hoarders.'[2]

When the SA Law Reform Commission reviewed the Protection of Personal Information Bill, it said: 'The most effective means of protecting a person's privacy rights is, furthermore, to limit access to the person's information. If the information is destroyed or permanently de-identified, the information self-evidently cannot be accessed or misused. Information should, therefore, not be kept longer than is necessary for the purpose for which it is processed.'[3]

One of the most common questions we get is 'How long can we keep information for?', followed by 'Can a data subject force us to delete their personal information?' That is what this chapter is about.

The wording of section 14(1), (3) and (4) of POPIA closely follows the wording of the Commonwealth Model Bill on the Protection of Personal Information and the Model Bill on Privacy.[4] The concept that personal information can be retained for historical, statistical and research purposes was recognised in article 6 of the Data Protection Directive of the EU and was retained and expanded on in the storage limitation principle of the EU GDPR.[5] POPIA closely follows the wording of article 18 of the EU GDPR in section 14(6), (7) and (8). This means that we can learn from how these provisions are interpreted in the EU.[6]

---

2 See '17 Marie Kondo quotes that will help you organise and get control of your life and work', available at https://www.inc.com/peter-economy/17-marie-kondo-quotes-that-will-help-you-organize-get-control-of-your-life-work.html.

3 SA Law Reform Commission Project 124 on Privacy and Data Protection (2009 Report) 203–204.

4 Available at https://thecommonwealth.org/sites/default/files/key_reform_pdfs/P15370_6_ROL_Model_Bill_Protection_Personal_Information_2.pdf.

5 Article 5(1)*(e)*.

6 We realise we didn't mention section 14(5) in this paragraph. Section 14(5) was adopted.

Key point: Records management is just as much about keeping personal information as it is about getting rid of it. When POPIA was being drafted there were concerns that 'over zealous application of [the storage limitation] principle might lead to premature destruction of records which may in fact turn out to be useful to the responsible party and able to be used both lawfully and in accordance with the information privacy principles'.[7] So, proceed with caution. We have found that the best way to do this, is to study the related discipline of 'records management'. Good records management ensures that a responsible party maintains records that:

- are transparent, consistent, and accountable
- meet legal, regulatory, fiscal, operational, and historical requirements
- support the efficient conduct of its business; and
- ensure the preservation of archives documenting its history and development.

As we discuss in chapter 20 paragraph 20.2.5, a records management policy applies to all types of information, not just personal information. However, in this chapter we focus on those records-management rules created by POPIA for personal information.

Now, let's get on with it.

In this chapter we discuss the following:

- What is a record?
- Destruction or de-identification of records
- Restriction of processing

17.2 WHAT IS A RECORD?

Section 14 deals with the retention, restriction, and destruction of records. POPIA defines a 'record' in section 1. Here is an abbreviated version: 'Any recorded information, regardless of form or medium, in the possession or under the control of the responsible party, whether or not it was created by a responsible party, and regardless of when it came into existence'. While this is undoubtedly an important definition, it is not appropriate in the context of

7 SA Law Reform Commission Project 124 on Privacy and Data Protection (2009 Report) 198.

records management.[8] We define a record as information created, received and maintained by an organisation as evidence of actions or decisions, to meet legal, regulatory, fiscal, operational and historical requirements.[9]

The definition of a record specifically includes the personal information that the responsible party creates. This means that a responsible party must consider how long they may retain personal information that was, for example, generated during profiling activities. Just because the responsible party created something, does not mean it belongs to them and they can keep it forever.

17.3 WHEN CAN RECORDS BE RETAINED?

Section 14 provides that a responsible party can retain a record of personal information for as long as they need it to achieve the purpose for which the information was collected or subsequently processed. Again, the importance of documenting processing activities is highlighted.[10] If the responsible party did not document the purpose for which personal information was collected, and any purposes for further processing, they will struggle to determine when the personal information is no longer required for those purposes.

Key point: Responsible parties must take care not to destroy records prematurely. For instance, a responsible party must not destroy personal information to prevent a data subject from exercising their rights.[11]

---

[8] The definition of 'record' in section 1 of POPIA is used to determine the application of POPIA in section 3. The application of POPIA is discussed in chapter 3.

[9] We borrowed heavily from ISO 15489 which is the standard for Records Management Systems.

[10] We discuss this in chapter 1 paragraph 1.4.

[11] SA Law Reform Commission Project 124 on Privacy and Data Protection (2009 Report) 198. The Danish Data Protection Authority proposed a fine against a Danish recruitment company because the company erased personal information of a data subject during the period after a request for access was submitted and prior to the company answering the request. See the story at https://edpb.europa.eu/news/national-news/2020/fine-proposed-danish-recruitment-company_en. The SA Law Reform Commission lists other instances where premature destruction can actually infringe on a data subject's privacy and autonomy such as destruction of the sole repository of a person's origins (e.g. 'information about a birth parent in an adoption context or about donor gametes in relation to offspring born through assisted human reproduction'); or information on which a judicial or administrative decision was based to prevent a review of that decision (e.g. 'information which would have indicated unlawful discrimination in an employment decision'). The European Data Protection Board has also pointed out that 'measures and safeguards that implement the principle of storage limitation shall complement the rights and freedoms of the data subjects, specifically, the right to erasure and the right to object'. See European Data Protection Board *Guidelines 4/2019 on Article 25 Data Protection by Design and by Default*, available at https://edpb.europa.eu/our-work-tools/our-documents/guidelines/guidelines-42019-article-25-data-protection-design-and_en.

Once the purpose no longer requires the retention of the record, POPIA provides that the record may be retained if:

- it is required by a law
- the responsible party requires the record for lawful purposes related to their functions or activities
- retention is required by a contract
- the data subject consented that the responsible party can retain their record; or[12]
- the responsible party is keeping the record for historical, statistical or research purposes as long as the responsible party ensures that the record is not used for any other purpose.[13]

If the responsible party made a decision about a data subject based on a certain record, section 14(3) provides that that record must be retained for the period prescribed by law or a code of conduct.[14] Maintaining a record of decisions becomes important in cases of automated decisions where the data subject has a right to make representations about the decision. This is discussed in chapter 15 paragraph 15.3.1. However, section 14(3) applies to all decisions, not just automated decisions.

We discuss these justifications for retention in more detail below.

17.3.1 Required or authorised by law

All organisations will have some records that they must retain because legislation requires it. Some of the common examples applicable to most organisations are as follows:

Legislation	What records must be retained?	For how long must the records be retained?
Companies Act 71 of 2008	Every company must maintain (amongst others): • a copy of its Memorandum of Incorporation and any amendments thereto • copies of annual financial statements; and • securities register.	For the life of the company and seven years after that.

➡

[12] Section 14(1).

[13] Section 14(2).

[14] Section 14(3). We discuss codes of conduct in chapter 19 paragraph 19.5.

Legislation	What records must be retained?	For how long must the records be retained?
Basic Conditions of Employment Act 75 of 1997	Employers must maintain a register or record of earnings and other prescribed particulars of all employees.	For three years from the date of last entry in the record.
Employment Equity Act 55 of 1998	Employers must maintain a copy of their employment equity plan.	For the life of the plan and five years thereafter.

Responsible parties should record these legislated retention periods in their records retention schedule.[15] Of course, this presupposes that an organisation is aware of all of the laws and regulations that apply to it. Compliance specialists refer to the exercise of establishing regulatory compliance obligations as compiling a regulatory universe. Compiling a regulatory universe can be equal parts boring and terrifying. It is boring when it just confirms what you already knew and terrifying when you find out POPIA is not the piece of legislation you should be most worried about. We discussed the relationship between compliance management maturity and POPIA compliance in chapter 1 paragraph 1.2.2. Records retention is one of the areas of POPIA compliance that will be difficult for organisations with low compliance management maturity as they often will not have a clear idea of what records retention requirements apply to them.

Key point: Organisations should take care that they don't over-comply with legal and regulatory requirements for record keeping. For example, organisations often retain more personal information than the legislation requires or retain the personal information for longer than is necessary. This would infringe the principle of minimality.[16]

Once the legal and regulatory requirements for retaining a record of personal information expire, the organisation must destroy the record, unless it can rely on one of the other justifications in section 14(1) to (3) (discussed below) to keep the record.

---

15 We discuss compiling a records retention schedule in paragraph 17.5.1.

16 The principle is discussed in chapter 9.

17.3.2 Lawful purposes related to the responsible party's functions or activities

This exception gives the responsible party the right to keep personal information even after the purpose for collection or further processing has expired, but the responsible party needs the information for another lawful purpose related to its business. Keeping information 'just in case' won't cut it; the responsible party has to document the purpose.

Here are some examples of lawful purposes related to an organisation's functions or activities:[17]

- A bank may need to retain CCTV footage from a camera installed at an ATM for several weeks, since a suspicious transaction may only be discovered when the victim receives their bank statement. In contrast, a nightclub may only need CCTV footage for a short period because incidents will come to light very quickly. However, the nightclub may need to retain footage if a crime was reported to the police, at least until the police collect the footage.
- A business receives a request from a former customer to unsubscribe them from the business's newsletter. The business should keep enough information of the requester to ensure that they do not send any newsletters to that customer in future.
- Organisations should keep information that they might need to defend themselves in possible future legal claims. The Prescription Act[18] should be considered here.
- A retailer retains a record for purposes of honouring a warranty.
- Financial institutions may need to retain fraud information for an indefinite period.[19]

The responsible party must document the business reasons for retaining personal information in their records retention schedule.[20] It is not acceptable to keep information on the basis that it might possibly be useful in future without a view of how it will be used.[21]

Here is an example of what not to do. The French Data Protection Authority (CNIL) fined a retailer because they defined an excessive retention period for personal information of their customers who

Chapter 17

17 ICO 'Principle (e): Storage limitation', available at https://ico.org.uk/for-organisations/guide-to-data-protection/guide-to-the-general-data-protection-regulation-gdpr/principles/storage-limitation/.

18 Act 68 of 1969.

19 SA Law Reform Commission Project 124 on Privacy and Data Protection (2009 Report) 199.

20 We discuss compiling a records retention schedule in paragraph 17.6.1.

21 SA Law Reform Commission Project 124 on Privacy and Data Protection (2009 Report) 200.

are members of their loyalty programme. CNIL found that retaining information for four years after the last activity was excessive and that it should not have been kept for more than three years. CNIL also found that the retailer kept information for longer than their defined retention period. Lastly, the retailer asked for copies of customers' ID documents when data subjects exercised their data protection rights (e.g. right to access, correction and deletion). The copies of ID documents were stored for up to six years. CNIL found that as soon as a requester's identity is confirmed, the retailer no longer needs the copy of the ID document. The retailer should only have archived a copy of their response to the data subject for evidentiary purposes.[22] This finding should make any organisation that retains copies of IDs for compliance with FICA, RICA or any other security requirements nervous. Even though verifying the data subject's identity might be required, retaining a copy of the ID might breach section 14 as well as the principle of minimality. [23] For a further discussion of our pet hate of retaining copies of IDs for no good reason, see chapter 18 paragraph 18.2.5.

Key point: A responsible party must define the retention periods for information stored for business reasons in their records retention schedule AND then implement a process to delete the information once the retention period has expired. It is going to be vital that the responsible party has a concrete reason for the retention period. 'Just in case' just won't do!

17.3.3 Retention is required by a contract

Personal information may also be retained if it is 'required by a contract between the parties thereto'.[24] An example of where retention is required by a contract is when an attorney or a bank agrees to store their client's will until their death.

---

22 See https://www.legifrance.gouv.fr/cnil/id/CNILTEXT000042563756. Here is an English article about the decision: https://www.huntonprivacyblog.com/2020/12/01/cnil-fines-two-companies-of-the-carrefour-group-e3-05-million-for-gdpr-and-cookie-violations/.

23 The principle is discussed in chapter 9. Compliance with FICA or RICA will make the retention of *some* records justifiable under section 14(1)*(a)* (discussed in paragraph 17.3.1), but organisations must ensure that they don't over-comply. Always ask whether there is a way of complying while retaining less personal information, for shorter periods of time.

24 Section 14(1)*(c)*.

Tricky area: If we take the wording of POPIA here on face value it would seem that a contract could determine how long a record should be retained. It is not clear whether the contract must be with the data subject whose record is being retained. To shed some light on what the lawmakers were thinking we considered a previous version of POPIA, when it was still a Bill. The previous wording read, 'unless the record is retained in terms of contractual rights or obligations of the parties'.[25] It would seem that an organisation can rely on this exception if any potential future rights or obligations could still flow from a contract and it will need the personal information to exercise those rights and fulfil those obligations.

This section also should not be interpreted in isolation. Organisations should consider the principle of minimality, i.e. to only keep those records that are genuinely necessary for protecting rights and performing obligations of the contract.[26] What this means is that it will not be enough to write the retention period into the contract, you must also be able justify why that retention period is appropriate.

17.3.4 Consent for retention

As with many of the conditions for lawful processing of personal information in POPIA, a data subject can consent to the retention of their records. We discuss the requirements for valid consent in chapter 2 paragraph 2.6.6.

Key point: Consent cannot be hidden in contract terms. The Court of Justice of the European Union found that a clause in a contract stating that a customer has consented to the collection and storage of their identity document cannot demonstrate that the customer has validly given their consent where the box referring to that clause has been ticked by the data controller (responsible party) before the contract was signed.[27]

---

25 SA Law Reform Commission Project 124 on Privacy and Data Protection (2009 Report) 196.

26 See our discussion in chapter 6 that the purpose of processing will be lawful if it is necessary to conclude or perform in terms of a contract.

27 *Orange România SA v Autoritatea Nationala de Supraveghere a Prelucrarii* (Judgment in Case C-61/19), available at https://curia.europa.eu/jcms/upload/docs/application/pdf/2020-11/cp200137en.pdf.

Consent should be the last resort.[28] Only after all other justifications for keeping personal information have expired should the responsible party rely on consent and that consent has to be voluntary. If the data subject withdraws their consent, the responsible party must delete the data subject's personal information, including any personal information being processed by operators on the responsible party's behalf.

Tricky area: Section 11(3)*(b)* states that a data subject may withdraw consent provided in terms of section 11(1)*(a)* at any time. The right to withdraw consent is not mentioned in section 14(1)*(d)*. However, we believe that data subjects also have the right to withdraw these other consents due to the requirement that consent must be voluntary.[29] Can the responsible party refuse to continue to process the data subject's personal information, because they withhold consent to retain that information? Under the EU GDPR data subjects must be free to withdraw consent without undue effort and without any detrimental effects such as an increase in cost, a cessation of services or a decrease in service levels.[30]

17.3.5 Retention for historical, statistical or research purposes

A responsible party may retain records of personal information for historical, statistical or research purposes, even after the purpose for collection or use has expired, and none of the exceptions we discuss above apply. We discuss the meaning of 'historical, statistical and research purposes' in chapter 2 paragraph 2.6.7. If a responsible party keeps personal information for historical, statistical or research purposes, this must be the only purpose for retention. The responsible party must establish 'appropriate safeguards' against the records being used for any other purpose.[31]

This section in POPIA is very similar to the section on storage limitation in the EU GDPR,[32] so we can look at how 'appropriate safeguards' have been interpreted in the EU. The EU GDPR has a whole section on the safeguarding and derogations relating to processing for archiving purposes in the public interest, or for scientific or

28 We explain why this is the case in chapter 2 paragraph 2.6.6.

29 Section 1 of POPIA.

30 European Data Protection Board *Guidelines 05/2020 on Consent under Regulation 2016/679* 13, available at https://edpb.europa.eu/sites/edpb/files/files/file1/edpb_guidelines_202005_consent_en.pdf.

31 Section 14(2).

32 Article 5(1)(e).

historical research purposes or statistical purposes.[33] The safeguards must include technical and organisational measures to ensure respect for the principle of data minimisation. The EU GDPR mentions measures such as pseudonymisation. Pseudonymisation is discussed in chapter 3 paragraph 3.3.2.

17.3.6 Records that relate to decisions about the data subject

If a responsible party used personal information to make a decision about the data subject, they must retain the record for the period required by law or a code of conduct.[34] If no law or code of conduct prescribes a retention period, the responsible party must retain the record for a period which will afford the data subject a reasonable opportunity to request access to the record. The responsible party must take all considerations relating to the use of the personal information into account.[35]

If a responsible party makes an automated decision based on profiling of a data subject and the decision results in legal consequences for a data subject or it affects the data subject to a substantial degree, the responsible party must also remember the requirements of section 71. We discuss automated decisions and profiling in chapter 15.

17.4 DESTRUCTION OR DE-IDENTIFICATION OF RECORDS

When all the justifications for retaining records have expired the responsible party must either destroy, delete or de-identify the records as soon as reasonably practicable.[36] De-identification is defined in POPIA and discussed in chapter 3 paragraph 3.3.2.

For a record to be considered deleted or destroyed, it must not be possible to reconstruct the record in an intelligible form.[37] Pulping or incineration may be an appropriate way to destroy paper documents,[38] but the situation is less certain with electronic storage. The delete button on a keyboard is a misnomer. It should actually have been called the 'hide' button. Digital data is not

33 Article 89.

34 We discuss codes of conduct in chapter 19 paragraph 19.5.

35 Section 14(3).

36 Section 14(4).

37 Section 14(5).

38 But what about shredding, we hear you say? For a cautionary tale about shredding (and the committed people who put the pieces together again), see Sam Wolfson 'Donald Trump and Michael Cohen are destroying their documents all wrong' *The Guardian*, available at https://www.theguardian.com/us-news/2018/jun/12/michael-cohen-donald-trump-ripped-paper-shredder.

destroyed if it is merely 'deleted', it often has to be overwritten.[39] Until personal information is actually deleted or destroyed, the requirements of POPIA will continue to apply.

> **Tricky area:** Permanently deleting or destroying information is difficult. First, we are all hoarders and programmed to think 'but what if I need it in future?' Second, deleting information is technical – it is not as easy as pressing 'delete'. Third, very few organisations control the number of copies made of information; the information is not managed centrally. So, how sure is the organisation that it has deleted every copy of the information?

Due to the complexity of destruction, some regulators in other jurisdictions have followed a practical approach, rather than a strict approach, to similar requirements in their data protection legislation. For instance, the UK ICO recognises that deleting information from a system is not always straightforward, and that data compliance may be 'suspended' where appropriate safeguards are in place. Here are some of the examples mentioned where compliance may be 'suspended' as long as safeguards are in place:[40]

- Information has been deleted with no intention on the part of the responsible party to use or access it again, but the information may still exist in the electronic ether. For instance, the information could be waiting to be over-written with other data. Because the information is no longer 'live', data protection compliance may be suspended.
- Information should have been deleted but is still held on a live system because it is not possible to delete this information without also deleting other information held in the same batch for technical reasons.

The UK ICO describes the following safeguards which essentially put the information 'beyond use':[41]

- the responsible party is not able or will not attempt to use personal information to make a decision about a data subject
- the responsible party does not give anyone else access to the personal information

---

[39] The method you use to delete files also depends on the hardware you are using. For example, older mechanical (spinning) hard drives require that new data overwrites the old data. An internal Solid State Hard drive may use a TRIM system which actually deletes the data to speed up the hard drive. To add to it, the geeks can't seem to agree on any of this. Like lawyers, they are. For a list of data wiping /erasure standards see https://www.blancco.com/resources/blog-comprehensive-list-data-wiping-erasure-standards/

[40] ICO *Guidance on Deleting Data* 4, available at https://ico.org.uk/media/for-organisations/documents/1475/deleting_personal_data.pdf.

[41] ICO *Guidance on Deleting Data* 5, available at https://ico.org.uk/media/for-organisations/documents/1475/deleting_personal_data.pdf.

- the personal information is surrounded by appropriate technical and organisational security; and
- the responsible party commits to permanently delete the information as soon as this becomes possible.

Here is a recent example of how the retention restriction has been interpreted in the context of the EU GDPR: The Berlin commissioner fined a real estate company EUR14.5 million for storing personal information of tenants without a legal basis and for not implementing the EU GDPR principle of privacy by design. The Commissioner first investigated the company in 2017 and found that the company's data archiving system did not allow the company to delete obsolete personal information. It was also found that tenants' personal information was being stored without the company checking whether the information was obtained legally or if it was necessary for any purpose. The Commissioner recommended an urgent adjustment to the company's archiving system. When the Commissioner did a follow-up inspection in 2019 the deficiencies were still present. The Commissioner took the following mitigating factors into account when they determined the fine:

- that the systems did not contain special personal information
- that the data had not been transferred to third parties
- that it could not be proven that the company used the unlawfully stored personal information; and
- that the company had been co-operative during the investigation.

The supervisory authority considered the fact that the company set up the archive structure and that the personal information was processed in a non-compliant manner for a long time as an aggravating factor.[42]

17.5 RESTRICTION OF PROCESSING

17.5.1 When processing of personal information must be restricted

In certain circumstances a responsible party must restrict the processing of personal information.[43] Processing must be restricted in the following cases:

- The accuracy of the personal information is contested by the data subject. See chapter 18 paragraph 18.4 where we discuss the data subject's right to request the correction of their personal information. Processing must be restricted until the responsible party verifies the accuracy of the personal information.

---

[42] European Data Protection Board press release 'Berlin Commissioner for Data Protection imposes fine on real estate company', available at https://edpb.europa.eu/news/national-news/2019/berlin-commissioner-data-protection-imposes-fine-real-estate-company_en.

[43] Section 14(6).

- The responsible party no longer needs the personal information for the purpose that it was collected and further processed, but the responsible party needs the information for purposes of proof. In this context proof relates to the establishment, exercise or defence of legal claims. This is sometimes referred to as a legal or litigation hold or a preservation order. This is where the normal records management process and retention periods are over-ridden due to anticipated litigation.
- The processing is unlawful and the data subject opposes its destruction or deletion and requests the restriction of the processing of personal information instead. An example of unlawful processing would be if a responsible party relies on the consent of the data subject as a legal basis for processing, but the consent wording was hidden in contract terms and therefore did not constitute valid consent for purposes of section 11.[44]
- The data subject requests that their personal information be transferred to another automated processing system. This is discussed in chapter 18 paragraph 18.9 where we discuss whether POPIA actually establishes a right to data portability.

17.5.2 What is the restriction of processing?

Restricting processing means that personal information may not be processed other than storing. This usually means that the responsible party must:

- temporarily move the information to another (inactive) processing system
- make the information unavailable to users; or
- temporarily remove published data from a website.

In principle restriction requires that personal information may not be used for any further processing purposes and that it cannot be changed. The fact that processing of the information is restricted must be clearly indicated in the system or on the record.[45]

17.5.3 Processing allowed despite a restriction

There are some exceptional circumstances where a responsible party may process the personal information despite a restriction. The responsible party may still process personal information despite a restriction if:

- the information is processed for purposes of proof

44 We discuss the requirements for valid consent in chapter 2 paragraph 2.6.6.

45 Recital 67 of the EU GDPR.

- the data subject consented to the processing[46]
- the information is processed to protect the rights of another individual or legal person;[47] or
- the processing is in the public interest.[48]

Tricky area: What is processing in the public interest? As discussed in chapter 2, there is a public interest in:

- freedom of expression
- national security
- the prevention, detection and prosecution of offences
- public health and safety
- research; and
- important economic and financial interests of a public body.

17.6 PRACTICAL ADVICE

17.6.1 Records management policy and records retention schedule

Organisations should create and maintain a records management policy supported by a records retention schedule. We discuss the content of a records management policy in chapter 20 paragraph 20.2.5. These are the items to be addressed in a records management policy:

- comply with all legal and operational record-keeping requirements and create a records retention schedule
- secure destruction
- information security (cross-reference to the information security management policy)
- effective version control
- minimise duplication by identifying and controlling master records
- manage and preserve knowledge and intellectual property
- incident management and response (may be the same process as the one in the information security management policy)
- empowered and responsible users
- clear roles and responsibilities in the implementation of the policy; and
- records management assessments.

Chapter 17

---

46 Subject to the usual stringent requirements. See chapter 2 paragraph 2.6.6.

47 We think the drafters meant 'juristic person'.

48 Section 14(7).

A records retention schedule should contain:

- a list of the categories of records that must be maintained for legal, regulatory and business requirements
- a default retention rule for each category of records
- any exceptions to the default rules for specific records within a category
- the legal, regulatory or business requirement that necessitates the retention of a category of records or a specific record
- the period for which the category of records or specific record must be retained; and
- the event that triggers the start of the period.

Tricky area: Confession time again. We are not records management specialists.[49] There are many people who are and they wrote an ISO standard for it.[50] What is to follow in this chapter are just some things we picked up along the way.

[49] As Dr McCoy from Star Trek would say: 'Damnit Jim, I'm a lawyer not a marketer!'

[50] ISO 15489.

Here is an extract from a very basic records retention schedule:

Category of information assets[51]	Description of what belongs in the category	Information asset owner[52]	Default retention period[53]	(Some examples of) Exceptions to default retention period
Employees	Information relating to: • Recruitment and selection • Induction and training • Performance and reward • Employee assistance and counselling • Employee relations • Employee contract management • Equality and diversity statistics and submissions • Remuneration and benefits • All information housed in or extracted from the HR system; and • Policy and procedure development relating to human resources.	Director of HR	Term of employment + 3 years[54]	• Day-to-day employee records which do not form part of the central and local staff files – date of document creation + 3 years. • Cancelled or spoiled employees' tax certificates – keep until the Commissioner requests surrender. • Unsuccessful applications for employment – date of refusal + 1 year • Pension fund records – conclusion of pension fund liability + 3 years.

51 Records management cannot be done on a 'document-by-document' basis. Instead, we suggest managing it per information asset. An information asset is a body of information that is organised and managed as a unit. For example: a database, a folder or physical records kept in a filing cabinet. Even if you manage records at this level, it gets complicated quickly. That is why we identify categories of information assets. What these are will differ from organisation to organisation, but usually they are: customer, finance, infrastructure and operations, governance and employees.

52 'Information asset owners' are accountable to define the appropriate uses of the information, which includes records retention rules. We discussed roles and responsibilities in chapter 1 paragraph 1.3. Management (the first line of defense) are the information asset owners.

53 It is easier to have a default rule per category and then to define exceptions to that default retention period. Note that when you define a retention period you should define the period plus a trigger for when that period starts to run (in this example the period starts to run at the end of employment).

54 It is important to preserve the reason(ing) for the retention period whether it is a piece of legislation or a operational reason.

Records management policies are difficult to implement. Here is why:[55]

- It is difficult to decide what to delete and the exercise can be filled with paradoxes. While the information officer wants to eliminate unnecessary information, other parts of the organisation may want to keep as much data as possible for analysis.
- It is almost impossible to manage access to information in a siloed environment. In master data management, this is often referred to as a 'legacy state' which is characterised by separate systems and disparate data. We discuss master data management in chapter 9 paragraph 9.6.5.
- Maintaining complete audit trails is also impossible in a siloed environment. How do you keep track of changes, edits and ownership if copies of the information are kept in multiple places?
- How do you identify the 'junk content' that can be destroyed? Many records management policies and retention schedules presuppose that 'every single piece of data must be assessed in some way in order to determine its status'. That is an incredibly daunting thought.

When we are confronted with a seemingly insurmountable task, we draw inspiration from Gandalf the Grey who once advised a stressed out records manager that '[a]ll we have to decide is what to do with the time that is given to us'.[56] We talk some more about pragmatism and implementing POPIA in chapter 20, but the techniques discussed in the next paragraph will also help.

17.6.2 Data footprint reduction

Reducing an organisation's data footprint saves on storage cost, decreases risk, facilitates compliance with data protection regulations, enhances application service delivery (e.g. making your systems faster), reduces bandwidth needs and reduces the time employees spend looking for records. The 'collection of techniques, technologies, tools and best practices that are used to address data growth management challenges' is referred to as data footprint reduction (DFR).[57] Here are examples of DFR technologies and techniques:

---

[55] Kon Leon '4 challenges to realistic records management', available at https://gcn.com/articles/2016/01/12/4-records-management-challenges.aspx.

[56] J.R.R Tolkien *The Fellowship of the Ring*.

[57] Greg Schulz 'Data Footprint Reduction', available at http://www.ittoday.info/ITPerformanceImprovement/Articles/2011-11Schulz1.html.

Technique	What is it?
Archiving	'Archiving is the process by which inactive information, in any format, is securely stored for long periods of time.'[58] It can improve an organisation's information security in that it limits access to the information.[59]
Deduplication	This is 'the process of finding and eliminating duplicate pieces of data stored in different data sets'.[60] Deduplication assists organisations to comply with the principle of minimal processing.[61]
Policy-based tiering	This is 'the process of moving data to different classes of storage based on criteria such as its age, how often it is accessed or the speed at which it must be available'.[62]
Data purging	Data purging 'is a process involving methods that permanently erase and remove data from a storage space'.[63] This is typically done to personal information that is no longer in active use or is redundant. If we ever make a (horror) movie about records management, we will call it Purge.
Storage consolidation or storage convergence	Storage consolidation is a 'method of centralising data storage among multiple servers'.[64] We discussed the functions of master data management, data storage and operations and data warehousing in chapter 1.

17.6.3 Do a spring clean

POPIA should be used as an excuse to do a spring cleaning exercise. All too often, organisations keep copies of copies of copies of information. Ask yourself, how much of the floor space of your office is filled with filing cabinets? How many of those filing cabinets are filled with copies or printouts of information you have in a digital format?

58 Secure Data Management 'What is Archiving and Why is it Important?', available at https://www.securedatamgt.com/blog/what-is-archiving/.

59 Information security management is discussed in chapter 5.

60 Robert L Scheier '5 ways to cut your storage footprint', available at https://www.infoworld.com/article/2626302/5-ways-to-cut-your-storage-footprint.html; Greg Schulz 'Data footprint reduction', available at http://www.ittoday.info/ITPerformanceImprovement/Articles/2011-11Schulz1.html.

61 Minimality is discussed in chapter 9.

62 Robert L Scheier '5 ways to cut your storage footprint', available at https://www.infoworld.com/article/2626302/5-ways-to-cut-your-storage-footprint.html.

63 Ravi Kalavendi 'Importance of Data Purging', available at https://medium.com/@RKTECHNOGEEK/importance-of-data-purging-6e9d42d8102c.

64 Techopedia 'Storage consolidation', available at https://www.techopedia.com/definition/13736/storage-consolidation.

Just getting rid of the copies will drastically reduce the organisation's 'data footprint'. Turn it into a competition to see which teams can get rid of the most copies! We dare you. After all, Marie says: 'By starting with the easy things first and leaving the hardest for last, you can gradually hone your decision-making skills, so that by the end, it seems simple.'

18

Data subject rights

18.1 WHAT TO EXPECT IN THIS CHAPTER

C-3PO once famously said to Han Solo: 'Sir, the possibility of successfully navigating a data subject request is approximately 3 720 to 1.' To which Han said: 'Never tell me the odds.'[1]

POPIA gives data subjects the right to:

- access their information
- correct or delete their information
- object to the processing of their personal information
- withdraw consent previously given; and
- not be subject to a decision based solely on automated processing of their personal information profiles.

Key point: None of these rights are absolute. As always, there is lots of room to manoeuvre. So, if you can think of instances where giving effect to these rights will not be practical, have no fear and read on. Or, be afraid. Be very afraid. Up to you.

Many organisations will struggle with data subject requests due to poor data management. For instance, it is estimated that between 80 and 90% of data is 'dark data'; this is information that is gathered or generated during regular business activities, but never makes it into a structured environment. The data is stuck in Excel spreadsheets, multiple versions of old documents, email attachments, ignored downloads, inactive databases and log files.[2] The fact that organisations do not know what information they have and often do not even have a way of searching dark data, makes it difficult to answer questions from data subjects about what personal information the organisation has about them and makes it complicated to reliably update the information. Why does this

[1] This bit of dialogue is from our imminent reboot called 'Episode V – The Information Regulator Strikes Back'.

[2] IBM 'Extracting dark data', available at https://developer.ibm.com/technologies/analytics/articles/ba-data-becomes-knowledge-3.

matter? If a data subject is interested (or irritated) enough to exercise their data subject rights, they will definitely also be interested in lodging a complaint if they feel that they are being denied those rights.

Key point: Data subject requests can be potent. A lone data subject request exposed Cambridge Analytica.[3] Cases against the likes of Google and Facebook also often start with a data subject request.

Data subject rights are a way of giving data subjects more control over their personal information. On paper, this is grand, but as we discussed in chapter 2, control is an illusion.[4] However, given that sections 23 and 24 of POPIA are not an illusion, in this chapter we discuss the following:

- Data subject request procedures
- The right to access your personal information
- The right to correct or delete personal information
- The right to withdraw consent
- The right to object to processing
- The right not to be subject to automated decision-making
- The right to object in relation to directories
- Does POPIA give data subjects the right to data portability?
- Rights that are discussed in other chapters

18.2 DATA SUBJECT REQUEST PROCEDURES

Before we discuss the different data subject rights, it is important to look at the process of responding to data subject requests. The process outlined here applies regardless of which right the data subject is trying to exercise.

3 See 'The Great Hack: How a subject access request exposed Cambridge Analytica' *Tapmydata*, available at https://tapmydata.com/the-great-hack-how-a-subject-access-request-exposed-cambridge-analytica/. Or just watch the movie. For the cases against Facebook, just get to know Max Schrems and his non-profit organisation, My Privacy is None of Your Business (www.noyb.eu). For the cases against Google, DuckDuckGo, Dr Johnny Ryan. Actually, you should Brave him, he used to work there.

4 See chapter 2 paragraphs 2.6.4 and 2.6.5.

Key point: When it comes to requests for access to information (discussed in paragraph 18.3), note that PAIA contains extensive provisions on how these requests must be handled. We have not dealt with them in full here. Read Francis Cronje and Eddie Laubscher *PAIA: What You Need to Know* (2016) and Currie and Klaaren *The Promotion of Access to Information Act Commentary* for more.

18.2.1 Identify whether it is a data subject request

We made up the phrase 'data subject request'. It is used in the context of the EU GDPR, but usually to describe requests for deletion or erasure. We use it to describe any instance where a data subject is trying to exercise one of their data subject rights.

It is very important that an organisation learns to distinguish data subject requests from other types of interactions with data subjects such as day-to-day customer service, general complaints management or other Promotion of Access to Information Act (PAIA) requests. If employees are not trained to recognise them and follow the correct channels, an organisation's response to such requests might be inconsistent or, non-compliant with POPIA, a security compromise, or, worse yet, non-existent.

18.2.2 Identify the responsible party

The data subject must exercise their rights against the responsible party. This means that the first step when receiving a data subject request is to determine who the responsible party(s) is. We discussed this in chapter 4. As the sheer length of that chapter indicates, it is hardly ever straightforward. In many cases, there will be multiple responsible parties, co-responsible parties and operators involved in processing a data subject's personal information. When this is the case, it is important to have agreements in place that create procedures and mechanisms to jointly respond to data subject requests.[5]

[5] We discuss having appropriate contracts in place in chapter 4 paragraph 4.8.

Key point: Organisations should be careful not to send the data subject from pillar to post. If an organisation is not the responsible party, the organisation should refer the data subject request to the responsible party and co-ordinate a response.[6] This is not a provision in POPIA, but it is a principle of good complaints management.

18.2.3 Determine which data protection regulation applies

For many organisations, POPIA will not be the only data protection regulation that applies to the organisation.[7] Determining what laws apply to the request is vital, because different data protection regulations have different data subject rights.

As we discussed in chapter 14 paragraph 14.3, determining when other data protection regulations apply is a complex task fraught with danger. For instance, it would have been easy if the citizenship of the data subject determined which rights they have, but that is hardly ever the case. In most instances, what data protection regulation applies will depend on where the responsible party resides, where the personal information is processed by or on behalf of the responsible party or who the responsible party is targeting. The test differs from regulation to regulation, and it will often have to be assessed on a case-by-case basis. Not very practical.

Key point: Some organisations decide to simplify matters by giving all data subjects the same rights, even if that means that some data subjects have more rights than they would otherwise have.

18.2.4 Review the request and provide assistance

The responsible party must review the data subject request and determine whether it includes sufficient information to respond to the request.

6 Unless of course the organisation has no part in the processing activity whatsoever.

7 We discuss this in chapter 14 paragraph 14.3.

Tricky area: Some organisations process only online identifiers, such as cookie identifiers or IP addresses. Without other data points such as an email address, it may be difficult to identify the data subject and even know that they have someone's personal information. Should the organisation collect additional personal information in order to make the information they have identifiable? In the EU an organisation does not have to process additional personal information to identify a data subject for the sole purpose of complying with the EU GDPR. However, if a data subject wishes to exercise their rights in terms of the EU GDPR, the organisation must use any additional information provided by the data subject to facilitate the data subject's request.[8]

Here are the forms prescribed by these Acts:

The right to	The form	Comments
Access to a record of personal information[9]	Form 2 of the PAIA regulations[10]	**Key point:** This form is not only used for data subject access requests, but for all requests for access to information in terms of PAIA. However, this chapter is limited to requests made by (or for) a data subject for access to their own personal information.

[8] Article 11(1) and (2) and recital 64 of the EU GDPR.

[9] The details relating to this right are discussed in paragraph 18.3.

[10] PAIA regulations were published on 27 August 2021. See GN 757 in *GG* 45057 of 27 August 2021.

The right to	The form	Comments
		The form requires that the data subject (or the person making the request on behalf of the data subject) must provide: • their full name • ID number • postal address • street address • email address • business telephone number • cell phone number • facsimile • description of the record or relevant part of the record • reference number • further particulars of the record • the type of record (e.g. written, electronic, video, sound) • the manner in which the data subject wants access (e.g. which address to send or fax it to) • preferred language • particulars of right to be exercised or protected • whether they qualify for an exemption from any fees that may be payable • manner of correspondence; and • signature.

The right to	The form	Comments
		Tricky area: The irony of having to provide more personal information than the responsible party had in the first place in order to exercise a data subject right is not lost on us. In some instances, the responsible party will not need all of this information in order to process the data subject's request. In such cases, collecting all of this personal information will be a breach of the principle of minimality.[11] This means that the PAIA regulations are probably not POPIA compliant. An example of how the principle of minimality could be applied here is to first ask how the data subject wants to receive the record and then to only ask enough information to honour the request. For instance, if the data subject only wants to correspond via email and wants the record to be made available via email, it is not necessary to collect all of the other addresses and contact details. This form only caters for requests for access to the record of the personal information. POPIA also provides the data subject with the right to enquire whether the responsible party has any personal information relating to the data subject. This is discussed in paragraph 18.3.2.2. There is no prescribed form to request this confirmation.

11 The principle of minimality is discussed in chapter 9.

The right to	The form	Comments
Correct or delete personal information[12]	Form 2 of the 2018 POPIA Regulations[13]	The form requires that the data subject must provide: • their full (or registered) name • a unique identifier (e.g. an ID number or registration number) • an address • contact numbers • an email address or fax number • information about the personal information that must be corrected or deleted • reasons for the correction or deletion of the personal information; and • the signature of the data subject.[14] **Tricky area:** Again, the irony.[15] The 2018 POPIA Regulations themselves are probably not POPIA compliant either. In order to only ask the necessary personal information, responsible parties should follow a two-step process where minimal information is required during step 1 and more information is only required if necessary.

[12] The details relating to this right are discussed in paragraph 18.4.

[13] As we were reading the final proofs of this edition the Information Regulator published draft amendments to Form 2 for comment (GN 45120, GoN 829). Some changes to Form 2 were proposed. For instance, the form no longer requires a unique identifier.

[14] We discussed the signature requirement in the context of Form 4 (consent for direct marketing) in chapter 16 paragraph 16.4.2. The long and short of it is that POPIA does not require that the signature must be in writing and it also does not require an advanced electronic signature.

[15] The principle of minimality is discussed in chapter 9.

The right to	The form	Comments
Withdraw consent[16]	None	If the responsible party is relying on consent from the data subject for any aspect of the processing activity, the data subject has the right to withdraw consent at any time.[17] There is no prescribed form for this.
Object to processing[18]	Form 1 of the 2018 POPIA Regulations	Despite its title, this form only applies to objections made in terms of section 11(3)*(a)*. That is, objections to processing where the responsible party is relying on legitimate interest or where the responsible party is a public body performing a public law duty.[19] It does not have to be used for objections to direct marketing.[20] Unsubscribing from direct marketing is discussed in chapter 16 paragraph 16.6.
Make representations for automated decisions[21]	None	If a data subject is being subjected to automated decisions, they have additional rights to receive information and make representations in terms of section 71(3). That is if the automated decision is justified at all. We discuss when automated decisions are allowed and these additional rights in chapter 15.

16 The details relating to this right are discussed in paragraph 18.5.

17 See chapter 2 paragraph 2.6.6 for a discussion on consent.

18 The details relating to this right are discussed in paragraph 18.6.

19 Legal justifications are discussed in chapter 6.

20 This might change. As we were reading the final proofs of this edition the Information Regulator published draft amendments to the Regulations for comment (GN 45120, GoN 829). The draft Regulations now specify that Form 1 must be used for objections to direct marketing in terms of section 11(3)(b).

21 The details relating to this right are discussed in chapter 15 paragraph 15.3.

Tricky area: What if the data subject does not use the right form? Can the responsible party refuse the data subject's request because it does not meet formal requirements? Must the responsible party provide assistance to the data subject? The rules on providing assistance to the data subject are inconsistent. PAIA provides that a data subject may make an oral request for access to information to a public body if they are illiterate or cannot make the request on the prescribed form due to a disability.[22] Interestingly, PAIA does not have similar provisions for requests to private bodies. Similarly, the information officer of a public body must assist the data subject with their request for access, whereas the information officer of a private body has no obligation to assist.[23] The 2018 POPIA Regulations provide that the forms used by the responsible party must be 'substantially similar' to those prescribed in the regulation.[24] In addition, the regulations provide that the responsible party must 'render such reasonable assistance, as is necessary free of charge'.[25] Making life too hard for data subjects will probably be seen as a denial of data subject rights. Of course, the irony is that the prescribed forms are complex, not in plain language and require knowledge about the processing activities of the responsible party that a data subject is unlikely to have.

18.2.5 Confirm the identity of the data subject

Before the responsible party considers a request for access to information, they must confirm the identity of the data subject by asking for 'adequate proof'.[26] Why? First, because POPIA provides that the data subject must provide 'adequate proof of identity'.[27] Second, not verifying the identity of a third party who is about to gain access to personal information may be construed as a failure to provide satisfactory information security measures.[28] Data subject requests can be used by malicious

22 Section 18(3) of PAIA.

23 Section 19 of PAIA.

24 See the definition of 'form(s)' and regulation 1 of the 2018 POPIA Regulations. We discussed this in the context of Form 4 (direct marketing consent) in chapter 16 paragraph 16.4.2.

25 Regulations 2 and 3 of the 2018 POPIA Regulations. This might change. As we were reading the final proofs of this edition the Information Regulator published draft amendments to the Regulations for comment (GN 45120, GoN 829). Strangely, the draft Regulations removed the requirement that the responsible party must render reasonable assistence from regulation 2 and 3.

26 Section 23(1).

27 POPIA does not state that the responsible party must insist on adequate proof of identity, but rather that the data subject must provide it.

28 Information security is discussed in chapter 5.

attackers to gain access to the personal information of data subjects.[29] If an unauthorised person makes a successful data subject request it will constitute a security compromise and the Information Regulator will have to be notified.[30] Worth avoiding.

For instance, the responsible party may confirm the identity of the data subject by:

- requiring the data subject to present an identification document[31]
- asking two or three security questions, such as asking the data subject to confirm their contact number, their address, or the bank from which they pay for the responsible party's service; or
- requiring a data subject to log into a platform or website that employs two-factor authentication in order to submit the request.

Tricky area: What will be considered 'adequate proof'? The key to determining the level of security measures put in place and determining whether the evidence is reasonably necessary is proportionality. If the data subject is requesting access to sensitive personal information, for instance health information, the responsible party should ask for more evidence than when a data subject asks for information that is publicly available. The security of the information must be weighed up against ensuring effective access free of excessively onerous requirements. The EU GDPR also does not provide specific guidance, but does say that if the data controller has 'reasonable doubts concerning the identity of the data subject' the data controller may request additional information and that 'the controller should use all reasonable measures to verify the identity of a data subject who requests access, in particular in the context of online services and online identifiers'.[32] For an extremely practical article on the do's and don'ts of verifying data subject requests, see Piotr Foitzik 'How to verify identity of data subject for DSARs under the GDPR'.[33]

29 Wondering how to do it? See James Pavur and Casey Knerr 'GDPRArrrrr: Using privacy laws to steal identities', available at https://arxiv.org/abs/1912.00731.

30 Section 22(1). Security compromises are discussed in chapter 5 paragraph 5.6.

31 Asking a person to submit a copy of their ID is effective in a face-to-face setting where the identity of the person producing the ID can be verified. In an online setting, the ability of a person to produce an identification document does not necessarily mean that they are who they say they are. In any event, requiring copies of identification documents *solely* for the purpose of verifying the identity of the data subject will be considered excessive.

32 Article 12(6) read with recital 64.

33 Available at https://iapp.org/news/a/how-to-verify-identity-of-data-subjects-for-dsars-under-the-gdpr/.

Responsible parties should also carefully consider what proof of the verification process they want to retain, in order to comply with the principles of minimality while still maintaining adequate records. For instance, retaining copies of ID documents indefinitely as proof that a person's identity was verified is not appropriate. We can't put it better than Piotr:[34]

> 'Asking for a copy of ID document, passport or other official, government-issued document, such as a birth certificate, as a standard way of verifying the identity of data subjects should be definitely avoided. [YES! Amen!][35]
>
> The obvious reason why is because it is disproportionate and not always relevant. The less obvious reason is that this is not considered a secure and efficient method of authentication, and the level of assurance as to the real identity of a person, in contrast to what some might think, is quite low.
>
> Authentication in an online environment is widely disputed, and most people will tell you that you should not use the information that basically stays the same for all your life or for a period of time, such as Social Security numbers or government issued identifiers, as it is likely that such data may already be in possession of unauthorised persons,[36] simply because they exist for a long time. Also, if this would be a prevalent practice, many companies would be, and sometimes already are, in possession of such information, and they often fall pray [sic] to breaches and hacker attacks.
>
> Last but not least, by collecting such information, you will create additional risks for data subjects, as such data may be used, for identity theft or fraud, for example, and you will need to protect it with higher security measures than for the innocuous data that is subject to the request itself, e.g., history of purchased items or the like. Quite likely you would need, under the GDPR, to conduct the data protection impact assessment before implementing such method of authentication.'

We sincerely hope this puts to bed this obsession of compliance folk with keeping a thousand copies of the ID of every person they meet. We also discussed this phenomenon (and the fines that resulted) in chapter 17 paragraph 17.3.2.

A request can be made on behalf of someone else, for instance an attorney can make the request on behalf of their client. The responsible party should ask for proof that the requester is authorised. Examples of proof include a letter of authority and a power of attorney.[37]

---

34 Piotr Foitzik 'How to verify identity of data subject for DSARs under the GDPR', available at https://iapp.org/news/a/how-to-verify-identity-of-data-subjects-for-dsars-under-the-gdpr/.

35 We really, really love this article.

36 Case in point: Almost all South African's ID numbers were compromised in 2017. See Andrew Fraser 'Revealed: The real source of SA's massive data breach' *Tech Central*, available at https://techcentral.co.za/revealed-real-source-sas-massive-data-breach/77626/.

37 Guide to the UK GDPR, available at https://ico.org.uk/for-organisations/guide-to-data-protection/guide-to-the-general-data-protection-regulation-gdpr/right-of-access/how-do-we-recognise-a-subject-access-request-sar/.

18.2.6 Finally, respond (but be careful)

Once the identity of the data subject has been verified, the responsible party can respond to the request. The responses to the various types of data subject requests will be discussed from paragraph 18.3 below. Responsible parties should define a process for investigating, formulating and approving a response to a data subject request.

Key point: None of the data subject rights are absolute. Responsible parties will have some discretion in how to respond. With this discretion comes the increased potential for mistakes and disputes. Responsible parties should have procedures in place for how to respond to ensure consistency and to proactively manage any disputes that may arise. This procedure should be tested and monitored by the information officer of the responsible party.[38]

18.2.7 Time waits for no responsible party

POPIA does not give a deadline for responding to data subject requests. It does state that the responsible party must respond to requests for access to information within a reasonable time.[39] In respect of the right to correct, delete or destroy information, POPIA states that it must be done 'as soon as reasonably practicable'.[40]

---

[38] Responding to data subject requests is an important duty of the information officer. We discuss the responsibilities of the information officer in chapter 1 paragraph 1.3. Defining a procedure for the processing of data subject rights is one of the express responsibilities of the information officer. See section 55(1)*(b)* and regulation 4(1)*(d)* of the POPIA Regulations.

[39] Section 23(1)*(b)*(i).

[40] Section 24(2). This might change. As we were reading the final proofs of this edition the Information Regulator published draft amendments to the Regulations for comment (GN 45120, GoN 829). The draft Regulation provides that a responsible party must respond to requests for correction, destruction or deletion within 14 days.

Tricky area: What is a reasonable time period to respond to a data subject request? Because data subject access requests are also covered by PAIA, the timelines provided by PAIA should be considered. The default period in PAIA is 30 days.[41] If an information officer misses the deadlines referred to in PAIA it is seen as a deemed refusal of the access request.[42] Given that POPIA only refers to a 'reasonable time', missing the deadlines in PAIA would probably also be seen as a breach of POPIA.[43] We can also look at the timelines provided by other jurisdictions. The EU GDPR requires a controller to take action on a request for access without undue delay, within one month of receipt of the request.[44] The California Consumer Privacy Act (CCPA) Regulations require a business to respond to consumer access requests within 45 days.[45]

What about other data subject rights? It is probably not a good idea to adopt 30 days as the standard for what is reasonable. Responsible parties should test their data subject request procedures and define a standard for different types of requests.

18.3 THE RIGHT TO ACCESS YOUR PERSONAL INFORMATION

18.3.1 The relationship between the right to access to personal information and the right to privacy

The right to access to information is not only a human right, but also enables data subjects to exercise or protect other rights, such as their right to privacy.[46] Without having access to their personal information, data subjects cannot hold responsible parties to account. In the words of Privacy International:[47]

41 See section 25 (in respect of public bodies) and section 56 (in respect of private bodies) of PAIA. There are exceptions to the default rule or instances when it can be extended.

42 See sections 27 and 58 of PAIA.

43 This might change. As we were reading the final proofs of this edition the Information Regulator published draft amendments to the Regulations for comment (GN 45120, GoN 829). The draft Regulation provides that a responsible party must respond to requests for correction, destruction or deletion within 14 days.

44 Article 12(3) of the EU GDPR.

45 Section 1798.130 of the California Consumer Privacy Act Regulations.

46 Section 14 of the Constitution enshrines the right to privacy and section 32(1)*(a)* and *(b)* the right to access to information. In this context, it is helpful to read these sections with the preamble to PAIA.

47 Privacy International *Rights of Data Subjects*, available at https://privacyinternational.org/sites/default/files/2018-08/Part%204%20-%20Rights%20of%20Data%20Subjects.pdf%C2%A7.pdf.

> 'The right of access is an essential right for individuals [and, in South Africa, organisations] to understand what data is being processed about them and how. Accessing their data enables then [*sic*] people to check whether their data is being processed in line with the law and their expectations, whether it's accurate and whether they want to take further action, such as exercising their right to object.'

The right to access to your own personal information is closely connected to the obligation on responsible parties to maintain documentation of their processing activities and to notify data subjects of these activities.[48]

18.3.2 What information does the data subject have a right to?

Data subjects have the right to request a responsible party to:[49]

- confirm whether or not a responsible party holds personal information about them
- provide a record or a description of their personal information in the responsible party's possession; and
- provide information about the identity of all third parties, or categories of third parties, who have, or have had, access to their personal information.

18.3.2.1 Confirmation of whether the responsible party has the data subject's personal information

This type of request seems very simple. A data subject will ask a responsible party whether they have information about them. The responsible party will check and say 'yes' or 'no'. It is so simple that neither the 2018 POPIA Regulations nor the PAIA Regulations provide a prescribed form for it. The responsible party may not charge the data subject a fee to provide a response.[50]

Of course, nothing in POPIA is simple.[51] Responsible parties should check carefully before answering, particularly if the answer is 'no'. If this turns out to be incorrect and the person making the statement was acting intentionally, they could face a fine (in their personal capacity) or a prison sentence of up

48 Sections 17 and 18. The duty to notify is discussed in chapter 11. The requirement to document processing activities is discussed throughout the book, but we summarise it in chapter 1 paragraph 1.4.

49 Section 23(1).

50 Section 23(1)*(a)*.

51 We found out the hard way.

to two years.[52] Even if it was not intentional, the responsible party may face an investigation and enforcement action.[53]

18.3.2.2 Providing a record or description of the data subject's personal information

The data subject may ask the responsible party to provide a record or a description of the data subject's personal information.[54]

Tricky area: Who decides whether the data subject receives a full record or merely a description? Section 23 says that data subjects have the right to request the record or a description of their personal information from the responsible party. It seems like it is the data subject's choice, but neither POPIA nor PAIA says this explicitly. We do not think that a responsible party can refuse a data subject's request for a record and offer them a description instead, unless one of the grounds for refusing access in PAIA applies. They are discussed in paragraph 18.3.3.

But, what is a:

- description of the data subject's personal information, versus
- a record of the data subject's personal information?

A description of the data subject's personal information would include details of the record(s) held by the responsible party without actually providing the personal information within that record. When a responsible party provides a record, the data subject gets access to a copy of the personal information. In this regard, the EU GDPR states that a responsible party 'shall provide a copy of the personal data undergoing processing'.[55]

Is providing a copy the same as providing a record? A 'record' is defined by both POPIA and PAIA, but POPIA takes things a bit further.[56] A record is defined as 'any recorded information

Chapter 18

---

52 Section 90(1) of PAIA. The offence relates to destroying, damaging, altering, concealing or falsifying a record with the intent to deny a data subject's right to access to information.

53 This is discussed in chapter 19.

54 Section 23(1)*(b)*.

55 Article 15.

56 Section 1 of POPIA.

... regardless of form or medium ... in the possession or under the control of a responsible party ... whether or not it was created by a responsible party ... regardless of when it came into existence'. A record includes:

- writing on any material
- information produced, recorded or stored by means of a tape-recorder,[57] a computer or other device (hardware or software) and 'any material subsequently derived from information'
- labels, markings or other writing that 'describes anything of which it forms part, or to which it is attached by any means'
- books, maps, plans, graphs or drawings
- photograph, film, negative, tape; and
- cave paintings, clay tablets and smoke signals.[58]

The definition of 'record' is primarily used to determine when POPIA applies. This was discussed in chapter 3 paragraph 3.2.2.

PAIA defines a record as 'any recorded information *(a)* regardless of form or medium; *(b)* in the possession or under the control of that public or private body, respectively; and whether or not it was created by that public or private body, respectively'.[59]

Key point: A data subject is in principle entitled to a record (or call it a copy) of all of the personal information a responsible party has about them, whether that information is in a system, in an email or on a piece of paper. At this point, one starts to realise how challenging data subject requests can become for responsible parties who do not manage their information properly; finding all relevant records could be a mammoth task. A search must be performed for personal information of the data subject held in email, all systems used by the responsible party, personal computers of employees, computer recycle bins that have not been permanently deleted, archives, physical records in filing cabinets, drawers, document storage facilities, etc.

[57] Remember those?

[58] We made up this last bullet. The rest is listed in the definition of 'record' in section 1 of POPIA.

[59] See the definition of 'record' in section 1 of PAIA.

When a data subject requests a record or a description, the responsible party is entitled to charge a fee.[60] These fees are prescribed by PAIA.[61] This record of personal information must be provided in a reasonable manner and format and in a form that is generally understandable.[62] PAIA also provides that its purpose is to enable 'persons to obtain access to records of public and private bodies as swiftly, inexpensively and effortlessly as reasonably possible'. The form allows the data subject to select the format in which the record must be provided. Whether the form is 'effortless' is debatable.

18.3.2.3 Information about the identity of third parties who have, or have had, access to the data subject's personal information

The data subject also has a right to 'information about the identity of all third parties, or categories of third parties, who have, or have had, access to the information'.[63] Luckily the drafters did not subject us to Back-to-the-Future Tense.[64] Then it would have read 'who have, or have had, or will have had access to the information'. In all seriousness, we do not believe that responsible parties can be taken to task if they did not retain a record of third parties who have had access to personal information before the effective date.[65]

60 Section 23(1)*(b)*(ii).

61 Sections 22 and 54 of PAIA read with Annexure B of the PAIA Regulations.

62 See section 23(1)*(b)*.

63 Section 23(1)*(b)*.

64 *The Big Bang Theory* 'The Focus Attenuation' Episode 8 of Season 5.

65 We discuss retro-POPIA in chapter 3 paragraph 3.5.

Tricky area: There is also a big difference between listing the identity of all third parties and listing categories of third parties. There is a similar provision in section 18(1)*(h)* which provides that a responsible party may have to notify the data subject of the 'recipient or category of recipients' of the personal information.[66] As we have pointed out in chapter 11 paragraph 11.3.2, it is not clear under what circumstances a responsible party may be required to disclose the actual identity of all third parties who had access to personal information as opposed to just the 'category' of third parties. Having said that, responsible parties should maintain a detailed record of all internal and external parties who had access in order to satisfy the information security management requirements in POPIA.[67] In addition, the principle of accountability dictates that a responsible party must have contracts in place with all operators who have access to personal information.[68] We believe that publishing the identity of all internal and external parties who had access will not be practical, because this might change fairly often. However, a full record should be available in the event that a data subject or the Information Regulator requests them.

The responsible party must respond to a data subject's request for access within a reasonable time, and as soon as reasonably possible after the fee has been paid.[69] If the responsible party provides access they must also tell the data subject about their right, in terms of section 24, to correct their personal information.[70]

18.3.3 When may a responsible party refuse access?

The right of a data subject to access their personal information is not absolute. The responsible party is entitled to refuse access to the records on the grounds set out in PAIA.[71]

[66] This is discussed in chapter 11 paragraph 11.3.2. We say 'may have to notify', because whether the duty exists is dependent on 'the specific circumstances in which the information is or is not to be processed' and whether it is 'reasonable' to notify (see section 18(1)*(h)*). In addition, section 18(4) contains a list of exemptions that may apply.

[67] Information security management is discussed in chapter 5.

[68] This is discussed in chapter 4 paragraph 4.4.

[69] Section 23(1)*(b)*.

[70] Section 23(2).

[71] Chapter 4 of Part 2 (public bodies) and Chapter 4 of Part 3 (private bodies) of PAIA.

Key point: These grounds for refusal apply to all requests for information; not just data subject requests in terms of POPIA. We mention all of them below (heavily simplified) for the sake of completeness even though some are not relevant when considering whether a data subject should be granted access to their own personal information, but we have not discussed them all in detail or included all of the relevant case law. Read Francis Cronje and Eddie Laubscher *PAIA: What You Need to Know* (2016) and Currie and Klaaren *The Promotion of Access to Information Act Commentary* for more.

18.3.3.1 A summary of the grounds for refusal

This section contains a summary of the grounds for rejecting a request for access to personal information.

Key point: Data subject access requests are not 'all or nothing'. All records that contain personal information of the data subject must be reviewed and any information about data subjects other than the requester, or for which the responsible party has reason to refuse access, or which does not fall within the definition of personal information of the data subject, must be redacted. If the responsible party has reason to refuse access to some of the information, that information must be severed from the information where access can be provided. The responsible party must then provide access to part of the record.[72]

The grounds differ slightly depending on whether the responsible party is a public or a private body. We will discuss some of the most relevant grounds for refusal in more detail in the rest of this section.

Key point: Note the use of must and may in the table below. Some of the grounds for refusal are mandatory (access must be refused) or optional (access may be refused).[73] We referred to the public or private body receiving the request for access as the responsible party.

72 Sections 28 and 59 of PAIA and section 23(5) of POPIA.

73 Section 33 of PAIA (in respect of public bodies) and the headings of sections 63 to 70 (in respect of private bodies).

Ground for refusal	Public body	Private body
If disclosure would involve the unreasonable disclosure of personal information about a third party, access *must* be denied, subject to a substantial list of exceptions. Because it relates specifically to personal information, we discuss this ground for refusal and the exceptions in more detail in paragraph 18.3.3.2.	Yes[74]	Yes[75]
SARS *must* not disclose a record if it contains records of someone other than the requester.	Yes[76]	No
A responsible party *must* not disclose: • trade secrets of a third party • financial, commercial, scientific or technical information (excluding trade secrets) if the disclosure would cause harm to the commercial or financial interest of the third party; or • information supplied in confidence to the responsible party by a third party if the disclosure would put the third party at a disadvantage in contractual or other negotiations or would prejudice the third party in commercial competition. This is subject to some exceptions.[77]	Yes[78]	Yes[79]

➡

[74] Section 34 of PAIA.

[75] Section 63 of PAIA.

[76] Section 35 of PAIA.

[77] Disclosing the information is permitted if the third party consents to the disclosure or if the information is about the results of any product or environmental testing or other investigation and its disclosure would reveal a serious public safety or environmental risk. If the responsible party is a public body, it must also disclose the information if the information is already public.

[78] Section 36 of PAIA.

[79] Section 64 of PAIA.

Ground for refusal	Public body	Private body
Information *must* not be supplied in breach of a contractual duty of confidence with a third party. If the responsible party is a public body, it *may* deny a request for access even if there is no contractual duty of confidence, but where the information was provided in confidence and the disclosure would prejudice the future supply of similar information and it is in the public interest that the supply of the information should continue. In other words, a public body can 'protect its sources' to a degree. This ground for refusal does not apply if the responsible party is a public body and the information is either already publicly available or the third party has consented to the disclosure.	Yes[80]	Yes[81]
Disclosure *must* be refused if it would endanger the life or safety of an individual. It *may* be refused if disclosure would impair the security of a building, structure or system (e.g. a computer or communication system), means of transport or other property. This includes disclosures of methods, systems, plans or procedures aimed at the protection of an individual in a witness protection scheme or the safety of the public.	Yes[82]	Yes[83]
If the data subject is an accused in bail proceedings, they *must* not get access to 'any information, record or document relating to the offence in question, which is contained in, or forms part of the police docket, including any information, record or document which is held by any police official charged with the investigation in question, unless the prosecutor otherwise directs'.[84] A public body *may* also refuse access to information which may prejudice the effectiveness of law enforcement and prosecution (i.e. methods, techniques, procedures or guidelines for the prevention, detection, curtailment, prosecution or investigation of crimes). The information officer can even refuse to confirm or deny the existence of a record.	Yes[85]	No

➥

80 Section 37.

81 Section 65.

82 Section 38 of PAIA.

83 Section 66 of PAIA.

84 Section 60(14) of the Criminal Procedure Act 51 of 1977.

85 Section 39 of PAIA.

Ground for refusal	Public body	Private body
Privileged documents (in the context of legal proceedings) *must* not be disclosed, unless the person entitled to the privilege has waived it.	Yes[86]	Yes[87]
Disclosure *may* be refused if it would prejudice the defence, security or international relations of South Africa. E.g. records containing information relating to military tactics, weapons, intelligence or intelligence gathering.	Yes[88]	No
Disclosure *may* be refused if it would materially jeopardise the economic interests or financial welfare of South Africa or the ability of the government to manage the economy. E.g. information relating to a contemplated change that might affect the currency, interest rate, taxes, regulation of financial institutions or contemplated international trade agreements.	Yes[89]	No
A responsible party *may* refuse to disclose: • trade secrets of the state, a public body or a private body • financial, commercial, scientific or technical information (excluding trade secrets) if the disclosure would cause harm to the commercial or financial interest of the state, a public body or a private body • if the disclosure would put a public body or a private body at a disadvantage in contractual or other negotiations or would prejudice the public body in commercial competition; or • a record which is a computer programme as defined in the Copyright Act 98 of 1978. This is subject to some exceptions.[90]	Yes[91]	Yes[92]

86 Section 40 of PAIA.

87 Section 67 of PAIA.

88 Section 41 of PAIA.

89 Section 42(1) of PAIA.

90 Disclosing the information is permitted if the information is about the results of any product or environmental testing or other investigation and its disclosure would reveal a serious public safety or environmental risk. If the responsible party is a public body, the responsible party must also disclose the information if the information is already public or if it consents to the disclosure.

91 Section 42(3) of PAIA.

92 Section 68 of PAIA.

Ground for refusal	Public body	Private body
The responsible party *must* refuse to disclose records that contain information about research carried out by or on behalf of a third party if the disclosure would expose the third party, the person carrying out the research on behalf of the third party or the subject matter of the research to serious disadvantage. Access *may* be refused if that research is being carried out by the responsible party.	Yes[93]	Yes[94]
A responsible party *may* refuse access to records that contain information (e.g. opinions, advice, reports, minutes of meetings) that was used to formulate a policy, to make a decision, to exercise a power or to perform a duty imposed by law if the disclosure would frustrate the deliberative process or if the premature disclosure of the information would frustrate the success of the policy.	Yes[95]	No
A responsible party *may* refuse access if the request is made manifestly frivolous or vexatious; or the work involved in processing the request would substantially and unreasonably divert the resources of the responsible party. We often hear public and private bodies complain about the amount of effort it takes to respond to data subject access requests and speculate about how these requests might be abused by data subjects, so we expect that this ground for refusal will be popular. We will discuss this in more detail in paragraph 18.3.3.3.	Yes[96]	Not in so many words[97]

Even when these grounds for refusal apply, the responsible party *must* give access to the information if:[98]

- the disclosure would reveal evidence of a substantial contravention of, or failure to comply with the law or imminent and serious public safety or environmental risk; and

93 Section 43 of PAIA.

94 Section 69 of PAIA.

95 Section 44 of PAIA.

96 Section 45 of PAIA.

97 There is no equivalent of this section for private bodies, but they can reject frivolous or vexatious requests based on section 50(1)*(a)*. See the discussion in paragraph 18.3.3.3.

98 Sections 46 and 70 of PAIA.

- the public interest in the disclosure or the record outweighs the harm contemplated in the provision in question.

Key point: Cronje and Laubscher note that this public interest section is 'most commonly used to justify making available the record(s) requested'.[99]

18.3.3.2 Unreasonable disclosure of personal information about a third party

If disclosure would involve the unreasonable disclosure of personal information about a third party, access must be denied, subject to a substantial list of exceptions.[100] What this ground for refusal illustrates is that generally, a data subject will be entitled to access to a record of their *own* personal information, but not to the personal information of someone else.

Tricky area: According to the definition of personal information in PAIA, 'personal information' is 'information relating to an identifiable natural person ... but excludes information of an individual who has been dead for more than 20 years'. It differs from the definition of personal information in POPIA in two ways: it excludes juristic persons and it includes the personal information of deceased individuals (for 20 years after their death).[101] In addition, the definition of 'third party' for purposes of this ground of refusal confirms that it only relates to 'natural persons'.[102] This means that:

[99] Francis Cronje and Eddie Laubscher *PAIA: What You Need to Know* (2016) 79.

[100] Section 34 (in respect of public bodies) and section 63 (in respect of private bodies).

[101] The definition of 'personal information' in section 1 of POPIA only includes the information of living individuals.

[102] The definitions of 'personal information' and 'third party' in section 1 of PAIA.

- If the third party is a deceased person, PAIA will protect their personal information from data subject access requests for 20 years.[103] POPIA does not apply to the personal information of deceased individuals at all. So, PAIA gives more protection than POPIA.
- If the third party is a juristic person, PAIA will not protect their personal information from data subject access requests. POPIA protects the personal information of juristic persons. So, POPIA gives more protection than PAIA.

In chapter 2 paragraph 2.7 we discuss conflicts between POPIA and other legislation. For instance, if POPIA provides more protection to a 'third party' than PAIA, POPIA will prevail. However, POPIA amended the definition of personal information in PAIA and left these discrepancies. Where does this leave third parties who are juristic persons? We honestly are not sure.

While the ground for refusal is mandatory (access must be refused), it is qualified by the fact that it only applies if the disclosure would be 'unreasonable'. This is how this requirement was interpreted in *Centre for Social Accountability v Secretary of Parliament*:[104]

> 'If the reasonable expectation test referred to by Ackermann J in *Bernstein* (*Bernstein v Bester NO and Others* 1996 (4) BCLR 449 (CC)) and followed by most other countries is used to determine the scope and content of the right to privacy, then the meaning of the words "*the unreasonable disclosure of personal information*" as used in section 34(1) do not constitute any interpretational problems. The first step is to ask if the information said to be "*personal*" is covered by the principle of freedom of identity. If so, does the individual objectively harbour a legitimate and reasonable expectation that such information will be protected by the right to privacy? If both questions are answered in the affirmative, then the enquiry proceeds to the second stage by determining whether or not society has a legitimate and reasonable expectation, objectively, that such information is protectable. If so, the disclosure of the information will be "*unreasonable*" within the meaning of that expression in section 34(1). This is so because personal

Chapter 18

[103] We discussed deceased data subjects in chapter 3 paragraph 3.2.1.1. For many organisations it will not be feasible to keep track of who is alive or deceased. This means that they will protect the personal information of all individuals, living or dead.

[104] 2011 (5) SA 279 (ECG) paragraph 74.

> information which may be reasonably disclosed is not recognised by society as personal, and no longer enjoys the protection of the right to privacy under section 14 of the Constitution. In this sense, such information falls outside the scope of protectable information, notwithstanding that such information may be personal in nature.'

Key point: Has the subsequent enactment of POPIA changed this test? We would think so, because POPIA has now given content to the legitimate and reasonable expectations of society regarding what is private. If the disclosure of the personal information of a third party would constitute an infringement of POPIA, then surely that disclosure is unreasonable.

There is a substantial list of instances when the personal information of a third party can be disclosed:

When access to the personal information of a third party can be disclosed	Public body	Private body
If the third party consents to the disclosure.	Yes[105]	Yes[106]
If the third party: • gave the personal information to the responsible party; and • the responsible party informed the third party that the information would be made available to the public.	Yes[107]	Yes[108]

[105] Section 34(2)*(a)* of PAIA.

[106] Section 63(2)*(a)* of PAIA.

[107] Section 34(2)*(b)* of PAIA.

[108] Section 63(2)*(c)* of PAIA.

When access to the personal information of a third party can be disclosed	Public body	Private body
If the personal information of the third party is already publicly available. **Tricky area:** 'Publicly available' is not defined in PAIA. In terms of POPIA, certain requirements are relaxed if personal information is derived from a public record or from information that the data subject deliberately made public.[109] 'Publicly available' is considerably wider and could include information that is available on the internet (for instance).	Yes[110]	Yes[111]
If the person is requesting information about the third party's physical or mental health or well-being if: • the person is caring for the third party • the third party is under the age of 18 years or incapable of understanding the nature of the request; and • if giving access to the information is in the third party's best interests.	Yes[112]	Yes[113]

109 These concepts are discussed in chapter 10 paragraphs 10.4.1 and 10.4.2.

110 Section 34(2)*(c)* of PAIA.

111 Section 63(2)*(b)* of PAIA.

112 Section 34(2)*(d)* of PAIA.

113 Section 63(2)*(d)* of PAIA.

When access to the personal information of a third party can be disclosed	Public body	Private body
If the third party is deceased and the person making the request is the third party's next of kin or making the request on behalf of the third party's next of kin. **Tricky area: If the third party has been deceased for longer than 20 years, their information no longer falls within the definition of personal information. This means that the 'unreasonable disclosure of the personal information of a third party' ground for refusal will no longer apply.**	Yes[114]	Yes[115]
If the third party is or was an official of a public or private body and the information relates to the position or functions of the third party. For example: • the fact that the individual is or was an official • the title, work address, work phone number and other similar particulars of the official • the classification, salary scale, remuneration and responsibilities of the third party's position; and • the name of the third party on records prepared by the individual in the course of employment.	Yes[116]	Yes[117]

➡

[114] Section 34(2)*(e)* of PAIA.

[115] Section 63(2)*(e)* of PAIA.

[116] Section 34(2)*(f)* of PAIA.

[117] Section 63(2)*(f)* of PAIA.

When access to the personal information of a third party can be disclosed	Public body	Private body
Tricky area: This is a very wide exemption to the mandatory refusal to give access to personal information of a third party. 'Official' is defined in section 1 of PAIA as any person who is in the employ of or a member of a public or private body. This is a significant erosion of the privacy of employees. In chapter 2 paragraph 2.7 we discuss conflicts between POPIA and other legislation. If POPIA provides more protection to an employee than PAIA, POPIA will prevail.		

18.3.3.3 Frivolous or vexatious requests for access to information

Section 45 of PAIA provides that a responsible party who is a public body *may* refuse access to a record if the request is 'manifestly frivolous or vexatious' or if 'the work involved in processing the request would substantially and unreasonably divert the resources of the public body'.

What will be considered 'manifestly frivolous or vexatious'? Currie and Klaaren point out that 'the ground is likely to have little practical utility because requesters are not required to state any reasons for their request'. They ask:[118]

> 'In the absence of such reasons what might evidence a "manifest" frivolous or vexatious request? It is not of much assistance to read the two terms separately. Frivolity, read on its own, seems to suggest that an applicant has light-hearted motivations for a request, or at least lacks the kind of seriousness appropriate for such matters. Vexatiousness, on the other hand, is something quite specific – a desire to vex, to annoy the target of the information request. Read together, the terms are little more helpful, indicating a desire to prevent misuse of the Act, an abuse of the rights granted by the Act for purposes other than those that the Act seeks to achieve.

118 Currie and Klaaren *The Promotion of Access to Information Act Commentary* at 191.

> Some assistance can be obtained from comparative sources. One model for s 45 is the Ontario Freedom of Information and Protection of Privacy Act. Section 10 of that Act provides a right of access to records in the custody or control of government agencies "unless ... the head [of an agency] is of the opinion on reasonable grounds that the request for access is frivolous or vexatious". Regulations have amplified this provision by laying down standards as to what constitutes reasonable grounds for such a refusal. In essence, a request can be treated as frivolous or vexatious if it is part of a pattern of conduct that suggests an abuse of the right of access to information, or that would interfere with the operations of the institution. Alternatively, the request may be refused if there is evidence that the request has been made in bad faith or for a purpose other than to obtain access. A reasonably clear case of manifest vexatiousness might be the making of repeated requests for the same records, or requests for records already in the possession of the requester.'

Article 12(5) of the EU GDPR contains a similar provision. A data subject request must be 'manifestly unfounded or excessive, in particular because of their repetitive character'. While the wording is quite different, we can take guidance from how other regulators have interpreted the provision. The ICO states that 'a request may be manifestly unfounded if the individual has no clear intention to access the information or is malicious in intent and is using the request to harass an organisation with no real purposes other than to cause disruption'. The ICO considers the following factors as indications of a malicious intent:[119]

- the data subject said that they intend to cause disruption
- the data subject makes unsubstantiated accusations against the responsible party or specific employees
- the data subject is targeting a specific employee of the responsible party against whom they have a personal grudge; or
- the data subject frequently sends different requests as part of a campaign aimed at causing disruption.

When will 'the work involved in processing the request [...] substantially and unreasonably divert the resources of the public body'? According to Currie and Klaaren 'the diversion of resources [must] be considerable and not merely an inconvenience for the body concerned'. They point out that:[120]

---

[119] ICO *Guide to Data Protection*, available at https://ico.org.uk/for-organisations/guide-to-data-protection/guide-to-law-enforcement-processing/individual-rights/manifestly-unfounded-and-excessive-requests/#mu2.

[120] Currie and Klaaren *The Promotion of Access to Information Act Commentary* at 192.

> 'The aim of the exclusion is probably to cater for the rare situation of a request that would have the effect of disrupting the operations of a body by requiring undue expenditure of time and use of staff and physical resources on research and collation of information. Unreasonableness in this regard must be interpreted in light of the purposes of the Act. The Act is intended to promote open government. Obviously, a reasonable degree of positive effort and expenditure by public bodies to achieve this goal can be expected and is part of its ordinary functions. If a request requires more than this effort and expenditure it will be unreasonably diverting.'

Key point: It will not be easy for public bodies to rely on these exceptions. If the responsible party is a private body, it will be impossible as there is no corollary for private bodies. Or can they? Section 50(1)*(a)* provides that 'a requester must be given access to any record of a private body if ... that record is required for the exercise or protection of any rights'. According to Currie and Klaaren '[m]anifestly frivolous or vexatious requests would not comply with this requirement and need not be entertained'.[121] Interestingly, section 77(1)*(c)* of POPIA gives the Information Regulator the discretion to decline to investigate a complaint by a data subject if it is 'frivolous or vexatious or is not made in good faith'. This is discussed in chapter 19.

So far so good for private bodies. However, private bodies will not have the option to reject a request for access because the work involved in processing the request would substantially and unreasonably divert the resources of the private body.

18.3.4 The continued role of the PAIA manual

We discussed the continued role of PAIA manuals and how POPIA amended sections 14 and 51 in chapter 11 paragraph 11.3.3.

The POPIA Regulations require that information officers must ensure that a PAIA manual is developed, monitored, maintained and made available and that 'internal measures are developed together with adequate systems to process requests for information or access thereto'.[122] What these internal measures and adequate systems might include is discussed in paragraph 18.11 below.

---

121 Currie and Klaaren *The Promotion of Access to Information Act Commentary* at 190.

122 Regulation 4 of the POPIA Regulations.

Key point: For a very long time small to medium sized private bodies were exempt from compiling and publishing a PAIA manual. That exemption was extended to 31 December 2021.[123] Not publishing a PAIA manual can land information officers (personally!) in hot water.[124]

18.4 THE RIGHT TO CORRECT OR DELETE PERSONAL INFORMATION

In addition to having access to their information, data subjects have the right to request a responsible party to: [125]

- correct or delete their personal information that is inaccurate, irrelevant, excessive, out of date, incomplete, misleading or obtained unlawfully; or
- destroy or delete their personal information that the responsible party is no longer authorised to retain.

These rights are closely related to the responsible party's obligation to take 'reasonably practicable steps to ensure that the personal information is complete, accurate, not misleading and updated where necessary'[126] and the principle that the responsible party must not retain records of personal information 'any longer than is necessary for achieving the purpose for which the information was collected or subsequently processed'.[127] These rights are also a means of enforcing the principle of minimal processing.[128]

---

[123] GN 397 in *GG* 44785 of 30 June 2021.

[124] The offences and penalties created by POPIA and PAIA are discussed in chapter 19 paragraph 19.10.

[125] Section 24.

[126] Information quality is discussed in chapter 9.

[127] See chapter 17.

[128] See chapter 9.

Tricky area: A responsible party will be responsible for corrections to or deletions of personal information 'in its possession or under its control'.[129] This test is different to the one for accountability discussed in chapter 4, but the same as the test to determine who is responsible for information security. See the discussion in chapter 5 paragraph 5.3. Where does the responsible party's control end? For instance, are responsible parties responsible to ensure that the corrections or deletions are made by an operator who is processing personal information on behalf of the responsible party? We think so. What about other third parties? Where the responsible party has shared the personal information with third parties who use that personal information to make decisions, responsible parties must 'if reasonably practicable, inform' these third parties.[130] The fact that this is a tricky area is yet another reason why third-party risk management and comprehensive agreements are important.[131]

18.4.1 The right to correct personal information

A data subject may ask a responsible party to correct the personal information of the data subject in its possession or under its control, if the information is inaccurate, irrelevant, excessive, out of date, incomplete, misleading or obtained unlawfully.[132] A data subject must use the prescribed form to request the correction of their personal information.[133]

Responsible parties do not have to take data subjects at their word that their personal information should be corrected; the data subject may be asked to provide documentary evidence in support of their request.[134] However, the responsible party also has a duty to provide 'credible evidence in support of the information'.[135] If the responsible party and the data subject cannot reach an agreement about the data

129 Section 24(1)*(a)*.

130 Section 24(3). This is discussed in paragraph 18.4.1.

131 See chapter 4 paragraph 4.8.1.

132 Section 24(1)*(a)*.

133 Regulation 3 and Form 2 of the Regulations Relating to the Protection of Personal Information, No. R. 1383, 14 December 2018. As we were reading the final proofs of this edition the Information Regulator published draft amendments to Form 2 for comment (GN 45120, GoN 829). Some changes to Form 2 were proposed.

134 Form 2 in POPIA allows for the inclusion of an affidavit or other evidence in support of the request.

135 Section 24(2)*(c)*.

subject's request, the data subject can request that the responsible party 'take such steps as are reasonable in the circumstances, to attach to the information in such a manner that it will always be read with the information, an indication that a correction of the information has been requested but has not been made'.[136] In other words, the data subject can ask that the allegedly incorrect or out of date personal information be flagged.

Key point: If a data subject contests the accuracy of their personal information, the responsible party must restrict the processing of the information while they verify the accuracy of the information.[137] The restriction of records is discussed in chapter 17 paragraph 17.5.

The responsible party must respond to the request as soon as reasonably practicable.[138] In the EU GDPR, the request must be processed 'without undue delay'. The ICO has interpreted this to mean within one month.[139]

The data subject must be notified of the responsible party's decision.[140] The responsible party must also notify its operators (anyone that has the information, but is still under the control of the responsible party) of the correction of the personal information. To enable compliance with this requirement, the responsible party must keep an up-to-date record of all third parties with whom they share personal information.[141]

In addition, if the responsible party corrects personal information that was or will be used to make a decision about the data subject and the correction could impact the decision, the responsible party must inform each third party to whom the personal information was disclosed about the correction, if it is reasonably practicable to do so.[142] This obligation will be challenging for responsible parties, such as

---

136 Section 24(2)*(d)*.

137 Section 14(6)*(a)*.

138 Section 24(2). As we were reading the final proofs of this edition the Information Regulator published draft amendments to Form 2 for comment (GN 45120, GoN 829). There is a proposal to amend the POPIA Regulations to require a response in 14 days.

139 ICO *Guide to Data Protection*, available at https://ico.org.uk/for-organisations/guide-to-data-protection/guide-to-the-general-data-protection-regulation-gdpr/individual-rights/right-to-rectification/#ib3.

140 Section 24(4).

141 Maintaining such a record is also necessary to comply with section 18 and with section 23. See the discussion in paragraph 18.3.2 above.

142 Section 24(3).

verification agencies and credit bureaus, that make a living providing personal information to third parties. The importance of discharging this duty (and what can be expected of the responsible party) will be determined by the seriousness of the decision that the third party is making about the data subject. If the decision has legal consequences and has been automated, the third party making the decision must also give the data subject the opportunity to make representations. This is discussed in chapter 15.

18.4.2 The right to delete information

The data subject may request a responsible party to:

- delete their personal information in its possession or under its control that is inaccurate, excessive, out of date, incomplete, misleading or obtained unlawfully; or
- destroy or delete their record of personal information that the responsible party is no longer authorised to retain.[143] We discuss the retention and destruction of records in chapter 17.

A data subject must use the prescribed form to request the deletion of their personal information and the responsible party must provide reasonable assistance to the data subject to complete the form.[144] The form indicates that the data subject may submit affidavits or other documentary evidence to support their request. The responsible party must respond to the request as soon as reasonably practicable.[145] The ICO has interpreted this to mean within one month.[146]

143 Section 24(1).

144 Regulation 3 and Form 2 of the Regulations Relating to the Protection of Personal Information, No. R. 1383, 14 December 2018. As we were reading the final proofs of this edition the Information Regulator published draft amendments to Form 2 for comment (GN 45120, GoN 829). Some changes to Form 2 have been proposed.

145 Section 24(2).

146 ICO *Guide to Data Protection*, available at https://ico.org.uk/for-organisations/guide-to-data-protection/guide-to-the-general-data-protection-regulation-gdpr/individual-rights/right-to-erasure/. As we were reading the final proofs of this edition the Information Regulator published draft amendments to Form 2 for comment (GN 45120, GoN 829). There is a proposal to amend the POPIA Regulations to require a response in 14 days.

Key point: The data subject's right to force a responsible party to destroy or delete their personal information is not absolute: far from it. There are a number of reasons why the responsible party can refuse a request to destroy or delete personal information. The retention of personal information is discussed in chapter 17. In addition, responsible parties must consider what personal information they must retain to document their compliance with POPIA itself!

The data subject must be notified of the responsible party's decision to delete or not to delete the personal information.[147]

Key point: Do data subjects have the right to be forgotten under POPIA? We discuss this in chapter 9 in the context of minimality.[148] Spoiler alert: We think they do.

18.5 THE RIGHT TO WITHDRAW CONSENT

POPIA gives data subjects the right to withdraw consent.[149] If a responsible party relied on consent as legal justification to process personal information or to send the data subject direct marketing, they must have procedures in place to deal with a withdrawal of consent. A data subject can withdraw consent 'at any time'.

Tricky area: Section 11(3)*(b)* states that a data subject may withdraw consent provided in terms of section 11(1)*(a)* at any time. Of course, consent features in many other sections of POPIA. See chapter 2 paragraph 2.6.6 for a full list. We are of the view that data subjects also have the right to withdraw these other consents due to the requirement that consent must be voluntary.[150]

Any processing activities that happened before consent was withdrawn stay legitimate, but the responsible party must stop any processing that was covered by the consent. However, the responsible party does not necessarily have to delete the data subject's information. The processing was lawful before the consent was withdrawn and the responsible party may retain personal information if the

147 Section 24(4).

148 Paragraph 8.3.2.

149 Sections 11(2)*(b)*, 69(3)*(c)*, and 5*(e)* and *(f)*.

150 See the definition of consent in section 1.

responsible party 'reasonably requires the record for lawful purposes relating to its functions or activities' (e.g. keeping a record of the processing) or if it is 'required or authorised by law' to keep the personal information.[151]

A responsible party cannot swop to a different legal justification for this processing.[152] This is why it is so important for a responsible party to consider the legal justification before they start processing personal information, and not to rely on consent unless no other justification is available. We discuss consent as a legal justification in chapters 2[153] and 6.[154]

Although the POPIA Regulations provide a prescribed form that must be used by data subjects to object to the processing of their personal information,[155] and a form to obtain consent for purposes of electronic direct marketing,[156] they do not prescribe how a responsible party should allow a data subject to withdraw consent. Much has been written about managing consent in other jurisdictions. The European Data Protection Board's guidance is that withdrawing consent must be as easy as giving it, but it does not necessarily have to be through the same action.[157] However, if consent was obtained through a service-specific interface, such as an app, the data subject must be able to withdraw consent via the same interface.

Data subjects must be free to withdraw consent without undue effort and without any detrimental effects such as an increase in cost, a cessation of services or a decrease in service levels.[158] Consent would not be valid in the first place if there is a penalty for withdrawing it.[159] However, it may still be possible to incentivise consent, but it must not rise to the level of unfairly penalising data subjects who refuse or withdraw consent.

Key point: A responsible party cannot refuse to allow the data subject to withdraw their consent.

151 Section 14(1).

152 See chapter 6 paragraph 6.3.

153 See paragraph 2.6.6.

154 See paragraph 6.3.6.

155 Form 1. As we were reading the final proofs of this edition the Information Regulator published draft amendments to Form 1 for comment (GN 45120, GoN 829).

156 Form 4. As we were reading the final proofs of this edition the Information Regulator published draft amendments to Form 4 for comment (GN 45120, GoN 829).

157 European Data Protection Board *Guidelines 05/2020 on Consent under Regulation 2016/679* 23, available at https://edpb.europa.eu/sites/edpb/files/files/file1/edpb_guidelines_202005_consent_en.pdf.

158 European Data Protection Board *Guidelines 05/2020 on Consent under Regulation 2016/679* 13, available at https://edpb.europa.eu/sites/edpb/files/files/file1/edpb_guidelines_202005_consent_en.pdf.

159 ICO 'How should we obtain, record and manage consent?', available at https://ico.org.uk/for-organisations/guide-to-data-protection/guide-to-the-general-data-protection-regulation-gdpr/consent/how-should-we-obtain-record-and-manage-consent/#how6.

18.6 THE RIGHT TO OBJECT TO PROCESSING

A data subject can object to the processing of their personal information if the responsible party processes their personal information to:

- protect the legitimate interest of the data subject
- comply with a public law duty; or
- pursue the legitimate interests of the responsible party or a third party to whom the information is supplied.[160]

Key point: We are not discussing the right to unsubscribe from direct marketing here. This is discussed in chapter 16 paragraph 16.6.

The data subject can object at any time using the prescribed form.[161] The responsible party must provide the data subject with reasonable assistance to make an objection free of charge.[162] POPIA provides that the data subject may object on 'reasonable grounds relating to his, her or its situation'.

Tricky area: What does 'reasonable grounds relating to his situation' mean? The EU GDPR says that if a data subject objects to processing based 'on grounds relating to his or her particular situation', the controller must stop the processing unless the controller demonstrates compelling legitimate grounds for the processing which overrides the interests, rights, and freedoms of the data subject, or for the establishment, exercise or defence of legal claims.[163] We discuss when the legitimate interest of a responsible party outweighs the interests, rights, and freedoms of a data subject in chapter 2.[164] A responsible party can also refuse an objection that is manifestly unfounded or excessive, because the request will then not be reasonable.[165]

Once the data subject has objected and that objection is reasonable, the responsible party must stop processing the personal information, unless the

---

160 Section 11(3)*(a)*.

161 Form 1 in the Regulations. As we were reading the final proofs of this edition the Information Regulator published draft amendments to Form 1 for comment (GN 45120, GoN 829).

162 Regulation 2 of the POPIA Regulations. As we were reading the final proofs of this edition the Information Regulator published draft amendments to regulation 2 for comment (GN 45120, GoN 829). The amendments would remove the requirement to provide reasonable assistance.

163 Article 21(1).

164 Paragraph 2.6.3.

165 ICO 'Right to object', available at https://ico.org.uk/for-organisations/guide-to-data-protection/guide-to-the-general-data-protection-regulation-gdpr/individual-rights/right-to-object/.

processing of the personal information is justified by legislation.[166] In addition, if an organisation performs any of the 'relevant functions' in section 38, the data subject does not have the right to object to the processing even if the responsible party relied on one of the justifications listed above.[167] The 'relevant functions' are functions that protect members of the public against:

- financial loss due to dishonesty, malpractice or other seriously improper conduct by, or the unfitness or incompetence of, persons providing banking, insurance, investment or other financial services or the management of bodies corporate; or
- dishonesty, malpractice or other seriously improper conduct by, or the unfitness or incompetence of, persons authorised to carry on any profession or other activity.

This exemption only applies to public bodies[168] or to other organisations who must perform these functions 'in terms of the law'.[169] It also only applies to the extent that the function is 'performed with the view to protecting members of the public'.

Tricky area: What does 'performed with the view to protecting members of the public' mean? First off, the exemption will not apply to functions performed by a responsible party to protect itself. For instance, it will certainly cover the Financial Sector Conduct Authority when it polices compliance with the fit and proper requirements imposed on intermediaries in terms of the Financial Advisory and Intermediary Services Act (FAIS).[170] However, will it cover a financial services provider when its human resources department uses the same information in its recruitment process for purposes of deciding between candidates for employment? Given that exemptions will be interpreted narrowly, the financial service provider will only be covered for activities that are necessary for its own compliance with FAIS. The minute an activity is performed for purposes other than complying with FAIS, the exemption will no longer apply.

Chapter 18

[166] The inclusion of the limitation of the right to object in cases where the processing is 'justified by legislation' is strange. If the processing is justified by legislation, the responsible party should simply rely on section 11(1)*(c)* (the processing complies with an obligation imposed by law), in which case there is no right to object.

[167] Section 38(1).

[168] See the definition of 'public body' in section 1.

[169] Section 38(2).

[170] Act 37 of 2002.

A data subject may also always object to (or withdraw their consent for) direct marketing. In this context, the right to object is absolute; the data subject does not have to show 'reasonable grounds relating to his, her or its situation, unless legislation provides for such processing'. We discuss direct marketing in chapter 16.

18.7 THE RIGHT NOT TO BE SUBJECT TO AUTOMATED DECISION-MAKING

Data subjects that are subject to automated decisions made in connection with the conclusion or execution of a contract and the decision has legal consequences or that can have a substantial effect on them, have the right to:[171]

- sufficient information about the underlying logic of the automated processing; and
- to make representations about the decision.

Profiling and automated decisions are discussed in detail in chapter 15.

18.8 THE RIGHT TO OBJECT IN RELATION TO DIRECTORIES

18.8.1 What is a directory for purposes of this section (and what is not)?

Remember 'let your fingers do the walking'?[172] Section 70 gives data subjects certain rights in relation to directories. The section protects data subjects who are:[173]

- subscribers to
- printed or electronic directories
- available to the public or obtainable through directory enquiry services
- in which the data subject's personal information is included.

[171] Section 71.

[172] This was the advertising slogan for the Yellow Pages (a telephone directory).

[173] Section 70(1). This section comes from Directive 2002/58/EC of the European Parliament and of the Council of 12 July 2002 concerning the processing of personal data and the protection of privacy in the electronic communications section (Directive on privacy and electronic communications). See article 12 and the discussion in the SA Law Reform Commission Project 124 on data Protection (2009 Report) from 345.

Tricky area: What does 'available to the public' mean? For instance, must access be unfettered, or will records that are available for a fee still be seen as accessible in the public domain? What if there is no fee, but you need to register an account? We are of the view that if there is any impediment (e.g. a paywall or a data wall) to the accessibility of the information it is not accessible in the public domain. However, this view may not be correct. In New Zealand, for instance, 'publicly available information' means personal information published in a publication '(including a register, list, or roll of data) in printed or electronic form that is, or will be, generally available to members of the public free of charge or on payment of a fee'.[174] POPIA is not explicit in this regard.

A subscriber is defined as 'any person who is party to a contract with the provider of publicly available electronic communications services for the supply of such services'.[175]

This section does not apply to editions of directories that were produced in printed or off-line electronic form prior to the commencement of this section.[176]

18.8.2 What are the data subject's rights?

Before a data subject's personal information is included in a directory, the data subject must be informed (free of charge) about:[177]

- the purpose of the directory; and
- any further uses to which the directory may possibly be put, based on search functions embedded in electronic versions of the directory.

174 Section 7 (Interpretation), available at https://www.legislation.govt.nz/act/public/2020/0031/latest/LMS23312.html. This position is confirmed in Case note 100413 [2007] NZ PrivCmr 20, available at https://privacy.org.nz/publications/case-notes-and-court-decisions/case-note-100413-2007-nz-privcmr-20-google-search-reveals-personal-information-on-law-firm-website/.

175 Section 70(5). Section 1 of the Electronic Communications Act defines an 'electronic communications service' as 'any service provided to the public, sections of the public, the State, or the subscribers to such service, which consists wholly or mainly of the conveyance by any means of electronic communications over an electronic communications network, but excludes broadcasting services'.

176 Section 70(3). This section commenced on 30 June 2020 (see *GG* 43461, RG 11136 at 21).

177 Section 70(1).

What is meant by 'based on search functions embedded in electronic versions'? If one reads recital 38 of the EU Directive on privacy and electronic communications on which this section is based, it refers to 'reverse search functions enabling users of the directory to discover the name and address of the subscriber on the basis of telephone number only' as an example.

In addition to being informed, data subjects must be given the right to:[178]

- object (free of charge and in a manner free of unnecessary formality) to the use of their personal information in the directory; and
- request verification, confirmation or withdrawal of their information from the directory.

Tricky area: The scourge of passive voice in legislation strikes again. The section does not say who must make the notification and ensure that these data subject rights are respected. Recital 39 of the EU Directive on privacy and electronic communications states that the obligation to inform should be on the party collecting the information for inclusion in the directory. We would suggest that this would be the duty of the 'responsible party' that decided to compile the directory.[179]

18.9 DOES POPIA GIVE DATA SUBJECTS THE RIGHT TO DATA PORTABILITY?

18.9.1 What is data portability?

The EU GDPR creates a right to data portability.[180] This right did not form part of the Data Privacy Directive, the EU GDPR's predecessor. However, a form of data portability has existed in the telecommunications sector for a while with number portability. Before the EU GDPR came into force, the Article 29 Data Protection Working Party published an opinion on purpose limitation that included a section on using big data to make automated decisions and the ideal safeguards that should be in place. One of the safeguards they recommended is to allow data subjects to have direct access to their information in a portable, user-friendly and machine-readable format in order to empower them.

[178] Section 70(2).

[179] See chapter 4 for how to determine accountability.

[180] Article 20 of the EU GDPR.

The idea is that data portability could enable businesses and data subjects to maximise the benefits of big data in a more balanced and transparent way.[181]

The EU GDPR provides that a data subject should be allowed to receive their personal information that they themselves provided to the controller, from a controller in a structured, commonly used, machine-readable and interoperable format, and to transmit it to another controller. This right is only applicable where processing is carried out by automated means and where the data subject provided their personal information on the basis of consent or where processing is necessary for the performance of a contract. Where technically feasible, the data subject has the right to have their personal information transmitted directly from one controller to another.[182]

18.9.2 Are there similar provisions in POPIA? (this whole paragraph is a tricky area)

If we were in Thailand we would say: 'same same but different'.[183] Hidden in the section that deals with the retention and restriction of records, you find an obligation on a responsible party to restrict the processing of personal information if 'the data subject requests to transmit the personal data into another automated processing system'.[184] Clearly the drafters of POPIA considered the possibility that a data subject can request that their information be transferred to another system, but for some reason did not include it as a data subject right, nor the circumstances in which a responsible party must comply with such a request.

Where does this leave us? If we read sections 14(6)*(d)* and 23(1)*(b)* together we could say that a data subject has the right to a record of their personal information held by a responsible party in a reasonable manner and format which could include the transmission of personal information into another automated processing system. However, we may be reading too much into it and it could be that the drafters of POPIA considered including the right to data portability or something

Chapter 18

[181] Available at https://ec.europa.eu/justice/article-29/documentation/opinion-recommendation/files/2013/wp203_en.pdf.

[182] Recital 68 to the EU GDPR and Article 29 Data Protection Working Party *Guidelines on the Right to Data Portability*, available at https://iapp.org/media/pdf/resource_center/WP242rev.01.pdf.

[183] For the origin of the Tinglish phrase, see https://theculturetrip.com/asia/thailand/articles/same-same-but-different-the-origins-of-thailands-tourist-catchphrase/.

[184] Section 14(6)*(d)*. Section 14 is discussed in chapter 17.

similar, but then decided against it and neglected to delete section 14(6)*(d)* from the final text. Another curiosity is that the section refers to 'personal data' and not 'personal information'.

Key point: Organisations that use big data and make automated decisions about data subjects should be prepared to respond to these requests.

18.10 RIGHTS THAT ARE DISCUSSED IN OTHER CHAPTERS

Data subjects have a number of other rights which we discuss in other parts of this book. They are the right:

- to be notified that their personal information is being collected, as discussed in chapter 11
- to be notified that their personal information was accessed or acquired by an unauthorised person, as discussed in chapter 5
- to have the processing of their personal information restricted in certain circumstances, as discussed in chapter 17
- not to have their personal information processed for unsolicited electronic direct marketing purposes, as discussed in chapter 16
- to complain to the Information Regulator regarding the alleged interference with the protection of their personal information, as discussed in chapter 19; and
- to institute civil proceedings regarding the alleged interference with the protection of their personal information, as discussed in chapter 19.

When an organisation is designing the processes and systems to process data subject requests, they should cater for these rights too to ensure that the organisation responds appropriately and on time.

18.11 PRACTICAL ADVICE

Responsible parties should consider how to best deal with these requests and implement a clear, documented process. This is also the area where technology can help most to be POPIA compliant. In a recent study by the IAPP and BigID, half of the respondents indicated that data discovery/inventory/mapping is the top area for additional future data rights investments.[185]

[185] Margaret Honda and Christelle Kamaliza 'The State of Data Rights', available at https://iapp.org/media/pdf/resource_center/iapp_bigID_state_of_data_rights_report.pdf.

We discuss the phases of this process in paragraph 18.2, but it is important to see it in a larger context. Access requests are really just a part of access control, but the procedure will differ depending on the identity of the requester. When it is:

- an employee of the responsible party, the organisation must give them access to the information they need to do their job (also referred to as roles-based access)[186]
- an organisation that the responsible party is working with, the right contracts must be in place depending on the relationship (responsible party-operator, co-responsible parties or independent responsible parties)[187]
- a data subject requesting access to their own information, the responsible party must consider sections 23 and 25 of POPIA and the applicable sections of PAIA; or
- someone else bringing a PAIA request for access to personal information, the responsible party must refuse if the information is still identifiable, unless the data subject gives their permission for the information to be shared.

These processes are easier to manage if they are centralised. Ideally an organisation would want to streamline the request process using dynamic forms that route requests to the right people quickly. Automated back-end workflows can help automate, process and respond to requests. eDiscovery tools could help to scan datasets, classify information, and even redact necessary information. Using technology will also help the responsible party to keep records of communication, create dashboards and allow them to spot trends.

Where possible, data subjects should have remote access to a secure system which provides them direct access to their personal information.[188] Allowing data subjects to update their details easily online could save an organisation a lot of time and resources. Just remember, self-service will only work if the organisation also has effective master data management.[189] If self-service only allows a data subject to update their information on one system, the organisation would still have to rectify the information on all other systems that are not connected.

186 Access control is discussed in chapter 5.

187 Accountability when different organisations are involved in the processing activity is discussed in chapter 4. When independent responsible parties are sharing information, consider chapter 13.

188 Recital 63 to the EU GDPR.

189 Master data management is discussed in chapter 9 paragraph 9.6.5.

Not only will effective master data management help an organisation respond to data subject requests, it will also assist with:

- standardising concepts
- meeting organisational data requirements
- managing data quality
- managing the cost of data integration
- reducing risk; and
- eliminating redundancies.[190]

[190] Michelle Knight 'What is Master Data Management (MDM)?' *Dataversity*, available at https://www.dataversity.net/what-is-master-data-management/.

19 Enforcement of POPIA

19.1 WHAT TO EXPECT IN THIS CHAPTER

Our go-to authority on all matters relating to enforcement is the inimitable Michael Scott, who once said: 'Would I rather be feared or loved? Easy. Both. I want people to be afraid of how much they love me.'[1] We get that same feeling when we read the enforcement provisions of POPIA.

When the SA Law Reform Commission was first investigating the case for enacting data privacy legislation in South Africa (as far back as 2005), there was a lot of debate about what the regulatory oversight model should look like.[2] Should there be a dedicated regulator to oversee data protection, should there be self-regulation, or both? In the end, POPIA created a specific regulatory oversight body for data privacy – the Information Regulator.[3]

1 Michael Scott *The Office* 'The Fight' (2005).

2 SA Law Reform Commission Project 124 on Privacy and Data Protection (2005 Discussion Paper) paragraph 5.1.6.

3 Section 39 of POPIA.

But, the Information Regulator also has the power to issue codes of conduct, which is a form of self-regulation.[4]

In this chapter, we discuss the following:

- Is it a bird? Is it a plane? No, it's the Information Regulator!
- The powers, duties and functions of the Information Regulator
- The status of guidance notes issued by the Regulator
- Codes of conduct
- Investigating complaints
- Investigations initiated by the Information Regulator
- Assessments by the Information Regulator
- Enforcement of PAIA: Here be dragons
- Offences, penalties and fines
- Civil liability

19.2 IS IT A BIRD? IS IT A PLANE? NO, IT'S THE INFORMATION REGULATOR!

The heading should actually read 'Is it a Chapter 9 Institution? Is it a National Public Entity? No, it's the Information Regulator!' Would you have read the paragraph? Probably not. In this paragraph we discuss the composition of the Information Regulator and the Enforcement Committee.

Section 39 of POPIA establishes the Information Regulator as a juristic person who is independent (subject only to the Constitution) and is accountable to the National Assembly. The Information Regulator is a unique type of regulatory oversight mechanism in South Africa. Unlike the previous regulatory oversight body for PAIA (the South Africa Human Rights Commission) the Information Regulator is not a Chapter 9 institution. The Information Regulator is also not listed as a Schedule 3 'National Public Entity' under the Public Finance Management Act (PFMA).[5] This was viewed as slightly controversial in 2018 when the Information Regulator's office was being established for the first time.[6] It is also different from the models adopted under other consumer, competition and credit statutes – the Competition Commission, the Competition Tribunal, the National Credit Regulator, the National Consumer Commission

Chapter 19

4 Section 60(3) of POPIA. Breaching the provisions of a POPIA Code of Conduct is the same as breaching POPIA (section 68).

5 1 of 1999.

6 *News24* 'Information Regulator struggles to take off almost 18 months later' dated 1 May 2018, available at https://www.news24.com/citypress/news/information-regulator-struggles-to-take-off-almost-18-months-later-20180501.

and the National Consumer Tribunal are all listed as 'National Public Entities' under Schedule 3 of the PFMA. At the time, the chairperson of the Information Regulator submitted to Parliament that the Information Regulator should not be defined as a 'National Public Entity', because: [7]

- The legislature intended to create an oversight body for POPIA which is completely independent, like the SAHRC.[8] That is why POPIA states that the CEO of the Information Regulator is the accounting officer of the Information Regulator for the purposes of the PFMA.[9]
- The Information Regulator could not be a 'National Public Entity' because it functions outside the spheres of the national and provincial governments. [10]

Key point: POPIA applies to both private and public bodies – and the Information Regulator has jurisdiction over POPIA compliance matters for both.

While this issue resulted in an administrative deadlock back in 2018, it has subsequently been resolved. The Information Regulator appointed its first CEO and CFO in mid-2019.[11] The Information Regulator has not been declared a 'National Public Entity' under Schedule 3 of the PFMA, and lists its CEO as an 'accounting officer' under the PFMA as opposed to having an 'accounting authority'.[12]

---

7 *News24* 'Information Regulator struggles to take off almost 18 months later', 1 May 2018, available at https://www.news24.com/citypress/news/information-regulator-struggles-to-take-off-almost-18-months-later-20180501.

8 *Mail & Guardian* 'Another day, another data breach' dated 22 June 2018, available at https://mg.co.za/article/2018-06-22-another-day-another-data-breach/. This is in direct conflict with the PFMA, which states that all 'National Public Entities' as defined under Schedule 3 of the PFMA, must have an 'accounting authority' (which is usually a board or controlling body of that 'National Public Entity', but can be the CEO where there is none) (section 49(1) and (2) of the PFMA). Chapter 9 institutions such as the SAHRC, on the other hand, are required to have an 'accounting officer' under the PFMA (section 36 of the PFMA).

9 Section 52(3) of POPIA.

10 *Mail & Guardian* 'Another day, another data breach' dated 22 June 2018, available at https://mg.co.za/article/2018-06-22-another-day-another-data-breach/.

11 Information Regulator 'Annual Report 2018/19 financial year', available at https://www.justice.gov.za/inforeg/docs.html.

12 Information Regulator ''Annual Report 2019/20 financial year', available at https://www.justice.gov.za/inforeg/docs.html.

The Information Regulator consists of the following personnel and committees:

- the chairperson
- a group of four ordinary members, two of which must be full-time and two of which can be full-time or part-time members
- administration staff
- the chief executive officer; and
- other committees, such as the Enforcement Committee.[13]

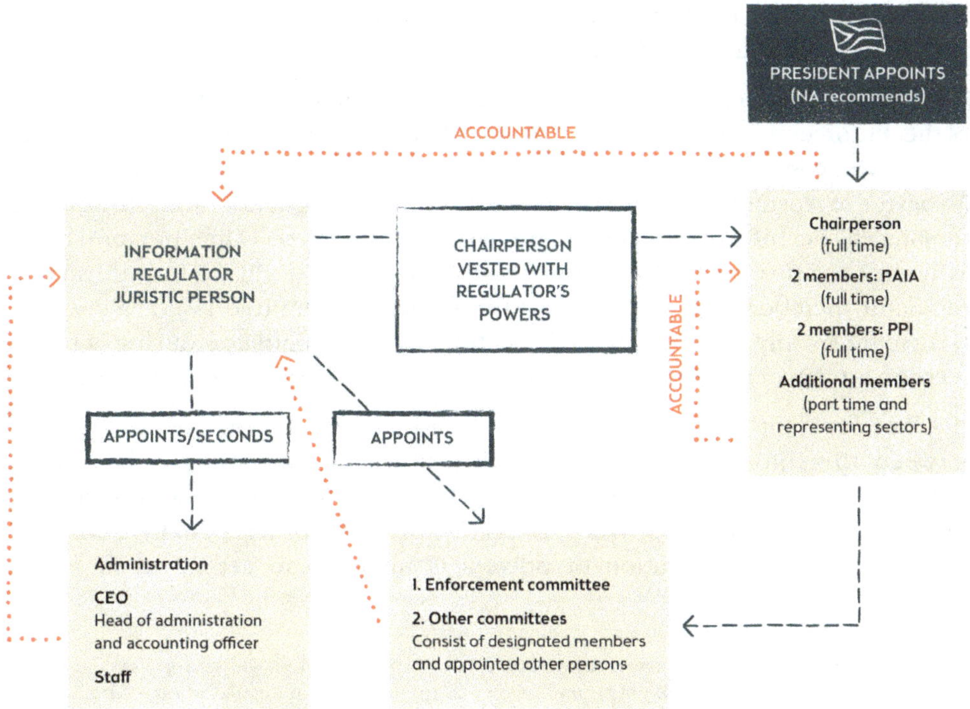

The President of South Africa appoints the chairperson and other members of the Information Regulator upon recommendation by the National Assembly.[14] The National Assembly's recommendation must include which members of the Information Regulator are to be appointed on a full-time and part-time basis. Appointments of the chairperson and other members of the Information Regulator expire after a term of five years, after which the chairperson and other members of the Information Regulator are eligible for re-appointment.[15]

Chapter 19

13 Sections 41 to 50.

14 Section 41(2)*(a)*.

15 Section 41(3). POPIA does not limit this re-appointment. Michael Scott would approve.

The ability of the Information Regulator to enforce its decisions properly is very important, especially considering how the SAHRC (the body who previously dealt with PAIA and privacy rights infringements) has faced chronic non-compliance with the implementation of its recommendations in the past.[16] POPIA has created an Enforcement Committee tasked with considering complaints that the Information Regulator refers to it after the Information Regulator has concluded its investigation.[17] The function of the Enforcement Committee is to consider the matters referred to it by the Information Regulator and to make recommendations about any action that should be taken against the responsible party or an information officer.[18]

The Information Regulator appoints the Enforcement Committee.[19] According to the Enforcement Committee's 'Terms of Reference', the Enforcement Committee must consist of a chairperson (who must be a judge, magistrate or senior advocate), a formal member of the Information Regulator and three other persons.[20] The Information Regulator will appoint these other persons on an ad hoc or temporary basis as provided for in section 47(7).[21] The Information Regulator member who sits on the Enforcement Committee is not allowed to participate in any proceedings of the Information Regulator during which a decision is taken concerning a recommendation by the Enforcement Committee.[22]

The Enforcement Committee creates a separation of powers (so-to-speak) between the Information Regulator's legislative, investigative, prosecutorial, and adjudicative[23] (in relation to complaints) powers, and the Information Regulator's enforcement powers to issue fines and other penalties for non-compliance.[24] This separation of powers is intended to act as an important

16 R Adams and F Adeleke 'Protecting information rights in South Africa: The strategic oversight roles of the South African Human Rights Commission and the Information Regulator' *International Data Privacy Law*, available at https://academic.oup.com/idpl/article/10/2/146/5700632.

17 Sections 92 and 93.

18 Section 93.

19 Section 50.

20 Information Regulator 'Enforcement Committee: Terms of Reference', available at https://www.justice.gov.za/inforeg/docs.html. While the Information Regulator has a free hand when appointing members of other committees, the Information Regulator must discuss the appointment of the chairperson of the Enforcement Committee with the Minister of Justice and the Chief Justice. See section 50(2).

21 Section 50(1)*(a)* and *(b)*.

22 Section 50(4)*(a)*.

23 The power to judge something. Don't worry, we looked it up too. Available at https://dictionary.cambridge.org/dictionary/english/adjudication.

24 Parliamentary Monitoring Group 'Information Regulator: Structure', available at https://webcache.googleusercontent.com/search?q=cache:kgQrpy0DK28J:https://pmg.org.za/files/docs/110919annexureB_0.doc+&cd=14&hl=en&ct=clnk&gl=za. This does not mean that the Information Regulator cannot participate in the discussions, simply that it cannot participate in the decisions. Obviously this raises the concern that – by means of influence rather than means of law – the Information Regulator can unduly influence the decision of the Enforcement Committee,

guarantee in ensuring the Information Regulator's impartiality when exercising its wide array of different powers and performing its various duties. Essentially this segregates the process so that the Information Regulator is not 'the judge, jury and executioner' in all matters.[25]

19.3 THE POWERS, DUTIES AND FUNCTIONS OF THE INFORMATION REGULATOR

They are to:

- provide education
- monitor and enforce compliance
- consult with interested parties
- handle complaints
- conduct research
- facilitate cross-border co-operation
- perform powers and duties in terms of PAIA; and
- make regulations.

Section 40 of POPIA includes extensive provisions under each of these functions. We have decided not to paraphrase them here, but will discuss them where they are relevant in the remaining parts of this chapter.

19.4 THE STATUS OF GUIDANCE NOTES ISSUED BY THE REGULATOR

While we were writing this book, the Information Regulator issued several guidance notes and we assume even more have been published since.[26] This is in addition to the regulations made by the Information Regulator in terms of section 112 and the guidelines issued in terms of section 63(2)*(a)*(ii).

We assume that these guidance notes are developed as part of the Information Regulator's duty to provide education by 'providing advice, upon request or on its own initiative, to a Minister or a public or private body on their obligations under the provisions, and generally on any matter relevant to the operation, of this Act'.[27] These guidance notes were (thus far) not published for comment, nor were they gazetted.

---

particularly if the Enforcement Committee's deliberations are not transparent to the public. The Information Regulator should be aware of this danger and consider itself to be more of a spectator that can correct manifest errors rather than an active participant in Enforcement Committee matters.

25 This concept dates as far back as the Roman times, where the saying went 'Nemo judex in causa sua, bro'. This means that no-one must judge their own case.

26 They are available on the Information Regulator's website: https://www.justice.gov.za/inforeg/docs.html.

27 Section 40(1)*(a)*(v). The only other reference to guidelines in POPIA is section 65 which relates to the guidelines for issuing Codes of Conduct.

Tricky area: Are these 'guidance notes' binding and what happens if a responsible party does not agree with them?[28] POPIA is silent on the status of this advice and how it must be published. We are of the view that these guidance notes are similar to the 'interpretation notes' issued by the South African Revenue Service. In a 2018 Constitutional Court judgment, the court asked

> '[w]hy a unilateral practice of one part of the executive arm of government play[s] a role in the determination of the reasonable meaning to be given to a statutory provision? It might conceivably be justified, where the practice is evidence of an impartial application of a custom recognised by all concerned, but not where the practice is unilaterally established by one of the litigation parties. In those circumstances it is difficult to see what advantage evidence of the unilateral practice [the interpretation note] will have for the objective and independent interpretation by the courts of the meaning of legislation, in accordance with constitutionally compliant precepts. It is best avoided.'[29]

19.5 CODES OF CONDUCT

Jurisdictions which use the 'regulatory system model' for regulatory oversight also incorporate some elements of self-regulation, where industries or professions can draw up codes of conduct for their specific sectors, in co-operation with the relevant information regulator.[30] In the regulatory system model codes of conduct are developed to implement or supplement the data protection legislation they fall under.[31]

---

28 Asking for a friend. According to our friend some of the advice goes beyond the provisions of POPIA and, at times, unfortunately, contradicts POPIA.

29 *Marshall NO v Commissioner for SARS* (CCT208/17) [2018] ZACC 11 (25 April 2018) at paragraph 10, available at https://collections.concourt.org.za/bitstream/handle/20.500.12144/34612/Full%20judgment%20Official%20version%2025%20April%202018.pdf?sequence=25. If we are being generous, the Supreme Court of Appeal (in the same case) held that 'though not binding on the courts or a taxpayer, [the interpretation notes] constitute persuasive explanations in relation to the interpretation and application of the statutory provision in question'. See *Commissioner for SARS v Marshall NO* (816/2015) [2016] ZASCA 158 (3 October 2016). However, the Constitutional Court took a different view. As South Africa's apex court the Constitutional Court decision is preferred.

30 SA Law Reform Commission Project 124 on Privacy and Data Protection (2005 Discussion Paper) paragraph 5.2.10.

31 SA Law Reform Commission Project 124 on Privacy and Data Protection (2005 Discussion Paper) footnote 99 at 2.

The benefit of Codes of Conduct was well described by David Stevens, the Chairman of the Belgian Data Protection Authority:[32]

> 'Not only are codes of conduct an efficient way to ensure the effective implementation of the GDPR in a specific sector, they also help build confidence between the sector and the data subjects. We hope to see more initiatives to create codes of conducts, especially for sectors that regularly collect and process sensitive data or large amounts of personal data.'

19.5.1 Who may issue a code?

POPIA provides that the Information Regulator may issue a code of conduct:[33]

- on its own initiative (but after consulting with affected stakeholders or a body representing the stakeholders); or
- on application by 'a body which is, in the opinion of the Regulator, sufficiently representative of any class of bodies, or of any industry, profession, or vocation as defined in the code'.

19.5.2 Who or what do codes apply to?

Codes of conduct could apply to:[34]

- any specified information or class of information
- any specified body or class of bodies
- any specified activity or class of activities; or
- any specified industry, profession, or vocation or class of industries, professions, or vocations.

Tricky area: A code in terms of POPIA, is not necessarily an 'industry code'. It could also apply across industries if its scope is defined by the type of personal information that is processed (e.g. health information), or by the type of processing activity (e.g. direct marketing). This means that responsible parties could find themselves subject to several codes at a time. One can only hope that the Information Regulator will keep very careful tabs on the scope and content of the different codes it issues.

[32] See 'The BE DPA approves its first European code of conduct', available at https://www.dataprotectionauthority.be/the-be-dpa-approves-its-first-european-code-of-conduct.

[33] Section 61(1).

[34] Section 60(3).

19.5.3 How do codes get issued?

South Africa's approach to codes of conduct is very similar to the approach of New Zealand. Firstly, there is a formal ratification process which needs to be followed for a code of conduct to be officially recognised.[35]

There are also stringent requirements for the content of a code as set out in section 60(2), (3) and (4) and the Information Regulator's extensive 'Guidelines to Develop Codes of Conduct in terms of Section 65 of the Protection of Personal Information Act, 2013 (No. 4 of 2013)' ('code guidelines').[36]

Key point: A code cannot contradict POPIA or provide less protection than POPIA does. Section 60(2) provides that a code must 'incorporate all the conditions for the lawful processing of personal information or set out obligations that provide a functional equivalent of all the obligations set out in those conditions'. However, the purpose of a code is not to simply repeat POPIA (there would be little point in that), but to 'prescribe how the conditions for the lawful processing of personal information are to be applied, or are to be complied with, given the particular features of the sector or sectors of society in which the relevant responsible parties are operating'. The code guidelines state that if the code covers the 'same matters' this may 'negate the need to develop the code'.[37] Section 5(7) puts it a bit more simply by stating that a code may be developed 'for purposes of clarifying how the conditions ... are to be applied, or are to be complied with within a particular sector'. If a code simply restates POPIA, the Information Regulator should not issue it.

POPIA also provides that codes of conduct *may* set out a complaints adjudication procedure, where complainants alleging a breach of the relevant code of conduct can seek redress.[38] Section 63(2) of POPIA sets out the requirements a complaints adjudication procedure in a

---

35 SA Law Reform Commission Project 124 on Privacy and Data Protection (2005 Discussion Paper) paragraph 5.2.13.

36 Information Regulator 'Documents', available at https://www.justice.gov.za/inforeg/docs.html.

37 Paragraph 7.2.

38 Section 63(1) of POPIA. The code guidelines confirm in paragraph 14 that a code *may* consider a process for dealing with complaints. However paragraph 24 implies that relevant bodies *must* have processes in place that outline how complaints will be handled. It is therefore uncertain whether a code that does not make provision for a complaints adjudication procedure will be accredited.

code of conduct must meet and the Information Regulator has also issued a 'Standard for making and dealing with complaints under approved codes of conduct'. [39]

Key point: If a data subject or responsible party is aggrieved by the determination made by an adjudicator under a code of conduct in relation to a complaint, the data subject or responsible party may submit a complaint about the determination to the Information Regulator.[40] When this happens, the Information Regulator can consider the determinations by adjudicators under a code 'afresh'.[41] In other words, the adjudication process in terms of the code does not replace the enforcement mechanisms in POPIA.

Before a code is formally accredited, a notice must be published in the *Gazette* making the proposed code available and inviting public submissions.[42] The Information Regulator must consider the submissions and must be satisfied that all persons affected by the proposed code have had a reasonable opportunity to be heard.[43]

Once a code is issued, it must be published in the *Gazette*.[44] The code will come into force on the 28th day after its publication in the *Gazette* or on the commencement date stated in the Code of Conduct.[45]

19.5.4 A code has been issued ... now what?

Codes of conduct that are issued formally under POPIA have the force of law.[46] A breach of an issued code is considered an 'interference with the protection of the personal information of a data subject' under section 73 of POPIA and is the same as breaching a section of POPIA.[47]

39 Information Regulator 'Documents', available at https://www.justice.gov.za/inforeg/docs.html.

40 Section 63(3) of POPIA.

41 Section 40(1)*(f)*.

42 Section 61(2).

43 Section 61(3). The failure to have proper public consultation can be fatal to the operation of the Code of Conduct. For instance see *National Credit Regulator v Getbucks (Pty) Ltd* (140/2020) [2021] ZASCA 28 (26 March 2021), available at http://www.saflii.org/za/cases/ZASCA/2021/28.html, where the failure to have proper public consultation resulted in the invalidity of Regulations published in terms of the National Credit Act.

44 Section 62(1).

45 Section 62(2).

46 Section 68.

47 Section 73*(c)*.

Key point: This is reinforced in section 1 of POPIA. Codes are included in the definition of 'this Act' and 'prescribed'.

So, a code may not make compliance with POPIA easier for the responsible parties governed by it. Except in one respect. If a responsible party is subject to a code, it is not required to apply for prior authorisation in terms of section 57(1).[48]

19.6 INVESTIGATING COMPLAINTS

POPIA is enforced through two mechanisms:

- investigating complaints; and
- conducting assessments.

In this section, we will discuss investigating complaints. Assessments are discussed in paragraph 19.8.

19.6.1 When can a complaint be lodged?

Section 73 of POPIA provides that complaints can be lodged for 'the interference with the protection of the personal information of a data subject'. POPIA defines 'interference with the protection of the personal information of a data subject' as: [49]

- any breach of the conditions for the lawful processing of personal information set out in sections 8 to 35; or
- non-compliance with sections 22 ('notification of security compromise'), 54 ('duty of confidentiality'), 69 ('direct marketing by means of unsolicited electronic communication'), 70 ('directories'), 71 ('automated decision-making') or 72 ('transfers of personal information outside the Republic'); or
- a breach of the provisions of a POPIA code of conduct.

Key point: No 'interference with the personal information of a data subject', no cry. Doesn't quite have the same ring to it, does it? If there was no interference, there are no grounds for a complaint. Of course, complaints are not the only way to trigger enforcement action. We discuss the actions the Information Regulator can take on its own initiative in paragraph 19.7.

[48] Prior authorisation is discussed in chapter 8.

[49] Section 73 of POPIA.

A person can also lodge a complaint if they are 'aggrieved by the determination of an adjudicator'.[50] This is a reference to an independent adjudicator appointed in terms of an accredited Code of Conduct.[51] This means that the Information Regulator also acts as an appeal forum for a data subject or responsible party who is aggrieved by an adjudicator's decision in terms of a POPIA code of conduct.[52]

19.6.2 Who can lodge a complaint?

According to section 73 'any person' can submit a complaint.

Tricky area: Section 74(1) allows 'any person' to make a complaint for the 'interference with the protection of the personal information of a data subject', but Form 5 of the POPIA Regulations assumes that the complainant will be the data subject. The form asks for the 'particulars of complainant', but then asks for the name and surname of the data subject. As we were reading the final proofs of this edition the Information Regulator published draft amendments to the Regulations for comment (GN 45120, GoN 829). The draft regulations did not change any of our conclusions about Form 5. Perhaps the form makes this assumption, because the Information Regulator is allowed to refuse to consider a complaint if the 'complainant does not have a sufficient personal interest in the subject matter of the complaint' which suggests that data subjects should object on their own behalf. This raises the following questions:

- Can another responsible party make a complaint? Their 'personal interest' would be the unequal playing field created by a competitor who is not playing by the POPIA rules.
- Can a data subject be represented by a third party? What if the complaint is being brought on behalf of a yet to be determined class of data subjects? Surely the 'personal interest' of a data subject can be pursued by a representative?

[50] Section 74(2).

[51] Section 63. Codes of Conduct are discussed in paragraph 19.5.

[52] Section 74(2).

Form 5 appears to be more limited than section 74(1). Given that regulations are subordinate legislation, the provisions of POPIA will prevail. So, all persons with a sufficient personal interest, come forth and complain. But what does 'sufficient personal interest' mean? Section 77(1)*(e)* was based on section 71(1)*(e)* of the 1993 New Zealand Privacy Act. When considering whether to retain this provision in the 2020 New Zealand Privacy Act, the New Zealand Law Commission stated that despite the provision '[t]here is no requirement that the complainant and the person whose privacy has been interfered with be the same person, although the Commissioner does have a discretion to take no action if the complainant lacks a sufficient personal interest in the subject matter of the complaint'. They state that section 71(1)*(e)* should be used to weed out 'officious bystanders with no real interest'.[53] The definition of 'officious' given by Merriam-Webster is 'volunteering one's services where they are neither asked nor needed; meddlesome'. We believe that POPIA should be interpreted in the same way as the New Zealand Privacy Act to ensure that socio-economically vulnerable data subjects can be assisted by civil society and other representatives.

Our conclusion that the complainant does not have to be the data subject is also supported by section 79 (pre-investigation proceedings)[54] which provides that the Information Regulator must inform 'the complainant, the data subject to whom the investigation relates (if not the complainant) and any person alleged to be aggrieved (if not the complainant), of the Regulator's intention to conduct the investigation'. This section clearly caters for the possibility that the complainant might not be the data subject.

[53] See the New Zealand Law Commission's *Review of the Privacy Act 1993* from 185, available at https://www.lawcom.govt.nz/sites/default/files/projectAvailableFormats/NZLC%20R123.pdf.

[54] Pre-investigation proceedings are discussed in paragraph 19.6.5.

19.6.3 How to make a complaint

A complaint is made by submitting Form 5 of the 2018 POPIA Regulations.

19.6.4 When can the Information Regulator decide not to take action?

There are certain instances when the Information Regulator may decide 'to take no action or, as the case may be, require no further action'.[55]

Tricky area: It is not entirely clear at which stage the Information Regulator can make this decision. For instance, can the Information Regulator take this decision without conducting a full investigation? One would think so, given that the purpose of this section is to ensure that the Information Regulator does not waste public resources on certain complaints. Section 74(1) lists the decision not to take action as an alternative to conducting an investigation,[56] but section 77(1) states that the Information Regulator may decide 'after investigating a complaint'. In addition, section 77(2) provides that the Information Regulator can decide that any further action is 'unnecessary or inappropriate' at any point during the investigation. The nature of the grounds on which the Information Regulator can decline to proceed does suggest that some investigation will be required.

[55] Section 77.

[56] Note the use of the conjunction 'or' in section 74(1).

The Information Regulator may decide to take no action under these circumstances:

When can the Information Regulator decide not to take action?	What does *that* mean?
The investigation is no longer practicable or desirable due to the length of time that has passed between the date on which the subject matter of the complaint arose and when the complaint was made.[57]	Oh the joy of a vague time bar clause! How long will this 'length of time' be?[58] This section was based on section 71(1)*(a)* of the 1993 New Zealand Privacy Act.[59] The reason for the provision is that when '[many] years have elapsed since an incident that triggers a complaint, it becomes difficult for [the Regulator's] investigators to collect evidence to determine the facts. It is also unfair to [responsible parties] to raise matters and ask them to respond to events that happened years ago'.[60] In the case the quote refers to, five years had lapsed. The 1993 Privacy Act was repealed by the Privacy Act 31 of 2020. Section 74(1)*(e)* now provides that the Commissioner can decide not to investigate a complaint if 'the aggrieved individual or aggrieved individuals knew about the action that is the subject of the complaint for 12 months or more before the complaint was made'. We would suggest based on this that the Information Regulator should also decline to investigate if more than a year has lapsed since the data subject became aware of the infringement.

57 Section 77(1)*(a)*.

58 Remember that POPIA does not apply retrospectively. We discuss this in chapter 3 paragraph 3.5.

59 Act 28 of 1993. Available at https://www.legislation.govt.nz/act/public/1993/0028/latest/whole.html#DLM297448. We could not find confirmation that the SA Law Reform Commission based section 77 of POPIA on this legislation, but the wording is identical.

60 Privacy Commissioner 'No judgment due to elapse of time – *Watson v Employers Mutual Limited*', available at https://privacy.org.nz/blog/no-judgement-due-to-elapse-of-time/.

When can the Information Regulator decide not to take action?	What does *that* mean?
The subject matter of the complaint is trivial.[61]	This section is identical to section 71(1)*(b)* the 1993 New Zealand Privacy Act. There is an important difference between POPIA and both the 1993 and 2020 New Zealand Acts: The New Zealand Acts contain a so-called 'harm threshold'. A breach of these Acts is not considered an 'interference with the privacy of an individual' unless the action has:[62] • caused (or will cause) loss, detriment, damage or injury to the data subject • adversely affected (or will adversely affect) the rights, benefits, privileges, obligations or interests of the data subject; or • resulted in (or will result in) significant humiliation, significant loss of dignity, or significant injury to the feelings of the data subject. Section 73 of POPIA does not include a harm threshold.[63] However, we believe that section 77(1)*(b)* does allow the Information Regulator to consider whether the data subject was harmed or will be harmed.

➡

61 Section 77(1)*(b)*.

62 Section 66 of the 1993 Privacy Act.

63 The other place in POPIA where a harm threshold was omitted is in the definition of reportable security compromises in section 22. This is discussed in chapter 5 paragraph 5.6.1. The extent of the 'damage or distress, including injury to feelings or anxiety suffered by data subjects' is relevant when the Information Regulator determines the appropriate fine in the event that the responsible party is guilty of an offence. Administrative fines are discussed in paragraph 19.10.3.

When can the Information Regulator decide not to take action?	What does *that* mean?
	Key point: Where the interference complained of does not harm the data subject in any way, the Information Regulator should consider whether investigating the complaint is the best application of its (public) resources. For a fascinating discussion of the policy decisions behind introducing a harm threshold, see the New Zealand Law Commission's *Review of the Privacy Act 1993*.[64]
The complaint is frivolous or vexatious or is not made in good faith.[65]	This ground for not taking action is similar to the ground for refusing access to information in section 45 of PAIA which is discussed in chapter 18 paragraph 18.3.3.3. Section 46(3) of New South Wales' Privacy and Personal Information Act[66] is virtually identical. The New South Wales Information and Privacy Commission lists the following examples:[67] • The data subject is bringing the complaint 'for some purpose other than a genuine concern about his or her privacy'. • They state that 'a complaint will not be made in "good faith" if complainant does not have honest intentions. A subjective assessment will need to be made as to whether the complainant shows honesty and sincerity in making the complaints.'

[64] From 179, available at https://www.lawcom.govt.nz/sites/default/files/projectAvailableFormats/NZLC%20R123.pdf.

[65] Section 77(1)*(c)*.

[66] Act 133 of 1998.

[67] Information and Privacy Commission: New South Wales *Protocol for Handling Privacy Complaints*, available at https://www.ipc.nsw.gov.au/protocol-handling-privacy-complaints.

When can the Information Regulator decide not to take action?	What does *that* mean?
The complainant does not want action to be taken or continued.[68]	We can take this one at face value. However, always remember that the Information Regulator can decide to assess or investigate a responsible party on its own initiative.[69]
The complainant does not have a sufficient personal interest in the subject matter of the complaint.[70]	We discussed this ground in paragraph 19.6.2.
The complaint relates to a matter that is covered in a code of conduct which provides for a complaints procedure, and the data subject has not fully pursued 'an avenue of redress available under that complaints procedure that it would be reasonable for the complainant to pursue'.[71]	Presumably, the Information Regulator would then refer the complaint to the relevant body. Codes of conduct are discussed in paragraph 19.5.
If, in the course of the investigation of the complaint, 'it appears to the Information Regulator that, having regard to all the circumstances of the case, any further action is unnecessary or inappropriate'.[72]	This is a catch-all provision that enables the Information Regulator to decline to take action when none of the other grounds apply.

68 Section 77(1)*(d)*.

69 See sections 89 and 76(3).

70 Section 77(1)*(e)*.

71 Section 77(1)*(f)*.

72 Section 77(2).

Can the responsible party raise one of the grounds in section 77(1) as a defence to a complaint? Section 77(1) provides that the Information Regulator 'may decide'. This means that they are not absolute defences. However, responsible parties would be well advised to make representations to the Information Regulator if they feel that one of these grounds applies in relation to a complaint when the responsible party is given an opportunity to respond during the pre-investigation proceedings.[73]

19.6.5 What is the pre-investigation?

Section 76 provides that the Information Regulator '*may* conduct a pre-investigation as referred to in section 79'.[74] Section 79 refers to 'pre-investigation proceedings' and requires that the Information Regulator *must* inform the following parties of the Information Regulator's intention to conduct an investigation:[75]

- the complainant
- the data subject to whom the investigation relates (if not the complainant); and
- any person alleged to be aggrieved (if not the complainant).

The Information Regulator must also inform the responsible party to whom the investigation relates of:[76]

- the details of the complaint or subject matter of the investigation;[77] and
- the responsible party's right to submit a written response within a reasonable period.

The Information Regulator will give the responsible party a deadline for the written response in the notification.[78]

73 Section 79.

74 Section 76(1)*(a)*.

75 Section 79*(a)*.

76 Section 79*(b)*.

77 The reference to the 'subject matter of the investigation' is included, because the Information Regulator does not have to wait for a complaint to commence an investigation. It can do so on its own initiative. Section 76(3).

78 Form 8 of the 2018 POPIA Regulations prescribes the form of the notification.

Key point: Even though section 76 provides that the Information Regulator *may* choose to do a pre-investigation, it would appear that if the Information Regulator decides to proceed with the investigation, these pre-investigation steps *must* be taken. This is confirmed in regulation 9 of the 2018 POPIA Regulations which provides that '[i]f the Regulator intends to investigate any matter contemplated in Chapter 10 of the Act, the Regulator must in terms of section 79 notify the parties to whom the investigation relates of such intention'.[79]

19.6.6 When can the Information Regulator act as a conciliator or attempt a settlement?

19.6.6.1 Conciliation

Section 76(1)*(b)* provides that when the Information Regulator receives a complaint, the Information Regulator can 'act, at any time during the investigation and where appropriate, as a conciliator' in relation to the complaint.

Tricky area: When will it be 'appropriate' for the Information Regulator to attempt conciliation? Regulation 8 of the 2018 POPIA Regulations refers to the process the Information Regulator must follow, but also does not state when it will be considered appropriate. It therefore does not appear that the Information Regulator can be forced to attempt conciliation.[80]

If the conciliation is successful, the Information Regulator will issue a conciliation certificate.[81]

Chapter 19

[79] As we were reading the final proofs of this edition the Information Regulator published draft amendments to the Regulations for comment (GN 45120, GoN 829). The draft regulations did not change any of our conclusions about regulation 9.

[80] As we were reading the final proofs of this edition the Information Regulator published draft amendments to the Regulations for comment (GN 45120, GoN 829). The draft regulations did not change any of our conclusions about regulation 8.

[81] Regulation 8(4) and Form 7 of the 2018 POPIA Regulations.

19.6.6.2 Settlement

Section 80 of POPIA relates to the settlement of complaints and provides that once the responsible party has provided its written response during the pre-investigation proceedings,[82] the Information Regulator may 'without investigating the complaint or, as the case may be, investigating the complaint further' attempt to secure a settlement if:

- the Information Regulator believes that it may be possible to secure a settlement; and
- the responsible party has given 'satisfactory assurance against the repetition of any action that is the subject matter of the complaint or the doing of further actions of a similar kind'.

Key point: Responsible parties who do not want an investigation to proceed further would be well advised to give the assurance that they will not 'do it again' in their written response to a complaint during the pre-investigation proceedings. Of course, this will horrify attorneys who will view this as an admission of guilt, so do be careful when wording this response.[83]

If the conciliation is successful, the Information Regulator will issue a settlement certificate.[84]

19.6.7 When must the Information Regulator refer the matter to another regulatory body?

Section 78 of POPIA provides for the referral of the complaint to another 'regulatory body established in terms of any law' if the Information Regulator believes that the complaint relates 'in whole, or in part, to a matter that is more properly within [the other regulatory body's] jurisdiction'. The Information Regulator must consult with the other regulatory body in this decision.

---

82 Section 79*(b)*(ii) is discussed in paragraph 19.6.5.

83 Winston Churchill once said 'Lawyers occasionally stumble over the truth, but most of them pick themselves up and hurry off as if nothing had happened.'

84 Regulation 10(4) and Form 10 of the 2018 POPIA Regulations.

Tricky area: What happens if the Information Regulator receives a complaint which falls within the jurisdiction of an independent adjudicator in terms of an accredited Code of Conduct? Section 76 of POPIA does not list referral to an independent adjudicator as one of the actions the Information Regulator can take on receipt of a complaint. However, section 77 provides that the Information Regulator may decline to take action if the complaint relates to a matter that is covered in a code of conduct which provides for a complaints procedure, and the data subject has not fully pursued 'an avenue of redress available under that complaints procedure that it would be reasonable for the complainant to pursue'.[85] Section 78 allows the regulator to refer the matter to another regulatory body which is established in terms of any law. Is an Adjudicator established in terms of an accredited POPIA Code of Conduct considered to be a 'Regulatory Body'? Since it is established in terms of a law (POPIA) and specifically given the force of law (in terms of section 68) there seems to be a decent argument that it is.

19.6.8 How a full investigation is conducted

The Information Regulator may decide to launch a full investigation into the complaint. Before launching the investigation, the Information Regulator must complete the pre-investigation procedure.

Tricky area: Section 76, which lists the different actions the Regulator may take on receipt of a complaint, is misleading. This is because it creates the impression that these actions are alternatives that the Information Regulator can choose from. For instance, it states that the Information Regulator can conduct a pre-investigation, conduct a full investigation *or* refer the complaint to the Enforcement Committee. This is not the case. The Information Regulator:

- must always conduct the pre-investigation proceedings '[b]efore proceeding to investigate any matter';[86] and
- can only refer a matter to the Enforcement Committee 'after completing the investigation of a complaint'.[87]

In the remainder of this section, we will discuss aspects of the investigation process.

---

85 Section 77(1)*(f)*.

86 Section 79.

87 Section 92.

19.6.8.1 The powers of the Information Regulator during an investigation

The powers of the Information Regulator in relation to conducting investigations are quite wide. The Information Regulator can:

- summon and force persons to testify before the Information Regulator either via oral or written evidence in the same manner that a High Court can[88]
- administer oaths[89]
- issue information notices (we discuss them in detail in paragraph 19.6.8.2)[90]
- 'receive and accept' any evidence and other information 'that the Regulator sees fit, whether or not it is or would be admissible in a court of law'[91]

Tricky area: Section 81*(c)* is a bit scary. Apart from issuing summons, the Information Regulator can also gather evidence by issuing information notices in terms of section 90. They are discussed in paragraph 19.6.8.2. Section 90 makes it very clear that certain types of information are off limits. For example, the Information Regulator is not entitled to communication between the responsible party and their professional legal adviser or 'information that would, by revealing evidence of the commission of any offence other than an offence under this Act, expose the responsible party to criminal proceedings'.[92] Section 86 and 87 of POPIA also excludes communication between a professional legal adviser and the responsible party from search and seizure in terms of a warrant. We cannot imagine that these restrictions do not apply to evidence 'received' for purposes of section 81*(c)*.

88 Section 81*(a)*.

89 Section 81*(b)*

90 Section 90.

91 Section 81*(c)*.

92 Section 90(7) and (8).

- conduct a search of the premises the responsible party occupies or conduct interviews with persons at the premises in terms of a warrant issued by the High Court, a regional magistrate or a magistrate;[93] and

Key point: The Information Regulator will have to demonstrate that it has reasonable grounds for suspecting that the responsible party is interfering with the protection of the personal information of a data subject or that an offence (in terms of POPIA) is being committed and that evidence is to be found at the premises.[94] Requirements for issuing of the warrant and the execution of the warrant are set out in sections 83 and 84 of POPIA respectively.

- conduct a private interview with any person in any premises the Information Regulator has a warrant to search.[95]

19.6.8.2 Information notices

The Information Regulator may issue an information notice in terms of section 90(1)*(b)* if it 'reasonably requires any information for the purpose of determining whether the responsible party has interfered or is interfering with the personal information of a data subject'.

Tricky area: Knowingly or recklessly making false statements in response to an information notice is an offence which could lead to imprisonment, a penalty, or an administrative fine.[96] Curiously, not responding to an information notice at all, is not an offence in terms of section 103(2). We would still advise against it. If a responsible party does not want to comply with an information notice, its only recourse is to lodge an appeal with the High Court within 30 days of receiving the notice.[97]

Chapter 19

93 Sections 81*(d)* and 82. Section 81*(d)* actually says that the Information Regulator may 'at any reasonable time, subject to section 81, enter and search any premises occupied by a responsible party'. We believe that the reference to section 81, should have referred to section 84, but we are not sure.

94 Section 82(1).

95 Section 81*(e)*.

96 Section 103(1) read with section 107.

97 Section 97.

Responsible parties must be given at least 30 days to comply with the information notice, unless the Information Regulator is of the opinion that the 'information is required as a matter of urgency'. If the Information Regulator does believe that there is urgency, it must provide reasons in the notice. The responsible party must be given at least three days to provide the information.

Tricky area: There is no indication in POPIA of what would constitute urgency. In this regard, we believe that the well-established factors considered by the High Court when determining whether urgency is required in the context of urgent applications should be used. This means that the Information Regulator would have to explicitly show why the normal 30-day period needs to be dispensed with. It is imaginable that the Information Regulator could demonstrate that data subjects would suffer serious prejudice and that this prejudice cannot be prevented in any other way. Even if the Information Regulator can show urgency, the response period may not be shorter than three days.

If the responsible party has lodged an appeal, the responsible party does not have to comply with the information notice until the appeal has been concluded or withdrawn.[98]

Information notices cannot compel a responsible party to provide communication between a 'professional legal adviser and his or her client'[99] if the communication is:[100]

- 'in connection with the giving of legal advice on the client's obligations, liabilities or rights in terms of this Act';[101]
- 'in connection with or in contemplation of proceedings under or arising out of this Act (including proceedings before a court) and for the purposes of such proceedings'.[102]

98 Section 90(3).

99 'Client' includes any person representing the client (section 90(7)).

100 Section 90(6).

101 Remember that 'this Act' includes codes of conduct.

102 Section 90(6)*(b)* applies to the legal adviser's client 'or any other person'.

Tricky area: 'Professional legal adviser' is a defined term in POPIA. A 'professional legal adviser' is defined as 'any legally qualified person, whether in private practice or not, who lawfully provides a client, at his or her or its request with independent, confidential legal advice'.[103] This definition would cover legal advisers in private practice, in-house counsel[104] and legal consultants. If contentious issues have to be discussed (e.g. a data breach), invite the legal adviser to ensure that the record of the meeting is confidential.

19.6.8.3 Referring complaints to the Enforcement Committee

After completing the investigation, the Information Regulator *may* refer the complaint to the Enforcement Committee. We discussed the need for and significance of the Enforcement Committee briefly in paragraph 19.2.

Tricky area: Section 92(1) states that the Information Regulator *may* refer a complaint to the Enforcement Committee. Does this mean that the Information Regulator can bypass the Enforcement Committee and issue an enforcement notice? We do not think so. The 'may' refers to the fact that the Information Regulator could come to the conclusion that the complaint has no merit, and decide not to refer it to the Enforcement Committee. There is no requirement that the Enforcement Committee must confirm the Information Regulator's decision to take no further action in terms of section 77(2).[105] However, if the Information Regulator decides that further action is required, and investigates the complaint, the complaint along with the factual findings of the Information Regulator must be referred to the Enforcement Committee. But, we might be wrong.

The Enforcement Committee has two distinct roles in terms of section 93:

- It *must* consider and 'make a finding' in respect of any complaint referred to it by the Information Regulator.

[103] See the definition of 'professional legal adviser' in section 1.

[104] There have been several cases in which it was found that privilege attaches to in-house counsel. See *Van der Heever v Die Meester* 1997 (3) SA 93 (T) and *Mohamed v President of the Republic of South Africa* 2001 (2) SA 1145 (C).

[105] Section 77(2). This was discussed in paragraph 19.6.4.

Tricky area: We think that 'findings' refers to a decision by the Enforcement Committee about whether the responsible party has contravened POPIA. This is an application of the law to the facts gathered during the investigation by the Information Regulator. In this regard, we think of the Information Regulator as the prosecutor and the Enforcement Committee as the judge. This is borne out by the fact that the Enforcement Committee must be comprised of a chairperson (who must be a judge, magistrate or senior advocate), a POPIA expert, a PAIA expert and a senior legal practitioner.[106]

- It *may* make a recommendation to the Information Regulator regarding the action to be taken against a responsible party in terms of POPIA or the information officer or head of a private body in terms of PAIA.

Tricky area: Must the Information Regulator abide by the findings of the Enforcement Committee? Section 95(1) states that the Information Regulator can 'consider the recommendation' of the Enforcement Committee and if the Information Regulator 'is satisfied that a responsible party has interfered or is interfering with the protection of the personal information of a data subject' it can issue an enforcement notice. Does this mean that the Information Regulator can ignore the finding of the Enforcement Committee on whether POPIA has been contravened? We are not sure. How we read sections 93 and 95 is that the Information Regulator must abide by the findings of the Enforcement Committee. However, the Information Regulator does not have to follow the recommendations of the Enforcement Committee with regards to the action to be taken against the responsible party or information officer. Admittedly, we were filling in some blanks in coming to this conclusion. We seem to be doing that a lot in this chapter. If you feel unsettled by this, go back to the Introduction and read the Dunning-Kruger prayer.

When the Information Regulator decides to refer a matter to the Enforcement Committee, it must send a notice to the responsible party that is substantially similar to

[106] Section 50 read with the Enforcement Committee Terms of Reference, available at https://www.justice.gov.za/inforeg/docs/pptr/InfoRegSA-TOR-EFcommittee.pdf.

Form 14 of the 2018 POPIA Regulations.[107] The form does not provide for a response by the responsible party. However, section 92(2) provides that the Information Regulator 'may prescribe the procedure to be followed by the Enforcement Committee' including:

- the manner in which the responsible party and data subject may make submissions
- whether the 'parties who make submissions' can make use of legal or other representation
- the period within which the Enforcement Committee must make a finding and submit a recommendation to the Information Regulator; and
- how the Enforcement Committee must finalise urgent matters.

> **Tricky area:** Section 92 is not listed as one of the areas in which the Information Regulator can make regulations. So, it is not clear whether the procedural aspects will be prescribed on a case-by-base basis or whether the Information Regulator would provide general prescriptions on how proceedings before the Enforcement Committee would work. It does seem that responsible parties can make submissions on the law.

19.6.8.4 Enforcement notices

Once the Information Regulator is satisfied that a responsible party has interfered or is interfering with the protection of the personal information of a data subject, the Information Regulator can serve the enforcement notice on the relevant responsible party.[108]

The following issues must be addressed in an enforcement notice:

- that the responsible party must take or refrain from taking certain steps in a specific time period; or
- that the responsible party must stop processing the personal information in question entirely or for a specific purpose, or in a specific way within a specific time period.[109]

[107] Section 94*(b)*. As we were reading the final proofs of this edition the Information Regulator published draft amendments to the Regulations for comment (GN 45120, GoN 829). The draft regulations did not change any of our conclusions about Form 14.

[108] Section 95(1).

[109] Section 95(2).

POPIA contains specific rules about the time periods within which the Information Regulator can require a responsible party to comply with the provisions set out in an enforcement notice.[110] For example, the enforcement notice cannot require that the responsible party comply with the provisions set out in the enforcement notice before the end of the period within which an appeal may be brought against the notice.[111] This effectively means that the responsible party must be given longer than 30 days to comply with the provisions of the enforcement notice, unless the Information Regulator determines that the enforcement notice must be complied with urgently. If that is the case, the Information Regulator must provide reasons and the responsible party must still be afforded at least three days to comply with the enforcement notice.

Tricky area: There is no indication in POPIA of what would constitute urgency. In this regard, we believe that the well-established factors considered by the High Court when determining whether urgency is required in the context of urgent applications should be followed. This means that the Information Regulator would have to explicitly show why the normal 30-day period needs to be dispensed with. It is imaginable that the Information Regulator could demonstrate that data subjects would suffer serious prejudice and that this prejudice cannot be prevented in any other way. Even if the Information Regulator can show urgency, the response period may not be shorter than three days.[112]

If an appeal is lodged, then the enforcement notice does not need to be complied with until the outcome of the appeal is determined.[113]

---

110 Section 95(3)–(5).

111 Section 95(3).

112 Section 95(5).

113 Section 95(3).

Key point: The consequences of non-compliance with an enforcement notice are severe. It constitutes an offence.[114] This means that the responsible party could face an administrative fine or criminal prosecution.[115]

19.6.8.5 Appeals to the High Court

If a responsible party on whom an information or enforcement notice was served wants to appeal this notice (either to have the contents of the notice varied or have the notice set aside completely), the responsible party must appeal to the relevant High Court.[116] This appeal must be lodged within 30 days of the information or enforcement notice being received.

A data subject has 180 days to appeal a decision by the Information Regulator:

- not to take action (e.g. because the claim is frivolous)[117]
- not to take further action (e.g. if after the investigation the Regulator decides not to refer the matter to the Enforcement Committee);[118] or
- if the Information Regulator cancels an enforcement notice.[119]

19.6.8.6 Application for the cancellation or variation of an enforcement notice

Once the 30-day period to appeal an enforcement notice to the High Court has lapsed, a responsible party can apply to the Information Regulator for the cancellation or variation of an enforcement notice if 'by reason of a change of circumstances, all or any of the provisions of that notice need not be complied with' in order to ensure compliance with POPIA.[120]

114 Section 103(1).

115 Section 103(1) read with section 107.

116 Section 97(1).

117 The other grounds on which the Information Regulator can decide not to take action are listed in section 77(1). They are discussed in paragraph 19.6.4.

118 Section 92(1).

119 Section 96.

120 Section 96(1).

19.7 INVESTIGATIONS INITIATED BY THE INFORMATION REGULATOR

In paragraph 19.6 we dealt with the scenario where 'a person' lodges a complaint against a responsible party. However, the Information Regulator does not have to wait for a complaint to commence an investigation. It can do so on its own initiative.[121] When the Information Regulator decides to commence an investigation, it must notify the responsible party of the subject matter of the investigation and specify by when the responsible party must provide a written response to the subject matter of the complaint. These 'pre-investigation proceedings' are discussed in paragraph 19.6.5.

Can the Information Regulator commence an investigation for no reason or on a whim? No. In *The National Credit Regulator v Capitec Bank Ltd*[122] the court held that:

> 'The NCR in initiating a complaint exercises a public power which must comply with the Constitution, which is the supreme law and the doctrine of legality, which is part of that law (*Pharmaceutical Manufacturers Association of SA and Another: In regard Ex parte President of the Republic of South Africa and Others* 2000 (2) SA 674 (CC) / 2000 (3) BCLR 241; [2000] ZACC 1) para 20). The NCR accordingly cannot arbitrarily, without a reasonable suspicion, initiate a complaint, generally against what it perceives to constitute a prohibited practice. The sanctioning thereof will widely open doors to all kinds of abuse.
>
> It is clear from the provisions of S136 of the NCA that the complaint must be initiated against "an alleged prohibited practice". The investigation by the NCR following upon the initiation of a complaint must be focussed on the complaint in respect of which a reasonable suspicion is held or relate to the information available to the NCR in respect of which a reasonable suspicion exists. It is that complaint which will be referred to the tribunal. As is the case with the Commission, the NCR's far reaching powers may not be abused:
>
> > "For purposes of a fishing expedition without first having initiated a valid complaint based on a reasonable suspicion. It would otherwise mean that the exercise of power would be unrestricted because there is no prior judicial scrutiny as is the case with a search warrant."
>
> (per Harms DP in *Woodlands,* para 20 with reference to *Sappi Fine Paper (Pty) Ltd v Competition Commission and Another* [2003] 2 CPLR 272 (CAC) ([2003] ZACAC 5) paras 35 and 39).'

So, no fishing expeditions.

---

[121] Section 76(3).

[122] (A440/2014) [2016] ZAGPPHC 125 (23 March 2016), paragraphs 10 and 11. Also see *Dacqup Finances CC v National Credit Regulator* [2021] ZAGPPHC 32 (8 January 2021).

Key point: Section 136 of the NCA and section 74 of POPIA are similar enough to apply the reasoning of the court to POPIA. This means that the Information Regulator must have a reasonable suspicion that there has been an 'interference with the protection of the personal information of a data subject' before it can initiate a complaint in its own name. There must be objective facts to support the suspicion *before* the complaint is initiated.

19.8 ASSESSMENTS BY THE INFORMATION REGULATOR

19.8.1 When can the Information Regulator conduct an assessment?

POPIA also provides for assessments.[123] An assessment can be initiated by the Information Regulator or it can be requested by:

- the responsible party
- a data subject; or
- any other person.

Key point: Can the Information Regulator initiate an assessment for no reason? No. POPIA just says that the Regulator must conduct the assessment 'if it appears to be appropriate'. Section 89(3) provides that when the Regulator considers whether an assessment would be appropriate, it can take into account:

- whether the request raises an issue of substance
- if there has been an undue delay in making the request; and
- whether or not the requester has the right to access, or request a correction or the deletion the personal information in question in terms of sections 23 or 24.

When the Information Regulator is initiating an assessment of its own accord, we are of the view that the Information Regulator should at least be acting on a reasonable suspicion given the fact that an assessment can culminate in an enforcement notice. This was discussed in the context of investigations in paragraph 19.7.

If the assessment is being requested, the Information Regulator must only initiate the assessment if it has enough information to identify the person making the request and to 'identify the action in question'. Form 11 of the 2018 POPIA Regulations sheds some light on what

[123] Section 76(3).

'the action in question' means.[124] The form requires that when an assessment is being requested, the requester must provide the following information:

- the information processing to be assessed
- persons affected by the relevant information processing practices
- the reason why an assessment is requested
- specific aspects of the processing of information that the assessment should address
- when the requester became aware that the processing of information should be assessed
- the reason for the delay (if any) in requesting the assessment; and
- whether the requester has the right to access, or request a correction or the deletion the personal information held by the responsible party in terms of sections 23 or 24.

Tricky area: Why the references to whether the requester has the right to access or correct the personal information in question?[125] Perhaps it is because a data subject who can utilize these rights will be able lodge a complaint rather than a request for an assessment either because the responsible party failed to afford him these rights, or the information provided by the responsible party would prove that they breached POPIA. We are not sure.

If the Information Regulator is initiating the assessment, the responsible party must also be notified. The second part of Form 11 contains this notification. It must also indicate the information processing to be assessed, the persons affected, the reason why an assessment is requested and the specific aspects of the processing that need to be assessed.

19.8.2 How are assessments conducted?

It is not clear whether assessments will work in the same way as full investigations as discussed in paragraph 19.6.8 above. Section 90, which governs information notices, refers explicitly to section 89 assessments, but it is the only section that does so.

---

[124] As we were reading the final proofs of this edition the Information Regulator published draft amendments to the Regulations for comment (GN 45120, GoN 829). The draft regulations did not change any of our conclusions about Form 11.

[125] These rights are discussed in chapter 18. Why does form 11 not mention the right to request a deletion of personal information in terms of section 24? Section 89(3)*(c)* refers to both section 23 and 24, so there deletion is included.

Tricky area: For instance, is the Enforcement Committee part of this process? Section 92 says that the Information Regulator may refer a matter to the Enforcement Committee '[a]fter completing the investigation of a complaint *or other matter* in terms of this Act'. Does an assessment qualify as an investigation *or other matter*? We think it does as an assessment could easily result in a finding that the responsible party is not complying with POPIA and it may then be appropriate for the enforcement committee to decide what type of action should be taken.

19.8.3 This culminates in a report

The Information Regulator must inform all the parties involved of its final decision or recommendations in the form of a report once the assessment has been concluded. The Information Regulator can make recommendations in this report of what actions the responsible party should take to remedy the situation if appropriate. This report is deemed to be the equivalent of an enforcement notice.[126]

Tricky area: The final report which the Information Regulator issues at the end of an assessment has the status of an enforcement notice.[127] While a party can appeal an enforcement notice to the relevant High Court, not complying with an enforcement notice is an offence in terms of section 103(1) of POPIA. However, section 91(1) refers to 'recommendations that the Regulator considers appropriate'. 'Recommendations' are not generally considered binding; the definition of recommendations is suggestions.[128] Does this mean that the final report is not binding? Or is the only recourse for a responsible party who does not agree with the Information Regulator's recommendations to appeal the notice to the High Court in terms of section 97? In our view, it does not make sense for a final report in an assessment to carry the same weight as an enforcement notice; why then define a different process?

126 Section 91(3).

127 Section 91(3).

128 Oxford Languages.

19.9 ENFORCEMENT OF PAIA: HERE BE DRAGONS

The enforcement provisions in PAIA were amended by POPIA and Information Regulator is charged with enforcing PAIA.[129] In this section we will briefly discuss the differences between the enforcement of PAIA and POPIA. Be warned, 'Here Be Dragons'.[130]

19.9.1 When will the enforcement provisions of PAIA apply

The most important question is when the enforcement provisions of PAIA will apply. This is important because PAIA has fewer teeth than POPIA. For instance, PAIA does not provide for an administrative fine against the responsible party like POPIA does.[131]

Tricky area: Sections 23 and 25 of POPIA provide that several sections of PAIA apply to access requests by data subjects. Does this mean that if a data subject is alleging that a responsible party infringed one of these provisions, the enforcement provisions of PAIA will apply? We think it does. This means that a responsible party that infringes these provisions will not be subject to an administrative fine, but the information officer or head of a private body may be guilty of an offence in terms of PAIA.[132] If the Information Regulator relies on the incorrect Act's enforcement mechanisms, a responsible party can raise this as a defence.

In the remainder of this paragraph we will focus on how the enforcement provisions of PAIA differ to those in POPIA. It mirrors the structure of paragraphs 19.6 to 19.8 and where the provisions of the two pieces of legislation are identical, the analysis in those paragraphs will also apply to the provisions in PAIA.

---

[129] See Francis Cronje and Eddie Laubscher *PAIA: What You Need to Know* (2016). The text shows exactly which provisions in PAIA were changed or inserted by POPIA.

[130] This phrase appeared in Latin (*Hic Sunt Dracones*) on medieval maps to indicate unchartered territory. It was also the working title of this book.

[131] Administrative fines are discussed in paragraph 19.10.3.

[132] Offences in terms of both POPIA and PAIA are discussed in paragraph 19.10.1.

19.9.2 Investigating complaints

19.9.2.1 When can a complaint be lodged?

Key point: PAIA allows for an extensive internal appeal procedure when it comes to access requests against public bodies. This process has to be exhausted before a requester or a third party can lodge a complaint.

In terms of POPIA, 'any person' can complain about the 'interference with the personal information of a data subject'.[133] In terms of PAIA, a 'requester or third party' can lodge complaints if the requester or a third party:[134]

- was unsuccessful in appealing the decision of a public body internally[135]
- feels aggrieved by a decision by a relevant authority of a public body not to allow an internal appeal[136]
- feels aggrieved by the decision of the information officer of a 'any department of state or administration in the national or provincial sphere of government or any municipality in the local sphere of government'[137] to:
  - refuse access to information
  - charge a fee[138]
  - extend the 30-day period within which the public body must respond to a request for access[139]
  - not give access to the record in the form the requester asked for;[140] or
- feels aggrieved by a decision of the head of a private body to:
  - refuse access to information
  - charge a fee[141]

133 Section 73 of POPIA.

134 Section 77A of PAIA.

135 Section 74 and 75 of PAIA. This only applies to public bodies.

136 Section 75(2) of PAIA.

137 Paragraph *(a)* of the definition of 'public body' in section 1 of PAIA

138 Section 22 of PAIA.

139 Section 26(1) of PAIA.

140 Section 29(3) of PAIA.

141 Section 54(1) of PAIA.

- extend the 30-day period within which the private body must respond to a request for access; or[142]
- not give access to the record in the form the requester asked for.[143]

The requester or third party has 180 days from the decision within which to complain to the Information Regulator.

19.9.2.2 Who can lodge a complaint?

Complaints can be lodged by:

- The requester: This is the individual or organisation making the request to access their personal information.[144]
- A third party: A third party can lodge a complaint against an information officer or head of a private body's decision to grant access to a record. However, this only applies to public bodies if the public body in question is 'any department of state or administration in the national or provincial sphere of government or any municipality in the local sphere of government'.[145] A third party cannot lodge a complaint about the decision by the public or private body to charge a fee, extend the 30-day period or give access in a different format.[146]

Key point: We discussed the ground for refusal if a record contains the information of a third party in chapter 18 paragraph 18.3.3.2. Presumably, a third party will complain if they feel that the responsible party should not have granted access.

19.9.2.3 How to make a complaint

Lodging complaints is governed by section 77B and regulation 10 of the PAIA regulations.[147] Complaints must be lodged using Form 5 of the regulations.

142 Section 57(1) of PAIA.

143 Section 60 of PAIA.

144 The definition of 'requester' in section 1 of PAIA read with section 77A(1) and (2).

145 Section 74 of PAIA.

146 Section 77A(3) of PAIA.

147 Updated PAIA regulations were published on 27 August 2021. See GG 45057, GoN 757 of 27 August 2021.

19.9.2.4 When can the Information Regulator decide not to take action?

The Information Regulator has fewer grounds based on which to decide not to take action in respect of a complaint in terms of PAIA. They are if the:[148]

- complainant did not bring the complaint within 180 days from the date of the decision
- complaint is frivolous or vexatious; or
- Information Regulator is of the view that any further action is unnecessary or inappropriate.

19.9.2.5 What is the pre-investigation?

The requirements of PAIA in respect of the pre-investigation proceedings are identical to POPIA requirements.[149]

19.9.2.6 When can the Information Regulator act as a conciliator or attempt a settlement?

Section 77C(2) of PAIA also provides that the Information Regulator may act as a conciliator. Regulation 13 adds that the Information Regulator may conduct conciliation proceedings 'if it becomes clear to the Information Regulator that the complaint, or certain aspects of the complaint, could successfully be settled'. It would therefore appear that conciliation is not a mandatory step in the complaint resolution process.

Section 77F of PAIA also provides that the Information Regulator may attempt to secure a settlement. It does not provide that the public or private body must give a satisfactory assurance that it will not happen again.

19.9.2.7 When must the Information Regulator refer the matter to another regulatory body?

There is no provision in PAIA to refer a complaint to another regulatory body.

[148] Section 77D of PAIA.

[149] Section 77E of PAIA.

19.9.2.8 How a full investigation is conducted

Section 77G(1) of PAIA provides that when the Information Regulator conducts an investigation into a PAIA complaint, the Information Regulator has the same powers as a court in terms of section 80 of PAIA. When you replace the word 'court' with 'Information Regulator' in section 80(1) it provides that the [Information Regulator] may 'examine any record of a public or private body to which [PAIA] applies, and no such record may be withheld from [the Information Regulator] on any grounds'. The remainder of the section contains several measures aimed at protecting the confidentiality of the record.[150]

In terms of PAIA, the Information Regulator can also:

- issue information notices; and[151]
- issue enforcement notices.[152]

Tricky area: The provisions of PAIA and POPIA in relation to information notices and enforcement notices are identical, in fact, in many cases PAIA simply refers to the corresponding provisions in POPIA. However, the consequences of non-compliance are different. Not responding to or making false statements in response to an information notice is not an offence in terms of PAIA. Non-compliance with an enforcement notice is an offence which can land the information officer or head of a private body a fine or imprisonment of three years. However, PAIA does not contain a provision for administrative fines against a private or public body at all. Having said that, regulation 4(1)*(d)* of the 2018 POPIA Regulations does provide that it is the duty of the information officer or head of a private body to ensure that 'internal measures are developed together with adequate systems to process requests for information or access thereto'. Does this mean that the administrative fine for offences in terms of POPIA might apply?

---

150 This section was discussed extensively in *President of the Republic of South Africa v M & G Media Ltd* 2011 (2) SA 1 (SCA).

151 Section 77I of PAIA.

152 Section 77J of PAIA.

We think that it might. In the draft POPIA regulations, section 4(1)*(c)* has been deleted. That was the section that stated that the information officer must ensure that a PAIA manual is published. Presumably, this was deleted because it is already governed by PAIA. Section 4(1)*(d)* has been retained. Seems deliberate?[153]

PAIA investigations can also be referred to the Enforcement Committee.[154]

Tricky area: The PAIA Regulations contain a very curious provision. Regulation 11(6) states that 'if it appears that the Enforcement Committee is better suited to investigate the complaint, [the Information Regulator may] refer the complaint to the Enforcement Committee, and must in writing inform the complainant accordingly'. Section 92 of POPIA makes it clear that a referral to the Enforcement Committee only happens after the Information Regulator has completed their investigation. The Enforcement Committee does not investigate complaints; they make legal findings based on the facts gathered by the Information Regulator.

19.9.2.9 Appeals to the High Court

If the requester or the public or private body is 'aggrieved by any decision of the Information Regulator', they can apply to a court within 180 days for the appropriate relief.[155] This is a broader right than the right to appeal in terms of section 97 of POPIA which only provides a right to responsible parties to appeal information or enforcement notices.

19.9.3 Investigations initiated by the Information Regulator

PAIA does not have an equivalent section 76(3) of POPIA. In other words, the Information Regulator must receive a complaint before launching an investigation. However, the Information Regulator can conduct an assessment.[156]

Chapter 19

153 As we were reading the final proofs of this edition the Information Regulator published draft amendments to the Regulations for comment (GN 45120, GoN 829). 'Bugger,' we all said, agreeing, for once.

154 Section 77C*(b)*.

155 Sections 80 and 82 of PAIA.

156 Section 77H of PAIA.

19.9.4 Assessments by the Information Regulator

Section 77H of PAIA provides that the Information Regulator can assess 'whether a public or private body generally complies with the provisions of [PAIA] insofar as its policies and implementation procedures are concerned'.

The assessment can be triggered by:

- the Information Regulator
- an information officer or head of a private body; or
- any other person.

> **Tricky area:** POPIA states that the Information Regulator must conduct the assessment 'if it appears to be appropriate' and proceeds to list instances when this will be the case.[157] PAIA does not contain a similar provision. In addition, section 77H provides that what the Information Regulator is assessing is the public or private body's 'policies and implementation procedures'. This sounds a lot like the responsibility of the information officer in terms of POPIA to ensure that 'internal measures are developed together with adequate systems to process requests for information or access thereto'.[158] Perhaps this assessment is how the Information Regulator will determine whether the information officer has discharged this duty. However, it is not clear what will happen if the policies and implementation procedures are found wanting. Section 91(3) of POPIA states that the Information Regulator must issue a report which is the equivalent of an enforcement notice. PAIA does not contain such a provision, and so the implications of such an assessment are not clear.

19.10 OFFENCES, PENALTIES AND FINES

19.10.1 Offences and penalties created by POPIA

Just because a responsible party is non-compliant with POPIA, does not mean that the responsible party has committed an offence. Non-compliance will be an 'interference with the protection of personal information of a data subject' in terms of section 73. This triggers either an investigation or an assessment, as discussed in paragraph 19.6, but does not constitute an 'offence', even if the investigation or assessment results in an enforcement notice.

---

157 Section 89(3) of POPIA.

158 Regulation 4(1)*(d)* of the 2018 POPIA Regulations.

Here are the offences created by POPIA and PAIA:

Type of offence	Possible consequences (imprisonment/ fine)	Who's going to the slammer
Destroying, damaging, altering, concealing or falsifying a record with the intent to deny a data subject's right to access to information.[159]	A fine or imprisonment for a period not exceeding two years.	A person
Failing to make a complete PAIA manual available wilfully or in a grossly negligent manner.[160]	A fine or imprisonment for a period not exceeding two years.	Information officer or head of a private body (as defined in PAIA)
Charging a fee other than as prescribed by PAIA.[161]	A fine or imprisonment for a period not exceeding two years.	Information officer or head of a private body (as defined in PAIA)
Failing to comply with an enforcement notice in terms of PAIA.[162]	A fine or imprisonment for a period not exceeding three years.	Information officer or head of a private body (as defined in PAIA)
Failing to comply with an enforcement notice in terms of POPIA.[163]	A fine, imprisonment for a period not exceeding ten years, or both.[164]	A responsible party
Knowingly or recklessly making false statements in response to an information notice.[165]	A fine, imprisonment for a period not exceeding 12 months, or both.[166]	A responsible party

➡

159 Section 90(1) of PAIA.

160 Section 90(2) and (3) of PAIA.

161 Regulation 16 of the PAIA Regulations published on 27 August 2021. See GG 45057, GoN 757 of 27 August 2021.

162 Section 77K of PAIA.

163 Section 103(1).

164 Section 107*(a)*.

165 Section 103(2).

166 Section 107*(b)*.

Type of offence	Possible consequences (imprisonment/ fine)	Who's going to the slammer
A failure to treat personal information which comes to his or her knowledge in the course of the performance of his or her official duties as confidential.[167]	A fine, imprisonment for a period not exceeding 12 months, or both.[168]	A person acting on behalf of or under the direction of the Regulator
Hindering, obstructing or unlawfully influencing the Information Regulator or any person acting on behalf of the Regulator.[169]	A fine, imprisonment for a period not exceeding ten years, or both.[170]	Any person
Intentionally obstructing a person executing a warrant or failing (without a reasonable excuse) to provide assistance to a person executing a warrant.[171]	A fine, imprisonment for a period not exceeding 12 months, or both.[172]	Any person
Failing to appear or produce information if summoned by the Information Regulator.[173]	A fine, imprisonment for a period not exceeding 12 months, or both.[174]	Any person
Giving false evidence under oath.[175]	A fine, imprisonment for a period not exceeding ten years, or both.[176]	Any person
Failing to ensure that the conditions for the lawful processing of personal information are complied with in relation to account numbers assigned by a financial institution (in certain circumstances).[178]	A fine, imprisonment for a period not exceeding ten years, or both.[177]	A responsible party

167 Section 54 read with section 101.

168 Section 107*(b)*.

169 Section 100.

170 Section 107*(a)*.

171 Section 102.

172 Section 107*(b)*.

173 Section 104(1).

174 Section 107*(b)*.

175 Section 104(2).

176 Section 107*(a)*.

177 Section 107*(a)*.

178 Section 105(1). Read the special word of warning in paragraph 19.10.2.

Type of offence	Possible consequences (imprisonment/ fine)	Who?
Obtaining, disclosing, selling or trying to sell an account number assigned by a financial institution without the permission of the responsible party or getting someone else to obtain or disclose an account number.[179]	A fine, imprisonment for a period not exceeding ten years, or both.[180]	Any person

Tricky area: Who will be imprisoned? Unlike PAIA, which sometimes refers to the imprisonment of the information officer or head of a private body (as defined in PAIA),[180] POPIA sometimes refers to 'any person'. In the case of obstruction, breaches of confidentiality, witnesses giving false evidence and offences relating to account numbers, it will be the person actually perpetrating the act. Other offences refer to the 'responsible party', which is the public or private body; while there may be employees making decisions about how and why personal information is processed, they are acting in the course and scope of their employment.[181] In the case of offences that refer to 'responsible party', a fine will be the appropriate sanction – either a criminal fine in terms of section 107 or an administrative fine in terms of section 109. Section 332 of the Criminal Procedure Act 51 of 1977 allows for the criminal prosecution of a 'corporate body' through the citation of a 'director or servant of the corporate body' as a representative. The director or servant cannot be imprisoned, but can only be fined and the fine is payable by the corporate body.[182] Administrative fines are imposed on the responsible party and are discussed in paragraph 19.10.3.

179 Section 106(1), (3) and (4) read with the definition of 'account number' in section 105(5). Read the special word of warning in paragraph 19.10.2.

180 Section 107*(a)*.

181 See section 90 of PAIA.

182 See the definition of 'responsible party' in section 1 of POPIA. Also see the definition of 'private body' and 'public body'. Identifying the 'responsible party' is discussed in chapter 4.

183 Section 332(2).

19.10.2 A special word of warning about offences relating to account numbers

Due to the extreme sensitivity of bank account information, especially with the rise of online and banking fraud schemes in the digital age, POPIA creates two new offences for the commission of unlawful acts in connection with an account number.[184]

Section 105(4) of POPIA defines an 'account number' for the purposes of sections 105 and 106 of POPIA as meaning:

> 'any unique identifier that has been assigned—*(a)* to one data subject only; or *(b)* jointly to more than one data subject, by a financial or other institution which enables the data subject, referred to in paragraph *(a)*, to access his, her or its own funds or to access credit facilities or which enables a data subject, referred to in paragraph *(b)*, to access joint funds or to access joint credit facilities.'

Key point: 'Account number' therefore refers to account numbers that gives access to an account that the data subject can use to pay for things.

Section 105 of POPIA makes it an offence for a responsible party to contravene the provisions of section 8 of POPIA in connection to the processing of an account number. Under section 8 of POPIA, the responsible party must ensure that all the lawful conditions for processing personal information set out in Chapter 3 are complied with in connection to an account number (at the time of the determination of the purpose and means of the processing and during the processing itself).

184 Sections 105 and 106 of POPIA.

Key point: Normally, even in relation to the processing of special personal information or children's personal information, if a responsible party fails to comply with one of the lawful conditions for processing personal information, the failure of the responsible party to comply is not an automatic offence under POPIA. Rather, the responsible party would have to actually fail to comply with an enforcement notice issued by the Information Regulator in relation to the POPIA breach to potentially be guilty of an offence. Only then can the responsible party be fined or face imprisonment (or both) for contravening POPIA – the responsible party is essentially given a chance by the Information Regulator to rectify their conduct. However, given the potential serious harm that the confidentiality of a data subject's account number being compromised can cause,[184] there are no second or third chances in relation to the processing of account numbers. Here, a responsible party will be charged with an offence under POPIA, if they are found guilty of failing to comply with the lawful conditions of the processing of personal information in connection to an account number.[185] Section 332 of the Criminal Procedure Act 51 of 1977 allows for the criminal prosecution of a 'corporate body' through the citation of a 'director or servant of the corporate body' as a representative. The director or servant cannot be imprisoned, but can only be fined and the fine is payable by the corporate body.[186] The other alternative is to impose an administrative fine on the responsible party. Administrative fines are imposed on the responsible party and are discussed in paragraph 19.10.3.

If one thinks about it, it can be quite easy for a responsible party to contravene section 8 in connection to an account number. Therefore, in order for the contravention of section 8 by a responsible party in connection to an account number to meet the criteria of constituting an offence under section 105, the contravention must be 'of a serious or persistent nature' and 'likely cause substantial damage or distress to the data subject'.[188] Additionally, the responsible party must have known or ought to have known that:

[185] Have a read of the examples of the serious harm caused by the confidentiality of data subjects' bank details being breached through simple clerical errors in the UK, here: https://www.financial-ombudsman.org.uk/files/2832/45.pdf.

[186] Section 105(1) of POPIA.

[187] Section 332(2).

[188] Section 105(2) of POPIA.

- there was a risk that the contravention would occur; or
- that such contravention would likely cause substantial damage or distress to the data subject; and
- have failed to take reasonable steps to prevent the contravention.[189]

Key point: POPIA notes that it is a valid defence to such a charge, for the responsible party to contend that they have taken all reasonable steps to comply with the provisions of section 8 in connection to an account number.[189]

Additionally, section 106 creates a special offence for 'unlawful acts by third parties in connection with account numbers'.[191] A third party is acting unlawfully if it knowingly or recklessly does any of the following without the consent of the responsible party:

- obtains an account number (e.g. stealing it)
- discloses an account number (e.g. shares it with someone else); or
- procures the disclosure of an account number (e.g. gets someone else to do the dirty work).[192]

There are some defences available to third parties:

- obtaining or disclosing the account number was necessary to prevent, detect, investigate or prove an offence
- obtaining or disclosing the account number was required or authorised in terms of the law or a court order
- the third party held a 'reasonable belief' that they were legally entitled to obtain or disclose the account number
- the third party held a 'reasonable belief' that the responsible party would have consented had they known about the processing of the account number; or
- obtaining or disclosing the account number was in the public interest.[193]

Selling, or merely advertising or offering to sell, an account number which was obtained unlawfully is also an offence.[194]

189 Section 105(3) of POPIA.

190 Section 105(4) of POPIA.

191 Section 106.

192 Section 106(1) of POPIA.

193 Section 106(2) of POPIA.

194 Section 106(3) to (5).

Key point: Responsible parties who process, store or transmit credit card numbers also have to comply with the Payment Card Industry Data Security Standard (PCI DSS).

19.10.3 Administrative fines

An offence could also lead to an administrative fine.[195] We listed all the offences created by the legislation in paragraph 19.10.1.

Tricky area: Having a security compromise will not necessarily result in an administrative fine. When a responsible party brings a 'security compromise' to the Information Regulator's attention as is required in terms of section 22, the Information Regulator can commence an investigation into the security compromise.[195] Such an investigation would culminate in the issuing of an enforcement notice. It is only if the responsible party does not comply with the enforcement notice, that it becomes an 'offence' in terms of POPIA.[196] Or does it? Section 109(1) provides that '[i]f a responsible party is *alleged to have committed an offence*', the Information Regulator may deliver an infringement notice to the responsible party. Does this mean that a responsible party could receive an infringement notice, before an enforcement notice is issued? No, because having a security compromise (or any other infringement of POPIA) is not an offence as listed in section 107; it only becomes an offence if the responsible party does not comply with an enforcement notice. This argument holds true for all instances of non-compliance that are not listed in paragraph 19.10.1.

The requirements for a valid infringement notice are listed in section 109(2).

When faced with an infringement notice, a responsible party (the infringer) has the following options:[198]

- pay the administrative fine
- make payment arrangements with the Information Regulator to pay the administrative fine; or

[195] Section 109(1).

[196] Section 76(3).

[197] Section 103(1).

[198] Section 109(2)*(d)*.

- elect to rather be tried in court for the offence. If an infringer elects to do this, the Information Regulator will hand the matter over to the South African Police Service.[199]

A responsible party cannot be charged with an offence *and* be hit with an administrative fine.[200] It is either one or the other.

Tricky area: There is no provision for an appeal against an infringement notice in POPIA. If an infringer fails to pay, the Regulator will file the notice with the registrar of any competent court and it will have the effect of a civil judgment.[200] Presumably, this is because by this time, the responsible party will already have had the opportunity to appeal the enforcement notice? But what of the other types of offences listed in section 107? If an infringer is unhappy with the administrative fine, they will have to elect to be tried in court.

The maximum administrative fine is R10 million per offence.[202]

Tricky area: What is 'an offence'? For instance, if a responsible party interferes with the protection of the personal information of 100 data subjects, will the responsible party be liable for R1000 000 000? Remember that an administrative fine can only be imposed if the responsible party is guilty of an offence. Interfering with the protection of the personal information of a data subject is not an offence in and of itself; a responsible party will get fined per offence (e.g. non-compliance with an enforcement notice), not per data subject.

But what if the offence relates to an account number? In paragraph 19.10.2 we discuss the special offences created for the mishandling of account numbers. There the offence is not non-compliance with an enforcement notice, but the compromise of the account number. Does this mean that a responsible party can be fined per account number? It just might.[202]

---

199 Section 109(4).

200 Section 109(6) and (7).

201 Section 109(5).

202 Section 109(2)*(c)*.

203 This question is not new to criminal law and was considered in the light of the crime of robbery in *Dlamini v S* 2012 (2) SACR 1 (SCA) where the Supreme Court of Appeal found that the accused should be convicted of three robberies rather than one robbery even though the events occurred at the same time albeit with three different victims.

How does this amount compare to the fines in other jurisdictions? In terms of the EU GDPR certain infringements attract a maximum fine of EUR20 million or 4% of the total worldwide annual turnover of the controller for the preceding financial year. In Brazil, fines can reach BRL50 million. In New Zealand, the fines are relatively low at NZD10 000 and in China it is CNY50 million or 5% of global annual turnover.[204] So, South Africa is at the lower end of the spectrum and bucks the trend of associating the fine with the turnover of the responsible party.[205]

POPIA does allow for an increase in the administrative fine, but the adjustment must be 'in accordance with the average of the consumer price index'.[206] If the amount has not been updated for a number of years, the Minister must use the CPI for the immediately preceding period of 12 months multiplied by the number of years for which the maximum fine has remained the same.[207] In other words, the ability to adjust the maximum fine is not unfettered.

When determining the 'appropriate fine', the Information Regulator must consider the following wide array of factors:[208]

- the nature of the personal information
- the duration and extent of the contravention
- the number of data subjects affected or potentially affected
- whether or not the contravention raises an issue of public importance
- the likelihood of substantial damage or distress, including injury to feelings or anxiety suffered by data subjects

204 See Dan Simmons '12 countries with GDPR-like data privacy laws', available at https://insights.comforte.com/12-countries-with-gdpr-like-data-privacy-laws.

205 This section of POPIA is very curious as it not only goes against the prevailing international practice of associating the fine with the turnover of the company but also goes against similar consumer-facing legislation such as the National Credit Act 34 of 2005 which allows for a fine of the 'greater' R1 million or 10% of the Respondent's turnover (section 151(2) of the National Credit Act 34 of 2005). The decision to limit this amount is most unfortunate as it opens the door for large organisations to intentionally breach POPIA and simply absorb the R10 million fine as part of the cost of doing business. This approach is not available to smaller companies with smaller turnovers and so the playing field is not level. Having said that, the concept of a fine based on turnover is not without its problems as well. Consider *Shoprite Investments Limited v National Credit Regulator* (A509/2107) [2019] ZAGPPHC 956 (18 December 2019) available at http://www.saflii.org/za/cases/ZAGPPHC/2019/956.html, where the National Consumer Tribunal had no information on the turnover of Shoprite and as a result defaulted to the R1 million fine.

206 Section 109(10).

207 Section 109(10).

208 Section 109(3).

- whether the responsible party or a third party could have prevented the contravention from occurring
- any failure to carry out a risk assessment or a failure to operate good policies, procedures and practices to protect personal information; and
- whether the responsible party has previously committed an offence in terms of POPIA.

Key point: These factors should inform a responsible party's strategy to implement POPIA. The factors underscore the need for a risk-based approach to POPIA compliance.[208] For instance, factors such as the number of data subjects affected, the public importance of the processing and the level of harm or distress should be factored in when doing risk assessments. In addition, being able to demonstrate compliance through policies, procedures and practices will assist responsible parties in managing the fallout of incidents.[209]

19.11 CIVIL LIABILITY

19.11.1 Who can institute an action

Data subjects have the right to institute civil action against a responsible party for 'interference with the protection of the personal information of a data subject' as defined in section 73.[211] Data subjects can also request that the Information Regulator institutes civil action.[212]

19.11.2 Strict civil liability (but not that strict)

Section 99(1) provides that data subjects or the Information Regulator can institute action 'whether or not there is intent or negligence on the part of the responsible party'. In other words, the liability is 'strict'. However, the words 'reasonable' and 'reasonably' appear 78 times in POPIA.[213] As we discussed in chapter 2 paragraph 2.6.1, reasonableness and the principles of necessity and proportionality will have a place in determining whether the protection of personal information of a data subject has been interfered with in the first place. In addition, section 99(2) lists the following defences:

209 We discuss risk assessments in chapter 20 paragraph 20.3.

210 The benefits of well-written and well-implemented policies are discussed in chapter 20 paragraph 20.2.5.

211 This was discussed in paragraph 19.6.1.

212 Section 99(1).

213 Yes, we counted.

- **Vis major**:[214] It will be a defence if the interference was caused by *vis major*. *Vis major* or *casus fortuitus* is some unforeseen and extraordinary accident or circumstance which would make it impossible for a responsible party to comply with POPIA. However, the responsible party would still have to show that the impossibility was not self-created or the fault of the responsible party.

Key point: We have argued that the 'satisfactory safeguard' standard in section 19 may require that responsible parties should plan for disasters and ensure that their information infrastructure is resilient by doing business continuity management. Not doing so would prevent a responsible party from relying on *vis major* if disaster does strike, because the responsible party should have foreseen the disaster.

- **Consent of the plaintiff**: It seems that a data subject can waive or limit their right to claim compensation for an infringement of their privacy.[215]

Tricky area: Does it open the door for a person to contract out of the right to claim damages? Or even to the infringement of their privacy? Under the common law, it is possible for a person to consent to an infringement of their privacy if that consent is voluntary, revocable and not contrary to public policy or *contra bonos mores*.[216] [The question of whether a person can 'waive rights that were conferred by law solely for his or her benefit' was considered in *The Council of Medical Schemes v Genesis Medical Scheme*.[217] The court observed that the general principle that rights can be waived does not apply in matters 'involving public interest and in respect of which public policy requires compliance'. The court quotes the famous speech of Lord Hailsham in *Johnson v Moreton*:[218]

➡

214 If you prefer French, *force majeure*. If you prefer high drama, Act of God.

215 We do not think this is a reference to consent as a legal justification (see chapter 2 paragraph 2.6.6.). If a responsible party obtained a valid consent to use the data subject's personal information in a certain way, that is not an infringement of their privacy.

216 SA Law Reform Commission Project 124 on Privacy and Data Protection (2009 Report) 48.

217 2016 (1) SA 429 (SCA).

218 1980 AC 37 (HL).

> '[I]t can no longer be treated as axiomatic that, in the absence of explicit language, the Courts will permit contracting out of the provisions of an Act of Parliament where that Act, though silent as to the possibility of contracting out, nevertheless is manifestly passed for the protection of a class of persons who do not negotiate from a position of equal strength, but in whose well-being there is a public as well as a private interest. Such acts are not necessarily to be treated as simply *jus pro se introduction*, a "private remedy and a private right" which an individual member of the class may simply bargain away by reason of his freedom of contract. It is precisely his weakness as a negotiating party from which Parliament wishes to protect him.'

Of course, POPIA is not silent on waiver. Could section 99 be an attempt to do just that! Just that? In any event, in cases where the data subject is also a 'consumer' for purposes of the Consumer Protection Act 68 of 2008, one has to comply with the provisions of the CPA that ensure the right to fair, just and reasonable terms and conditions.[219] For instance:

- the waiver must be in plain language[220]
- it must not be unfair, unjust or unreasonable (e.g. by being excessively one-sided or if the data subjects are vulnerable)[221]
- the data subject cannot waive liability for gross negligence[222]
- the fact, nature and effect of the waiver needs to be drawn to the attention of the data subject in a conspicuous manner and form before the data subject shares their personal information with the responsible party[223]
- the data subject must be given sufficient time to understand the waiver;[224] and
- the data subject must sign the waiver.[225]

- **Fault on the part of the plaintiff**: If a data subject intentionally or negligently caused the infringement of the protection of their own personal information, the responsible party can raise this as a defence. Will this defence be absolute? Presumably, the principles of contributory negligence will be followed here; that is that the data subject's claim will be reduced based on his or her fault.[226]

219 Sections 48 to 52.

220 Section 49(3) read with section 22.

221 Section 48 read with the factors in section 52.

222 Section 51(1)*(c)*(i).

223 Section 49(4).

224 Section 49(5).

225 Section 49(2).

226 Does the Apportionment of Damages Act 34 of 1956 apply to cases where there is strict liability? According to De Stadler and Du Plessis: '[T]he possibility of apportionment in respect of such action

- **Compliance was not reasonably practicable in the circumstances of the case**: We discuss the concept of 'reasonably practicable' in chapter 2 paragraph 2.6.2. Do not get too excited, the inclusion of this defence does not mean that this defence is available to justify non-compliance with POPIA. It is merely a defence against a claim for damages.
- **The Information Regulator has granted an exemption in terms of section 37**: This defence is a bit odd. If an exemption was granted, the responsible party is not interfering with the protection of personal information. We do not think a responsible party would be able to apply for an exemption after the horse has bolted.

19.11.3 What can data subjects claim?

Data subjects can claim for:[227]

- patrimonial loss (such as financial loss and loss of income)
- non-patrimonial loss (such as damage to reputation and pain and suffering)
- aggravated damages

Key point: 'Aggravated damages' is not previously recognised by South African law and POPIA does not provide assistance on how it should be calculated. Here is what the SA Law Reform Commission had to say:

> 'It further recommends that a court may, apart from compensatory damages for patrimonial and non-patrimonial loss, also award aggravated damages that are just and equitable ... It should be noted that the meaning of the expression "punitive (penal) damages" is damages awarded to punish the defendant. Aggravated damages, on the other hand, may include punitive damages but may basically only be compensatory damages and may therefore differ from punitive damages.'[228]

- interest; and
- legal costs on a scale determined by a court.

has not been specifically excluded. The problem of applying apportionment in strict liability cases is that apportionment is normally based on comparative degrees of fault, whereas fault is not assessed for the purposes of strict liability. It is impossible, therefore, to measure the relative contribution made by the negligence on the part of one or more of the defendants, when they, notionally at least, are not being assessed in such terms.' See De Stadler & Du Plessis 'Section 61' in *Commentary on the Consumer Protection Act* at 61-28. But, as we pointed out, civil liability in terms of POPIA is not strict.

[227] Section 99(3).

[228] SA Law Reform Commission Project 124 on Privacy and Data Protection (2009 Report) 599.

19.11.4 POPIA and class action lawsuits

As large-scale data breaches have become more commonplace internationally, so have the subsequent privacy rights' class actions lawsuits which have been launched against the various companies housing the compromised personal information.[229] For example, in October 2020, international law firm Pinsent Masons reported that the trends are pointing to a rise in data breach claims.[230] Pinsent Masons said that in their team's experience working on a significant number of data breach response matters, in cases where data subjects are notified about a data breach, around 20% have resulted in actual or threatened claims of legal action from data subjects.[231]

On a global scale, one of the biggest legal settlements seen so far in this arena has been for the Equifax data breach in 2017.[232] Here, the international credit bureau settled with various regulators and over 24 consolidated class action lawsuits, to the total tune of around USD700 million.[233]

So, what are the chances of a privacy rights' class action lawsuit being launched against a South African organisation as the result of the organisation suffering a data breach?

Class actions are recognised in South African law, and have become more frequent in the post-1994 constitutional era.[234] The foundation for class actions in South Africa is laid down in section 38*(c)* of the Constitution which states:

> '[A]nyone acting as a member of, or in the interests of, a group or class of persons has the right to approach a competent court to allege that a right in the Bill of Rights has been infringed or threatened.'[235]

---

229 CSO 'The biggest data breach fines, penalties and settlements so far', available at https://www.csoonline.com/article/3410278/the-biggest-data-breach-fines-penalties-and-settlements-so-far.html.

230 Pinsent Masons 'Trends point to a rise in data breach claims', available at https://www.pinsentmasons.com/out-law/analysis/trends-rise-data-breach-claims.

231 Pinsent Masons.

232 Federal Trade Commission 'Equifax to pay $575 million as part of settlement with FTC, CFPB, and states related to 2017 data breach', available at https://www.ftc.gov/news-events/press-releases/2019/07/equifax-pay-575-million-part-settlement-ftc-cfpb-states-related.

233 CNN 'Equifax will pay up to $700 million over its data breach. Here's how to claim your money', available at https://edition.cnn.com/2019/07/25/us/equifax-700-million-settlement-data-breach-trnd/index.html.

234 For example, in 2019, the South Gauteng High Court approved a R5 billion class action lawsuit settlement, reached between old mining companies and law firms representing thousands of miners who contracted the fatal lung diseases silicosis and tuberculosis. See *africanews.com* 'South African court approves $353 million class action settlement', available at https://www.africanews.com/2019/07/28/south-african-court-approves-353-million-class-action-settlement/.

235 Section 38*(c)* of the Constitution of the Republic of South Africa, 1996.

From a purely procedural perspective, in the case of *FirstRand Bank Ltd v Chaucer Publications (Pty) Ltd*,[236] it was held that the following steps must be taken to launch a class action suit:

- Leave must be sought from the High Court to embark on a representative basis prior to actually embarking on that road.
- The determination of a common interest sufficient to justify a class action takes place prior to the institution of the proceedings.[237]
- The representing party must give sufficient notice to all the affected parties so that they may associate or disassociate themselves from the proposed litigation.[238]

Then in 2012, *Children's Resource Centre Trust v Pioneer Foods (Pty) Ltd*[239] *(Children's Resource Centre)* widened the scope for class action suits in South Africa. This judgment extended class action litigation to include civil damages claims which fall outside the scope of the Bill of Rights, and established the criteria for the certification of a class action claim in South Africa.[240]

The court in *Children's Resource Centre* held that the following criteria are the core considerations that need to be taken into account in a class action certification inquiry (i.e. the court must be satisfied that):

- The class must be defined with enough precision to allow for the objective determination that an individual falls into the class.
- The cause of action raises a triable issue.
- The right to relief depends on the determination of issues of law and/or fact that are common to all members of the class.
- The relief sought or damages claimed flow from the cause of action and are ascertainable and capable of determination.
- Where the claim is for damages, there is an appropriate procedure for allocating the damages to the members of the class.
- The representative should not have any conflict of interest with the class and must have the capacity to conduct the litigation properly.

236 2008 (2) SA 592 (C).

237 Please note that in the case of *Nkala v Harmony Gold Mining Co* 2016 (5) SA 240 (GJ) it was held that a certification was not dependent on each class member's case being fully and finally determined once the common issues were determined in favour of the class. As long as it could be shown that determination of the common issues would allow the cases of the individual class members to move forward without duplication of the judicial analysis, a certification of the intended class action would be justified and would be in the interests of justice.

238 *FirstRand Bank Ltd v Chaucer Publications (Pty) Ltd* at paragraph 26.

239 2013 (2) SA 213 (SCA).

240 Bowmans 'Guide – Class action litigation in South Africa', available at https://www.bowmanslaw.com/wp-content/uploads/2017/01/Class-Action-Litigation-Guide.pdf.

- The tool of a class action must be the most appropriate procedure to adopt for adjudication of the underlying claims (given the composition of the class and the nature of the proposed action).[241]

In the case of *Mukaddam v Pioneer Foods (Pty) Ltd*[242] it was held 'that a class action ought to be certified if it were in the interests of justice to do so'.[243] The court further held that the core considerations for class action lawsuits outlined in the *Children's Resource Centre*:

> 'must serve as factors to be taken into account in determining where the interests of justice lie in a particular case. They must not be treated as conditions precedent or jurisdictional facts which must be present before an application for certification may succeed. The absence of one or another requirement must not oblige a court to refuse certification where the interests of justice demand otherwise.'[244]

It is clear that the legal position in South Africa on class action lawsuits is by no means settled. Nevertheless, on the basis of the above, it is clear that data subjects whose privacy rights have been infringed in a data breach (or the Information Regulator on their behalf) can probably bring a class action suit against the responsible party in a South African court.

19.12 PRACTICAL ADVICE

19.12.1 Do not get caught

Of course, this is a joke. As we have said before, POPIA risks are here to stay, because it is unlikely that any organisation will be 100% POPIA compliant 100% of the time. So, what are the things organisations can do to mitigate the seriousness of non-compliance when it does occur and the Information Regulator has gotten wind of it?

19.12.2 Manage complaints

Many POPIA enforcement actions will start with a complaint from a data subject. In many instances, the data subject would have complained to the responsible party or tried to exercise their data subject rights first and will resort to a complaint with the Information Regulator if the responsible party does not respond adequately or in time.

---

241 Dentons 'The difficulties of class action claims in South Africa', available at https://www.dentons.com/en/insights/newsletters/2019/june/27/south-africa-newsletter/south-africa-newsletter-june-2019-2nd-edition/the-difficulties-of-class-action-claims-in-south-africa, read with the *Children's Resource Centre* case at paras [23], [26] and [28] at 226H–227B, 228B–E and 229C–E.

242 2013 (5) SA 89 (CC).

243 *Mukaddam v Pioneer Foods (Pty) Ltd* at [A] on 90.

244 *Mukaddam v Pioneer Foods (Pty) Ltd* at paragraph 35.

Every time a data subject tries to exercise their rights or complains, it is an opportunity for a responsible party to prevent a complaint with the Information Regulator.

Responsible parties should make sure that they have a user-friendly data subject request process and that it has been well implemented, tested and that employees are trained. Data subject rights are discussed in chapter 18.

19.12.3 Hope for the best, plan for the worst

In chapter 5 paragraph 5.6 we discussed the importance of incident response planning. The act of planning incident response is just as important when it comes to other types of non-compliance with POPIA. It is important to rehearse how the responsible party would respond to an information notice, a warrant and a summons.

19.12.4 Document decisions

We have mentioned the concept of unconscious incompetence a couple of times now. The key to POPIA compliance is to move to a state of conscious incompetence. What we mean by that is that organisations should be deliberate in how they manage POPIA risk. When enforcement action begins, those organisations who have the ammunition to defend their decisions and priorities will be in a good position to demonstrate that they behaved reasonably. This means that how well you documented POPIA compliance will be pivotal. We discuss this in chapter 1 paragraph 1.4.

20

How to implement a POPIA Programme

20.1 WHAT TO EXPECT IN THIS CHAPTER

Many information officers want to reduce POPIA to a once-off, tick-box exercise. While the sentiment is understandable, it could not be further from the truth. As the ICO points out in its Accountability Framework:[1] 'Accountability is **not about ticking boxes**. While there are some accountability measures that you must take, such as conducting a data protection impact assessment for high-risk processing, there isn't a "one size fits all" approach' (their emphasis).

A POPIA Programme is a set of activities to be undertaken by the information officer within a certain period (e.g. annually). This includes the review of specific policies and procedures, completing personal information impact assessments and monitoring POPIA compliance. It becomes a permanent fixture at an organisation.[2] A POPIA Programme is governed by a (POPIA) compliance framework.[3] It is not necessarily a document. Rather, it is comprised of all of the strategies, initiatives, policies, procedures, standards and guidelines that work together to achieve POPIA compliance. However, it is a good idea to create a document that ties all of this together as it will make it easier to audit POPIA compliance and to demonstrate compliance to the Information Regulator.

Key point: There is neither a right way nor a wrong way to implement POPIA (yet). This chapter sets out our approach to compliance with POPIA, but other specialists adopt other approaches. Ours is underpinned by compliance and risk management theory and benchmarking against what responsible parties have done in other parts of the world. Use it, don't use it; it is up to you.

In this chapter we discuss the following:

- An overview of a (POPIA) compliance framework
- Personal information impact assessments
- Internal measures to process requests for information or access thereto
- Providing training
- Privacy management software
- How on Earth must a small business do this?

---

1 ICO *Accountability Framework*, available at https://ico.org.uk/for-organisations/accountability-framework/.

2 This definition is borrowed and adapted from the Generally Accepted Compliance Practice framework of the Compliance Institute of Southern Africa ('GACP') definition of 'compliance programme'. By contrast, a POPIA Project has a defined beginning and end, with a defined scope, resources and deliverables. The aim of a POPIA Project will often be to establish a POPIA Programme.

3 It is referred to in regulation 4(1)*(a)* of the POPIA Regulations.

20.2 AN OVERVIEW OF A (POPIA) COMPLIANCE FRAMEWORK

One of the responsibilities of an information officer is to 'ensure that ... a compliance framework is developed, implemented, monitored and maintained'.[4] Compliance officers will not be strangers to this obligation as it bears an uncanny resemblance to the definition of a 'compliance framework' in the *Generally Accepted Compliance Practice Framework* issued by the Compliance Institute Southern Africa. With some minor adjustments, a POPIA compliance framework could therefore be defined as:

> 'all of the interrelated and/or interacting components within an organisation that:
>
> - Set out the organisation's approach to the management of [POPIA] risk. The framework addresses aspects such as compliance strategy, objectives, governance, policy, roles and responsibilities, compliance risk appetite, process and techniques and reporting.
> - Establish and maintain (or contribute to, support, facilitate or enabling establishing and maintaining) [POPIA] related objectives and the activities, policies, procedures, processes and practices to achieve those objectives; and
> - Direct, guide, contribute to, facilitate, enable or support [POPIA] related practices and activities.'[5]

For organisations who already have a compliance framework, POPIA and personal information risk, as a category of 'compliance risk' would form part of that larger framework. In fact, in the words of Dr Coombs, the NSW Privacy Commissioner: 'Privacy is easiest when it is the organisation's standard mode of operation and monitoring is mainstreamed through existing governance mechanisms such as the Board, Executive or Senior Management meetings. Monitoring and review can be achieved through existing mechanisms such as the Audit and Risk Committee or Customer and other Advisory Committees.'

The verbs used to describe an information officer's responsibilities in relation to the POPIA Compliance Framework are important:[6]

- **Develop**: The information officer must ensure that the framework is created. This is done through obtaining executive sponsorship, doing stakeholder consultation, defining roles and responsibilities and policy development.
- **Implement**: This is done by implementing the policies created during the development phase.

[4] Regulation 4(1)*(a)* of the POPIA Regulations.

[5] This definition is borrowed and adapted from the definition of 'compliance framework' in the GACP.

[6] Regulation 4(1)*(a)* of the POPIA Regulations.

- **Monitor and maintain**: This is done through compliance monitoring and audits and by responding to the findings made.

> **Key point:** The POPIA Regulations provide that the information officer must 'ensure' that a compliance framework is developed etc.[7] This does not mean that the information officer must do all of the work themselves. In fact, doing so may well compromise their independence. Instead, the information officer should provide advice to management on POPIA obligations, oversee implementation of compliance-related procedures (e.g. a personal information impact assessment procedure), report to the governing body on the level of compliance being achieved, liaise with the Information Regulator, resolve issues of non-compliance, and assist with investigations and providing training. See the discussion of roles and responsibilities in chapter 1 paragraph 1.3.

This image represents a POPIA Compliance Framework. It is also a roadmap to creating a sustainable POPIA Programme.

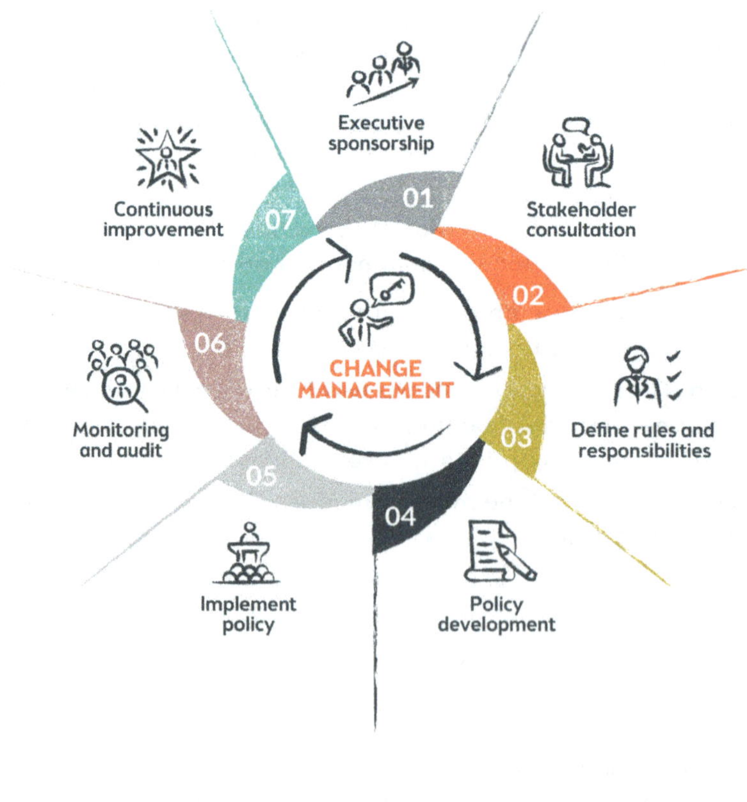

7 Regulation 4(1) of the POPIA Regulations.

An organisation's approach to each phase in the POPIA Programme life cycle should be documented in its POPIA compliance framework.

In this section, we will discuss each phase in this POPIA Programme life cycle.

20.2.1 Change management

POPIA is a people problem. First, to become POPIA compliant, organisations have to make changes to how they operate. If people do not adopt these changes, POPIA compliance will remain elusive. Second, human error is one of the leading causes of data breaches.[8] This means that training should be a large component of a POPIA Programme. Third, some employees will have new roles that will require new skills. The worst outcome is if nothing changes.

This is where change management comes in. It is a set of practices based on an understanding of how people respond to change, to effectively prepare, equip and support people through change. Not unlike project management, change management requires a plan. While project management focuses on costs and deliverables, a change management plan focuses on the changes in mindsets, skills and knowledge that will be required to achieve POPIA compliance.

Effective change management centres around answering these questions:

- **Why** should the organisation become POPIA compliant? The key is to understand that different organisations and different groups of people within organisations are motivated by different things. In paragraph 20.2.2 some of these motivations are discussed in the context of getting executive sponsorship.
- **What** needs to change to achieve POPIA compliance? This will depend on the outcomes of the personal information impact assessments we discuss in paragraph 20.3.
- **Who** needs to be involved in the POPIA Programme? This is also referred to as stakeholder engagement, which is discussed in paragraph 20.2.3.
- **How** and **when** do things need to change? A communication and training plan is essential to achieve POPIA compliance. This is discussed in paragraph 20.5.

[8] IBM Security *Cost of a Data Breach Report 2020*, available at https://www.ibm.com/security/digital-assets/cost-data-breach-report/#/.

20.2.2 Executive sponsorship: Why POPIA Programmes are worth investing in

POPIA affects most processes in an organisation. This means that having the support of the leadership of the organisation is vital in establishing a sustainable, and well-funded, POPIA Programme. Here is some ammunition which can be used to convince executives that POPIA Programmes are worth investing in:

- The cost of data breaches can be astronomical. IBM and the Ponemon Institute calculate the average cost of data breaches annually.[9] In 2020, the average cost stood at USD3.9 million. These costs are comprised of regulatory fines, civil liability in the form of class actions, disruptions in operations due to investigations and regulatory interventions, business continuity risk due to lost or inaccessible information, unexpected financial expenditure to remedy shortcomings, and the loss of goodwill. The good news is that having an incident response plan and team, and testing them from time to time, would in 2020 have saved an organisation USD2 million.
- A POPIA Programme can have a positive return on investment. In 2020, on average, for every dollar spent on privacy, organisations receive USD2.70 in benefits.[10] POPIA Programmes can reduce sales delays, mitigate losses from data breaches, enable agility and innovation, achieve operational efficiency from data controls, make organisations more attractive to investors, and build loyalty and trust with consumers.
- Consumer surveys are showing that consumers increasingly care enough about their privacy that they will switch to another service provider if they feel that their privacy is not a priority. This market segment is often referred to as 'privacy actives'. Organisations can attract this market segment by embedding privacy in their overall customer experience and by fixing the transparency gap.[11]

---

[9] IBM Security *Cost of a Data Breach Report 2020*, available at https://www.ibm.com/security/digital-assets/cost-data-breach-report/#/.

[10] CISCO *From Privacy to Profit: Achieving Positive Returns on Privacy Investments*, available at https://www.cisco.com/c/dam/global/en_uk/products/collateral/security/2020-data-privacy-cybersecurity-series-jan-2020.pdf.

[11] Thomas C Redman and Robert M Waitman 'Do you care about privacy as much as your customers do?' *Harvard Business Review*, available at https://hbr.org/2020/01/do-you-care-about-privacy-as-much-as-your-customers-do.

- Other organisations are investing in privacy. If all else fails, business leaders may be persuaded by the 'keeping up with the Joneses' argument. Each year, Ernst & Young measures what organisations are spending on privacy.[12] In 2019, when the EU GDPR dust had settled, organisations were spending USD128 per employee per year.

20.2.3 Stakeholder consultation

POPIA compliance, and by extension, a POPIA Programme, is a massive exercise in teamwork and co-ordination. This means that stakeholder consultation is extremely important. Unsuck-it.com, a jargon dictionary, quips that 'stakeholders are anyone in an organisation who will kill a good idea out of spite or political ill will'.[13] Truth be told, failing to manage important stakeholders can undermine a POPIA Programme.

It is important to identify the following types of stakeholders:

- Those who **govern** the change: Who are the decision-makers? Who approves new policies? Who are the leaders?
- Those who must give **input**: Who will help to develop new policies and procedures? Who understands the impacts of new policies and procedures?
- Those who are **impacted** by the change: Who will need to change how they work?
- Those whose **support** you need: Who in the organisation already has some of the skills needed to implement a POPIA Programme?

One method used to identify stakeholders is to make a chart of the different functional areas within an organisation. Here is a typical one:

[12] IAPP-EY Annual Governance Report 2019, available at https://iapp.org/store/books/a191P000003Qv5xQAC/.

[13] http://unsuck-it.com/.

Ask the following question of each business area:

- How are they impacted by POPIA?
- Do they already fulfil some of the functions required by POPIA?
- Can they assist in the POPIA Programme?
- How can the POPIA Programme assist them?

Once the stakeholders have been identified, the impact of the POPIA Programme on each of them should be assessed. This ultimately leads to a stakeholder engagement plan. In this image, the level of influence of a stakeholder and the level of the impact the POPIA Programme will have on them is used to determine how the stakeholder should be engaged:

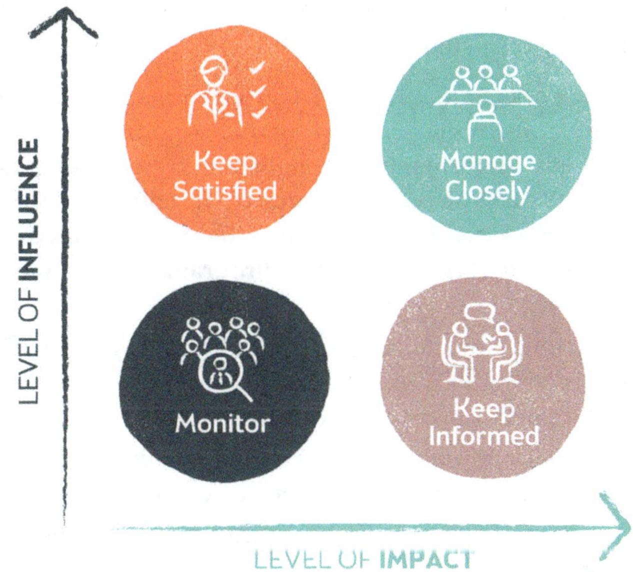

* Influence means the capacity of the stakeholder to affect the behaviour, development or culture of the organisation and its employees.

** Impact means the level of change to which the stakeholder will be subjected to by POPIA.

20.2.4 Define roles and responsibilities

In risk and compliance management it is considered best practice to follow the three lines of defence model. To properly comply with POPIA and manage POPIA risk, all three lines need to be functioning optimally.

As discussed in chapter 1, this is how the three lines of defence model operates in the POPIA context:[14]

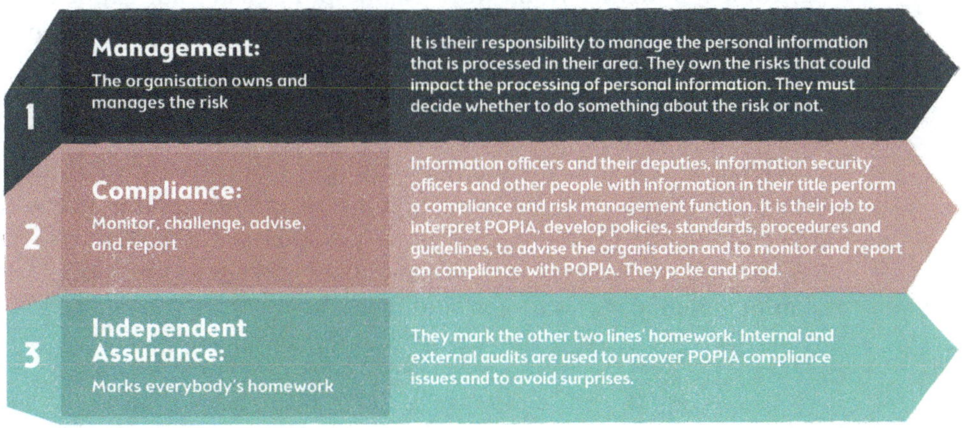

[14] See the discussion of roles and responsibilities in chapter 1 paragraph 1.3.

The different roles and responsibilities required for POPIA compliance were discussed in chapter 1.

To establish a sustainable POPIA Programme, it is essential to ensure that the responsibilities created by the programme are included in the organisation's performance management system. What is performance management? In the POPIA context, it could be described as the continuous process of improving the performance of individuals in their roles within the POPIA Programme. It should include the following steps:

- Individual and team goals should be aligned with the strategic goals of the POPIA Programme and should be documented (e.g. in key performance indicators).
- Plans should be developed to achieve these goals and individual and team progress should be reviewed and assessed.
- The knowledge, skills and abilities of the individuals should be developed.

20.2.5 Policy development

A policy is a formal, high-level statement that applies throughout an organisation. It generally promotes operational efficiencies, enhances an organisation's mission or reduces risk. It states required actions and may be implemented through standards, procedures and other supporting documents.

Key point: POPIA does not require that an organisation must have policies that ensure the protection of personal information. However, we view (well-drafted) policies as an indispensable part of a compliance framework. While policies are not explicitly required in POPIA, it is one of the factors the Information Regulator will take into account when determining the size of the administrative fine against a responsible party who is guilty of an offence (see chapter 19 paragraph 19.10.3). Section 109(3)*(g)* provides that the Information Regulator must consider 'any failure to carry out a risk assessment or a failure to operate good policies, procedures and practices to protect personal information'. The European Data Protection Board also lists policies as an example of appropriate organisational measures.[15]

15 European Data Protection Board *Guidelines 4/2019 on Article 25 Data Protection by Design and by Default* 8, available at https://edpb.europa.eu/sites/default/files/files/file1/edpb_guidelines_201904_dataprotection_by_design_and_by_default_v2.0_en.pdf.

Generally speaking, the compliance obligations imposed by POPIA will be met by implementing 'compliance controls'. These controls are 'generally incorporated in an organisation's policies, procedures, processes, people practices and structures, systems and technology'.[16] We believe that policies play an important role in the broader discipline of information governance, but also assist organisations to demonstrate compliance with legislation such as POPIA. As discussed in chapter 1, one of the principles of information governance is 'standardisation'; the extent to which an organisation has an agreed way of working.[17] Policies are a way of defining and documenting an organisation's way of working transparently.

What policies need to be in place to manage POPIA risk, how they are structured and who the policy owners will be will differ from organisation to organisation. Three policy areas need to be covered to achieve full POPIA compliance:

- information security management
- privacy; and
- records management.

They are distinct from one another because they apply to different classes of information. While the Protection of Personal Information Policy only applies to personal information, the Information Security Management Policy and Records Management Policy applies to all types of information. Often, organisations will make the information officer or a specific deputy information officer the policy owner, but not always. This is another reason to keep the policies separate.

Here are the principles we often include in our policies:

16 See the definition of 'compliance control' in the GACP.

17 Chapter 1 paragraph 1.3.3.

<table>
<tr><th>Name and scope of the policy</th><th>Topics which should be addressed</th></tr>
<tr><td>Information Security Management Policy
This policy describes how personal information is secured against:<ul><li>breaches of confidentiality</li><li>failures of integrity; and</li><li>interruptions to the availability of information.</li></ul>This policy applies to all types of information, not just personal information.</td><td><ul><li>information classification</li><li>access control</li><li>third-party management</li><li>information integrity</li><li>availability and business continuity management</li><li>compliance with binding rules that govern information security (e.g. all relevant privacy regulations, corporate governance standards, internal policies and contractual obligations)</li><li>incident management and response</li><li>empowered and responsible users</li><li>clear roles and responsibilities in the implementation of the policy; and</li><li>information security assessments.[18]</li></ul></td></tr>
<tr><td>Protection of Personal Information Policy
This policy ensures that the organisation proactively complies with all relevant privacy regulations and respects the right to privacy of its data subjects.
This policy only applies to personal information.</td><td><ul><li>information classification</li><li>documenting personal information processing activities</li><li>purpose specification</li><li>legal basis for processing</li><li>assess further processing</li><li>minimality</li><li>lawful sources</li><li>transparency</li><li>information quality</li><li>limit sharing with third parties</li><li>information security (a cross-reference to the Information Security Management Policy)</li><li>incident management and response (may be the same process as the one in the Information Security Management Policy)</li><li>respect data subject rights</li><li>empowered and responsible users</li><li>clear roles and responsibilities in the implementation of the policy; and</li><li>personal information impact assessments.</li></ul></td></tr>
</table>

➥

[18] Information security assessments assess whether a business process (activity) complies with the principles in the Information Security Management Policy. When doing a personal information impact assessment, the assessments for all three policies can be consolidated. They also exist separately, because this policy also applies to other types of information.

Name and scope of the policy	Topics which should be addressed
Records Management Policy This policy ensures that the organisation's recordkeeping: • is transparent, consistent, and accountable • meets legal, regulatory, fiscal, operational, and historical requirements • supports the efficient conduct of its business; and • ensures the preservation of archives documenting its history and development. This policy applies to all types of information, not just personal information.	• comply with all legal and operational record-keeping requirements and create a records retention schedule • secure destruction of records • information security (a cross-reference to the Information Security Management Policy) • effective version control • minimise duplication by identifying and controlling master records • manage and preserve knowledge and intellectual property • incident management and response (may be the same process as the one in the Information Security Management Policy) • empowered and responsible users • clear roles and responsibilities in the implementation of the policy; and • records management assessments.[19]

When new policies are introduced, or existing policies are amended, the policy owner should support management to develop implementation plans. Policy implementation is discussed in the next section.

20.2.6 Policy implementation

Policies get a bad rap because '[n]obody reads it, nobody owns it, nobody updates it, nobody tests compliance against it. It is a hostage of fortune at best, a ticking time bomb at worst. It adds no value, it gives no help. Why bother?'[20] It is true – too many organisations are content to have their policies gather dust in a folder somewhere. It is essential that once they are approved, policies should be successfully implemented. A policy is considered successfully implemented once compliance with the policy is measured (usually through an internal or external audit) and non-compliance is routinely addressed.

19 Records management assessments assess whether a business process (activity) complies with the principles in the Records Management Policy. When doing a personal information impact assessment, the assessments for all three policies can be consolidated. They also exist separately, because this policy also applies to other types of information.

20 Howard Walwyn 'What makes a good policy: Five watchwords', available at https://prism-clarity.com/2016/07/makes-good-policy-5-watchwords/.

How a policy will be implemented is something which should be considered when the policy is drafted. Often, organisations adopt policies that are not practical or the organisation lacks the resources to implement it.

A policy implementation plan is comprised of the following elements:

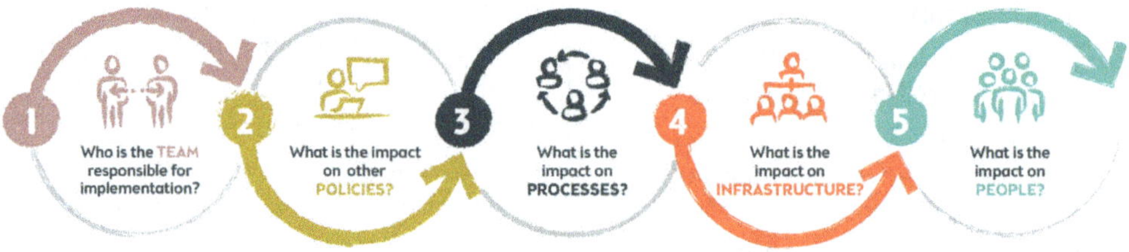

Usually, the **team** responsible for implementation will be comprised of the policy owner (usually the information officer or a deputy information officers) and representatives of senior management. They should involve other people as and when specific skillsets are required.

Policies rarely stand in isolation. They are often referenced in **other policies and supporting documents**. When a new policy is adopted the policy implementation team should assess whether other policies must be amended. This will be the case if other policies govern specific personal information processing activities or if there is an opportunity to insert POPIA controls in processes governed by other policies (e.g. HR and procurement policies).

A policy is comprised of high-level policy statements, but does not in and of itself answer the questions 'what is required?' and 'how do we do it?' Usually policies have to be supported by supporting documents:

- Procedures: The processes required to implement a policy and which describe who does what, when they do it and under what criteria (e.g. conduct a personal information impact assessment).
- Standards: A set of mandatory rules or specifications that give effect to the principles in the policy (e.g. technical standards for the configuration of systems).
- Guidelines: General statements, recommendations or instructions to achieve a policy's objectives. They are not mandatory and can change more frequently than procedures and standards.

A new Protection of Personal Information Policy will have an **impact on any business process** that involves personal information. A business process is a collection of related tasks aimed at a specific outcome (e.g. onboarding a new customer or employee). The impact of the policy on these processes will be assessed by doing personal information impact assessments. The aim of these assessments is to identify instances where the process does not comply with the policy and to manage the POPIA risk that is caused by that non-compliance. The implementation plan must also include a plan for how changes to processes or the introduction of new processes will be assessed to ensure that new POPIA risks are not introduced. This is discussed in paragraph 20.3 below.

Be on the lookout for any **infrastructure or equipment requirements**. For instance, one of the policy statements of the Records Management Policy is that personal information must be destroyed securely. How will the organisation do this? The organisation will need special software for digital information and shredders for paper records. If the Information Security Management Policy provides that access to personal information must be restricted to employees who 'need to know', is it still appropriate for the organisation to have an open-plan office? If sending personal information via email is not permitted, how must employees share personal information? If employees are not provided with the infrastructure, equipment, hardware, software and other tools to comply with new policies, they will continue to work the way they are used to.

Last, but definitely not least, it is vital to assess the impact of the new policy on people. Who will have to do something different tomorrow? Do they have the knowledge and skills to make these changes? If they do not, what kind of training or skills development will they require? What else might they need to make the changes that the policy requires? Chocolates or wine?

20.2.7 Compliance monitoring and continuous improvement

The information officer must ensure that the performance and effectiveness of the POPIA compliance framework are evaluated and that shortcomings are addressed. POPIA does not expressly state how the POPIA compliance framework must be monitored, but as was discussed in chapter 1, compliance management best practice indicates that it should be a combination of self-assessments by the information officer and independent reviews by internal auditors, external auditors or both.

Organisations should agree and document a monitoring plan and procedure. According to ISO 27001 this includes determining:[21]

- what needs to be monitored and measured (usually processes and controls)
- methods for monitoring and measurement
- when the monitoring and measurement must take place
- who will do it (often internal or external auditors)
- when the results will be analysed and evaluated; and
- who will analyse and evaluate the results.

According to the GACP, this is what should be assessed:[22]

- 'The overall integrity and effectiveness of the compliance programme
- The adequacy of the compliance resources
- Whether the responsibility for compliance has been appropriately assigned and whether the activities of the overall compliance function are being coordinated. This would be particularly important in an organisation with numerous compliance departments
- The adequacy of the compliance policy, framework, associated objectives and compliance methodologies
- An evaluation of the compliance policies, procedures and controls put in place to identify, assess, monitor and report on compliance with compliance obligations
- The extent to which any specific objectives or targets relating to the compliance function for the period under review have been met
- The adherence to any compliance principles, standards, codes or other requirements adopted by the organisation
- The extent to which any previously identified weaknesses or agreed action arising from previous independent reviews have been attended to
- The level of compliance with any relevant compliance obligations relating to the organisation, and
- The findings and recommendations arising from the review should be documented and provided to the governing body and any relevant assurance committees.'

21 Section 9.1.

22 GACP 80.

20.3 PERSONAL INFORMATION IMPACT ASSESSMENTS

20.3.1 What is a personal information impact assessment?

Information officers must also ensure that 'a personal information impact assessment is done to ensure that adequate measures and standards exist to comply with the lawful processing of personal information'.[23]

'Personal information impact assessment' is not defined in POPIA. However, the concept is not a novel one. In the context of data protection, the EU GDPR refers to data protection impact assessment (or DPIAs).[24] It is seen as an assessment of compliance with existing laws. There is also the broader 'privacy impact assessment' (or PIA) which is a crucial component of 'privacy by design'. PIAs are not just about compliance with regulations, but are aimed at:

- identifying and evaluating the impact of a particular project, initiative or system on the privacy of all stakeholders; and
- searching for ways to avoid or mitigate these impacts.[25]

While embracing the principles of privacy by design is as laudable, it appears that personal information impact assessments are closer to the DPIAs referred to in the EU GDPR; an assessment which is used to assess whether a process complies with POPIA.

---

[23] Regulation 4(1)*(b)* of the POPIA Regulations.

[24] Article 35 of the EU GDPR.

[25] Roger Clarke 'An evaluation of privacy impact assessment guidance documents' (March 2011) *International Data Privacy Law* 111–120. For the foundational principles of privacy by design, see Ann Cavoukian 'Privacy by Design: The 7 Foundational Principles' available at https://www.ipc.on.ca/wp-content/uploads/resources/7foundationalprinciples.pdf.

Tricky area: Some specialists say that the assessment referred to in regulation 4(1)*(b)* is not the same as a DPIA; partly because it is referred to as a singular assessment. We do not mind admitting that we are not sure what the intention of the Information Regulator was, but we think it is safe to assume that it is an assessment aimed at identifying non-compliance with POPIA. It is dangerous to blindly equate the EU GDPR's DPIA to POPIA's 'personal information impact assessments'. DPIAs are not always required, only '[w]here a type of processing in particular using new technologies, and taking into account the nature, scope, context and purposes of the processing, is likely to result in a high risk to the rights and freedoms of natural persons'.[26] It goes on to list certain types of automated processing and decision-making, large-scale processing of special categories of data or data relating to criminal convictions and offences and systematic monitoring of publicly accessible areas as specific activities that require a DPIA. POPIA does not contain similar qualifications – personal information impact assessments are always required. This will often be impractical for organisations to achieve, which is why a risk-based approach is essential. See paragraph 20.3.4 below.

Article 35(1) of the EU GDPR provides that the assessment must include:

- a description of the envisaged processing operations and the purposes of the processing (this includes the 'nature, scope, context and purposes of the processing')[27]
- an assessment of the necessity and proportionality of the processing
- an assessment of the risks to the rights and freedoms of data subjects (this includes the 'origin, nature, particularity and severity of that risk');[28] and
- the measures envisaged to address the risks and demonstrate compliance.

In the context of compliance in general, the notion of doing 'risk assessments' as 'the overall process of risk identification, risk analysis and risk evaluation' as 'a basis for determining how risks should be managed', is as old as the mountains (or at least as old as ISO 31 000).[29]

---

[26] Article 35(1) of the EU GDPR.

[27] Recital 90.

[28] Recital 84.

[29] See the definition of 'risk assessment' in the GACP. ISO 31 000 refers to the family of standards relating to risk management.

Following a risk-based approach to POPIA will ensure that information officers and deputy information officers focus on the most pertinent threats. In short, and adapted slightly for the context, '[o]ne of the main [POPIA] risks is to think that they don't exist. The other is to try and treat all potential risks. Fix the basics, protect first what matters to your business and be ready to react to pertinent threats.'[30]

This image is often used to depict the risk management process:[31]

Here is a brief explanation of what each of these phases means:[32]

- **Communication and consultation:** Effective risk management relies on effective communication and consultation. Stakeholders will make decisions based on the perceptions they have about certain risks and ineffective or incomplete communication can undermine these decisions. In addition, informed stakeholders can help identify risks.
- **Establishing the context:** Risks should be mentioned keeping the objectives and the operating model (how it will achieve those objectives) of the organisation in mind. Before risks can be identified, the organisation should identify those internal and external factors which could keep it from achieving its goals. During these steps, it is important to consider whether the specific type of risk being managed requires different risk

30 Stephane Nappo, Global Chief Information Security Officer, 2018 Global CISO of the year.

31 See *The IRMSA Guide to Risk Management* 9.

32 See *The IRMSA Guide to Risk Management* 34.

evaluation criteria than the broader criteria established in the organisation's risk management framework.

- **Risk identification:** During this phase the organisation uses various approaches (quantitative, qualitative, or semi-quantitative) and tools (risk registers, competitor analysis, market trend research, SWOT analysis, internal questionnaires, sales performance reports) to identify risks and lost opportunities.
- **Risk analysis:** During this phase, the aim is to understand the risk. This is done by analysing the causes and sources of the risk and by obtaining the information required to do a risk evaluation. It includes assessing existing controls, analysing the consequences of a particular risk for the organisation, analysing likelihood and estimating probability, doing probability monitoring, obtaining expert opinions, completing risk registers and accounting for uncertainties.
- **Risk evaluation:** The risk is then compared against pre-determined criteria in order to determine how significant it is to the organisation. It involves assigning a rating to the risk comprised of the likelihood or probability of the risk, the impact or severity and an assessment of existing controls. At this stage some risks may be immediately accepted 'as is' or immediate steps could be taken to avoid the risk.
- **Risk treatment:** This phase involves deciding what to do about the risks that have been identified. Generally, an organisation has to choose between accepting or tolerating the risk, avoiding the risk, removing the source of the risk, changing the likelihood of the risk, changing the consequences, transferring the risk or exploiting an opportunity. During this step risk response plans are developed and implemented.
- **Monitoring and review:** This is a continuous process aimed at ensuring that the risk management process actually works. It involves planning, examining and evaluating information, recording the results, communicating them and improving the process.

Note that this methodology applies not only to risks, but also to lost opportunities. These may be opportunities to:

- create a new process, product or service
- improve existing processes, products or services
- improve the reputation and trust in the organisation; or
- build or strengthen relationships with new and existing stakeholders.

20.3.2 What is being assessed?

We assess business processes or processing activities against POPIA. A process is a collection of interrelated tasks that achieve a specific result during which personal information is created, collected, used, shared, transformed, stored or destroyed.

When a responsible party is implementing a POPIA Programme for the first time, the first step should be to create a process universe. Remember this picture that we used in the stakeholder engagement discussion?

When you compile your process universe, you can ask the following question of each business area:

- What does this business area do? What activities or tasks do they perform? Hint: look for the forms they use to collect information.
- Which of the processes involve personal information?
- Are these processes documented?
- Is the documentation up to date?
- Is the documentation detailed enough to perform an inherent risk-rating?[34]

20.3.3 When a personal information impact assessment should be performed

POPIA does not say when personal information impact assessments should be performed. For many organisations, their POPIA Programme will be the first time they are implementing policies aimed at the protection of personal information. Personal information impact assessments can be used to bring business processes in line with new policies. For others, they will already have implemented some policies, but they may be based on other data protection legislation or standards, in which case there will be gaps. Personal information impact assessments can be used to identify these gaps.

Lastly, personal information impact assessments should be used to ensure that new data protection or privacy risks are not introduced into the organisation when the way in which personal information is processed changes. The following changes could trigger a personal information impact assessment:

- processing personal information for a new purpose[35]
- launching new products or services
- expanding into other countries
- new systems, software or hardware which is used for processing
- sharing personal information with third parties
- using a new service provider or supplier; or
- changes to privacy regulations.

---

33 You made it to page 666. To mark this auspicious occasion we thought this completely irrelevant quote from Good Omens (Neil Gaiman and Terry Pratchett) would be fitting: 'It is said that the devil has all the best tunes. This is broadly true. But Heaven has the best choreographers.'

34 See paragraph 20.3.4. The inherent risk-rating is the second step.

35 The requirements that apply when purposes shift are discussed in chapter 12.

Key point: Information officers and deputy information officers are often the last people to know if one of these trigger events take place. We have often had to do PIIAs after the POPIA horse has bolted. This has led to wasted capital investments, wounded egos and eons of wasted time and energy. The key is to insert a PIIA requirement early on and train staff in key business processes. For instance, we are big fans of inserting a PIIA requirement in the following processes: IT project start-up, procurement, business (or investment) case development and project management. Most organisations have some approvals that need to take place before money and time is spent on something – this is where the PIIA should go and why it is called 'privacy by design' and not privacy as an afterthought.

20.3.4 How to perform personal information impact assessments

The following eight-step approach is an amalgamation of several guidelines, risk management best practice and some practical experience:[36]

What to do	How to do it
Determine whether a personal information impact assessment is required.	If a process, project, initiative, contract or activity involves personal information, a personal information impact assessment should be performed. The way to implement this is to train employees in key positions to recognise these processes, projects, initiatives, contracts or activities to recognise personal information so they can trigger a personal information impact assessment. For instance, asking whether personal information is involved should be a standard part of your project management life cycle and your procurement process.

➥

[36] UCISA *Privacy Impact Assessment Toolkit*, available at https://www.ucisa.ac.uk/Resources/Privacy-Impact-Assessment-Toolkit; Article 29 Data Protection Working Party *Guidelines on Data Protection Impact Assessment (DPIA) and determining whether processing is 'likely to result in a high risk' for the purposes of Regulation 2016/679* (4 October 2017); ICO *Sample DPIA Template*, available at https://gdpr.eu/wp-content/uploads/2019/03/dpia-template-v1.pdf.

What to do	How to do it
Perform an inherent risk-rating: determine the level of personal information impact assessment required.	Is the process, project, initiative, contract or activity inherently high risk? Doing an inherent risk-rating will help the organisation to spend the bulk of its resources on the significant data protection or privacy risks. This is implemented by creating a short questionnaire designed to identify processes or activities that have inherently high data protection or privacy risks. Generally, the following factors could be taken into account: • the volume of personal information • whether there is any special personal information involved • whether it is 'further processing' • whether it involves profiling or automated decision-making • whether the processing is invisible (i.e. the data subject is not aware of the processing) • whether it involves any form of processing that requires prior authorisation (e.g. the further processing of unique identifiers with the aim of linking information or processing information for the purposes of credit reporting) • the value of the personal information (e.g. what would it cost to replace the personal information if it was lost) • how disruptive would it be if the processing activity was interrupted or if the personal information was no longer available (i.e. how important is this processing activity to the organisation); and • how valuable would the personal information be to a bad actor. The inherent risk-rating would determine the level of personal information impact assessment required and who can sign off on the assessment. This ensures that organisations apply most of their resources to high-risk activities.

➥

What to do	How to do it
Describe the processing activity.	Remember that the organisation is assessing a processing activity to determine whether it complies with POPIA. This means that knowing the ins and outs of the processing activity is vital. This is done through an activity called data flow mapping. Data flow maps are used to document the collection, use, transfer, archiving or destruction of personal information. This is also called 'tracking the lifecycle of data'.[37]
Identify privacy risks.	The methodology used in this phase ranges from questionnaires to face-to-face interactions. During this phase, the processing activity is assessed against the policy statements in the Information Security Management Policy, the Protection of Personal Information Policy and the Records Management Policy. The purpose of this process is to provide a list of all possible POPIA risks, regardless of whether there are existing controls that already address them. It is appropriate to include both risks to the data subject and the organisation.

➥

[37] Jeremy Berkowitz, Michael Mangold & Stephen Sharon 'Data flow maps—increasing data processing transparency and privacy compliance in the enterprise' (2017) 73(2) *Washington and Lee Law Review Online* 802, available at https://scholarlycommons.law.wlu.edu/wlulr-online/vol73/iss2/11. We discuss data flow mapping and records of processing activities (or ROPA's) in chapter 1 paragraph 1.4.

What to do	How to do it
Identify and evaluate privacy solutions.	The aim is to identify solutions that eliminate the risks or reduce it to a level that is acceptable to the organisation. These steps are then recorded in a risk response plan. Here are some examples of solutions: • some risks may be acceptable without further action, because they are unlikely or low impact • a contractual arrangement which provides assurance or transfers the liability • improving transparency by developing a privacy notice • introducing a new policy or amending an existing one • introducing a procedure to manage the risk • disabling certain features of a product or service • training people to be aware of the risk and to avoid it • technical measures like enforcing strong encryption or preventing certain actions; and • abandoning the processing activity. These solutions may not entirely eliminate the POPIA risk. The residual risks should be identified and rated to ensure that the organisation is comfortable with the level of residual risk. There will always be a myriad of ways to address a risk. POPIA by and large requires organisations to act reasonably.

➡

What to do	How to do it
Sign off and record the outcomes.	Depending on how an organisation has defined roles and responsibilities, senior management would have to decide how to treat the POPIA risks involved and which solutions to implement. This is based on the view that senior management is the first line of defence. See the discussion in paragraph 20.2.4 above. The information officer is in the second line of defence, which means that their primary role is to advise, monitor and report. In other words, it is the information officer's role to ensure that there is a personal information impact assessment procedure in place, but it is senior management's responsibility to follow the procedure and to respond to the POPIA risks that are identified. While the information officer plays a supporting role, that is not to say that they do not have a say in the solutions that are proposed and accepted. This is part of their advisory and monitoring role. It is vital to ensure that there is a permanent record of who signed off the solutions and when this took place.
Integrate the outcomes into a project plan	To ensure that the risk response plan is implemented, it should be integrated into a project plan. This will ensure that there is a clear plan, an implementation timeline and that actions are assigned to a responsible person.
Agree on a monitoring plan	The information officer, the relevant members of senior management and internal audit should agree on a monitoring plan to assess whether the agreed solutions have been implemented and to ensure that the risk does not recur and that new risks are managed in future.

20.4 INTERNAL MEASURES TO PROCESS REQUESTS FOR INFORMATION OR ACCESS THERETO

The information officer must ensure that 'internal measures are developed together with adequate systems to process requests for information and access thereto.'[38] This duty refers to requests for access to information which is one of the data subject rights in terms of section 23 of POPIA. It may also refer to the information officer's duties in terms of the Promotion of Access to Information Act, where the data subject is not the requester and which may relate to information other than personal information.

Data subject requests (which include requests for access) are discussed in chapter 18.

[38] Regulation 4(1)*(d)* of the POPIA Regulations.

20.5 PROVIDING TRAINING

The information officer must ensure that 'internal awareness sessions are conducted regarding the provisions of the Act, regulations made in terms of the Act, codes of conduct, or information obtained from the Regulator.'[39]

The importance of training in the context of POPIA cannot be over-stated. Kevin Mitnick, a convicted hacker, once remarked that '[t]he methods that will most effectively minimise the ability of intruders to compromise security are comprehensive user training and education. Enacting policies and procedures simply won't suffice'.

POPIA does not specify who must receive what training. To determine this, a training plan should be developed by:

- applying the principles of change management discussed in paragraph 20.2.1
- considering the different groups of stakeholders identified during the stakeholder consultation process discussed in paragraph 20.2.3; and
- taking the outcome of the policy impact assessment described in paragraph 20.2.6 into account.

When these three sets of data are combined it is possible to develop a communication and training plan which will ensure that the appropriate individuals within the organisation develop the knowledge and skills regarding POPIA that are appropriate for their position. The training plan should also consider how the employees will be trained. There are four important considerations when determining how training should take place:

- The characteristics of the audience: How sophisticated is the audience? How busy are they (i.e. how much time do they have for training)? When is a good time for the training to take place? How are they usually trained? Does a replacement need to be arranged to do their job while they receive training?
- The level of knowledge or skill they require: Do they just need to know something? Or do they need to acquire a new skill? Should they be tested at the end of the training to ensure that they have actually developed the new skill?
- Infrastructure limitations: What kind of equipment do they have access to? E.g. do they have easy access to computers for online training or will the training have to take place face-to-face?
- Proof of training: How will the information officer prove that training took place, should the Regulator request the information?

---

[39] Regulation 4(1)*(e)* of the POPIA Regulations.

Information officers should work closely with their learning and development specialists in Human Resources as compliance training should not be treated differently to any other form of training.

Always consider that training is not a once-off exercise. Not only will information officers have to consider how they will ensure that new employees or employees who move to new positions are trained (i.e. induction training or 'onboarding'), but employees will likely also require refresher training as time goes by.

20.6 PRIVACY MANAGEMENT SOFTWARE

Many information officers will be looking around feverishly for software that can make their new role easier. And, yes, there is a lot of privacy management software out there. A lot. So much, that the International Association of Privacy Professionals (the IAPP) publishes an annual *Privacy Tech Vendor Report* of about 200 pages![40] Here are the categories the IAPP use to organise the vendors:

- Assessment managers: Here the focus is on automating personal information impact assessments and managing risks.
- Consent managers: If you do need consent for a processing activity, there is technology that will help you manage those consents.
- Data mapping: The software in this category helps organisations to determine how information flows through the organisation.
- Data subject requests: If an organisation has a high volume of data subject requests, there is software available to help automate the process.
- Incident response: Incident response software helps organisations to respond to data breaches quickly by automating the flow of information to stakeholders.
- Privacy information managers: There are a lot of privacy laws to keep track of. Organisations who are subject to multiple privacy laws make use of privacy information managers to get information on the latest privacy laws across the world and to keep up with changes in the regulatory landscape.
- Website scanning: The software in this category can determine what cookies, beacons and other trackers are being used on a website to ensure compliance with cookie laws.
- Activity monitoring: The software in this category helps organisations to keep track of who had access to personal information, when the information was accessed and what was done to the information.

[40] International Association of Privacy Practitioners *Privacy Tech Vendor Report*, available at https://iapp.org/resources/article/privacy-tech-vendor-report/.

- Data discovery: Finding and correctly classifying information can be a laborious task. The software in this category identifies and classifies personal information.
- De-identification and pseudonymisation: De-identification and pseudonymisation[41] are not as easy as hitting the delete button. The software in this category helps organisations to execute de-identification and pseudonymisation.
- Enterprise communications: There are so many ways to communicate within an organisation other than email. The technology in this category offers alternatives to email which are more secure and prevent leaks of employee communications.

Before you get too excited, there are no technologies that will magically make an organisation POPIA compliant. At best, they can automate some of the tasks which the organisation has to perform to become, and remain, compliant. At worst, they become expensive boondoggles that nobody uses.

In order to understand what a successful adoption of privacy technology looks like, think about digital transformation in general. It is not about blindly adding technology to processes; it is about transforming those processes. Richard Susskind (legal futurist and author of *The Future of Law*) said: 'Grafting technology on to processes that can date as far back as 900 years is not the answer ... The point is not to computerise current practices. The great power of technology lies in transformation, not in automation.' George Westerman (Principle Research Scientist at MIT Sloan Initiative on the Digital Economy) adds a bit of levity: 'When digital transformation is done right, it's like a caterpillar turning into a butterfly, but when done wrong, all you have is a really fast caterpillar.'

Before considering technology, first ensure that you have processes that work, and people who can do the work. When these two elements of digital transformation are in place, an organisation is mature enough to add technology to help people perform the work.

41 De-identification/anonymisation and pseudonymisation was discussed in chapter 3.

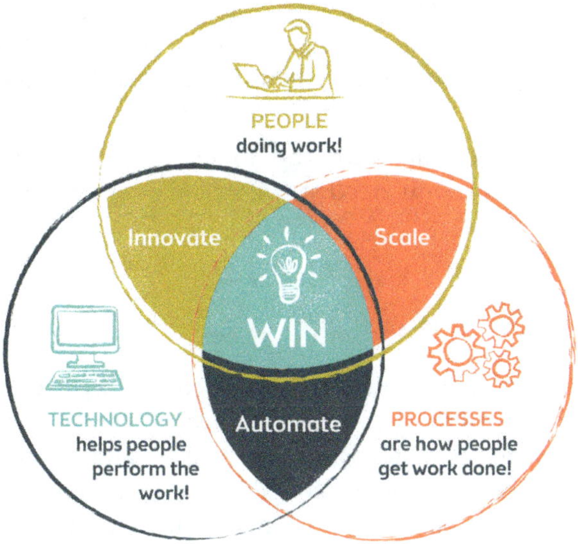

If you feel that you are ready to graduate from manual processes, here are some things you should keep in mind when you decide whether to use technology and what to use:

- Know what the problem is that you want to solve. Albert Einstein said: 'It's not that I'm so smart, it's just that I stay with problems longer.' When you deploy technology without analysing the problem, you may be treating the symptoms of the problem without identifying the root cause. The problem might be the people or the process!
- Be user-centric. Listen to the people who will be using the technology and their requirements. If the technology is not user-friendly, they will not use it.
- Focus on change management. If you do not ensure that people know why they have to use the technology and how to use it, they will not use it.
- Know that technology will not do the work for you. Most of the privacy technology out there automates existing processes; it is not 'plug in and play'. The organisation still has to develop the process and then integrate the technology.
- Follow the KISS[42] principle. If the technology is more complicated than the manual process that went before it, people will not use it.
- First, look at the technology you already have. Many organisations already have software that can automate processes. It might not be specifically designed for compliance or data protection processes, but it will do the job just as well.

42 KISS stands for 'Keep It Simple, Stupid'.

- The EU GDPR and POPIA are not identical. Much of the software out there was developed with the EU GDPR or another privacy law in mind. If you want to use it to enable POPIA compliance, make sure it can be customised.
- Stop trying to keep up with the Joneses. Are you buying the latest technology because you need it, or because everybody on LinkedIn is talking about it?

20.7 HOW ON EARTH MUST A SMALL BUSINESS DO THIS?

Information officers at small, medium and micro enterprises will be thinking 'that's nice, how do I do all this in a small business?'[43] POPIA does not distinguish between different types of enterprises, by size or any other metric. In other words, small businesses are subject to the same compliance requirements. In addition, small businesses may even be more vulnerable than big businesses, because their ability to absorb the losses that come with data breaches will be more limited. All is not lost though as POPIA is likely to give small businesses some slack when considering what is 'reasonable'.

Here are the actions which we think small businesses should focus on:

<table>
<tr><td>Assess your risk</td><td>Just because the business is small, does not mean that it is low risk from a POPIA perspective. Some products or services are inherently invasive (e.g. lead generation, profiling and predictive analytics, unsolicited direct marketing, services involving special personal information or the information of children). Businesses big and small that are engaged in high-risk activities should make sure that their business model is still viable.

Other small businesses process personal information on behalf of bigger businesses. They are high risk, because their clients will force them to be POPIA compliant. If they are not, the damage to their reputation will be severe and many of their clients will cancel their agreements.

A small business that is high risk, or processes information on behalf of bigger businesses, should invest in POPIA compliance.</td></tr>
</table>

[43] In South Africa, SMMEs are classified according to their turnover and differ depending on the sector they trade in. The thresholds are determined by the Department of Trade and Industry and can be found in Schedule 1 of the National Small Business Act of 1996 (as amended): https://www.gov.za/sites/default/files/gcis_document/201409/act102of1996.pdf. This classification is also used by Statistics South Africa.

Adopt a POPIA policy	Small businesses are not big on policies. But, it is important to document who your information officer is, that you will adhere to the principles of POPIA (and that you know what they are) and that you will assess the business from time to time.
Train the information officer	In small businesses, there will probably not be a team of people looking after POPIA compliance or the luxury of three lines of defence[44] – it will just be the information officer. Small businesses should make sure that their information officer is aware that he or she is the information officer and what that means. While it may be impractical to make your CEO (who is your information officer) a POPIA expert, they should certainly know who to call when a data protection issue crops up.
Train the rest of the employees	At a small business, every employee is a line of defence. Make sure that they can spot non-compliance and know when it is serious. Remember, do not train everybody on everything!
Review your forms	Review the forms you use to collect personal information and make sure you are using all of it. If you are not, stop collecting it.
Have a privacy notice and a PAIA manual[45]	Small businesses should be transparent. Make sure that people know what information you collect and what you do with it.

➡

44 The three lines of defence are discussed in paragraph 20.2.4.

45 Not all small businesses were required to have PAIA manuals in the past. GN 1222 in *GG* 39504 of 11 December 2015 and GN 1354 in *GG* 44003 of 18 December 2020 exempted certain private bodies from compiling a PAIA manual. The exemption has been extended to 31 December 2021 by GN 397 in *GG* 44785 of 30 June 2021.

Look after information security	Data breaches are a big risk to small businesses. They are an attractive target, because they do not have the resources to manage information security that their bigger counterparts have. The ICO suggests that small businesses should take the following practical steps:[46] • back up your data • use strong passwords • take care when working remotely • be wary of suspicious emails • install anti-virus and malware protection • do not leave paperwork or laptops unattended • make sure your Wi-Fi is secure • lock your screen when you are away from your desk • keep on top of who has access to what • do not keep data for longer than you need it • dispose of old computer equipment and records securely; and • get a shredder.
Get together once a year (or if something big changes) and do a PIIA	Small businesses usually don't have well-documented standard operating procedures, but they should – small businesses also need to be efficient. Have a workshop once a year where the organisation does some training, talks through their business processes and map how personal information flows through the business using a personal information impact assessment.
Beg, borrow and steal	There are lots of free guidelines out there for small businesses. One of the best examples is the ICO's *Data Protection Hub for Small Businesses*.[47]

20.8 (SOME LAST) PRACTICAL ADVICE

Given that POPIA is a people problem,[48] it seems appropriate that the last piece of practical advice should be about change management and the interpersonal skills[49] required from the POPIA compliance team. Information officers and their deputies should ask themselves the following questions:

46 ICO '11 practical ways to keep your IT systems safe and secure', available at https://ico.org.uk/for-organisations/data-protection-advice-for-small-organisations/whats-new/blogs/11-practical-ways-to-keep-your-it-systems-safe-and-secure/.

47 ICO *Data Protection Hub for Small Businesses*, available at https://ico.org.uk/for-organisations/data-protection-advice-for-small-organisations/guide-to-the-data-protection-hub-for-small-organisations. Just be careful; POPIA and the EU GDPR are not identical.

48 See paragraph 20.2.1.

49 We refuse to call these soft skills. It is an antiquated term coined by the US Army in the late 1960s as a way to refer to any skill that does not require the use of machines. The terminology is roundly criticised, because of the connotation that soft skills are somehow inferior to hard skills.

- Does my POPIA compliance strategy align with the organisation's strategy?
- Am I following a risk-based approach to make sure that my risk appetite matches the organisation's risk appetite and to stop myself from sweating the small stuff?
- Do I stop myself from assuming that non-compliance is the product of ignorance or stupidity? Do I always ask why the organisation is doing something in a certain (perhaps non-compliant) way, before giving my opinion?
- Do I always do a cost-benefit analysis before making recommendations?
- Do people read what I write? And, if they do, will they understand it? Do I speak like a normal person or do I use the technical language in POPIA?
- Am I always making sure that what I am saying is relevant to the people I am speaking to?
- Am I sensitive to the changes I am asking people to make? Am I supporting them through those changes?

What we are talking about here are soft skills. A horrible misnomer, because they are actually the hardest skills of all. Nicola Askham, the 'Data Governance Coach', writes about the six vital characteristics of a successful data governance manager, but she might as well have been writing about information officers.[50] Here they are (edited a bit for context):

- Passion: If the information officer believes that privacy is important and that the POPIA Programme will make a difference, others will believe this as well. In the words of Simon Sinek, 'There are only two ways to influence human behaviour: you can manipulate it or you can inspire it.'
- Communication: The information officer has to sell POPIA to the organisation. The best way to do this is to focus on your audience at all times and to connect what is important to you (hopefully the protection of personal information) to what they are passionate about.
- Influence: An information officer has to have 'the capacity to have an effect on the character, development, or behaviour of someone or something'.[51] The name of the game is stakeholder management. We spoke about it earlier in this chapter.[52]

---

50 Nicola Askham *The Six Vital Characteristics of a Successful Data Governance Manager*, available at https://static1.squarespace.com/static/52ed2570e4b02079a82e6ff3/t/55f04428e4b096103647ceb5/1441809448449/6+Vital+Characteristics+ebook.pdf.

51 *Oxford English Dictionary*.

52 See paragraph 20.2.3.

- Pragmatism: An information officer has to be sensitive to the organisation's history, issues, work culture and strategies. Above all, any POPIA compliance strategy needs to be grounded in reality.
- Persistence: POPIA compliance is very, very hard to achieve. There will be trials, tribulations, setbacks and in our experience, tears. Information officers need grit.
- Patience: POPIA compliance takes a long time. Information officers first have to convince the organisation that it is necessary, and then they have to implement new processes, change mindsets and often transform the old way of working.

We leave you with the words of the inimitable Dolly Parton: 'Find out who you are and do it on purpose.'

TABLE OF CASES

S

T

V

TABLE OF STATUTES

MODEL LAWS

SUBORDINATE LEGISLATION

FOREIGN REGULATIONS

European Union

GUIDELINES

Article 29 Data Protection Working Party Guidelines

European Data Protection Board Guidelines

OPINIONS

Article 29 Data Protection Working Party opinions

INDEX

Note: Page numbers in *italics* refer to text boxes.

C

www.ingramcontent.com/pod-product-compliance
Lightning Source LLC
LaVergne TN
LVHW060008210926
848481LV00013B/3670
* 9 7 8 1 4 8 5 1 3 6 8 2 8 *